The McGraw-Hill Series on Computer Communications (J. Ranade, Series Advisor)

0-07-019022-4	Edmunds	*SAA/LU6.2 Distributed Networks and Applications*
0-07-054418-2	Sackett	*IBM's Token-Ring Networking Handbook*
0-07-004128-8	Bates	*Disaster Recovery Planning: Networks, Telecommunications, and Data Communications*
0-07-020346-6	Feit	*TCP/IP: Architecture, Protocols, and Implementation*
0-07-005075-9	Berson	*APPC: Introduction to LU6.2*
0-07-005076-7	Berson	*Client/Server Architecture*
0-07-012926-6	Cooper	*Computer and Communications Security*
0-07-016189-5	Dayton	*Telecommunications*
0-07-016196-8	Dayton	*Multi-Vendor Networks: Planning, Selecting, and Maintenance*
0-07-034242-3	Kessler	*ISDN*
0-07-034243-1	Kessler/Train	*Metropolitan Area Networks: Concepts, Standards, and Service*

Other Related Titles

0-07-051144-6	Ranade/Sackett	*Introduction to SNA Networking: A Guide for Using VTAM/NCP*
0-07-051143-8	Ranade/Sackett	*Advanced SNA Networking: A Professional's Guide to VTAM/NCP*
0-07-033727-6	Kapoor	*SNA: Architecture, Protocols, and Implementation*
0-07-005553-X	Black	*TCP/IP and Related Protocols*
0-07-005554-8	Black	*Network Management Standards: SNMP, CMOT, and OSI*
0-07-021625-8	Fortier	*Handbook of LAN Technology, 2/e*
0-07-063636-2	Terplan	*Effective Management of Local Area Networks: Functions, Instruments, and People*
0-07-004563-1	Baker	*Downsizing: How to Get Big Gains from Smaller Computer Systems*

TCP/IP

Architecture, Protocols, and Implementation

Sidnie Feit

McGraw-Hill, Inc.
New York St. Louis San Francisco Auckland Bogotá
Caracas Lisbon London Madrid Mexico Milan
Montreal New Delhi Paris San Juan São Paulo
Singapore Sydney Tokyo Toronto

TCP/IP : Architecture, Protocols, and Implementation
International Editions 1993

Exclusive rights by McGraw-Hill Book Co. - Singapore for manufacture and export. This book cannot be re-exported from the country to which it is consigned by McGraw-Hill.

Copyright © 1993 by McGraw-Hill, Inc. All rights reserved. Except as permitted under the United States Copyright Act of 1976, no part of this publication may be reproduced or distributed in any form or by any means, or stored in a data base or retrieval system, without the prior written permission of the publisher.

4 5 6 7 8 9 0 BJE UPE 9 8 7 6 5

The sponsoring editor for this book was Jerry Papke.

Library of Congress Cataloging-in-Publication Data

Feit, Sidnie.
   TCP/IP : architecture, protocols, and implementation / Sidnie Feit
     p.   cm.
   Includes bibliographical references and index.
   ISBN 0-07-020346-6
   1. TCP/IP (Computer network protocol).   I. Title.
TK5105.5.F423   1993
                                                      92-25977
                                                            CIP

Trademarks. The following products are copyrighted by the companies that produce them. cisco is a trademark of cisco Systems, Inc. DEC, VAX, VMS, ULTRIX, DIGITAL, and DECnet are trademarks of Digital Equipment Corporation. HP, Hewlett-Packard, Network Computing System are trademarks of Hewlett-Packard Corporation. NetWare is a trademark of Novell, Inc. LANWatch, PC/TCP, and FTP Software are registered trademarks of FTP Software, Inc. MS-DOS is a registered trademark of Microsoft Corporation. AIX, RISC System/6000, IBM, MVS, OS/2, PC DOS are trademarks of International Business Machines Corporation. IBM PC is a registered trademark of International Business Machines Corporation. Intel is a trademark of Intel Corporation. AFS and Transarc are registered trademarks of the Transarc Corporation. OSF/1 is a trademark of the Open Software Foundation. X/Open is a trademark of X/Open Company Limited. UNIX is a registered trademark of UNIX System Laboratories, Inc. Macintosh is a registered trademark of Apple Computer, Inc. Sniffer is a registered trademark of Network General Corporation. NFS, Network File System, Sun and SunOS are trademarks of Sun Microsystems, Inc. TransLAN is a registered trademark of Vitalink Communications Corporation. Ethernet is a registered trademark of Xerox Corporation. Netwise System and Netwise RPC TOOL are trademarks of Netwise, Inc.

Information contained in this work has been obtained by McGraw-Hill, Inc., from sources believed to be reliable. However, neither McGraw-Hill nor its authors guarantee the accuracy or completeness of any information published herein and neither McGraw-Hill nor its authors shall be responsible for any errors, omissions, or damages arising out of this information. This work is published with the understanding that McGraw-Hill and its authors are supplying information but are not attempting to render engineering or other professional services. If such services are required, the assistance of an appropriate professional should be sought.

When ordering this title, use ISBN 0-07-113304-6

Printed in Singapore

*This book is dedicated to my husband and friend,
Walter*

Contents

Preface xxi
Acknowledgments xxiii

Introduction 1

I.1 Background 1
I.2 Terminology 2
    I.2.1 Bytes and Octets 3
    I.2.2 Big Endians and Little Endians 3
    I.2.3 Protocols, Stacks, and Suites 3
    I.2.4 Hosts, Routers, and Others 3
    I.2.5 Notational Conventions 4
I.3 References 4

Chapter 1. TCP/IP: What It Is and Where It Came From 5

1.1 Introduction 5
    1.1.1 The Birth of TCP/IP 5
    1.1.2 TCP/IP Characteristics 6
    1.1.3 Acceptance of the Protocols 7
    1.1.4 Availability of TCP/IP 7
1.2 The Internet 8
    1.2.1 The Internet Activities Board 8
    1.2.2 Task Forces and Protocol Development 9
    1.2.3 Other Sources of Internet Protocols 9
    1.2.4 TCP/IP and the Distributed Computing Environment 10
1.3 Requests for Comments 10
    1.3.1 State and Status of Standards 11
    1.3.2 Assigned Numbers 11
    1.3.3 RFCs That Promote Multivendor Interworking 12
    1.3.4 Related Documents 13
1.4 Functions of the NIC 13
    1.4.1 Online Information 14

viii Contents

| 1.5 | Other Information Resources | 14 |
| 1.6 | Open Systems Interconnection | 15 |

Chapter 2. TCP/IP Suite Service Overview 17

2.1	Introduction		17
2.2	Application-to-Application Communication		17
	2.2.1	Connection-oriented Communication	17
	2.2.2	Connectionless Communication	17
	2.2.3	Socket Programming Interface	18
	2.2.4	Remote Procedure Call Programming Interface	18
2.3	Basic Services		18
	2.3.1	File Transfer	19
	2.3.2	Terminal Access	19
	2.3.3	Mail	19
2.4	Additional Services		20
	2.4.1	File Access	20
	2.4.2	Domain Name System Name Service	20
	2.4.3	Commercial Software	21
	2.4.4	Network Management	21
2.5	Dialogues		21
	2.5.1	Terminal Access Dialogue	22
	2.5.2	Looking Up a Name in the Domain Name System Database	22
	2.5.3	File Transfer Dialogue	23
	2.5.4	File Access Dialogue	24

Chapter 3. TCP/IP Architecture 25

3.1	Introduction		25
3.2	Layering		26
	3.2.1	Lower Layers (Layers 1 and 2)	27
	3.2.2	IP and OSI Network Layers (Layer 3)	28
	3.2.3	TCP and OSI Transport Layers (Layer 4)	28
	3.2.4	User Datagram Protocol (Layer 4)	28
	3.2.5	Application Services	29
3.3	Protocol Overview		29
3.4	Topologies		31
3.5	IP Architecture		33
	3.5.1	IP Actions	34
	3.5.2	Routing Table Information	34
3.6	TCP Architecture		35
3.7	UDP Architecture		37
3.8	Protocol Data Units		38
	3.8.1	Peer to Peer Interactions	39
3.9	Looking Ahead		40

Chapter 4. Physical and Data Link Technologies — 41

- 4.1 Introduction — 41
- 4.2 Point-to-Point Protocols — 42
- 4.3 HDLC — 44
  - 4.3.1 HDLC Frame Format — 44
  - 4.3.2 The Internet Point-to-Point Protocol — 45
  - 4.3.3 Serial Line Interface Protocol — 46
- 4.4 Packet Networks — 47
  - 4.4.1 X.25 Networks — 47
  - 4.4.2 X.25 and IP — 48
  - 4.4.3 Frame Relay — 49
- 4.5 The 802 Networks — 51
  - 4.5.1 Layering for 802 Networks — 51
  - 4.5.2 Ethernet and 802.3 — 51
  - 4.5.3 Coax Media — 52
  - 4.5.4 Other 802.3 Media Choices — 53
  - 4.5.5 Connecting to the Medium — 53
  - 4.5.6 Ethernet and 802.3 Media Access Control Protocols — 54
  - 4.5.7 Ethernet Media Access Control Frames — 54
  - 4.5.8 802.3 Media Access Control Frames — 55
  - 4.5.9 802.5 Token-Ring Configuration and Media — 56
  - 4.5.10 802.5 Media Access Control Protocol — 57
  - 4.5.11 Other 802.X Technologies — 57
  - 4.5.12 IEEE 802.2 — 57
  - 4.5.13 Logical Link Control Header — 58
  - 4.5.14 Fiber Distributed Data Interface — 59
  - 4.5.15 Switched Multimegabit Data Service — 59
  - 4.5.16 Some Sample Frame Sizes and Maximum Datagram Sizes — 59
  - 4.5.17 Broadcasting and Multicasting — 60
  - 4.5.18 Tunneling — 61
- 4.6 Network Interfaces — 61
- 4.7 Link Layer Issues — 63
- 4.8 Relation to OSI — 63
- 4.9 Recommended Reading — 64

Chapter 5. Naming and Addressing — 65

- 5.1 Introduction — 65
- 5.2 Naming — 65
- 5.3 Examples of Internet Names — 66
  - 5.3.1 The NIC Naming Tree — 66
  - 5.3.2 Structure of Names — 67
- 5.4 Addresses — 69
  - 5.4.1 Address Formats — 69
  - 5.4.2 Assigning Class C Addresses to Networks — 72
  - 5.4.3 Assigning Class B Addresses to Networks — 72
  - 5.4.4 Assigning Class A Addresses to Networks — 72
  - 5.4.5 Network Address Spaces — 73

Contents

5.5	Subnets		73
	5.5.1	Subnet Masks	74
5.6	Special Addresses		75
	5.6.1	Identifying Networks	75
	5.6.2	Broadcasts to Networks	75
	5.6.3	Broadcasts to Subnets	76
	5.6.4	Loopback Address	76
	5.6.5	This Host and This Network	76
5.7	The Domain Name System		76
	5.7.1	Looking up Host Addresses	77
5.8	Address Resolution Protocol		78
	5.8.1	ARP Message Contents	79
	5.8.2	The ARP Table	81
	5.8.3	Reverse ARP	81
5.9	Multihoming		82
5.10	The Relationship Between Names and Addresses		84
5.11	Multicasting		84
	5.11.1	Multicast Groups	84
	5.11.2	Translating to Physical Multicast Addresses	86
5.12	Recommended Reading		87

Chapter 6. Internet Protocol — 89

6.1	Introduction		89
6.2	Operational Model		91
	6.2.1	Routing Operations	91
	6.2.2	Frame Encapsulation and Maximum Transmission Unit	92
6.3	Functions		93
	6.3.1	Primary Function	94
	6.3.2	Subnetwork Mask	94
	6.3.3	Looking Up Addresses and Masks	94
	6.3.4	Routing Table	95
	6.3.5	Routing Protocols	97
	6.3.6	Router Tables	97
	6.3.7	Host Tables	98
	6.3.8	Fragmentation	98
	6.3.9	Type of Service	98
	6.3.10	Time-to-Live	98
	6.3.11	Checksum	99
	6.3.12	Options	99
6.4	IP Protocol Mechanisms		100
	6.4.1	Datagram Header	100
	6.4.2	Type of Service	101
	6.4.3	Total Length Field	102
	6.4.4	Fragmentation Fields	102
	6.4.5	Reconstructing a Fragmented Datagram	103
	6.4.6	Time-to-Live	104
	6.4.7	Protocol	104
	6.4.8	Header Checksum	104
	6.4.9	Source Address and Destination Address	105

Contents   xi

	6.4.10	Options	105
	6.4.11	Strict Source Route	105
	6.4.12	Loose Source Route	106
	6.4.13	Record Route	106
	6.4.14	Timestamp	107
	6.4.15	Department of Defense Basic and Extended Security	107
	6.4.16	No Operation and End of Option List	107
	6.4.17	Encoding Options	108
	6.4.18	Encoding a Strict Source Route	108
	6.4.19	Encoding a Loose Source Route	110
	6.4.20	Encoding Record Route	110
	6.4.21	Encoding a Timestamp	110
	6.4.22	Encoding Basic and Extended Security Options	110
	6.4.23	Sample IP Header	111
6.5	Datagram Processing Scenarios		113
	6.5.1	Router Processing	114
	6.5.2	Destination Host Processing	115
6.6	IP Performance Issues		115
	6.6.1	Transmission Bandwidth	115
	6.6.2	Buffer Utilization	118
	6.6.3	CPU Processing	119
6.7	Service Interface		119
	6.7.1	Service Interface Requests	120
	6.7.2	Events at the Interface	120
6.8	Relationship to OSI		120
6.9	Recommended Reading		121

Chapter 7. Internet Control Message Protocol   123

7.1	Introduction		123
7.2	ICMP Error Messages		124
	7.2.1	Types of Error Messages	125
	7.2.2	ICMP Message Format	126
	7.2.3	Destination Unreachable Message	127
	7.2.4	Time Exceeded Message	128
	7.2.5	Parameter Problem	128
	7.2.6	Source Quench	129
	7.2.7	Redirect	130
7.3	ICMP Query Messages		131
	7.3.1	Echo or Echo Reply	132
	7.3.2	Timestamp and Timestamp Reply	134
	7.3.3	Address Mask	134
7.4	Viewing ICMP Activities		135
7.5	Relationship to OSI		136
7.6	Recommended Reading		137

Chapter 8. IP Routing — 139

- 8.1 Introduction — 139
- 8.2 IP Routing — 140
  - 8.2.1 Routing Tables — 140
  - 8.2.2 Routing Protocols — 141
  - 8.2.3 Routing Metrics — 142
- 8.3 Routing Information Protocol (RIP) — 143
  - 8.3.1 RIP Routing — 144
  - 8.3.2 Recovering from Network Disturbances — 145
  - 8.3.3 Timing Out Unreachable Routers — 146
  - 8.3.4 Split Horizon and Poisoned Reverse — 147
  - 8.3.5 Triggered Updates and Hold Down — 148
  - 8.3.6 RIP Message Protocol — 148
- 8.4 Open Shortest Path First — 149
  - 8.4.1 OSPF Model — 150
- 8.5 Areas and Databases — 152
  - 8.5.1 The Backbone of an Area — 152
- 8.6 Building the Routing Database for an Area — 154
  - 8.6.1 Hello Messages — 154
  - 8.6.2 The Designated Router — 154
  - 8.6.3 Initializing a Routing Database — 155
  - 8.6.4 Message Types — 155
- 8.7 Routing Across an Area Border — 156
  - 8.7.1 Routing to Other Autonomous Systems — 157
- 8.8 OSPF Protocol — 158
  - 8.8.1 OSPF Message Header — 158
  - 8.8.2 Contents of a Link State Update — 159
  - 8.8.3 Router Links — 160
  - 8.8.4 Network Links — 160
  - 8.8.5 Summary Link to a Network — 160
  - 8.8.6 Summary Link to a Boundary Router — 160
  - 8.8.7 Autonomous System External Link — 161
- 8.9 Important Features of OSPF — 161
- 8.10 Other Interior Gateway Protocols — 162
  - 8.10.1 Cisco Systems IGRP — 162
  - 8.10.2 OSI Routing — 162
- 8.11 External Gateway Protocols — 162
  - 8.11.1 The Exterior Gateway Protocol — 163
  - 8.11.2 EGP Model — 163
  - 8.11.3 Border Gateway Protocol — 164
- 8.12 Recommended Reading — 164

Chapter 9. User Datagram Protocol — 165

- 9.1 Introduction — 165
- 9.2 Ports — 166
- 9.3 UDP Protocol Mechanisms — 168

		9.3.1	UDP Header	169
		9.3.2	Checksum	170
		9.3.3	Other UDP Functions	170
		9.3.4	UDP Overflows	172
	9.4	Recommended Reading		172

Chapter 10. Transmission Control Protocol   173

	10.1	Introduction		173
		10.1.1	Major TCP Services	173
		10.1.2	TCP and the Client/Server Model	174
	10.2	TCP Concepts		174
		10.2.1	Outgoing and Incoming Data Streams	175
		10.2.2	Segments	175
		10.2.3	Push and Urgent Data	175
		10.2.4	Type of Service and Security	176
		10.2.5	Relationship to IP	177
		10.2.6	Ports	177
		10.2.7	Socket Addresses	178
	10.3	TCP Mechanisms		179
		10.3.1	Numbering and Acknowledgment	179
		10.3.2	TCP Header Fields for Ports, Sequencing, and ACKs	180
		10.3.3	Establishing a Connection	181
		10.3.4	A Connection Scenario	181
		10.3.5	Simultaneous Connection Establishment	183
		10.3.6	Support for Type of Service	183
		10.3.7	Support for Security	183
		10.3.8	Data Transfer	183
		10.3.9	Closing a Connection	185
		10.3.10	Abrupt Close	187
		10.3.11	Maximum Segment Size	187
	10.4	Flow Control		188
		10.4.1	Receive Window	188
		10.4.2	Send Window	190
		10.4.3	Checksum	191
	10.5	TCP Header		192
		10.5.1	Use of Header Fields During Connection Setup	192
		10.5.2	Choosing the Initial Sequence Number	194
		10.5.3	General Field Usage	194
		10.5.4	Sample TCP Segment	195
		10.5.5	Timing Out	195
		10.5.6	Error and Problem Handling	196
	10.6	Performance		197
		10.6.1	Silly Window Syndrome	199
		10.6.2	Nagle Algorithm	199
		10.6.3	Retransmission Timeout	200
		10.6.4	Treating Congestion	204
		10.6.5	Slow Start	205
		10.6.6	Vendor Conformance	205
		10.6.7	Vendor's Choice	205

xiv   Contents

		10.6.8	Ongoing Performance Research	206
		10.6.9	TCP Functions	207
		10.6.10	TCP States	208
		10.6.11	Viewing the States of TCP Connections	210
	10.7	Relationship to OSI		210
		10.7.1	TCP and OSI Transport Class 4	211
		10.7.2	OSI Connection Request PDU	212
		10.7.3	OSI TP4 Data and ACK PDUs	214
		10.7.4	OSI TP4 Acknowledgment PDU	215
	10.8	Recommended Reading		215

Chapter 11. File Transfer Protocol 217

	11.1	Introduction		217
	11.2	FTP Scenario		218
	11.3	FTP Model		220
		11.3.1	FTP Commands	220
	11.4	The FTP Protocol		225
		11.4.1	Data Format Issues	225
		11.4.2	Data Type	225
		11.4.3	File Structure	226
		11.4.4	Transmission Mode	226
		11.4.5	Error Recovery and Restart	227
		11.4.6	Reply Codes	228
	11.5	An FTP Session		228
	11.6	Commands		231
		11.6.1	Access Control Commands	231
		11.6.2	File Management Commands	232
		11.6.3	Commands That Set Data Formats	233
		11.6.4	File Transfer Commands	233
		11.6.5	Miscellaneous Commands	234
	11.7	Performance Issues		234
	11.8	Relationship of FTP to OSI		235
	11.9	Trivial File Transfer Protocol (TFTP)		235
		11.9.1	TFTP Protocol	236
		11.9.2	Protocol Data Units	236
	11.10	Scenarios		238
	11.11	Recommended Reading		239

Chapter 12. NFS, RPC, and NIS 241

	12.1	Introduction		241
		12.1.1	NFS Structure	243
	12.2	Remote Procedure Call		244
		12.2.1	RPC Model	245
		12.2.2	Programs, Procedures, and Versions	246
		12.2.3	Typical RPC Programs	246
		12.2.4	RPC Portmapper	247

	12.2.5	Viewing Portmapper RPC Services	248
	12.2.6	RPC Message Formats	250
	12.2.7	RPC Authentication	250
	12.2.8	Dealing With Duplicate Requests	254
12.3	XDR		256
	12.3.1	XDR Data Description Language	256
	12.3.2	XDR Encoding	257
	12.3.3	RPC and XDR Programming Interface	258
	12.3.4	Other Remote Procedure Call Facilities	258
12.4	NFS Model		259
12.5	The Mount Protocol		260
12.6	NFS Protocol		262
	12.6.1	File Handles	262
	12.6.2	NFS Procedures	263
	12.6.3	Special NFS Services	264
	12.6.4	File Locking	265
	12.6.5	NFS Implementation Issues	265
	12.6.6	Monitoring NFS	266
12.7	Network Information Service		266
	12.7.1	Network Information Service Protocol	269
12.8	Recommended Reading		270

Chapter 13. Telnet 271

13.1	Introduction		271
	13.1.1	Network Virtual Terminal	271
13.2	Telnet Model		272
	13.2.1	NVT Keyboard	273
	13.2.2	Dealing With Control Codes	273
	13.2.3	Using Telnet	274
	13.2.4	Control Codes Sent from the Telnet Server	274
	13.2.5	Options	275
13.3	TELNET Command Protocol		276
	13.3.1	The Telnet Synch	276
	13.3.2	Negotiating Options	277
	13.3.3	Encoding Option Requests	278
13.4	TELNET Dialogues		279
	13.4.1	3270 Logons	281
13.5	Relationship to OSI		282
	13.5.1	Other Technologies	282
13.6	Recommended Reading		283

Chapter 14. Electronic Mail 285

14.1	Introduction		285
14.2	Model for Mail Operations		287
	14.2.1	Relaying Mail	288
	14.2.2	A Mail Relay Scenario	288

14.3	Names and Mail Domains		289
	14.3.1	The Mail Domain Tree	290
	14.3.2	Role of a Mail Exchanger	290
14.4	SMTP Mail Transfer Protocol		292
	14.4.1	Mail Scenario	292
	14.4.2	Timestamps and Return Address	294
	14.4.3	SMTP Commands	295
	14.4.4	Reply Codes	296
14.5	Internet Message Format		296
	14.5.1	The Post Office Protocol	297
14.6	Mail Issues		298
	14.6.1	Performance	298
	14.6.2	Deficiencies in the Internet Standards	298
14.7	X.400		298
	14.7.1	X.400 Message	299
	14.7.2	X.400 Naming	301
	14.7.3	Interworking Between X.400 and Internet Mail	301
14.8	ISO/CCITT Directory		302
	14.8.1	The X.500 Directory Information Tree	303
	14.8.2	Directory Model	305
14.9	Recommended Reading		308

Chapter 15. Network Management — 309

15.1	Introduction		309
	15.1.1	Results of IAB Adoption of SNMP	310
	15.1.2	CMOT	310
15.2	SNMP Model		312
	15.2.1	Roles of Managers and Agents	312
	15.2.2	Proxy Agents	313
15.3	SNMP Messages		314
	15.3.1	Communities	315
	15.3.2	SNMP Message Protocol	315
15.4	Structure of Management Information		317
	15.4.1	Object Identifiers	317
	15.4.2	Vendor Variables	319
	15.4.3	Categories of MIB Information	319
	15.4.4	MIB Extensions	319
15.5	Defining MIB Variables		319
	15.5.1	SNMP Datatypes and Abstract Syntax Notation One	321
	15.5.2	SNMP Datatypes	322
	15.5.3	Sample IP Datatypes	323
15.6	SNMP Message Format		323
15.7	ASN.1 Encoding		324
	15.7.1	Identifiers Used in SNMP Datatypes	326
	15.7.2	Encoding Object Identifiers	326
	15.7.3	Format of SNMP Messages	327
	15.7.4	Get Next Requests	330

	15.7.5	Tables and Get Next Requests	331
	15.7.6	The RMON MIB	331
	15.7.7	What Next?	332
15.8	Recommended Reading		332

Chapter 16. Administering a TCP/IP Network   333

16.1	Introduction		333
16.2	Topology		334
	16.2.1	Connecting LANs with Bridges	336
	16.2.2	Splitting LANS with Bridges	338
	16.2.3	Backup Bridges and Network Loops	338
	16.2.4	Routers	339
	16.2.5	Router Capabilities	339
	16.2.6	Router Security Features	341
	16.2.7	Routers with Proxy ARP	341
	16.2.8	Brouters and Multiprotocol Routing	342
16.3	Configuration		343
	16.3.1	Installing Interfaces	343
	16.3.2	Configuring Interface Addresses and Masks	344
	16.3.3	Other Interface Parameters	345
	16.3.4	Running Multiple Subnets on one LAN	346
	16.3.5	Interfaces With More Than One Name	347
	16.3.6	Configuring Point-to-Point Links	347
	16.3.7	Serial Interfaces without IP Addresses	348
	16.3.8	Configuration Parameters and Commands	348
	16.3.9	Configuring System Names	350
	16.3.10	IP Routing Tables	350
	16.3.11	Accessing Routers	351
	16.3.12	DDN IP Security	351
	16.3.13	IP Parameters	352
	16.3.14	Dynamic Configuration	352
	16.3.15	External Routing	353
	16.3.16	Name to Address Translation	355
	16.3.17	Using the Domain Name System	355
	16.3.18	Getting All of the IP Addresses for a System	356
	16.3.19	Setting Up Domain Name Servers	357
	16.3.20	Configuring TCP	359
	16.3.21	Configuring Services	360
	16.3.22	Configuring Anonymous FTP	361
	16.3.23	Running Services	361
	16.3.24	Mail	363
	16.3.25	Remote Procedure Call Services	363
	16.3.26	NFS	364
	16.3.27	Configuring Network Management	364
	16.3.28	General TCP/IP Configuration	364
	16.3.29	The System Startup Procedure	365
16.4	Maintenance, Monitoring, and Troubleshooting		365
	16.4.1	SNMP Facilities	366
	16.4.2	Network Monitors	366

xviii Contents

		16.4.3	Ping, Spray, and Traceroute	367
		16.4.4	Netstat for General Networking Status	369
		16.4.5	Checking the Status of Computers	372
		16.4.6	Checking Telnet, Mail, and FTP	373
		16.4.7	Monitoring Remote Procedure Call Services	374
		16.4.8	Monitoring NFS	375
		16.4.9	Simple Troubleshooting	377
	16.5	Security		378
		16.5.1	Audit Trails	379
		16.5.2	Kerberos	379
	16.6	Recommended Reading		383

Chapter 17. The Socket Programming Interface 385

	17.1	Introduction		385
	17.2	UNIX Orientation		386
		17.2.1	Socket Services	386
	17.3	The TCP Service Interface		387
		17.3.1	Opening a Connection	388
		17.3.2	Transmission Control Block (TCB)	388
		17.3.3	OPEN Command	389
		17.3.4	OPEN Command and the Socket Interface	389
		17.3.5	Sending and Receiving Data	390
		17.3.6	SEND/RECEIVE Primitives and the Socket Interface	390
		17.3.7	Other Commands	390
		17.3.8	Relation to the Socket Interface	391
		17.3.9	Blocking and Nonblocking Calls	391
	17.4	The TCP Socket Programming Interface		392
		17.4.1	TCP Server Model	392
		17.4.2	TCP Server Passive Open	393
		17.4.3	TCP Client Active OPEN	393
		17.4.4	Other Calls	394
		17.4.5	A TCP Server Program	395
		17.4.6	Calls Used in the TCP Server Program	399
		17.4.7	A TCP Client Program	402
		17.4.8	Calls Used in the TCP Client Program	403
		17.4.9	A Simpler Server	404
	17.5	The UDP Socket Programming Interface		407
		17.5.1	A UDP Server Program	407
		17.5.2	Calls Used in the UDP Server Program	409
		17.5.3	A UDP Client Program	410
		17.5.4	Calls used in the UDP Client Program	412
	17.6	Recommended Reading		412

Appendix A. Abbreviations and Acronyms 413

Appendix B. RFCs and Other NIC Documents 419

Appendix C. Dialogues 435

Appendix D. Review of Commands	441
Glossary	443
Bibliography	453
Index	457

Preface

This book provides a general introduction to TCP/IP. It also contains a body of specific reference information for those who will continue to use or support TCP/IP. The book is intended to be a practical guide to TCP/IP, and contains detailed information on how to get started on a real network — how to tie together existing local and wide area networks, how to choose system names, who to call to get network addresses, where to get advice on administration and security, and what to expect from current TCP/IP products.

The book is intended for those who need to learn about TCP/IP, either as planners, network managers, network administrators, software developers, technical support, or as end-users who like to understand their operating environment.

This book explains TCP/IP terminology, concepts, and mechanisms. It describes the standards that define the TCP/IP protocol suite. It contains interactive online dialogues that show how to use TCP/IP applications, how to peek at what is going on in the background, and how to check up on the health of network resources. For those who need a truly detailed level of understanding, there are traces that show the byte-by-byte structure of network messages and the interactive flow of these messages. Finally, the standard socket programming interface is explained, and several sample client/server programs are included.

Looking to the future, Open Systems Interconnect (OSI) features are discussed and similarities and differences with the TCP/IP suite are pointed out. The book deals with migration issues, but also points out reasons to expect that TCP/IP will be the prevalent communications protocol suite for a long time to come.

This book was written after performing months of on-the-road TCP/IP seminar training, and the author has attempted to include answers to most of the questions that attendees asked, and to explain the issues that seemed to concern people most.

Sidnie M. Feit

Acknowledgments

I would like to thank the Yale University mathematics department for their invitation to spend a term as visiting faculty. The opportunity to use the diverse computer systems on the Yale computer network and to study their documentation has been invaluable. H. Morrow Long, Manager of Development for the Yale Computer Science department, and Edward Anselmo, Senior Software Systems Programmer for the Yale Computer Science department, have pointed me toward a wealth of interesting information, and provided helpful insights into what works and what does not.

Gary C. Kessler reviewed the draft for this book, and made many comments that improved its completeness, usefulness, and readability. Edward Anselmo contributed many helpful suggestions and corrections. Jay Ranade, editor of this series, always has offered positive encouragement and has maintained his patience as both this book and our production schedule lengthened beyond our original plan.

Many vendors contributed product and technical information. Karen Anderson and her colleagues at Network General provided product information and many megabytes of protocol traces. Paula Burke of FTP Software, Inc. contributed software and documentation for their DOS product set. Vendors including Cisco Systems, Vitalink, Ungermann-Bass, and Retix, among others, answered questions diligently, and responded quickly with product information.

TCP/IP

Introduction

I.1 BACKGROUND

In the early days of computing, hosts exchanged information with directly attached devices, such as card readers and printers. Interactive use of computers first required local and then remote attachment of end-user terminals. When an organization had acquired several computers, often there would be a need to transfer data between computers or to allow users attached to one computer to access another computer.

Computer vendors responded to these requirements by developing communications hardware and software. Unfortunately, this hardware and software:

- Was proprietary, and worked only with the vendor's equipment.
- Supported only a limited number of local and wide area network types.
- Sometimes was extremely complex, requiring different software dialects for each device and each application.
- Lacked the flexibility that would enable previously independent networks to be connected to each other easily and inexpensively.

In the 1990's, connectivity needs have become urgent. Organizations need to combine desktop workstations, servers, and hosts into Local Area Network (LAN) communities. They want to connect LANs to other LANs and to Wide Area Networks (WANs). They wish to enable any pair of systems to communicate when they need to, without regard for where they may be located in the network. They also wish to take advantage of new, cost-effective network technologies as quickly as possible.

These requirements are similar to those set forth in the 1970's by the United States Defense Advanced Research Projects Agency, or DARPA. TCP/IP was shaped by these needs, and evolved under DARPA sponsorship.

From the start, it was intended that TCP/IP would be the basis for several important generic services:

- Terminal access to any host.
- The ability to copy files from one host to another.
- Electronic mail between any pair of users.

Many useful facilities have been added to the TCP/IP suite since then. For example:

- The ability to discover the physical addresses of nodes on a LAN.
- Directory services for mapping user-friendly host names to network addresses.
- Transparent access to remote files as if they are local.
- Network Management for hosts, routers, and other network devices.
- X Windows for concurrent access to applications running on multiple hosts.

The TCP/IP family is alive, well, and growing. Its user community is expanding at an almost explosive rate, and new services are being developed and modularly integrated into TCP/IP product offerings. TCP/IP is an integral part of the *Distributed Computing Environment* that has been defined by the Open Software Foundation.

Concurrently, the International Organization for Standardization (ISO) has been engaged in specifying standards for Open Systems Interconnect (OSI). The OSI layered model for communications is known to virtually every networking professional. In this text we shall introduce and discuss the OSI counterpart for each TCP/IP service.

1.2 TERMINOLOGY

Like many technical disciplines, data communications has a language all its own. Everyone in the field uses the same vocabulary. The only problem is that groups within the profession use the same words to mean different things, and different words to mean the same thing!

We have made an effort to select a fairly simple vocabulary and use it consistently within this text. Some of the options and choices are discussed in the sections that follow.

The glossary at the end of this book contains definitions of the technical terms that are used in the text. Acronyms and abbreviations are expanded in Appendix A.

I.2.1 Bytes and Octets

Most of us use the word *byte* to mean an 8-bit quantity. However, byte also has been used to mean the smallest addressable unit in a computer, and at one time or another, computer designers have produced machines with all sorts of byte sizes.

OSI standards writers have finessed the problem by using the term *octet* to mean an 8-bit quantity. In this text, we will use octet and byte interchangeably, and will use the term *logical byte* when the size of an addressable unit in a computer is other than eight bits.

I.2.2 Big Endians and Little Endians

Some computers store data with the most significant byte first. This is called the *Big Endian* style of data representation. Some computers store data with the least significant byte first, in a *Little Endian* style.

Similarly, there are Big Endian data communications standards that represent transmitted data with the most significant bit and byte first. Internet protocol standards writers are Big Endians. However, keep in mind that there are other groups that represent transmitted data with the least significant bit and byte first.

I.2.3 Protocols, Stacks, and Suites

A *protocol* is a set of rules governing the operation of some communications function. For example, IP consists of a set of rules for routing data, and TCP includes rules for reliable, in-sequence delivery of data.

A *protocol stack* is a layered set of protocols that work together to provide communication between applications. For example, TCP, IP, and Ethernet make up a protocol stack.

A *protocol suite* is a family of protocols that work together in a consistent fashion. The TCP/IP protocol suite encompasses a large number of functions, ranging from dynamic discovery of the physical address on a network interface board to a directory service that reveals how electronic mail should be routed.

I.2.4 Hosts, Routers, and Others

A *host* is a computer with one or more users. A host that supports TCP/IP can act as the endpoint of a communication. Note that PCs, workstations, minicomputers, and mainframes all satisfy the definition of host, and all can run TCP/IP!

The text also uses the terms station, computer, and computer system synonymously with host.

A *router* routes data through a network. Back in the early days,

4 Introduction

TCP/IP standards writers adopted the word *gateway* for what the commercial marketplace now calls a router. Elsewhere in the communications world, the term gateway came to mean a system that performs some kind of protocol translation.

We have chosen to use the term router throughout this book. However, if you go back and read TCP/IP standards documents, keep in mind that they frequently use the term gateway.

Finally, *node* or *network element* will be used to refer to a communicating entity in the network without specifying whether it is a host, a router, or another device, such as a bridge. For example:

> "The goal of network management is to control and monitor all of the nodes in a network."

I.2.5 Notational Conventions

There are many interactive dialogues in this text. They were generated on a Sun Microsystems computer running SunOS Release 4.1.1. TCP/IP has been implemented with very similar user interfaces and command sets across many types of computers. Hence, the dialogues are close to or identical to what you will experience across a wide range of systems. In the dialogues, end-user input is represented in **bold** text, while computer prompts and responses appear without emphasis.

Several chapters describe the formal interactions between protocol layers, showing the commands and parameters that are passed back and forth. Formal commands will be printed in capital letters. Optional parameters will be placed within brackets, [].

I.3 REFERENCES

Like many works whose subject is data communications, this book is peppered with acronyms. Appendix A contains a list of acronyms and their translations. A separate Glossary contains full definitions.

Appendix B includes an extensive list of documents that define TCP/IP and related facilities. Appendix C contains detailed dialogues showing how users with online or electronic mail access to the Internet can obtain free information. Chapter 1 contains information about gaining access to Internet resources.

Appendix D describes commands that frequently are part of a TCP/IP product.

Chapter 1

TCP/IP: What It Is and Where It Came From

1.1 INTRODUCTION

In the late 1960s, the Advanced Research Projects Agency of the U.S. Department of Defense, or ARPA (later changed to "DARPA") began a partnership with U.S. universities and other research organizations to investigate new data communications technologies.

Together, the participants built ARPANET, the first packet switching network. An experimental four-node version of the ARPANET went into operation in 1969. The experiment was a success, and the testbed facility evolved into a network spanning the United States from coast to coast. In 1975, the Defense Communications Agency (DCA) assumed responsibility for operating the network, which still was considered a research network.

1.1.1 The Birth of TCP/IP

The early ARPANET protocols were slow and subject to frequent network crashes. By 1974, the design for a new set of core protocols was proposed in a paper by Vinton G. Cerf and Robert E. Kahn.[1]

The Cerf/Kahn design provided the basis for the subsequent development of the Internet Protocol (IP) and Transmission Control Protocol (TCP). It took three years to convert the ARPANET hosts, then numbering over one hundred, to the new protocol suite.

The versatility of the new protocols was illustrated in a 1978 demonstration in which a terminal in a mobile van driving along California's

---

[1] *A Protocol for Packet Network Interconnections*, IEEE Transactions of Communications, May 1974.

6   Chapter One

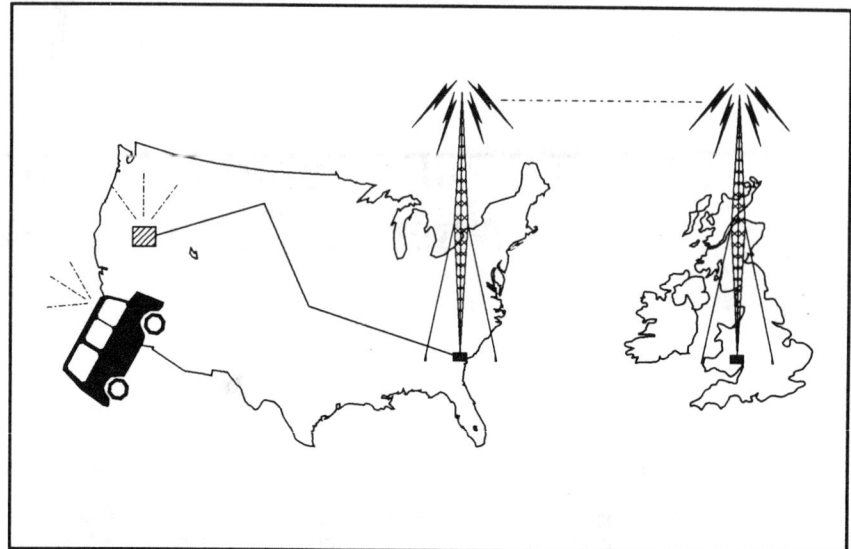

Figure 1.1 Demonstration of TCP/IP across a mixture of technologies.

Highway 101 transmitted data via packet radio to a node at SRI International, across the continent via ARPANET, and then over a satellite network to login to a host in London (see Figure 1.1).

By 1983, the ARPANET included over three hundred computers, and had become an invaluable resource to its users. In 1984, the original ARPANET was split into two pieces. One, still called ARPANET, was dedicated to research and development. The other, called MILNET, was an unclassified military network. The original ARPANET finally was dissolved in 1990.

1.1.2 TCP/IP Characteristics

TCP/IP has some unique characteristics that account for its durability. The TCP/IP architecture glues clusters of networks together, creating a larger network called an internet. To a user, an internet simply appears to be a single network, composed of all of the hosts connected to any of the constituent networks.

The TCP/IP protocols were designed to be independent of host hardware or operating system, as well as media and data link technologies. The protocols were required to be robust, surviving high network error rates and supporting transparent adaptive routing in case network nodes or lines were lost.

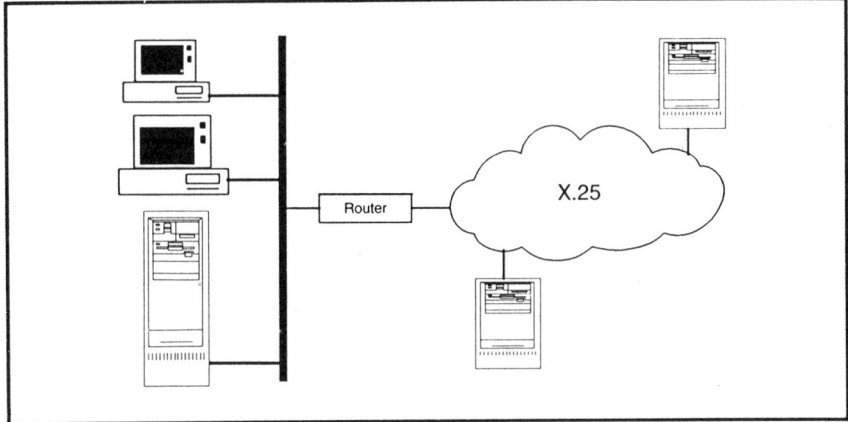

Figure 1.2 TCP/IP multivendor and multinetwork environment.

1.1.3 Acceptance of the Protocols

In 1982, the U.S. Department of Defense issued a policy statement adopting a single set of communications protocols based on the ARPANET protocols, and created the Defense Data Network (DDN) as the parent entity uniting its distributed operational networks.

In 1983, the Department of Defense adopted the TCP/IP protocol suite as its standard. Acceptance of TCP/IP spread to other government departments, creating a large market for the technology.

1.1.4 Availability of TCP/IP

When the TCP/IP protocols became a requirement in computer procurements by the U.S. Department of Defense and other government agencies, vendors needed to implement TCP/IP in order to compete in government bids. Figure 1.2 illustrates how different systems, local area networks, and wide area networks can be combined in a TCP/IP environment.

The U.S. Department of Defense encouraged the availability of TCP/IP by funding Bolt, Beranek, and Newman (BBN) to implement TCP/IP for UNIX, and the University of California at Berkeley to incorporate the BBN code into the Berkeley Software Distribution (BSD) 4.2 UNIX operating system. This operating system and its successor, BSD 4.3, have been migrated to many hardware bases. Later, TCP/IP was added to AT&T's System V UNIX.

Recently, TCP/IP has moved into the commercial world. It is the most universally available networking software for the multivendor environment. There is support for TCP/IP over an ever increasing selection of transmission technologies. We will explore a number of these technologies in Chapter 4.

1.2 THE INTERNET

The ease of gluing TCP/IP networks together combined with an open door policy that allowed academic and commercial research networks to connect to the ARPANET spawned a new supernetwork called the Internet.[2] Throughout the 1980s, the ARPANET was maintained as a backbone of this flourishing network.

Because of the characteristics of the TCP/IP protocols, Internet growth was steady and non-disruptive. The Internet became the world's largest network, comprising substantial government, military research, academic, and commercial networks, each containing hundreds of subnetworks. In the late 1980s, a new backbone net, the National Science Foundation Net (NSFNET), was incorporated to accommodate high speed links to research sites and supercomputer facilities.

A plan already is in place for the next generation of the Internet. The proposed National Research and Education Network (NREN) will be a testbed for new information services running over high-speed, high-capacity networks.

Although the Internet long ago grew far beyond the scope of being a military research network, the Department of Defense retains an important coordination role. Currently, the Defense Information Systems Agency (DISA) is responsible for determining the official DDN protocols, architecture, policy guidelines, management strategies, and operations procedures. The DDN Network Information Center (DDN NIC) provides services to users, host administrators, site coordinators, and network managers.

The Internet continues to be a testbed for new technology. Its mail, news, and bulletin board services provide a public forum in which ideas are debated and refined. Researchers, systems programmers, and network administrators exchange software bug corrections, solutions to interworking problems, and hints for improving performance.

1.2.1 The Internet Architecture Board

Development of new TCP/IP protocols and maintenance of old protocols is coordinated by an independent organization called the Internet

---

[2]While an internet, with a small "i," is any network created by joining two or more TCP/IP nets, the Internet is a specific network.

Architecture Board (IAB), formerly known as the Internet Activities Board. The IAB identifies technical areas that need study. For example, in recent years, the IAB has spearheaded efforts to develop new network management protocols and more functional routing protocols.

The IAB oversees two important bodies. The Internet Research Task Force (IRTF) establishes working groups for long term research. The Internet Engineering Task Force (IETF) handles immediate needs. Activities of the IETF working groups are coordinated by the Internet Engineering Steering Group (IESG).

1.2.2 Task Forces and Protocol Development

Task Force members are research volunteers. To tackle a specific problem, a working group whose members have appropriate technical expertise is formed. Participants in a working group use a methodology that combines theory with immediate implementation.

In fact, a group usually tests the validity and completeness of a protocol specification by creating at least two independent implementations. An iterative *design-implement-experiment-review* process is used to evolve and enhance protocols, and to improve the performance of the implementations.

This practical, hands-on approach to protocol development uncovers many flaws and oversights before a protocol is adopted. Features that make impossible demands on system resources or cause very poor performance can be prevented from being incorporated into a protocol's architecture.

1.2.3 Other Sources of Internet Protocols

Although many of the protocols in the TCP/IP suite were designed and implemented by IAB-sponsored working groups, university research groups and commercial organizations also have made significant contributions. To be accepted, contributions must have been implemented and shown to be useful and usable.

Source code for new protocols often is placed in public databases on the Internet. Vendors can use this code as the starting point for new products. This has many benefits. Product development is rapid and less costly. Starting from a common source framework promotes interoperability.

Users also may copy and install public code on their own systems. Of course, when using free code, users lose the benefit of the support and maintenance services provided by a vendor.

1.2.4 TCP/IP and the Distributed Computing Environment

The Open Software Foundation (OSF) is a consortium of computer vendors. The goal of the OSF is to build technologies that enable systems and applications to interwork across local and wide area networks. The TCP/IP protocol suite is an integral part of the OSF/1 operating system.

The OSF Distributed Computing Environment (DCE) defines operating system elements, application programming interfaces, and tools that support distributed client/server computing and access to distributed data. The current OSF DCE is built on top of TCP/IP, and many DCE features are based on the TCP/IP protocol suite.

1.3 REQUESTS FOR COMMENTS

After a new protocol has been proved to be useful and implementable, it is circulated in a document called a Request For Comments (RFC). RFC documents are numbered in sequence. Currently, more than 1300 of these documents have been defined.

Users can obtain RFC documents from the DDN NIC (see Section 1.3.4). Copies of RFC documents have been stored at many public computer directories at sites all around the world, and may be copied from any one of these sites by means of electronic file transfer.

Sometimes protocol specifications are updated to correct errors, improve performance, or add new features. Updated protocols are published with new RFC numbers.

The NIC maintains an index of RFCs, and entries for obsoleted RFCs contain the number(s) of the superseding documents. For example, the index entry below announces that RFC 1098 obsoletes the original Simple Network Management Protocol standard, and has itself been obsoleted by a later document, RFC 1157.

> 1098 Case, J.D.; Fedor, M.; Schoffstall, M.L.; Davin, C.
> Simple Network Management Protocol (SNMP). 1989 April; 34 p.
> (Format: TXT=71563 bytes) (Obsoletes RFC 1067; Obsoleted by RFC 1157)

Not all RFCs describe protocols. Some just organize and present insights that have evolved within the Internet community. For example, there is an RFC that gives advice on selecting names for computers. Other RFCs provide guidance on how to administer a TCP/IP network and how to implement security procedures. There are RFCs that suggest implementation strategies for better performance, describe experimental algorithms, and discuss ethics on the Internet.

1.3.1 State and Status of Standards

The NIC provides information on the progress of protocols as they move through several *states*:

- Experimental
- Proposed
- Draft
- Standard

Some protocols are required standards, while others are used where there is some special need. Some have outlived their usefulness and have been retired. The formal *status* of a protocol is defined by one of the levels:

- Required
- Recommended
- Elective
- Limited use
- Not recommended

The current state and status of Internet protocols is described in an RFC called *IAB Official Protocol Standards*. This document is updated periodically and released with a new RFC number.[3]

1.3.2 Assigned Numbers

Network parameters, special network addresses, service names, and standard identifiers for terminals and computer systems are listed in an RFC called *Assigned Numbers*.[4]

The Internet Assigned Numbers are managed by an administrator called the Internet Assigned Numbers Authority (IANA), currently located at the USC Information Services Institute.

The Assigned Numbers RFC includes an address, telephone number, and electronic mail address that protocol and application developers can use in order to register parameter information with this authority.

---

[3] At the time of writing, the current release of this document was RFC 1250.

[4] At the time of writing, this was RFC 1340.

1.3.3 RFCs That Promote Multivendor Interworking

The expectation that users would have needs that could not be met by a single computer architecture was a strong motivation for adoption of the TCP/IP communications standards by U.S. government organizations. These groups wanted to be able to purchase equipment in a competitive market, with several vendors able to satisfy requirements. They believed that the effort to establish and maintain standards would be repaid in lower costs and better service.

However, there are problems that can arise in a multivendor environment:

- Every standard includes optional features. By implementing different options, vendors can make interoperability very difficult.
- Vendors sometimes misunderstand the standards, and their products operate incorrectly.
- There are mistakes in standards.
- Some implementations, although fairly accurate, are inflexible, and don't allow a system administrator to tune configuration parameters to improve performance.
- A single system that uses poorly designed algorithms for pacing data transmission and retransmission can degrade performance for all of the systems on a network.

Two RFCs published in October of 1989 address many of these problems, correcting errors, clarifying definitions, specifying option support, listing configuration parameters, and identifying high performance algorithms. Most importantly, these RFCs state specific conformance requirements. This has been a major deficiency in the past. Correct operation, interworking capability, and performance are greatly improved by adherence to these RFCs, which are:

- *RFC 1122, Requirements for Internet Hosts — Communication Layers.* This document deals with link layer, IP, and TCP issues.
- *RFC 1123, Requirements for Internet Hosts — Application and Support.* This document covers remote login, file transfer, electronic mail, and various support services.

An RFC published in 1987 deals with equally important issues relating to the operation of routers:

- *RFC 1009, Requirements for Internet Gateways.* This document provides guidelines for the implementation of IP routers.

1.3.4 Related Documents

A series of RFCs that do not contain protocol specifications also were published as a separate set of For Your Information (FYI) documents. For example, RFC 1206 is an FYI: *Answers to commonly asked "new Internet user" questions.*

Another series, the Internet Engineering Notes (IEN) contains a set of discussion papers written in the early years of Internet protocol development.

1.4 FUNCTIONS OF THE NIC

The DDN Network Information Center (NIC) collects and distributes information about protocols. Users can request documents by telephone, U.S. postal mail, or electronic mail. The NIC also maintains a public database of documents that can be obtained by electronic file transfer.

The NIC is responsible for administering the assignment of names to networks and hosts, and for distributing blocks of network addresses to organizations. By registering with the NIC a company can be assured that their naming and addressing plan is globally unique and consistent.

Companies and individuals can join the Internet. There are several commercial services that provide access for anyone who wants to connect. The Network Information Center maintains a list of these services.

Formerly all NIC services were located at SRI International in Menlo Park, California. Late in 1991, Government Systems, Inc. took over responsibility for providing user services. The current NIC postal address is:

DDN Network Information Center
14200 Park Meadow Drive
Suite 200
Chantilly, VA 22021

The Government Systems NIC can be reached at an 800 number on Monday through Friday, 7 AM to 7 PM, Eastern Standard Time:

1-800-365-3642

There also is an international telephone number for the NIC:

1-703-802-4535

1.4.1 Online Information

For users with an Internet connection, online information is available at host NIC.DDN.MIL.[5] Online information can be obtained by file transfer or via mail. Chapter 11 of this book contains a detailed explanation of Internet file transfer. Appendix C contains a dialogue that demonstrates how you can copy files from the NIC. It also contains instructions on obtaining files by means of electronic mail.

The NIC distributes a free brochure listing NIC publications, online services, and online files. This information can be found online in file */netinfo/what-the-nic-does.txt.* An overview of NIC publications is stored in */netinfo/nic-pubs.txt.* An comprehensive index of RFCs is stored in */netinfo/rfc-index.txt.* The RFCs are online in directory */rfc.*[6]

There is a document listing TCP/IP-related products called the *DDN Protocol Implementations and Vendors Guide.* This is online in a large file called */netinfo/vendors-guide.doc.*

The NIC supports a number of online information services:

- A distributed database for translating host names to network addresses
- A database of Internet user names, addresses, and mail identifiers
- An online query database and a Defense Data Network news service

The query database is accessed by means of interactive login. See Chapter 13 for details on logging in using the TCP/IP Telnet service.

The NIC also acts as a clearinghouse for reporting and dealing with security incidents. Security bulletins are published online in the */scc* directory. The NIC's 800 number is used to report MILNET security-related incidents.

1.5 OTHER INFORMATION RESOURCES

There are many public file systems located at universities, research institutes, and commercial organizations attached to the Internet. These systems offer a variety of information, such as copies of RFCs, papers discussing new algorithms, performance test results, and source code for protocols and network management tools. Any Internet user whose host supports TCP/IP file transfer can copy documents or source code from these sites.

---

[5] Currently this is a UNIX host.
[6] See Appendix B for more details.

Some networks are connected to the Internet by means of electronic mail gateways. Users at hosts on these networks cannot perform file transfer. Fortunately, many public file systems also support an electronic mail document distribution service.

There are several useful database services on the Internet. For example, the Archie Archive Server Listing Service supported by the School of Computer Science at McGill University helps users to find software and documents on the Internet.

Appendix C contains information on how to locate and use the public Internet information archives and database facilities.

1.6 OPEN SYSTEMS INTERCONNECTION

Open Systems Interconnection (OSI) is an international effort to create standards for computer communications and generic application services. OSI is an activity of the International Organization for Standardization (ISO), founded to promote trade and cooperative advances in science and technology. Standards promoting OSI are published as ISO documents.

The TCP/IP protocol suite strongly influenced several of the OSI standards. OSI standards-makers added many new features to the communications protocols, and enhanced the functionality of the network applications. The United States government has mandated eventual migration to OSI. The United States Government OSI Profile (GOSIP) specification details the OSI protocols that are to be requested in government procurements.

August, 1990, was targeted as the time that United States government agencies would begin to integrate OSI into their networks. The migration is expected to take a long time. The OSI protocols are far more complex than the TCP/IP protocols. At this time, OSI protocol documents are costly to obtain, and the free flow of information that characterizes TCP/IP protocol development is missing from the OSI world.

OSI protocols are designed first, and implemented later. Computer vendors have discovered that implementing OSI and executing the tests that are needed to assure multivendor interworking is a time-consuming and costly undertaking. However, an interesting approach to OSI migration is provided by the ISO Development Environment (ISODE). ISODE software enables OSI applications to run on top of TCP/IP communications. True to the Internet spirit, ISODE software is freely available via file transfer from an Internet host.

Chapter

2

TCP/IP Suite Service Overview

2.1 INTRODUCTION

Why is the TCP/IP protocol family so widely used? Its ability to glue heterogeneous local and wide-area networks together makes it a capable integrator. Equally important, it provides the foundation for peer-to-peer communications, and then goes on to build generic services on top of this foundation.

2.2 APPLICATION-TO-APPLICATION COMMUNICATION

There are two styles of application-to-application interaction. *Connection-oriented* communication is appropriate when the applications need a sustained interchange of streams of data. In contrast, applications engaged in *connectionless* communication exchange standalone messages. This style is well suited to interactions that are sporadic and involve small amounts of data.

2.2.1 Connection-oriented Communication

The TCP in TCP/IP stands for *Transmission Control Protocol*, which provides reliable, connection-oriented, peer-to-peer communications. Terminal login sessions and file transfers are carried over TCP.

2.2.2 Connectionless Communication

Some data exchanges do not require a continuous interaction. For example, suppose that a database at a network server contains a table of names of company personnel and their telephone numbers. A telephone number might be looked up by sending a request message containing a person's name to the server. The server would respond with a message containing the matching telephone number. The User Datagram Protocol (UDP) supports this type of interaction.

2.2.3 Socket Programming Interface

Systems that implement TCP/IP usually provide a programming interface for peer-to-peer communications. Most of these closely imitate the *socket programming interface*, first defined for the Berkeley UNIX operating systems.

The socket programming interface includes simple subroutine calls that create, transmit, and receive the standalone messages used in connectionless communication. For connection-oriented interactions, there is a set of library routines that set up the connection, send and receive data, and close the connection.

2.2.4 Remote Procedure Call Programming Interface

Although not as prevalent as the socket programming interface, there is fairly wide availability of a programming interface for *Remote Procedure Call* (RPC) client/server interactions.[1]

A client using an RPC interface invokes a subroutine call that automatically causes a request to be sent to a server. The server carries out the real work of the subroutine and then returns the subroutine's output parameters to the client. This scenario is appropriately named a *Remote Procedure Call* because a locally invoked procedure is executed at a remote system.

For example, the telephone number lookup application described in Section 2.2.2 could be written using Remote Procedure Call routines.

2.3 BASIC SERVICES

Implementations of TCP/IP are expected to provide at least three basic services: file transfer, remote login, and electronic mail. It also has become routine to offer a remote printing service.

---

[1]The Remote Procedure Call interface introduced by Sun Microsystems has been ported to a very large number of platforms. The Open Software Foundation offers an alternative RPC programming interface with its Distributed Computing Environment. Additional RPC toolkits are offered by vendors such as NetWise.

2.3.1 File Transfer

File transfer was among the earliest services added to TCP/IP. The File Transfer Protocol (FTP) enables users to copy entire files from one system to another. FTP deals with simple types of files such as ASCII text or a sequence of binary data records. FTP also lets a user access a remote file system to perform housekeeping functions such as renaming files, deleting files or creating new directories.

2.3.2 Terminal Access

In the early 1970s, most computer vendors built proprietary terminals that could be used only with their own computer systems. The U.S. Department of Defense purchased systems from many different vendors, but wanted every user to be able to connect to any host on their network from a single terminal. The *Telnet* virtual terminal protocol was created to make this possible. Over the years Telnet has been enhanced to work with a large assortment of terminal displays and operating system types.

2.3.3 Mail

Mail has attracted many end users to TCP/IP. Two aspects of mail need to be standardized. An Internet text message protocol defines the format of the memos passed between users. Another protocol, the Simple Mail Transfer Protocol (SMTP), defines the mechanisms needed for direct or store-and-forward transfer of mail between hosts. One facet of mail that is deliberately *not* standardized is the user interface.

Many proprietary mail systems have been linked to Internet mail, enlarging the community of potential mail partners. Figure 2.1 illustrates interactions between hosts on a network.

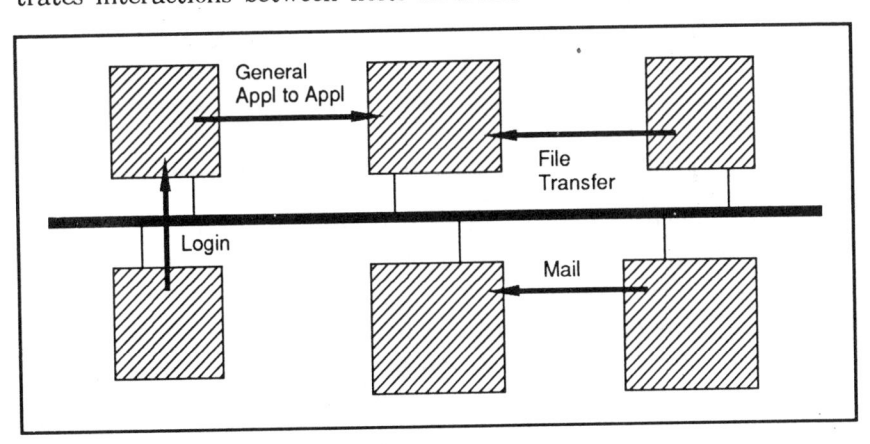

Figure 2.1 Basic services on a network.

2.4 ADDITIONAL SERVICES

Many other services have been added to the TCP/IP suite. The sections that follow describe those that are most popular and widely available.

2.4.1 File Access

File servers let users access remote files as if they are local. File servers first became popular in personal computer Local Area Network (LAN) environments as a means to share valuable disk resources and centralize maintenance and backup chores.

Many TCP/IP product families support the Network File System (NFS). The products provide one or both of the NFS roles:

- *File access client:* Lets a computer access remote files as if they are local. End users and local programs will be unaware of the actual location of these files.

- *File server:* Maintains directories at a server that can be accessed by specified computers on a network.

2.4.2 Domain Name System Name Service

In order to use any network service, you must be able to identify remote computers. Users and programs can identify a computer by a name that is easy to remember and easy to type.

To set up communication with a host, its name must be translated to a numeric address. Originally, each TCP/IP host kept a complete list of all of the names and addresses of all hosts on its network. It was impossible to keep these lists up to date on a dynamically growing network like the Internet, which contained hundreds — and later hundreds of thousands — of hosts.

The Domain Name System (DNS) was invented to solve this problem. DNS consists of a database of host names and addresses distributed across a set of servers. DNS protocols enable users to submit database queries and receive database responses.

There are products that provide one or both of the DNS roles:

- *System name to network address translation client:* Allows end users and programs to look up host names and obtain their network addresses.

- *System name to network address translation server:* Maintains the address translation database and responds to clients' queries.

In addition to host names and addresses, DNS servers also offer information about electronic mail routing and descriptions of host CPU and operating system types.

2.4.3 Commercial Software

Many third party vendors have built applications that run on top of TCP/IP. For example, database vendors link desktop clients to their servers by means of TCP/IP. There is a NETBIOS interface to TCP/IP, enabling many existing LAN applications to operate in this environment.

2.4.4 Network Management

Over the years, many network management tools have been developed for use with the TCP/IP protocol suite. For example, there are commands that enable a network manager to check if systems are active, view their current load, list logged-in users, and list services that are available.

These commands are very useful, but a lot more is needed to provide a consistent and comprehensive platform for centralized network management. The Internet community recently focused intense energy on the task of network management protocol development. There were several goals: to produce a simple standard that could be implemented rapidly, to encourage rapid evolutionary growth, and to create a framework that would ease migration to OSI network management.

The result was the Simple Network Management Protocol (SNMP). SNMP was designed to be both useful and easy to implement, and was brought to market in record time.

Products may embody one or both of the SNMP roles:

- *Network management agent:* Equips a system to record and report status and performance information. An agent also updates configuration information in response to direction from a remote manager.

- *Network manager:* Enables a system to monitor and configure network management agents at distributed systems.

2.5 DIALOGUES

The best way to become acquainted with TCP/IP services is to use them. We close this chapter with a few brief interactive dialogues that illustrate what some of these services are like. In all of the dialogues, the text entered by the user is displayed in bold face. This convention will be followed throughout the remainder of this book.

22   Chapter Two

The basic interactions are very simple.

Each service displays some messages as it does its work. End users ignore these most of the time. Later chapters will explain all of the mechanisms that underlie the services. We will discover that these messages are very informative when you want to know exactly what is going on!

2.5.1 Terminal Access Dialogue

Terminal access is the simplest service. Below we ask Telnet to connect us to a host named bulldog.[2] After a TCP connection has been set up, Telnet prints a reminder that the combination CONTROL-] is a *hot-key* that will take us back to the local login session. The remote host then prints its *login:* prompt. From that point on, the session becomes a normal interactive login at that host.

```
telnet bulldog
Trying 128.36.0.3 ...
Connected to bulldog.cs.yale.edu
Escape character is '^]'.

login:
```

Although this was a very simple dialogue, quite a lot was going on behind the scenes. Telnet looked up the host name, bulldog, in a Domain Name System database and found out that the system's full name is "bulldog.cs.yale.edu," and its address is 128.36.0.3. Telnet used this address to connect to the remote system.

The TCP/IP naming and numbering schemes will be explained in Chapter 5. However, we already can observe that names consist of several words separated by periods, and addresses consist of four numbers separated by periods.

2.5.2 Looking Up a Name in the Domain Name System Database

Like many TCP/IP systems, our host has a client application called *nslookup* (for "network server lookup") that lets a user query a Domain Name System database interactively.

Below, the name and address of the local default server is printed in response to an *nslookup* command. A database query is entered simply by typing the name of the host to be looked up. The response starts off by repeating the identity of the server that provided the

---

[2]Recall that user input is displayed in boldface.

answer. Keep in mind that this is a distributed database service, and there is a way for a user to switch to another server if the local one does not know the answer.

```
nslookup
Default Server:  DEPT-GW.CS.YALE.EDU
Address:  128.36.0.36

> bulldog
Server:  DEPT-GW.CS.YALE.EDU
Address:  128.36.0.36

Name:     bulldog.cs.yale.edu
Address:  128.36.0.3
```

2.5.3 File Transfer Dialogue

Next, we will use the File Transfer Protocol to copy a file named *chapter1* in directory *book* from a host named *golem* to the local host. Lines that start with numbers are messages from the file transfer server. The *cd* (change directory) command is used to change to directory *book* at the remote host. The *get* command is used to copy the file.

```
ftp golem
Connected to golem.cs.yale.edu.
220 golem FTP server (SunOS 4.1) ready.

Name : icarus
331: Password required for icarus

Password :
230 User icarus logged in.

ftp> cd book
250 CWD command successful.

ftp> get chapter1
200 PORT command successful.
150 ASCII data connection for chapter1 (130.132.23.16,3330) (32303 bytes).
226 ASCII Transfer complete.
32303 bytes received in 0.95 seconds (33 Kbytes/s)

ftp> quit
221 Goodbye.
```

2.5.4 File Access Dialogue

Let's look at one last dialogue. In this example, we are using a DOS PC which is attached to a TCP/IP network. We switch to device *d:* at our local host and list the contents of the root directory.

```
d:
d:\> dir
 Volume in drive D is SERVER
 Directory of   D:\

   .            <DIR>              10-25-90   8:03a
   ..           <DIR>              10-25-90   8:03a
 ALTB           WPM         711     2-18-89  12:53p
 EGA512         FRS        3584     9-16-88   3:57p
 WPRINT1        ABK      344392    11-05-9   13:28p
 README         WPD        5492     9-16-88   3:57p
 SPELL          EXE       40448     9-16-88   3:55p
 WP             EXE      252416    11-15-88   4:51p
 . . .
```

There is nothing about this that looks special — but that is the point! The files that appear to be on local device *d:* actually are read from a remote Network File System server.

Chapter 3

TCP/IP Architecture

3.1 INTRODUCTION

TCP/IP was designed for an environment that was quite unusual in the 1970s, but now is the norm. The TCP/IP protocols had to connect equipment from different vendors. They had to be capable of running over different types of media and data links. They had to unite sets of networks into a single *internet*,[1] all of whose users could access a set of generic services.

Furthermore, the academic, military, and government sponsors of TCP/IP wanted to be able to plug new networks into their internets without interruption of service to the rest of the network!

These requirements shaped the protocol architecture. The need for portability and independence of media technology made a layered structure attractive.

One layer was devoted to routing data. Inspired by the ARPANET's packet-switching model, the designers decided to move data across an internet by chopping it into pieces and routing each piece as an independent unit.

Another layer contained the functions that guaranteed reliable data transmission. These functions were placed only within source and destination hosts.

As it happens, the protocols turned out to scale well, running on systems ranging from mainframes to PCs. In fact, a useful subset that supports network management routinely is ported to "dumb" network devices such as bridges, multiplexers, and switches.

---

[1]Recall that an internet is a set of networks joined by one or more routers.

3.2 LAYERING

In order to achieve a reliable exchange of data between computers, there are many separate procedures that must be carried out:

- Format the data.
- Package the data.
- Determine the path that the data will follow.
- Regulate the rate of data transfer according to the available bandwidth and the capacity of the receiver to absorb data.
- Transmit the data on a physical medium.
- Assemble incoming data so that it is in sequence and there are no missing pieces.
- Check incoming data for duplicated pieces.
- Notify the sender of how much data has been received safely.
- Deliver data to the right application.
- Handle error or problem events.

The result is that communications software is complicated!

One motivation for following a layered model is to give communications software a structure that is rational, simple, and easy to modify.

The specific layering used for the TCP/IP protocols was dictated by requirements that evolved in the academic and defense communities. IP does what is needed to glue different types of networks into an internet. TCP provides reliable data transfer.

OSI layering subsequently was strongly influenced by the way that TCP/IP was organized. The OSI layering model and OSI terminology have become a standard part of the data communications culture.

Figure 3.1 shows the TCP/IP and OSI host layers. The bottom layers, depicted in the OSI model as the Physical and Data Link Layers, will be discussed in detail in Chapter 4. For convenience, we will refer to these layers as the *lower layers* within this text. Note that this differs from OSI terminology. OSI documents refer to layers 1 to 3 as lower layers.

Let us take a brief look what happens within each of the layers, starting from the bottom.

TCP/IP Architecture

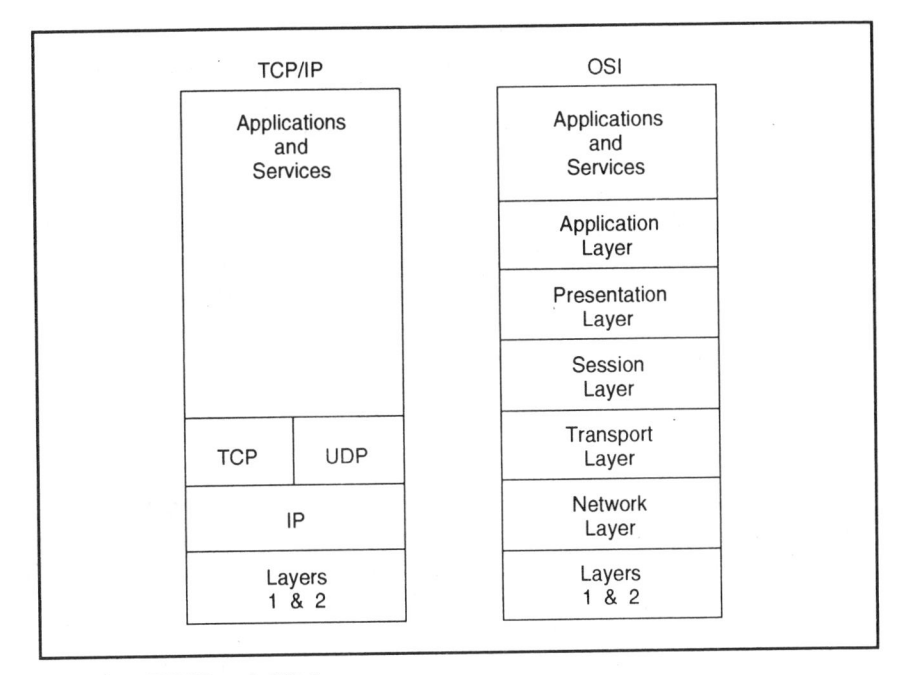

TCP/IP	OSI
Applications and Services	Applications and Services
	Application Layer
	Presentation Layer
	Session Layer
TCP | UDP	Transport Layer
IP	Network Layer
Layers 1 & 2	Layers 1 & 2

Figure 3.1 TCP/IP and OSI Layers.

3.2.1 Lower Layers (Layers 1 and 2)

The lower layers have to deal with the real world of device drivers, media access controls, physical attachments, and physical signals. They package data into units called *frames* or *packets* and send the data from an interface[2] on the local system to a destination interface attached to the same physical network. Local area networks (LANs) and wide area networks (WANs) provide these lower layer functions.

The boundary between IP and the lower layers is an important one. When a vendor implements this boundary well, then:

- A new type of network interface and medium for IP can be added to a computer without undue effort.

- IP can share a network interface and medium with other protocols. For example, both TCP/IP and DECnet traffic might share a single Ethernet interface.

---

[2]Examples of interfaces include Ethernet boards, Token-Ring boards, and serial line devices.

3.2.2 IP and OSI Network Layers (Layer 3)

The Internet Protocol (IP) layer routes data between hosts. The data may traverse a single network or may be relayed across several networks in an internet. Data is carried in units called *datagrams*.

The IP layer is called *connectionless* because every datagram is routed independently and IP does not guarantee reliable or in-sequence delivery of datagrams. IP routes its traffic without caring which application-to-application interaction a particular datagram belongs to.

The IP layer corresponds to OSI's network layer (layer 3). In fact, OSI provides a connectionless network service that closely resembles IP. OSI also defines a connection-oriented service at this layer. An X.25 connection is the prime example of this type of service.

3.2.3 TCP and OSI Transport Layers (Layer 4)

The Transmission Control Protocol (TCP) provides reliable data connection services to applications. TCP contains the mechanisms used to guarantee that data is error-free, complete, and in sequence.

TCP sends units called *segments* by passing them to IP, which routes them to the destination. TCP accepts incoming segments from IP, determines which application is the recipient, and passes data to that application in the order in which it was sent.

The connection-oriented OSI transport layer also guarantees reliable data transmission, but was not intended to interface directly with applications because there are other layers above it.

The higher OSI layers provide some interesting functions. The session layer sets up and terminates application-to-application communications. A pair of applications use session layer facilities to impose a structure on their conversation. For example, they may decide to take turns in sending data, or set synchronization points to establish that tasks have been completed. Applications use the presentation layer to negotiate a data transmission format that both partners can understand.

3.2.4 User Datagram Protocol (Layer 4)

Applications invoke the User Datagram Protocol (UDP) in order to send isolated messages to each other. UDP packages data into units called *User Datagrams* and passes them to IP for routing to a destination. UDP is a connectionless communication service that often is used for simple database lookups.

OSI has defined a specification for connectionless transport, but this has not been implemented in products.

3.2.5 Application Services

The TCP/IP protocol suite includes a set of standard application services including program-to-program communications, File Transfer Protocol (FTP), Simple Mail Transfer Protocol (SMTP), Telnet terminal access, and Domain Name System (DNS) directory services.

There are OSI versions of these services that offer enhancements of their TCP/IP counterparts. The OSI mail service in particular has very attractive features. However, OSI services are far more complex to build, support, maintain, and interconnect.

Most TCP/IP product families support Network File System (NFS) file servers and file clients, as well as a set of network functions that have been built using a facility called the *Remote Procedure Call* (RPC). Often these are optional features that require an additional license fee.

As a rule, products also include communications programming libraries that can be used by software developers. One of the standard programming libraries comprises the *socket programming interface*. The socket programming interface includes calls that enable applications to interact with TCP, UDP, or even directly with IP. Another library is used to write client/server applications based on the Remote Procedure Call facility.

3.3 PROTOCOL OVERVIEW

Figure 3.2 shows how parts of the TCP/IP protocol suite fit together.

Although the user interfaces for file transfer, terminal access, and Domain Name System name-to-address queries have not been formally standardized, most vendors offer command sets that copy the Berkeley Software Distribution UNIX end-user interfaces. Users who work with two or more types of hosts find it to be very helpful that the user interface stays pretty much the same as they move from system to system.

File transfer (FTP), mail (SMTP), and terminal access (Telnet) modules communicate with their peers via reliable TCP connections. Most NFS file servers exchange UDP messages with their clients, although there are a few NFS implementations that are built on top of TCP.

The Domain Name System (DNS) protocols provide TCP/IP network directory services. DNS servers carry out most of their transactions by means of UDP messages, but occasionally switch to TCP when larger amounts of data need to be moved.

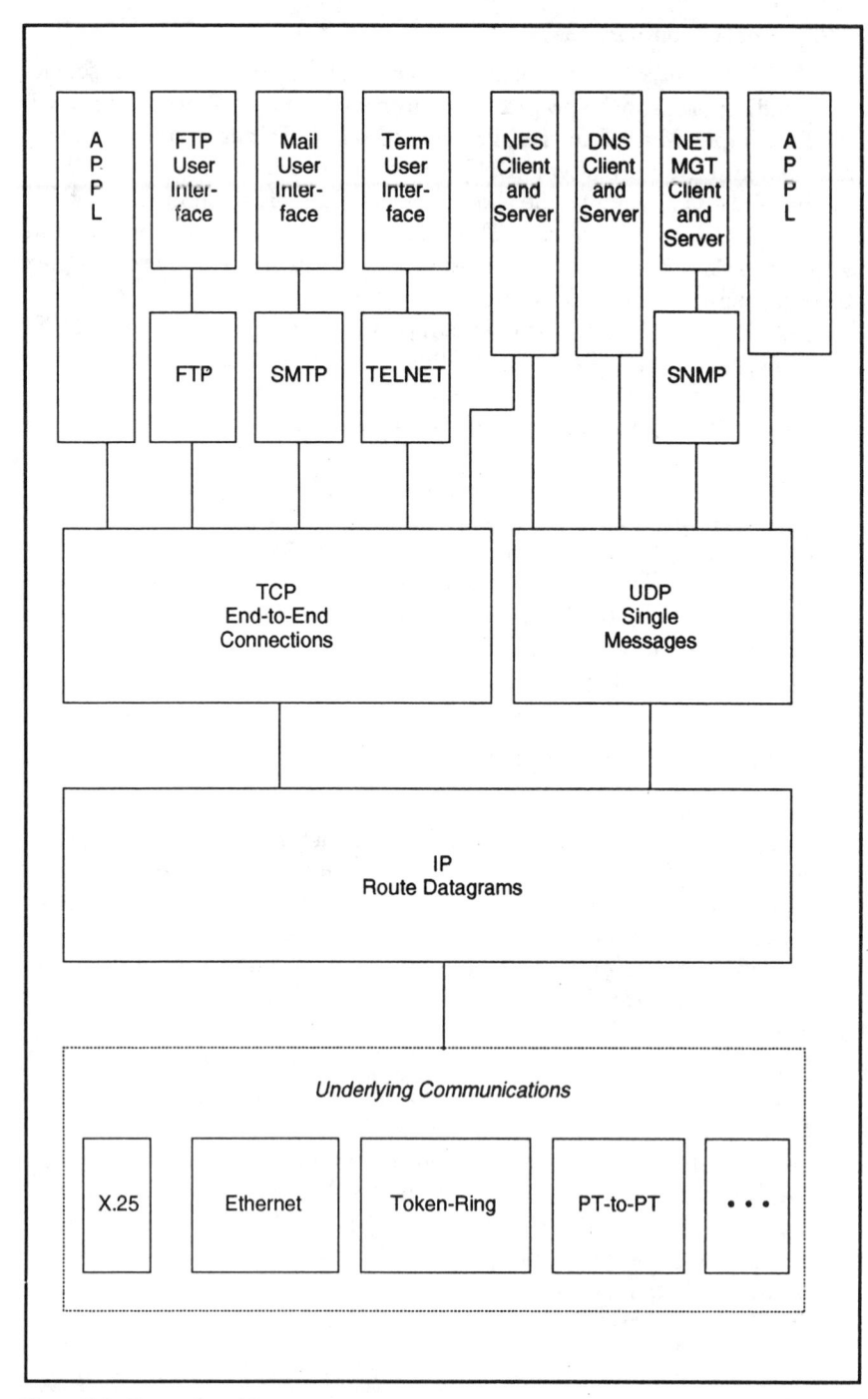

Figure 3.2 Protocol architecture overview.

3.4 TOPOLOGIES

The TCP/IP protocol suite can be used on standalone LANs and WANs or on complex internets created by gluing many networks together.

Figure 3.3 illustrates standalone networks. Any hosts that are equipped with TCP/IP can communicate with one another across a point-to-point line, local area network, or wide area network.

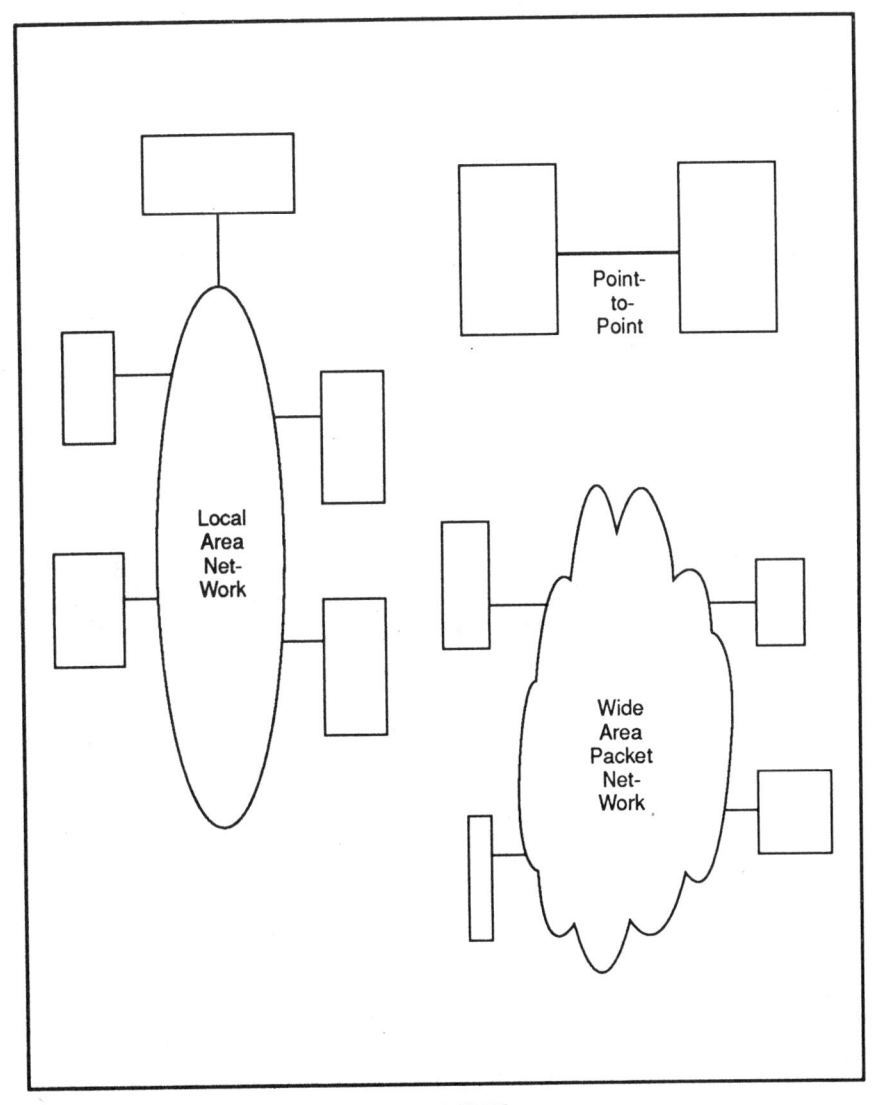

Figure 3.3 TCP/IP on standalone LANs and WANs.

32   Chapter Three

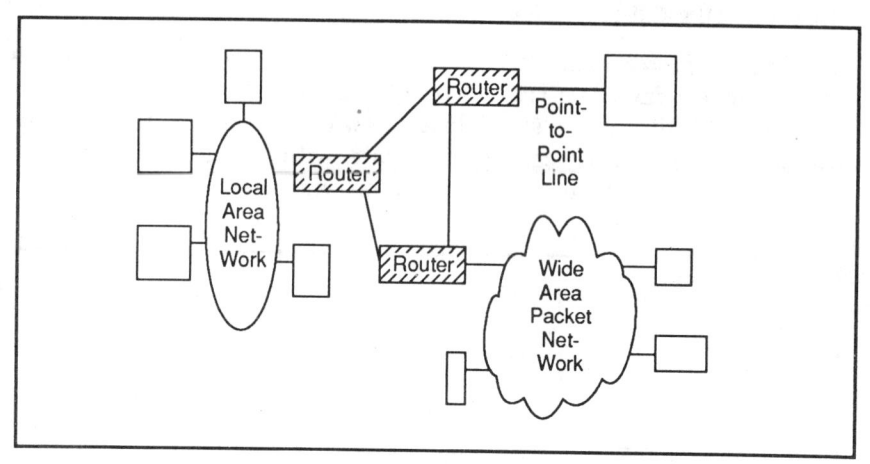

Figure 3.4 Creating an internet with IP routers.

Networks are joined into an *internet* by means of *IP routers*. Figure 3.4 illustrates an internet created using IP routers to link up a local area network, a wide area packet network, and a remote host system.

In addition to running IP software, routers typically employ a second protocol to exchange information with one another about the current status of their internet. Up-to-date knowledge helps routers to choose the best paths for datagrams to follow.

Traditionally, the Internet world has used the term *gateway* rather than IP router. RFC documents routinely use gateway in this manner. However, the data communications world has chosen the term gateway to refer to a system that performs protocol translation. In this book, we will follow the modern usage and use the term *router*. However, keep in mind that authors of much existing TCP/IP literature employ the term gateway!

The robust and competitive IP router market has helped to promote TCP/IP architecture. Router vendors are quick to implement new LAN and WAN technologies, widening their customers' connectivity options. The router price/performance ratio has decreased steadily over the past few years.

In theory, internets can have arbitrarily messy topologies. However, when an internet has a coherent structure, it is easier for routers to do their job efficiently and to react quickly to a failure in some part of the network, altering paths so that datagrams avoid a trouble-spot. An easy-to-understand logical design also helps network managers to diagnose, locate and repair network faults.

3.5 IP ARCHITECTURE

Internet Protocol software runs in hosts and in IP routers. In general, a computer's IP software will allow it to act as an IP host, an IP router, or both. Most organizations prefer to use specialized router equipment to join networks. However, it is convenient to be able to take an unused computer and press it into service as a router.

Figure 3.5 illustrates the protocol architecture of a dedicated router. There is no need for TCP, since application connections do not originate or terminate at the router.[3] A router is, of course, connected to at least two networks.

Modern router products are equipped with multiple interface hardware slots that can be configured with the combination of attachments that the customer needs: Ethernet, Token Ring, point-to-point synchronous, fiber optic, or whatever.

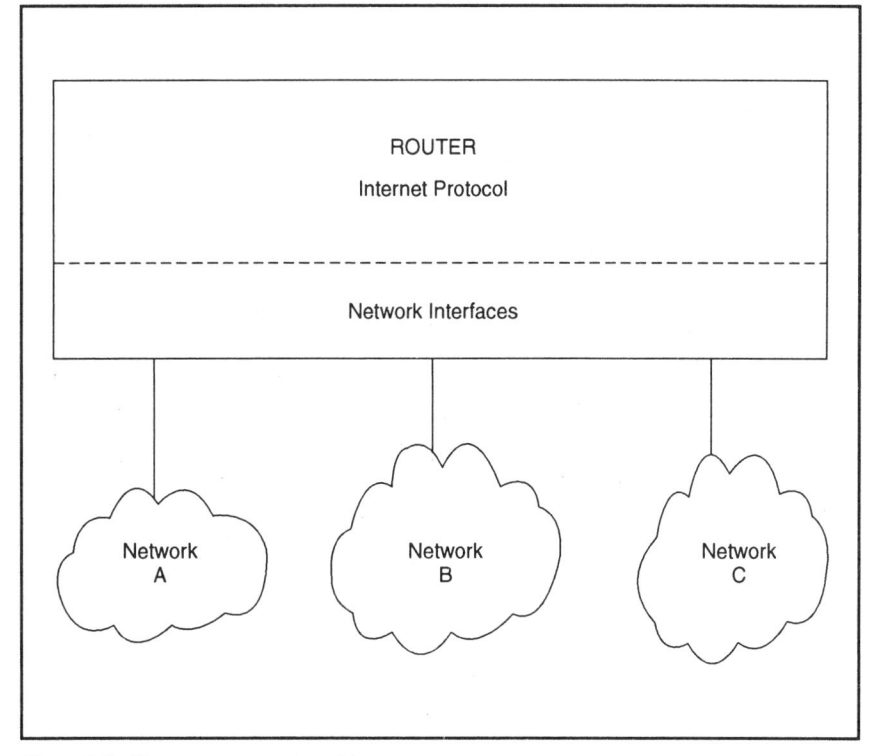

Figure 3.5 IP router protocol architecture.

---

[3]Sometimes an exception is made. TCP and Telnet terminal access may be supported in a router in order to let a network administrator login across an internet to perform configuration and maintenance tasks.

3.5.1 IP Actions

If the destination for a datagram is not on the same network as the source host, IP in the host directs the datagram to a local router. If that router is not connected to the destination network, the datagram must be sent on to another router. This continues until the destination network is reached.

IP makes a routing decision by looking up a remote destination in a routing table. IP looks for an entry in the routing table that matches the destination with the identity of the next router to which datagram traffic should be relayed.

3.5.2 Routing Table Information

In a small, static internet, routing tables can be entered and maintained manually. In larger internets, routers keep their tables up-to-date by exchanging information with one another. Routers can dynamically discover facts such as:

- A new network has been added to the internet.
- The path to a destination has been disrupted, and that network cannot be reached at this time.
- A new router has been added to the internet. This router provides a shorter path to certain destinations.

Surprisingly, there is no single required standard for router-to-router information exchange.

The routers under the control of an organization are called an *Autonomous System*. The organization can choose any router information exchange protocol that it wants within its own Autonomous System. A router information exchange protocol used within an Autonomous System is called an *Interior Gateway Protocol* or IGP.

The *Routing Information Protocol* (RIP) is a popular Interior Gateway Protocol. One reason for the popularity of RIP is that it is so widely available. However, the newer *Open Shortest Path First* (OSPF) protocol has a rich set of useful features. The availability and popularity of OSPF are growing steadily.

Some router vendors provide their own proprietary protocols for router-to-router information exchange as well as support for standard protocols. A number of vendors have the ability to run several protocols at the same time; their routers can exchange information with other routers using any of these protocols.

3.6 TCP ARCHITECTURE

TCP is implemented in hosts. The TCP entity at each end of a connection must insure that the data delivered to its local application is:

- Accurate
- In sequence
- Complete
- Free of duplicates

A sending application passes a stream of bytes to TCP. TCP breaks the stream into pieces and adds a header to each piece, forming *segments*. TCP then passes each segment to IP for transmission in a datagram (see Figure 3.6).

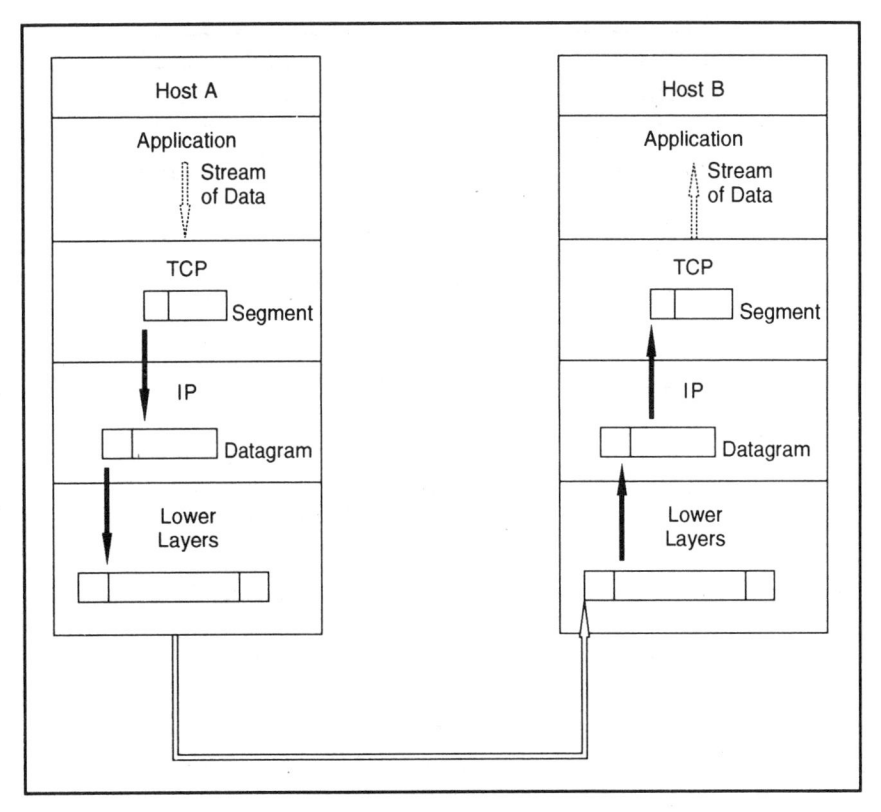

Figure 3.6 Packaging a stream of application data.

A receiving TCP has to keep its partner informed of how much correct data has arrived by means of acknowledgments (ACKs). If an ACK for a segment does not arrive within a timeout period, TCP resends the segment. This strategy is called retransmission with positive acknowledgment. Occasionally, a retransmission will cause duplicate segments to be delivered to the receiving TCP.

The receiving TCP must arrange incoming segments in the right order, discarding duplicates. TCP delivers data to its application in order, without any missing pieces.

So far we have made it sound as if one side sends and the other receives. TCP is a *full duplex* protocol; that is, both ends of a connection can send and receive at the same time, so there are in fact two streams of data being transmitted. TCP can play a sender role and a receiver role simultaneously, as illustrated in Figure 3.7.

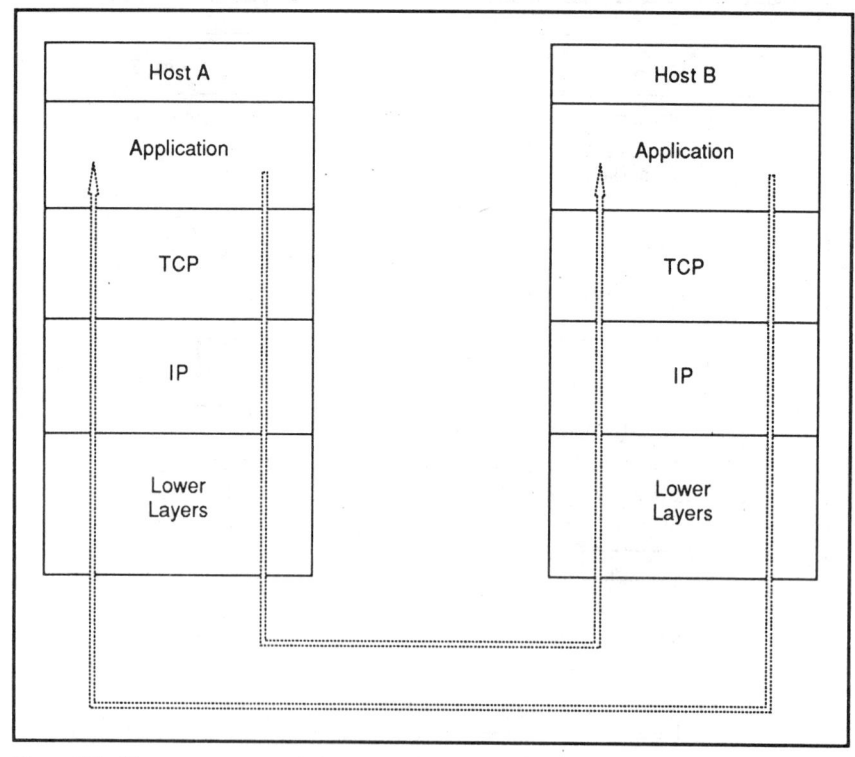

Figure 3.7 The two streams of data in a TCP connection.

3.7 UDP ARCHITECTURE

The UDP layer is implemented in host end systems. UDP makes no promise of guaranteed delivery, and it is up to the peer applications to exchange information that confirms that data has arrived safely.

An application that wants to send data via UDP passes a *block* of data to UDP. UDP adds a header to the block, forming a *User Datagram*. The User Datagram is then passed to IP and packaged in an IP datagram.

Figure 3.8 illustrates how a block of data is packaged and sent via UDP. Of course, UDP messages may be sent by either partner, and Host B could concurrently be in the process of preparing a block to be sent to A.

An application participating in UDP communications may send and receive User Datagram messages at any time. It is up to the clients and servers that are built on top of UDP to keep track of any relationship between the User Datagrams that are exchanged.

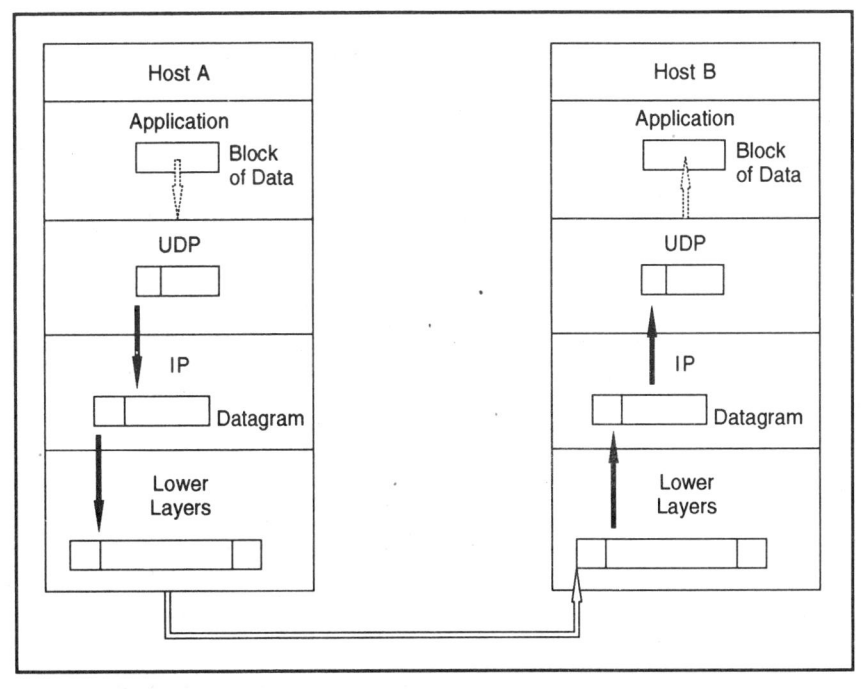

Figure 3.8 Packaging a block of application data.

3.8 PROTOCOL DATA UNITS

So far, we primarily have looked at the vertical relationships between the TCP/IP protocol layers. Let's take a closer look at the relationship between peer TCPs and peer IPs.

To be formal for a moment, the OSI model uses the term *Layer N protocol data unit* or *Layer N PDU* for the information unit that the *Nth* layer protocol deals with. A PDU consists of a header and (optionally) some enclosed data. Peers cooperate by exchanging PDUs.

TCP/IP uses a less ceremonious style of language. Rather than saying *Layer 4 PDU* or *Layer 3 PDU*, the TCP, UDP, and IP terms are *segment* or *User Datagram* at layer 4, and *datagram* at layer 3.

Figure 3.9 shows the headers that are successively added at each layer to form its protocol data units. User data from an application is passed to TCP or UDP. A TCP segment header contains information such as a sequence number used to keep data in order, an ACK for received data, and information identifying the sending and receiving applications that are using the connection. A UDP header contains fields that identify the sending and receiving UDP applications. An IP header contains information such as the source and destination network addresses for the data.

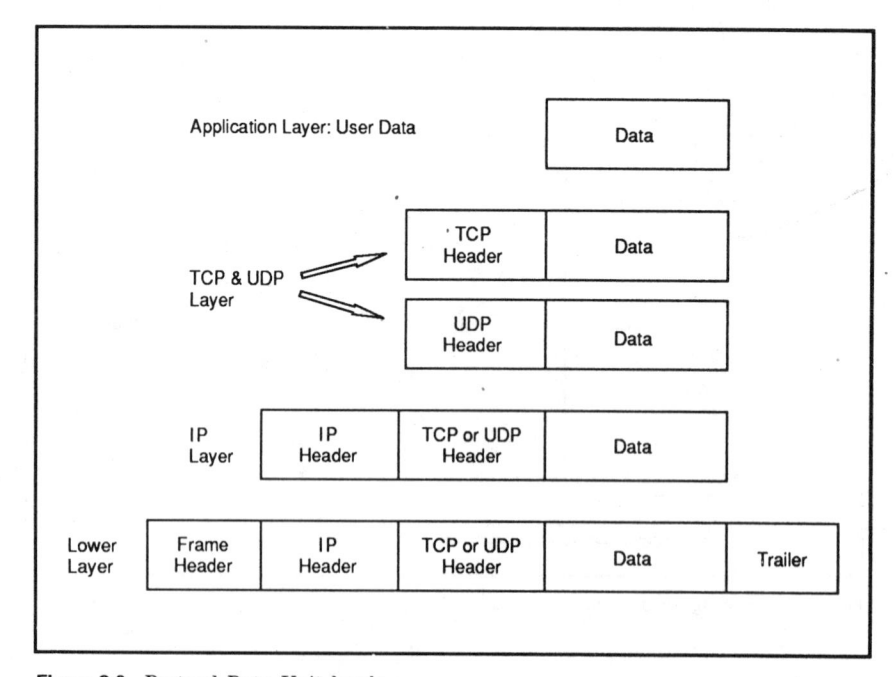

Figure 3.9 Protocol Data Unit headers.

Frame Header	Data Link Header	IP Header	TCP Header	Data	Frame Check Sequence

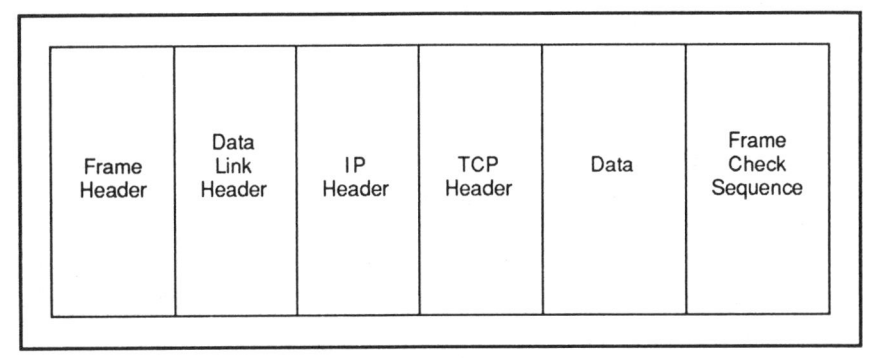

Figure 3.10 Full set of Protocol Data Unit headers.

Recall that a lower layer protocol data unit is called a *frame*. A frame header contains fields that identify the source and destination physical devices. In many instances, the frame header will be followed by a second header called a Logical Link Control header or Data Link header (see Figure 3.10).[4]

Most frames contain not only a header but also a trailer containing a *frame check sequence* that is used to detect transmission errors. A frame check sequence contains the result of a mathematical calculation that the sender performs on the bits of a message. The receiver performs the same calculation and compares the result with the value in the trailer. The calculation has been devised so that if the values agree, there is a very high probability that the integrity of the data was preserved during transmission.

3.8.1 Peer to Peer Interactions

The lower layers are responsible for transporting information across a single local or wide area network.[5]

The IP layers in systems that have a direct local or wide area network connections exchange IP datagrams with one another by wrapping them within frames. IP datagrams exchanged by hosts that are connected to different networks are relayed across an internet via one or more routers.

Figure 3.11 illustrates how the TCP/IP peer layers interact. Applications exchange information by making use of the end-to-end facilities

---

[4] Frame and data link headers will be described in detail in Chapter 4.

[5] We use the term network in a very broad sense here. Ethernets, point-to-point links, and X.25 public data facilities all are networks.

40 Chapter Three

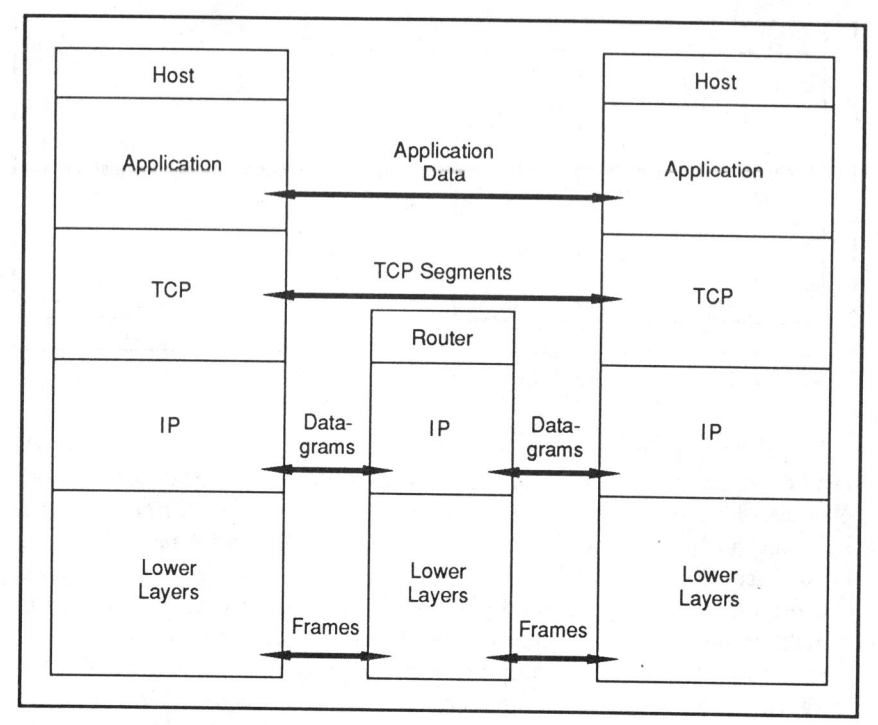

Figure 3.11 Relaying datagrams through a router.

provided by TCP. A TCP segment is wrapped inside an IP datagram and then it is routed from its source host to its destination host. Datagrams are embedded in frames and passed across a physical medium.

3.9 LOOKING AHEAD

The topics that we have met in this brief overview will be visited in detail in the chapters that follow. The mysteries of the lower layers are explored in Chapter 4. Chapter 5 explains naming and addressing. The IP protocol is mapped out in Chapter 6, while Chapter 8 focuses on routing. Chapter 7 deals with some error handling and query facilities associated with IP. UDP is described in Chapter 9. Chapter 10, one of the longest in this book, is devoted to TCP. Chapters 11 through 14 describe application services. Chapter 15 deals with network management, while Chapter 16 deals with administration. Finally, Chapter 17 introduces the socket programming interface.

Chapter 4

Physical and Data Link Technologies

4.1 INTRODUCTION

During the past few years an unprecedented number of innovative LAN and WAN networking technologies have been introduced and quickly absorbed into the marketplace. The use of twisted pair and fiber media and adoption of Token-Ring protocols have proceeded at a pace that no one could have predicted. T1, fractional T1, ISDN, Frame Relay, and Switched Multimegabit Data Service promise wide area connections that are faster, more flexible, and cheaper.

There are TCP/IP implementations that run over virtually every type of network technology. Most popular in the commercial world are:

- High-level Data Link Control (HDLC) over synchronous lines
- X.25
- Institute of Electrical and Electronics Engineers (IEEE) 802.3
- Ethernet
- Token-Ring

Emerging technologies that are used for TCP/IP include:

- Point-to-point connections using a new Point-to-Point Protocol
- Frame Relay
- Fiber Distributed Data Interface (FDDI)
- Switched Multimegabit Data Service (SMDS)
- Integrated Services Digital Network (ISDN)

Chapter Four

TCP/IP also runs over older or more specialized technologies, such as:

- Serial Line Interface Protocol (SLIP) point-to-point connections
- ARCNET
- HYPERchannel
- IEEE 802.4 broadband LAN
- Packet radio

4.2 POINT-TO-POINT PROTOCOLS

Point-to-point connections rely on physical layer and data link layer protocols. These layers are shown in Figure 4.1. The physical layer protocol specifies the hardware medium, connectors, and electrical characteristics of the equipment, as well as the rules for impressing data upon the medium. The data link layer defines units of data called frames,[1] and specifies frame delimiters, headers, and trailers.

IP datagrams can be sent across a point-to-point link between a pair of hosts, a pair of routers, or a host and a router. In any case, IP will transmit datagrams for many different TCP and UDP interactions across a single link.

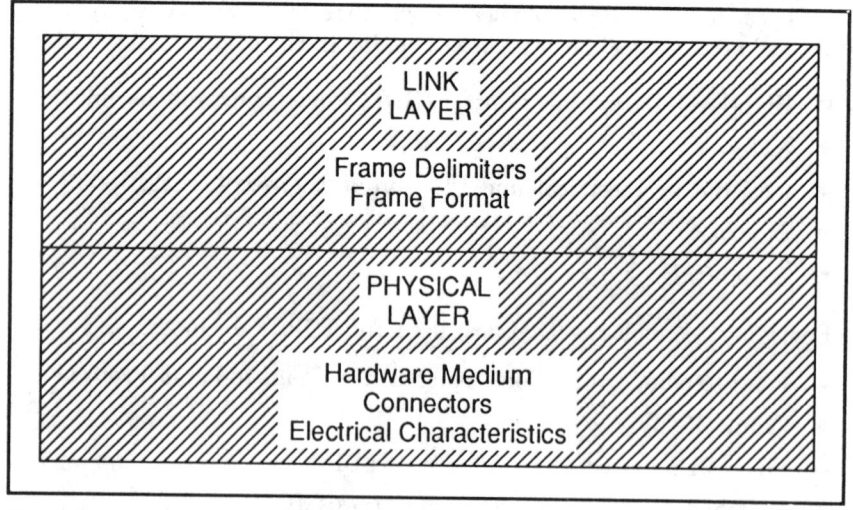

Figure 4.1 Lower layers for point-to-point connections.

---

[1] Note that some authors refer to these units as *packets*.

Recall that IP does not know or care about the identities of source or destination applications. Every time that IP is handed a datagram, it transmits the datagram as soon as it can. As a result, as illustrated in Figure 4.2, the traffic for many different application interactions is mingled on a link.

The sections that follow will describe link protocols used in many TCP/IP networks.

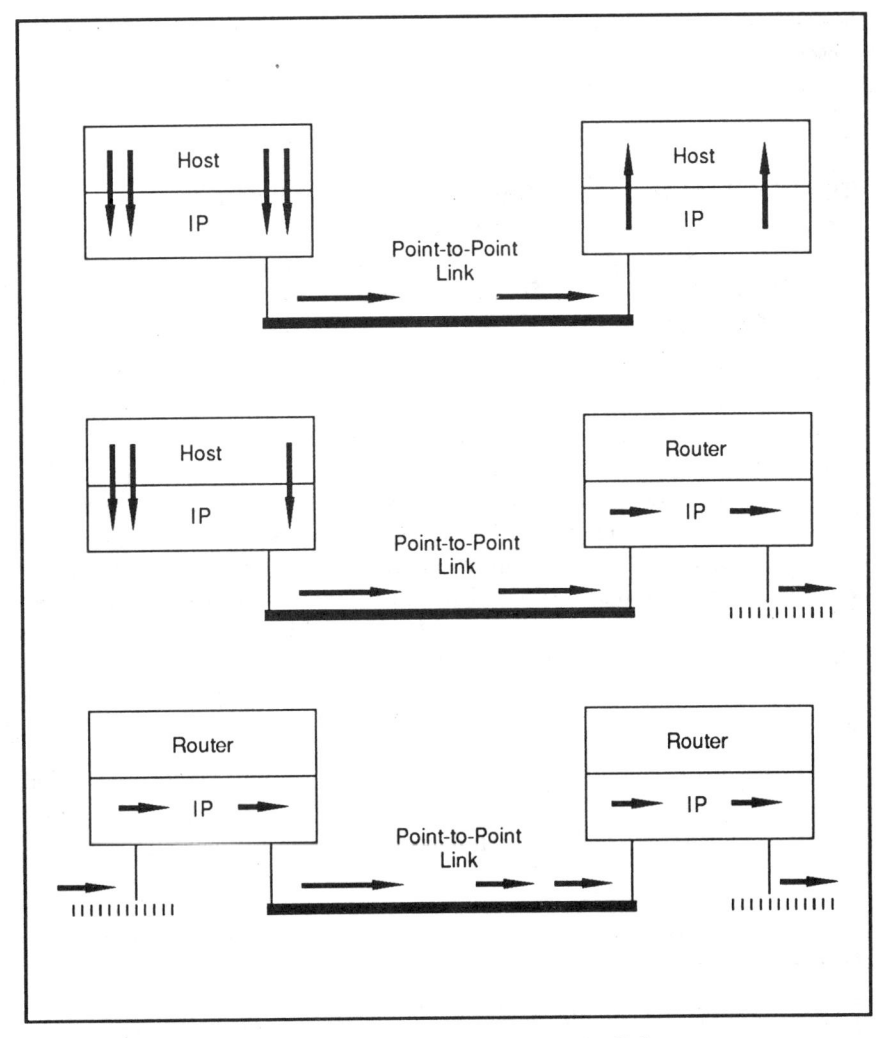

Figure 4.2 IP multiplexing datagrams across a point-to-point link.

44   Chapter Four

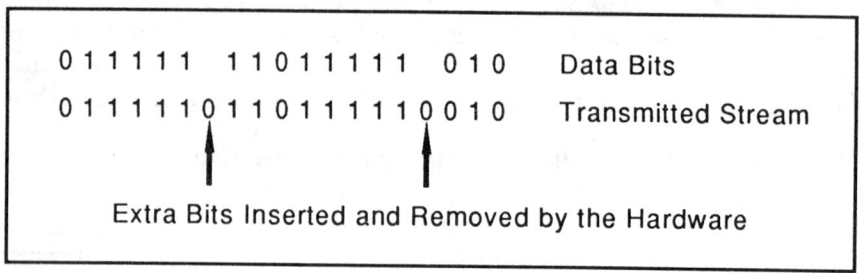

```
0 1 1 1 1 1   1 1 0 1 1 1 1 1   0 1 0         Data Bits

0 1 1 1 1 1 0 1 1 0 1 1 1 1 1 0 0 1 0         Transmitted Stream
            ↑             ↑
        Extra Bits Inserted and Removed by the Hardware
```

Figure 4.3   HDLC bit-stuffing.

4.3   HDLC

The High-level Data Link Control (HDLC) protocol is an international standard that defines facilities to be used in synchronous point-to-point connections. Serial data is sent as a clocked stream of bits which are partitioned into message frames. Every frame is delimited by the special *flag* pattern:

0 1 1 1 1 1 1 0

In order to recognize this pattern, it is necessary to prevent the flag pattern from appearing within the user's data. After transmitting the opening flag, the sending hardware will insert a 0 after any five consecutive ones in the data. This procedure is called *zero-bit insertion* or *bit-stuffing*. After recognizing an opening flag, the receiving hardware will remove a zero which appears after five consecutive ones.

The example in Figure 4.3 shows some sample data and the bits as they would be transmitted.

4.3.1   HDLC Frame Format

As shown in Figure 4.4, an HDLC frame is made up of a header, (optionally) some data, and a frame check sequence. The header contains an address field (which is useful for multipoint lines) and a control field.

Flag 01111110	Address	Control	...Data...	Frame Check Sequence	Flag 01111110

Figure 4.4   Format of an HDLC frame, with its flag delimiters.

There are many options defined within the HDLC standard, and many variants of HDLC exist. For example, the Link Access Procedures Balanced (LAPB) standard used in the X.25 protocol, the Link Access Procedures on the D-channel (LAPD) standard that supports ISDN, and IBM's Synchronous Data Link Protocol (SDLC) all are HDLC dialects.

Many vendors have added their own enhancements to implementations of point-to-point device drivers. The result is that there has not been a single standard for point-to-point communication, making it difficult to interwork equipment from different vendors.

4.3.2 The Internet Point-to-Point Protocol

The Point-to-Point Protocol (PPP) was defined by Internet researchers to remedy the lack of a real standard serial link protocol. PPP can be used over any duplex circuit, either synchronous bit-oriented or asynchronous (start/stop).

PPP was designed so that it could carry PDUs from other protocols such as DECnet or OSI as well as IP datagrams. In fact, PPP can be used to multiplex traffic from several protocols across a single link.

PPP includes several subprotocols. The Link Control Protocol sets up, tests, configures, and closes down a link. Network Control Protocols are used to initialize, configure, and terminate use of a particular network protocol. A separate Network Control Protocol is defined for IP, OSI, DECnet, and so forth.

Finally, there is a protocol for the exchange of actual information, such as IP datagrams or OSI PDUs.

A scenario for PPP usage is:

1. An originating PPP sends a series of Link Control Packets to configure and test the link.

2. Both ends exchange Link Control Packets to establish the facilities to be used.

3. The originating PPP sends Network Control Protocol messages to choose and configure the network layer protocols to be used.

4. IP Datagrams and Protocol Data Units for any other selected type of protocol are sent across the link.

5. Network Control and Link Control Protocol Packets are used to close the link down.

Like the HDLC header, the PPP header starts with an Address field and a Control field.

Flag	Address	Control	Protocol	Information	FCS	Flag
01111110	11111111	00000011	16 Bits		16 Bits	01111110

FCS = Frame Check Sequence

Figure 4.5 Format of a PPP frame.

The Address field contains the binary sequence 11111111 (or X'FF in hexadecimal) which, by convention, is known as the *All-Stations* or broadcast address. The Control field contains binary 00000011 (X'03) which identifies an HDLC *Unnumbered Information* frame.[2] It may seem wasteful to include two constant octets in every frame. In fact, the partners at each end of the PPP link can negotiate to operate in a compressed mode that eliminates these fields.

The value in the Protocol field indicates whether the information content is a Link Control Protocol message, a Network Control Protocol message, or information such as an IP datagram. The size of the protocol field can be negotiated down to 8 bits. A PPP frame has the format shown in Figure 4.5.

4.3.3 Serial Line Interface Protocol

The Serial Line Interface Protocol (SLIP) is surely the most rudimentary protocol ever invented! An IP datagram simply is transmitted, byte by byte, on a serial line. SLIP marks the end of a datagram with the delimiter byte, 11000000. SLIP also includes a mechanism for indicating when this byte is part of the information in a datagram, rather than a delimiter.

SLIP typically is used at speeds ranging from 1200 bits per second to 19.2 kilobits per second. However, there is inherent no speed limit, and SLIP can run at higher speeds. Either asynchronous (start/stop) or synchronous transmission can be used. Note that SLIP provides no frame check sequence, and leaves all error checking to higher layers. SLIP's most appealing feature is that it is widely available. (Its most appalling feature is its lack of error checking.)

---

[2] HDLC unnumbered information frames are used for connectionless layer 2 communications.

Physical and Data Link Technologies   47

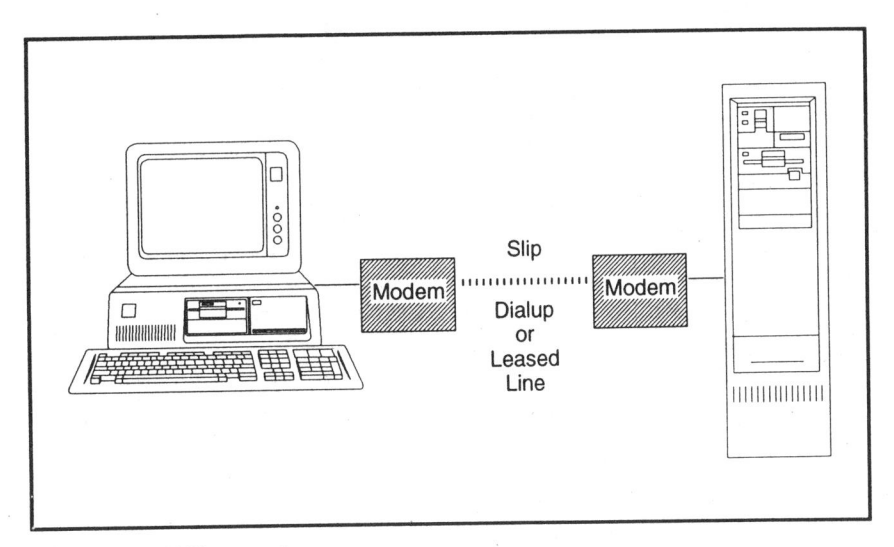

Figure 4.6 A SLIP connection.

SLIP can be used for host-to-host, host-to-router, or router-to-router communications. Figure 4.6 shows a SLIP connection between a workstation and a host. The modems may be asynchronous or synchronous — as long as they match.

4.4 PACKET NETWORKS

The packet-switching technology that was introduced in the experimental ARPANET has been reshaped and used in many of data communications facilities. X.25 packet networks gained wide use in the 1980s. The recently introduced Frame Relay packet switching technology has generated a lot of interest.

4.4.1 X.25 Networks

Our telephone network lets any telephone instrument place a call to any other phone in the world. The organization responsible for defining standards for plugging a phone into a national network and standards for joining national networks into a global network, is the *International Telegraph and Telephone Consultative Committee*, known as the *CCITT*. The CCITT calls its standards *recommendations*.

During the 1970s, the CCITT started work on a set of recommendations intended to create a global *data* network. These recommendations reached maturity during the 1980s. The most important of these is

X.25, which lays down the rules for connecting a computer to a data network. More specifically, X.25 defines the interface between a computer (called Data terminal equipment or DTE) and a communications element (data circuit-terminating equipment or DCE) that is part of the data network.

X.25 sets up reliable data circuits between computers. These are called *virtual circuits* because, unlike the phone system, a path for the exclusive use of the caller and called is not reserved throughout a call. Path segments usually are shared by a number of concurrent virtual circuits. However, the path sharing that takes place is invisible to the users of the circuits.

X.25 is popular worldwide, and there are many X.25 public data networks supporting connectivity between computers around the globe. These public data networks offer two types of connections. *Switched virtual circuits* are data calls that are set up just like a phone call. Participating computers are assigned numbers.[3] A caller enters the number of the computer to be reached, and the call is put through. Alternatively, a customer may acquire *permanent virtual circuits* that behave like dedicated leased lines.

The CCITT recommendations do not place constraints on the *internal* structure of a regional data network. However, many X.25 data networks use an internal packet-switching technology.

Private organizations sometimes purchase packet-switching equipment and build their own X.25 networks.

4.4.2 X.25 and IP

X.25 is one of the facilities used to transport IP datagrams. IP uses an X.25 virtual circuit in the same way that it uses a point-to-point line. That is, IP traffic exchanged by a pair of hosts or a pair of routers is multiplexed onto an X.25 virtual circuit.

The X.25 link (layer 2) and packet (layer 3) protocols go to a lot of trouble to make sure that data is transmitted in order and free of errors. The original intention was to provide an end-to-end data connection service that applications could rely on.

It might seem rather strange to run an unreliable IP datagram service on top of a hard-working protocol like X.25. It may seem even stranger when one realizes that both X.25 and IP provide layer 3 protocols! However, considerations of cost or convenience often override purity of layering.

---

[3]The 14-digit numbers used in X.25 calls are described in CCITT recommendation X.121.

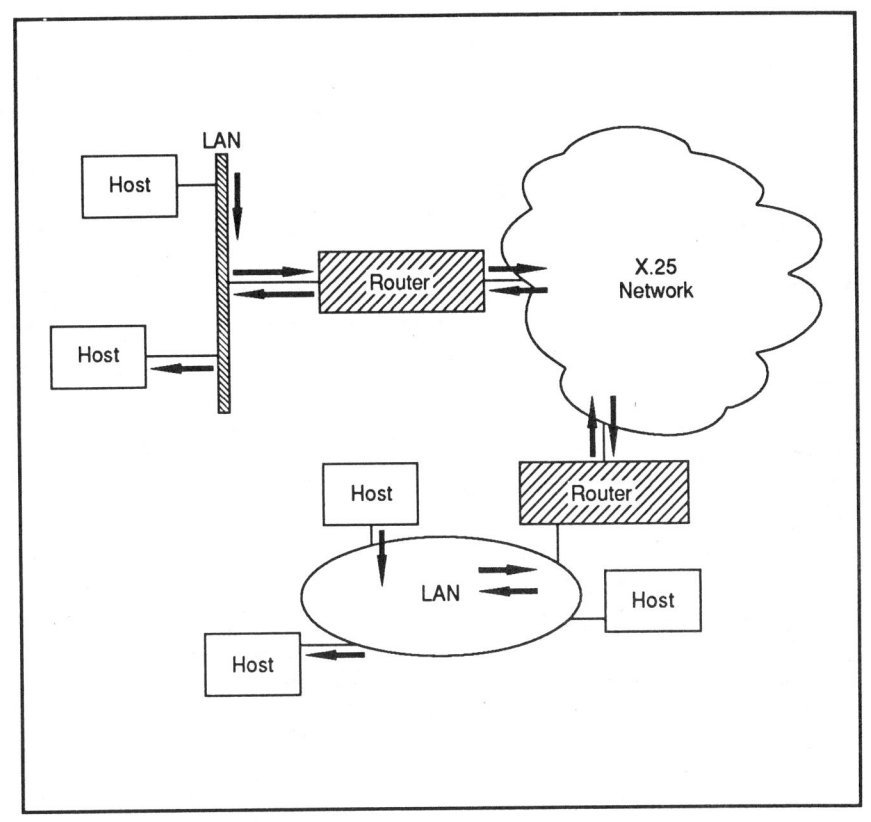

Figure 4.7 Use of an X.25 network for routing IP datagrams.

Figure 4.7 illustrates how IP traffic between multiple sources and destinations is multiplexed across an X.25 virtual circuit.

The use of X.25 to carry IP datagrams may gradually be displaced by a new service, Frame Relay, which is discussed in the next section.

4.4.3 Frame Relay

X.25 networks provide reliable, in-sequence transmission of data. There is a great deal of overhead involved in assuring the level of quality offered by X.25. When IP traffic is multiplexed across an X.25 virtual circuit, much of the X.25 overhead is wasted effort. The emerging Frame Relay technology is better suited to TCP/IP use.

Frame Relay is a layer two protocol. When using Frame Relay, only a simple link layer header and error checking trailer are added to a datagram.

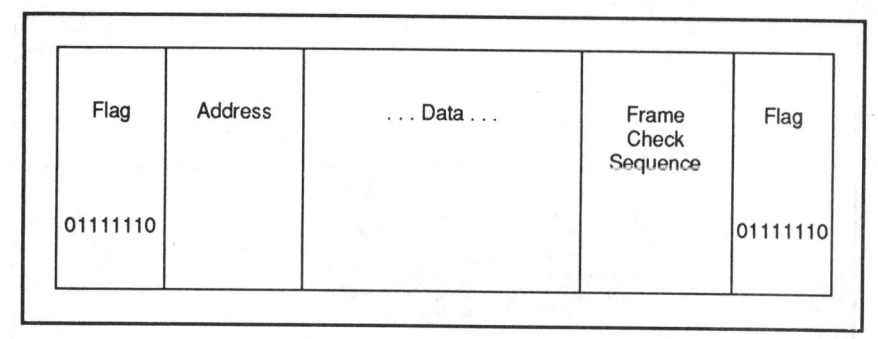

Flag	Address	...Data...	Frame Check Sequence	Flag
01111110				01111110

Figure 4.8 Format for a frame relay frame, with flag delimiters.

As shown in Figure 4.8, the header consists of a 2-octet address field. A few bits in the address field are used to signal congestion, and to indicate whether this frame should be given preferential treatment when frames are discarded due to congestion.

The frame is transmitted across the service provider's network. Frames whose frame check sequence values reveal that data has been corrupted are discarded.

X.25 saves messages until they are acknowledged, and retransmits if an ACK is not received. Unlike X.25, Frame Relay does *not* save messages, it does not wait for ACKs, and it does not retransmit datagrams. This results in the efficient use of the network memory buffers used to hold outgoing datagrams, and fuller use of the bandwidth that is available.

The initial Frame Relay standard defines service over permanent virtual circuits. This means that a user must contract with a service provider to obtain connectivity to prespecified sites at a set of agreed bandwidths. Many service providers offer bandwidths up to the T1 (1.544 megabits per second) rate. Generally, a customer pays a fixed monthly fee based on bandwidth and distance.

Work is proceeding on a standard for switched Frame Relay service. Supporting a switched service is more of a challenge because it will be hard to predict how much traffic users will present to the service at any given time, and networks may occasionally be flooded with sudden bursts of traffic.

Frame Relay offers excellent performance when compared to X.25, and has been well received. Some organizations are buying their own Frame Relay equipment, and are building private networks.

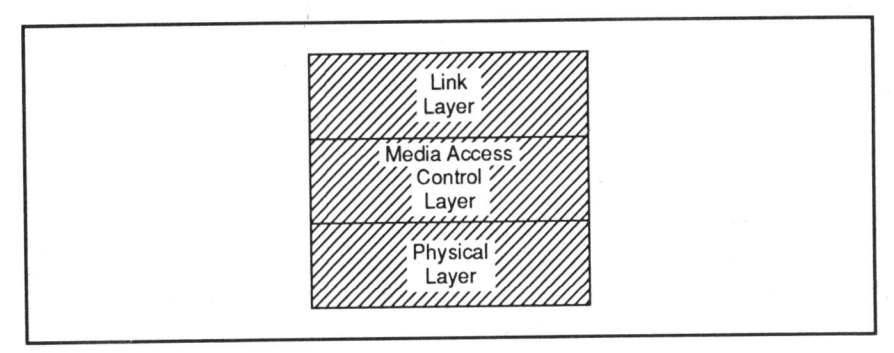

Figure 4.9 Lower layers, including media access control layer.

4.5 THE 802 NETWORKS

A committee of the Institute of Electrical and Electronics Engineers (IEEE) has been tasked with establishing and publishing standards for networking technologies. Standards in the 802 series have guided many vendor implementations, and these standards have been recognized by ISO and republished with ISO document numbers.

The 802 standards deal with physical media, media access controls, data link layer protocols, and internetworking issues.

4.5.1 Layering for 802 Networks

With the advent of LANs, a new sublayer was added to the lower layer protocols. Unlike point-to-point links, LANs connect to large communities of computers that share access to a transmission medium. The mechanisms that allow these communities to exchange data in an orderly manner are embedded in an additional layer, the *Media Access Control* (MAC) layer. The new layering is shown in Figure 4.9.

4.5.2 Ethernet and 802.3

Digital Equipment Corporation, Intel Corporation, and Xerox Corporation defined the original *"DIX" Ethernet* specification in 1980. This was revised as Version 2 in 1982.[4] An altered form of the protocol, 802.3, was later defined as a standard by the IEEE and adopted by ISO. A significant difference between DIX Ethernet and 802.3 is the inclusion of a Logical Link Control (LLC) header within 802.3 frames.

---

[4] Sometimes this protocol is called "DIX Ethernet," where DIX is an acronym for the sponsoring company names.

52   Chapter Four

It is expected that DIX Ethernet Version 2 gradually will be phased out, but there are many TCP/IP networks which run over the older DIX Ethernet protocol. It is unfortunate that the term *Ethernet* often is used indiscriminately for both the older implementations and the newer IEEE 802.3 version!

4.5.3 Coax Media

For both Ethernet and 802.3, the traditional backbone medium is baseband coaxial cable. Originally, only a heavy half-inch 50 ohm cable, often referred to as *goldenrod*, was used. Then a thinner, more flexible quarter-inch grade of coax, called *thinnet* or *cheapernet* was introduced. A 10 megabit per second signaling rate is popular.

A network may consist of a single section of cable or may include several sections that have been connected to one another. Figure 4.10 illustrates the components that are used to build a network.

A network *segment* may be an isolated section or can consist of one or more sections connected via passive hardware connectors. In the figure, a barrel connector combines two sections of cable into one segment.

Terminator hardware is attached to the ends of each segment. The two segments in the figure are joined together by an electronic *repeater*. The repeater retransmits the data bits that it hears on one segment onto the other.

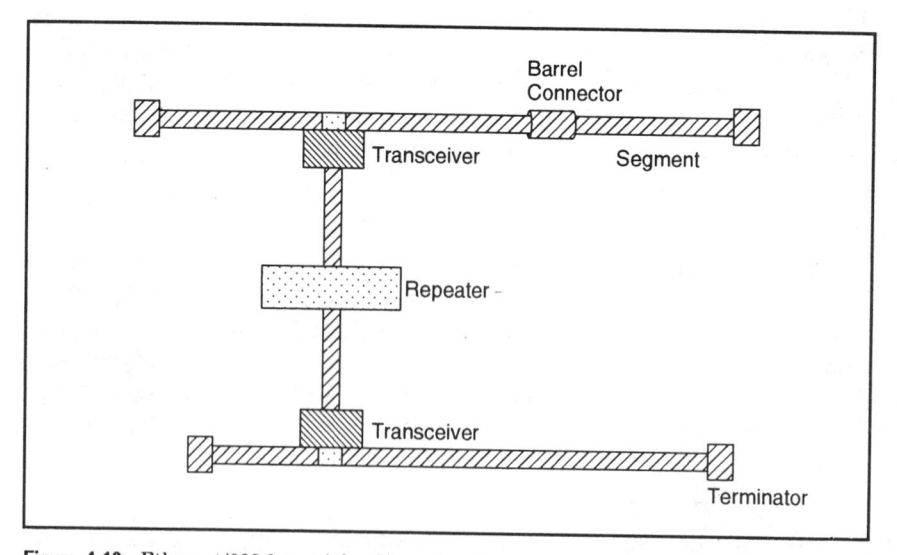

Figure 4.10 Ethernet/802.3 coaxial cable network.

4.5.4 Other 802.3 Media Choices

The IEEE 802.3 standard also encompasses specifications for broadband, twisted pair, and fiber-optic media. To distinguish between implementations, the following notation is used:

[Data Rate in Mbps] [Medium Type] [Maximum Cable Segment in 100-Meters]

Thus 10BASE5 means BASEband coax with a data rate of 10 megabits per second, and a maximum cable segment length of 500 meters. The thin cable specification is 10BASE2, which means BASEband coax with a data rate of 10 megabits per second, and a maximum cable segment size of 200 meters.

Similarly, 10BROAD36 is BROADband coax, 10 megabits per second, and a maximum cable segment length of 3600 meters. The recent twisted pair and fiber specifications are identified as 10BASET and 10BASEF, which do not quite match the pattern!

4.5.5 Connecting to the Medium

Figure 4.11 shows one of the configurations used to connect a station to a coax-based Ethernet or 802.3 LAN. A transceiver (transmitter-receiver) is connected to the medium by driving the prongs of a "vampire" tap into the LAN cable. An interface board in a station connects to a transceiver by means of a drop cable.

Each Ethernet or 802.3 interface board is preconfigured with a unique physical address. An administrator can override these preconfigured addresses and assign locally selected physical addresses, if desired.

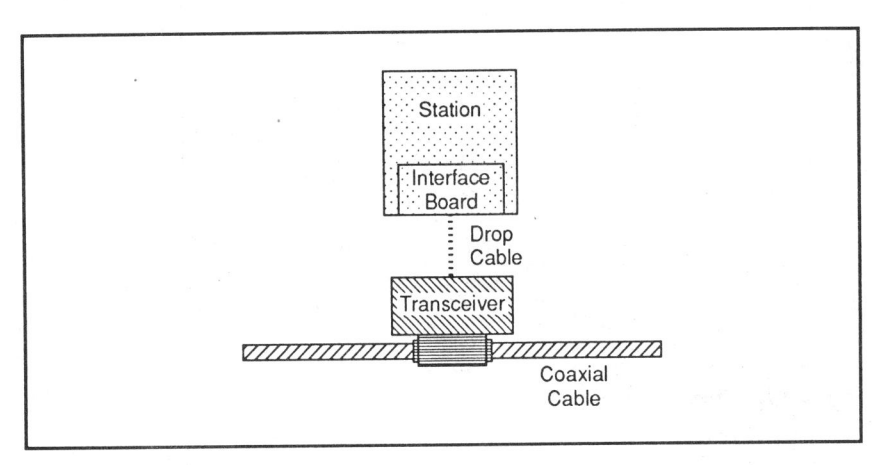

Figure 4.11 Connecting a station to an Ethernet.

4.5.6 Ethernet and 802.3 Media Access Control Protocols

The Ethernet and 802.3 Media Access Control (MAC) protocols are based on a very simple procedure with a long title: Carrier Sense Multiple Access with Collision Detection (CSMA/CD).

The interface hardware at each station on the LAN listens to the medium. An interface with data to send wraps the data in a frame header and listens to the medium. If the medium is not in use, the interface transmits.

> LISTEN ...
> Quiet?
> SEND!

The frame header contains the physical address of the destination interface. The system with that physical address absorbs the frame and processes it. If two or more stations transmit at the same time, they can hear their frames *collide*, and they back off for a random amount of time and try again.

4.5.7 Ethernet Media Access Control Frames

Ethernet and 802.3 use very simple MAC frames consisting of a header, data, and a trailer. The format of an Ethernet frame that is carrying an IP datagram is shown in Figure 4.12.

```
Destination
Address
------------
Source
Address
------------
Ethernet
X'0800
------------
("Data" Field)
IP DATAGRAM
------------
(Padding if Needed)
------------
Frame Check Sequence
```

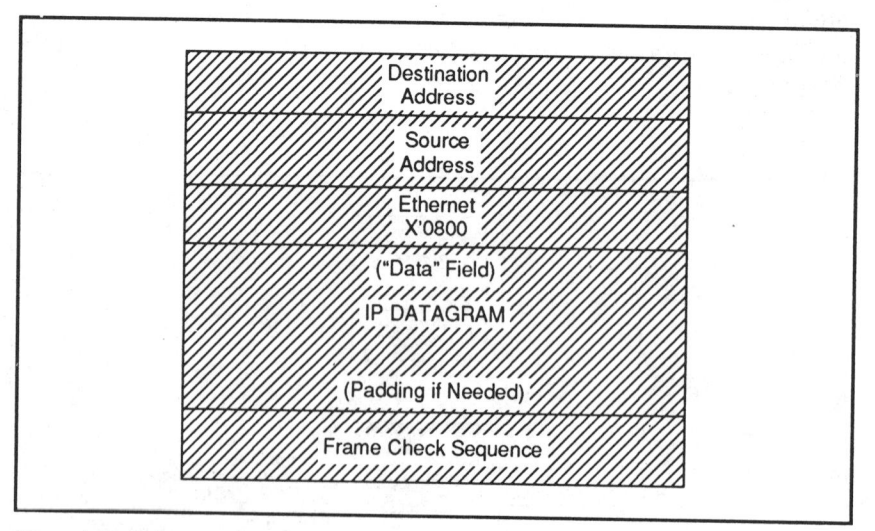

Figure 4.12 Ethernet frame carrying an IP datagram.

The destination and source addresses are six octets long.[5] The type code, X'0800, signals that the data content of this frame is a datagram that should be passed to IP. There are type codes that identify other protocols (for example, *DECnet*). The cable can be shared by several protocols because the type code identifies the protocol that should receive the data.

The data field contains whatever information the frame carries. This information will include the headers used in the remaining protocol layers. In order to operate correctly, the CSMA/CD protocol requires frames to be at least 64 octets in length. It might be necessary to add padding after a very short datagram.

4.5.8 802.3 Media Access Control Frames

The format of an 802.3 frame that is carrying an IP datagram is shown in Figure 4.13.

The third field of the 802.3 frame header contains the length of the data field (exclusive of padding). As is common for the 802.X family, the data field contains an 802.2 Logical Link Control (LLC) header as well as a datagram.

An interface can distinguish between an 802.3 frame and an Ethernet frame because type field values are much larger than the maximum allowed data length.

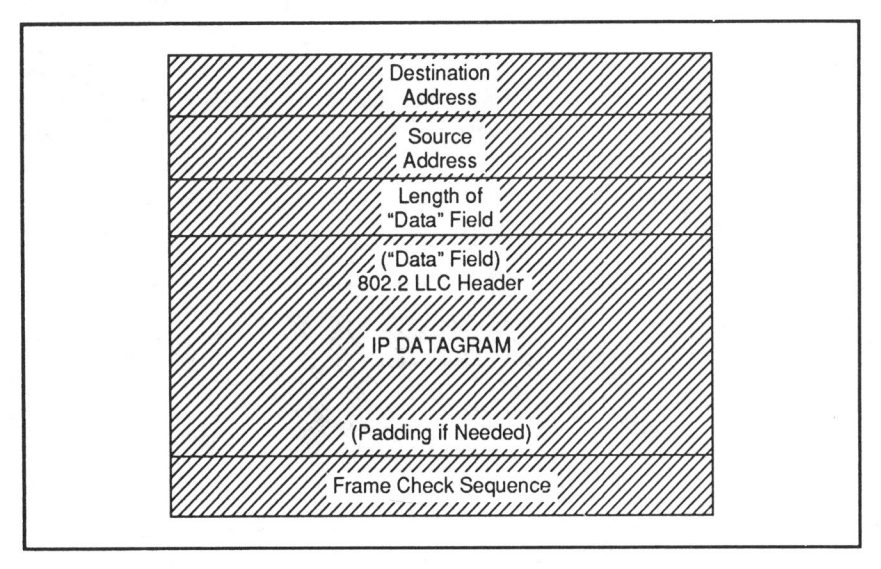

Figure 4.13 802.3 frame carrying an IP datagram.

---

[5]Two octet addresses used to be allowed but rarely were used.

56 Chapter Four

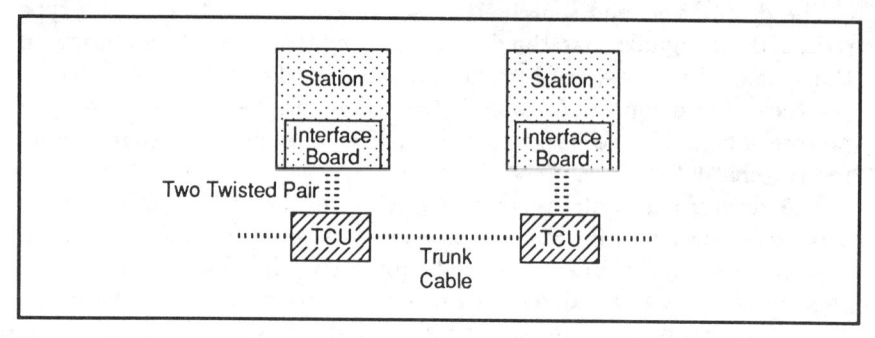

Figure 4.14 Token-Ring architecture.

4.5.9 802.5 Token-Ring Configuration and Media

Token-Ring LANs are becoming increasingly popular. IEEE 802.5 defines the Token-Ring physical and Media Access Control protocols. Stations on a Token-Ring are configured as a physical ring.

As shown in Figure 4.14, a station's interface board is attached to a very simple device called a *Trunk Coupling Unit* or TCU by means of two twisted pair wiring. The job of the TCU is to sense if the station is active. If not, it causes signals to bypass the station.

TCUs are connected by lengths of trunk cable which can be shielded twisted pair, coax, or optical fiber. Typical speeds are 4 and 16 megabits per second.

In current implementations, several Token-Ring TCUs are packaged within a single hardware unit. For example, IBM's original Multistation Access Unit provided attachments for up to 8 stations, while the newer, modular Controlled Access Unit can be connected to up to 80 stations. Figure 4.15 shows a multiaccess unit and its cables to stations and to other units.

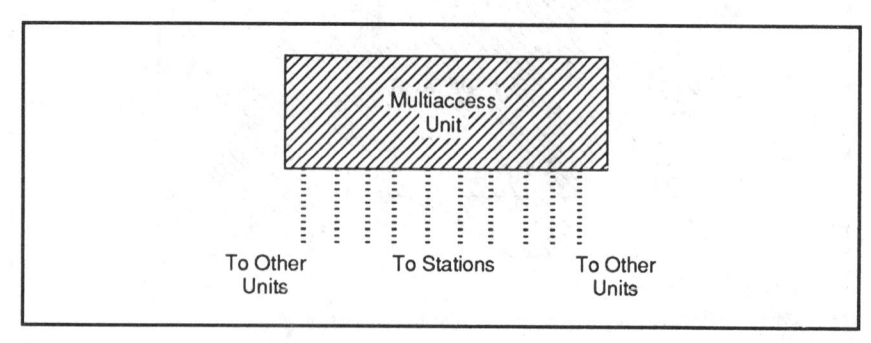

Figure 4.15 Hardware for a Token-Ring network.

4.5.10 802.5 Media Access Control Protocol

The idea behind token-based Media Access Control protocols for rings is simple. A special frame called the token is passed from station to station, around the ring. When a station receives the token, it has the right to transmit data for a limited period of time. When that time expires, the token-holder must pass the token to the next station.

Although the basic idea is straightforward, a ring protocol needs many more mechanisms than CSMA/CD requires. In particular, the MAC layer protocol for 802.5 includes mechanisms for joining or leaving the Token-Ring, detecting a lost station or lost token, and preventing data from cycling forever. There are different MAC layer headers defined for each of the 802.5 functions.

4.5.11 Other 802.X Technologies

Other 802 technologies have been defined. The 802.4 standard contains specifications for a broadband coax based bus LAN that uses token-passing to control access to the medium. 802.4 was adopted for use within the Manufacturing Automation Protocol suite, which was defined for use in industrial facilities. Its broadband coax medium resists the electronic disruptions common in a factory environment. Its use of a token-passing protocol provides the predictable scheduling of LAN access that manufacturers require.

802.6 describes a Metropolitan Area Network that can serve a large area and provide speeds ranging from 34 to 155 megabits per second. An interesting aspect of this standard is that it is able to support applications like voice that require reserved bandwidth, as well as bursty data traffic.

Like 802.5, both 802.4 and 802.6 have been assigned a set of MAC headers and a set of rules controlling access to their media.

4.5.12 IEEE 802.2

A single Logical Link Control (LLC) protocol, defined in the IEEE 802.2 standard, is used by the entire 802 family. The 802.2 standard defines several types of link interactions. A Type 1 link is used to send standalone messages called *unacknowledged frames*. A connection-oriented Type 2 link is used to reliably send a sequence of messages across a link.

4.5.13 Logical Link Control Header

Currently, a Type 1 Logical Link Control (LLC) header is the standard packaging for the transmission of IP datagrams. A Type 1 LLC header containing a datagram effectively accomplishes only one thing: it announces that its contents should be passed to IP. However, we include a brief technical discussion that describes this header in detail.

A Type 1 LLC header contains a Destination Service Access Point (DSAP) code, Source Service Access Point (SSAP) code, and a control field. A Type 1 header used to carry an IP datagram has a Control field that is set to X'03.[6]

Service Access Point codes are used to identify the source and destination protocol entities for the message. Both the DSAP and SSAP fields are set to X'AA (decimal 170), which signals that another 5-byte field called the Sub-Network Access Protocol (SNAP) header follows immediately after the control field.

The SNAP header starts with a protocol identifier code. In this case, the code is zero, indicating that the next field contains an Ether type code. The last two bytes of the SNAP header contain the characteristic X'0800 code that signals that an IP datagram is enclosed.

Figure 4.16 displays the format of the LLC Type 1 header and the SNAP subheader.

LLC Header

DSAP X'AA	SSAP X'AA	Control X'03

Snap Header

Protocol ID X'00	X'00	X'00	Ether-Type X'08	X'00

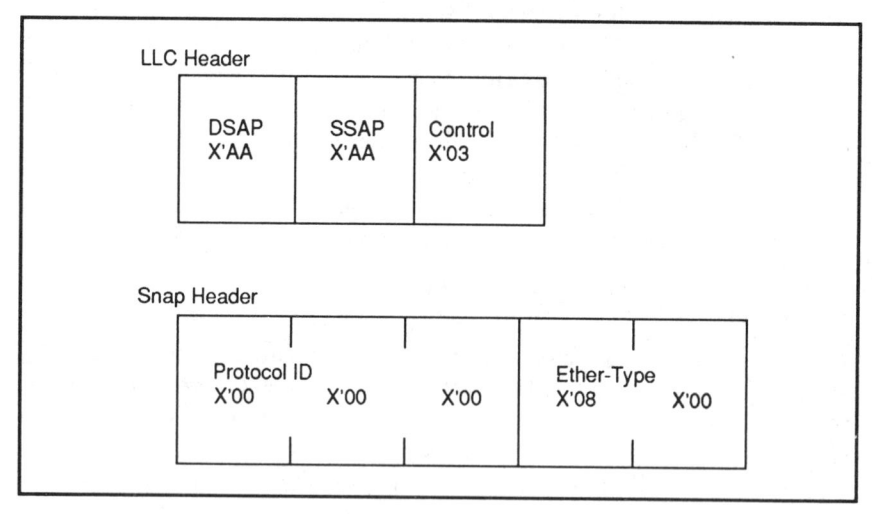

Figure 4.16 LLC and SNAP headers.

---

[6]IEEE standards documents write these values in binary with the least significant bit first, while Internet documents write them with the most significant bit first. Thus IEEE writes 3 in binary as 11000000, while RFCs write 3 as 00000011.

4.5.14 Fiber Distributed Data Interface

The Fiber Distributed Data Interface (FDDI) standards define a token-passing network based on fiber optic media.[7] To ensure robustness, FDDI networks are wired as dual rings. FDDI networks can carry data at 100 megabits per second.

The maximum FDDI frame size is 4500 octets.[8] A frame has a MAC header and trailer, and when used to carry IP, contains the same 802.2 and SNAP headers that were discussed earlier. A generous amount of space has been allowed for future MAC header extensions, so the largest datagram that can be carried via FDDI is limited to 4352 octets.

The original FDDI standard effort has reached its completion point. However, a new version is being developed. The improved version includes important features such as expanding to a spectrum of higher speeds, integrating a reserved bandwidth protocol for carrying digitized voice, and implementing the protocol over twisted pair wire.

4.5.15 Switched Multimegabit Data Service

Switched Multimegabit Data Service (SMDS) is an emerging regional Bell operating company (RBOC) public packet-switching service. SMDS offers high speed switched digital transmission. Typical rates are expected to include T1 speed (1.544 megabits per second), 4, 10, 16, 25, 34, and 45 megabits per second. Services at the new telephony SONET rate of 155.52 megabits per second are being defined.

The SMDS interface protocol is based on IEEE Standard 802.6, *Distributed Queue Dual Bus Connectionless MAC protocol*. An SMDS frame has a MAC header and trailer, and, when used to carry IP, contains 802.2 and SNAP headers. The largest datagram that can be carried via SMDS is 9180 octets.

4.5.16 Some Sample Frame Sizes and Maximum Datagram Sizes

Each of the technologies that we have discussed has a different maximum limit on the size of its frames. Some technologies have limits that depend on implementation parameters. For example, the maximum size for an 802.5 Token-Ring depends on the transmission speed and token holding time. The optimal size limit for a point-to-point line depends on the line's error rate.

---

[7]There are some new products that use the FDDI MAC protocol, but operate over twisted pair or coaxial cable.

[8] FDDI-II will allow larger frames.

TABLE 4.1 Maximum Frame and Datagram Sizes

Protocol	Maximum Frame Octets	Maximum Datagram Octets
Ethernet 10BASE5	1518	1500
802.3 10BASE5	1518	1492
802.4	8191	8166
802.5 4 Mbit/Sec, 9 Ms Hold	4508	4464
FDDI	4500	4352

Table 4.1 summarizes maximum frame and datagram sizes for Ethernet, 802.3, 802.4, 802.5, and FDDI.

The size of the datagram part of a message is calculated by subtracting the number of octets in the MAC header, MAC trailer, Logical Link Control and SNAP headers (if present) from the total frame size.

For example, the maximum frame size for an 802.3 10BASE5 network is 1518 octets. Subtracting the MAC header and trailer (18 octets) and the Type 1 link control and SNAP headers (8 octets), we get a maximum datagram size of 1492 octets.

4.5.17 Broadcasting and Multicasting

A multiaccess LAN technology easily supports broadcasting. An all-ones destination physical address is used to indicate that every interface attached to a LAN should absorb a frame.

Physical addresses often are expressed as a sequence of hexadecimal octets separated by colons. Thus, the broadcast address can be written as FF:FF:FF:FF:FF:FF.

An interface also can be configured to absorb frames sent to one or more *multicast* addresses. Multicasting allows frames to be sent to a selected set of systems. A multicast address always has a one in the low-order bit of its first byte — that is, in position 01:00:00:00:00:00. The other bits will be set to values that have been picked for some multicast-based service.

More information about multicast addresses will be presented in Chapter 5.

The Internet Assigned Numbers Authority has reserved a list of multicast addresses for a number of its services. For example, a multicast address is used to send a message to every router. An organization may choose to select some multicasting addresses to meet its own specific needs.

4.5.18 Tunneling

Adhering to a layered structure is a worthy goal, but sometimes the easiest way to get data from one place to another is to hitch a ride with another protocol. This process is called tunneling, probably because data temporarily disappears into the depths of another protocol until it pops out at some exit point.

Making tunneling work is not complicated — you simply wrap the header for another protocol around your data unit, route it using the other protocol, and unwrap it at the destination.

In fact, we already have seen an example of tunneling. When IP datagrams are moved across an X.25 network, they are wrapped inside X.25 network layer headers. In this case, IP traffic is tunneled through X.25.

There are many other examples of tunneling current today. Novell NetWare IPX traffic is tunneled through an IP network. A NetWare message is wrapped in IP and UDP headers, routed through the IP network, and delivered to a remote NetWare server. A number of vendors offer products that tunnel IP traffic through an SNA network — or SNA traffic through an IP network!

4.6 NETWORK INTERFACES

Today it is not unusual to find that a LAN or WAN is being used for several protocols at once. In fact, a single node sometimes sends and receives a mixture of protocols on its network interface. How can this be done?

To keep the discussion simple, let's consider a specific interface, say for an 802.3 LAN. A PC or server may wish to use the 802.3 interface for TCP/IP, OSI, and DECnet. Can these protocols coexist?

We already have seen some evidence that they can. The link layer header will contain a field that identifies the network layer (layer 3) protocol for the message.

Each of the layer 3 protocols accessing the network interface has a different network layer addressing scheme for identifying its destination on the LAN. This network layer address must be translated to the 6-octet Ethernet physical address before data is transmitted.

62 Chapter Four

Who should do this translation? The most efficient method is to build the translation task into the interface software.

This accomplishes several things:

- The higher layer protocols don't have to know any physical addresses.

- The higher layers don't have to know anything about the internal workings of the interface. If you removed an 802.3 card and replaced it with 802.5, there would be no change to the higher layer software. The only value of interest to the IP layer that would change would be the maximum datagram size.

- It is possible to introduce an efficient, multiprotocol approach to translation between network layer addresses and physical addresses. The Address Resolution Protocol, a popular method for doing this, will be described in Chapter 5.

Figure 4.17 shows how an 802.3 interface might be shared by DECnet, TCP/IP, and OSI protocol stacks. The intervening layer of interface software hides the detailed hardware I/O interactions from the higher level protocol users.

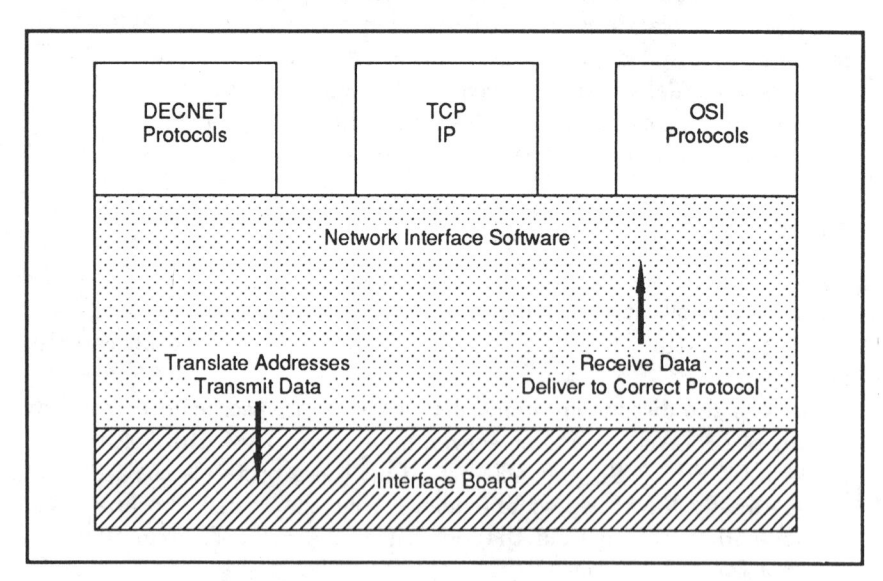

Figure 4.17 Protocols sharing a network interface.

4.7 LINK LAYER ISSUES

An IP datagram header contains between 20 and 60 octets.[9] The percentage of a datagram that is header information impacts throughput. Obviously, it is best to carry as much data as possible in a datagram.

However, we have seen that there are different maximum data field sizes for various network types. In Chapter 6, we shall see that IP provides a mechanism for fragmenting large datagrams when passing into a network with a small datagram size. As might be expected, this mechanism slows down network response time.

When a pair of communicating hosts are attached to the same LAN, they will wish to optimize data transfers by using the largest possible datagrams. When transmitting data to a remote host across unknown network types, it is best to use a conservative size that can be handled by any network.

A troublesome issue is the use of nonstandard protocol formats by some obsolete versions of TCP/IP. The Berkeley Software Distribution 4.2 implementation introduced a nonstandard format for Ethernet MAC frames that moved the frame type field and layer three and four header information into a trailer. Some commercial products incorporated this feature. Fortunately, its use is becoming quite rare. If possible, the use of trailers should be avoided.

4.8 RELATION TO OSI

Several Data Link protocols and physical media used for TCP/IP and OSI are the same. For example, both run over 802.2, 802.3, 802.4, 802.5, and X.25. Of course, fields (such as the Logical Link Control and SNAP headers) identifying the higher level protocol of a message will differentiate between TCP/IP and OSI traffic. The convergence between TCP/IP and OSI at this level makes it possible for them to share physical facilities.

There is one important difference between TCP/IP and OSI over X.25. OSI provides several classes of service at the transport (TCP) layer. It is possible to set up a single reliable X.25 virtual circuit for a single OSI connection, and then use an extremely simple class of transport protocol directly over this circuit. This makes use of the fact that X.25 is a network layer protocol that already has done the work of making a connection reliable.

---

[9] As we shall see later, 20-octet headers are the norm.

4.9 RECOMMENDED READING

The UNIX System Administration Handbook, by E. Nemeth, G. Snyder, and S. Seebass, contains a very lively and detailed account of setting up and configuring an Ethernet network.

RFC 1172 describes the Point-to-Point protocol. There are several RFCs that describe how to transmit IP datagrams over lower layer facilities: RFC 1209 for SMDS, RFC 1188 for FDDI, RFC 1088 for NetBIOS, RFC 1055 for SLIP, RFC 1201 for ARCNET, RFC 1042 for IEEE 802 networks, RFC 894 for Ethernet, and RFC 877 for public data networks.

Information about HDLC can be found in ISO 3309, 4335, and 7809. The IEEE 802 series and ISO 8802 series describe physical, media access, and logical link protocols for local area networks and metropolitan area networks.

CCITT Recommendation X.25 can be found in the 1984 CCITT red books. There are several standards documents relating to Frame Relay. A good place to start is with ANSI T1.606 and CCITT Recommendation I.122.

RFC 893 discusses trailer encapsulations.

Chapter 5

Naming and Addressing

5.1 INTRODUCTION

Every node in a network needs to be given a name and address. How should this be done? It may not be much of a problem on a stand-alone LAN with a handful of hosts, but when dealing with hundreds or thousands of hosts, starting off with a good name and address plan saves a ton of headache remedies when hosts, routers, and networks are added, removed, or relocated.

Internet administrators have had to cope with name and address management for a facility whose size has doubled every thirteen months or so. They came up with a practical strategy — delegate! They use a scheme of name and address management that:

- Allows names to reflect the logical structure of an organization.
- Assigns addresses that reflect the physical topology within an organization's network.
- Makes it possible to delegate name and address assignment to someone in charge of part of a network.

We shall see that the Internet's naming method also enables administrators to construct descriptive, easy-to-remember names.

5.2 NAMING

Both the structure of Internet names and the administrative system used to assign the names are hierarchical. The Internet is divided into partitions called *domains*.

Responsibility for assigning names within a domain is delegated to a designated domain administrator. This administrator can create subdomains and delegate naming authority to someone in each subdomain. Subdomains can be partitioned further to any required depth.

We shall see that every domain is assigned a label, and names are constructed by concatenating the labels for the chain of domains that they belong to.

5.3 EXAMPLES OF INTERNET NAMES

An Internet name can describe a system very appropriately. For example, the DDN Network Information Center (NIC) host is called NIC.DDN.MIL or nic.ddn.mil. Internet host names are not case sensitive. Usually an end user will type host names in lower case, while tables list names in upper case. Throughout this text you will see both upper and lower case names.

Some names are whimsical, such as the hosts in the MED.YALE.EDU subdomain which have been called:

```
BLINTZ.MED.YALE.EDU
BORSCHT.MED.YALE.EDU
COUSCOUS.MED.YALE.EDU
GAZPACHO.MED.YALE.EDU
LASAGNE.MED.YALE.EDU
PAELLA.MED.YALE.EDU
SUKIYAKI.MED.YALE.EDU
STRUDEL.MED.YALE.EDU
```

It is easy to understand the hierarchical structure for these names. All educational institutions are in the EDU domain of the Internet. YALE is a second level domain, under the first level domain, EDU. MED is one of the domains within YALE. Finally, the host name is prefixed to identify an individual system. A period is used to separate adjacent parts of a name.

5.3.1 The NIC Naming Tree

The overall Internet naming scheme is administered out of the NIC. It is a good idea for an organization to coordinate its name assignments with the NIC in order to reserve names that are unique and are consistent with what other organizations expect. Even if your organization engages in no outside communication today, it may do so in the future.

NIC names are organized in a tree, and each node in the tree corresponds to a domain. The NIC has defined the nodes located at the top of the tree. Names derived from the NIC tree are called *Domain Names*.

Naming and Addressing   67

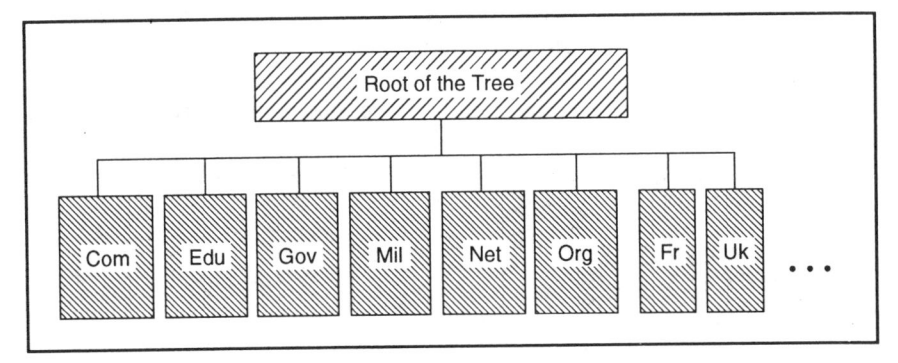

[Figure: tree diagram with "Root of the Tree" at top and children: Com, Edu, Gov, Mil, Net, Org, Fr, Uk, ...]

Figure 5.1 The NIC naming tree.

The top level domains in the tree (as shown in Figure 5.1) are:

- COM for commercial organizations
- EDU for educational institutions
- GOV for government bodies
- MIL for military organizations
- NET for systems performing network services
- ORG for organizations that don't fit into COM
- INT for international groups
- NATO for the North Atlantic Treaty Organization

There also are domains for each country: France, Great Britain, and so forth. Thus, there are organizations whose names end in a country code. For example, NRI.RESTON.VA.US and BROUILLY.INRIA.FR.

An organization may fit into more than one category, and can choose whichever naming domain it prefers.

5.3.2 Structure of Names

It is not uncommon to see names made up of two, three, four, or five labels. All of the following are legitimate Internet names:

BELLCORE.COM
NIC.DDN.MIL
BLINTZ.MED.YALE.EDU
LION.ZOO.CS.YALE.EDU

68 Chapter Five

Names that are longer than this may be difficult for users to remember and type. However, Internet naming standards permit labels of up to 63 characters and names of up to 255 characters.

Names are constructed by reading the node labels in the naming tree, starting from the bottom. The labels are concatenated, using "." as a separator. Some nodes of the Internet tree sprouting from EDU and shown in Figure 5.2 are:

SUN.DEPT.CS.YALE.EDU
RA.DEPT.CS.YALE.EDU
LION.ZOO.CS.YALE.EDU
TIGER.ZOO.CS.YALE.EDU
APPLECIDER.CS.YALE.EDU
DIOR.STAT.YALE.EDU
HERMES.STAT.YALE.EDU
BATSTATION.PSYCH.YALE.EDU

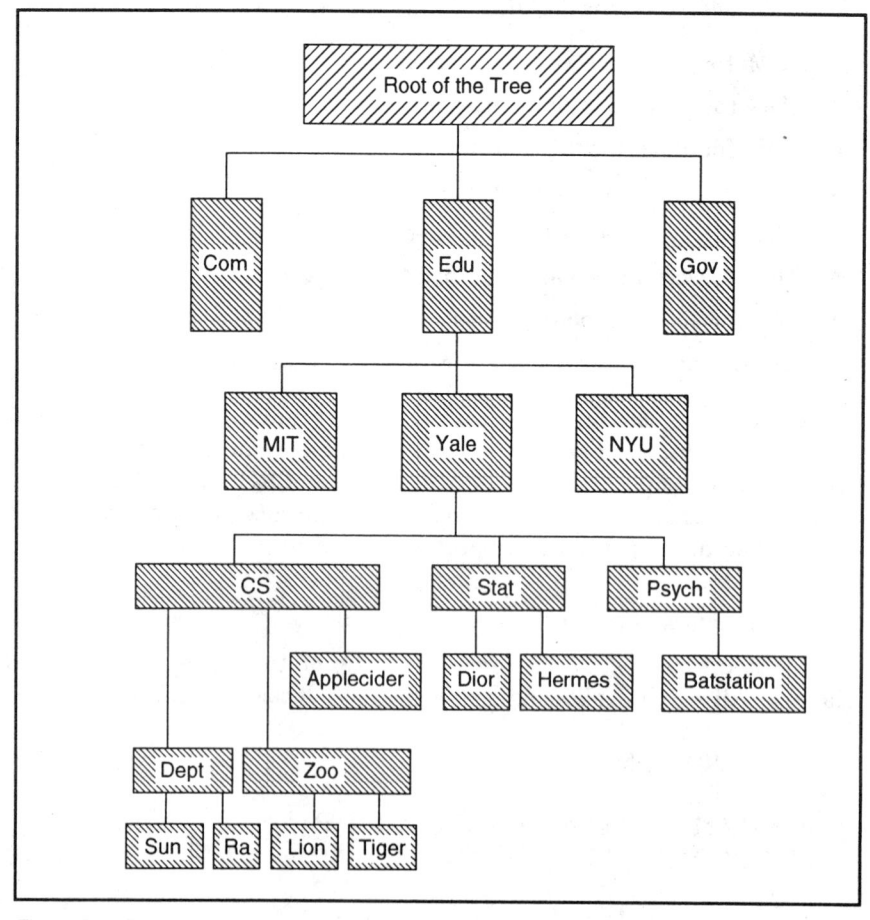

Figure 5.2 Part of the Internet naming tree.

Four-label names are quite common. The Yale Computer Science department decided to use five-deep labels for some *dept* machines, and for the *zoo* machines, which are used by students. In any case, the names are meaningful to their users, and are easy to remember.

5.4 ADDRESSES

The IP protocol uses addresses to identify hosts and to route data to them. Every host must be assigned an IP address that can be used in actual communications. A host name is translated into its IP address by looking up the name in a table of name-address pairs.

An IP address is a 32-bit (4-octet) binary value. This defines the overall *address space* which is the set of address numbers. The total IP address space contains 2^{32} numbers.

The *dot* notation is a popular way of expressing an IP address so that users can read and write it easily. Each octet of the address is converted into a decimal number and the numbers are separated by dots.

For example, the address for BLINTZ.MED.YALE.EDU in 32-bit binary and dot notation is:

10000010 10000100 00001011 00011111
130.132.11.31

Note that the biggest number that can appear in a dotted address is 255, which corresponds to the binary number 11111111.

5.4.1 Address Formats

An IP address has a two part format consisting of a *network address* and a *local address*. The network address identifies the network to which the node is attached. The local address identifies an individual node.

Network Address	Local Address

Networks vary in size. There are three Internet address formats defined for use with large, medium, and small networks. These are:

- Class A for large networks
- Class B for medium sized networks
- Class C for small networks

In addition to Classes A, B, and C, there are two special address formats, Class D and Class E. Class D addresses are used for IP *multicasting*. Multicasting is used to distribute a single message to a group of systems dispersed across the Internet. Class E addresses are reserved for experimental use.

The five address formats are displayed in Figure 5.3. The first four bits of each address identify its class. The patterns are:

INITIAL BITS	CLASS
0xxx	Class A
10xx	Class B
110x	Class C
1110	Class D
1111	Class E

Note that when written in dot notation:

- Class A addresses start with a number between 0 and 127
- Class B addresses start with a number between 128 and 191
- Class C addresses start with a number between 192 and 223
- Class D addresses start with a number between 224 and 239
- Class E addresses start with a number between 240 and 255

Organizations with private TCP/IP internets generally adhere to Internet conventions and use the Class A, B, and C address formats.

In fact, organizations usually ask the DDN Network Information Center for a block of network addresses in order to be sure that their addresses will be globally unique. The Class of address assigned depends on the size of the organization's network.

Class A Format

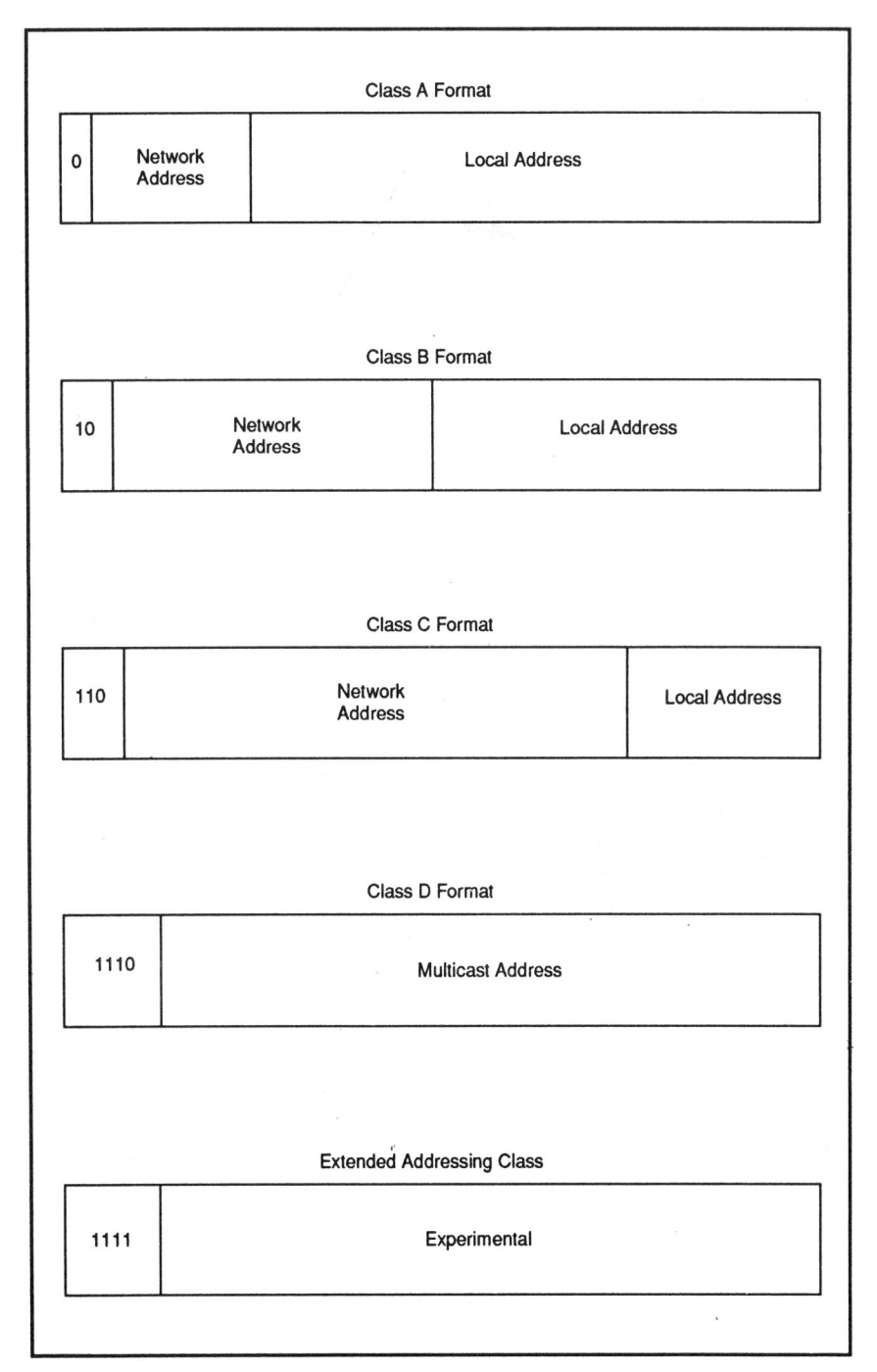

| 0 | Network Address | Local Address |

Class B Format

| 10 | Network Address | Local Address |

Class C Format

| 110 | Network Address | Local Address |

Class D Format

| 1110 | Multicast Address |

Extended Addressing Class

| 1111 | Experimental |

Figure 5.3 IP address formats.

5.4.2 Assigning Class C Addresses to Networks

An organization with a small network is given one or more Class C addresses. This means that the NIC assigns one or more fixed values to be used in the first three bytes of the organization's addresses. The organization has control of the last byte. For example, the following addresses and host names belong to an organization that was assigned the Class C address 192.31.235.

192.31.235.67	terra.sca.com
192.31.235.68	luna.sca.com
192.31.235.69	moon.sca.com

This organization owns the numbers from 192.31.235.0 to 192.31.235.255. These numbers make up the organization's *address space*.

5.4.3 Assigning Class B Addresses to Networks

A medium to large-sized network is given a Class B address. The NIC assigns a fixed value to the first two bytes of the address. The last two bytes can be managed by the organization. For example, the following addresses and host names belong to an organization that was assigned the Class B address 131.146.

131.146.8.29	daffodil.tymnet.com
131.146.8.26	petunia.tymnet.com
131.146.2.111	bcool.tymnet.com
131.146.2.150	smurf.tymnet.com

Class B addresses are very popular and many organizations have requested and received them. Although there are more than 16,000 possible Class B network identifiers, the supply is running out.

5.4.4 Assigning Class A Addresses to Networks

Some very large organizations have Class A addresses. The NIC has assigned a fixed value to the first byte of the address and the last three bytes are managed by the organization. For example, the following addresses and host names belong to an organization that was assigned the Class A address 26.

26.5.0.63	longbeach-bumed.navy.mil
26.11.0.3	pendleton-bumed.navy.mil
26.15.0.50	quantico-bumed.navy.mil

5.4.5 Network Address Spaces

When an organization is assigned a block of addresses, it takes charge of part of the overall address space. The address space sizes[1] for the three classes of network are:

NETWORK CLASS	ADDRESS SPACE SIZE
A	2^{24} = 16777216 Addresses
B	2^{16} = 65536 Addresses
C	2^{8} = 256 Addresses

Note that the term *network* has a special connotation in the TCP/IP world. A *network* consists of all of the systems with addresses in a particular Class A, B, or C address space. For example, all systems whose addresses start with 26. form a network, as do all systems whose addresses start with 192.31.235.

5.5 SUBNETS

An organization that has a Class A or Class B network address is very likely to have a fairly complex network made up of several LANs and WANs. It makes sense to partition the address space in a way that matches the network's structure as a family of subnets. To do this, the local part of the address is broken into pieces in any convenient way:

Network Address	Subnet Address	Host Address

The size of the subnet part of an address and the assignment of numbers to subnets is the responsibility of the organization that "owns" that part of the address space.

---

[1] A few address values have special meanings and are reserved, so that the number of addresses that can be assigned to systems is slightly less than these quantities.

Subnet addressing often is done at a byte boundary. An organization with a Class B address such as 156.33 might use its third byte to identify subnets. For example:

    156.33.1
    156.33.2
    156.33.3

The fourth byte would then be used to identify individual hosts on a subnet.

On the other hand, an organization with a Class C address has only a 1-byte address space and might use 4 bits for subnet addresses and 4 bits for host addresses.

5.5.1 Subnet Masks

Traffic is routed to a host by looking at the network and subnet part of its IP address. It is easy to tell how much of an address is the network part because of the strictly defined Class A, B, and C formats.

Organizations choose their own subnet field sizes, so how can hosts and routers recognize this field? The answer is that there is a configuration parameter called the *subnet mask*. This is a sequence of 32 bits. The bits covering the network and subnet part of an address are set to 1. (Another way to view the subnet mask is that zero bits are used to *mask out* the host number in the IP address!)

For example, if the administrator of Class B network 156.33 has chosen to use the third octet of all addresses to identify subnets, then the network's subnet mask is:

A Mask for a Class B Network With 8-bit Subnets
11111111   11111111   11111111   00000000

Subnet masks often are expressed in dotted decimal notation. The mask above can be written as 255.255.255.0.

Routers directly connected to a subnet are configured with the mask for the subnetwork. It is common practice to use a single subnet mask throughout an organization's internet.

If a network contains a large number of point-to-point lines, subnet numbers will be used up very wastefully since there are only two systems on each point-to-point subnetwork. An organization may decide to use 14-bit masks (255.255.255.252) for its point-to-point lines.

The subnet mask for a network usually is known only to routers directly attached to the network. When traditional routing protocols are used, the outside world cannot tell how a network has been subnetted.[2]

5.6 SPECIAL ADDRESSES

5.6.1 Identifying Networks

It is convenient to have a way to use a dotted IP address to refer to a network.[3] By convention, this is done by filling in the local part of the address with zeroes. For example, 5.0.0.0 identifies a Class A network, 131.18.0.0 identifies a Class B network, and 201.49.16.0 identifies a Class C network.

The same convention is used to identify a subnet. For example, if network 131.18.0.0 uses an 8-bit subnet mask, then 131.18.5.0 and 131.18.6.0 refer to subnets. The price of this convenience is that addresses of this form must never be assigned to hosts or routers because of the confusion that this would cause.

5.6.2 Broadcasts to Networks

IP address 255.255.255.255 (i.e., an address consisting of 32 ones) has a special purpose. It is used to send a message to every host on the local network. A broadcast often is used when a host needs to locate a server.

It also is possible to send a message to every host on a selected remote network. This is done by setting the local part of the address to ones. For example, suppose that a user wants to send a message to all nodes on a Class C Ethernet network 201.49.16.0. The address used for broadcasting is:

201.49.16.255

The result of sending an IP datagram to this address is that the datagram would be relayed to a router attached to network 201.49.16.0. The router would then do a MAC layer broadcast to deliver the message to all hosts on the network. Note that no host can be given the address 201.49.16.255!

---

[2] A new routing protocol will change this picture. The Open Shortest Path First (OSPF) protocol makes it easy to use different mask sizes within a network and makes subnets visible throughout an internet. This protocol will be described in Chapter 8.

[3] For example, in routing tables.

5.6.3 Broadcasts to Subnets

A broadcast also can be directed to a specific subnet. For example if 131.18.7.0 is a subnet of a Class B network, then address 131.18.7.255 is used to broadcast a message to all nodes on this subnet.

Address 131.18.255.255 still can be used to aim a message at every node in the entire Class B network. The routers within the organization will have to be smart enough to distribute the message to each subnet. If one of the subnets had been assigned subnet number 255, we would have a problem. It would not be clear whether a broadcast to 131.18.255.255 was intended for the subnet or for the whole network. The way to avoid this is never to assign an all-ones address (like 255) to a subnet.

5.6.4 Loopback Address

At the opposite extreme to broadcasting are messages that never leave the local host. It is useful to have a loopback address that means "this node" for the purpose of testing network software. By convention, any address starting with 127 is reserved for this purpose. An example of a loopback address is:

127.0.0.1

Note that a Class A address space of 2^{16} numbers has been reserved for loopback addresses!

5.6.5 This Host and This Network

There are some special address formats that are used only during system initialization. These forms are reserved and cannot be used to identify destinations. By convention, address 0.0.0.0 stands for *this host on this network*. Other hosts on the local network are denoted by filling in just the host part of the address. For example, 0.0.0.5 means host 5 on this network.

5.7 THE DOMAIN NAME SYSTEM

It is necessary to know a host's address in order to communicate with the host. Often an end user will know a host's name, but not its address. In this case, either the end user or the application that the end user has invoked needs a way to look up the address.

Small, isolated networks can meet this need by keeping a centrally maintained host name-to-address translation table. Individual hosts on the network stay up-to-date by copying this table periodically. This method was used in the early days of the Internet. The NIC maintained the master version of the translation table, and other systems received a copy on a regular basis. As time went by, this method became burdensome and inefficient.

The Domain Name System was set up to provide a better method of keeping track of Internet names and addresses. Names and addresses now are kept at name servers spread through the Internet.[4]

These name servers are updated locally, so node additions, deletions, and moves are recorded quickly and accurately at a *primary authoritative server*. Because name to address translation is so important, the information is copied to one or more *secondary authoritative servers*.

Many vendors provide software that lets a system function as a name server. Often this software has been adapted from the Berkeley Internet Domain ("BIND") package. An organization can use this software to run its own private name service, and optionally may connect its name service to the Internet Domain Name System.

A client program capable of performing Domain Name System lookups is a standard part of TCP/IP products, and is called a *resolver*.

5.7.1 Looking up Host Addresses

The dialogue that follows shows a user interacting with a domain name server to get the IP addresses for several hosts. The user's home computer supports the widely available *nslookup* user interface. (Another user interface named *DIG* sometimes is provided.)

Immediately after the user types *nslookup*, the local default server identifies itself, displaying its name and address. In this case, the server's name is DEPT-GW.CS.YALE.EDU and the server's address is 128.36.0.36.

Thereafter, the user simply types in the name of a host whose address is desired. The request is sent to the default server. After each query, the server identifies itself and then provides the answer. If the user has asked for local information, the server extracts the answer from its own data base. If not, the server first checks a cache of recent queries to see if the information is available, and if not, interacts with an authoritative server to get the answer.

Each step in the dialogue that follows is explained by comments on the right. Note that the local server transparently consults with other servers to get address information for lots of remote computers.

---

[4]Later, we shall see that name servers also contain mail routing information as well as data describing the types of host systems on a network.

78 Chapter Five

```
nslookup
Default Server:
DEPT-GW.CS.YALE.EDU
server ID
Address:   128.36.0.36

> golem.cs.yale.edu
Server:   DEPT-GW.CS.YALE.EDU
Address:   128.36.0.36

Name:     golem.cs.yale.edu
Address:   128.36.0.36

> daffodil.tymnet.com
Server:   DEPT-GW.CS.YALE.EDU
Address:   128.36.0.36

Name:     daffodil.tymnet.com
Address:   131.146.8.29

> longbeach-bumed.navy.mil
Server:   DEPT-GW.CS.YALE.EDU
Address:   128.36.0.36

Name:
longbeach-bumed.navy.mil
Address:   26.5.0.63
```

Request Domain Name Service

Responds with
default server ID
and its address

User makes a local query
Server ID again
Server's address

The name in the query
The answer

User makes a remote query
Server ID again
Server's address

The name in the query
The answer

User makes a remote query
Server ID again
Server's address

The name in the query
The answer

5.8 ADDRESS RESOLUTION PROTOCOL

The preceding dialogue translated node names into IP addresses. Before data can be sent between two stations on a LAN, a second translation must be performed. The physical address of the destination node must be discovered. There are three methods used for providing this information:

- Configure a table of values directly into each node.
- Configure a table of values onto a server which the nodes consult.
- Discover values by broadcasting a query on the LAN.

The Address Resolution Protocol (ARP) defines a broadcast-based method for dynamically translating between IP addresses and physical addresses. ARP lets a network administrator add nodes to a local network or change a node's interface boards without needing to manually update address translation tables.

The systems on the local network can use ARP to discover physical address information for themselves.[5] When a host wants to start communicating with a local partner, it looks up the partner's IP address in its ARP table. If there is no entry for that IP address, the host broadcasts an ARP request containing the destination IP address (see Figure 5.4).

The target host recognizes its IP address and reads the request. The first thing that the target host does is update its own address translation table with the IP address and physical address of the sender. This is prudent, because it is likely that the target soon will be conversing with the sender! The target host then sends back a reply containing its own hardware interface address.

When the source receives the reply, it updates its ARP table and is ready to transmit data across the LAN.

5.8.1 ARP Message Contents

ARP initially was used on Ethernet LANs, but its design is general so that it can be used with other types of networks such as Token-Rings, FDDI LANs, and networks providing SMDS. ARP even has been adapted for wide area networks (such as frame relay) by sending ARP messages via a limited multicast rather than a broadcast.

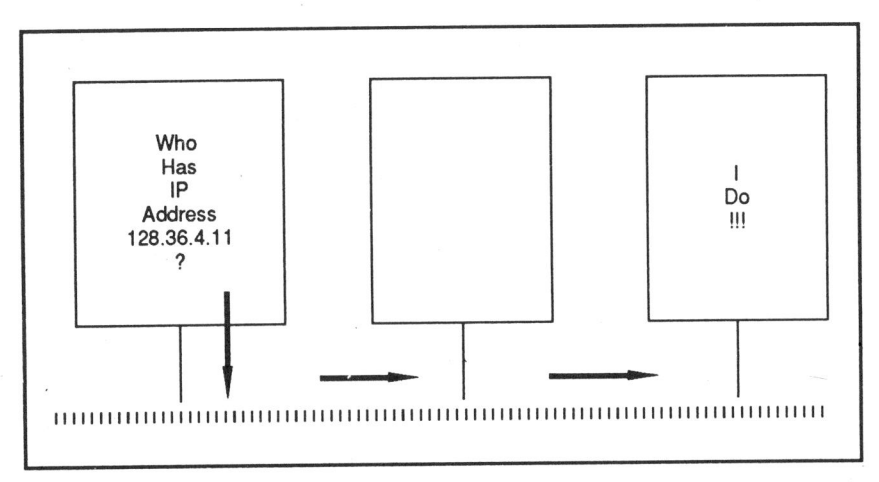

Figure 5.4 Discovering the physical address of a system with a known IP address.

---

[5]An administrator also can manually enter some permanent address translation entries into the ARP table, if desired.

An ARP message is placed in the data field of a frame, following the lower layer header(s).[6] The ARP message fields are:

NUMBER OF OCTETS	FIELD
2	Type of hardware address
2	Higher layer addressing protocol
1	Length of hardware address
1	Length of higher layer address
2	Type of message (00 01 = request, 00 02 = response)
*	Source hardware address
*	Source higher layer address
*	Destination hardware address
*	Destination higher layer address

The lengths of the last four fields depend on the technology and protocol in use. Hardware addresses for 802.X LANs contain 6 octets, and IP addresses are 4 octets long. For example, a message requesting translation of an IP address to an Ethernet address would have the (hexadecimal) form:

NUMBER OF OCTETS	FIELD	DESCRIPTION
2	00 01	Ethernet
2	08 00	IP
1	06	Ethernet 6 octet physical address
1	04	IP protocol
2	00 01	Request
6	02 07 01 00 53 23	Source hardware address
4	80 04 0C 1B	Source higher layer address
6	00 00 00 00 00 00	Destination hardware address
4	80 04 0C 08	Destination higher layer address

Note that ARP is not exclusively owned by TCP/IP, since the second field identifies the protocol that is using ARP.

Since the original ARP request is broadcast, any system on the LAN could use the information in the ARP message to update its table entry for the requester. However, usually a system only enters an update when it is the target of an ARP message.

---

[6]For example, for an Ethernet, an ARP message follows the MAC header, while for an 802.5 network, the ARP message follows the MAC header, LLC header, and SNAP subheader.

5.8.2 The ARP Table

Most systems provide a command that allows an administrator to:

- View the local ARP table
- Manually add or delete table entries
- Load a table with entries from a configuration file

The dialogue below uses the *arp -a* command to show how the local ARP table changes after a Telnet connection is set up to host *popeye*, which is not currently in the table. Note that the output displays the IP addresses in dot format, and displays the six octets of the physical addresses as hexadecimal numbers separated by a ":" delimiter.

```
arp -a
casper.na.cs.yale.edu   (128.36.12.1)    at    8:0:20:8:59:ec
cantor.cs.yale.edu      (128.36.12.26)   at    8:0:20:8:6e:a0

telnet popeye.na.cs.yale.edu

Trying 128.36.12.8
Connected to popeye.na.cs.yale.edu.
login:
 . . .
 . . .
 . . .
logout

arp -a
casper.na.cs.yale.edu   (128.36.12.1)    at    8:0:20:8:59:ec
cantor.cs.yale.edu      (128.36.12.26)   at    8:0:20:8:6e:a0
popeye.na.cs.yale.edu   (128.36.12.8)    at    8:0:20:7:c7:b7
```

5.8.3 Reverse ARP

A variant of ARP called *reverse ARP* (RARP) helps a node to find out its own IP address. This is useful for diskless workstations which need to get configuration information from the network.

A station using the reverse ARP protocol broadcasts a query stating its *physical address* and requests its *IP address*. A server on the network that is configured with a table of physical addresses and matching IP addresses can respond to the query.

5.9 MULTIHOMING

Identifying networks (and subnets) directly within an IP address has many benefits:

- It simplifies the job of assigning addresses. A block of addresses can be delegated to the administrator of a particular network or subnet.
- It helps keep routing tables short. A routing table needs to contain only a brief list of networks and subnets, rather than a list including every host in an internet.
- It simplifies the job of routing. Table lookups of network or subnet numbers can be carried out quickly and efficiently.

These are important advantages. Unfortunately, there is one complication introduced by using an address format that contains a clue to routing.

A host may be connected to more than one network. For example, a host might have interfaces to a Token-Ring LAN and to an X.25 WAN. Since these are different nets, a separate internet address is required for each of these attachments! Of course, by definition, a router has two or more network interfaces, and a separate internet address is required for each of these.

In Figure 5.5, an X.25 network is connected to a Token-Ring LAN and to an Ethernet LAN by routers. Each router has two IP addresses. The X.25 network has a Class A network address of 27.0.0.0. The Token-Ring and Ethernet are subnets of Class B networks with network addresses 130.40.0.0 and 128.36.0.0 respectively. Each router network interface is assigned a different IP address.

There is a host in the figure that has connections both to a Token-Ring and to an Ethernet. This host also would need to be assigned two IP addresses.

Multihoming introduces some complications into network routing. For example, data may be routed to a multihomed host differently depending on which of its IP addresses is chosen for communication. It may in fact be helpful to associate two names to the host, corresponding to its two network interfaces.

In spite of the drawbacks that result from multihoming, the inclusion of a network and subnet identifiers within an address has contributed greatly to the efficiency of routers, and to the ease with which a TCP/IP internet can be enlarged.

Naming and Addressing 83

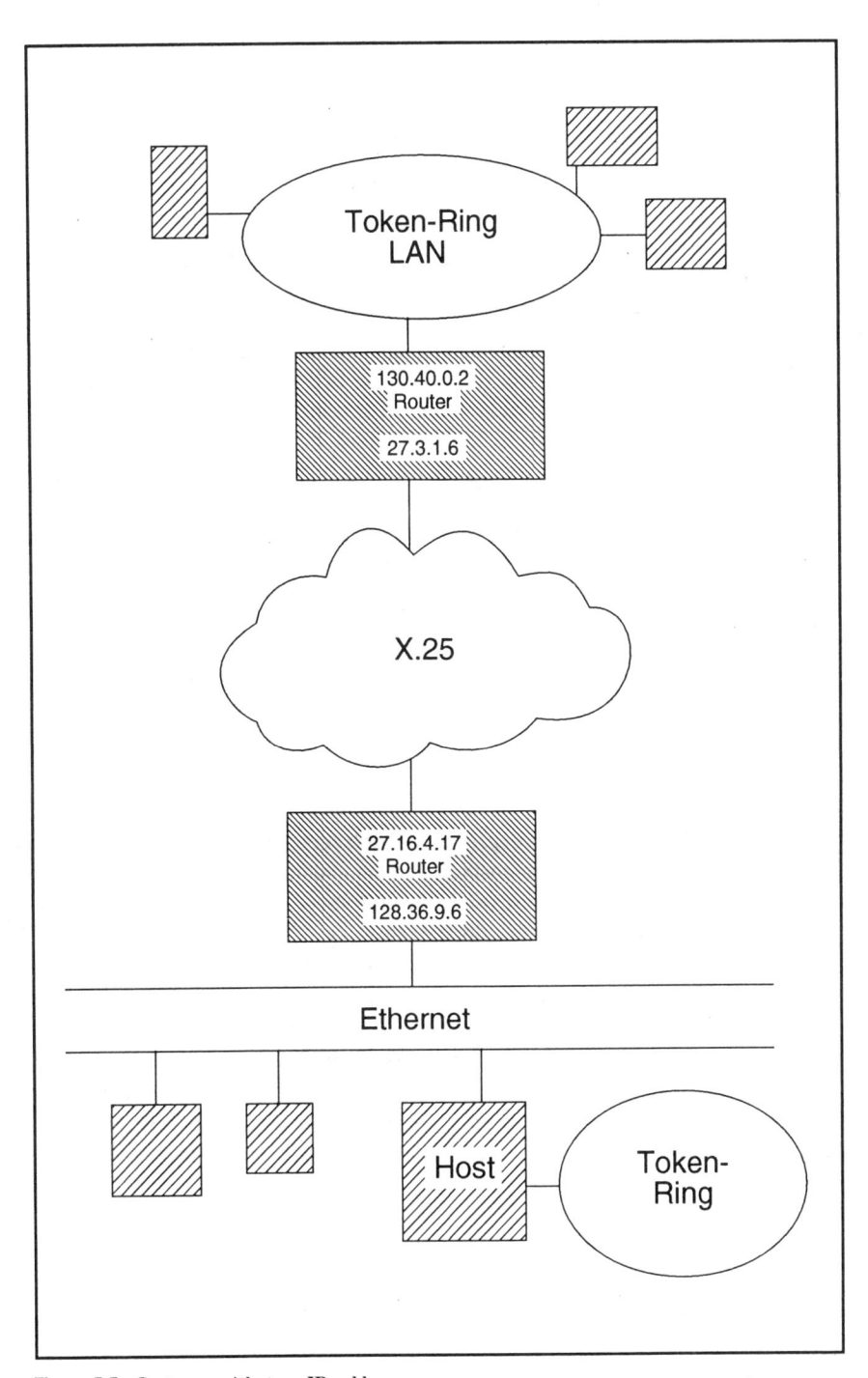

Figure 5.5 Systems with two IP addresses.

5.10 THE RELATIONSHIP BETWEEN NAMES AND ADDRESSES

Users who look at a system name like FRACTAL.ENG.YALE.EDU and its IP address in dot format, 130.132.20.253, can easily get the idea that parts of names always must correspond to numbers in the dotted address. This is definitely not the case!

It is true that sometimes names are constructed so that the name hierarchy matches the address hierarchy up to some point. If this is the case, it is important to keep in mind that the sizes of the network and subnet parts of IP addresses vary.

Moreover, even when an organization correlates network and subnet IDs with name labels, it may still wish to branch off more domains at the bottom of its naming tree. For example, if departments such as SALES and ADMIN share a LAN, it may be convenient to create a separate naming domain for each, although they belong to the same subnet.

But the fact is that there is no requirement for system names to depend in any way on their physical network attachments. For example, the host NIC.DDN.MIL recently was moved from the west coast of the United States to the east coast! Routing is based on addresses, not names, and a system's address always is looked up before data is sent to it. Organizations are free to design a flexible naming plan that best meets their needs.

5.11 MULTICASTING

Broadcasting causes a datagram to be delivered to every system on a network or subnet. A more restricted form of multiple delivery, called *multicasting*, causes a datagram to be delivered to a group of systems. Multicasting can be a very useful facility. For example, a single message can be used to simultaneously update configuration data across a homogeneous group of hosts, or to poll a group of routers for their status.

A multicasting protocol standard has been defined, but the number of available hosts and routers that support the standard currently is limited. However, its use is likely to grow over the next few years, so that it is worthwhile to examine its major features here.

5.11.1 Multicast Groups

A *multicast group* is a set of systems with an assigned multicast IP address. Members of the group still retain their own IP addresses, but also have the ability to absorb data that has been sent to the multicast address. Any system may belong to zero or more multicast groups.

Recall that Class D addresses are used for multicasting, and these addresses start with numbers ranging from 224 to 239. Some multicast addresses are permanent, and are listed in the Internet Assigned Numbers RFC. Some examples of permanently defined multicast addresses include:

224.0.0.1	All hosts on a local subnet
224.0.0.2	All routers on a local subnet
224.0.0.5	All routers supporting the open shortest path first protocol
224.0.0.6	Designated routers supporting the open shortest path first protocol

Multicast addresses also may be assigned to temporary groups that are formed and dissolved on an as-needed basis.

A number of functions must be supported within a host that is a member of one or more multicast groups:

- There must be a command that identifies the multicast address of a group that the host wishes to join, and the interface that should listen for this address.
- A host's IP layer must be able to recognize multicast addresses for incoming and outgoing datagrams.
- There must be a command that allows a host to cancel its membership in a multicast group.

Multicasting is not restricted to a local network. Routers with multicasting software will be able to propagate multicast datagrams to systems across an internet.

In order to do this efficiently, a router needs to know whether there are hosts on its locally attached networks that belong to a particular multicasting group. Routers also will need to exchange information with other routers so that they can find out whether there are group members on remote networks to whom they should forward multicast datagrams.

Hosts use the Internet Group Management Protocol (IGMP) to report their group memberships to neighboring routers that support multicast routing. The reports are sent to the IP multicast address that belongs to the group that the host is joining.[7]

---

[7] Routers will not forward this report out of the local network, so it will be heard only by routers and by other local members of the group.

To assure that their membership information is complete, the IGMP protocol enables routers to poll hosts periodically, asking for reports of their current memberships. The polls are sent to the all-hosts multicast IP address, 224.0.0.1.

5.11.2 Translating to Physical Multicast Addresses

Recall that the physical interfaces to Ethernet and 802.X LANs optionally can be assigned one or more multicast addresses. These are logical assignments, and any convenient values can be selected. This fact is used to make it easy to translate an IP multicast address to a multicast physical address.[8]

The following rule, specified for Ethernet, can be used for any of the 802.X networks that have 6-octet physical addresses:

- The first 3 octets of the physical multicast address should be set to 01:00:5e

- The next bit should be set to 0, and the final 23 bits should be set to the low-order 23 bits of the IP multicast address.

In other words, the bits from the IP multicast address below that have been marked "x" are borrowed and put into the low order bits of the physical multicast address:

IP Multicast Address:
                1110????   ?xxxxxxx xxxxxxxx xxxxxxxx

Physical Multicast Address:
00000001 00000000 01011110 0xxxxxxx xxxxxxxx xxxxxxxx

What about the positions marked "?" in the IP multicast address? Any values could have been selected for these positions, and these values will not appear in the physical multicast address. The result is that the physical interface might pick up multicasts that this host does not want. The host's IP layer will discard the extraneous multicasts.

A good way to avoid this extra processing is to restrict multicast addresses by setting the "?" positions to zero. This still leaves 2^{23} or over eight million multicast addresses, which should be enough to meet all needs!

---

[8]Note that ARP is *not* used to translate multicast addresses.

5.12 RECOMMENDED READING

The address classes and special addresses are defined in RFC 1060. Subnetting is described in RFC 950. RFC 1219 introduces some ideas for improved flexibility in the use of subnet masks, including assignment of masks of different sizes within a single network. RFC 1112 describes IP multicasting.

The Address Resolution Protocol was defined for Ethernets in RFC 826. RFC 925 defined Multi-LAN Address Resolution. Reverse ARP is described in RFC 903.

RFC 1178 contains both sound and entertaining advice on how to choose a name for your computer. RFC 1034 contains a comprehensive exposition of domain naming. RFC 1035 describes the protocols used to build the Domain Name System and discusses the implementation of this system.

Chapter

6

Internet Protocol

6.1 INTRODUCTION

An internet is a set of networks connected by routers.[1] The Internet Protocol (IP) is a network layer protocol that routes data across an internet. The researchers and designers who created IP were responding to U.S. Department of Defense requirements for a protocol that could:

- Accommodate the use of hosts built by different vendors.
- Accommodate the use of routers built by different vendors.
- Encompass a growing variety of network types.
- Be adaptable to network growth and change.
- Interwork older technologies with newer, more capable technologies.
- Support higher layer connectionless and connection-oriented services.

A connectionless network layer architecture was selected as the best way to meet these needs. The IP protocol provides the mechanisms needed to transport units called *datagrams* across an internet.

It turns out that the use of IP gives network builders a great deal of flexibility in constructing the topologies that meet their needs. Furthermore, IP networks can grow without disrupting what already is in place.

There is a good selection of capable IP router products available, and router performance has been steadily improving.

---

[1] Recall that most RFC documents use the term gateway rather than router.

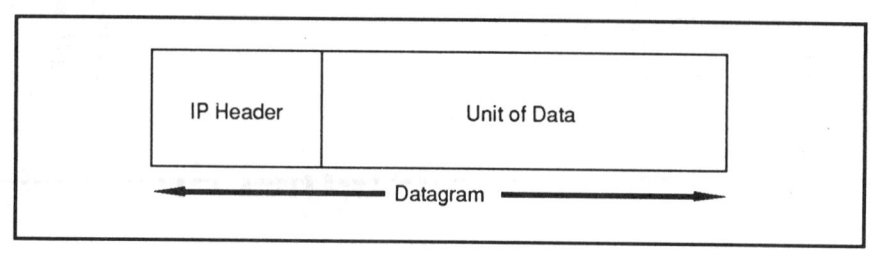

Figure 6.1 Datagram format.

As shown in Figure 6.1, a datagram is made up of an IP header and a unit of data to be delivered.

Each IP datagram is routed independently. One result of this is that the order in which datagrams arrive may not be the same as the order in which they were sent.

IP is a "best effort" protocol. This means that IP does not guarantee that a datagram will be delivered safely to its destination. All that is guaranteed is that a best effort will be made (see Figure 6.2). A datagram may be destroyed along the way because:

- Bit errors occurred during transmission across a medium.
- A congested router discarded the datagram because of a shortage of buffer space.
- Temporarily, there was no usable path to the destination.

Figure 6.2 IP best effort delivery.

All of the features that assure reliability have been concentrated within the TCP layer. Recovery from destroyed data depends on TCP actions.

6.2 OPERATIONAL MODEL

Hosts are the sources and destinations for information. Routers select the paths that datagrams follow and relay data between networks. The function of a router is to perform routing!

6.2.1 Routing Operations

Figure 6.3 illustrates IP routing operations. When TCP or UDP at Host A wishes to send data to its peer at Host B, the sender passes its data to IP, along with the destination host's IP address and some handling parameters.

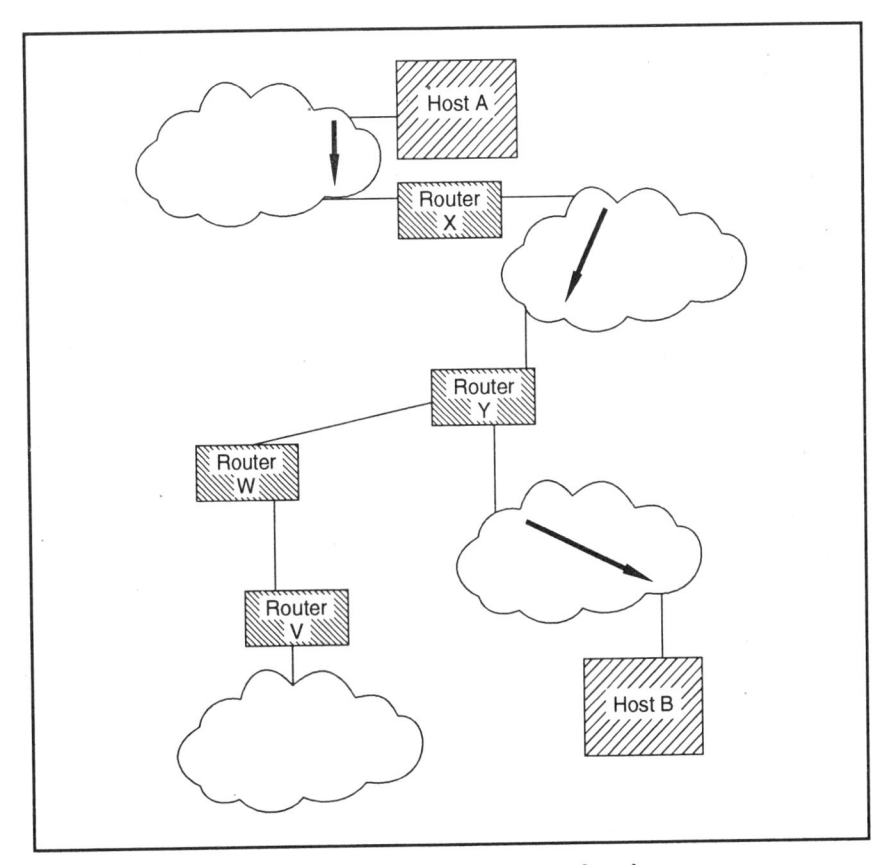

Figure 6.3 Routing a datagram to its destination across three hops.

IP adds a header to the data and forms a datagram. IP examines the destination address and uses a routing procedure to determine that the datagram should be sent to router X. At X, the routing procedure is repeated, and the datagram is sent to router Y. Router Y recognizes that host B is on a directly connected network, and delivers the datagram to host B. This route from host A to host B consists of 3 *hops*: A to X, X to Y, and Y to B.

6.2.2 Frame Encapsulation and Maximum Transmission Unit

Before a datagram can be transmitted across a network hop, it must be encapsulated within the header(s) required for the network technology, as shown in Figure 6.4. For example, to traverse an 802.3 or 802.5 network, a datagram is embedded within data link and MAC headers and a MAC trailer.

As we have seen in Chapter 4, each LAN and WAN technology imposes a different size limit on its frames. IP transmits an entire datagram in a single frame, so the maximum frame size restricts the size of the datagrams that IP can send across a particular medium. The size of a datagram is equal to:

[*Frame Size*]-[*MAC Header Size*]-[*Link Layer Header Size*]-[*MAC Trailer Size*]

The biggest datagram size for a type of network is called its *maximum transmission unit* or MTU. For example, Ethernet has an MTU of 1500 octets, 802.3 has an MTU of 1492 octets, FDDI has an MTU of 4352 octets, 802.4 has an MTU of 8166 octets, and SMDS has an MTU of 9180 octets.

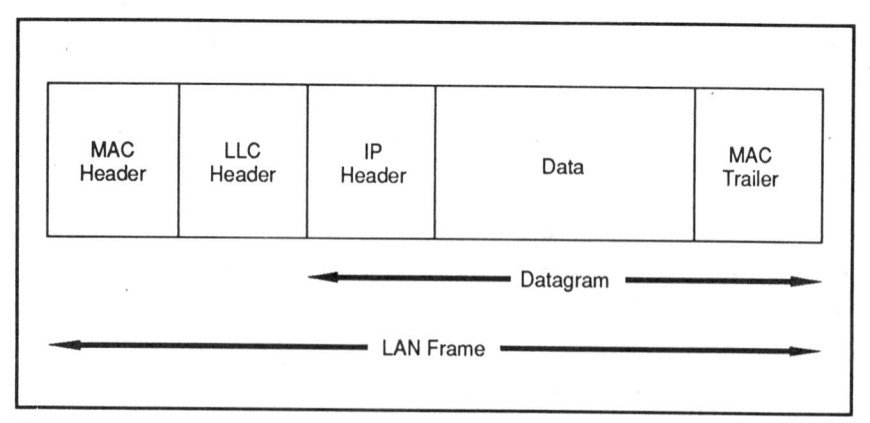

Figure 6.4 Transmission format.

6.3 FUNCTIONS

This section describes *what* the IP layer does. Figure 6.5 summarizes the functions that IP performs. We will illustrate some of the nuts and bolts behind IP's implementation by means of some interactive dialogues on a Sun Microsystems UNIX workstation. Commands that are identical or similar to the commands in these dialogues are available on many other types of computer systems.

In the next section, we will investigate *how* IP carries out its mission.

How Route?
- Check Options for Source Route
- Next Hop

Handling
- Precedence
- Delay
- Throughput
- Reliability

Time to Live

Checksum

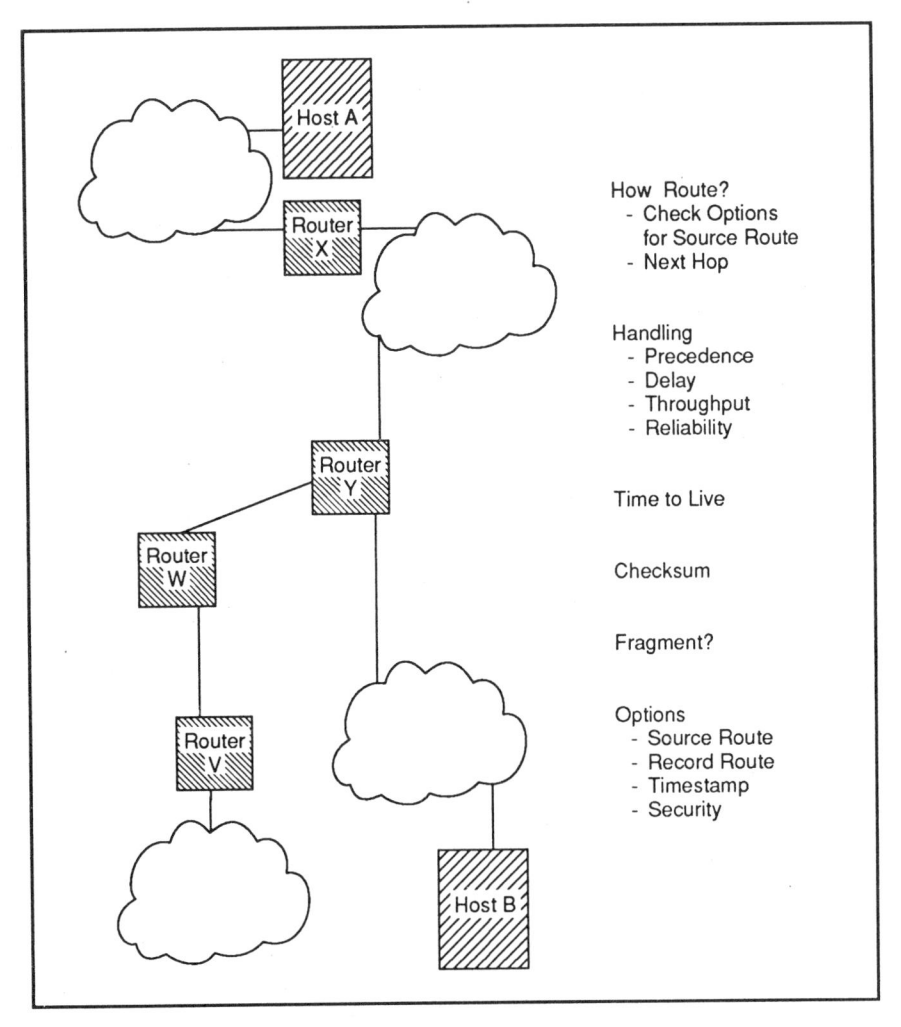

Fragment?

Options
- Source Route
- Record Route
- Timestamp
- Security

Figure 6.5 IP functions.

6.3.1 Primary Function

The primary IP function is to accept data from TCP or UDP at a source host, create a datagram, and route the datagram through the network. IP at the destination host delivers the data to the recipient TCP or UDP. IP software routes data to a destinations using two mechanisms:

- The subnetwork mask
- A routing table

6.3.2 Subnetwork Mask

Recall that a subnetwork mask is a sequence of 32 bits with 1s in the positions that cover the network and subnet portions and 0s covering the host address field. Instead of expressing the mask as 1s and 0s, we can write it in hexadecimal notation, or in a "friendly" dot notation. Thus if we have a subnet mask of:

11111111 11111111 11111111 00000000

It can be written in hex as:

ffffff00

Alternatively, it can be written in dot notation as:

255.255.255.0

To see how the mask is used, suppose that our host is attached to a LAN and has IP address 128.36.12.27 with subnet mask ffffff00. If we want to send data to a host with IP address 128.36.12.14, then the mask tells us that both the source and destination belong to the same subnet — 128.36.12. Hence, they can exchange traffic directly across the subnet.

Before our host can send data, the destination's IP address must be translated to its LAN physical address. IP addresses and matching physical addresses are stored in the ARP translation table. If the destination's physical address is not currently in this table, our system uses the ARP protocol to broadcast a request for the information.

6.3.3 Looking Up Addresses and Masks

How can we find out what our IP address and subnet mask are? These parameters are part of the configuration data for the interface that attaches to the subnet. For example, suppose that our host is attached to an Ethernet via a network interface named *le0*.

Let's examine the configuration data for that interface. On our sample system, the *ifconfig* command is used to set or view interface configuration information.

```
ifconfig le0
le0: flags=63<UP,BROADCAST,NOTRAILERS,RUNNING>
     inet 128.36.12.27 netmask ffffff00 broadcast 128.36.12.255
```

The response shows that the IP address associated with this interface is 128.36.12.27. The subnet mask has been expressed in hexadecimal as ffffff00, which is 255.255.255.0 when written in user-friendly dot notation. We also are reminded that address 128.36.12.255 should be used to transmit broadcasts on this subnet.[2]

You should expect to find an *ifconfig* command on any UNIX system, and the command also has been ported to other operating systems. For example, FTP Software's DOS PC/TCP product includes an *ifconfig* command that defines and shows the characteristics of LAN, serial, and X.25 interfaces.

On the other hand, interfaces on an IBM AS/400 are configured by means of menus, while an IBM VM system combines interface data with other TCP and IP parameters in a single file.

6.3.4 Routing Table

Now suppose that we want to communicate with a host whose IP address is 192.35.89.5. Clearly this is not on our local network. In this case IP must consult its routing table.

What does this table look like? To find out, we can use the command *netstat -nr*[3] to get a printout of the routing table at our local host[4] (whose IP address is 128.36.12.27):

---

[2] Berkeley 4.2 TCP/IP and some products based on it used 0s instead of 1s for broadcasting. This is a non-standard practice, and over time, these systems should be obsoleted and replaced.

[3] The netstat command is widely available. The flags or subcommands used to display information vary from vendor to vendor.

[4] Other computers may respond with tables that are formatted a little differently. They will contain similar, but not necessarily identical information. For example, some systems may provide a column that displays a distance associated with each destination.

96 Chapter Six

```
netstat -nr
Destination    Gateway        Flags Refcnt  Use      Interface
127.0.0.1      127.0.0.1      UH    1       130      lo0
128.36.12.0    128.36.12.27   U     20      22199    le0
192.35.89.0    128.36.12.1    UG    0       29       le0
130.132.0.0    128.36.12.2    UG    3       26621    le0
128.36.17.0    128.36.12.1    UG    0       0        le0
default        128.36.12.1    UG    0       21325    le0
```

Each entry provides information about routing to an individual destination. A destination can be a network, a subnet, or an individual host. A default or "wildcard" entry also can be included and used to route to any destination that is not explicitly listed in the table.

Lets take a closer look at the individual entries in the table:

- Recall that all addresses starting with 127 are used for loopback testing. We can see that the first destination in the table is a loopback address.

- Destination 128.36.12.0 is the local network to which this host is attached. The Gateway (router) column contains the address of this host. Note that if the host had several network interfaces, there would be an entry for each of these.

- The next destination, 192.35.89.0, identifies a remote Class C network. This network is reached via a gateway at address 128.36.12.1. The host that we originally wanted to reach has an IP address of 192.35.89.5 and is on this network, so traffic to that host should be sent via this gateway.

- Destination 130.132.0.0 is a remote Class B network and is reached via a gateway with IP address 128.36.12.2.

- Destination 128.36.17.0 is a subnet of the same Class B network as the local subnet. It is reached via the gateway at IP address 128.36.12.1.

- The entry labeled **default** is the most important of all. Any traffic not specifically routed by another table entry is sent to this default address.

Flags tell whether a route is up (usable), and whether the destination is a host (H) or gateway (G).

REFcnt tracks the number of currently active uses of the route. The Use column contains counts of the number of packets sent on the route. Interface lo0 is a logical interface used for loopback testing. All external traffic passes through the single Ethernet interface, le0.

Note that hosts on a LAN which has a single router often get by with exactly three entries: a loopback destination, an entry for the local LAN, and a default for all non-local traffic.

When IP looks up the address of a destination host, it first searches through the table to see if there is an entry for the full IP address. If there is, then this entry is used to route traffic. If not, then IP searches for an entry corresponding to the destination network. If this cannot be found, the default is used.

6.3.5 Routing Protocols

Ordinarily, datagram routing is adaptive. That is, the best choice for the next hop is made by checking the routing table at the source host and at each router along the way. Adaptive routing builds in flexibility and robustness:

> *A change in network topology just causes datagrams to be rerouted automatically.*

6.3.6 Router Tables

How are the tables in routers constructed and maintained? Initially, each table is manually configured with a few known entries and a default next hop for any destinations that are not listed. For small networks, only these static entries are needed.

Medium and large-sized networks need routing tables that change dynamically during operation. Change is automated by means of a *routing information protocol*. A routing information protocol enables routers to exchange information with one another and to automatically recompute their routing table entries.

There is no single required routing information protocol. The Internet philosophy gives any organization the freedom to choose whatever *internal* routing protocol that it wants. This has encouraged experimentation and the invention of many improvements.

Chapter 8 will describe two important routing protocols:

- Routing Information Protocol, a simple, widely available protocol
- Open Shortest Path First, a new and highly capable protocol

Chapter 8 also will discuss the Internet protocols that are used to learn and distribute the routing information that is needed in order to transmit datagrams between different organizations.

6.3.7 Host Tables

Hosts usually are initialized with a few static entries. Can these entries change dynamically? We shall see in Chapter 7 that a router will automatically notify a host of the existence of another router that provides better paths to specific destinations.

In addition, a host needs to be smart enough to notice when a local router has crashed and either compute new routes or mark all routes through the router as down.

A host can optionally participate in dynamic routing by running a process that eavesdrops on update messages broadcast by local routers. The host can use this information to update its own routing table. However, keep in mind that doing this uses up system resources; a host may end up storing a lot of extraneous information that does not result in better routing decisions and slows down table searches.

Now let's take a look at the rest of the IP functions.

6.3.8 Fragmentation

In a large internet, an originating host may not know all of the size limits that a datagram will meet along its path. What happens if the source host has sent out a datagram that is too large for some intermediate network?

When the datagram arrives at the router that is attached to that intermediate network, IP solves the size problem by fragmenting the datagram into several smaller datagrams. It is up to the destination host to gather up incoming fragments and rebuild the original datagram.

Fragmentation usually is performed only in a router. However, a UDP application might send a large message that causes the sending host to fragment a datagram.

6.3.9 Type of Service

Applications can select Type of Service features such as precedence (priority) level, reliability of delivery, need for low delay, and requirement for high throughput. An increasing number of products are able to respond to Type of Service selections.

6.3.10 Time-to-Live

A datagram's route may be changed due to router failures or traffic congestion. A datagram might be diverted onto an indirect path and arrive very late, or even get into a repeating loop. The Time-to-Live mechanism makes sure that old datagrams are removed from the network. A maximum lifetime limit is included in the datagram header and is decreased at each router. If the value reaches zero, the datagram is discarded.

6.3.11 Checksum

The IP header carries a checksum field. The checksum is calculated from the remaining header fields. It might seem unnecessary to compute another checksum when a layer 2 Frame Check Sequence is calculated at every hop. However, interface board faults and bus errors when transferring the datagram to computer memory happen often enough to make this advisable. Also, note that at least one lower layer protocol, SLIP, does not include a Frame Check Sequence.[5]

The IP header checksum must be recomputed at every hop, because the header is constantly being updated. At the least, the Time-to-Live is reduced at each hop. Some of the optional fields described next also are updated at each hop.

6.3.12 Options

IP offers a number of service options that can be invoked by a communicating application.

The *Strict Source Route* option mandates a complete path to be followed from source to destination. This service might be used as part of a security program, or could be invoked by a network management program that tests whether a route is available.

The *Loose Source Route* option provides *landmark* destinations along the way. The datagram will visit the landmarks, but there may be intermediate hops on the way to each landmark. This option can be helpful when trying to route to remote parts of an internet.

The *Record Route* and *Timestamp* options are useful for network management. The address of each router visited is added to a Record Route field. A Timestamp Field records a sequence of 32-bit timestamps, and optionally, the route too.

An IP *Security* option was defined to satisfy the needs of military and other government users, and the contents of the Security field were set by the U.S. Department of Defense. This option often is omitted from commercial IP implementations.

---

[5]Higher layer checksums provide the only protection for protocol information and user data when SLIP is used.

6.4 IP PROTOCOL MECHANISMS

6.4.1 Datagram Header

A datagram header is formatted as 5 or more 32-bit words. The maximum size for a header is 15 words (that is, 60 octets), but in practice, most datagram headers have the minimum length of 5 words (20 octets). Header fields are displayed in Figure 6.6.

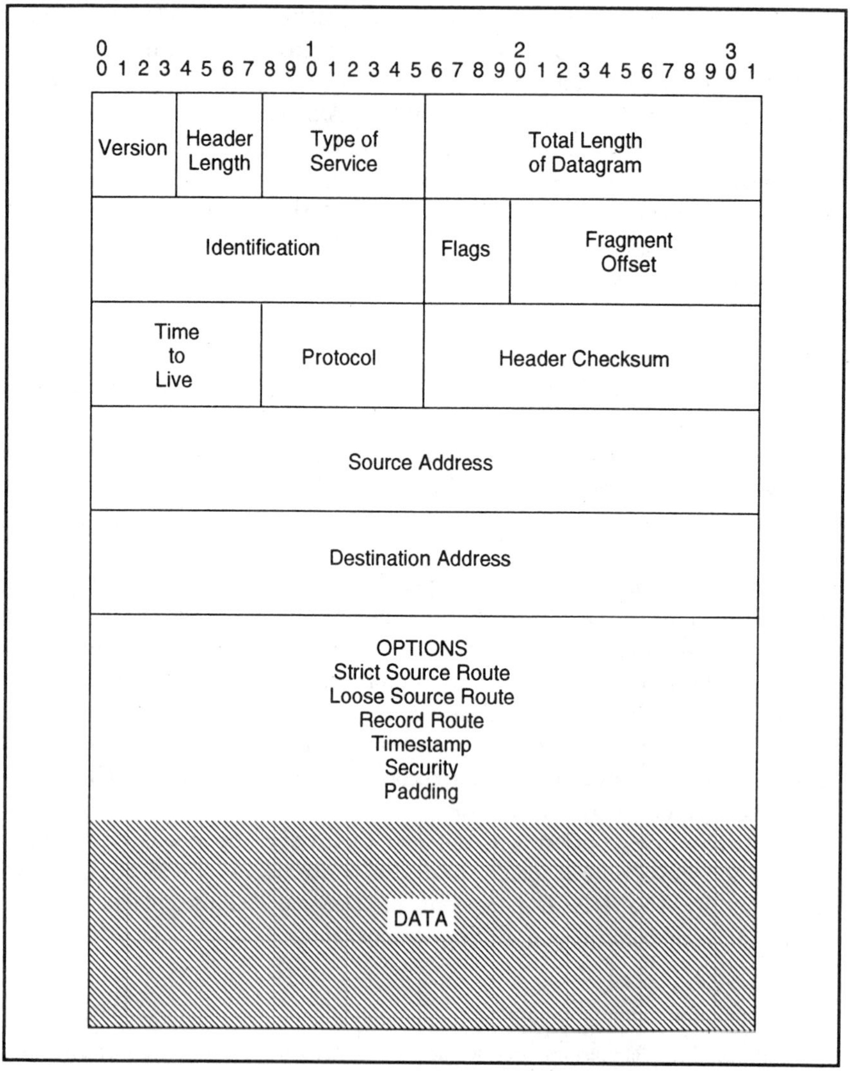

0 1 2 3	4 5 6 7	8 9 0 1 2 3 4 5	6 7 8 9 0 1 2 3 4 5 6 7 8 9 0 1
Version	Header Length	Type of Service	Total Length of Datagram
	Identification	Flags	Fragment Offset
Time to Live		Protocol	Header Checksum
	Source Address		
	Destination Address		
	OPTIONS Strict Source Route Loose Source Route Record Route Timestamp Security Padding		
	DATA		

Figure 6.6 IP datagram header and data.

The first word in the header contains the Version, Header Length, Type of Service, and Total Length fields of the datagram.

The current version of IP is 4. This version does not interwork with any earlier versions. An incoming datagram with an earlier version is discarded by current software.

The header length is measured in 32-bit words. If there are no options, the header length is 5 words (that is, 20 octets). If one or more options are included, the header may need to be padded with 0s so that it ends at a 32-bit word boundary.

6.4.2 Type of Service

The Type of Service field contains quality of service information that can affect how a datagram is handled. The field contains eight bits, whose meaning is explained below.

BITS	DESCRIPTION	
0-2	Precedence: Level 0 is normal. Level 7 provides the highest priority.	Levels 0 - 7.
3	Delay indication:	0 = normal, 1 = low
4	Throughput indication:	0 = normal, 1 = high
5	Reliability indication:	0 = normal, 1 = high
6-7	Reserved for future use.	

The IP standard does not mandate the specific actions that are caused by the values in the Type of Service field. It was originally intended that IP would map the Type of Service settings onto similar options for the subnet to be crossed on the next hop. For example, access to a Token-Ring can be scheduled based on a precedence level. IP could map its precedence level to a corresponding Token-Ring precedence level.

Some hosts and routers ignore the Type of Service field entirely, while others use the field in making routing decisions, or in deciding which traffic should be protected against discard when memory is in short supply.

6.4.3 Total Length Field

The Total Length field contains the length of the datagram measured in octets, including both the header and the data portions of the datagram. This 16-bit field can express values up to a maximum of $2^{16} - 1 = 65,535$ octets. Currently there is no MTU close to this value.

Network technologies are not the only reason to limit datagram size. The diverse types of computers that support IP have different limits on the sizes of the memory buffers that they use for network traffic.

The IP standard requires that all hosts must be able to accept datagrams of up to 576 octets.

6.4.4 Fragmentation Fields

The Identification, Flags, and Fragment Offset fields play a major role in datagram fragmentation and reassembly. The Identification field contains a 16-bit number. This number helps the destination host to recognize datagram fragments that belong together. The Flag field contains three bits, as shown below:

Bit 0 is reserved, and must be 0. The sender can set the next bit to 1 to prevent the datagram from being fragmented. If a router could not deliver a datagram without fragmentation and this bit were set to one, then the datagram would have to be discarded and an error message would be sent back to the source. A network manager can use this facility to test the size at which datagrams addressed to different parts of an internet are fragmented.

Bit 2 is set to 0 if this is the last — or the only — component of a datagram. Bit 2 is set to 1 if the datagram has been fragmented and more fragments follow.

BITS 0	1	2
(Reserved) 0	0 = May Fragment 1 = Don't Fragment	0 = Last Fragment 1 = More Fragments

When a router fragments a datagram, each break must be aligned with an eight-octet boundary. Eight-octet units are called *Fragment Blocks*. The Offset Field contains the distance of this fragment's data from the start of the original datagram, measured in Fragment Blocks.

The Offset field is 13 bits long, so that offsets can range from 0 to 8192 fragment blocks, corresponding to 0 to 65528 octets.

For example, suppose that a router fragments a datagram with identifier = 348 containing 3000 octets of data into 3 datagrams, each including its own header and 1000 octets (125 Fragment Blocks) of data. The contents of the Identification, Flags, and Offset fields would be:

	ID	FLAGS	FRAGMENT OFFSET
Fragment 1	348	May Fragment, More	0 Blocks From Start
Fragment 2	348	May Fragment, More	125 Blocks (1000 octets) From Start
Fragment 3	348	May Fragment, Last	250 Blocks (2000 octets) From Start

On the other hand, if the datagram had been delivered without fragmentation, it would have the following fields:

ID	FLAGS	FRAGMENT OFFSET
348	May Fragment, Last	0 Blocks From Start

In the latter case, the recipient host can tell that the incoming datagram was not fragmented because an offset of 0 shows that it contains the start of the data, while the flag set to "last" shows that it contains the end of the data.

6.4.5 Reconstructing a Fragmented Datagram

A fragmented datagram is reconstructed at the recipient host. The pieces of a fragmented datagram can arrive out-of-order. When the first piece arrives at the destination host, IP allocates reassembly resources. The Fragment Offset field indicates the byte boundary where the data in this fragment should be placed.

Fragments with matching Identification, Source, Destination, and Protocol fields belong together and are merged in as they arrive. There is one inconvenient omission in the IP protocol; the recipient has no way of knowing how long the entire datagram will be until the end fragment arrives. The Total Length field in a fragment reveals only the length of *that* datagram fragment.

This means that the recipient system has to do some guesswork about how much buffer space to reserve for an incoming datagram. Vendors handle this problem in different ways. Some allocate small incremental buffers to hold incoming fragments, while others have a single, fixed-sized buffer for incoming datagrams. In any case, all implementations are required to handle incoming datagrams whose total length is up to 576 octets.

6.4.6 Time-to-Live

The Time-to-Live (TTL) field contains the maximum number of seconds (up to 255, which is 4.25 minutes) that a datagram will be allowed to remain in the internet before reaching its destination. The TTL is set by the originating host, and decremented at each router that handles the datagram. A datagram that has not yet reached the destination host when the TTL expires is discarded.

In reality, there is no accurate way to keep track of this time. TTL usually is implemented as a simple hop counter and typically the TTL is decremented by one at each router. Optionally, a larger decrement can be applied to a datagram that has just crossed a very slow link.

A recommended default value for the initial TTL setting is approximately twice the longest path in the internet that is being traversed. The length of the longest path is sometimes called the *diameter* of the internet.

6.4.7 Protocol

This field contains an 8-bit number that identifies the upper layer protocol which is to receive the data portion of the datagram. The identifier for TCP is 6 and for UDP is 17.

6.4.8 Header Checksum

This 16-bit field contains a checksum that is computed on the fields[6] of the IP header. The checksum must be updated as the datagram is forwarded because the Time-to-Live field changes at each router. Other header values also may change because of fragmentation, or due to values written into option fields.

---

[6]The checksum is the 16-bit one's complement of the one's complement sum of all 16-bit words in the header. Prior to the calculation, the checksum field is set to 0.

6.4.9 Source Address and Destination Address

A 32-bit value was chosen for IP addressing. The formats for this field were discussed in Chapter 5. In the 1970s, when the IP address field was defined, this size seemed sufficient for all conceivable networks. However, because addresses must be assigned in blocks, the supply of Class A and Class B addresses is dwindling.

OSI network addresses will allow for variable lengths and a wider range of formats. However, note that a fixed length and restricted formats make addressing and routing easier to implement, and enable routers to process datagrams very quickly.

6.4.10 Options

Up to 40 IP header octets are available to carry one or more options. The options that are included in a datagram are chosen by the communicating applications. The options currently in use consist of:

- Strict Source Route
- Loose Source Route
- Record Route
- Timestamp
- Department of Defense Basic Security
- Department of Defense Extended Security
- No Operation
- End of Option List (Padding)

6.4.11 Strict Source Route

A Strict Source Route consists a sequence of IP addresses of routers to be visited on the way to a destination. Strict source routes are sometimes used to improve data security. Naturally, the traffic flowing back from the destination to the source should follow the same route; i.e., should visit the same set of routers in reverse order!

There is one complication; the source and destination views of a router's address are not the same. Figure 6.7 shows a path through two routers. The route from host A to host B traverses routers whose IP addresses are known to host A as 130.132.9.29 and 130.132.4.11. The route from host B to host A traverses routers whose IP addresses are known to host B as 128.36.5.2 and 130.132.4.16. The addresses at each of a router's interfaces differ because the interfaces connect to different subnets, as shown in the figure.

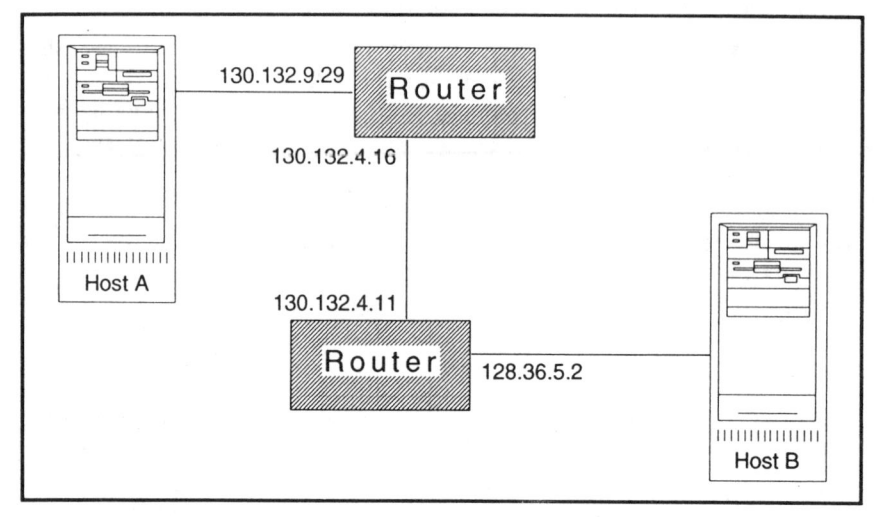

Figure 6.7 Routes from the point of view of host A and host B.

The solution is simple. As each router is visited, its incoming address is replaced by its outgoing address. The destination takes the resulting list, reverses its order, and uses it as the strict source route in the opposite direction.

6.4.12 Loose Source Route

A Loose Source Route is a list of IP addresses of routers to be visited on the way to a destination. Recall that a loose source route can be viewed as a set of landmarks that help to find the way to a target host. Traffic can pass through additional intermediate routers.

Just as for Strict Source Routes, return traffic is expected to follow a corresponding Loose Source Route back. As before, incoming router addresses are replaced by the outgoing router addresses that make sense to the destination node.

6.4.13 Record Route

A Record Route field contains a list of IP addresses of routers visited by the datagram. Each router along the way will try to add its outgoing IP address to the list.

The length of the field is preset by the sender, and it is possible that all of the space will be used up before the datagram reaches its destination. In this case, the router simply forwards the datagram without adding its address.

6.4.14 Timestamp

There are three formats for a Timestamp field. It may contain:

- A list of 32-bit timestamps.
- A list of IP address and corresponding timestamp pairs.
- A list of preselected addresses provided by the source, each followed by space in which to record a timestamp. A node records a timestamp only if its address is next on the list.

Space may run out if the first or second format is used. There is an overflow field that is used to count the number of nodes that could not record their timestamps.

6.4.15 Department of Defense Basic and Extended Security

The Basic Security option is used to assure that the source of a datagram is authorized to transmit it, intermediate routers may appropriately transmit it, and the destination should be allowed to receive it.

The Basic Security option parameters consist of a classification level that ranges from Unclassified to Top Secret, and flags that identify the protection authorities whose rules apply to the datagram. Protection authorities include organizations such as the U.S. National Security Agency, Central Intelligence Agency, and the Department of Energy.

A datagram carrying the Basic Security option may also include an Extended Security option field. There are several different subformats for this option, depending on the needs of various defining authorities.

A host or router must discard information that it has not been authorized to handle. Secure systems are configured with the range of classification levels that they may transmit and receive and the authority or authorities that are valid. Note that there are many commercial products that do not support secure operation.

6.4.16 No Operation and End of Option List

The No Operation option is used as a filler between options. For example, it is used if it is desirable to align the next option on a 16 or 32-bit boundary.

The End of Option List option is used to pad the end of the options field to a 32-bit boundary.

6.4.17 Encoding Options

There are two single-byte options which are encoded as follows:

No Operation	00000001
End of Option List	00000000

The remaining options consist of several bytes. Each starts with a type octet and a length octet.

One issue that must be considered for these options is: should the option be copied into the header of each fragment of a fragmented datagram? This must be done for security, strict source routing, and loose source routing. Record Route and Timestamp fields appear only in the first fragment.

The type octet can be broken down as follows:

BITS		
0	Copy flag:	Set to 1 if copied on fragmentation.
1-2	Option Class:	0 for datagram or network control. 2 for debugging and measurement.
3-7	Option Number:	Unique value for each option.

For example, the type field for the Strict Source Route option is equal to 10001001, or 137 in decimal. This code indicates that the field will be copied on fragmentation, has class 0, and is option number 5.

The length of each option field is preset by the sender. Hence, it is possible that a Timestamp or Record Route field might be filled up before reaching its destination.

The formats for the optional fields are displayed in Figure 6.8.

6.4.18 Encoding a Strict Source Route

A Strict Source Route option contains a pointer and a list of addresses. The pointer contains the position of the next address to be processed. Initially, the pointer starts out with a value of 4. It is incremented by 4 at each hop.

If the value of the pointer is greater than the length of the field, then all addresses have been consumed, and the remainder of the routing should be based on the destination address.

Internet Protocol 109

Strict Source Route: Type = 137

| 10001001 | Length | Pointer | List of Addresses |

Loose Source Route: Type = 131

| 10000011 | Length | Pointer | List of Addresses |

Record Route: Type = 7

| 00000111 | Length | Pointer | Address . . . Address |

Timestamp: Type = 68, Flag = 0

01000100	Length	Pointer oflw Flag
Timestamp		
Timestamp		
. . .		

Timestamp: Type = 68, Flag = 1

01000100	Length	Pointer oflw Flag
Internet Address		
Timestamp		
. . .		

Basic Security: Type = 130

| 10000010 | Length | Classification | Protection Level | Authority Flags |

Extended Security: Type = 133

| 10000101 | Length | Format Code | Additional Security Information |

Figure 6.8 Formats for optional fields.

6.4.19 Encoding a Loose Source Route

A Loose Source Route option contains a pointer and a list of addresses. Here again, the pointer indicates the position of the next address to be processed.

However, the datagram may traverse intermediate hops between addresses on the list. After the list is exhausted, the remainder of the routing should be based on the destination address.

6.4.20 Encoding Record Route

A Record Route option contains a pointer and space for addresses. Initially, the value of the pointer is set to 4. This is followed by unused space that is preallocated to hold addresses.

As each router is visited, its address is recorded at the location indicated by the pointer, and the pointer is incremented by 4. If all of the preallocated space gets used up, then the datagram is routed to the destination, and no more addresses are recorded.

6.4.21 Encoding a Timestamp

A Timestamp option contains a pointer, an overflow field, and a flag field. The flag field indicates which of the three possible formats is to be used in this timestamp option.

If the flag field contains a 0, then at each hop a timestamp will be recorded in the preallocated space and the pointer will be incremented by 4. If the preallocated space has been used up, then the overflow field will be incremented by 1. What happens if the overflow count overflows? The datagram is discarded.

If the flag field contains a 1, then at each hop, an IP address and a timestamp will be recorded in the preallocated space and the pointer will be incremented by 8. If the preallocated space has been used up, then the overflow field will be incremented by 1.

Suppose that the sender wants to record timestamps at a list of preselected nodes? In this case, the flag field is set to 3, and the sender fills in the selected internet addresses.

If the pointer is currently set at a router's address, the router fills in the timestamp field and increments the pointer by 8.

6.4.22 Encoding Basic and Extended Security Options

A Basic Security option contains a classification level and protection authority flags. The classification level is a 1-octet code that indicates whether the message is Top Secret, Secret, Confidential, or Unclassified.

Each protection authority is assigned a flag position, and the datagram is to be protected according to the rules for that authority if its flag is set to one. Multiple flags can be set to one.

An Extended Security option field can accompany a Basic Security option. It contains a format code field that determines the format of the remaining part of the option.

6.4.23 Sample IP Header

The display in Figure 6.9 shows a Network General *Sniffer* analysis of a DIX Ethernet MAC frame header and an IP header.

The MAC header starts out with the 6-byte physical addresses of the destination and source stations. Note that the Sniffer analyzer has replaced the first three bytes of each physical address with the name of the board manufacturer, which in this case is Sun. The type field contains the characteristic X'0800 code that says "deliver this information to IP."

In the display, an IP datagram follows immediately after the short DIX Ethernet MAC header. Recall that if this were an 802.3 frame, then an 8-byte Logical Link Control header and SNAP subheader would follow the MAC frame header.

The frame size is stated as 60 bytes. This includes the 14-byte MAC frame header but does not include the 4-byte MAC trailer, so that the complete frame originally was 64 bytes long. Ethernet or 802.3 frames on coax media must have a length of at least 64 bytes, so this frame has the minimum size. The datagram in this frame has a total length of only 40 bytes. This means that the frame had to be padded with 6 extra bytes to reach its required minimum size!

Like most IP headers, this one carries no options, and therefore has the standard 20-byte length. As is frequently the case, the Type of Service field has been set to 0.

We can tell that this datagram is not a fragment of a larger datagram because its fragment offset field is 0 — showing that this is the start of a datagram — and the second flag is set to 0 — indicating that this is the end of a datagram.

This datagram has 30 hops left in its Time-to-Live field. Since the protocol field has value 6, the datagram will be delivered to TCP at the destination host.

The Sniffer has translated the source and destination IP addresses into the convenient dot format.

The hexadecimal octets that made up the original MAC header and IP header are shown at the bottom of the display. The original Sniffer display of the hex fields has been altered to make it easier to match the hex codes to their interpretation.

Chapter Six

```
DLC:    ----- DLC Header -----
DLC:
DLC:    Frame 3 arrived at 10:24:42.5252; frame size is 60 bytes.
DLC:    Destination = Station Sun    07FD89, Sun Jupiter
DLC:    Source       = Station Sun    076A03, Sun Atlantis
DLC:    Ethertype    = 0800 (IP)
DLC:
IP:     ----- IP Header -----
IP:
IP:     Version = 4, header length = 20 bytes
IP:     Type of service = 00
IP:            000. .... = routine
IP:            ...0 .... = normal delay
IP:            .... 0... = normal throughput
IP:            .... .0.. = normal reliability
IP:     Total length = 40 bytes
IP:     Identification = 14503
IP:     Flags = 0X
IP:     .0.. .... = may fragment
IP:     ..0. .... = last fragment
IP:     Fragment offset = 0 bytes
IP:     Time to live = 30 seconds/hops
IP:     Protocol = 6 (TCP)
IP:     Header checksum = EBBD (correct)
IP:     Source address = [192.42.252.20]
IP:     Destination address = [192.42.252.1]
IP:     No options
IP:

HEX

MAC Header
08 00 20 07 FD 89    (Destination physical address in hex)
08 00 20 07 6A 03    (Source physical address in hex)
08 00                (Code for IP)

IP Header
45 00 00 28  (Version, Header Length, Type of Service, Total Length)
38 A7 00 00  (Identification, Flags, Fragment Offset)
1E 06 EB BD  (Time To Live, Protocol, Header Checksum)
C0 2A FC 14  (Source IP Address)
C0 2A FC 01  (Destination IP Address)
```

Figure 6.9 Interpretation of MAC header and IP header.

6.5 DATAGRAM PROCESSING SCENARIOS

To get a better understanding of IP, it is useful to walk through the steps carried out when a datagram is processed at a router and at a recipient host. Figure 6.10 summarizes these steps.

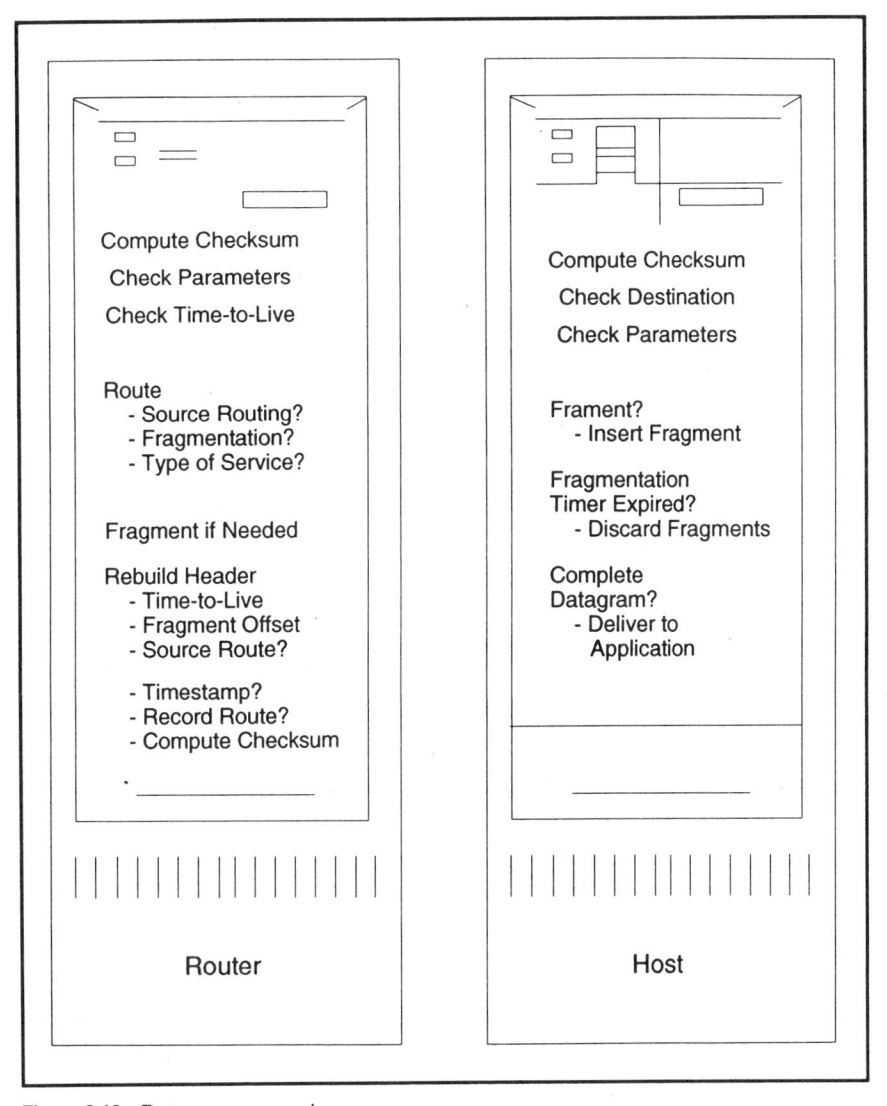

```
Router                              Host
Compute Checksum                    Compute Checksum
Check Parameters                    Check Destination
Check Time-to-Live                  Check Parameters

Route                               Frament?
  - Source Routing?                   - Insert Fragment
  - Fragmentation?
  - Type of Service?                Fragmentation
                                    Timer Expired?
Fragment if Needed                    - Discard Fragments

Rebuild Header                      Complete
  - Time-to-Live                    Datagram?
  - Fragment Offset                   - Deliver to
  - Source Route?                       Application

  - Timestamp?
  - Record Route?
  - Compute Checksum
```

Figure 6.10 Datagram processing.

114   Chapter Six

Problems or errors generally are handled by discarding the datagram and sending a report back to the source. These reports will be described in Chapter 7, which discusses the Internet Control Message Protocol (ICMP).

6.5.1 Router Processing

When a router receives a datagram, it first goes through a series of checks to see if the datagram should be discarded. The Header Checksum is recomputed and compared to the checksum field.

The Version, Header Length, Total Length and Protocol fields are screened to see that they make sense. The Time-to-Live is decremented. A checksum error, parameter error, or zero Time-to-Live cause the datagram to be discarded. Of course, the datagram also could get discarded if the router does not have enough free buffer space to continue processing the datagram.

Next, the router executes the routing procedure. A strict or loose source routing field will be consulted if it is present. An advanced router may consider the Type of Service and fragmentation permission settings. For example, if fragmentation is not permitted, a longer route whose next hop did not require fragmentation would be preferred to a shorter route whose next hop did require fragmentation. If no suitable next hop can be found, the datagram will have to be discarded.

If necessary, the datagram now is fragmented. When a datagram is fragmented, some options are carried only in the first fragment, while others must be copied into every fragment. Loose source routing, route recording, and timestamping appear only in the first fragment. Security and strict source routing must appear in every fragment.

An updated header must be built for each datagram or datagram fragment. The new Time-to-Live is recorded in the header. If a Source Route, Record Route, or Timestamp option is present, this field is updated. If the datagram has been fragmented, the last/more flag and fragment offset must be entered correctly. Finally, the header checksum is recalculated, and the datagram is forwarded to its next-hop system.[7]

---

[7] This is the common scenario for datagram processing at a router. However, there are times when a router will be the final destination for a datagram. For example, a request for network management information may be sent to a router. See Chapter 16.

6.5.2 Destination Host Processing

At the destination host, the checksum is computed and compared to the Header Checksum field. The Version, Header Length, Total Length and Protocol fields are screened for correctness. A datagram will be discarded if any of these are in error, or if the host does not have buffer space available to process the datagram.

If the datagram is a fragment, the host checks four fields: Identification, Source Address, Destination Address, and Protocol. Fragments with identical values in all of these fields belong to the same datagram. Next, the Fragment Offset is used to position this fragment correctly within the whole.

A host cannot wait indefinitely to complete the reassembly of a datagram. When the initial fragment arrives, a timer is set at a locally configured value between one and two minutes. All fragments are discarded when the timer expires.

6.6 IP PERFORMANCE ISSUES

The performance of an internet depends on the quantity of available resources in its hosts and routers and on how efficiently the resources are used. These resources are:

- Transmission bandwidth
- Buffer memory
- CPU processing

Perfect protocol mechanisms are unknown. Protocol design involves tradeoffs between gains and losses in efficiency. Figure 6.11 summarizes IP's positive and negative performance features. These features will be described in the sections that follow.

6.6.1 Transmission Bandwidth

IP makes efficient use of bandwidth. Datagrams queued for transport to their next hop can be transmitted as soon as any bandwidth is available. There is no waste due to having to reserve bandwidth for specific traffic or waiting for acknowledgments, as would be case for a connection-oriented layer 3 protocol.

Furthermore, there are new, more capable IP routing protocols that can split traffic over multiple paths and can choose routes dynamically so that they avoid a congested router or an overloaded link. Use of these protocols will help to maintain the best possible use of the available transmission resources.

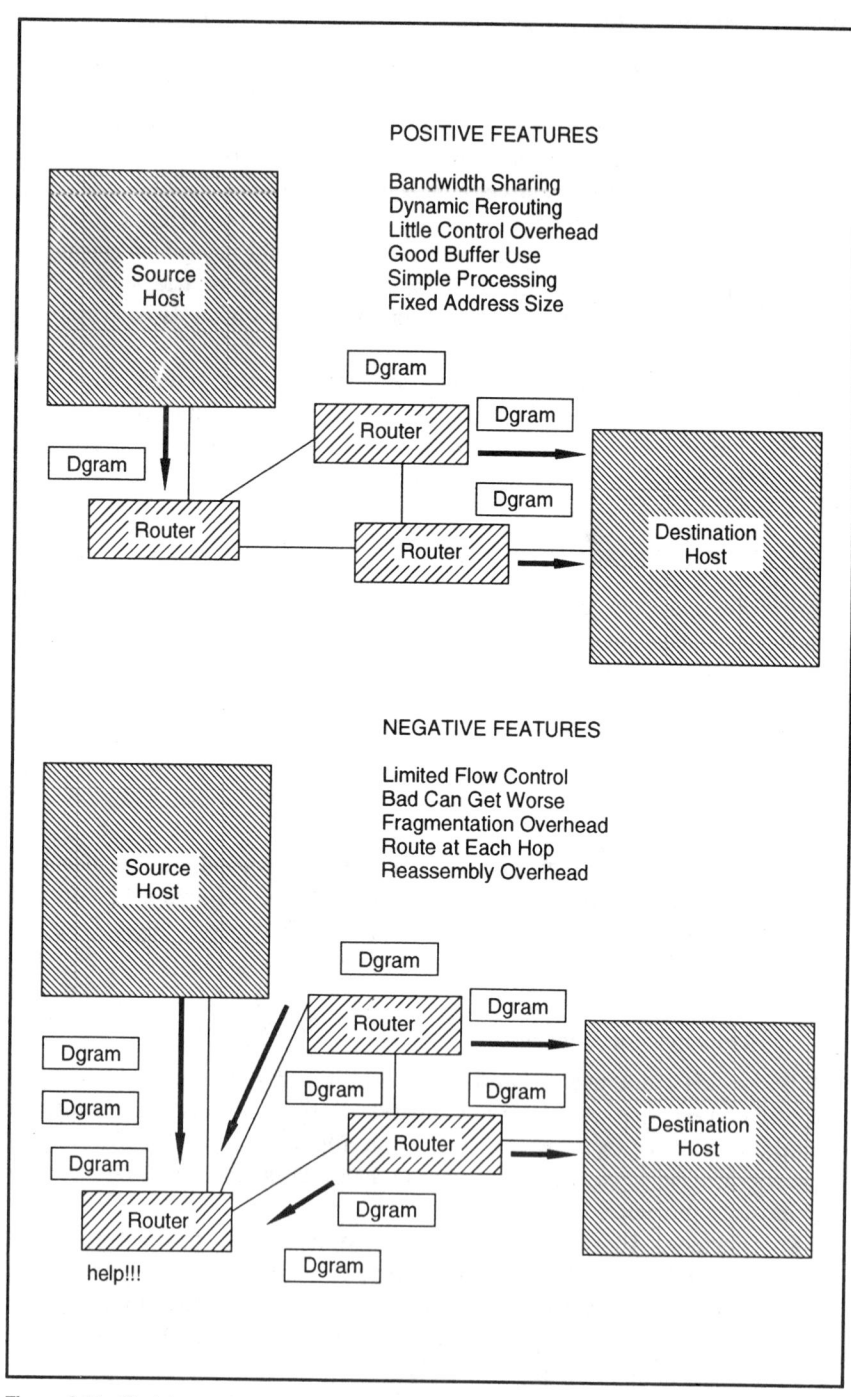

Figure 6.11 Positive and negative performance characteristics.

There is little overhead due to control messages. ICMP[8] error messages are the only source of control traffic.

There are some potentially negative features. Under heavy load, datagrams start to pile up in queues at routers. Delivery time from source to destination increases and some datagrams will be discarded. This will cause TCP to retransmit datagrams, increasing the load and decreasing the effective throughput.

Note that once a network becomes congested, datagram delivery becomes slow and less reliable. TCP retransmissions could have the effect of keeping the network congested.

Fortunately, some very effective algorithms developed by P. Karn and V. Jacobson cause TCP to respond to congestion immediately by throttling back the amount of data that is sent and slowing down the retransmission rate. These algorithms have a significant impact on network performance and have become a required part of the TCP standard. The Karn and Jacobson algorithms will be discussed in Chapter 10.

The ICMP protocol also provides some relief for network overload. During congestion, ICMP messages warn UDP and TCP data sources to slow down their rate of transmission.

Most importantly, router vendors are competing vigorously in offering ever more capable products, able to process thousands of datagrams per second. To assure smooth performance, it is safest to configure the network so that the maximum expected load on a router is approximately 50% of capacity.

6.6.2 Buffer Utilization

Once IP has transmitted a datagram, its responsibility for that datagram is over. The buffer that was occupied by the datagram is available for immediate reuse. However, IP at a destination host will have to tie up some of its buffer space while it is reassembling a fragmented datagram.

Congestion problems can arise when a router connects a fast network to a slow one. Datagrams from the fast network may flood the router's buffers. This commonly has occurred when connecting a LAN to a wide area circuit. New wide area network technologies — ISDN, T1, Frame Relay, SMDS, and others — offer flexible choices for LAN to LAN connectivity that can maintain sufficient bandwidth to handle the traffic.

---

[8]See Chapter 7.

6.6.3 CPU Processing

There is little CPU overhead in processing datagrams. Header analysis is straightforward. The 32-bit address size speeds table lookups used in selecting a next hop. There is no need for elaborate software to manage timeouts and retransmissions when a connection-oriented network layer is used.

However, because it is connectionless and dynamic, IP *does* require routing to be executed at each hop. The amount of router processing time consumed by routing depends on the sophistication of the routing algorithm. Routing that takes into account throughput and delay conditions, tries to balance traffic load, and acts on the user's Type of Service preferences requires much more processing power. Fortunately, processing power is becoming very cheap, while the performance and robustness gained by using smarter routing can be substantial.

6.7 SERVICE INTERFACE

The service interface (see Figure 6.12) describes the interactions between the IP layer and the upper layer protocols. Usually a service interface corresponds closely to system function calls or subroutine calls in programming libraries provided by vendors.

It is highly unusual for an application programmer to write code that interacts directly with IP. However, developers who implement protocols such as TCP and UDP must use this kind of programming interface.

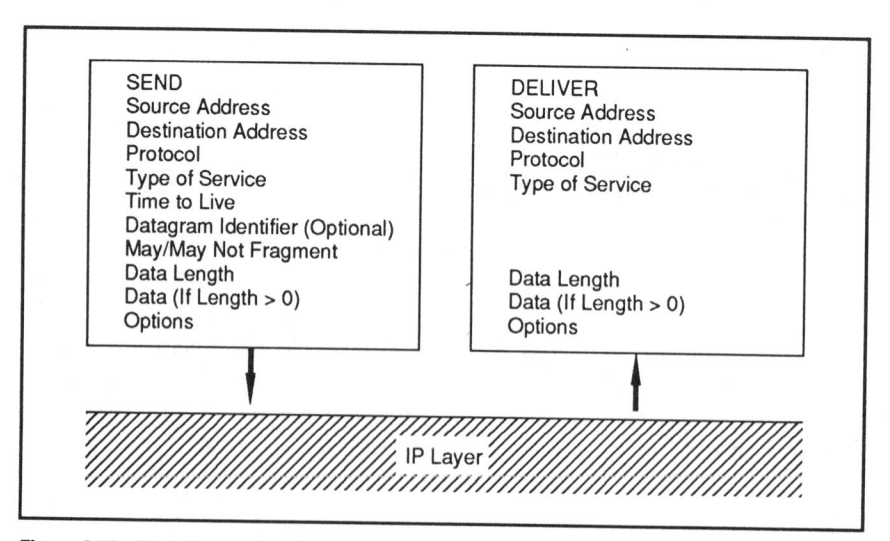

```
SEND                              DELIVER
Source Address                    Source Address
Destination Address               Destination Address
Protocol                          Protocol
Type of Service                   Type of Service
Time to Live
Datagram Identifier (Optional)
May/May Not Fragment
Data Length                       Data Length
Data (If Length > 0)              Data (If Length > 0)
Options                           Options

                    IP Layer
```

Figure 6.12 IP layer service interface.

6.7.1 Service Interface Requests

The service interface is very simple, and consists of a SEND request and a DELIVER request. The requests and their parameters are shown in Figure 6.12. If the program invoking a SEND request does not include a datagram identifier parameter, then IP generates the datagram identifier. The SEND and DELIVER parameters reveal that the layer 4 protocol knows all about a datagram's information.

6.7.2 Events at the Interface

A vendor should provide tracing to help administrators to track the activities at this interface. Tracing can be a useful problem-solving tool.

Keep in mind that turning on detailed tracing will affect performance. A computer can be kept quite busy writing log entries into a disk file every time any datagram is sent or received. Comprehensive tracing should be enabled only for a limited period for the purpose of troubleshooting. Usually tracing or auditing can be restricted to specific traffic, such as traffic from an individual network or to a given destination host.

6.8 RELATIONSHIP TO OSI

IP corresponds to the OSI Connectionless Network Layer Protocol (CNLP). Like IP, the OSI connectionless network protocol[9] is based on datagrams, and architecturally it is strikingly similar to IP.

OSI uses different terminology for a number of features, such as *network layer protocol data unit* for datagram, *lifetime* for Time-to-Live, *protocol data unit length* for Datagram Length, *segment* for fragment, and *quality-of-service* for Type of Service.

The OSI network layer protocol data unit carries the same kind of information that is contained in an IP datagram header. There are some differences in detail, namely:

- The data unit identifier, segment offset, and PDU total length fields will be included only if segmentation (fragmentation) is allowed. In this case, the PDU total length field in the OSI header informs the recipient of the total amount data to expect. In contrast, the recipient of a fragmented IP datagram does not know the total length until the last fragment arrives.

---

[9]OSI also defines a connection-oriented network layer protocol.

- The Type of Service field required by IP has become an optional quality-of-service field in the OSI PDU.

The difference in address structure is more significant:

- OSI addresses, called *Network Service Access Points* (NSAPs), are of variable length. The OSI address identifies the upper layer entity to which the data should be delivered, so no separate Protocol field is included.

- There are several very dissimilar OSI address formats. Unlike IP addresses, OSI addresses are administered by a number of different authorities, and each mandates a different address composition.

For example, there are addresses that start with an ISO Data Country Code that identifies each country. An addressing authority within each country then assigns subcodes to internal organizations, which further define the rest of the address format. There are a number of other address formats. Among them are X.121, international telephone Numbers, and ISDN numbers. These are used to assign a unique identifier to a system, and do not necessarily imply that the system can be reached via the corresponding network.

The U.S. GOSIP format follows a hierarchical pattern that identifies an administrative authority, an area, and an individual identifier. A GOSIP address is 20 bytes long and its contents can be used to assist in routing.

The OSI network layer protocol data unit is displayed in Figure 6.13.

6.9 RECOMMENDED READING

RFC 1180 contains an introductory TCP/IP tutorial. The IP protocol is defined in RFC 791. Updates, corrections, and conformance requirements are specified in RFC 1122. RFC 1009 details the requirements for Internet gateways (i.e., IP routers), and explains many details about the operation of these gateways.

Department of Defense security options are discussed in RFC 1108. RFC 1071 discusses computation of the Internet checksum. RFC 815 introduces an efficient algorithm for reassembling fragmented datagrams at a recipient host.

RFC 994 describes the ISO protocol for providing connectionless-mode Network Service. ISO 8348 Addendum 1 contains the Connectionless Network Service definition and ISO 8473 holds the protocol specification. RFC 1237 discusses guidelines for OSI NSAP address allocation on the Internet.

Internet Protocol 121

Octets	
1	Network Layer Protocol Identifier
1	Header Length
1	Version
1	Lifetime (Time-to-Live)
1	Flags
2	Segment (Fragment) Length
2	Checksum
1	Destination Address Length
Varies	Destination Address
1	Source Address Length
Varies	Source Address
2	Identification
2	Segment (Fragment) Offset
2	PDU Total Length
Varies	OPTIONS Padding Security Source Routing Recording of Route Quality (Type) of Sevice Priority
Varies	DATA

Figure 6.13 OSI network layer protocol data unit.

Chapter

7

Internet Control Message Protocol

7.1 INTRODUCTION

IP has a simple, elegant design; under normal conditions IP makes very efficient use of memory and transmission resources. But what happens when things go wrong? After a router has crashed and disrupted the network, what notice is given that datagrams are wandering around until their Times-to-Live expire? What warning is provided so that sources don't persist in sending information to an unreachable destination? How can a congested router warn traffic originators that the router is approaching or has reached a congested state?

The Internet Control Message Protocol (ICMP) offers remedies for these ills. ICMP also plays the role of network helper, assisting hosts with their IP routing and enabling network managers to discover the status of network nodes.

ICMP's functions are an essential part of IP. All hosts and routers must be able to generate ICMP messages as well as process the ICMP messages that they receive. Properly used, ICMP messages can contribute to smoother network operation.

ICMP messages are carried in IP datagrams which have ordinary IP headers (see Figure 7.1) for which:

- The Type of Service = 0. No special priority is given to ICMP messages.
- The Protocol code is set to 1.

```
┌─────────────────────────────────────────┐
│  ┌───────────────────────────────────┐  │
│  │           IP Header               │  │
│  │      ┌──────────────┐             │  │
│  │      │ Protocol = 1 │             │  │
│  │      └──────────────┘             │  │
│  ├───────────────────────────────────┤  │
│  │                                   │  │
│  │          ICMP Message             │  │
│  │                                   │  │
│  └───────────────────────────────────┘  │
└─────────────────────────────────────────┘
```

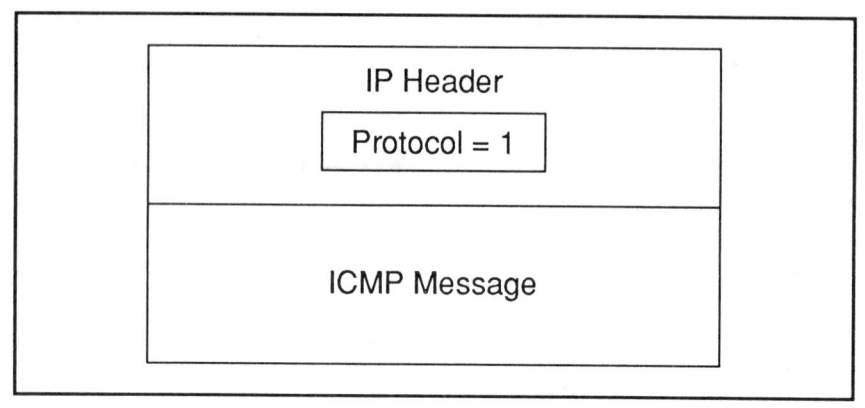

Figure 7.1 Packaging for an ICMP message.

7.2 ICMP ERROR MESSAGES

There are a number of situations that cause IP datagrams to be discarded. For example, a destination may be unreachable because a link is down. A router may be discarding datagrams because it is congested and its memory resources are exhausted. It might be impossible for a router to forward a large datagram because fragmentation was not enabled.

Immediately after a discard, ICMP can direct an error message back to the address that sent the datagram. Figure 7.2 shows ICMP messages being distributed to datagram sources.

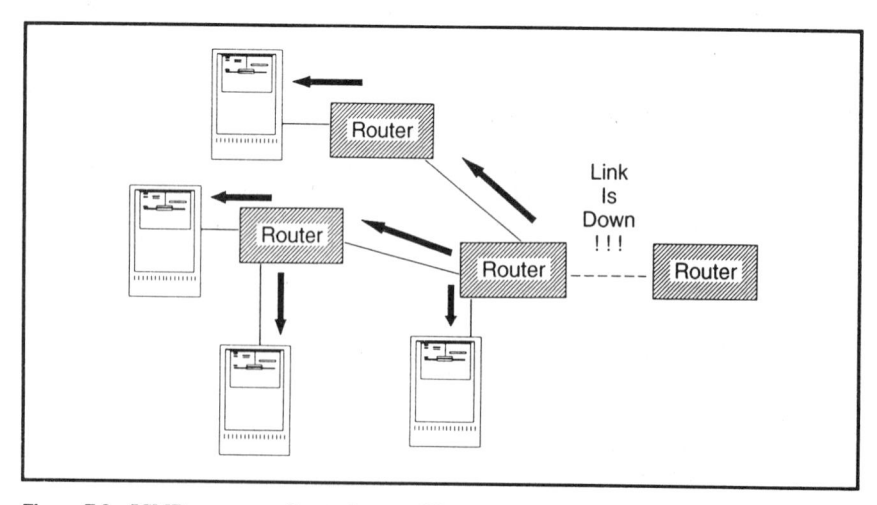

Figure 7.2 ICMP messages directed to traffic sources.

Internet Control Message Protocol 125

This assures that systems are notified of problems quickly. ICMP is a very robust protocol because error notification does not depend on the existence of a network management center.

There also are disadvantages. ICMP generates numerous network problem reports. For example, if a destination is not reachable, messages will be propagated to sources all over the network, rather than to selected network management stations.

In fact, ICMP has no facilities for reporting errors to a designated network operations center. This is left up to the Simple Network Management Protocol, which is presented in Chapter 16.

7.2.1 Types of Error Messages

Figure 7.3 summarizes the messages that routers and destination hosts send in order to report problems.

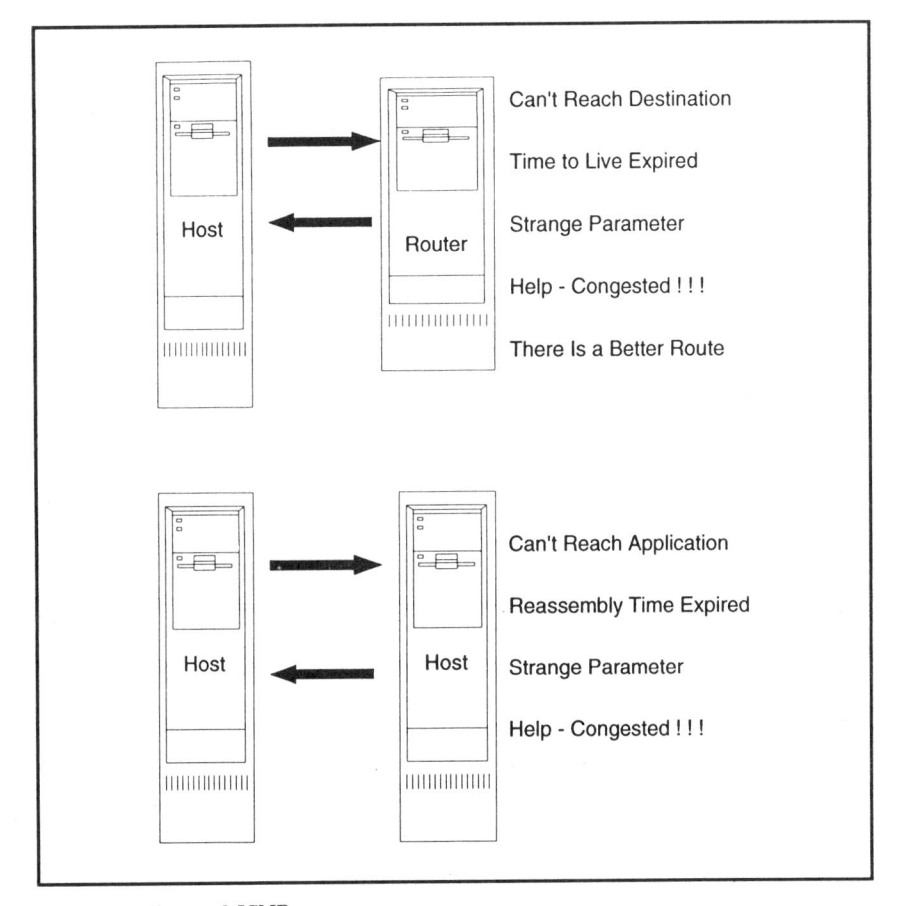

Figure 7.3 Types of ICMP messages.

ICMP error messages may be sent when:

- A datagram cannot reach its destination.
- The Time-to-Live has expired.
- There is a bad parameter in the IP header.
- A router or destination is congested.
- A host has routed a datagram to the wrong local router.
- The destination host's time to reassemble fragments has expired.

The ICMP protocol specifies that an ICMP message *should* or *may* be sent in each instance. It does not require that *every* error *must* result in an ICMP message.

Incoming ICMP error messages are passed to appropriate entities. For example, notification of inability to deliver datagrams must be passed to the traffic originator — a TCP or a UDP application. ICMP messages also should be logged for use by network management applications.

We can expect ICMP to send error messages when a network is under stress. It is important to assure that the ICMP traffic does not flood the network, making the situation much worse. Some obvious limits have been imposed on the protocol. ICMP must not report problems caused by:

- Routing or delivering ICMP messages.
- Broadcast or multicast datagrams.
- Datagram fragments other than the first.

7.2.2 ICMP Message Format

Recall that an ICMP message is carried in the data field of an IP datagram. Each ICMP message starts with the same three fields: a message type field, a code that provides a more specific description of the type, and a checksum that is applied to the message. The format of the rest of the message is determined by the type.

ICMP error messages enclose the IP header and first eight octets of the datagram that caused the error. This information can be the basis for problem-solving since it includes data such as the intended destination and the target layer 4 protocol. When we study the upper layer protocols, we will discover that the extra eight octets include information that identifies the communicating application entities.

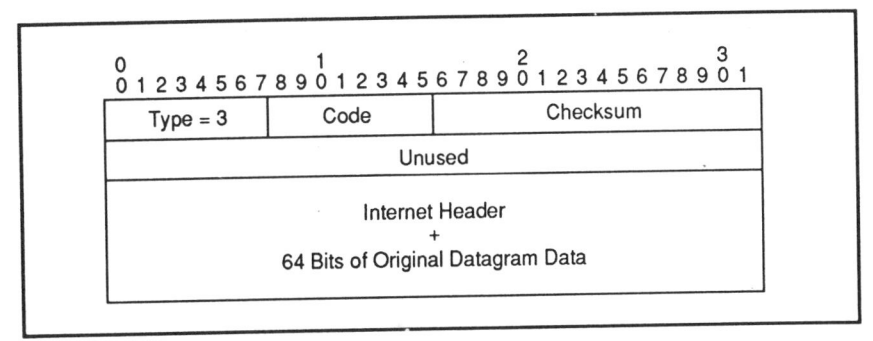

```
 0                   1                   2                   3
 0 1 2 3 4 5 6 7 8 9 0 1 2 3 4 5 6 7 8 9 0 1 2 3 4 5 6 7 8 9 0 1
+-------------+-------------+-------------------------------+
|  Type = 3   |    Code     |           Checksum            |
+-------------+-------------+-------------------------------+
|                           Unused                          |
+-----------------------------------------------------------+
|                      Internet Header                      |
|                             +                             |
|              64 Bits of Original Datagram Data            |
+-----------------------------------------------------------+
```

Figure 7.4 Format of the Destination Unreachable ICMP message.

7.2.3 Destination Unreachable Message

There are many stages at which delivery of a datagram can fail. Because of a broken link, a router may be physically unable to reach a destination subnet or to execute the next hop in a source route. A destination host may be unavailable because it is down for maintenance.

As we shall see in Chapter 16, modern routers have powerful security features. A router could be configured so that it selects which traffic is allowed to enter a network or reach a specific host. Thus, datagrams may be undeliverable because communication with the destination has been administratively prohibited.

The format of the Destination Unreachable message is shown in Figure 7.4. The type (3 in this case) identifies this as a Destination Unreachable message. The code indicates the reason. The full list of reasons is quite extensive:

Code	Meaning
0	Network is unreachable.
1	Host is unreachable.
2	Protocol at the destination is unreachable.
3	Port is unreachable.
4	Fragmentation is needed but the "Don't Fragment" flag is set.
5	Source route has failed.
6	Destination network is unknown.
7	Destination host is unknown.
8	Source host is isolated.
9	Communication with destination net is administratively forbidden.
10	Communication with destination host is administratively forbidden.
11	Network is unreachable for specified Type of Service.
12	Host is unreachable for specified Type of Service.

128 Chapter Seven

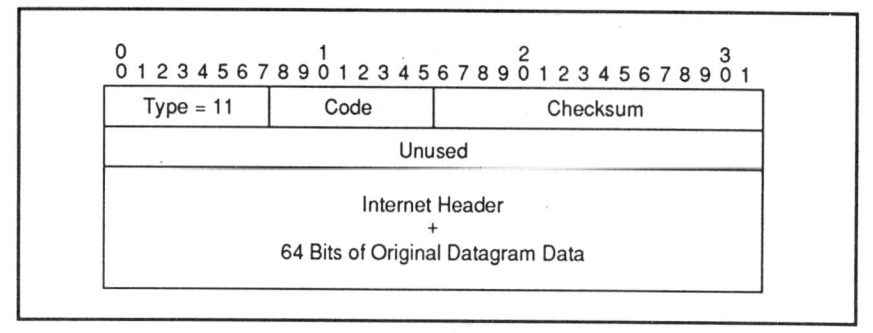

```
 0                   1                   2                   3
 0 1 2 3 4 5 6 7 8 9 0 1 2 3 4 5 6 7 8 9 0 1 2 3 4 5 6 7 8 9 0 1
+-------------------+-------------------+-------------------------------+
|    Type = 11      |      Code         |          Checksum             |
+-------------------+-------------------+-------------------------------+
|                              Unused                                   |
+-----------------------------------------------------------------------+
|                         Internet Header                               |
|                               +                                       |
|                  64 Bits of Original Datagram Data                    |
+-----------------------------------------------------------------------+
```

Figure 7.5 Format of the Time Exceeded ICMP message.

7.2.4 Time Exceeded Message

A datagram may time out because the Time-to-Live reached zero while the datagram was in transit. Another type of timeout occurs when a datagram has been fragmented and the destination host's reassembly timer expires before all of the pieces have arrived. In either case, an ICMP Time Exceeded message is sent to the datagram source. The format of the Time Exceeded message is shown in Figure 7.5.

The code indicates the nature of the timeout:

Code	Meaning
0	Time To Live exceeded
1	Fragment Reassembly Time exceeded

7.2.5 Parameter Problem

A router or host may encounter a problem with some header field that makes it impossible to process the datagram correctly, so that the datagram must be discarded. The ICMP Parameter Problem message can report the difficulty. Code values include:

Code	Meaning
0	The value in the pointer field identifies the octet where an error occurred.
1	A required option is missing (used in the military community to indicate a missing security option).

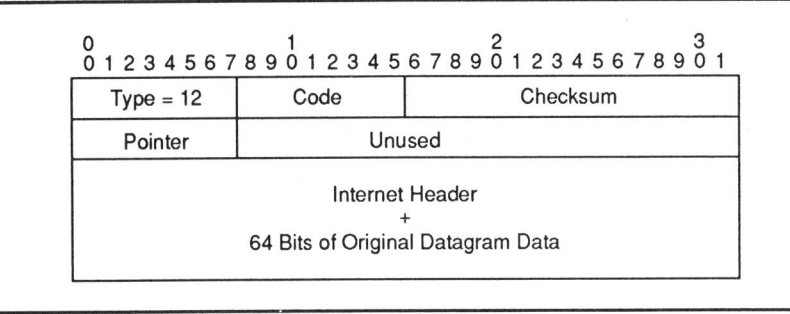

```
 0                   1                   2                   3
 0 1 2 3 4 5 6 7 8 9 0 1 2 3 4 5 6 7 8 9 0 1 2 3 4 5 6 7 8 9 0 1
```
| Type = 12 | Code | Checksum |
| Pointer | Unused |

Internet Header
+
64 Bits of Original Datagram Data

Figure 7.6 Format of the Parameter problem ICMP message.

Option fields (such as source route) are the most usual sources of trouble. The pointer field identifies the octet where the error was detected. Figure 7.6 displays the format of the Parameter Problem message.

7.2.6 Source Quench

The IP protocol is very simple; a host or router processes a datagram and sends it on as quickly as possible. However, delivery does not always proceed smoothly. A number of things can go wrong.

One or more hosts sending UDP traffic to a slow server may flood the server with UDP traffic. This will cause the server to discard the overflow traffic.

A router may run out of buffer space and be forced to discard some datagrams. A slow wide area connection, such as a 56 kilobit per second link between two 10-megabit per second LANs, can create a bottleneck.

Congestion causes datagrams to be discarded, resulting in retransmissions which produce even more traffic to handle. The Source Quench message shown in Figure 7.7 is intended to relieve this problem.

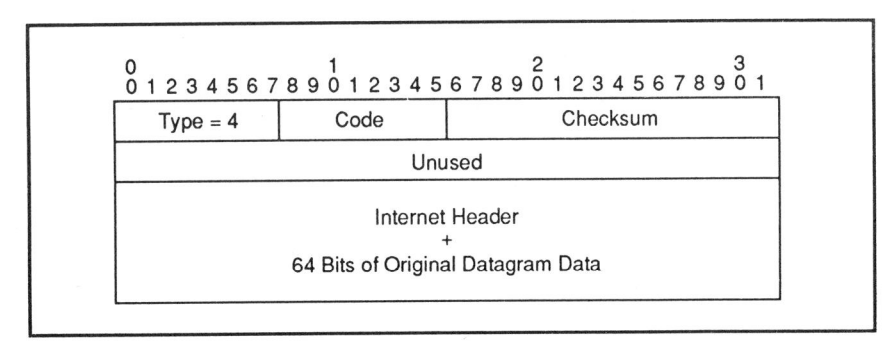

```
 0                   1                   2                   3
 0 1 2 3 4 5 6 7 8 9 0 1 2 3 4 5 6 7 8 9 0 1 2 3 4 5 6 7 8 9 0 1
```
| Type = 4 | Code | Checksum |
| Unused |

Internet Header
+
64 Bits of Original Datagram Data

Figure 7.7 Format of a Source Quench ICMP message.

A Source Quench should be delivered to the upper layer sender: that is, TCP or a UDP application. The sender is supposed to throttle back traffic for a while, and gradually build back to normal. The details of exactly how the congested system should execute a source quench are left to the implementor, leaving some important questions open:

- When should a router or host send a Source Quench message?
- To which sources should messages be sent?

Up until this point, the ICMP messages that we have described have been sent to notify a source host that one of its datagrams has been discarded. However, in a congestion situation, it is possible that the datagrams that happen to be discarded do not come from the hosts that are generating very heavy traffic!

In fact, it is probably best for the network if a system starts a source quench action before it is totally congested and needs to discard datagrams. Instead, action should be triggered when free buffer space reaches a preset low water mark. If the system keeps track of the systems that send it the most traffic, quenches can be targeted at these sources. Alternatively, quenches can be sent to every traffic source for some period of time.

7.2.7 Redirect

A host may have access to more than one local router. When a router receives a datagram that should have been sent to another router, it directs the datagram onward and sends a Redirect message to the host. The host should switch subsequent traffic to the shorter route. The redirect message has the format shown in Figure 7.8.

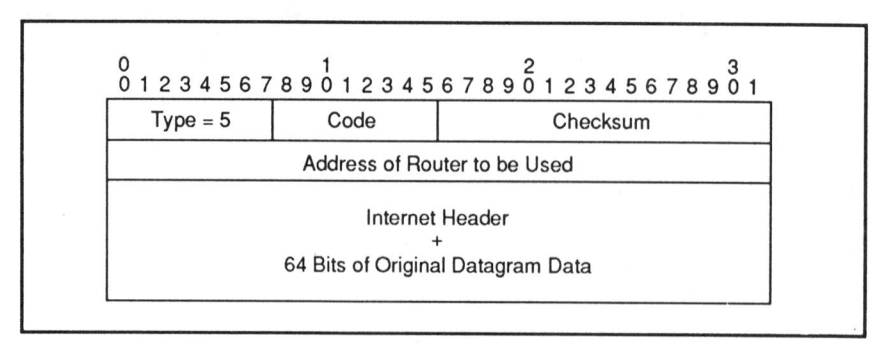

```
 0                   1                   2                   3
 0 1 2 3 4 5 6 7 8 9 0 1 2 3 4 5 6 7 8 9 0 1 2 3 4 5 6 7 8 9 0 1
+---------------+---------------+-------------------------------+
|    Type = 5   |     Code      |           Checksum            |
+---------------+---------------+-------------------------------+
|                   Address of Router to be Used                |
+---------------------------------------------------------------+
|                       Internet Header                         |
|                              +                                |
|                 64 Bits of Original Datagram Data             |
+---------------------------------------------------------------+
```

Figure 7.8 Format of the Redirect ICMP message.

Redirect messages can be used to cut down on manual network administration. A host can be configured with a single default router, and can learn dynamically about routes through other routers. The redirect codes are:

Code	Meaning
0	Redirect datagrams for the Network.
1	Redirect datagrams for the Host.
2	Redirect datagrams for the Type of Service and Network.
3	Redirect datagrams for the Type of Service and Host.

Recall that a routing table can contain entries for individual hosts as well as for networks.

Some routing protocols can choose a delivery path based on a datagram's Type of Service field. These codes provide advice that reflects these considerations.

7.3 ICMP QUERY MESSAGES

Not all ICMP messages signal errors. Some are used to probe the network for useful information. Is host X up? Is router Y running? How long does it take for a round trip to Z and back? What is my address mask?

Specifically, the ICMP query messages include:

- An "Are you alive?" Echo query and response that can be exchanged with hosts and routers.
- A Timestamp query and response that indicates the clock setting at a target system, and how long that system typically takes to process a datagram.
- An Address Mask query and response that allows a host to ask a server what subnet address mask should be assigned to an interface.

Figure 7.9 summarizes the ICMP query services. The "Are you alive?" echo message is used on a daily basis by network managers. The timestamp and address mask queries rarely are seen.

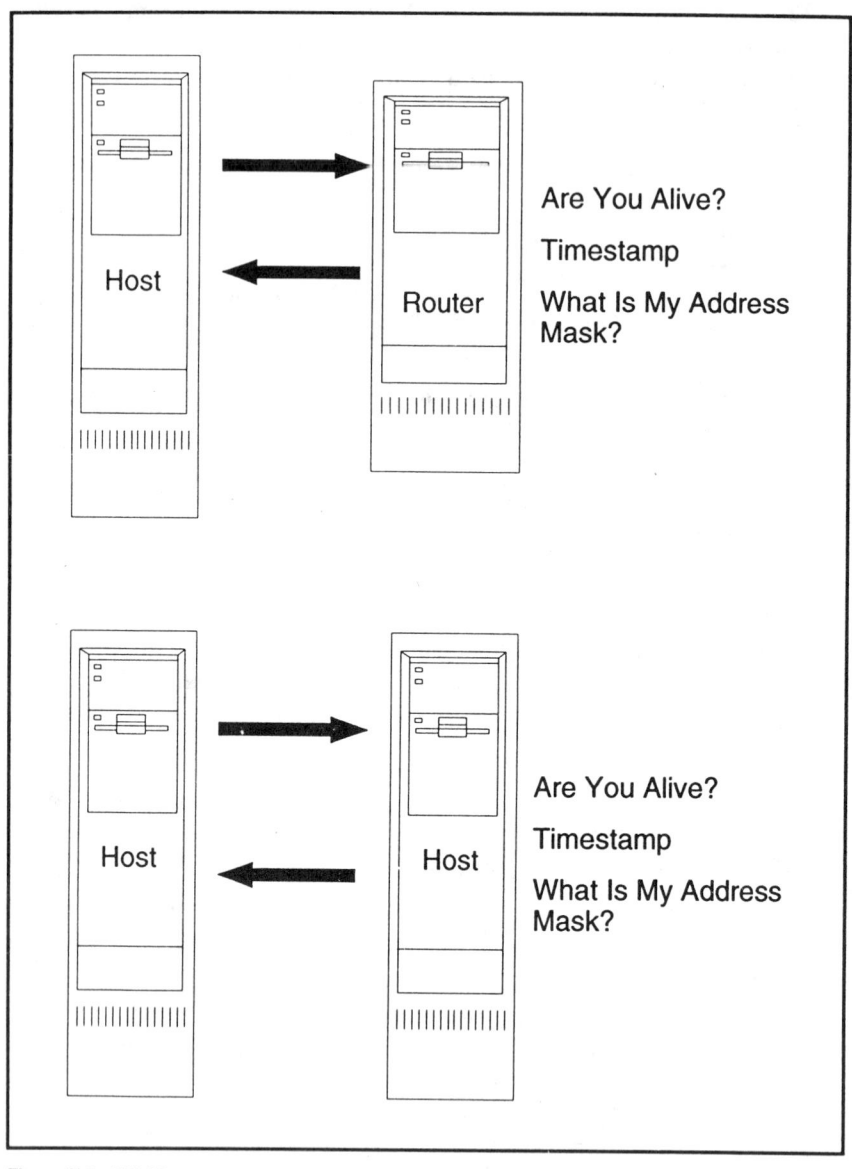

Figure 7.9 ICMP query messages.

7.3.1 Echo or Echo Reply

The Echo Request and Echo Reply are used to check whether systems are active. Type 8 is used for the request and type 0 for the reply. The number of octets in the Data field is variable, and can be selected by the sender.

```
 0                   1                   2                   3
 0 1 2 3 4 5 6 7 8 9 0 1 2 3 4 5 6 7 8 9 0 1 2 3 4 5 6 7 8 9 0 1
```
| Type = 8 or 0 | Code | Checksum |
| Identifier | Sequence Number |

DATA

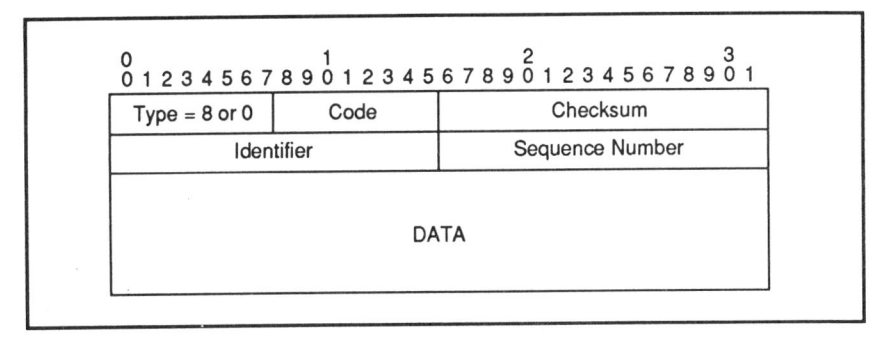

Figure 7.10 Format of the Echo and Echo Reply ICMP messages.

The responder must send back the same data it receives. The identifier is used to match a reply with its original request. A sequence of echo messages can be sent to test whether the network is dropping messages and to estimate average throughput and round trip time. In this case, the identifier is held fixed while the sequence number is incremented for each message. The format of the echo message is shown in Figure 7.10.

The famous *ping* command, available on just about every TCP/IP system, is built on the ICMP echo message. In the dialogue below, we first test that host ring.bell.com is alive. Then we send it a sequence of 14 messages, each containing 64 octets of data.

```
ping ring.bell.com
ring.bell.com is alive

ping -s ring.bell.com  64   14
64 bytes from ring.bell.com: icmp_seq=3. time=21. ms
64 bytes from ring.bell.com: icmp_seq=4. time=18. ms
64 bytes from ring.bell.com: icmp_seq=5. time=17. ms
64 bytes from ring.bell.com: icmp_seq=6. time=19. ms
64 bytes from ring.bell.com: icmp_seq=7. time=17. ms
64 bytes from ring.bell.com: icmp_seq=8. time=17. ms
64 bytes from ring.bell.com: icmp_seq=9. time=17. ms
64 bytes from ring.bell.com: icmp_seq=10. time=18. ms
64 bytes from ring.bell.com: icmp_seq=11. time=17. ms
64 bytes from ring.bell.com: icmp_seq=12. time=17. ms
64 bytes from ring.bell.com: icmp_seq=13. time=17. ms

----ring.bell.com PING Statistics----
14 packets transmitted, 11 packets received, 21% packet loss
round-trip (ms)  min/avg/max = 17/17/21
```

```
 0                   1                   2                   3
 0 1 2 3 4 5 6 7 8 9 0 1 2 3 4 5 6 7 8 9 0 1 2 3 4 5 6 7 8 9 0 1
+---------------+---------------+-------------------------------+
| Type = 13 or 14 |    Code     |           Checksum            |
+---------------+---------------+-------------------------------+
|           Identifier          |        Sequence Number        |
+-------------------------------+-------------------------------+
|                      Originate Timestamp                      |
+---------------------------------------------------------------+
|                       Receive Timestamp                       |
+---------------------------------------------------------------+
|                       Transmit Timestamp                      |
+---------------------------------------------------------------+
```

Figure 7.11 Format of the Timestamp request and reply.

7.3.2 Timestamp and Timestamp Reply

Timestamp messages provide more information than echo messages. They give a sense of how long the remote system spends buffering and processing a datagram. Note the fields:

- Originate timestamp: time the sender last touched the message
- Receive timestamp: time that the echoer first touched it
- Transmit timestamp: time that the echoer last touched it

The time is measured in milliseconds since midnight, Universal Time (formerly Greenwich Mean Time).

Note that this protocol also provides a very simple way for one system to synchronize its clock with another. Of course the synchronization will be a rough one because of possible network delays. There is a far more capable *Network Time Protocol* that has been defined for Internet time synchronization.

Type 13 is used for the timestamp query and 14 is used for the reply. The format of the message is shown in Figure 7.11.

7.3.3 Address Mask

Recall that an organization may choose to break up its local address field into a subnet part and a host part. When a host comes up, it may not be preconfigured to know how many bits have been assigned to the subnet address field. To find out, the host can broadcast an Address Mask Request.

The response will be sent by an authorized address mask server. Normally, we would expect that server to be a router, but a host might be used. The reply will put 1s into the network and subnet fields of a 32-bit address mask field.

```
 0                   1                   2                   3
 0 1 2 3 4 5 6 7 8 9 0 1 2 3 4 5 6 7 8 9 0 1 2 3 4 5 6 7 8 9 0 1
```

Type = 17 or 18	Code	Checksum
Identifier		Sequence Number
Address Mask		

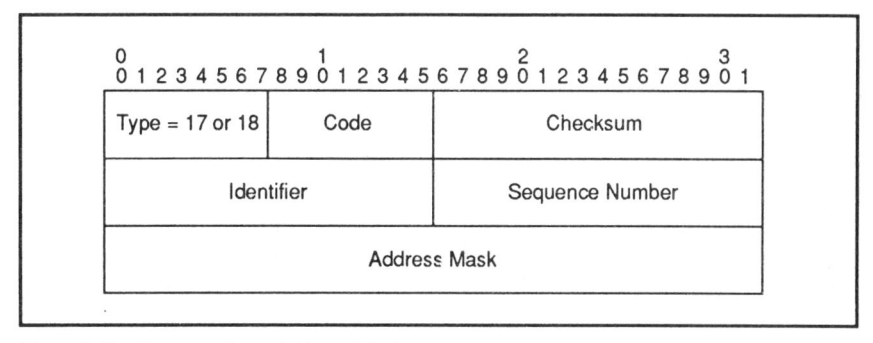

Figure 7.12 Format of an Address Mask message.

An address mask server that has been offline will broadcast an Address Mask Reply when it becomes active. This is done for the benefit of hosts that started up while the server was unavailable.

Figure 7.12 displays the format of the Address Mask Request and reply. The type is 17 for the Address Mask Request and 18 for the Reply. Generally, the identifier and sequence number can be ignored.

7.4 VIEWING ICMP ACTIVITIES

The *netstat* command is included with TCP/IP implementations for a very wide variety of system types. The command is used to obtain network-related information. The netstat command has many options and subcommands. Below we show the ICMP part of a *netstat* report on protocol statistics. This report shows ICMP activity since the last system initiation.

```
netstat -s

icmp:
  1075 calls to icmp_error

  Output histogram:
    echo reply: 231
    destination unreachable: 1075

  2 messages with bad code fields
  0 messages < minimum length
  21 bad checksums
  0 messages with bad length
```

```
Input histogram:
  echo reply: 26
  destination unreachable: 1269
  source quench: 2
  echo: 231

  231 message responses generated
```

The system has sent 1075 Destination Unreachable messages. There were 231 Echo Requests received, and all were answered. There were 26 echo replies received.

ICMP has recorded the fact that 21 messages were *received* with bad checksums. No ICMP message can be directed to a source that sent a datagram with a bad checksum because the source address may have been corrupted.

There were 1269 Destination Unreachable messages and two Source Quenches that were sent to this system.

The *netstat* report that follows includes information about routing. There were two routers that were discovered dynamically. From this report, we can see that all Destination Unreachable messages referred to 12 destinations. There were over 300 uses of *wildcard* or default route selections.

```
netstat -rs
routing:
   0 bad routing redirects
   0 dynamically created routes
   2 new routers due to redirects
  12 destinations found unreachable
 349 uses of a wildcard route
```

7.5 RELATIONSHIP TO OSI

As we have seen, the OSI connectionless network layer protocol is very similar to IP. OSI sends error messages that have a format similar to ICMP messages. The OSI header contains a type flag that indicates that a PDU contains an error message. OSI offers one small enhancement: the sender of a PDU can set a flag to authorize or prevent an error message from being returned if there is a problem in delivering the PDU.

The data field of the error report includes the header of the discarded PDU, and optionally may contain some of the headers from the discarded PDU. OSI needs to include more information than IP because there are *three* layers of headers embedded in messages carrying user data, rather than the single TCP or UDP header.

Conditions that might cause an OSI error PDU to be generated include:

- Destination address unreachable
- Destination address unknown
- Source routing problem
- Lifetime expired in transit
- Lifetime expired during reassembly
- Could not reassemble because of problem
- Unsupported option
- Unsupported protocol version
- Unsupported security option
- Unsupported recording of route option
- Protocol procedure error
- Incorrect checksum
- PDU discarded due to congestion
- Header syntax error
- Segmentation needed but not permitted
- Incomplete PDU
- Too much user data

Like IP, the OSI Network layer standard does not define any specific action to be taken at the network layer as a result of an error report. The report must be passed to an appropriate upper layer entity.

The format of the OSI layer three header and error report is displayed in Figure 7.13. Note that like an ICMP error message that reports a discard, the error protocol data unit is made up of a layer 3 header, the reason for the discard, and header information from the datagram that was discarded.

7.6 RECOMMENDED READING

ICMP is defined in RFC 792. RFC 1122 contains some useful clarifications. The ISO error PDU is defined in ISO 8473. RFC 1129 describes the Network Time Protocol.

138 Chapter Seven

Octets	
1	Network Layer Protocol Identifier
1	Header Length
1	Version
1	Lifetime (Time-to-Live)
1	Flags (Type = Error)
2	Segment (Fragment) Length
2	Checksum
1	Destination Address Length
Varies	Destination Address
1	Source Address Length
Varies	Source Address
2	Identification
2	Segment (Fragment) Offset
2	PDU Total Length
	Options
Varies	Reason for Discard
Varies	ERROR REPORT

Figure 7.13 OSI network layer error report.

Chapter 8

IP Routing

8.1 INTRODUCTION

Routing is the most important function that IP does. In large networks, IP routers exchange information that keeps their routing tables up-to-date. How is this done?

In fact, there is no single required protocol for updating routing information. Instead, there is the concept that within a locally administered and managed part of a network, any convenient routing protocol can be used. This may be one of the standard Internet protocols or a proprietary protocol supplied by a router vendor. Currently, use of the venerable *Routing Information Protocol* (RIP) predominates. The new *Open Shortest Path First* protocol (OSPF) is rapidly gaining acceptance.

The Internet model for routing partitions a large network into many separate autonomous routing regions. These are called *Autonomous Systems*. For example, a large division of a company might control its own Autonomous System. Personnel responsible for a region's network make their own decisions about the routers and the routing protocol that they will employ. A routing protocol that is used within an Autonomous System is called an *Interior Gateway Protocol* (IGP).[1]

How can separate Autonomous Systems be tied together? The Internet has been finding ways to do this for many years. The model and protocols that make this work are discussed later in this chapter.

---

[1] An Autonomous System is formally defined as a set of routers that are controlled by a single administrative authority and use a common Interior Gateway Protocol.

8.2 IP ROUTING

An IP datagram follows a path made up of a sequence of *hops*. A node is one hop away, or *adjacent*, if there is a direct LAN or WAN connection to the node. Routers that are separated by one hop are called *neighbors*.

A source route that lists a preselected list of hops can be embedded in an IP header. However, the use of source routes is not the norm. Usually a datagram is routed by choosing its next hop destination at each router along its path.

Next hop routing is flexible and robust. A permanent change in network topology usually can be configured by updating a few routers. Routers can be programmed to inform one another of temporary and permanent changes in the network, and dynamically can switch traffic onto alternative routes as needed.

8.2.1 Routing Tables

Routing is carried out in a host or a router by consulting a routing table. This table matches a destination with the address of the router to be used as the next hop. There is no unique format for routing tables, but a typical table entry contains items such as:

- Address of a destination network, subnet, or host
- IP address of a next hop router
- Network interface to be used
- Subnet mask for this interface
- Distance to the destination (e.g., number of hops to reach the destination)
- Number of seconds since the route was last updated

In order to keep routing tables small, most or all of the entries identify destination networks or subnets. The idea is that if you can get to a router on a host's network or subnet, you will be able to get to that host. Sometimes a few important host destinations are included in the table.

It may be helpful at this point to look at a typical routing table report. Most systems that run TCP/IP provide a *netstat* command that displays network information. The *netstat* command often includes a subcommand (*netstat -r* in UNIX) that displays selected routing table information. The output produced by this command will vary for different TCP/IP products. The format will depend on what each specific vendor has decided to include in the table.

Sample netstat output is shown below:

```
Destination     Gateway         Flags   Refcnt  Use     Interface
127.0.0.1       127.0.0.1       UH      1       422     lo0
128.36.16.0     128.36.12.1     UG      0       65      le0
192.35.89.0     128.36.12.5     UG      2       201     le0
default         128.36.12.1     UG      0       0       le0
```

The first destination is 127.0.0.1. By convention, all addresses starting with 127 mean *this host*. These addresses are used for testing network code by *looping* it back to the local computer. Interface *lo0* is the loopback interface; data never actually exits the computer. The Refcnt column shows that there is one active loopback user, and the Use column reports that 422 packets have been sent on this route.

This host is connected to an Ethernet LAN via interface le0. All destinations are reached through this hardware interface.

The address 128.36.16.0 identifies a subnet. Traffic bound for destinations on this subnet should be sent to 128.36.12.1, whose flags ("UG") identify it as a router that is up.[2] Class C network 192.35.89.0 is reached via router 128.36.12.5. The Refcnt indicates that there are 2 active users of the route to 192.35.89.0.

Any network not specifically mentioned in the table is reached through the default router, 128.36.12.1.

Routing tables can be made very small and efficient by including just a few network identifiers and a default. It is acceptable to list individual host addresses in a routing table, but including a large number of individual host addresses slows down routing lookups and complicates maintenance.

8.2.2 Routing Protocols

How are tables entered into hosts and routers? How are they kept up-to-date? How is the best choice for the next hop router discovered? These chores are the job of a routing protocol. The simplest routing protocol is:

- Study diagrams of your network to find the best paths. Choose the next hop so that these paths are followed.
- Enter your routing tables manually.
- Update your routing tables manually.

---

[2] U is for up and G is for gateway — i.e., router.

This is a reasonable choice for a small internet. For a more complex network that is growing and changing and has multiple potential routes to a destination, manual routing will be a nightmare. At some point it becomes impossible for humans to analyze and respond to network conditions. A routing protocol is needed to automate:

- Exchange of information between routers about the current state of the network
- Recomputation of the best next hop selection as changes occur

Over the years, there has been substantial research into routing protocols. Many have been implemented and their merits have been hotly debated. What are the characteristics of a winning protocol?

- When the network changes, it should respond quickly.
- It should compute optimal routes.
- It should scale up well as your network grows.
- It should be frugal in its use of computer resources.
- It should be frugal in its use of transmission resources.

But computing optimal routes in a large network may require considerable CPU and memory, and quick response may require immediate transmission of a mass of information. A good protocol design has to balance these requirements.

8.2.3 Routing Metrics

How do we decide that one route is better than another? There has to be some *metric* (distance measurement) that can be used to compare routes.

Very simple routing protocols just use end-to-end hop counts to compare routes. Some improvement is gained by using weighted hop counts; for example, a hop across a high speed LAN can be given weight 1, while a hop across a slow medium such as a 56-kilobit per second point-to-point line could be given a weight of 10.

More sophisticated metrics combine one or more of bandwidth, delay, Maximum Transmission Unit size, reliability, current load, or dollar cost into the calculation of a routing metric. Algorithms that base routing decisions entirely on the calculated metric values are called *distance vector* algorithms.

Currently, a lot of attention is focused on *link state* routing algorithms. Routers participating in a link state protocol maintain an up-to-date picture of the *complete topology* of the network by telling one another what is going on.

For example, if a link goes down, the news spreads quickly to routers throughout the Autonomous System. A router uses its knowledge of the current topology to plot all available paths to a destination, and then chooses the path whose metric is smallest.

Link state algorithms are sometimes called *Shortest Path First*, or SPF. (This term is not particularly descriptive of what these algorithms do.)

Note that most implementations of routing protocols allow a network manager to preconfigure a few static, permanent routes. The protocol is then applied to handle the bulk of the routing that remains.

8.3 ROUTING INFORMATION PROTOCOL (RIP)

The Interior Gateway Protocol in widest use today is RIP, which is derived from the Xerox Network Systems (XNS) routing protocol. RIP's popularity is based on its simplicity and availability.

RIP was included in the Berkeley Software Distribution TCP/IP implementation, and is still distributed with UNIX systems as program *routed*. A RIP *routed* program is a standard part of most vendors' host and router TCP/IP packages. RIP is included in a free bundle of software from Cornell University called *gated*. RIP was in widespread use for several years before being standardized in RFC 1058.

RIP computes routes using a simple *distance vector* routing algorithm. Every hop in the network is assigned a cost. The total metric for a path is the sum of the hop costs. RIP tries to choose the next hop so that datagrams will follow a least cost path.

RIP has some serious shortcomings. The maximum metric for any path is fifteen. For this reason, RIP usually is configured with a cost of one for each hop. After a disruption in the network, RIP is slow to find optimal routes.

In fact, datagrams may run around in a loop for a while. RIP cannot respond to changes in delay or load across links. Normally, it cannot split traffic to balance the load, although some router vendors have added facilities to do this in special cases.

Like all automated routing protocols, RIP has to send routing updates, receive routing updates, and recompute routes. A RIP router sends information to its neighbor routers every thirty seconds. If the neighbors are on a LAN, the update is broadcast. Sending out routing information is called *advertising routes*. A host on a LAN can eavesdrop on RIP broadcast advertisements, and use them to update its own routing table.

144 Chapter Eight

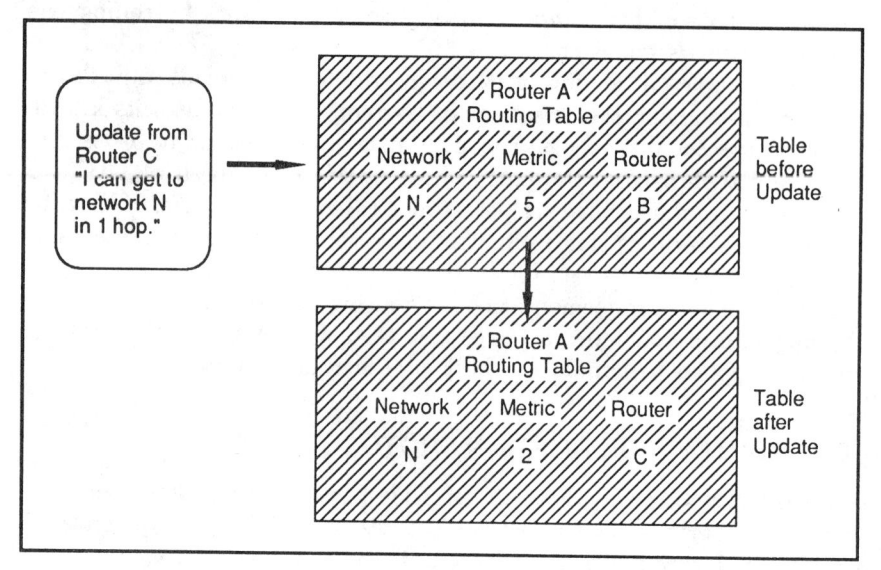

Figure 8.1 Updating routing tables with RIP.

In Figure 8.1, router A has been sending traffic to network N through router B. Router A receives an update from router C announcing a shorter route, and updates its routing table. Note that the hop from router A to router C is added to C's metric to get the distance from A to N.

8.3.1 RIP Routing

How does a system, say node i, compute the best route to node j? The best RIP route is defined as the one for which the distance is smallest.

We start our routing table off with distances that we know about. Then, whenever an update arrives from a neighbor, we recheck all of our distances. Sometimes, nodes in a network become *unreachable*. In RIP, a distance of 16 or larger indicates that a node is unreachable.

The steps in computing RIP distances are listed below. Note that a RIP node depends entirely on information received from its adjacent neighbors to update its routes to destinations that are more than one hop away.

Suppose that we are node i, and want to find out the distance to every node in the network.

1. Initially, we know the distances to each of our adjacent neighbors. Configure the distance to each adjacent neighbor k into variables called $d(i,k)$.
2. The variable $D(m,n)$ will hold the total distance between node m and node n. Initially, we fill in the values that we know about, namely $D(i,k) = d(i,k)$. We mark all other total distances as unreachable.
3. Now we are ready to find out about the rest of the world. We will be receiving regular bulletins from each adjacent neighbor. When neighbor k sends us its own estimate $D(k,j)$ of its distance to node j, we compute our distance to j through k:

$$D(i,j) = d(i,k) + D(k,j) = \text{total distance to } j \text{ through } k$$

If this is a reachable distance and is smaller than the current table entry (or if there is no current entry for j), we write $D(i,j)$ into the routing table and use neighbor k as the next hop destination on the way to j.
4. Routes don't always get shorter, sometimes they get longer. How can we adapt when routes get longer? If we are currently routing to j through neighbor k and we get an update from k so that the new $D(i,j)$ is larger than the entry in our table, we must write the new $D(i,j)$ into the table:

$$D(i,j) = d(i,k) + D(k,j) = \text{total distance}$$

If the new $D(i,j)$ is bigger than 15, j must be marked unreachable.

8.3.2 Recovering from Network Disturbances

When a destination becomes unreachable, it can take quite a long time for the news to get to all of the routers in the Autonomous System. At a remote router, what typically happens is that the metric for the unavailable network will increase gradually as a series of updates containing larger and larger metrics arrive.

This phenomenon, called counting to infinity, is caused by updates from neighbors that believe that they have a new route to the destination when in fact, their traffic is ending up in the same place. For a period of time, datagrams wander aimlessly through the network while routers exchange updates and make a series of adjustments in their metrics. Eventually, all of the routers realize that the destination is unreachable and their tables converge to correct values.

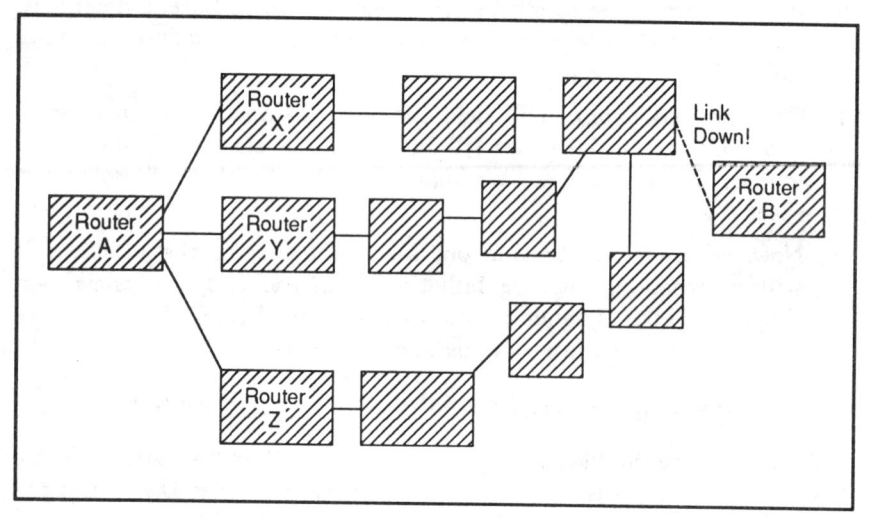

Figure 8.2 Inefficient routing updates.

Figure 8.2 shows a simple example of what can happen. Router A normally gets to router B in four hops. Router A discovers that it no longer can reach B through X. Router A switches its traffic to Y, which does not yet know that there is a problem. Later, Y discovers that it cannot reach B and A switches its traffic to Z.

In the meantime, router A is being told about longer routes to destination B. However, all of the traffic ends up in the same place, and is undeliverable.

The problem is caused by the fact that RIP knows the distance between a neighbor and a destination, but has no idea of the path that actually will be followed.

This is a case where we definitely want bad news to travel fast. The sections that follow will present a number of mechanisms that prevent RIP from choosing impossible paths and help RIP to discover and spread bad news quickly.

8.3.3 Timing Out Unreachable Routers

Suppose we are sending traffic via a router that crashes? A router expects to hear from a neighbor every 30 seconds. If 180 seconds pass without an update, routes through that neighbor are timed out and marked unreachable.

It doesn't make sense to include unreachable destinations in a routing table forever. However, they should be kept around for a while, so that updates sent to neighbors will warn them not to send traffic for the destination to this router. Usually defunct routes are kept for a minute or two. This period is called the *garbage collection* time.

8.3.4 Split Horizon and Poisoned Reverse

In Figure 8.3, router A normally reaches network N through router D. If the path between router D and network N is disrupted, then D will start looking around for an alternate route. If A advertises the fact that it knows how to get to network N, then D will start routing its traffic to A — who will send it right back!

The *split horizon* technique is used to prevent this. Router A simply does not include its route to N when advertising its routes on network M. While D's connection is up, the hosts and routers on M should be routing through router D anyway. When D's connection goes down, it will not help at all if systems on network M try to reach network N by sending their traffic to router A.

Split horizon with poisoned reverse is an even more effective solution. Router A includes an entry for network N in its advertisements on network M, but marks N as unreachable through A. This makes it very clear that systems on M should not try to route to N through router A.

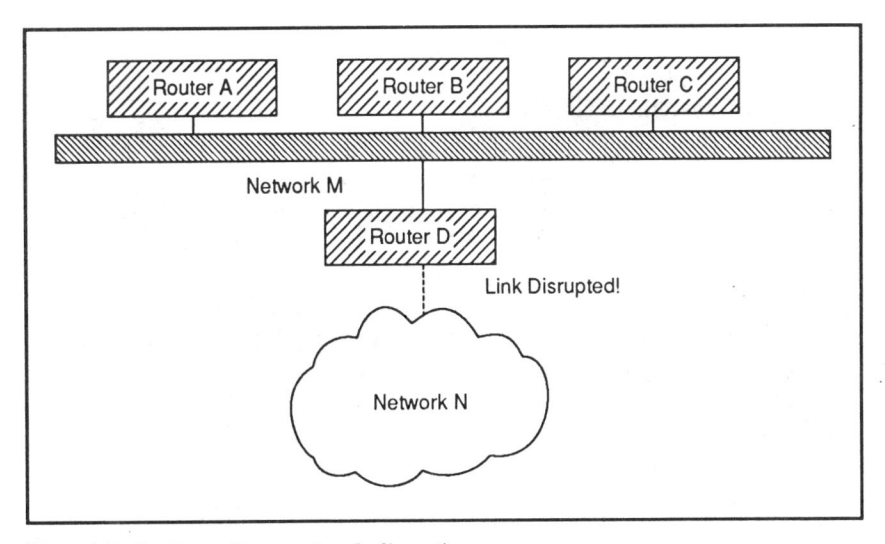

Figure 8.3 Routing after a network disruption.

8.3.5 Triggered Updates and Hold Down

Triggered updates are used to speed up the process of discovering changes. The triggered update rule requires a node to send updates almost immediately after changing its metric for a route.

Note that one new update will trigger others that may trigger others. However, this spurt of messages can prevent a lot of purposeless user traffic. One way to limit the bandwidth used by triggered updates is to send only those entries which actually have changed, rather than an entire routing table.

While adjustments are going on, a node that has discovered that a destination is unreachable may receive an obsolete update that indicates that a route is available.

The *hold down* rule sets a period of time during which updates are ignored for a destination that has just been marked unreachable. The time period is chosen large enough so that all of the routers in the domain will have had time to hear about the loss of connectivity to the destination.

8.3.6 RIP Message Protocol

As already noted, update messages (called *responses*) are sent between routers at regular intervals, and also are triggered by network changes. In addition, request messages may be sent to poll for routing information.

Typically, a system would send out requests:

- During system initialization.
- When performing a network monitoring function.

The format of the request and response messages is shown in Figure 8.4. A command field of 1 indicates a request and 2 indicates a response. The current version is 1.

When the RIP RFC was written, it was anticipated that RIP routing would be used for IP and for other network protocols, so an *address family identifier field* and space for up to 14 address octets were included.

The address family, IP address, and metric fields can be repeated so that the message can contain up to 25 address entries. The maximum message size is 512 octets. If more than 25 entries need to be sent, multiple messages can be used.

A request contains an entry for each address for which a metric is desired. A single entry with address 0 and metric of 16 asks for a complete routing table update.

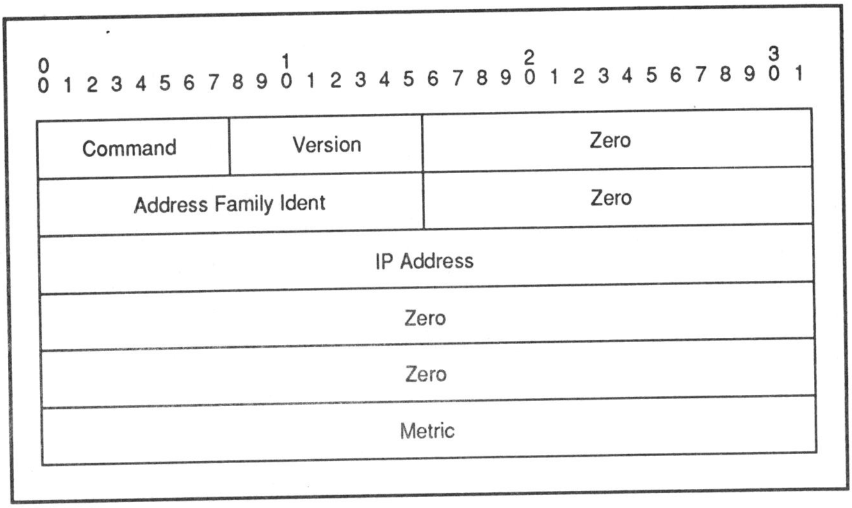

```
 0                   1                   2                   3
 0 1 2 3 4 5 6 7 8 9 0 1 2 3 4 5 6 7 8 9 0 1 2 3 4 5 6 7 8 9 0 1
+-------------------+-------------------+-------------------------------+
|      Command      |      Version      |             Zero              |
+-------------------+-------------------+-------------------------------+
|       Address Family Ident           |             Zero              |
+---------------------------------------+-------------------------------+
|                              IP Address                                |
+------------------------------------------------------------------------+
|                                 Zero                                   |
+------------------------------------------------------------------------+
|                                 Zero                                   |
+------------------------------------------------------------------------+
|                                Metric                                  |
+------------------------------------------------------------------------+
```

Figure 8.4 Format of RIP messages.

8.4 OPEN SHORTEST PATH FIRST

In 1988, the Internet Engineering Task Force started work on a new protocol to replace RIP. The result is the *Open Shortest Path First* (OSPF) Interior Gateway Protocol, a link state protocol intended for use within Autonomous Systems of all sizes. In 1990, OSPF was recommended as a proposed standard. It is freely available as a non-proprietary public technology.

OSPF is designed to scale well and to spread accurate routing information through an internet quickly. In addition, OSPF supports:

- Traffic splitting across multiple paths
- Routing based on Type of Service
- Authentication for routing update messages

In April of 1990, the NASA Science Internet converted to OSPF. Results have been encouraging. Routing traffic decreased. After a change or disruption in the network, globally correct routing information was reestablished very quickly — typically within a few seconds, as compared to minutes for other protocols!

Version 2 of OSPF was published in mid-1991, and experimental software versions quickly were made available. Because of the complexity of the OSPF protocol, minor revisions and bug fixes will continue for some period of time.

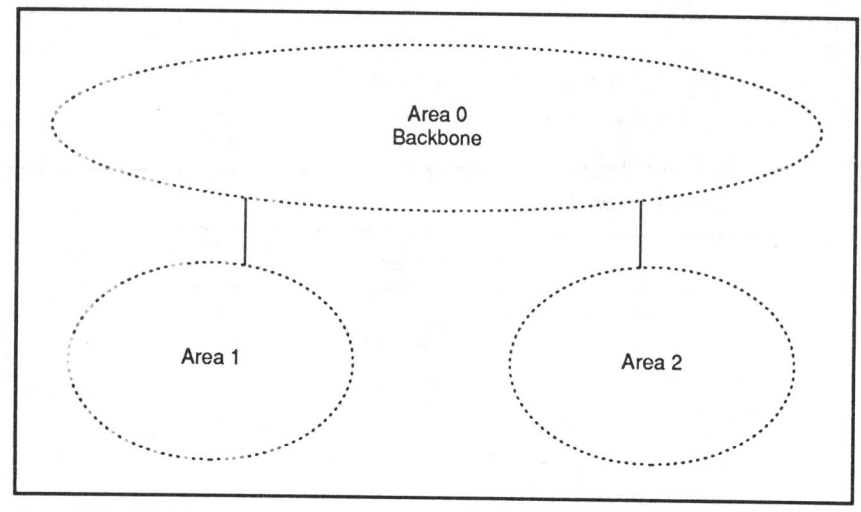

Figure 8.5 OSPF backbone and areas.

8.4.1 OSPF Model

In the OSPF standard, the term *network* means an IP network or a subnet. An *area* is a set of networks. An Autonomous System using OSPF is structured as a set of areas. Each area is assigned a number. Area 0 is a backbone that connects to all of the other areas and glues the Autonomous System together. Figure 8.5 illustrates this topology.

OSPF scales well because a router in an area needs to know detailed topology and metric information only about that area. A summary of distances from routers at an area's border to networks in other areas is used for routing to destinations in other areas. A summary of distances between routers at the boundary of an Autonomous System and external networks is used for routing to destinations in other Autonomous Systems.

A participating router in an area keeps a database describing the topology and status of all of the elements in the area. Whenever a change occurs (such as a link going down) this information is propagated through the area.

This promotes accurate routing and quick response to trouble. For example, if OSPF routing were used in the network in Figure 8.2, node A would be informed that the link to B was down, and would realize immediately that there was no usable route to B.

A node that is initializing obtains a copy of the current routing database from a neighbor. After that, only changes need to be communicated. Changes get known quickly because OSPF uses an efficient *flooding* algorithm to spread update information through the area: after receiving an update, a node sends the update to a selected set of neighbors.

Medin's Map Analogy[3] (illustrated in Figure 8.6) may help to understand the OSPF philosophy. If you were making a trip through your home town, you would look at a detailed street map to find the shortest route. Detailed routing is used within an OSPF area.

If you were going to some destination out of town but in the county, you would turn to a county map that shows major roads, and use the local map to decide which combination of local route and major road was the shortest. OSPF uses a combination of detailed routing and summary information to route between areas within an Autonomous System.

If you were going on a trip that crossed several states, you would use a national map to check the superhighways. If one superhighway was 400 miles shorter than another, that's the one you would use. OSPF uses summary information to route between Autonomous Systems.

There is an OSPF option that allows routes between Autonomous Systems to be treated as an order of magnitude larger that those within an Autonomous System. When picking the best route to a destination in a remote Autonomous System, OSPF could concentrate on finding the shortest way to get to that Autonomous System.

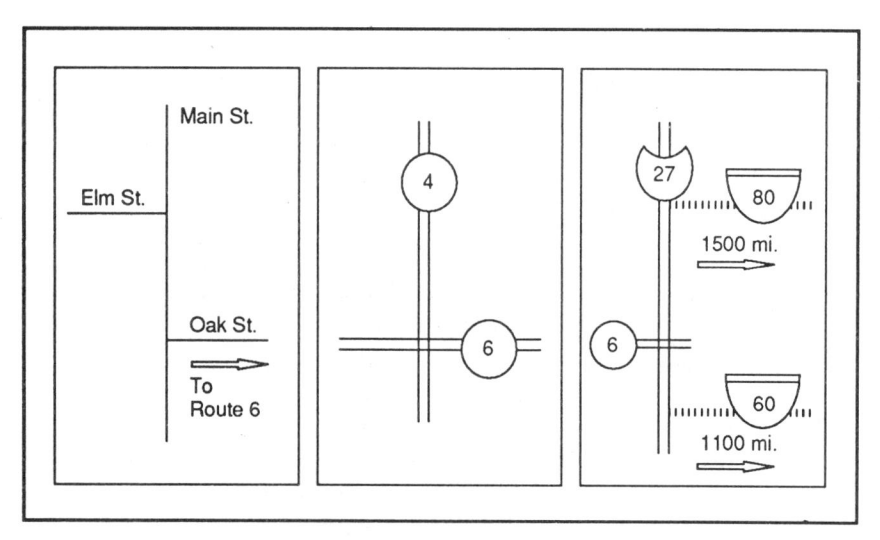

Figure 8.6 Medin's map analogy for routing.

---

[3]Created by Milo Medin, a member of the OSPF working group.

8.5 AREAS AND DATABASES

A small Autonomous System can consist of a single area. A medium to large sized Autonomous System can be broken into several areas, each consisting of one or more networks. For OSPF, a destination network is identified by its IP address and subnet mask, so that OSPF can route to subnets.

Every router in an area maintains an identical detailed database that describes the complete network topology of the area. This includes the state of every router, each router's usable interfaces, its connected networks, and its neighboring routers. Less detailed summary information in the database is used for routing to destinations outside the area. Hence, breaking an Autonomous System into areas substantially reduces the amount of information that a link state router needs to store and maintain.

A router uses its database to construct a tree of shortest paths with itself as the root. This tree is used to build the routing table. If Type of Service routing is supported in the area, a separate tree and set of routes is built for each Type of Service value.

8.5.1 The Backbone of an Area

Areas are glued together by the backbone, which is itself an area. The backbone contains *all routers that belong to multiple areas, as well as any networks and routers not assigned to any other area*. Recall that areas are numbered, with area 0 being the backbone.

The backbone is supposed to be contiguous. In cases where it is not, *virtual routes* must be defined to tie together the pieces of the backbone. Virtual routes also can be defined in order to provide backup paths in case of a backbone router or link failure.

In Figure 8.7, backbone area 0 includes routers A, B, and C. Area 1 includes routers B and D. Area 2 includes routers C and E. Routers B and C are *border routers*. In this simple configuration, areas 1 and 2 are *stub* networks — that is, they each have a single connection to the backbone. Router B knows the full topologies of area 1 and of the backbone. Similarly, router C knows the full topologies of area 2 and of the backbone.

In Figure 8.8, area 0 includes routers A, B, C, F, G, and H. Routers B, C, F, and G are *border routers*. *Boundary router* H connects this Autonomous System to external Autonomous Systems. Area 1 includes routers B, D, and F. Area 2 includes routers G, C and E. Normally, traffic from network M to network N follows the route B-A-C-E. If router A crashes, traffic entering router B that has destination network N can be sent along the virtual route B-D-F-G-E.

IP Routing   153

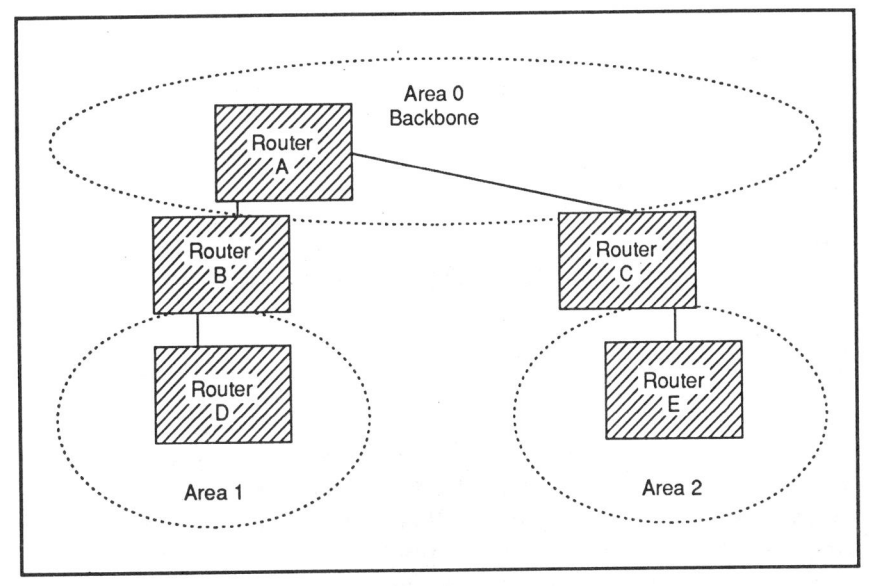

Figure 8.7 Autonomous System with a simple contiguous backbone.

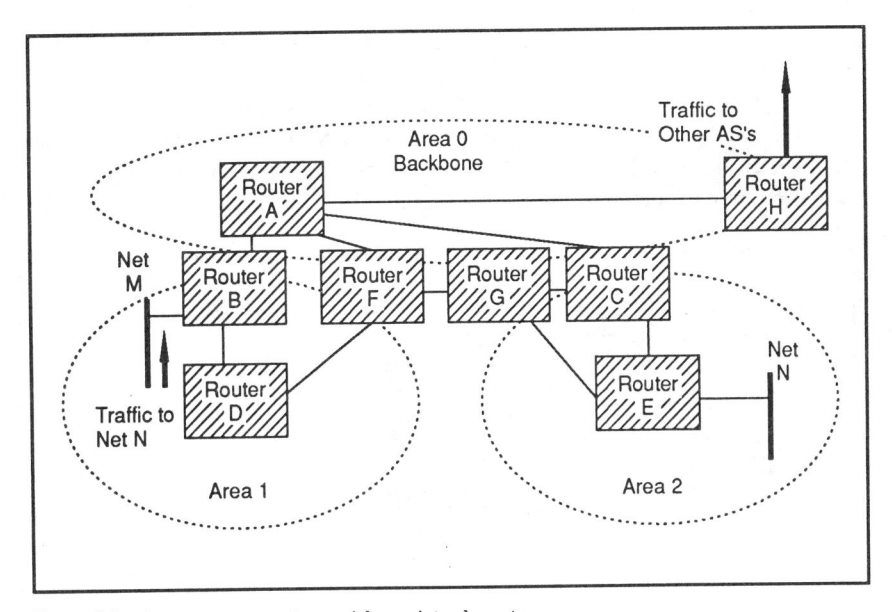

Figure 8.8 Autonomous system with a virtual route.

8.6 BUILDING THE ROUTING DATABASE FOR AN AREA

Every OSPF router maintains a detailed database of information needed to build the area routing tree, such as descriptions of:

- Each router's interfaces, connections, and associated metrics.
- Each multi-access network, and a list of all routers on the network.

How does a router get its information? It starts by finding out who its neighbors are by means of *Hello messages*.

8.6.1 Hello Messages

Every router periodically multicasts *Hello messages* on a multi-access network (such as an Ethernet or Token-Ring LAN) to let other routers know that it is active. It sends Hello messages to peers attached by point-to-point links to check if these neighbors are awake.

One reason that Hello works well is that a message contains lists of neighbors whose Hellos the sender already has heard. That way, every router knows whether its messages are getting through.

8.6.2 The Designated Router

On multi-access networks, the Hello protocol also is used to select a *Designated Router* that is responsible for reliably updating its adjacent neighbors with the latest network topology news.

In Figure 8.9, Designated Router A exchanges information with routers B, C, and D on its local area network, as well as with router E which is connected by a point-to-point link.

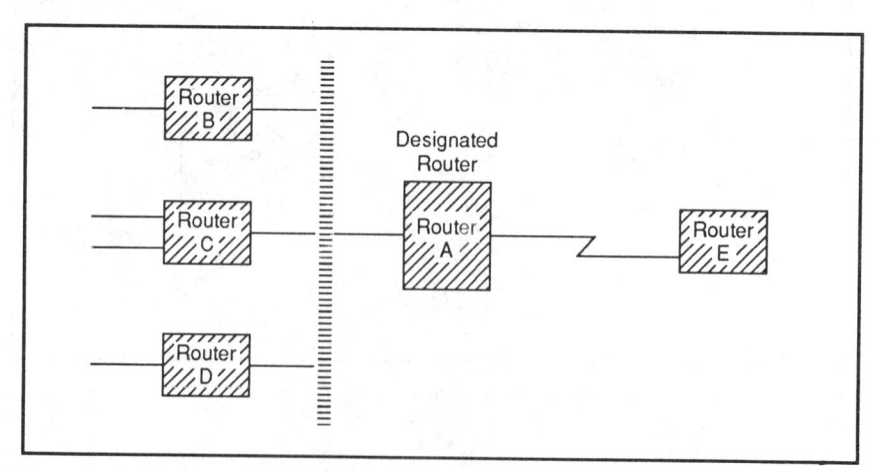

Figure 8.9 A Designated Router updates its neighbors.

Note that B does not have to coordinate with C or D, because A makes sure that they all have the same information.

8.6.3 Initializing a Routing Database

Now suppose that router B has just been restarted after being offline for maintenance. First B will discover its neighbors, and will find out that router A is the Designated Router, via Hellos. Next, B will bring itself up-to-date by talking to A.

More specifically, A and B will exchange *Database Description* messages. These messages contain a list of what each has in its database, and an indication of how fresh the information is.

After this exchange of information is complete, each has discovered:

- Which items are not yet in its local database.
- Which items are present, but out of date.

Link State Request messages are used to ask for data that is in need of an update. *Link State Update* messages respond to these requests. After a full (and acknowledged) exchange of information, the databases are in sync. Link State Update messages also are used to report changes in the area topology. Topology updates are flooded through an area, so that all databases are kept in synchronization.

8.6.4 Message Types

The five message types used in the OSPF protocol exchanges that we have described are:

1. *Hello:* Used to identify neighbors, to elect a Designated Router for a multi-access network, to find out about an existing Designated Router, and as an "I am alive" signal.
2. *Database Description:* During initialization, used to exchange information so that a router can find out what data is missing from its database.
3. *Link State Request:* Used to ask for data that a router has discovered is missing from its database.
4. *Link State Update:* Used to reply to a Link State Request, and also to dynamically report changes in network topology.
5. *Link State ACK:* Used to confirm receipt of a Link State Update. The sender will retransmit until an update is ACKed.

8.7 ROUTING ACROSS AN AREA BORDER

A border router knows the complete topology of each area to which it connects. Recall that every border router belongs to the backbone, and so it knows the full backbone topology.

A border router is responsible for summarizing what it knows and distributing the summary to the other backbone routers. A summarized item of information includes an IP network or subnet identifier, a subnet mask, and the distance from the router to that network. Routers on the backbone will use this information to deliver traffic to the areas served by the border router.

For example, in Figure 8.10, router A and router B each *advertise* (that is, report) their distances to net M and net N. This enables all of the backbone routers to calculate their shortest distances to net M and net N.

Information flows in both directions. Routers A and B tell the rest of the world about their connections to networks in area 1. Other backbone routers send the distances to networks in their own areas to routers A and B.

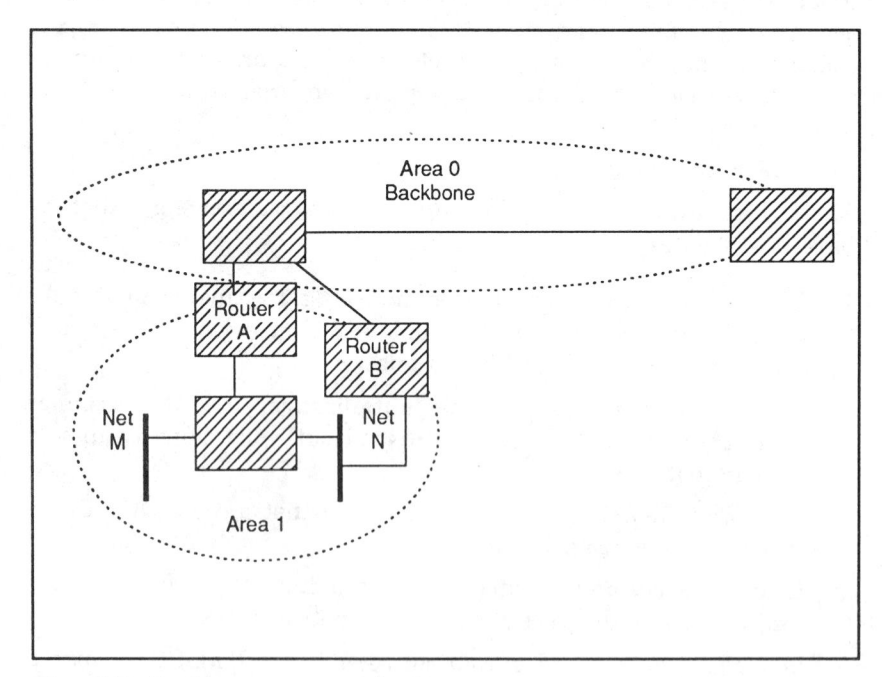

Figure 8.10 Routing across an area border.

After these exchanges of information, every area border router knows:

- The distance between any border router and its area's networks.
- The distance across the backbone to any border router.

By combining these distances, every border router can compute its shortest distance to every network in the Autonomous System.

A border router spreads this information through each of its connected areas. This enables every node to pick the best route to any network in the Autonomous System. For example, every node in area 1 of Figure 8.10 can decide whether to go through router A or router B to get to a particular network.

8.7.1 Routing to Other Autonomous Systems

An Autonomous System is connected to other Autonomous Systems by *boundary routers*. Each of these boundary routers generates summary reports indicating the distance to each known external destination. These reports are distributed to all of the backbone routers, and into all areas that connect to the backbone via more than one router.

When choosing a route to a network in a remote Autonomous System, often only the distance between boundary routers is looked at. There is no point in trying to add on the internal Autonomous System distance: if the metric used outside an Autonomous System is not the same as the one inside. Usually it is safest to assume that external routes are probably very long and are the ones that need to be optimized (see Figure 8.11).

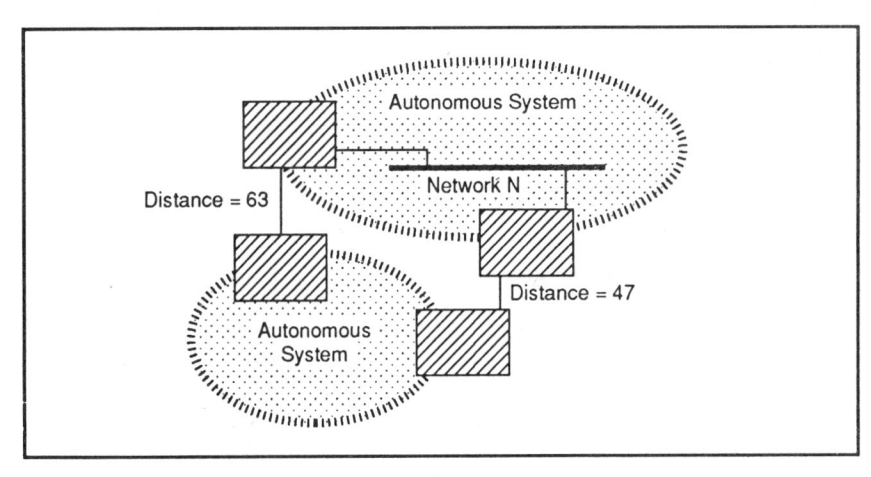

Figure 8.11 Routing between Autonomous Systems.

158   Chapter Eight

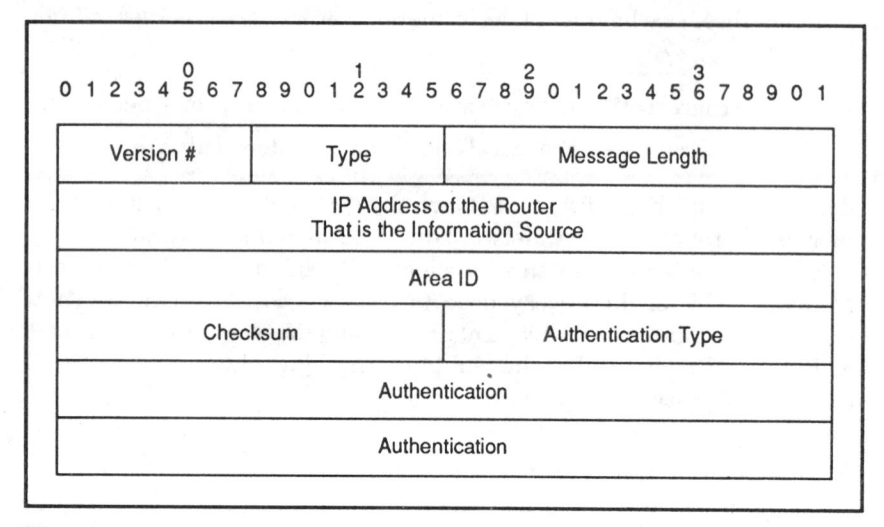

0 1 2 3 4 5 6 7 8 9	0 1 2 3 4 5 6 7 8 9	0 1 2 3 4 5 6 7 8 9	0 1
Version #	Type	Message Length	
IP Address of the Router That is the Information Source			
Area ID			
Checksum		Authentication Type	
Authentication			
Authentication			

Figure 8.12 The standard 24-octet OSPF message header.

8.8 OSPF PROTOCOL

The sections that follow contain more detailed information about some key elements of the OSPF protocol. The general reader may wish to skip them.

8.8.1 OSPF Message Header

All OSPF messages start with the 24-octet header that is shown in Figure 8.12. The current version is 2. The type field contains a number corresponding to the message type. There are five message types, namely:

1. Hello
2. Database Description
3. Link State Request
4. Link State Update
5. Link State Acknowledgment

The length is the total length, including the header. Room has been provided for the inclusion of authentication information in the header. Work on a defining a standard authentication protocol is in progress at the present time. Secure and authenticated transmission of routing information is especially important to the robustness of networks!

8.8.2 Contents of a Link State Update

The critical OSPF routing information is transmitted in Link State Update messages. The message contains items that are called *Advertisements*. Each message can include the following types of Advertisements:

TYPE OF ADVERTISEMENT	DESCRIPTION
Router Links	The state of each of the interfaces on a router. Each router provides this information.
Network Links	The list of routers connected to a multiaccess net. This is provided by the Designated Router on the net.
Summary Link to a Network	Indicates a route to a network outside the local area but in the Autonomous System. This is provided by a border router.
Summary Link to a Boundary Router	Indicates a route through the Autonomous System to a boundary of the Autonomous System. This is provided by a border router.
AS External Link	Indicates a route to a destination in another Autonomous System. This is provided by a boundary router.

A Link State Update message begins with the standard 24-octet header, with Type=4. The remainder of the message is made up of advertisements of the various types listed above. Each advertisement begins with the header shown in Figure 8.13.

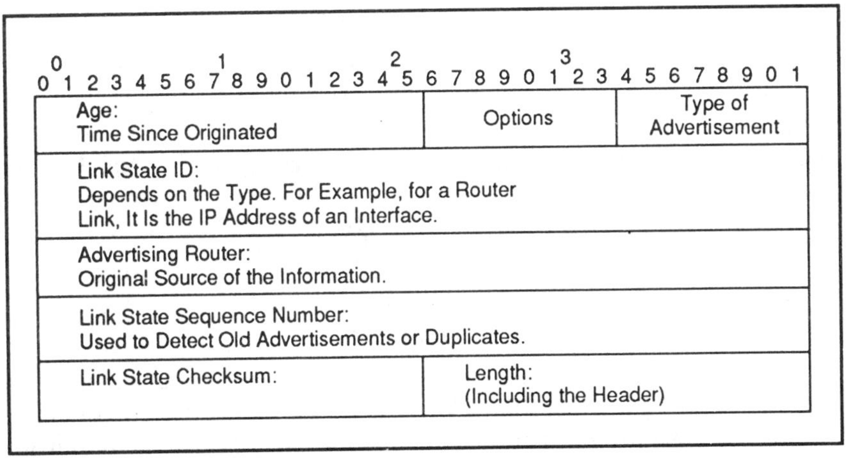

```
 0                   1                   2                   3
 0 1 2 3 4 5 6 7 8 9 0 1 2 3 4 5 6 7 8 9 0 1 2 3 4 5 6 7 8 9 0 1
```

Age: Time Since Originated		Options	Type of Advertisement
Link State ID: Depends on the Type. For Example, for a Router Link, It Is the IP Address of an Interface.			
Advertising Router: Original Source of the Information.			
Link State Sequence Number: Used to Detect Old Advertisements or Duplicates.			
Link State Checksum:		Length: (Including the Header)	

Figure 8.13 Header for the OSPF Link State Update message.

8.8.3 Router Links

Each router link advertisement includes information about the set of interfaces on the advertising router. Different information is provided depending on the type of interface:

TYPE	DESCRIPTION	VALUE
1	Point-to-point connection to another router	Neighbor's IP Address
2	Connection to a multiaccess network with several routers	Designated Router's IP Address
3	Connection to a stub network	Network or subnet number
4	Virtual link	Neighbor's IP Add.ess

At least one metric will be included for each router link. If Type of Service routing is supported, then separate metrics can be provided for each Type of Service value. Where it is appropriate, a subnet mask for the link is included.

8.8.4 Network Links

A network links advertisement is generated by the Designated Router on a multiaccess, multirouter network. The advertisement contains the subnet mask for the network and the IP addresses of each of its routers.

8.8.5 Summary Link to a Network

A summary link to a network is generated by an area border router. The Link State ID field contains the address of a destination network that is within the Autonomous System but is outside of this area. The advertisement contains a subnet mask and a metric giving the distance from the border router to the network. If Type of Service routing is supported, then separate metrics can be provided for each Type of Service value.

8.8.6 Summary Link to a Boundary Router

A summary link to a boundary router is generated by an area border router. The Link State ID field contains the address of a boundary router for the Autonomous System. The advertisement contains a metric giving the distance from the border router to the boundary router. If Type of Service routing is supported, then separate metrics can be provided for each Type of Service value.

8.8.7 Autonomous System External Link

External link advertisements are generated by an Autonomous System boundary router. The Link State ID field contains the address of a destination network that is external to this Autonomous System.

The advertisement contains a subnet mask and a metric giving the distance from the boundary router to the network. If Type of Service routing is supported, then separate metrics can be provided for each Type of Service value.

A flag indicates whether the metric is comparable to the metric used inside the Autonomous System. If not, then the metric is considered to be larger than any internal path.

The Link State ID optionally may contain a default address 0.0.0.0. In this case, the mask also is 0.0.0.0. This indicates that the boundary router can be used to reach networks for which no other specific path has been defined.

8.9 IMPORTANT FEATURES OF OSPF

Because routers know the actual topology of an area, they are able to adapt very quickly to a network change such as a new router coming up or the loss of a link. Routing overhead traffic is diminished because once initialization is complete, individual updates, rather than complete routing tables, are sent between routers. OSPF uses multicasting on LANs to cut down even more on message traffic.

Unlike other routing protocols, OSPF provides a framework for authentication, and even lets each area define its own authentication scheme. This means that an area can protect its routers from accepting spurious information that could disrupt the network.

OSPF specifies statistics that must be made available, and defines logging events. This will assist management of OSPF routers in a multivendor environment.

OSPF routers exchange and record subnet masks[4] as well as subnet addresses. This enables the routers to chart optimal paths to subnets both within and outside of the local network. Older routing protocols do not support the use of different network masks within a network, or knowledge of a subnet's mask outside of its network.

---

[4] OSPF supports the use of different subnet masks within a single network.

8.10 OTHER INTERIOR GATEWAY PROTOCOLS

8.10.1 Cisco Systems IGRP

Router vendors provide a variety of proprietary routing algorithms. A notable example is Cisco System's *Inter-Gateway Routing Protocol* (IGRP). IGRP is a distance vector routing protocol with a number of special features. IGRP's metric takes distance, delay, bandwidth, utilization level, and reliability into account. Traffic can be split among multiple routes whose metrics are close to the optimum value. IGRP is tuned to reduce message loops and to cut down on the traffic generated by routing update messages.

Like a number of other routing products, Cisco routers can be configured to prevent selected traffic from passing into or out of a network.

8.10.2 OSI Routing

OSI uses the term *Intermediate System* rather than router or gateway. The OSI routing protocol, IS-IS, has been extended to route IP traffic as well as OSI traffic. Like OSPF, IS-IS is a link state protocol, and supports hierarchical routing, Type of Service routing, splitting of traffic on multiple paths, and authentication.

There are a number of differences between the protocols. IS-IS has two types of routers: level 1 for routing within an area and level 2 for routing to destinations outside an area. Instead of spreading summary information through an area, IS-IS routes traffic bound for destinations outside of the area to the nearest level 2 router. After a change in an area, OSPF reports only the change, while IS-IS sends out the whole area database.

There is spirited competition between proponents of OSPF and IS-IS. One of the issues being debated is whether it is better to route IP and OSI traffic separately, or use a single integrated protocol.

8.11 EXTERNAL GATEWAY PROTOCOLS

Recall that by definition, an Interior Gateway Protocol is used within an Autonomous System. Different Autonomous Systems are free to choose the protocol and metric that suits them best. But how can we make reasonable routing decisions about traffic that travels between two different Autonomous Systems?

8.11.1 The Exterior Gateway Protocol

For many years, the *Exterior Gateway Protocol* (EGP) was used on the Internet to enable Autonomous Systems to exchange information about what networks were *reachable* within each system. EGP is widely available because it has been implemented by router vendors, and is included in the free *gated* routing software developed at Cornell University.

EGP has a number of shortcomings. EGP is not a proper routing protocol; it enables routers to exchange information, but does not specify how to use that information to build routes. It was designed in the early 1980s when the Internet was still fairly small and had a simple topology consisting of a backbone and a set of networks directly connected to the backbone. As the Internet evolved into its present, mesh-like topology, EGP's inability to function in a complex topology became a serious liability.

8.11.2 EGP Model

OSPF borrowed a number of concepts from EGP. Two routers are neighbors if they are connected to the same multiaccess network or are joined by a point-to-point link. Sometimes it also is necessary to consider a pair of routers to be neighbors when there is no direct connection between them. This is similar to the OSPF virtual route concept. EGP information is exchanged between neighboring routers.

Routers that belong to different Autonomous Systems are called *exterior neighbors*. EGP enables a router to find out which networks can be reached through its exterior neighbors.

The Exterior Gateway Protocol has three ingredients:

- *Neighbor acquisition:* A router acquires a neighbor by sending a Neighbor Acquisition Request and receiving a Neighbor Acquisition Response. Note that the neighbor also must send its request and get its response.

- *Neighbor reachability:* The relationship between acquired neighbors is kept alive by periodic exchanges of "Hello" and "I Heard You" messages.

- *Network reachability:* A router sends the neighbor a list of networks in its own Autonomous System; networks on the list can be reached through this router. Optionally, a metric to each network can be included. However, metrics in each autonomous system can be different. Since there is no standardized metric, EGP cannot combine distances provided by different Autonomous Systems.

An EGP router can assume a role similar to OSPF's Designated Router. The router can inform each neighbor of the reachability information for the other neighbors in the network.

Network Reachability messages usually are sent in response to a poll. However, between polls, a node is allowed to send one update in an unsolicited Network Reachability message. This permits some flexibility in reacting to change in the network.

8.11.3 Border Gateway Protocol

Research and debate on the best way to discover efficient routes between Autonomous Systems continues at the present time. Because of the problems caused by deficiencies in EGP, it was necessary to come up with an interim algorithm that would improve the situation.

The *Border Gateway Protocol* (BGP) is the result of that effort, and is currently in use in parts of the Internet. Some router vendors provide BGP software.

Like EGP, the purpose of BGP is to enable routers who are exterior neighbors to exchange reachability information. BGP permits an Autonomous System to carry traffic between other Autonomous Systems. BGP reachability information includes the entire chain of Autonomous Systems that are crossed on the way to a destination network. Routing loops are easily prevented by not allowing an Autonomous System to appear twice on a path.

BGP runs over TCP and uses connections to well-known port 179. A pair of systems open a connection and exchange complete information about reachability within their Autonomous Systems. The connection remains open, and the systems periodically exchange keep-alive messages and updates in the network configuration.

8.12 RECOMMENDED READING

RFC 1058 describes RIP and RFC 1247 contains Version 2 of OSPF. The Border Gateway Protocol can be found in RFC 1267, and the Exterior Gateway Protocol was defined in RFC 827. The ISO Open Systems Interconnect Routing Framework is described in ISO TR 9575. For ISO Open Systems Interconnect routing, see ISO 9542 and ISO 10589.

Chapter

9

User Datagram Protocol

9.1 INTRODUCTION

Now that we have dealt with the physical movement of bits across media and the routing of datagrams across an internet, we are ready to turn to the services that applications will use directly for the transfer of data. The first of these, User Datagram Protocol (UDP), is very straightforward. UDP enables applications to send individual messages to one another.

Why define this kind of service? There are many applications that can be built on top of User Datagrams in a very natural way. For example, a simple exchange of User Datagrams can be used to execute a quick database lookup. The overhead of sending and receiving the many messages required to set up and take down a connection is avoided by simply sending a query and a response. UDP also is a perfect building block for constructing monitoring, debugging, management, and software testing functions.

Let's look at some examples that illustrate typical UDP applications. In the first example, we will look up a user's mail identifier in a database that is located at a LAN server. The example is based on a Network Information Service (NIS) command and database; NIS LAN databases are used to centralize the maintenance of user and network information, and will be discussed in Chapter 12.

Below, the NIS *ypmatch* command is used to look up a user's mail identifier. The query and response are carried in User Datagrams.

```
ypmatch brown aliases
   'brown@plum.cs.yale.edu'
```

Another useful service that we already have met is also based on User Datagrams. This is the service that looks up the IP address for a given host name. The query is sent to a network name-to-address translation server. The response prints the name of the server and the answer to the query.

```
nslookup nic.ddn.mil

Server:    DEPT-GW.CS.YALE.EDU
Address:   128.36.0.36

Name:      nic.ddn.mil
Address:   192.112.36.5
```

UDP is a very simple service, simply passing individual messages to IP for transmission. Since IP is unreliable, there is no guarantee of delivery. If an application sends a query in a UDP Datagram and a response does not come back within a reasonable amount of time, it is up to the application to retransmit the query.

Sometimes this results in duplicate queries showing up at a server. The application needs to include a query transaction identifier within the message data, so that the server can recognize duplicates and discard them. This mechanism is the application's responsibility, not UDP's.[1]

9.2 PORTS

A host can be expected to participate in many simultaneous communications at any time. How do UDP datagrams get sorted out and assigned to appropriate recipients? The answer is that every UDP communication endpoint is assigned a 16-bit identifier called a *port* number.

Port numbers from 0 to 1023 are reserved for standard services. Standard ports are called *well-known* ports. For example, the UDP-based name-to-address translation service is accessed at well-known port 53.

How do well-known ports get assigned? The *Internet Assigned Numbers Authority* (IANA) is in charge of this function, and publishes information including protocol numbers, port assignments, and protocol parameter values in the *Assigned Numbers RFC*. Recall that this RFC is updated and released with a new RFC number every few months.

---

[1] In Chapter 12 we will discuss the Remote Procedure Call protocol, which supports client/server interactions by automatically providing elements such as transaction identifiers.

The IANA supervises port numbers. Port numbers that are reserved for specific applications are registered with the IANA and published in its Assigned Numbers RFC. A partial list of UDP ports taken from the current Assigned Numbers RFC document is displayed in Table 9.1.

Many of these services provide building blocks for testing, debugging, and measurement. For example, the echo service at port 7 does what its name implies — it returns any datagram that is sent to it. Discard at port 9, on the other hand, just throws datagrams away. A character generator responds to any message with a datagram containing between 0 and 512 bytes. The number of bytes is randomly chosen.

The quote of the day service responds to any datagram by sending back a message — for example, some fortune cookie wisdom to brighten your day when you log off.

A daytime server responds to any datagram with a message containing the current date and time in a readable ASCII format. In contrast, the Network Time Protocol provides a robust method for synchronizing the clocks at computers across a network.

TABLE 9.1 Examples of UDP Well-known Ports

Service	Port/Protocol	Description
Echo	7/udp	Echo User Datagram back to sender.
Discard	9/udp	Discard User Datagram.
Daytime	13/udp	Report time in a user-friendly way.
Quote	17/udp	Return a "quote of the day".
Chargen	19/udp	Character generator.
Nameserver	53/udp	Domain name server.
Bootps	67/udp	Server port used to download config. info.
Bootpc	68/udp	Client port used to receive config. info.
TFTP	69/udp	Trivial File Transfer Protocol port.
SunRPC	111/udp	Sun Remote Procedure Call.
NTP	123/udp	Network Time Protocol.
SNMP	161/udp	Used to receive net management queries.
SNMP-trap	162/udp	Used to receive network problem reports.

The bootp server and client ports are used for a protocol that initializes an unconfigured device, such as a diskless workstation. The workstation can find out its IP address, its address mask, the location of its default router, the addresses of its important servers, and the name and location of its software download file. The workstation's software is then downloaded using the Trivial File Transfer Protocol.[2]

We already have used the nameserver at port 53 via the *nslookup* command. Ports 161 and 162 are used by the Simple Network Management Protocol.

Apart from the official number assignments, any system running TCP/IP may reserve a range of numbers for important network services and applications. The remaining port numbers are allotted by a host's networking software on an as-needed basis. The scenario below indicates how this happens:

1. A user invokes a client program (such as *nslookup*).
2. The client process executes a system subroutine that says "I want to perform UDP communication. Give me a port."
3. The system subroutine selects an unused port from the pool of available ports and gives it to the client process.

We shall see that TCP also identifies its sources and destinations with 16-bit port identifiers. For example, port 21 is used to reach a File Transfer server and port 23 is used to reach a Telnet login server.

TCP and UDP numbers are independent of each other. One user may be sending messages from UDP port 1700 while another is engaged in a session at TCP port 1700. There are some services that can be accessed via both TCP and UDP. In this case, the IANA makes an effort to use the same number for both the UDP and the TCP ports assigned to a server.

The combination of the IP address and the port used for communication is called a *socket address*. The IP header for a UDP datagram contains its source and destination IP addresses. The UDP header contains the source and destination port numbers. Thus every UDP datagram carries the socket addresses for its source and destination.

9.3 UDP Protocol Mechanisms

What protocol mechanisms are needed to make the User Datagram service work? First of all, UDP has been assigned its unique protocol

---

[2]The Trivial File Transfer Protocol will be described in Chapter 11.

User Datagram Protocol 169

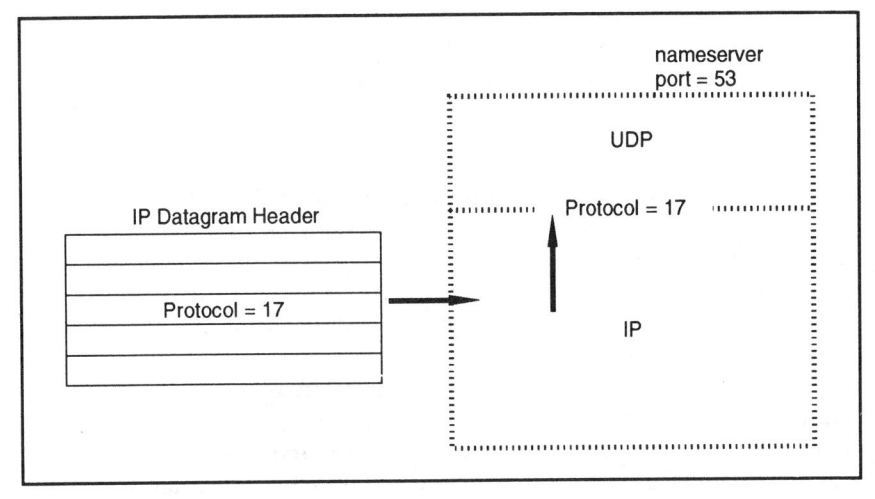

Figure 9.1 Protocol mechanisms for UDP.

identifier, 17. This number is placed in the IP protocol field for outgoing UDP messages. Incoming messages with 17 in the IP protocol field are delivered to UDP. UDP forms a message by adding a simple header to application data. This header contains the source and destination port numbers.

Figure 9.1 shows how an incoming IP datagram is directed to a UDP application. IP passes the datagram to UDP because the value in the protocol field is 17. UDP passes the datagram to the domain name server if the destination port number is 53.

9.3.1 UDP Header

Figure 9.2 displays the UDP header format. The header contains the 16-bit source and destination port numbers that identify the endpoints

Source Port	Destination Port
Length	Checksum

Figure 9.2 The UDP header.

of the communication. A length field indicates the total number of octets in the UDP header and data part of the message. A checksum field is provided to validate the contents of the message.

9.3.2 Checksum

Recall that the IP header contained a checksum field used to validate its fields. The purpose of the UDP checksum is to validate the *contents* of a datagram.

The UDP checksum is computed on the combination of a specially constructed *pseudo header* containing some IP information, the UDP header, and the message data.

The format of the pseudo header that is put together by the checksum function is shown in Figure 9.3. Note that the source address, destination address, and protocol field are taken from the IP header.

Use of the UDP checksum in a particular communication is optional. If unused, the field is 0. If a checksum has been computed and the value turns out to be 0, then this is represented as a field of 1s.

9.3.3 Other UDP Functions

Apart from submitting and accepting datagrams, UDP must obey the common sense rules of passing options down from an application to IP, and passing error notifications up from IP to the application.

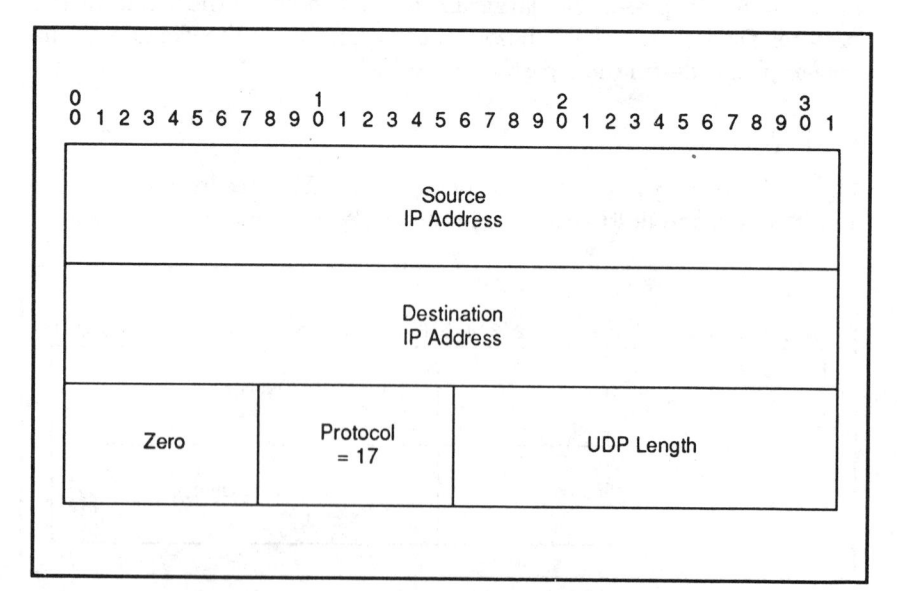

```
 0                   1                   2                   3
 0 1 2 3 4 5 6 7 8 9 0 1 2 3 4 5 6 7 8 9 0 1 2 3 4 5 6 7 8 9 0 1
+---------------------------------------------------------------+
|                         Source                                |
|                       IP Address                              |
+---------------------------------------------------------------+
|                       Destination                             |
|                       IP Address                              |
+---------------------------------------------------------------+
|        Zero        |   Protocol   |        UDP Length         |
|                    |     = 17     |                           |
+---------------------------------------------------------------+
```

Figure 9.3 UDP pseudo header, used in computing the UDP checksum.

Figure 9.4 contains side-by-side displays of the IP and UDP portions of a query and its corresponding response. The displays were generated by a Network General *Sniffer* LAN monitor. The query contained a request for status information and was sent to a host by a network management station. The data portions of the query and response messages are not displayed here.

The request was sent from IP address 130.128.1.40 and source UDP port 1112 to destination IP address 130.128.1.1 and destination UDP port 161. (Network management queries always are sent to UDP port 161.)

In both IP headers, the IP protocol field was set to 17, meaning "UDP." A UDP checksum was not computed for the request, but a checksum is included in the response.

The *Sniffer* analyzer recognizes that port 161 is a network management port. SNMP stands for *Simple Network Management Protocol*.

```
--- IP Header for the Request ---              --- IP Header for the Response ---

IP:   Version = 4, header length = 20 bytes    Version = 4, header length = 20 bytes
IP:   Type of service = 00                     Type of service = 00
IP:         000. .... = routine                      000. .... = routine
IP:         ...0 .... = normal delay                 ...0 .... = normal delay
IP:         .... 0... = normal throughput            .... 0... = normal throughput
IP:         .... .0.. = normal reliability           .... .0.. = normal reliability
IP:   Total length = 110 bytes                 Total length = 115 bytes
IP:   Identification = 14181                   Identification = 51523
IP:   Flags = 0X                               Flags = 0X
IP:   .0.. .... = may fragment                 .0.. .... = may fragment
IP:   ..0. .... = last fragment                ..0. .... = last fragment
IP:   Fragment offset = 0 bytes                Fragment offset = 0 bytes
IP:   Time to live = 255 seconds/hops          Time to live = 30 seconds/hops
IP:   Protocol = 17 (UDP)                      Protocol = 17 (UDP)
IP:   Header checksum = 7CF0 (correct)         Header checksum = CC0D (correct)
IP:   Source address = [130.128.1.40]          Source address = [130.128.1.1]
IP:   Destination address = [130.128.1.1]      Destination address = [130.128.1.40]
IP:   No options                               No options

--- UDP Header for the Request ---             --- UDP Header for the Response ---

UDP:  Source port = 1112                       Source port = 161 (SNMP)
UDP:  Destination port = 161 (SNMP)            Destination port = 1112
UDP:  Length = 90                              Length = 95
UDP:  No checksum                              Checksum = 0B1A (correct)
UDP:
```

Figure 9.4 IP and UDP headers for a request and a response.

9.3.4 UDP Overflows

When an application acquires a UDP port, the networking software will reserve some buffers to hold a queue of User Datagrams arriving at that port. Typically, a UDP-based server has no way to predict or control how many datagrams will be sent to it at any time.

If the server is bombarded with more datagrams than it can handle, the overflow simply will be discarded. The fact that this has happened will show up in networking statistics reports under a heading such as "UDP Socket Overflows." For example, the report below was produced by the *netstat* command,[3] which displays many interesting measurements of network activities.

```
netstat -s
udp:
    0 incomplete headers
    0 bad data length fields
    0 bad checksums
   17 socket overflows
```

9.4 RECOMMENDED READING

The User Datagram Protocol was defined in RFC 768. RFCs 862 to 865 discuss the echo, discard, character generator, and quote of the day services. RFC 867 describes the daytime utility and RFC 958 presents the network time service. The bootp protocol is discussed in RFCs 906, 951, and 1084. Additional UDP services are examined in other chapters.

---

[3] We already have met the *netstat* command in Chapter 6.

Chapter 10

Transmission Control Protocol

10.1 INTRODUCTION

IP was kept simple so that the network layer could focus on performing one important function — routing data from its source to its destination. The job of turning an exchange of datagram traffic into a solid, reliable application-to-application data connection is carried out by TCP, which is implemented in the end hosts. Services such as terminal logon, file transfer, and mail transfer are built on top of TCP.

10.1.1 Major TCP Services

We may view TCP as providing *data calls*, analogous to voice telephone calls. A caller identifies the destination. At the other end, a listening application is alerted that there is an incoming call and picks up the connection. The two ends exchange information for a while. When they are finished, both parties say "goodbye" and hang up.

IP makes a best effort attempt to deliver datagrams, but some may be destroyed along the way, while others can arrive out-of-order. A datagram may wander around the network for a long time, and turn up unexpectedly. It is up to TCP to assure that data is delivered *reliably, in sequence, and without confusion or error.*

An application in a fast, powerful host could swamp a slow recipient with data. TCP provides the *flow control* that enables the *receiver* to regulate the rate at which the sender may transmit data.

TCP also contains mechanisms that let it respond to network conditions, adjusting its own behavior to optimize performance.

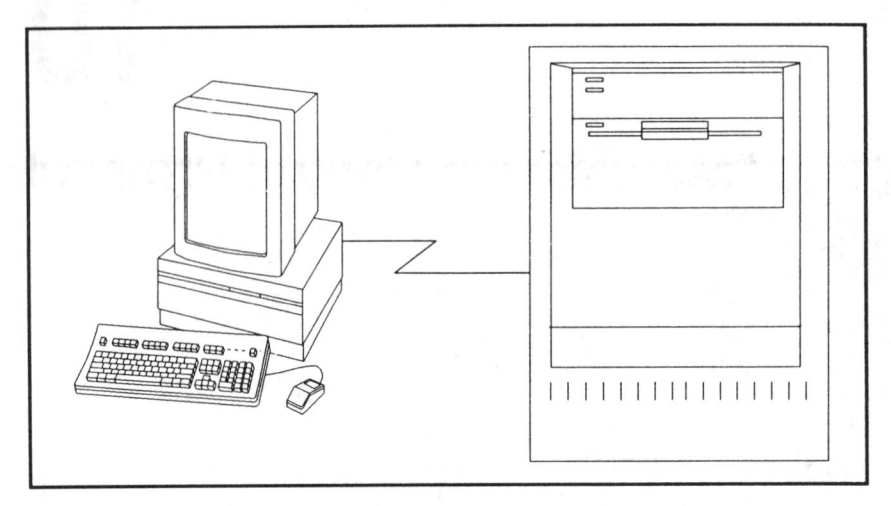

Figure 10.1 A client calling a server.

10.1.2 TCP and the Client/Server Model

TCP operates very naturally in a client/server environment (see Figure 10.1). A server application *listens* for incoming connection requests. For example, file transfer and terminal access servers listen for incoming clients. A client application initiates TCP communication by invoking communications routines that establish a connection with a server.[1]

The "client" may actually be another server; for example, a mail server connects to a peer mail server in order to transfer mail between computers. In fact, TCP is flexible enough to correctly establish a connection between two peer applications that happen to call each other at the same time. This probably will be a rare event, and we will continue to follow the more usual client/server model when discussing data calls.

10.2 TCP CONCEPTS

In what form does an application pass data to TCP? In what form does TCP pass data to IP? How do sending and receiving TCPs identify the specific application connection that a unit of data belongs to? These questions will be answered in the sections that follow, which deal with TCP's conceptual design.

---

[1] Chapter 17 describes the socket programming interface.

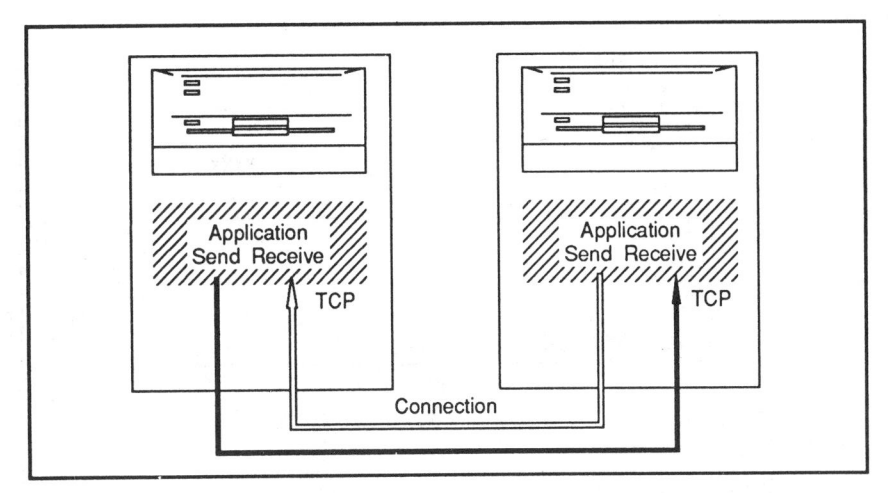

Figure 10.2 Applications exchanging streams of data.

10.2.1 Outgoing and Incoming Data Streams

During a TCP connection, an application sends a stream of data to a peer application. At the same time, it is receiving a stream of data from its peer. TCP provides a *full duplex* service that simultaneously manages *two streams* of data, as shown in Figure 10.2. This means that TCP concurrently acts as a sender and as a receiver.

10.2.2 Segments

TCP must convert an application's outgoing stream of data into a form that can be delivered in datagrams. How is this done?

The application passes data to TCP and TCP accumulates this data in a send buffer. Periodically, TCP slices off a chunk of data and adds a header, forming a *segment*.

Figure 10.3 shows how data in a TCP buffer is packaged into a segment. TCP passes the segment to IP for delivery in a single datagram. Sending data in good-sized chunks makes efficient use of transmission facilities, so TCP would like to wait until a reasonable amount of data has collected before creating a segment.

10.2.3 Push and Urgent Data

Sometimes big, efficient data chunks are not convenient for a TCP user. For example, suppose that an end user has initiated a connection for a remote login, and the user has just typed a command followed by *return*.

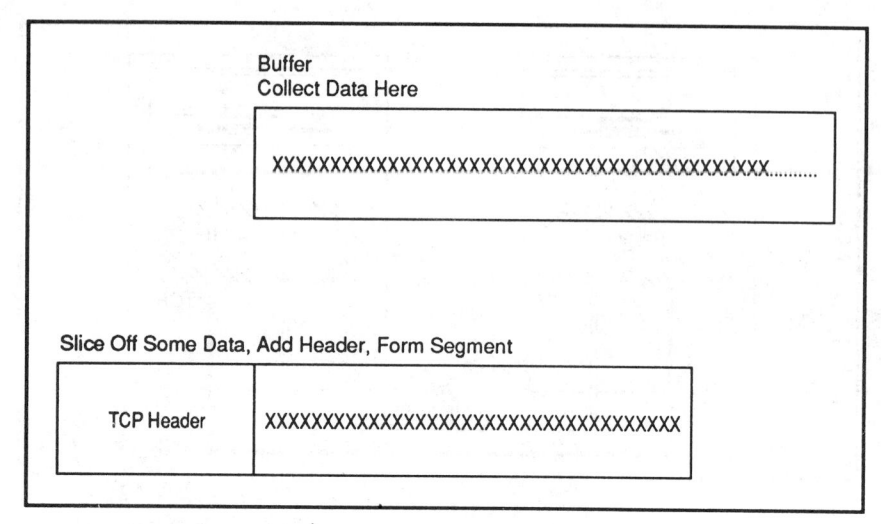

```
┌─────────────────────────────────────────────────────┐
│                    Buffer                           │
│                    Collect Data Here                │
│          ┌──────────────────────────────────────┐   │
│          │ XXXXXXXXXXXXXXXXXXXXXXXXXXXXXXXXXXXX.│   │
│          └──────────────────────────────────────┘   │
│                                                     │
│  Slice Off Some Data, Add Header, Form Segment      │
│  ┌──────────┬──────────────────────────────────┐    │
│  │TCP Header│ XXXXXXXXXXXXXXXXXXXXXXXXXXXXXXXX │    │
│  └──────────┴──────────────────────────────────┘    │
└─────────────────────────────────────────────────────┘
```

Figure 10.3 Creation of a TCP segment.

The user wants this data to be sent to the remote host right away. There is a TCP *push* function that makes this happen. The local software indicates a push after the user has pressed *return*. TCP promptly transmits the user's data to the peer TCP, which in turn promptly delivers the data to its application.

Another useful TCP function marks some information as *urgent*. Using the example of a remote login again, a user may have pressed an *attention* or *break* key. TCP communicates this to its peer, which notifies the destination application that urgent data has arrived.

10.2.4 Type of Service and Security

Recall that a datagram's Type of Service identifies its delivery priority as well as its delay, throughput, and reliability levels. The IP header contains a Type of Service field, and optionally may contain a Security field. Decisions about the Type of Service and Security that are appropriate for a connection are made by the applications using the connection. Each application passes its selections to TCP.[2] TCP cooperates with IP to support these functions. We will take a closer look at how this works later in this chapter.

---

[2] If no explicit values are passed to TCP, then preconfigured defaults are used on the connection.

10.2.5 Relationship to IP

TCP and IP rely on each other for information. IP forms its outgoing datagram headers based on information passed down from TCP. When an incoming datagram arrives, IP reports datagram header information such as the source address, Type of Service, data length, and options to TCP. Keep in mind that if IP knows anything that TCP might be interested in, TCP knows it too.

10.2.6 Ports

A client must identify the server that it wants to reach; this is done by specifying the server host's IP address and its TCP *port number*. Just as for UDP, TCP port numbers range from 0 to $2^{16} - 1$.

Ports in the range 0 to 1023 are *well-known* ports, used to access standardized services. The Internet Assigned Numbers Authority registers, tabulates, and publishes the list of well-known ports.[3] An operating system may be configured with additional services that are accessed at reserved ports within some range above 1023.

Some sample well-known TCP ports and their applications are listed in Table 10.1. *Discard* at port 9 and *chargen* at port 19 are TCP versions of the utility services already described for UDP. Keep in mind that traffic sent to TCP port 9 will be totally separate from traffic sent to UDP port 9.

TABLE 10.1 Well-known Ports and their Applications

Port	Application	Description
9	Discard	Discard all incoming data.
19	Chargen	Exchange streams of characters.
20	FTP-Data	File Transfer data transfer port.
21	FTP	File Transfer dialogue port.
23	TELNET	Telnet remote login port.
25	SMTP	Simple Mail Transfer Protocol port.
103	X400	Used for X400 mail service.
110	POP3	Used for PC mail service.

---

[3] See the *Assigned Numbers* RFC.

What about the ports used by clients? There are a few instances in which a client will operate out of a well-known port, but most of the time, a client who wants to open a connection just asks the operating system to assign it an unused, unreserved port number. At the end of the connection, the client will relinquish the port back to the system, and it can be reused by another client. Since there are more than 63,000 ports in the pool of unreserved numbers, there is no shortage of ports for clients!

10.2.7 Socket Addresses

Recall that the combination of the IP address and the port used for communication is called a *socket address*. A TCP connection is completely identified by the socket addresses at its two ends.

Figure 10.4 shows a connection between a client with socket address (128.36.1.24, 3358) and a server with socket address (130.42.88.22, 21). Every datagram header contains its source and destination IP addresses. As we shall see later, the source and destination port numbers are carried in the TCP segment header. Hence every TCP segment carries the socket addresses of the end points of a connection.

Usually a server is capable of handling many clients at the same time. The server's unique socket address is accessed simultaneously by all of its clients.

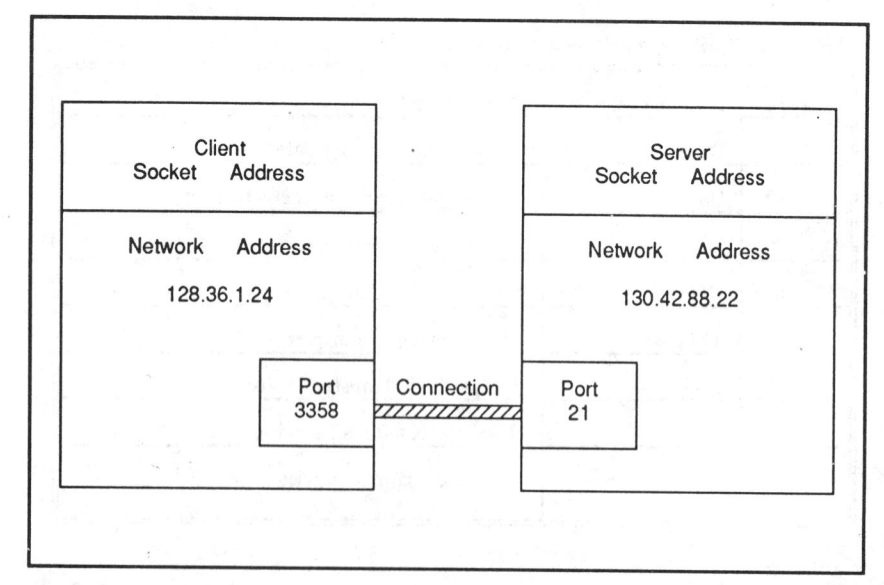

Figure 10.4 Socket addresses.

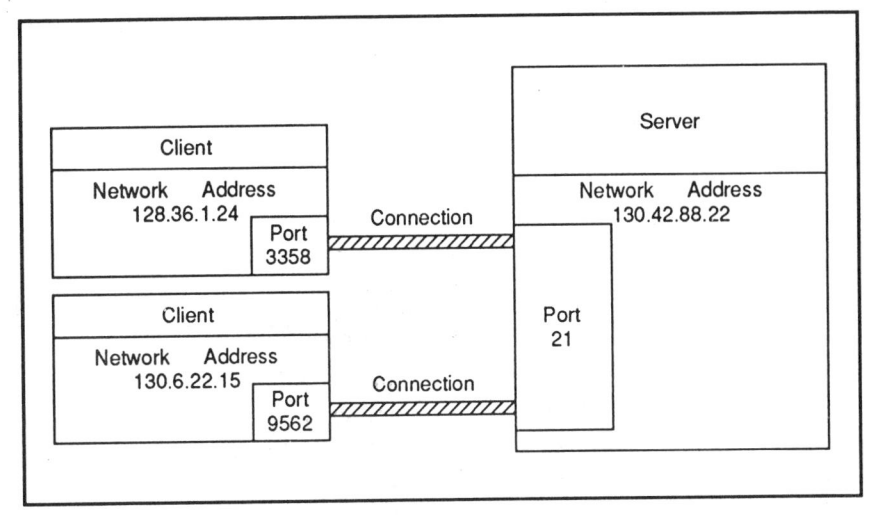

Figure 10.5 Multiple clients connecting to a server socket address.

Since data for a particular TCP connection always is identified by *both IP addresses* and *both ports*, it is easy for a server to keep track of multiple client connections, as shown in Figure 10.5.

10.3 TCP MECHANISMS

The sections that follow describe the mechanisms that TCP uses to deliver data reliably, in order, and without loss or duplication.

10.3.1 Numbering and Acknowledgment

TCP employs a numbering and acknowledgment scheme to transfer data reliably. The TCP numbering scheme is unusual: *every octet* sent on a TCP connection is viewed as having a sequence number. A segment's TCP header contains the sequence number *of the first octet of data in the segment.*

The receiver is expected to ACK received data. If an ACK does not arrive within a timeout interval, the data is retransmitted. This strategy is called *positive acknowledgment with retransmission.*

The receiving TCP keeps a close watch on incoming sequence numbers to keep arriving data in order, and to make sure that no data is missing. Since ACKs are occasionally lost, duplicate segments may occasionally arrive at the receiver. The sequence numbers pinpoint which data has been duplicated, so that it can be discarded.

180   Chapter Ten

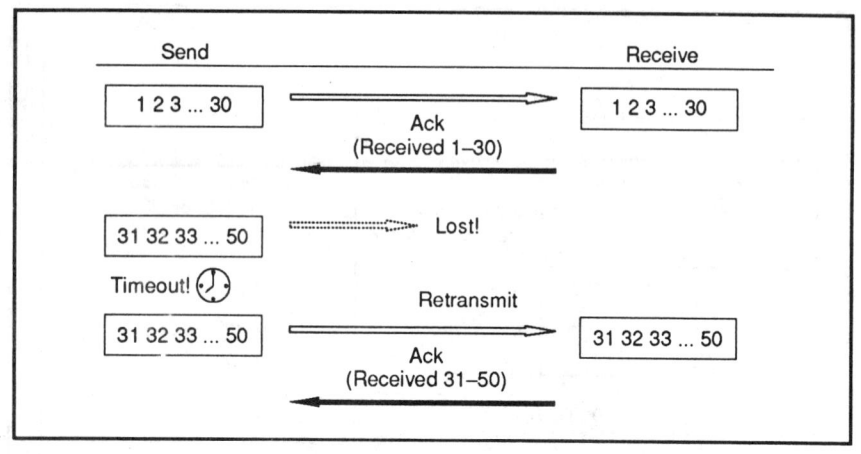

```
         Send                              Receive
    ┌─────────────┐                    ┌─────────────┐
    │ 1 2 3 ... 30│ ═══════════════▶   │ 1 2 3 ... 30│
    └─────────────┘       Ack          └─────────────┘
                     (Received 1–30)
                    ◀═══════════════

    ┌─────────────┐
    │31 32 33 ... 50│ ┈┈┈┈┈▷ Lost!
    └─────────────┘
     Timeout! 🕐        Retransmit
    ┌─────────────┐                    ┌─────────────┐
    │31 32 33 ... 50│ ═══════════════▶ │31 32 33 ... 50│
    └─────────────┘       Ack          └─────────────┘
                     (Received 31–50)
                    ◀═══════════════
```

Figure 10.6 TCP timeout and retransmission.

Figure 10.6 shows a simplified view of TCP retransmission and timeout.

10.3.2 TCP Header Fields for Ports, Sequencing, and ACKs

The sender fills in the source and destination ports and the sequence number of the first byte of enclosed data.

Remember that the flow is full duplex, and data may be arriving from the other end at the same time that this end is sending. The sender fills in the acknowledgment field, which contains the number of the *next* byte expected from the other end. In other words, if I have received all bytes up to 30, I would write 31 into the acknowledgment field of the next segment that I transmit to my partner. The first few fields of the TCP header are displayed in Figure 10.7.

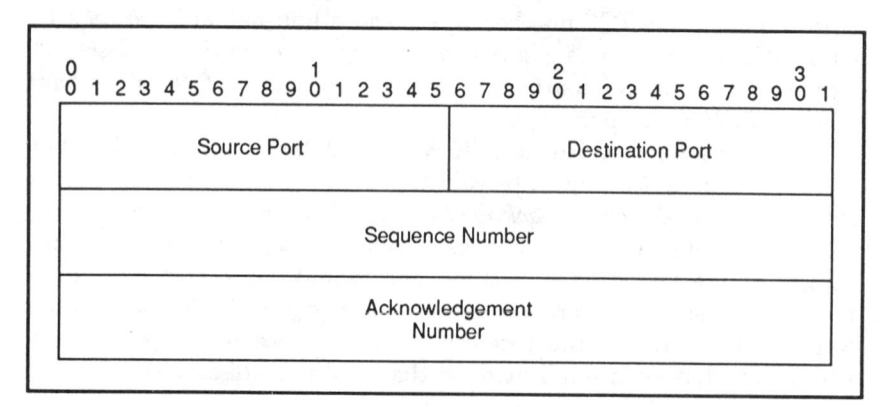

```
 0                   1                   2                   3
 0 1 2 3 4 5 6 7 8 9 0 1 2 3 4 5 6 7 8 9 0 1 2 3 4 5 6 7 8 9 0 1
┌───────────────────────────────┬───────────────────────────────┐
│         Source Port           │      Destination Port         │
├───────────────────────────────┴───────────────────────────────┤
│                        Sequence Number                        │
├───────────────────────────────────────────────────────────────┤
│                     Acknowledgement Number                    │
└───────────────────────────────────────────────────────────────┘
```

Figure 10.7 Initial fields of the TCP header.

10.3.3 Establishing a Connection

How do two processes start a connection? The common pattern is that one process is a server operating at a well-known or reserved port. The server issues a *passive* open which instructs its TCP to *listen* for clients. Later, a client issues an *active* open to its TCP, asking to be connected to the server's network address and port.

There is one technical point. Rather than starting their byte numbering at 1, each side picks an *initial sequence number* from a 32-bit internal clock. We will explain why this is a good idea later in this chapter.

10.3.4 A Connection Scenario

Figure 10.8 shows a complete connection scenario. The connection procedure is called a three-way handshake, because three messages (called SYN, SYN, and ACK) are exchanged to set up the connection. The precise steps are:

1. The server issues a passive open command that tells TCP that it is ready to accept connections from clients.
2. The client issues an active open command that tells TCP that it wants to open a connection to a server at a given port and IP address.
3. The client TCP picks an initial sequence number (700 in this case). The client TCP sends a *synchronize segment* (called a *SYN*) carrying this sequence number.
4. When the SYN arrives, the server TCP picks *its* initial sequence number (400 in this case). The server TCP sends a SYN segment containing initial sequence number 400 and an ACK of 701, meaning that the first data byte sent by the client should be numbered 701.
5. When the client TCP receives the server's SYN/ACK message, the client TCP sends back an ACK of 401, meaning that the first data byte sent by the server should be numbered 401.
6. The client TCP notifies its upper layer process that the connection is open.
7. When the server TCP receives the client TCP's ACK, the server TCP notifies its upper layer process that a connection is open.

The client and server have synchronized their sequence numbers and are ready to exchange data. Later, we will take a closer look at this

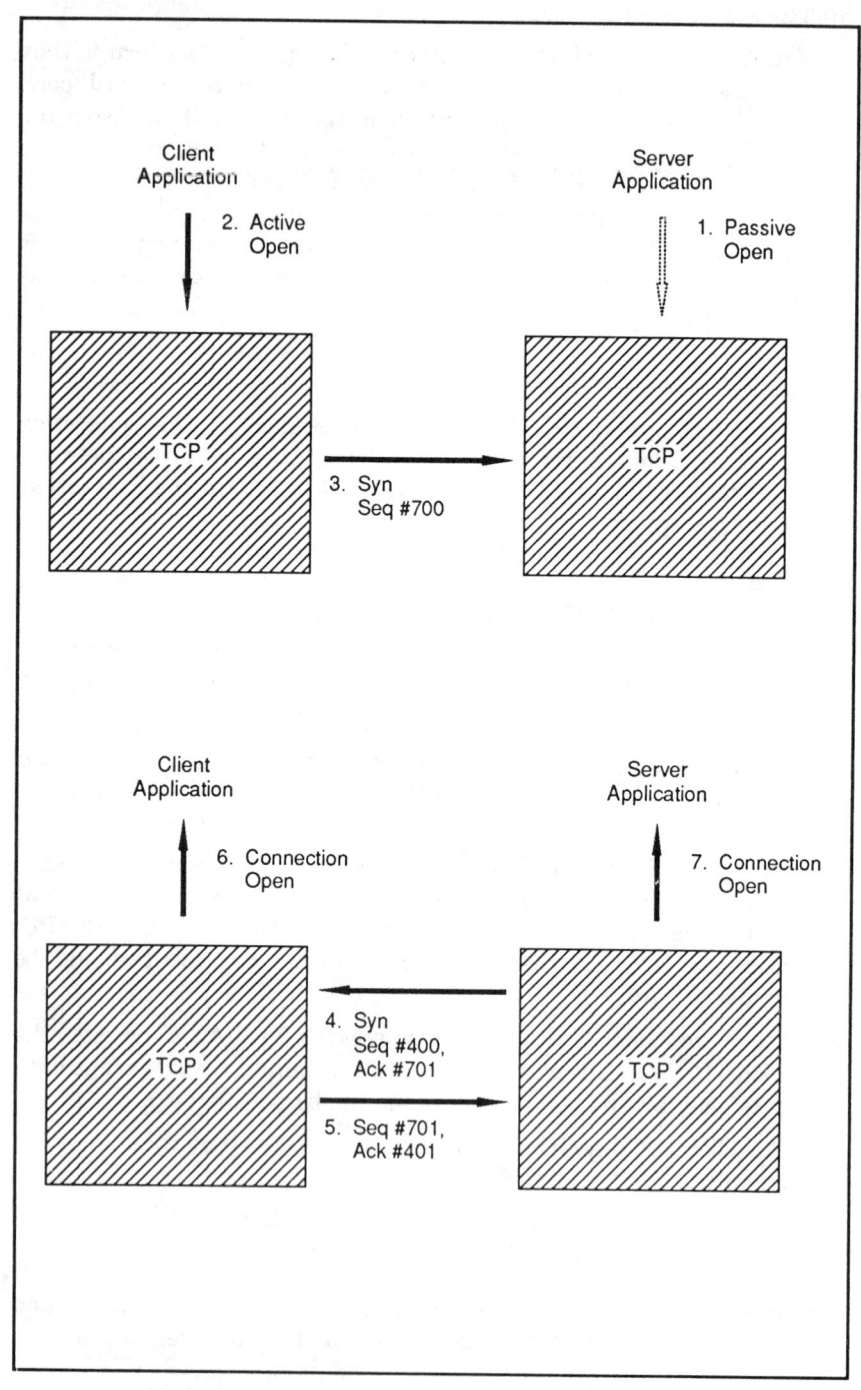

Figure 10.8 Setting up a connection.

dialogue and discover that each has told the other the total size of its receive buffer and the size of the biggest segment that it can handle.

10.3.5 Simultaneous Connection Establishment

Although the scenario shown in Figure 10.8 is the most usual, occasionally two processes will simultaneously send SYN messages to each other. Each TCP will return an ACK to its partner, which will complete the connection setup process.

10.3.6 Support for Type of Service

An application informs TCP of the Type of Service that it wants for the connection.[4] TCP notifies IP of the Type of Service that was picked. IP should use that Type of Service for its outgoing datagrams. Each end of a connection chooses its own Type of Service independently. These can be different for the two directions of data flow!

10.3.7 Support for Security

If applications wish to use the IP security option, both ends of the connection must agree on the same security level. TCP informs IP of the requested security level and IP includes the security option in the IP header for the SYN message. The security option primarily is used by government and military organizations.

10.3.8 Data Transfer

Data transfer begins after completion of the three-way handshake.[5] Figure 10.9 shows a one-way transfer of data. In order to keep the example simple, 100 bytes are sent in each message. Every segment header includes an ACK identifying the sequence number of the next byte expected from the partner.

The first segment sent by the client contains bytes 701 to 800. The ACK field announces that 401 is the sequence number of the next byte expected from the server. The server responds with an ACK that indicates that bytes 701 to 800 have been received, so that the sequence number of the next byte expected from the client is 801.

---

[4] Often a default value is used.

[5] The TCP standard actually allows inclusion of data in the handshake segments. This data will not be delivered to an application until the handshake is complete.

184   Chapter Ten

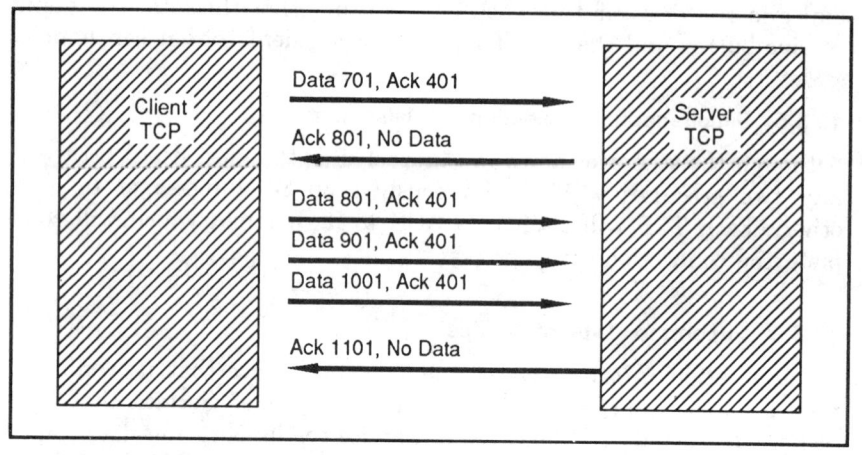

```
Client TCP  →  Data 701, Ack 401       →  Server TCP
            ←  Ack 801, No Data        ←
            →  Data 801, Ack 401       →
            →  Data 901, Ack 401       →
            →  Data 1001, Ack 401      →
            ←  Ack 1101, No Data       ←
```

Figure 10.9 Simple flow of data and ACKs.

Note that a sender does not have to wait for an ACK before sending more data.[6] In the dialogue, the client sends segments starting at bytes 801, 901, and 1001 in quick succession. The responding ACK from the server indicates that all were received.

Figure 10.10 shows a transfer in which the first segment is lost. After a timeout period, the segment is retransmitted. Note that once the missing segment arrives, the receiver sends a single ACK that confirms that all three segments have arrived safely.

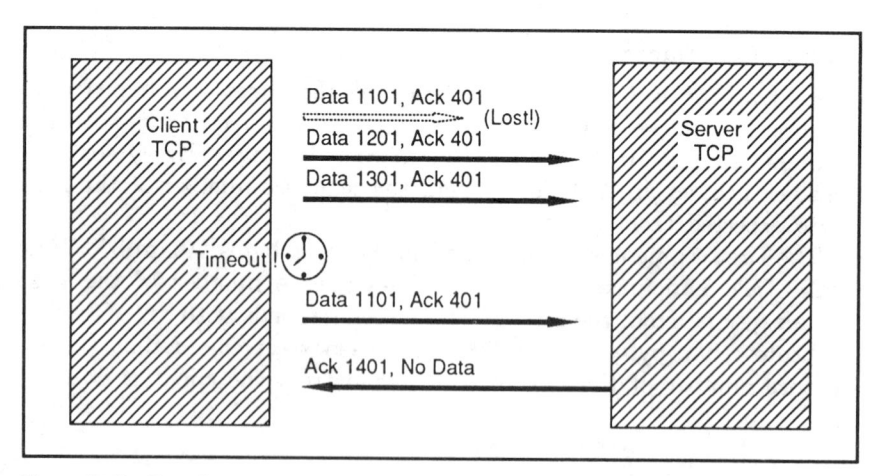

```
Client TCP  →  Data 1101, Ack 401  (Lost!)
            →  Data 1201, Ack 401       →  Server TCP
            →  Data 1301, Ack 401       →
  Timeout!
            →  Data 1101, Ack 401       →
            ←  Ack 1401, No Data        ←
```

Figure 10.10 Data loss and retransmission.

---

[6]Later we shall see that the receiver controls the amount of data that can be sent at any time.

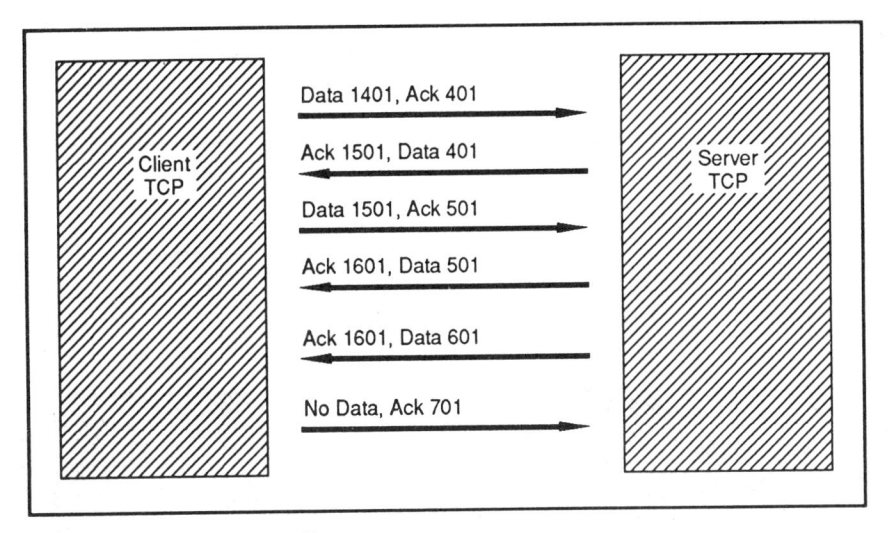

```
                    Data 1401, Ack 401
                 ──────────────────────▶
                    Ack 1501, Data 401
                 ◀──────────────────────
   Client                                    Server
    TCP             Data 1501, Ack 501        TCP
                 ──────────────────────▶
                    Ack 1601, Data 501
                 ◀──────────────────────
                    Ack 1601, Data 601
                 ◀──────────────────────
                    No Data, Ack 701
                 ──────────────────────▶
```

Figure 10.11 Two-way data flow.

The dialogue continues in Figure 10.11 with a two-way exchange of data. Each side numbers its own data and ACKs the data that it has received. For the sake of simplicity, we continue to use segments containing 100 bytes of data.

The first segment contains bytes 1401 to 1500. The client still is waiting to receive byte 401 from the server. The server responds with a segment containing bytes 401 to 500. Both client and server continue to transmit data to one another.

10.3.9 Closing a Connection

The normal termination of a connection is carried out by means of a three-way handshake similar to the connection opening. Either side can launch the close, which usually follows the pattern:

A: "I'm finished - I have no more data to send."
B: "OK."
B: "I'm finished too."
A: "OK."

Or the pattern:

A: "I'm finished - I have no more data to send."
B: "Here is some data."
B: "I'm finished too."
A: "OK."

186 Chapter Ten

Both sides may initiate a close simultaneously. In this case the normal close is completed when each partner has sent an ACK.

Figure 10.12 shows a normal close between a client and server.

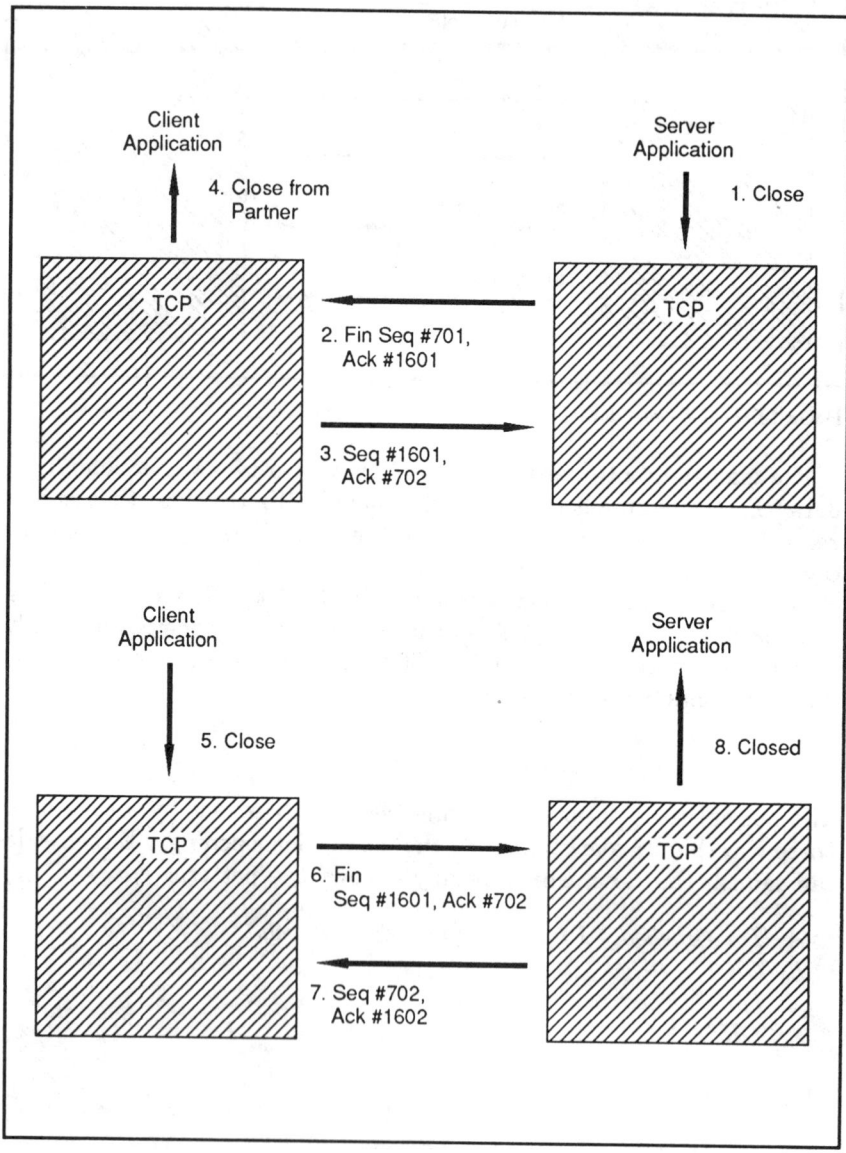

Figure 10.12 Closing a connection.

In the example, the server initiates the close. This often is the case in real client/server interactions. For example, after a Telnet user types "logout," the server will invoke a call to close the connection. The steps shown in Figure 10.12 are:

1. The server has finished its work and tells TCP to close the connection.
2. The server TCP sends a FIN segment, informing the partner that it will send no more data.
3. The client TCP acknowledges receipt of the FIN segment.
4. The client TCP notifies its application that the server wishes to close.
5. The client tells its TCP to close.
6. The client TCP sends a FIN message.
7. The server TCP receives the client's FIN, and responds with an ACK.
8. The server TCP notifies its application that the connection is closed.

10.3.10 Abrupt Close

Either side can call for an abrupt close. This may be done because the application wishes to abort the connection, or because TCP has detected a serious communication problem that cannot be resolved. An abrupt close is signaled by sending a "reset" to the partner. This is done by means of a flag in the TCP header.

10.3.11 Maximum Segment Size

Large segments give better performance during bulk data transfers, because a smaller percentage of bandwidth and memory resources are used for headers. For example, if a datagram has a 20-octet IP header, 20-octet TCP header, and 60 octets of data, then overhead consumes 40% of the resources.

However, not all computers can handle very large segments. A small desktop station might be able to process incoming segments whose size is at most one kilobyte. A midrange computer might manage incoming four kilobyte segments. A supercomputer might be able to handle sixty kilobyte segments.

In choosing segment sizes, maximum datagram transmission limits also must be considered. For example, Ethernet sets a maximum datagram size of 1500 octets. Recall that a segment must fit into a single datagram.

How does a computer warn its partner of the limit that should be imposed on the size of segments that the partner transmits? During connection setup, each party can declare the *maximum segment size* (MSS) that it is willing to receive. To be more precise, each party declares the maximum amount of data that can be carried in a segment; the size of the TCP header is not included in the MSS value.

Choosing an appropriate MSS is a bit of a problem, since an IP header may vary between 20 and 60 octets. Currently, TCP headers only carry an option during connection setup, and so it is reasonable to assume that they will consist of 20 octets. The most common assumption is that the IP header also is most likely to hold 20 octets.

For a destination on a local network, the MSS usually is set at 40 less that the maximum transmission unit for the system's network interface. An estimated MSS of 576 − 40 = 536 often is used for remote destinations.

10.4 FLOW CONTROL

The TCP data receiver is in charge of its incoming flow of data. The receiver decides how much data it is willing to accept, and the sender must stay within this limit. The discussion that follows describes at a conceptual level the way that this is done; vendors can implement these mechanisms in any way that is convenient for them.

During connection setup, each partner assigns receive buffer space to the connection and announces, "Here's how many bytes you can send me!" This number is usually an integer multiple of the maximum segment size.

Incoming data flows into the receive buffer and stays there until it is absorbed by the application associated with that TCP port. Figure 10.13 shows a receive buffer that can hold 300 bytes.

Buffer space is used up as data arrives. When the receiving application removes data, space is cleared for more incoming data.

10.4.1 Receive Window

The *receive window* consists of any space in the receive buffer that is not occupied by data. Data will remain in a receive buffer until the targeted application accepts it. Why wouldn't an application remove its data immediately? A simple example should help to explain this. Suppose that a client is transferring a file to a file server process. The server program will read data from the receive buffer and write it out to disk. When the server performs a disk I/O, it will have to

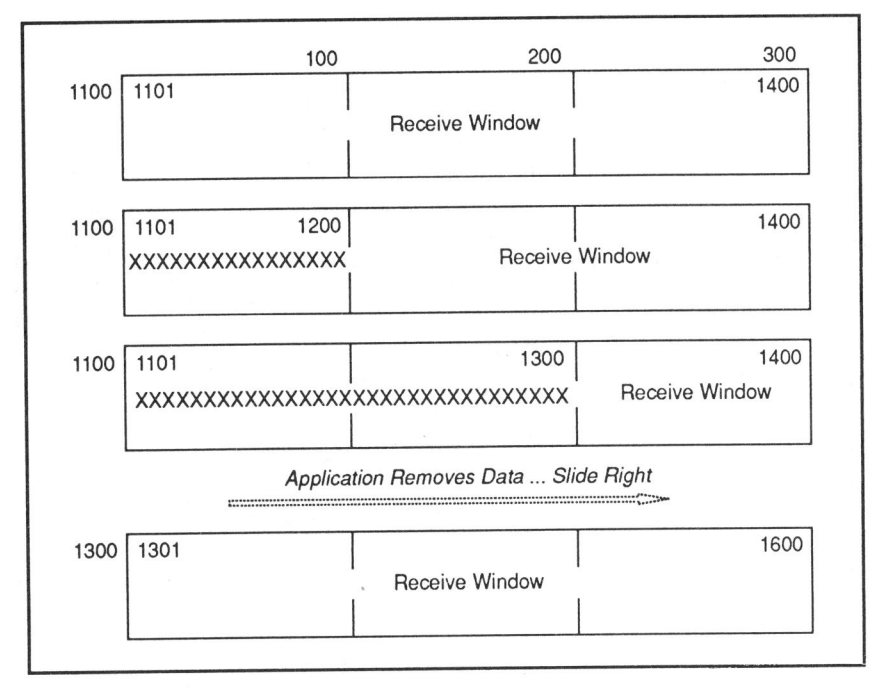

Figure 10.13 The receive window within a receive buffer.

wait for the I/O to complete. In the meantime, other programs will be scheduled and run by the operating system. More data may arrive while the file server process is waiting to run again.

The receive window extends from the last acknowledged byte to the end of the buffer. In Figure 10.13, initially the whole buffer is available, and so there is a 300-byte receive window. The sequence number of the last acknowledged byte was 1100, so that bytes 1101 to 1400 will fit into the window. One hundred bytes arrive and are ACKed, and the receive window shrinks to 200 bytes, extending from 1201 to 1400. Another one hundred bytes arrive, causing the receive window to shrink to 100 bytes, extending from 1301 to 1400.

Finally, the application absorbs the 200 bytes of data in the buffer, making space available for more incoming data. This is visualized by *sliding* the window to the right. Now all 300 buffer bytes are available and the window spans sequence numbers 1301 to 1600.

Every ACK sent by the receiver contains an update on the current state of its receive window. The flow of data from the sender is regulated according to these window updates.

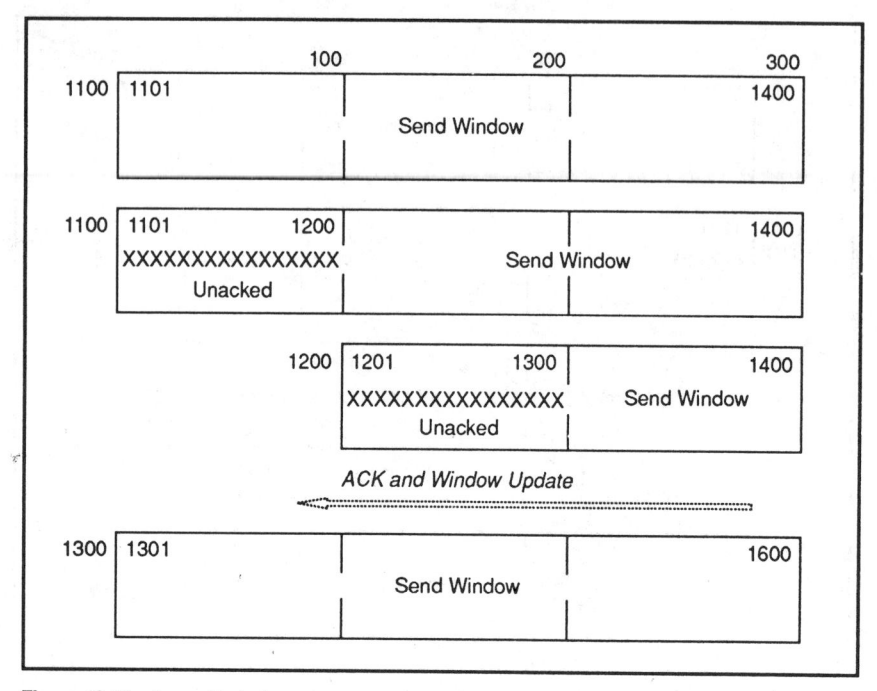

Figure 10.14 A send window.

10.4.2 Send Window

The data transmitter maintains a *send buffer* that tracks two things; how much data has been sent and acknowledged, and the size of the partner's receive window. The send buffer extends from the first unacknowledged octet to the right edge of the current receive window. The *send window* covers the unused part of the buffer.

The initial sequence number and initial receive window size are announced during connection setup. In Figure 10.14, the sender tracks the receive window shown previously, and starts out with a 300 byte send window. The sender transmits 100 bytes, numbered 1101 to 1200. A copy of these bytes must be kept in the send buffer until the bytes have been acknowledged, since they may have to be retransmitted.

Next, two events happen: an ACK arrives for the first 100 bytes, and another 100 bytes are sent. The result is shown in the third part of the figure. Bytes 1201 to 1300 are kept in the send buffer and the send window now extends from 1301 to 1400.

Finally, an ACK arrives for the bytes up to 1300, along with an updated window size of 300. The new send window extends from 1301 to 1600.

Most of the time, the receive buffer size set at startup is maintained throughout the connection. However, the TCP standard does not restrict the way that an implementation manages its buffers. The receive buffer size can grow or to shrink, as long as the receiver never "takes back" an allowance that it has granted the sender.

For example, in the last step above, the receiver could have shrunk the window after the application absorbed the waiting data. The receiver could have sent an update of only 200 bytes, rather than 300.

What happens when segments arrive which are in the window, but are out of order? The TCP standard leaves it up to the implementer! Virtually all implementations hold onto any data falling within the window, and ACK the entire block of contiguous data when the missing bytes arrive. This is fortunate, since throwing away data would lead to poor performance.

10.4.3 Checksum

The IP checksum was applied only to the IP header. A checksum in the TCP header is applied to the entire TCP segment,[7] as well as to a pseudo header made up of information extracted from the IP header. The pseudo header shown in Figure 10.15 is similar to that used for the UDP checksum.

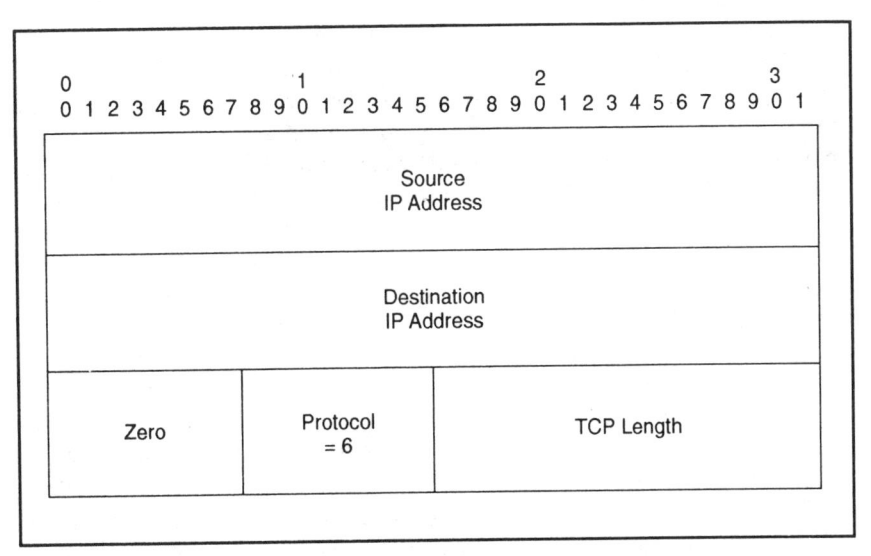

```
 0                   1                   2                   3
 0 1 2 3 4 5 6 7 8 9 0 1 2 3 4 5 6 7 8 9 0 1 2 3 4 5 6 7 8 9 0 1
+---------------------------------------------------------------+
|                        Source                                 |
|                       IP Address                              |
+---------------------------------------------------------------+
|                      Destination                              |
|                       IP Address                              |
+---------------------------------------------------------------+
|      Zero       |   Protocol    |         TCP Length          |
|                 |     = 6       |                             |
+---------------------------------------------------------------+
```

Figure 10.15 Pseudo header used in the TCP checksum.

---

[7]The checksum field in the TCP header is set to 0 during the checksum computation.

The TCP length is computed by adding the length of the TCP header to the length of the data. The TCP checksum is *required*, not optional as in UDP. The checksum for an incoming segment is computed and compared to the checksum field in the TCP header. If the values do not match, then the segment is discarded.

10.5 TCP HEADER

Figure 10.16 displays a segment — that is, a TCP header and data. The TCP header starts with its source and destination port identifiers. The Sequence Number field identifies the position in the outgoing data stream held by the data in this segment. The ACK field identifies where we expect the next incoming segment to be located in the incoming data stream.

10.5.1 Use of Header Fields During Connection Setup

The first segment sent to start a connection has SYN flag set to 1 and ACK flag set to 0. The initial SYN is the only segment that will have an ACK field of 0.

The Sequence Number field contains the *initial sequence number*. The Window field contains the initial *receive window* size. The Options field can contain the maximum segment size (MSS) that the initiator is willing to receive. This is the only TCP option, and it is used in virtually all implementations.

In a response accepting the connection, both the SYN and ACK flags are 1. The responder's initial sequence number is in the Sequence Number field and the receive window size is in the Window field. The Options field can contain the maximum segment size that the responder is willing to receive. This can be different from the initiator's size — there is no reason why they should be the same.

A connection attempt can be rejected by sending a response whose reset flag, RST, is equal to 1.

The Data Offset field contains the TCP header length, measured in 32-bit words. The TCP header must end on a 32-bit boundary. The only option currently defined is the maximum segment size and that occupies 32 bits. Thus the length of a TCP SYN header that contains the MSS option is 24 bytes.

The maximum segment size currently is encoded with a 2-byte introducer followed by a 2-byte value, so the biggest size possible is $2^{16} - 1$, or 65,535 bytes. Where no maximum segment size is included, a default maximum size of 536 bytes will be assumed.

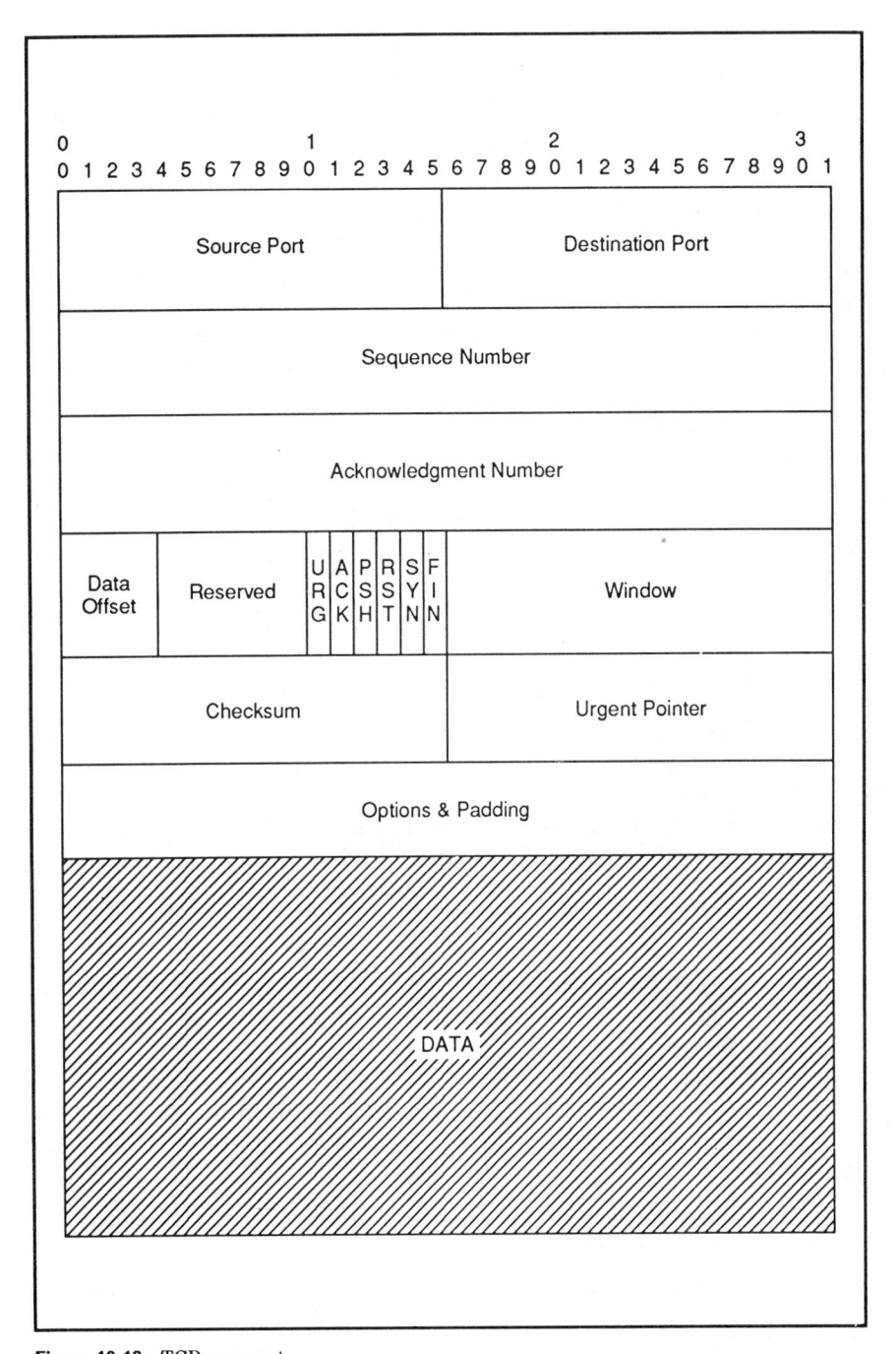

Figure 10.16 TCP segment.

10.5.2 Choosing the Initial Sequence Number

During connection startup, each end of the connection picks an *initial sequence number* from a 32-bit internal clock. Why bother to do this?

Imagine what happens after a system has crashed. Suppose that a user has opened a connection just before the crash and has sent a small amount of data.

After it recovers, the system does not remember anything that it was doing before the crash — including the connections that were running and the port numbers that were assigned. Users will have to start their connections again. Port numbers will be handed out on a first-come first-served basis, and some of these may be ports that were in use for other connections just a few seconds earlier.

In the meantime, a system at the far end of a connection may be totally unaware that its partner has crashed and restarted. There could be a lot of confusion as old data that took a long time coming through the network gets intermingled with data from fresh connections. Hitching fresh starts to clock values helps to avoid this problem. Old data is likely to be numbered with values that are outside of the new sequence number range.[8]

10.5.3 General Field Usage

During data transfer, the sequence number of the first octet of enclosed data[9] is entered into the Sequence Number field. The number of the next octet expected from the partner is filled into the Acknowledgment Number field, and the ACK bit is set to 1. The Window field contains the updated size of the receive window; that is, the number of bytes, starting from the acknowledgment number, that can be received.

If the application has signaled a push to TCP, then the PUSH flag is set to 1. The receiving TCP is supposed to react to the PUSH flag by delivering the data to its application promptly when the application is willing to receive it.

An URG flag set to 1 indicates that urgent data is included, and the Urgent Pointer points to the last octet of urgent data. Recall that a typical use of urgent data is to send a break or interrupt signal from a terminal.

---

[8] A second mechanism can be used to prevent confusion. By performing no communication during the first few minutes after a crash recovery, a host enables all of its in-flight datagrams to be cleared from the internet.

[9] If the segment is an ACK containing no data, then the sequence number belongs to the next octet to be sent at some future time.

Urgent data is sometimes referred to as *out-of-band* data. This term is a little misleading. Urgent data is sent within the TCP data stream. A pointer in the header pinpoints the location of the urgent data. It is up to the local TCP implementation to provide some mechanism that lets an application examine the urgent data before it has read all of the bytes that lead up to this data.

The RST (reset) flag is set to 1 to abort a connection. It also can be set in response to a segment that does not make sense for any current connection that TCP is managing.

The FIN flag is set to 1 in the messages that are used to close a connection.

10.5.4 Sample TCP Segment

The display in Figure 10.17 shows a Network General *Sniffer* analysis of a TCP segment, as well as the hex form in which the segment is transmitted. This segment was sent from a file transfer client to a file transfer server. The *Sniffer* analyzer translates *most* numbers to decimal form. However, the flags values are reported in hex so that Flags=18 means flag pattern 0 1 1 0 0 0. The checksum also is reported in hex.

The segment's data consists of 11 ASCII characters: the text "USER demo" followed by a carriage return and line feed.

10.5.5 Timing Out

A partner's system may crash, or the route to the partner may be totally disrupted by loss of a gateway or link. What prevents TCP from retransmitting the same data forever? There are several mechanisms.

After reaching a first threshold number of retransmissions, TCP notifies the application that there is a problem. TCP proceeds to transmit until a second threshold is reached; then it breaks the connection.

Of course, before all this happens, an ICMP message may arrive stating that the destination was unreachable for some reason. Transient problems are reported to the application, which then must decide what to do; more serious conditions cause the connection to be broken automatically by TCP.

An application also can place its own time limit on data delivery, along with an action to be taken when the time expires; typically, the action is to break the connection.

```
TCP:     ----- TCP header -----
TCP:
TCP:     Source port = 2916
TCP:     Destination port = 21 (FTP)
TCP:     Sequence number = 1533632001
TCP:     Acknowledgment number = 38080040
TCP:     Data offset = 20 bytes
TCP:     Flags = 18
TCP:     ..0. .... = (No urgent pointer)
TCP:     ...1 .... = Acknowledgment
TCP:     .... 1... = Push
TCP:     .... .0.. = (No reset)
TCP:     .... ..0. = (No SYN)
TCP:     .... ...0 = (No FIN)
TCP:     Window = 4096
TCP:     Checksum = B880 (correct)
TCP:     No TCP options
TCP:     [11 byte(s) of data]
TCP:
FTP:     ----- FTP data -----
FTP:
FTP:     USER demo<0D><0A>
FTP:

HEX EXPANSION:

Source   Dest    Sequence       Ack
 Port    Port    Number         Number
0B 64    00 15   5B 69 5E 01    02 45 0E 28

Data     Flags   Window         Checksum    Urgent
Offset                                      Pointer
& Reserved
Bits
50       18      10 00          B8 80       00 00

              DATA
     U  S  E  R     d  e  m  o
     55 53 45 52 20 64 65 6D 6F 0D 0A
```

Figure 10.17 "Sniffer" analyzer display and hex expansion of a TCP segment.

10.5.6 Error and Problem Handling

"If anything can go wrong, it will." Handling errors is a thorny part of an implementation. Some error conditions are handled entirely by TCP; sometimes TCP passes responsibility back to an upper layer application.

To summarize the actions that TCP will take in response to errors and problems, TCP will:

- Discard segments with a bad checksum.
- Notify the application when the connection has been broken because of excessive retransmissions or because a user-specified timeout has expired.
- Slow down in response to an ICMP source quench, and after retransmissions.[10]
- Pass ICMP reports of transient problems to the application.
- Abort the connection if an ICMP message indicates that the destination cannot be reached because of a permanent problem.
- Send resets when segments arrive that cannot legitimately be part of current connection data.

10.6 PERFORMANCE

How well can TCP perform? There are many factors that affect performance. Most basic are resources such as memory and bandwidth. Figure 10.18 summarizes the elements that have an impact on performance.

The bandwidth and delay of the underlying network impose limits

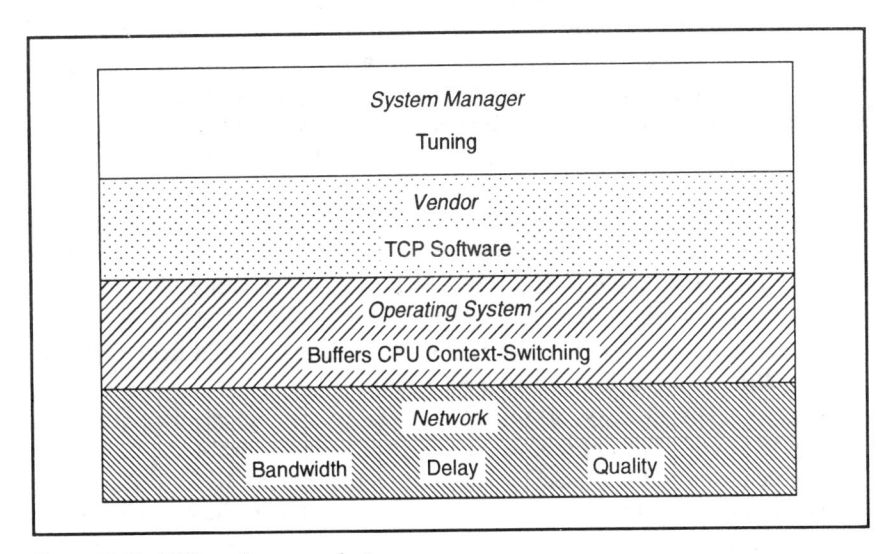

Figure 10.18 TCP performance factors.

---

[10]Backoff after a retransmission will be discussed in the next section.

on throughput. Poor transmission quality causes lots of discarded datagrams. Discards provoke retransmissions, with the result that effective bandwidth is cut. For example, if the bandwidth is 3 megabits per second and half of the data must be retransmitted, then bandwidth effectively is cut to 2 megabits per second.

A receiver that provides lots of input buffer space allows a sender to keep transmitting without pause. This is especially important for networks with large delays, where a long time elapses between sending data and receiving an ACK and window update. To support a steady flow of data from a source, the destination needs a receive window whose size is at least (Bandwidth × Delay).

For example, if you can send data at 10,000 bytes per second, and it takes 2 seconds for an ACK to arrive, the receiver must provide a receive buffer of at least 20,000 bytes in order to maintain an steady flow of data. A receive buffer that could hold only 10,000 bytes would cut throughput in half.

Another factor that has an impact on performance is a host's ability to react to high priority events and rapidly *switch context* — that is, stop doing one thing and take care of another. A host may be supporting many local interactive users, background batch processes, and dozens of communications connections. Switching context to take care of communications housekeeping is a hidden overhead. An implementation that integrates TCP/IP with the operating system kernel can cut back significantly on context switching overhead.

Capable CPU resources are needed to quickly carry out the steps required to process the TCP header. A CPU that cannot compute checksum values rapidly can slow down data transmission.

Finally, vendors should make it easy to set configuration parameters so that network managers can tune TCP to local conditions. For example, the ability to match segment sizes to the networks to be crossed, and buffer sizes to bandwidth and delay can improve throughput substantially. Unfortunately, there are many implementations that hard code fixed configuration choices into the software.

Now suppose that your environment is perfect — lots of resources, and the host switches contexts faster than Billy the Kid ever drew his gun. Will you get wonderful performance?

Maybe. The quality of the TCP software is important. Over the many years of TCP experience, many performance problems have been diagnosed and solved. Software that conforms to RFC 1122, which defines requirements for the communications layers in Internet hosts, encompasses these solutions. Silly Window Syndrome avoidance and the algorithms of Karn and Jacobson are especially important. These important algorithms are discussed in the sections that follow.

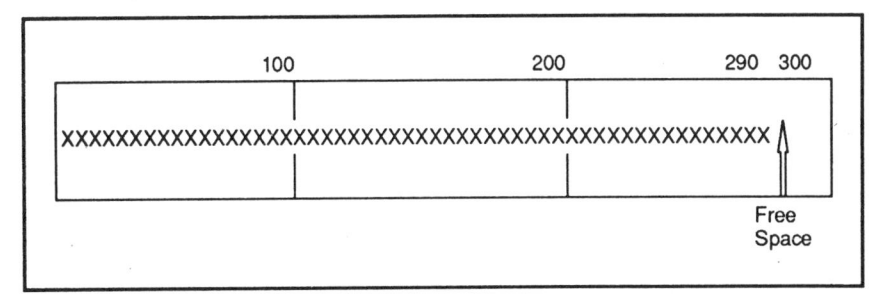

```
        100              200          290  300
XXXXXXXXXXXXXXXXXXXXXXXXXXXXXXXXXXXXXXXXXXXXXX ↑
                                              Free
                                              Space
```

Figure 10.19 Buffer with a very small receive window.

10.6.1 Silly Window Syndrome

Recall that the data receiver checks its window and sends back a credit based on how many window octets are free. From the time of the earliest implementations of TCP/IP, a phenomenon called *Silly Window Syndrome* was observed to happen fairly frequently.

In a typical Silly Window situation, an application is slowly removing small amounts of data from a full receive buffer − say 10 bytes at a time. If the receiving TCP sends a corresponding window credit of 10 bytes every time this occurs, the sender will fall into a pattern of sending lots of tiny segments, making very poor use of the connection. Figure 10.19 shows a buffer whose condition could trigger Silly Window Syndrome.

The solution that RFC 1122 mandates is simple. Let the sender fill up the current receive window. Then, don't slide the buffer to the right until there is a substantial amount of buffer space available. The recommended amount is:

minimum (1/2 Receive-Buffer-Size, Maximum Segment Size)

The receiver will have to "lie" to the sender by reporting a zero window size in its segment headers until a good-sized chunk of buffer space has been cleared. Notice that no harm is being done by holding back transmission since the application has not absorbed most of the data that already is waiting for it!

10.6.2 Nagle Algorithm

The sender should independently avoid transmitting short segments by accumulating data for a while before dispatching it. The Nagle algorithm introduces a very simple idea that reduces the number of tiny datagrams presented to a network.

Nagle recommends holding back transmission (even of pushed data!) if the sender is waiting for an ACK of some previously transferred data. More generally, the TCP standard recommends that data be sent when a either a maximum sized segment or a preset fraction of the receiver's full buffer size can be sent. Otherwise, if data has not been pushed, the sender should continue to accumulate data locally.

10.6.3 Retransmission Timeout

After sending a segment, TCP sets a timer and listens for an ACK. If the ACK does not arrive within the timeout period, TCP retransmits the segment. But how long should the timeout be?

If the retransmission timeout is too short, the sender will clutter the network with unnecessary segments, and burden the receiver with extraneous duplicates. But timeouts that are too long prevent brisk recovery when a segment really has been destroyed, and will decrease throughput.

How do you choose an ideal timeout? A value that works well on a high speed LAN would be disastrous for a multi-hop long-distance connection, so it is clear that "one size fits all" will not work here. Moreover, even during a single connection, network conditions may change and delays may increase or decrease. Algorithms of Karn and Jacobson enable TCP to adapt to changing conditions, and are now mandated for TCP implementations. These algorithms are sketched below.

Common sense tells us that the best basis for estimating a good retransmission timeout is to keep a watch on the connection, recording the *round trip times* that elapse between the transmission of data and the arrival of matching acknowledgments.

In order to get a feel for how round trip times can vary, let's look at some samples.

Recall that the *ping* command causes an ICMP echo message to make a round trip between systems. On my computer, *ping -s* causes one echo message to be sent each second. The default message length is 64 bytes, but this can be changed. The display below shows a single complete line of output from the *ping -s* command. The round trip time (RTT) to ucbvax.Berkeley.EDU was 156 milliseconds.

```
ping -s berkeley.edu
64 bytes from ucbvax.Berkeley.EDU(128.32.133.1):icmp_seq=0.time=156.ms
```

Table 10.2 displays the sequence numbers and round trip times (RTTs) from two sample *ping -s* outputs. The average round trip time for each sample also is reported.

TABLE 10.2 Sample Round Trip Times

| Sample 1 || Sample 2 ||
ICMP_seq	Time	ICMP_seq	Time
0.	156. ms	0.	294. ms
1.	170. ms	1.	264. ms
2.	161. ms	2.	340. ms
3.	287. ms	3.	246. ms
4.	156. ms	4.	201. ms
5.	158. ms	5.	340. ms
6.	170. ms	6.	272. ms
7.	185. ms	7.	311. ms
8.	162. ms	8.	282. ms
9.	158. ms	9.	246. ms
10.	164. ms	10.	304. ms
11.	171. ms	11.	308. ms
12.	154. ms	12.	230. ms
13.	161. ms	13.	328. ms
14.	152. ms	14.	266. ms
15.	172. ms	15.	257. ms
16.	160. ms	16.	305. ms
	MEAN RTT=170		MEAN RTT=282

The first sample corresponds to round trip times that were obtained early in a connection. The means is 170, the minimum is 152, and the maximum is 287. Later on, network conditions caused the longer delays exhibited in the second sample, whose mean is 282, minimum is 201, and maximum is 340.

If we kept a running average of all round trip times, and the session started with 1,000 fairly short times, a significant increase in delays would not make much of a dent on the running average.

For example, if 1,000 values with average 170 were followed by 50 values with average 282, the running average would be

$$170 \times 1000/1050 + 282 \times 50/1050 = 175$$

A more responsive measure is to use a weighted sum, computing a Smoothed Round Trip Time (SRTT):

$$New\ SRTT = (1-\alpha) \times (Old\ SRTT) + \alpha \times (Latest\ Round\ Trip\ Time)$$

The value of α lies between 0 and 1. Increasing α causes the current round trip time to have a greater effect on the smoothed average. Since computers can divide by powers of 2 very quickly by shifting binary numbers to the right, a value of $(1/2)^n$ is always chosen for α, typically 1/8, so that we have:

$$New\ SRTT = (7/8) \times (Old\ SRTT) + (1/8) \times (Latest\ Round\ Trip\ Time)$$

Table 10.3 shows how quickly the SRTT adjusts if the current SRTT is 230, and a change in network conditions causes a sequence of longer round trip times (RTTs).

TABLE 10.3 Computing the Smoothed Round Trip Time

Old SRTT	Latest RTT	(7/8)(Old SRTT)+(1/8)(RTT)
230.00	294	238.00
238.00	264	241.25
241.25	340	253.59
253.59	246	252.64
252.64	201	246.19
246.19	340	257.92
257.92	272	259.68
259.68	311	266.10
266.10	282	268.09
268.09	246	265.33
265.33	304	270.16
270.16	308	274.89
274.89	230	269.28
269.28	328	276.62
276.62	266	275.29
275.29	257	273.00
273.00	305	277.00

Now what value should be chosen for the retransmission timeout? A look at the sample round trip times shows that there are fairly large deviations between individual times and the current average. It makes sense to allow a good-sized margin for deviations. If we can come up with a reasonable estimate for a smoothed deviation (SDEV), then the formula below would provide a good retransmission timeout value:

$$TIMEOUT = SRTT + 2 \times SDEV$$

To compute SDEV, first calculate the absolute value of the current deviation:

$$DEV = |\ Latest\ Round\ Trip\ Time\ -\ Old\ SRTT\ |$$

Next, use a smoothing formula to weight in this latest value:

$$New\ SDEV = (3/4) \times (Old\ SDEV) + (1/4) \times (DEV)$$

One question remains — how do we get started? Initially set SRTT=0, and choose a value for SDEV so that TIMEOUT is 3 seconds. Since we used a factor of 2 in the TIMEOUT formula, an initial SDEV of 1.5 seconds will get us off to the right start.

The TCP/IP community is indebted to V. Jacobson for the algorithm for computing the smoothed round trip time. The basic retransmission timeout formula works quite well until there is a sudden change to very long round trip times or problems in the network cause datagrams to be destroyed. When a retransmission timeout occurs, we immediately switch over to Karn's algorithm to compute the next timeout.

Karn's algorithm is based on the assumption that the expiration of a retransmission timer probably indicates a condition of congestion in the network. The reasonable thing to do is to apply a large increase to the duration of the retransmission timer. This is usually done via a multiplicative factor:

$$New\ TIMEOUT = Factor \times Old\ TIMEOUT$$

The most popular choice for a backoff factor is 2:

$$New\ TIMEOUT = 2 \times Old\ TIMEOUT$$

If the new timeout expires, we increase again. Of course two limiting values are needed:

- Timeouts will increase up to a prespecified maximum, and then stay there.

- There will be a limit on the total number of unacknowledged retransmission attempts. When this limit is reached, the connection will be aborted.

Note that the new timeout applies to the retransmitted data, and to subsequent data that is sent on the TCP connection. Suppose that data was indeed delayed by a temporary condition of congestion. How do we get back to the normal computation of timeout values?

This is simple. As soon as acknowledgements begin to arrive before timeouts expire, we can go back to the Jacobson estimation technique.

These algorithms of Karn and Jacobson prevent retransmissions from crippling a congested network. Further mechanisms are needed to reduce the total amount of TCP traffic presented to the network until normal operation can be restored. The next section describes the congestion avoidance algorithms introduced by V. Jacobson.

10.6.4 Treating Congestion

Growth in round trip times or the arrival of ICMP Source Quench messages are indicators of congestion in the network. Increasing the retransmission timeout helps to reduce the amount of duplicate traffic on a congested network, but a more drastic temporary cutback in load is needed to let the network recover.

The mechanism for doing this is to define a *congestion window* and to restrict a sender to transmitting data that lies within the congestion window. During normal transfer, the congestion window is the same size as the send window. When a retransmission occurs or an ICMP Source Quench is received, the congestion window is resized to:

maximum(1/2 × current congestion window size, single segment size)

A sequence of retransmissions or source quenches will cause the congestion window to be cut down until it is the size of a single segment.

How do we get back to normal? When an ACK arrives, the congestion window is increased by the size of one segment. Growth continues every time a segment is ACKed within the timeout period until the normal window size is reached.

What do these algorithms achieve? When a traffic jam builds up on an internet, retransmission timers will expire and source quenches will be sent out. We can imagine this resulting in connections all across the network going into *red alert* status. When this happens, the congestion algorithm says, in effect, "Will half of the traffic please get off the freeway?" If the network stays congested, the request is repeated.

10.6.5 Slow Start

New connections that immediately start to transfer bulk data across a network can cause stress. *Slow start* prevents this by initializing every connection with a congestion window of one segment, and growing the window as ACKs arrive, just as was done above during congestion recovery. Of course, the maximum window size will be defined by the limit set by the receiver.

10.6.6 Vendor Conformance

The current TCP standard requires conformant implementations to adhere to slow start when initiating a connection, to use the algorithms of Karn and Jacobson to estimate retransmission timeouts, and to control congestion by implementing the congestion window. Tests have shown that these mechanisms produce significant improvement in performance.

What happens when you install a system that does not adhere to these standards? Not only does it provide poorer performance for its own users, but it will be a bad neighbor for the other systems on the network, hampering recovery from temporary congestion, and producing excessive traffic that causes datagram discards.

10.6.7 Vendor's Choice

The TCP specification leaves many internal actions up to the implementor. Some choices that a vendor makes can have an impact on performance, namely:

- While a sending TCP waits for an ACK, more data may be added to the send buffer. If TCP needs to retransmit a small segment, it can repackage the segment so that the new data is included.
- When segments arrive out of order, the receiving TCP has the choice of saving or discarding them. Discarding out-of-order segments burdens the network.
- A receiver may delay sending an ACK for a period of time (which must be less than 0.5 second). The purpose is to try to combine multiple ACKs, window update information, and outgoing data into a single segment.

10.6.8 Ongoing Performance Research

TCP has proved to be very flexible, running over networks that carry hundreds of bits per second or millions of bits per second. The protocol has achieved acceptable results on modern Ethernet,[11] Token-Ring, and FDDI LANS, as well as low bandwidth paths and paths with long delays (such as satellite links).

TCP has been tuned so that it is responsive to abnormal conditions such as congestion or temporary loss of a route.

However, there are features in the current protocol that limit TCP throughput over emerging technologies that offer bandwidth in the hundreds and thousands of megabytes. To understand the problem, let's look at a simple example.

Suppose that we are performing a file transfer between two systems, and want to send the data out in a steady stream as efficiently as possible. Suppose that:

- The receiver's maximum segment size is 1 kilobyte.
- The receive window is 4 kilobytes.
- There is enough bandwidth to send 2 segments per second.
- The receive application is absorbing the data as soon as it arrives.
- ACKs arrive within 2 seconds.

The sender will be able to send data steadily, because just as the window allocation becomes exhausted, an ACK arrives that allows another segment to be sent:

SEND SEGMENT 1.
SEND SEGMENT 2.
SEND SEGMENT 3.
SEND SEGMENT 4.
Two seconds have elapsed.
RECEIVE ACK OF SEGMENT 1, CAN SEND SEGMENT 5.
RECEIVE ACK OF SEGMENT 2, CAN SEND SEGMENT 6.
RECEIVE ACK OF SEGMENT 3, CAN SEND SEGMENT 7.
RECEIVE ACK OF SEGMENT 4, CAN SEND SEGMENT 8.
Two more seconds have elapsed.
RECEIVE ACK OF SEGMENT 5, CAN SEND SEGMENT 9.
. . .

---

[11] V. Jacobson performed an FTP file transfer between two Sun/60s on an Ethernet whose throughput was 816,000 bytes per second.

If the receive window had been only 2 kilobytes, then the sender would have been forced to wait 1 second out of every 2 before sending more data. In fact, to keep a steady flow going, the receive window must have a size that is at least:

$$WINDOW = BANDWIDTH \times DELAY$$

For example, if the bandwidth were 1 megabyte per second and the delay was 100 milliseconds (1/10 second) then a steady-flow receive window needs to hold at least 100 kilobytes. But the largest number that can be written in the window field in the TCP header is $(2^{16}-1)$ — that is, one less than 64 kilobytes!

Another problem can arise at very high transmission rates because sequence numbers get used up very quickly. If we could transmit data at 4 gigabytes per second, then the sequence numbers would wrap around in 1 second. It would not be possible to distinguish old duplicate datagrams that had been delayed for more than a second while crossing an internet from fresh new data.

There is active ongoing research into enhancing TCP to remove these barriers.

10.6.9 TCP Functions

TCP is a protocol of considerable size. This chapter has dealt with the many jobs that TCP has to perform. The list below summarizes TCP's functions:

- Associating ports with connections.
- Establishing connections by means of a three-way handshake.
- Segmenting data for transmission.
- Numbering data.
- Positive acknowledgment with retransmission.
- Handling duplicate segments.
- Computing checksums.
- Regulating the flow of data with receive and send windows.
- Terminating connections in an orderly fashion.
- Aborting connections.
- Interacting with upper layer applications.
- Pushing data.
- Signaling urgent data.

- Error checking and error reporting.
- Adjusting to network congestion.

10.6.10 TCP States

A TCP connection passes through a number of stages. First the connection is set up by means of an exchange of messages, then data is transmitted, and then it is closed by means of an exchange of messages. Each step in the progress of a connection corresponds to a connection *state*. The TCP software at each end of a connection keeps track of the state at its end of the connection at all times.

Below, we sketch a typical progression of states at the server and client ends of a connection. This is not intended to represent an exhaustive investigation of all possible state transitions. See RFC 793 for a complete discussion of TCP states.

During connection setup, the sequence of states is slightly different at the server and client ends. The server states during setup are:

Server State	Description
CLOSED:	A fictitious state, prior to starting the connection.
LISTEN:	The server waits for a connection from a client.
SYN-RECEIVED:	The server has received a SYN. It sent a SYN/ACK, and is waiting for an ACK.
ESTABLISHED:	The ACK has been received and the connection is open.

The client states during setup are:

Client State	Description
CLOSED:	A fictitious state, prior to starting the connection.
SYN-SENT:	The client has sent a SYN to the server.
ESTABLISHED:	The client has received a SYN/ACK from the server, and has sent back an ACK. Data transfer can proceed.

There are cases when peers may simultaneously actively initiate a connection. For example, a pair of mail servers may try to reach one another at the same time. In this case, each passes through the states

CLOSED, SYN-SENT, SYN-RECEIVED, and ESTABLISHED.

The ends of a connection remain in ESTABLISHED state until one end initiates a close by sending a FIN segment. The closer passes through the states:

Closer State	Description
FIN-WAIT-1:	The closer is waiting for the partner to send a FIN. Recall that fresh data may still arrive from the partner at this stage.
FIN-WAIT-2:	The closer has received an ACK from the partner, but not a FIN. The closer waits for the FIN, accepting incoming data in the meantime.
CLOSING:	A FIN/ACK has arrived. The closer sends an ACK. This state can be reached from either FIN-WAIT-1 or FIN-WAIT-2.
TIMED WAIT:	The connection is held in limbo for sufficient time until all connection messages (e.g., late duplicates) that may still exist out in the network have perished. If any messages arrive, TCP will know that they belong to a defunct connection and will discard them. The timeout period is twice the estimated maximum segment lifetime.
CLOSE:	All information about the connection is deleted.

The closer's partner passes through the states:

Partner State	Description
CLOSE WAIT:	A FIN has arrived. The application may optionally send more data. TCP sends an ACK and waits for its application to issue a close.
LAST ACK:	The application has issued a close, and TCP has sent a FIN. It is waiting for an ACK of the termination. This state will persist for the timeout period.
CLOSE:	All information about the connection is deleted.

10.6.11 Viewing the States of TCP Connections

The *netstat* command can be used to examine the current state of connections. In the display below, two connections are timing out, and two are in an active data exchange state.

Note that the connection port number is tacked onto the end of each local and foreign address. The computer is lightly loaded, and so there is no traffic backed up on either send queues or receive queues.

```
netstat -n
Active Internet connections
Proto  Recv-Q  Send-Q  Local Address       Foreign Address      (state)
tcp    0       0       128.36.12.27.939    128.36.12.26.111     TIME_WAIT
tcp    0       0       128.36.12.27.936    128.36.12.1.111      TIME_WAIT
tcp    0       0       128.36.12.27.513    130.132.23.16.102    ESTABLISHED
tcp    0       0       128.36.12.27.794    130.132.23.16.513    ESTABLISHED
```

10.7 RELATIONSHIP TO OSI

TCP and the OSI transport layer have the same overall function — to provide reliable end-to-end data transfer. The OSI transport layer specification was strongly influenced by TCP. However, there are a number of significant differences.

If the underlying network service is in fact a reliable connection-oriented facility (e.g., an end-to-end X.25 circuit), then why bother with retransmission, ACKs, and all of the other error correction facilities? OSI allows for 5 different classes of service, ranging from Class 0, which assumes a very reliable underlying connection and adds negligible overhead, to Class 4, which can operate over a connectionless network, as TCP does. The classes are sketched below:

Class 0:   Used over a reliable connection-oriented network layer. The transport layer has little to do other than packaging and unpackaging transport PDUs.

Class 1:   Used over a connection-oriented network that may be subject to occasional loss of data sequencing or loss of a connection. Class 1 provides the ability to recover from these problems.

Class 2:   Used over a reliable connection-oriented network. A Class 2 transport can multiplex several transport connections onto a single network connection. In addition, flow control is available at the option of the service users.

Class 3:   Provides the capabilities of both Class 1 and Class 2.

Class 4:   Used over an unreliable network layer (for example, a connectionless datagram facility). Class 4 provides the same kinds of services supported by TCP.

10.7.1 TCP and OSI Transport Class 4

OSI Transport Protocol Class 4 (TP4) is a very complex protocol intended to operate in a connectionless network environment, just as TCP does. OSI TP4 borrowed many ideas from TCP, but there are important differences between them. Some of the most significant are listed below:

- TCP uses one header format. OSI TP4 has separate headers for a whole array of protocol data units (Connection Request and Confirm, Data, Acknowledgment, Expedited Data and Expedited Data Acknowledgment, Disconnect Request and Confirm, and Error). These protocol data units provide a compatible match with the various protocol data units that are used in the X.25 packet layer (layer 3).
- TCP numbers data octets. OSI numbers protocol data units in sequence. If transmission rates of 4 gigabytes per second are attained in the future, the current TCP sequence numbering field would be exhausted within one second, which would be unacceptable. OSI numbering is robust at high speeds.
- The maximum receive window that can be expressed in the current TCP header is 65,535 bytes. TP4 supports receive windows of up to 32,767 *data units*. Large buffer sizes are needed to sustain very high transmission bandwidths.
- OSI TP4 has a complex set of rules for packaging transport PDUs together into a single network layer PDU.
- There is an OSI transport layer PDU that is used to carry a small amount of expedited data. This PDU provides true out-of-band data transmission.
- TCP provides a graceful close procedure for connections. OSI TP4 connections close abruptly; graceful close is handled by the OSI session layer.

The OSI Connection Request and Data PDU headers that follow illustrate some of the similarities and differences between the protocols.

An important distinction is in the way that applications are identified. In TCP, a 16-bit port number in the header is used to direct data to an application. In OSI, the application is not identified until you have climbed up some more layers. At the transport layer, a Transport Service Access Point (TSAP) field identifies a session layer entity. At the higher layers, a Session Service Access Point, Presentation Layer Service Access Point, and Application Entity Title are used to identify the ultimate user of the connection.

Fortunately, OSI TP4 does not have to worry about all of these names during a connection. Once a TP4 connection is set up, a 16-bit reference number is assigned to each end of the connection and is used by TP4 much as a port number is used by TCP.

Reference numbers are assigned dynamically and are not reused for a period of minutes after a connection ends; hence data from an old connection will not be confused with data from a current connection.

The class for the connection is negotiated at setup time; if the first choice cannot be supported at the called end, there is a field to indicate preferred alternatives.

Some of the fields in OSI connection setup protocol data unit headers are optional. Space is available to exchange quite a bit of information about each partner's wishes and capabilities for the connection.

Note that the data PDU header is quite short. The connection is identified simply by the reference integer assigned by the partner's end. ACK and window information are carried in a separate PDU. Often an ACK and a data PDU are bundled together, with joint header length similar to TCP's.

10.7.2 OSI Connection Request PDU

Recall that TP4 uses many different protocol data units. The Connection Request PDU is shown in Figure 10.20.

Both the Connection Request and Connection Response can be fairly long, but of course they are used only at connection setup.

Some of the fields in these protocol data units are optional. In some cases, OSI has offered alternative options for the lengths of fields. This is the case, for example, for the data numbering and window credit fields.

Since our purpose here is to provide a general feel for TP4, we omit many details here. The fields and lengths displayed below are those recommended by the United States *Government OSI Profile* (GOSIP). GOSIP prefers the *extended format* which selects large fields for sequence numbering and window credit.

Transmission Control Protocol 213

Octets	OSI Connection Request PDU
1	Length of Header
1	Type of PDU (Connection Request) and Initial Credit (Number of PDUs)
2	Destination Reference Placeholder (0 Here)
2	Source Reference
1	Options First Choice for Class Indicate Choice of Normal or Extended Format
4	Calling Transport Service Access Point
4	Called Transport Service Access Point
3	Maximum PDU Size
3	Version
4	Checksum
3	Options (e.g., Use Checksums or Not)
2 + 1 Byte for Each Class	Alternative Protocol Classes
4	(Optional) Maximum Acknowledge Time

Figure 10.20 OSI Connection Request PDU.

10.7.3 OSI TP4 Data and ACK PDUs

The header for data transmission (see Figure 10.21) is quite straightforward. TP4 differs significantly from TCP in the fact that TP4 may take a unit of transport layer data and break it into pieces. The end flag below signals whether this is the final piece. A 16-bit checksum is used. The first two octets of the checksum field contain an ID and length for the field.

OSI TP4 Data PDU

Octets	
1	Length of Header
1	Type of PDU (Data)
2	Destination Reference
1	TPDU Number End Flag
4	Checksum
	Data

OSI TP4 Acknowledgment PDU

Octets	
1	Length of Header
1	Type of PDU (Ack)
2	Destination Reference
4	Ack: Seq Number of Next Data PDU Expected
2	Credit (Window)
4	Checksum
N	Options

Figure 10.21 OSI TP4 Data and Acknowledgement PDUs.

10.7.4 OSI TP4 Acknowledgment PDU

Acknowledgments and credit updates are handled by a separate ACK protocol data unit (see Figure 10.21). The ACK has a number of optional embellishments. For example, a sequence of ACKs can be sent signaling receipt of the same data, but containing changes to the size of the receive window. A field containing a secondary sequence number is included to sort out which credit is the most recent.

10.8 RECOMMENDED READING

The original TCP standard is defined in RFC 793. Updates, corrections, and conformance requirements are specified in RFC 1122. Karn and Partridge published their article, *Improving Round-Trip Estimates in Reliable Transport Protocols*, in the Proceedings of the ACM SIGCOMM 1987. The Jacobson article, *Congestion Avoidance and Control*, appeared in the Proceedings of the ACM SIGCOMM 1988 Workshop.

Chapter

11

File Transfer Protocol

11.1 INTRODUCTION

In a networked environment, it is natural to wish to copy files between computer systems. Why isn't it always easy to do this? Computer vendors have devised hundreds of file systems. These file systems differ in dozens of minor ways, and in quite a few drastic major ways too!

This is not just a multivendor problem. Sometimes it is difficult to copy files between two different types of computers manufactured by the same vendor.

Among the problems that may be encountered when dealing with a multisystem environment are:

- Different conventions for naming files.
- Different rules for traversing file directory systems.
- File access restrictions.
- Different ways to represent text and numeric data within files.

The designers of the TCP/IP protocol suite did not try to create a very complicated general solution to every file transfer problem. Instead, they evolved a fairly basic but elegant File Transfer Protocol (FTP) that is serviceable and easy to use.

The File Transfer Protocol is designed to be operated by interactive end users or by application programs. We will confine the discussion here to the familiar interactive FTP end-user service that is universally available with TCP/IP implementations. The user interface developed for Berkeley UNIX has been ported to many types of computers. In this chapter we will see end-user dialogues based on that interface.

The core file transfer functions enable users to copy files between systems, view directory listings, and perform housekeeping chores such as renaming or deleting files. These functions are part of the standard TCP/IP protocol suite.

There are some optional functions that are not so generally available. One of these is *third party transfer* in which a user at one host causes a file to be copied between two other remote hosts. Another service that frequently is omitted is *restart recovery* — the ability to restart a failed file transfer where it left off.

The Trivial File Transfer Protocol (TFTP), discussed at the end of this chapter, is a bare-bones file transfer protocol used for special situations such as downloading software to a diskless workstation.

11.2 FTP SCENARIO

How can we move around in directories, identify files, and manipulate them at a computer whose organization is different from our own?

A standard set of commands is used to communicate with any remote FTP server, but a user identifies directories and files at the server's computer using the naming conventions of the remote system.

Computers usually do not let outsiders view or manipulate their files. However, there are times when it is useful to create a public file area. FTP accommodates both public information sharing and private file system security by offering two kinds of services:

- Access to public files by means of *anonymous* logins
- Access to private files, which is restricted to users with system login identifiers and passwords

The dialogue that follows demonstrates how a file may be copied from the public repository of RFC documents at the Network Information Center (NIC).[1] We will connect to the NIC with login identifier *anonymous*. Some public systems prefer login identifier *guest*. Public file systems generally expect a password which either is *guest*, or else is the user's electronic mail identifier.

The initial connection to the server is called the *control connection*. The control connection is used to send commands to the file server and to carry the server's responses back.

---

[1] We have omitted the banner messages displayed by the NIC. See Appendix C for a login that displays the full opening message from the NIC.

`ftp nic.ddn.mil`	*ftp starts the FTP user interface program. The user wants to work with remote host nic.ddn.mil.*
`Connected to nic.ddn.mil.`	*A successful connection is reported by the local FTP.*
`220 nic FTP server (SunOS 4.1) ready.`	*This message comes directly from the remote system.*

`Name : anonymous`
`331 Guest login ok,`
`send ident as password.`
	The local FTP prompts for a userid. The NIC is not too picky - they let anyone in.

`Password:`
`brown@plum.math.yale.edu`
`230 Guest login ok,`
`access restrictions apply.`
	The local FTP prompts for a password. We give the polite response, which is our mail identifier.

`ftp>`
 	
`ftp> cd rfc`
	The ftp> prompt means "What do you want to do next?" The user changes to the remote directory, rfc, that contains RFC documents.

`250 CWD command successful.`	*The cd command entered by the user was sent to the server as FTP's formal CWD (change working directory) command. The server directory has been changed to rfc and we are ready to get an rfc document.*
`ftp> get rfc1261.txt nicinfo` `200 PORT command successful.`	*We ask for a copy of rfc1261.txt. A second connection will be created to copy the file. The local FTP has obtained a second port and has told the server to connect to this port.*
`150 ASCII data connection for rfc1261.txt (128.36.12.27,1401) (4318 bytes).`	*At this point, the data connection has been opened for the file transfer.*

`226 ASCII Transfer complete.`
`local: nicinfo remote: rfc1261-.txt`
`4488 bytes received in`
`15 seconds (0.3 Kbytes/s)`
	The transfer is complete and a new local file has been created.

`ftp> quit` `221 Goodbye.`	*Enough work for now.*

Our first command asked the server to change to directory *rfc*. Then we copied the remote document rfc1261.txt to local file nicinfo. If we had not entered a filename, the local file would have been assigned the same name as the remote file.

Note that FTP allows us to talk the remote host's language when identifying its files. We use local file conventions to name the files at our end.

The prompt ftp> is displayed whenever the local FTP application is waiting for user input. On the other hand, lines that start with numbers contain messages from the remote file server.

The File Transfer Protocol has a distinctive style of operation. Whenever a file is copied, *a second connection is opened up and used to transfer the data*. After the *get* command in the dialogue, the local FTP acquires a second port and tells the server about it. We do not see this outgoing message, but we do see the response:

```
200 PORT command successful.
150 ASCII data connection for rfc1261.txt (128.36.12.27,1401)
```

The last response tells us that the local FTP at our own IP address, 128.36.12.27, has acquired port 1401 for the data connection.

11.3 FTP MODEL

As we can see from the dialogue, the user interacts with a local client FTP process. The local client software conducts a formal conversation with remote server FTP software over the control connection.[2]

During the dialogue in the previous section, the end user entered requests to change directories and copy a file. These were translated to formal FTP commands and passed across the control connection to the remote FTP server. Actual transfers of data take place over the separate data connection which is created for the purpose. There is a Data Transfer Protocol that is used over the data connection. Figure 11.1 illustrates this model.

11.3.1 FTP Commands

What types of commands can be passed on the control connection? There are authentication commands that enable a user to identify the userid, password, and account to be used for a set of FTP activities.

---

[2] The control connection has the characteristics of a basic Telnet Network Virtual Terminal protocol. See Chapter 13 for a description of the behavior of this protocol.

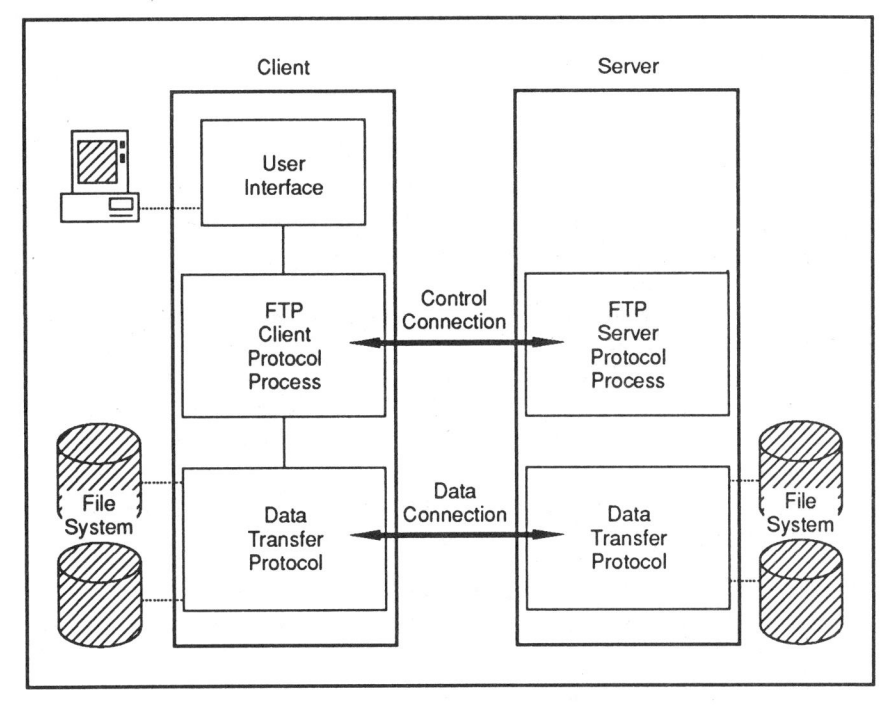

Figure 11.1 FTP control and data connections.

There are file transfer commands that enable a user to:

- Copy a single file between hosts.
- Copy multiple files between hosts.
- Append a local file to a remote file.
- Copy a file and append a number to its name so that the name is unique.[3]

There are file management commands that enable the user to:

- List the files in a directory.
- Identify the current directory and change directories.
- Create and remove directories.
- Rename or delete files.

---

[3]For example, a daily log file could be retrieved and automatically called log.1, log.2, and so forth.

222 Chapter Eleven

There are control commands that enable the user to:

- Identify whether ASCII text, EBCDIC text, or binary data is to be transferred.
- Establish whether the file is structured as a series of bytes or as a sequence of records.
- Describe how the file will be transferred — as a stream of octets, a sequence of blocks, or in a compressed format.

The commands that are sent across the control connection have a fixed format. For example, STOR is sent to copy a file to the remote site. The Berkeley user interface, which has been adopted by most vendors, lets end users type *put* or *send*, which is felt to be more user-friendly than STOR. FTP puts no restrictions on the kind of user interface that any vendor may provide.

The user interface generally includes additional commands that let the user customize the local environment, such as:

- Ask FTP to ring a bell at the end of a transfer.
- Ask FTP to print a *hash symbol*, "#," for each block of data transferred.
- Set up automatic translation of the case of letters in a filename, or set up a table for automatically translating characters in the names of transferred files.

The complete set of functions supported by a particular host can be viewed by entering the FTP application and typing *help*. A terse description of a command is obtained by typing *help "commandname."* Consult your host's manuals for full information.

The dialogue that follows starts with a *help* display. There are a number of commands that have synonyms, such as *ls* or *dir* to ask for directory information, *put* or *send* to copy a file to a remote host, *get* or *recv* to copy a file from the remote host, and *bye* or *quit* to leave FTP.

Multiple files can be copied using *mget* or *mput* using "global wild card" naming. For example, *mget a** retrieves a copy of every file whose name starts with the letter *a*. This will work if *globbing* is on; you turn global wildcard naming on and off by typing *glob*.

In the dialogue, we turn *debugging* on in order to get some insight into how the protocol works. Lines starting with —> show the messages that the local host sends across the control connection. Lines starting with a number show the messages sent from the remote host to report the outcome of a command.

File Transfer Protocol

```
ftp
ftp> help
Commands may be abbreviated.  Commands are:

!            cr           macdef       proxy        send
$            delete       mdelete      sendport     status
account      debug        mdir         put          struct
append       dir          mget         pwd          sunique
ascii        disconnect   mkdir        quit         tenex
bell         form         mls          quote        trace
binary       get          mode         recv         type
bye          glob         mput         remotehelp   user
case         hash         nmap         rename       verbose
cd           help         ntrans       reset        ?
cdup         lcd          open         rmdir
close        ls           prompt       runique

ftp> help account
account          send account command to remote server

ftp> help append
append           append to a file

ftp> debug
Debugging on (debug=1).


ftp> open plum
Connected to plum.math.yale.edu.
220 plum FTP server (Version 4.7
Sun Sep 14 12:44:57 PDT 1986)
ready.

Name : brown
---> USER brown
331 Password required for brown.
Password:
---> PASS pudding
230 User brown logged in.


ftp> status
Connected to plum.math.yale.edu.

Mode: stream; Type: ascii; Form:
non-print; Structure: file
Verbose: on; Bell: off; Prompt-
ing: on; Globbing: on
Store    unique:    off;    Receive
unique: off Case: off; CR strip-
ping: on Ntrans: off
Nmap: off Hash mark printing:
off; Use of PORT cmds: on
```

We open a connection to host plum, which is on our local area network.

A real userid and password are entered so that private files can be accessed.

This displays the complete list of current settings for the FTP environment. Many of these will be explained later in this chapter.

```
ftp> ls
```
We request a directory listing. Directory listings can be long, so FTP sends directory listings on a data connection!

```
---> PORT 128,36,12,27,5,123
200 PORT command okay.
```
We need a port for the data transfer. The local host sends a message with its IP address (4 bytes) and a new port (2 bytes) to be used for data transfer. The bytes are translated to decimal and separated by commas.

```
---> NLST
```
NLST is the formal message that asks for a directory listing.

```
150 Opening data connection for
/bin/ls (128.36.12.27,1403) asn-
1.txt
mbox
snmp.txt
226 Transfer complete.
```
A brand new connection to client port 1403 has been opened to transfer the directory.

```
ftp> get asn1.txt
---> PORT 128,36,12,27,5,124
200 PORT command okay.

---> RETR asn1.txt
150 Opening data connection for
asn1.txt    (128.36.12.27,1404)
(4535 bytes).

226 Transfer complete.
local: asn1.txt remote: asn1.txt
4680 bytes received in 0.2 sec-
onds (23 Kbytes/s)
```
It is not unusual for FTP to start a new data connection for each data transfer operation, and close the connection at the end of the operation. This time the server connects to client port 1404.

```
ftp> put rfc1261
---> PORT 128,36,12,27,5,125
200 PORT command okay.
```
Next we copy a local file to the remote system. Once again, a new connection will be opened.

```
---> STOR rfc1261
150 Opening data connection for
rfc1261 (128.36.12.27,1405).
226 Transfer complete.
local: rfc1261 remote: rfc1261
4488 bytes sent in 0.037 seconds
(1.2e+02 Kbytes/s)

ftp> quit
---> QUIT
221 Goodbye.
```

Note that the scenario for the data connection was:

- The local client got a new port and used the control connection to tell the server FTP what the port number was.
- The FTP server connected to the client's new data port.
- The data was transferred.
- The connection was closed.

An alternative scenario is possible. If the port number is sent by means of the *PASV* command, then the server listens for a data connection that originates from the client's port. By convention, a server uses port 20 for its end of a data connection.

11.4 THE FTP PROTOCOL

There are several elements that make up the file transfer protocol, including:

- The format of the data to be transferred.
- The command words and related parameters sent on the control connection.
- The numeric codes returned in response to the commands.

11.4.1 Data Format Issues

The two ends of a file transfer dialogue need a common understanding of the format of the data that will be transferred. Is it text or binary? Is there any structuring of the data into records or blocks?

Three attributes are used to define the transfer format: data type, file structure, and transmission mode. The values that can be assigned to these attributes are described in the sections that follow.

11.4.2 Data Type

A file may contain ASCII text, EBCDIC text, or binary image data. There also is a type called *logical byte* to accommodate computers that have unusual byte sizes such as 11-bit bytes.

A text file may contain ordinary text or text formatted for a printer. A print text file contains format codes that are either:

- Telnet vertical format controls (i.e. <CR>, <LF>, <NL>, <VT>, <FF>)
- ASA (FORTRAN) vertical format controls

11.4.3 File Structure

The most common structure assigned to a file is called *file-structure*, which means no structure at all! The file is viewed as a sequence of bytes. This is the default for the protocol.

A *record-structure* file is naturally made up of a sequence of records. A third type, *page-structure*, was introduced to accommodate DEC TOPS-20 files and now is obsolete.

11.4.4 Transmission Mode

The transmission mode combined with the file structure determines how the data will be formatted for transfer. The three transmission modes are *stream, block,* and *compressed.*

For *stream* mode and *file-structure*, the file is transmitted as a stream of bytes. FTP relies on TCP to provide data integrity, and no headers or delimiters are inserted into the data. The only way to signal that the end of the file has been reached is by a normal close of the data connection!

For *stream mode and record-structure*, each record is delimited by a 2-byte End Of Record (EOR) control code. Another 2-byte code is used to represent End Of File (EOF).

In *block mode*, a file is transmitted as a series of data blocks. Each block starts with a three-byte header. The header has the format shown in Figure 11.2.

A block may contain an entire record, or a record can span several blocks. Note that the descriptor contains an End Of Record (EOR) flag that is used to identify record boundaries. The End Of File (EOF) flag in the descriptor indicates that the block is the last one in the file transfer.

8 Bits	16 Bits
Descriptor Flags	Byte Count
End of Block is EOR End of Block is EOF Restart Marker	Number of Data Bytes That Follow

Figure 11.2 Header format used for FTP block mode transfers.

Compressed mode offers a very basic form of data compression. When a file is transferred in compressed mode, repeated characters are transmitted efficiently. Special encoding is used to signal that a particular character should be expanded so that it repeats up to 63 times. In addition, control sequences containing descriptor bytes and restart markers can be embedded in the data.

An advantage of using record structure, block mode, or compressed mode is that the end of the file will be marked clearly so that a data connection could be held and reused for multiple transfers.

In the dialogue shown earlier, the response to the status command included the statement:

```
Mode: stream; Type: ascii; Form: non-print; Structure: file
```

That is, the default setting for data transfer mode was *stream*, the data type was *ASCII non-print*, and the organization of the file was *file-structure*, which really means unstructured. Defaults at your host will match the data type, file structure, and transmission mode that best match your local environment.

11.4.5 Error Recovery and Restart

While transmission rates and computer storage resources have increased steadily, so have the needs of user applications. Many organizations have a need to transfer very large files. Suppose that a system that is executing the transfer of a very large file fails? If an ordinary FTP transfer was in progress, either the transfer must be started over or the user will have to manually reconstruct the file.

The restart service is designed to solve this problem. If block or compressed mode transfer is used and the restart service is supported, then the sending FTP has the ability to insert restart markers in the data stream. Each marker is a printable text string. For example, successive markers could be 1, 2, 3, ... Whenever the receiver gets a marker, the receiver writes the data onto non-volatile storage and keeps track of the marker's position in the data.

If the receiving system is local, the end user is notified of each marker as soon as the data has been stored. If the receiving system is remote, a message is sent back to the user on the control connection indicating that data up to the marker has been safe-stored.

After a system failure, the user can invoke a restart command with a marker value as its argument. This is followed by the command that was being executed (get or put) when the system failed.

Implementation of the restart service is optional. Unfortunately, few if any TCP/IP products include this service.

11.4.6 Reply Codes

Each command in a dialogue is answered with a reply code and message. For example:

```
ftp> get asn1.txt
  --> PORT 128,36,12,27,5,124
200 PORT command okay.
---> RETR asn1.txt
150 Opening data connection for asn1.txt (128.36.12.27,1404) (4535
bytes). 226 Transfer complete.
```

Reply codes consist of three digits. Each has a specific purpose. Codes in the 200s indicate successful completion of a command. The 100s indicate that an action is being started and the 300s indicate that an intermediate point has been reached successfully. Codes in the 400s signal transient errors, while the 500s are really bad news and announce a permanent error. The second and third digits of a reply code classify the reply more precisely.

11.5 AN FTP SESSION

The trace that follows was captured by FTP Software's *LANWatch* Network Analyzer product.[4] The trace illustrates the actions of the FTP and TCP protocols.

The client, at port 12533, sends a SYN to well-known FTP port 21. The initial sequence number (in hex) is 0b540100, and the initial credit window size is 1024. The header length of six 32-bit words (24 octets) indicates that the maximum segment size option is present. The maximum segment size is, in fact, 1024.

```
1
TCP:   12533 -> ftp(21)       seq: 0b540100  ack:   ----
win: 1024   hl:6    xsum: 0x9452  urg: 0   flags: <SYN>  mss: 1024
```

The FTP server offers a larger initial credit window of 4096 octets, but its maximum segment size also is 1024. When the client ACKs, the connection is established.

```
2
TCP:   ftp(21) -> 12533       seq: 008d32c1  ack: 0b540101
win: 4096   hl:6    xsum: 0x3613  urg: 0   flags: <ACK><SYN>  mss: 1024
```

---

[4]The LANWatch output provides more detail. The trace shows an excerpt.

```
3
TCP:  12533 -> ftp(21)        seq: 0b540101  ack: 008d32c2
win: 1024   hl:5   xsum: 0x3f35  urg: 0   flags: <ACK>
```

The FTP server sends a positive 220 message indicating that it is ready. The trace prints only part of the data field; 55/70 means that 55 of the 70 bytes in the message are displayed. Watch for the PUSH flag with every message.

```
4
TCP:  ftp(21) -> 12533        seq: 008d32c2  ack: 0b540101
win: 4096   hl:5   xsum: 0xab30  urg: 0   flags: <ACK><PUSH>
data (55/70): 220 ftp FTP server Version 4.10 Thu Apr 2 21:49:18 EST
```

The client ACKs. Note that the client's window has shrunk by 70 bytes.

```
5
TCP:  12533 -> ftp(21)        seq: 0b540101  ack: 008d3308
win: 954   hl:5   xsum: 0x3f35  urg: 0   flags: <ACK>
```

The client software collects the user's ID and password, and then sends them to the server.

```
6
TCP:  12533 -> ftp(21)        seq: 0b540101  ack: 008d3308
win: 954   hl:5   xsum: 0xc124  urg: 0   flags: <ACK><PUSH>
data (14/14): USER testing
```

```
7
TCP:  ftp(21) -> 12533        seq: 008d3308  ack: 0b54010f
win: 4096   hl:5   xsum: 0xeb28  urg: 0   flags: <ACK>
```

```
8
TCP:  ftp(21) -> 12533        seq: 008d3308  ack: 0b54010f
win: 4096   hl:5   xsum: 0xdfa6  urg: 0   flags: <ACK><PUSH>
data (36/36): 331 Password required for testing.
```

```
9
TCP:  12533 -> ftp(21)        seq: 0b54010f  ack: 008d332c
win: 988   hl:5   xsum: 0xeb34  urg: 0   flags: <ACK>
```

```
10
TCP:  12533 -> ftp(21)        seq: 0b54010f  ack: 008d332c
win: 988   hl:5   xsum: 0x7e1b  urg: 0   flags: <ACK><PUSH>
data (14/14): PASS testing
```

230 Chapter Eleven

```
11=========================================================
TCP:   ftp(21) -> 12533          seq: 008d332c  ack: 0b54011d
win: 4096   hl:5    xsum: 0xb928  urg: 0    flags: <ACK>
```

The user with ID "testing" has been logged in to the FTP server.

```
12=========================================================
TCP:   ftp(21) -> 12533          seq: 008d332c  ack: 0b54011d
win: 4096   hl:5    xsum: 0xcda5  urg: 0    flags: <ACK><PUSH>
 data (29/29): 230 User testing logged in.
```

```
13=========================================================
TCP:   12533 -> ftp(21)          seq: 0b54011d  ack: 008d3349
win: 995    hl:5    xsum: 0xb934  urg: 0    flags: <ACK>
```

The user has issued a *get* command. The client obtains a data port and asks the server to open a connection. The six numbers in the PORT command are the four octets of the IP address and the two octets of the port number, where each octet has been translated to decimal. After the PORT command succeeds, the client sends a RETR command.

```
14=========================================================
TCP:   12533 -> ftp(21)          seq: 0b54011d  ack: 008d3349
win: 995    hl:5    xsum: 0xe87e  urg: 0    flags: <ACK><PUSH>
 data (27/27): PORT 128,127,2,133,48,246
```

```
15=========================================================
TCP:   ftp(21) -> 12533          seq: 008d3349  ack: 0b540138
win: 4096   hl:5    xsum: 0xcda5  urg: 0    flags: <ACK><PUSH>
 data (24/24): 200 PORT command okay.
```

```
16=========================================================
TCP:   12533 -> ftp(21)          seq: 0b540138  ack: 008d3361
win: 1000   hl:5    xsum: 0xb9e0  urg: 0    flags: <ACK><PUSH>
 data (19/19): RETR /etc/termcap
```

```
17=========================================================
TCP:   ftp(21) -> 12533          seq: 008d3361  ack: 0b54014b
win: 4096   hl:5    xsum: 0x59e2  urg: 0    flags: <ACK><PUSH>
 data (60/83): 150 Opening data connection for /etc/termcap
  (128.127.2.133,
```

The server reacts by initiating a new connection. Port 20 is the usual choice for the server end of a data connection. Note that port 12534 is used at the client end.

```
18
TCP:  ftp-data(20) -> 12534    seq: 008d4141  ack:     ----
win: 4096   hl:6   xsum: 0x1b11  urg: 0   flags: <SYN>  mss: 1024

19
TCP:  12533 -> ftp(21)          seq: 0b54014b  ack: 008d33b4
win: 941    hl:5   xsum: 0x5634  urg: 0   flags: <ACK>

20
TCP:  12534 -> ftp-data(20)     seq: 06a81434  ack: 008d4142
win: 1024   hl:6   xsum: 0x2e02  urg: 0   flags: <ACK><SYN>  mss: 1024

21
TCP:  ftp-data(20) -> 12534     seq: 008d4142  ack: 06a81435
win: 4096   hl:5   xsum: 0x370c  urg: 0   flags: <ACK>
```

The transfer of the file begins.

```
22
TCP:  ftp-data(20) -> 12534     seq: 008d4142  ack: 06a81435
win: 4096   hl:5   xsum: 0xd0e0  urg: 0   flags: <ACK>
 data (60/1024): #
#
#
#@(#)termcap.src      1.14      (ULTRIX)       3/18/87
#
#
```

The file transfer would now proceed to completion.

11.6 COMMANDS

The set of FTP commands that can be sent over the control connection is summarized in the sections that follow. The set of commands has been growing steadily for years, and has become quite large. However, only a small subset is mandatory. Hosts need not implement all of the commands listed below.

11.6.1 Access Control Commands

The commands and parameters that define a user's access to a remote host's filestore are defined in Table 11.1.

TABLE 11.1 Commands Authorizing a User to Access a Filestore

Command	Definition	Parameter(s)
USER	Identify the user.	Userid
PASS	Provide a password.	Password
ACCT	Provide an account to be charged.	Accountid
REIN	Reinitialize to start state.	None
QUIT	Logout.	None
ABOR	Abort the previous command and its associated data transfer.	None

11.6.2 File Management Commands

The commands in Table 11.2 permit the user to execute typical directory positioning and file management functions at a remote host. The *working directory* is the one in which you are currently located.

TABLE 11.2 Directory Selection and File Management Commands

Command	Definition	Parameter(s)
CWD	Change to another server directory.	Directory name
CDUP	Change to the parent directory.	None.
DELE	Delete a file.	Filename
LIST	List information about files.	Directory name, list of files, or else none to get information about the working directory.
MKD	Make a directory.	Directory name
NLST	List the files in a directory.	Directory name or none for the working directory.
PWD	Print the name of working directory.	None
RMD	Remove a directory.	Directory name
RNFR	Identify a file to be renamed.	Filename
RNTO	Rename the file.	Filename
SMNT	Mount a different file system.	Identifier

TABLE 11.3 Commands That Define the Type, Structure, and Mode

Command	Definition	Parameter(s)
TYPE	Identify the data type and print format (if any) for the transfer.	ASCII, EBCDIC Image/Binary, Non-print, Telnet, ASA
STRU	Organization of the file.	File or Record
MODE	Transmission format.	Stream, Block, or Compressed

11.6.3 Commands That Set Data Formats

The commands in Table 11.3 are used to establish the combination of data format, file format, and transmission format that will be used when copying files.

11.6.4 File Transfer Commands

The commands in Table 11.4 set up data connections, copy files, and support restart recovery.

TABLE 11.4 Commands That Support File Transfer

Command	Definition	Parameter(s)
ALLO	Allocate (reserve) enough storage for data that follows.	Integer number of bytes
APPE	Append a local file to a remote file.	Filenames
PASV	Identify a network address and port to be used for a data connection to be initiated by the client.	IP Address and Port number
PORT	Identify a network address and port to be used for a data connection to be initiated by the server.	IP Address and Port number
REST	Identify a restart marker (to be followed by the transfer command to be restarted).	Marker value
RETR	Retrieve or get a file.	Filename(s)
STOR	Store or put a file.	Filename(s)
STOU	Store unique: create a version of a file with a unique name.	Filename

TABLE 11.5 Miscellaneous User Information Commands

Command	Definition	Parameter(s)
HELP	Return information about the server implementation.	None
NOOP	Asks server to return an "OK" reply.	None
SITE	Used for server-specific subcommands that are not part of the standard, but may be needed at the server's site.	None
SYST	Asks the server to identify its operating system.	None
STAT	Requests parameter information and connection status.	None

11.6.5 Miscellaneous Commands

The final set of commands in Table 11.5 provide helpful information to an end user.

11.7 PERFORMANCE ISSUES

The efficiency of file transfer operations depends on a number of factors:

- Host file system access efficiency
- Processing required to reformat data
- Underlying TCP service

It is very important that an implementation include some internal checking of the status of FTP connections. Systems and communications connections do fail. An FTP process may be orphaned and left hanging for a long time tying up a lot of resources, if the service does not check itself and terminate idle connections.

Note that a brief throughput report usually is printed at the end of a file transfer.

```
226 Transfer complete.
local: rfc1261 remote: rfc1261
4488 bytes sent in 0.037 seconds (1.2e+02 Kbytes/s)
```

A bulk transfer can be initiated in order to obtain a rough measure of TCP and FTP performance.

11.8 RELATIONSHIP OF FTP TO OSI

The OSI File Transfer, Access, and Management (FTAM) standard defines a far higher level of functionality than FTP. Differences in file systems are overcome by defining a generic virtual filestore. The attributes of files are defined in a system-invariant manner.

Some of the FTAM enhancements include:

- FTAM supports the transfer of individual units of data. For example, selected records can be read, updated, added, or deleted.
- Complex file structures such as hierarchical files or files accessed via keys can be defined and used.
- There are commands that enable a user to navigate the file in order to reach specific data to be read or written.
- Rich data structures can be defined, embracing virtually any data type. A unit of data might be a record, a table, or a subtree of information.
- There are mechanisms that support sensitive access control. For example, some users may be able to read only a file's attributes, others may have read access, while others may be able to read and write. Restrictions on concurrent access can be imposed.

The price is that FTAM is complex and difficult to develop. There is a great deal of overhead involved in using FTAM, and its high level of resource utilization is likely to make it a slow performer in its first few implementations.

11.9 TRIVIAL FILE TRANSFER PROTOCOL (TFTP)

There are file copying applications that require a very simple level of functionality.

For example, an initial download of software and configuration files to a diskless workstation or an unconfigured PC is best carried out using a very simple protocol.

The Trivial File Transfer Protocol (TFTP) has proved to be very useful for basic file copying between computers. TFTP transfers data via UDP datagrams. Very little communications software — only IP and UDP — need be running in a computer that participates in a TFTP download. TFTP has proved to be very useful for initializing network devices such as bridges and hubs.

The Trivial File Transfer Protocol:

- Sends 512-octet blocks of data (except for the last).
- Numbers the blocks starting with one.
- Supports ASCII or binary transfers.
- Can be used to read or write a remote file.
- Uses a simple header.
- Has no provision for user authentication!

One partner in a TFTP interaction sends numbered, uniformly sized blocks of data, and the other partner ACKs the data as it arrives. The sender must wait for an ACK of a block before sending the next block. If no ACK arrives within a timeout period, the current block is resent. Similarly, if the receiver does not get any data during a timeout period, an ACK is retransmitted.

11.9.1 TFTP Protocol

A TFTP session starts with a read request or a write request. The TFTP client starts off by obtaining a port and then sends the Read Request or Write Request message to port 69 at the server. The server has the option of choosing a new port to be used for the remainder of the file transfer. The server directs its messages to the client's port. Data transfer proceeds with an exchange of data blocks and ACKs.

A data block consists of a 4-octet header and data. All blocks except for the last must contain 512 octets of data, and this is how end-of-file is signaled. If the file's length is a multiple of 512, then the final block consists of a header and no data. Data blocks are numbered, starting with one. Each ACK contains the block number of the data that it is acknowledging.

11.9.2 Protocol Data Units

There are five types of protocol data units.

1. Read Request (RRQ)
2. Write Request (WRQ)
3. Data (DATA)
4. Acknowledgment (ACK)
5. Error (ERROR)

Error messages signal conditions such as "file not found" or "no space to write file on disk." In most cases, an error message terminates the TFTP transfer.

Each TFTP protocol data unit starts with an operation code identifying its PDU type. The formats for the protocol data units are displayed in Figure 11.3.

Note that the lengths of Read Requests and Write Requests vary, depending on the length of the file name and mode fields, each of which contains an ASCII text string terminated by a 0 byte. The mode field contains "netascii" or "octet."

Read Request:

2 Octets	String	1 Octet	String	1 Octet
Opcode=1	Filename	0	Mode	0

Write Request:

2 Octets	String	1 Octet	String	1 Octet
Opcode=2	Filename	0	Mode	0

Data:

2 Octets	2 Octets	
Opcode=3	Block #	Data

Acknowledgement:

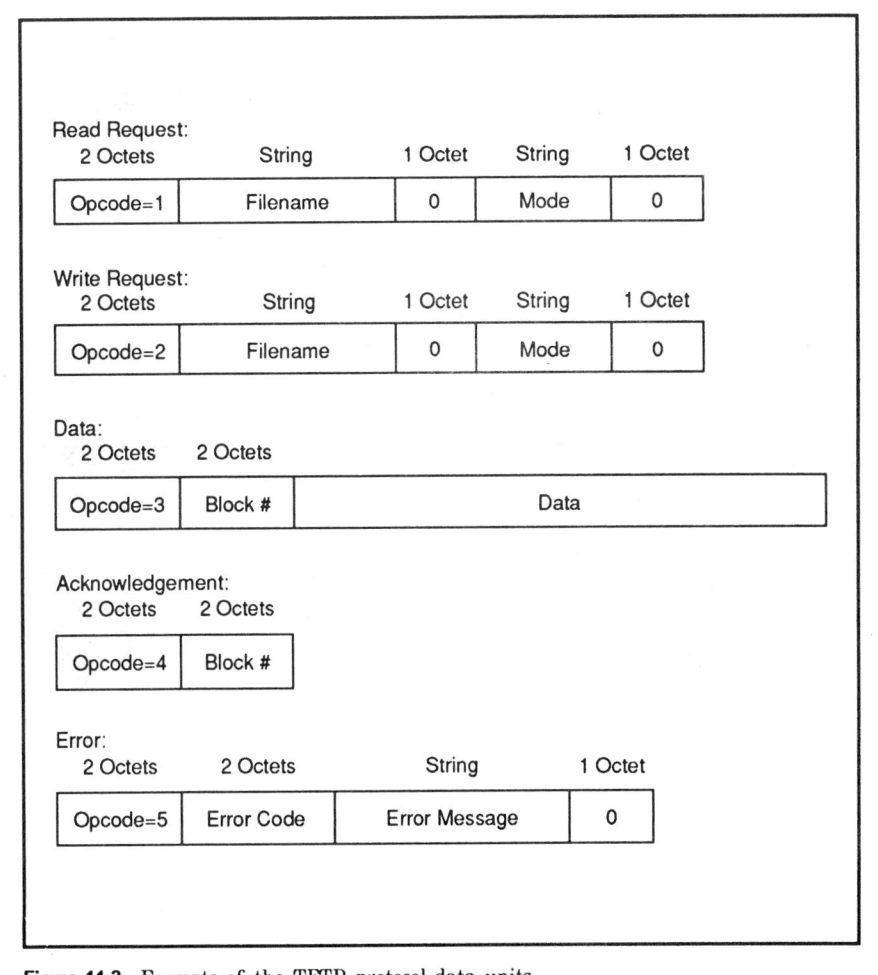

2 Octets	2 Octets
Opcode=4	Block #

Error:

2 Octets	2 Octets	String	1 Octet
Opcode=5	Error Code	Error Message	0

Figure 11.3 Formats of the TFTP protocol data units.

11.10 SCENARIOS

The protocol can be illustrated by means of simple scenarios. The scenario in Figure 11.4 illustrates how a TFTP originator reads a remote file. After the responder sends a block to the reader, the responder will wait until an ACK for the block arrives before sending the next block.

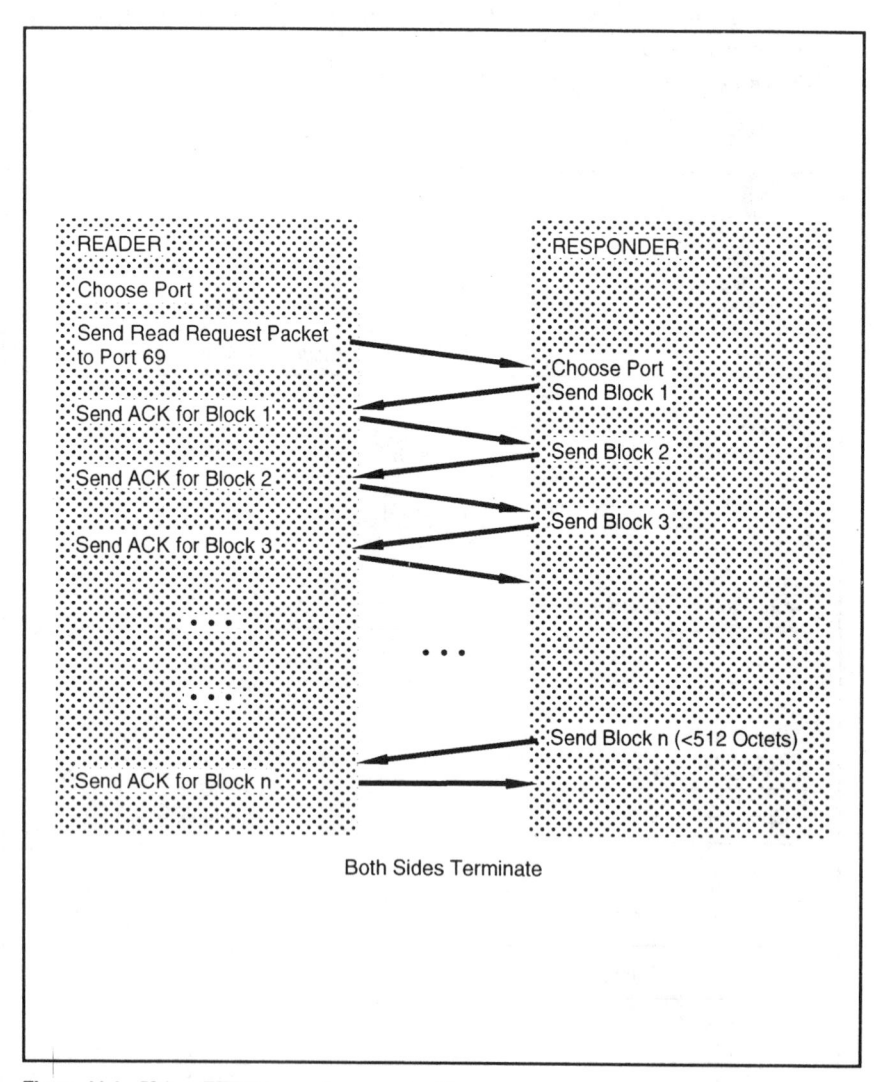

```
READER                                    RESPONDER
Choose Port
Send Read Request Packet
to Port 69
                                          Choose Port
                                          Send Block 1
Send ACK for Block 1
                                          Send Block 2
Send ACK for Block 2
                                          Send Block 3
Send ACK for Block 3
       . . .                                   . . .

                                          Send Block n (<512 Octets)
Send ACK for Block n

                    Both Sides Terminate
```

Figure 11.4 Using TFTP to read a remote file.

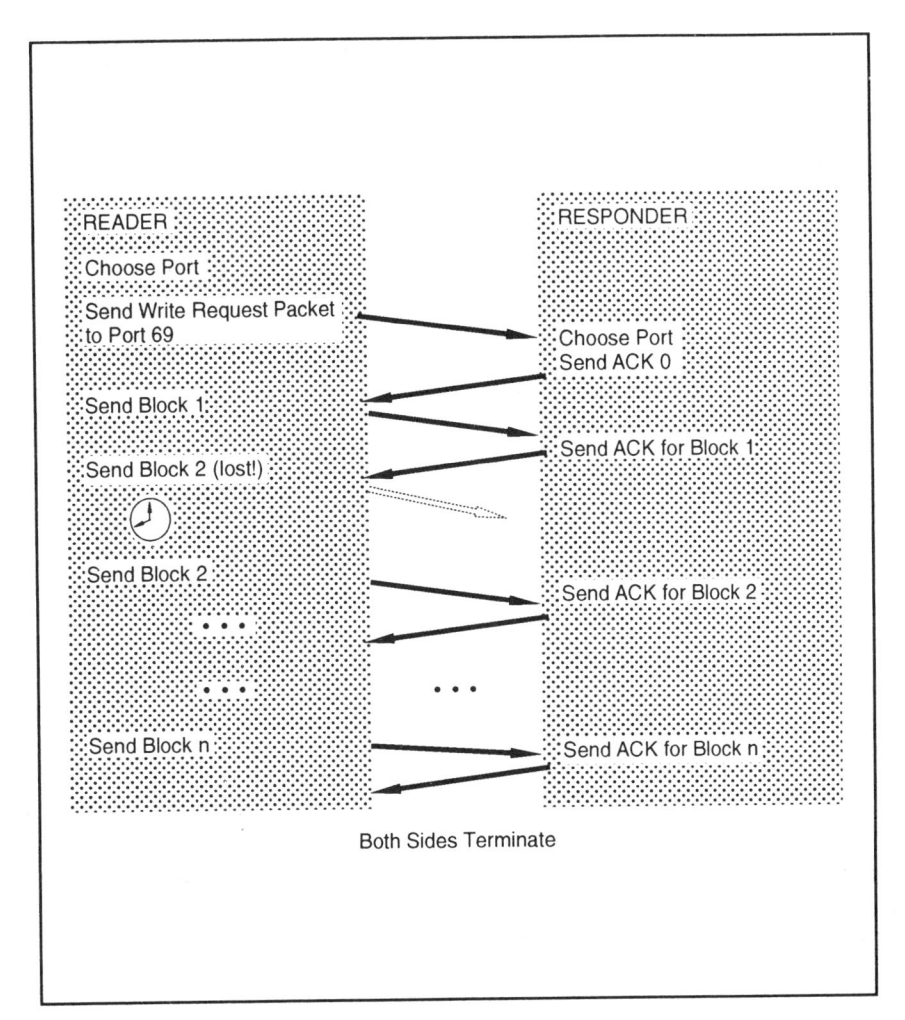

```
                READER                    RESPONDER
                Choose Port
                Send Write Request Packet
                to Port 69       ─────────▶
                                           Choose Port
                                           Send ACK 0
                Send Block 1    ◀─────────
                                 ─────────▶ Send ACK for Block 1
                Send Block 2 (lost!)
                  🕐            ┈┈┈┈┈┈┈▶
                Send Block 2    ─────────▶
                                 ◀───────── Send ACK for Block 2
                     ...                          ...
                     ...                          ...
                Send Block n    ─────────▶
                                 ◀───────── Send ACK for Block n
                          Both Sides Terminate
```

Figure 11.5 Using TFTP to write a remote file.

The next scenario (see Figure 11.5) illustrates a TFTP write. In this example, block 2 is lost, and is resent after a timeout.

11.11 RECOMMENDED READING

RFC 959 defines the File Transfer Protocol, and RFC 783 describes the Trivial File Transfer Protocol. RFC 1068 discusses background file transfer. The ISO File Transfer, Access, and Management protocols were published in ISO 8571.

Chapter

12

NFS, RPC, and NIS

12.1 INTRODUCTION

The computer environment is changing. Instead of dumb terminals tied to a central computer, we find desktop stations, one or more servers, and local area networks.

Users like the convenience, availability, and control that comes with a personal system. But they also want to access common information and share printers. End users generally do not want to be burdened with configuration, update, or backup chores. As a result, today's systems managers coordinate software updates, supervise resources, schedule backups, and configure network parameters for large numbers of computers.

Many organizations have turned to a network operating system for resource sharing and central management. For example, Novell's *NetWare* is a very popular network operating system for DOS computers. Sun Microsystems originally introduced its *Network File System* (NFS) and *Network Information Service* (NIS) to provide resource sharing and configuration services for UNIX workstation LANs.

NFS makes remote file directories appear to be part of the local directory system − remote files are accessed by end users and programs exactly as if they were local. NFS offers many benefits. For example, a single copy of software can be kept at a server and shared by all users. Software updates can be installed at the server, rather than at multiple computers across the network.

NIS provides simple directory services that enable a UNIX administrator to maintain network configuration data at a central server. Figure 12.1 shows a LAN with one central server that provides NFS and NIS services.

241

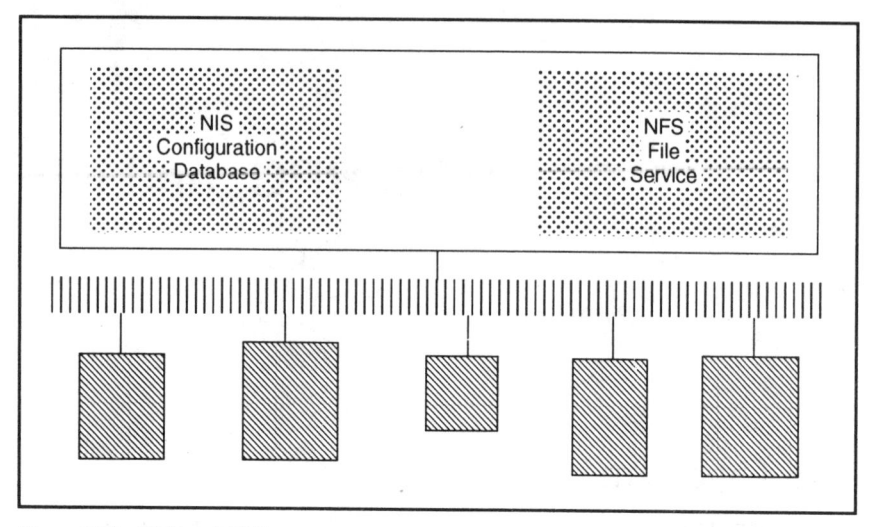

Figure 12.1 NFS and NIS servers.

Sun Microsystems published the protocol specifications for NFS in an RFC,[1] and Sun licenses NFS and NIS software. NFS and NIS have been implemented by most UNIX vendors, and NFS has been ported to many proprietary operating systems. For example, IBM VM, IBM MVS, and DEC VAX VMS systems can act as NFS file servers.

Some vendors bundle NFS client or server software with their TCP/IP products, while others market NFS as an option available for an additional fee.

NFS is built on top of a *Remote Procedure Call* (RPC) facility that supports general client/server applications. Many vendor NFS products include an RPC programming library.

Most TCP/IP products for DOS offer an option that lets a DOS system be an NFS client. Recent releases of Novell's NetWare support both NetWare and NFS file services. Any client that knows either of these protocols can access the server. In particular, both DOS and UNIX clients are supported.

The Open Software Foundation has integrated NFS into its UNIX operating system, OSF/1. The Open Software Foundation also offers a wide area file access protocol, the Distributed File Service (DFS). DFS is part of the Open Software Foundation's Distributed Computing Environment (DCE) and includes a number of advanced features.

---

[1]RFC 1094, Sun Microsystems, Inc., *NFS: Network File System Protocol specification.*

For example, copies of a DFS file can be cached at several locations. This makes it possible to use DFS across an internet as well as on a LAN. A DFS server keeps track of the locations of file copies. There are mechanisms that allows a DFS server to maintain the integrity of distributed files during updates.

12.1.1 NFS Structure

NFS is portable across different hardware, operating systems, transport protocols, and network technologies. However, it was designed with the UNIX file system in mind. UNIX files are stored in a hierarchical tree of directories. A UNIX file is accessed as a sequential stream of bytes. NFS follows this model.

An NFS client host *mounts* a remote directory subtree into its own directory system. This is accomplished by a mount protocol exchange between the client host and server host.

A user or application is not aware of using NFS. When a call is made to perform a file operation (such as open, read, write, copy, rename, delete, etc.) and the file happens to be located at a remote computer, the operating system redirects the request to NFS.

NFS is built on top of the Remote Procedure Call (RPC) protocol, which is important in its own right. RPC enables a client to call a subroutine that is executed at a remote server. RPC has been used to write network versions of many common operating systems calls. For example, a user or program can ask a remote system for the time of day, for a list of logged-on users, or for the length of time the system has been running. NIS services also are built on top of RPC. RPC is defined in RFC 1094 and is an elective Internet protocol.

The final protocol in this family is External Data Representation (XDR). XDR provides a generic way to define and encode parameters so that different types of hosts can understand them. When a client sends an RPC request to a server, the parameters in the request are encoded using XDR. XDR is described in RFC 1014.

Figure 12.2 shows components that support NFS. NFS usually is implemented over UDP, but some recent products are based on TCP connections.

In the sections that follow, we will explore these components from the bottom up. First RPC and XDR, then mount, and finally NFS. We will end the chapter with a description of NIS services.

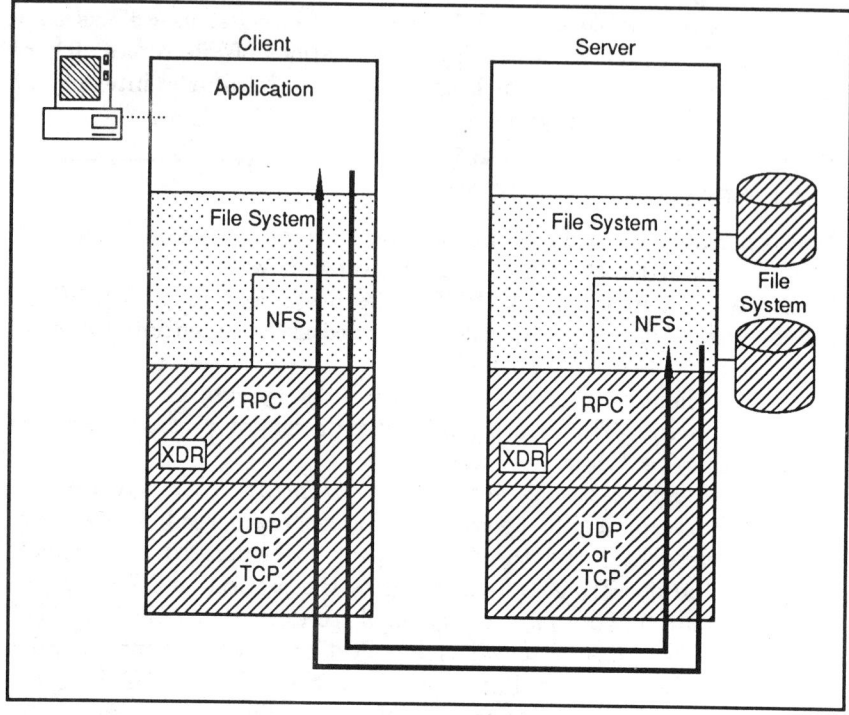

Figure 12.2 Components supporting NFS.

12.2 REMOTE PROCEDURE CALL

Modern client/server applications often are built on top of remote procedure calls. A remote procedure call is modeled on an ordinary subroutine call. For example, in the C programming language, an ordinary subroutine procedure call commonly has the form:

```
return_code = procedure_name(input_parameters, output_parameters)
```

When the procedure is invoked, the code executes using the values stored in the input parameters. If the procedure completes successfully, new values will be stored into the output parameters. The return_code can be used to indicate whether the procedure completed successfully.

When a remote procedure call is used, the local system transmits a request to run the procedure, along with the input parameters, to a remote server that executes the procedure. When its work is complete, the remote server replies, indicating whether the procedure succeeded. If the procedure completed successfully, the response contains the procedure's output parameters.

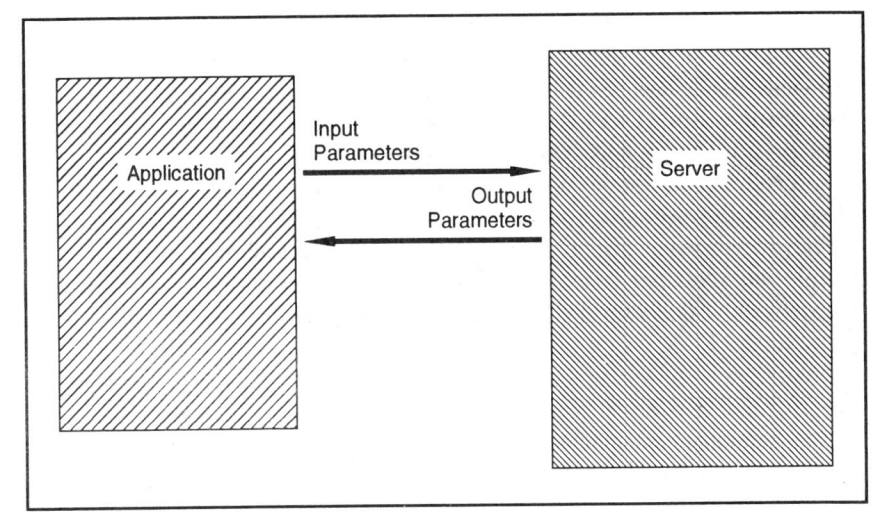

Figure 12.3 A remote procedure call interaction.

Figure 12.3 illustrates this interaction. The Remote Procedure Call protocol defines the mechanisms that make this happen.

12.2.1 RPC Model

A remote procedure call is sent from a client to a server in a formatted message.

An RPC interaction can be *synchronous* or *asynchronous*.[2] In a synchronous interaction, the client waits for the server's reply. Most clients interact in a synchronous manner with their servers. This matches what usually happens when program makes a local subroutine call.

In an asynchronous interaction, the client program does not wait for a response, but continues to execute. The client is notified of the reply by some local mechanism, such as an interrupt.

RPC does not care what transport protocol is used to carry its messages. In the TCP/IP world, RPC runs over both TCP and UDP. RPC could be implemented over other transports, such as ISO TP0 or TP4. RPC hides the actual transport from higher level services like NFS or NIS. This means that client/server applications built on top of RPC are portable. They can run anywhere that RPC can run.

---

[2]Sometimes the terms blocking and non-blocking are used instead of synchronous and asynchronous.

12.2.2 Programs, Procedures, and Versions

An RPC server application is called a *program*. Programs are assigned numeric identifiers. Sun Microsystems assigns program numbers in the (hex) range 0 to 1FFFFFFF. End-user organizations may assign numbers in the range 20000000 to 3FFFFFFF.

A program is made up of a set of *procedures*. A client request identifies the procedure to be run. For example, *read* and *rename* are NFS procedures. The idea is that a procedure should perform one simple well-defined function. The procedures are labeled with integer identifiers. For example, *read* is NFS procedure 6 and *rename* is NFS procedure 11.

Experience shows that over time, programs change. The procedures are refined and more procedures are added. For this reason, a program's version is identified in RPC calls. It is not unusual for more than one version of an RPC service to be running at a server host.

12.2.3 Typical RPC Programs

NFS is probably the best known RPC program. The mount command that is used to glue a remote directory into a local directory system also is implemented as an RPC program. There are lock manager and status programs that provide a crude locking apparatus when users want to update shared files at an NFS server.

Spray is an example of a very simple RPC program. A spray client sends a batch of messages to a remote system and gets a report on the result. The command below sends 100 datagrams to host plum:

```
spray -c 100 plum
sending 100 packets of lnth 86 to plum ...
   in 10.1 seconds elapsed time,
   29 packets (29.00%) dropped by plum
Sent:   9 packets/sec, 851 bytes/sec
Rcvd:   7 packets/sec, 604 bytes/sec
```

The *rusers* program finds out who is logged on at either a selected list of hosts, or at all hosts on the local network. An rusers client broadcasts its RPC call on the LAN. Responses contain a hostname and the host's logged-in users.

```
rusers
zonker.num.cs.yale.edu       leonard  jones  harris
mark.num.cs.yale.edu         davis    sherman
duke.num.cs.yale.edu         burry    victor
. . .
```

12.2.4 RPC Portmapper

An abundance of RPC client/server programs has been written, and more are being written all the time. Well-known ports are becoming hard to get, so how will clients be able to identify this growing family of servers?

The RPC protocol specification introduced a method for dynamically finding out what port a service is using. At each server host, a single RPC program, called the *portmapper*, acts as a clearinghouse for information about the ports that *other* RPC programs use. The portmapper maintains a list of the local active RPC programs, their version numbers, transport protocols, and the ports at which they are operating.

The portmapper program is started up when a server computer initializes. As other RPC services are started, each gets an unused port from the operating system and then tells the portmapper that it is ready to go to work; that is, each registers its port, program number, and version with the portmapper (see Figure 12.4).

The portmapper listens at well-known port 111. When a client wants to access an RPC service, the client sends an RPC message to the portmapper at port 111. The message contains the service's program number, version, and transport protocol (UDP or TCP). The portmapper responds, giving the current port for the service.

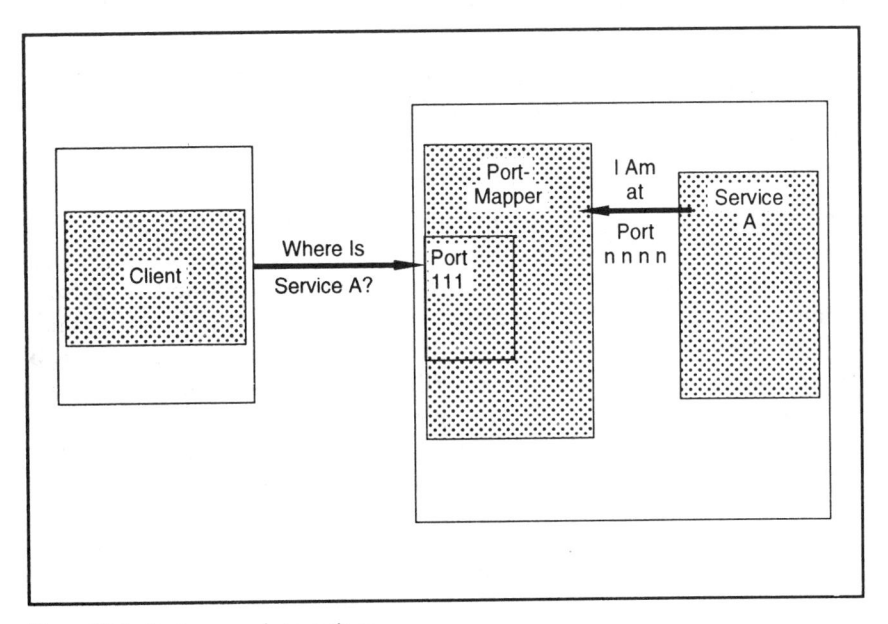

Figure 12.4 Portmapper interactions.

The portmapper also enables some RPC services to be based on broadcast; that is, a client broadcasts an RPC call on a subnet or network. For example, the *rusers* RPC call asks *every* machine on a LAN to report its logged-on users.

But note that the rusers program at each host could be operating out of a different port! What port number should a client put into a call message that it broadcasts?

The answer is that the client wraps its request inside a special call to the portmapper and sends this to port 111. The portmapper relays the request to the service, and then relays the response back to the client. The port number for the service is added to the response, so that future (individual) calls could be sent directly.

The full set of procedures executed by a portmapper program are:

- Return a response that shows that the portmapper is active.

- Return a list of all local RPC programs, their versions, their communications protocols, and their ports.

- Given a specific program number, version, and protocol, return its port.

- Relay an incoming client's request to a local RPC service. Return the result and the program's port number.

- Add a local program, version, protocol, and port number to the list of active servers.

- Remove a local program, version, protocol, and port number from the list of active servers.

12.2.5 Viewing Portmapper RPC Services

The UNIX *rpcinfo* command displays useful information about RPC programs. Other operating systems that support RPC clients provide a similar command. The UNIX version provides a number of subcommands. Each subcommand responds with different information.

The *rpcinfo -p* command shown below gets its information from a portmapper. In fact, *rpcinfo* is a client application that uses remote procedure calls to interact with portmappers and with other RPC servers. Thus, we are using a remote procedure call application to find out about the activities of other remote procedure call applications!

The *rpcinfo -p* command that follows asks the portmapper at host BULLDOG.CS.YALE.EDU for a list of the remote procedure call programs that are running at that host.

The output includes the program number, version, transport protocol, port, and identifier for each program at the server. Note that the portmapper itself is listed first!

```
rpcinfo -p bulldog.cs.yale.edu

   program vers proto    port
    100000   2   tcp      111    portmapper
    100000   2   udp      111    portmapper
    100029   1   udp      657    keyserv
    100005   1   udp      746    mountd
    100005   2   udp      746    mountd
    100005   1   tcp      749    mountd
    100003   2   udp     2049    nfs
    100005   2   tcp      749    mountd
    100026   1   udp      761    bootparam
    100024   1   udp      764    status
    100024   1   tcp      766    status
    100021   1   tcp      767    nlockmgr
    100021   1   udp     1033    nlockmgr
    100021   3   tcp      771    nlockmgr
    100021   3   udp     1034    nlockmgr
    100020   1   udp     1035    llockmgr
    100020   1   tcp      776    llockmgr
    100021   2   tcp      779    nlockmgr
    100021   2   udp     1036    nlockmgr
    100011   1   udp     1070    rquotad
    100001   2   udp     1111    rstatd
    100001   3   udp     1111    rstatd
    100001   4   udp     1111    rstatd
    100002   1   udp     1124    rusersd
    100002   2   udp     1124    rusersd
    100012   1   udp     1127    sprayd
    100008   1   udp     1132    walld
    100068   2   udp     1133
```

The *rpcinfo -b* command broadcasts on the network, asking for all servers running a specific program and version. Below, we ask about version 1 of spray. Spray is program number 100012.

```
rpcinfo -b 100012 1

128.36.12.1      casper.na.cs.yale.edu
128.36.12.28     tesla.math.yale.edu
128.36.12.6      bink.na.cs.yale.edu
. . .
```

RPC programs have a null *procedure 0*, which does nothing but return an "I am alive" response. The *rpcinfo -u* command sends a message to the null procedure of the UDP based spray program, which is program number 100012.

```
rpcinfo -u bulldog.cs.yale.edu 100012
program 100012 version 1 ready and waiting
```

12.2.6 RPC Message Formats

An RPC client sends a call message to a server, and gets back a corresponding reply message. What do these messages need to contain so that the client and server understand each other?

A transaction identifier is needed to match a reply with its call. The client's call must identify the program and procedure that it wants to run. The client needs some way to identify itself and provide credentials that prove its right to invoke the service. Finally, the client's call will carry input parameters. For example, an NFS *read* call identifies the name of a file to be accessed and the number of bytes to be read.

In addition to reporting the results of successful calls, the server must be able to let the client know when its requests are rejected and why. A call may be rejected for reasons such as mismatched versions or a client authentication failure. The server needs to report errors caused by a bad parameter, or a failure such as "unable to find file."

Figure 12.5 illustrates a client interacting with a server program. The client sends a call. When the requested procedure completes, the server program returns a reply.

12.2.7 RPC Authentication

Some services do not need any security protection. An RPC service that lets users find out the time of day at a server can safely be left open to the public. However, services that read and write private files should protect users' data. Some kind of authentication information must be included in file access requests.

RPC authentication information is carried in two fields. The first contains credentials that identify a caller. The second provides space for a verifier that can be used by a caller or responder to prove their identity. For example the verifier could contain an encrypted password and timestamp.

There is no single standard for credentials. It is left to each program's designer to decide what is needed for that program. However, there is an ongoing effort to provide standards in this area.

NFS, RPC, and NIS

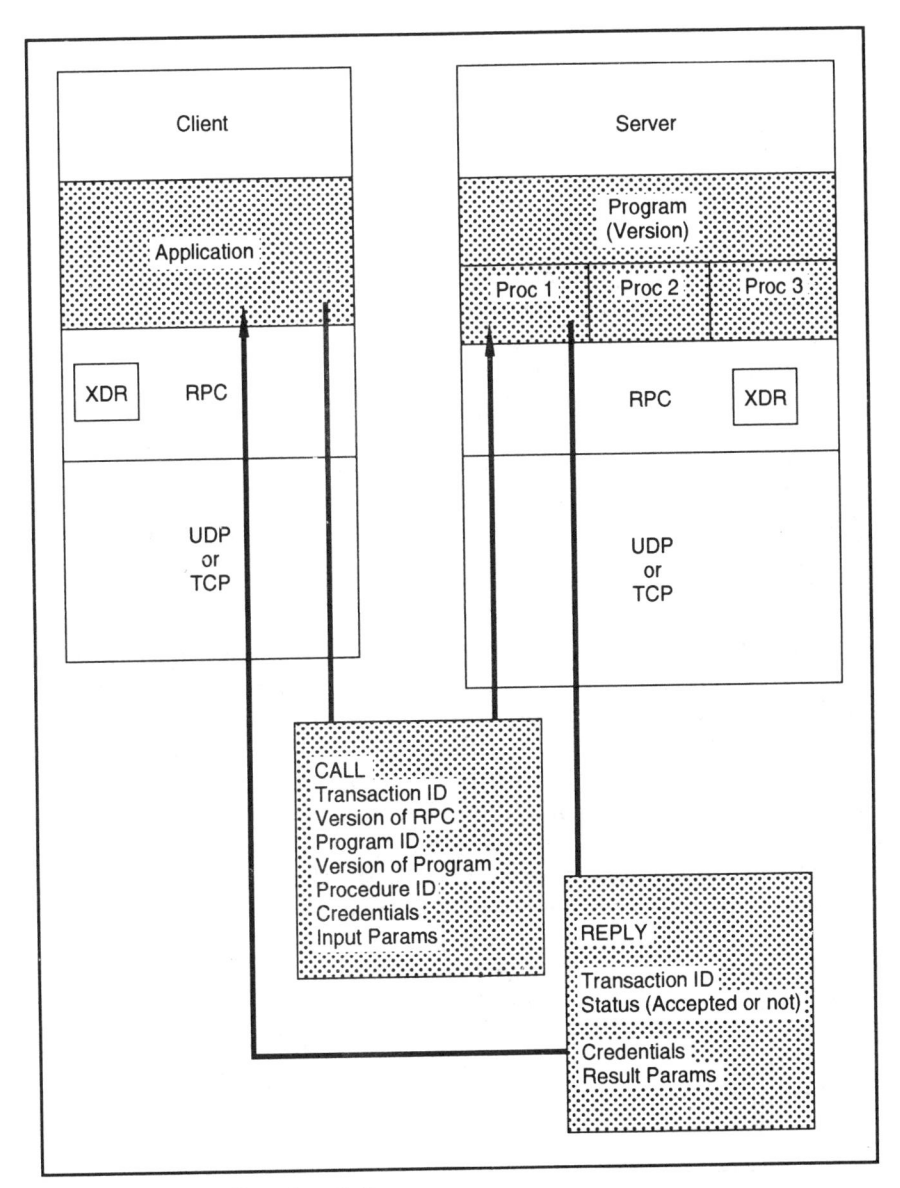

Figure 12.5 Remote Procedure Call messages.

Types of credentials that were described in the original RPC specification are sketched below:

- *NONE:* Access is open.

- *UNIX:* This type is appropriate for access to a UNIX NFS file server. The call contains the name of the caller's machine and a UNIX userid and groupid that are valid at the server machine.[3] Other fields contain anything that the implementer wants to add to improve security.
- *SHORT:* This can contain anything that an implementer wants.
- *DES:*[4] A call message includes a client userid that is designed to be unique across the network, and an encrypted timestamp. The client uses a public encryption key[5] to pass a session key to the server in the first message. Subsequent messages contain a timestamp encrypted with the session key by means of the *Data Encryption Standard* (DES) algorithm.

It is very likely that future versions of Sun's RPC will embrace the Kerberos authentication scheme developed at the Massachusetts Institute of Technology (MIT). The Open Software Foundation supports an RPC that incorporates Kerberos support. Kerberos is described in Chapter 16.

There is a tradeoff between providing secure RPC services and achieving satisfactory performance. Secure RPC is provided through the use of encryption. However, encryption of even a single field can inflict a substantial overhead burden on a service.

Figure 12.6 shows a Sniffer display of the UDP header and RPC fields for an NFS call message that is asking about the attributes of a file. The data link and IP headers have been omitted from the display.

Note that a call is a message of *type 0.* The reply will have *type 1.* The RPC protocol is periodically updated, and so the RPC protocol version is stated. In this call, the version is 2.

The caller uses *UNIX credentials,* which identify its machine and include a UNIX userid and groupid. The *stamp* is an arbitrary identifier created by the caller. The *verifier* field for UNIX authentication is left empty in this message. NFS often is implemented with sketchy authentication because fuller protection would slow down performance.

---

[3]As we shall see later in this chapter, NIS allows a single userid and password to be valid across a selected set of computers on a LAN.

[4]DES stands for *Data Encryption Standard,* which is an encryption algorithm defined by the U.S. government.

[5]In Public Key Encryption, the decryption key is different from the encryption key. As long as the owner keeps the decryption key secret, the encryption key can be made public. Anybody can encrypt a message and send it to the key owner, but only the key owner will be able to decrypt the message.

```
UDP:    ----- UDP Header -----
UDP:
UDP:    Source port = 1023 (Sun RPC)
UDP:    Destination port = 2049
UDP:    Length = 124
UDP:    No checksum
UDP:

RPC:    ----- SUN RPC header -----
RPC:
RPC:    Transaction id = 641815012
RPC:    Type = 0 (Call)
RPC:    RPC version = 2
RPC:    Program = 100003 (NFS), version = 2
RPC:    Procedure = 4 (Look up file name)
RPC:    Credentials: authorization flavor = 1 (Unix)
RPC:      len = 32, stamp = 642455371
RPC:      machine = atlantis
RPC:      uid = 0, gid = 1
RPC:      1 other group id(s):
RPC:        gid 1
RPC:    Verifier: authorization flavor = 0 (Null)
RPC:    [Verifier: 0 byte(s) of authorization data]
RPC:
RPC:    [Normal end of "SUN RPC header".]
RPC:
NFS:    ----- SUN NFS -----
NFS:
NFS:    [Paramaters for Proc = 4 (Look up file name) follow]
NFS:    File handle = 0000070A00000001000A0000000091E3
NFS:                  5E707D6A000A0000000044C018F294BE
NFS:    File name = README
NFS:
NFS:    [Normal end of "SUN NFS".]
NFS:

ADDR    HEX                                             ASCII
0000            DATA LINK AND IP HEADER OMITTED
0010            <-------U   D   P-------->
0020            03 FF 08 01 00 7C  00 00 26 41 51 E4 00 00    .....|..&AQ...
0030    00 00 00 00 00 02 00 01  86 A3 00 00 00 02 00 00    ................
0040    00 04 00 00 00 01 00 00  00 20 26 4B 17 4B 00 00    ......... &K.K..
0050    00 08 61 74 6C 61 6E 74  69 73 00 00 00 00 00 00    ..atlantis......
0060    00 01 00 00 00 01 00 00  00 01 00 00 00 00 00 00    ................
0070    00 00 00 00 07 0A 00 00  00 01 00 0A 00 00 00 00    ................
0080    91 E3 5E 70 7D 6A 00 0A  00 00 00 00 44 C0 18 F2    ..^p}j......D...
0090    94 BE 00 00 00 06 52 45  41 44 4D 45 00 00          ......README..
```

Figure 12.6 Format of an RPC message carrying an NFS request.

254 Chapter Twelve

The parameters for program 100003 (NFS) procedure 4 (look up file name) appear next in the message. The parameters are a file handle and a file name.

A *file handle* is a special identifier associated with a directory or file at the server. We are interested in a file named *README* located in the directory identified by the file handle.

The fields in the call message are encoded using simple XDR format rules which will be discussed in the next section. We can get a feeling for the way that XDR works by looking at some of the examples in the call message. The encodings for two integers and an ASCII text string are shown. The sample fields appear in bold typeface at the bottom of Figure 12.6.

Type = 0 is encoded (in hex) as:

00 00 00 00

RPC version =2 is encoded as:

00 00 00 02

Machine = atlantis is encoded as:

```
(length of string = 8)    a  t  l  a  n  t  i  s
     00 00 00 08         61 74 6C 61 6E 74 69 73
```

The reply shown in Figure 12.7 has a matching transaction identifier. No authentication information is included. The call has been accepted and has completed successfully.

The reply contains a lot of useful information about file *README*. A 32-byte identifier for the file — its *file handle* — is returned. Any further operations on this file will refer to the file using this file handle.

The *mode* is a UNIX field that describes the file type and indicates who may access the file. The mode also declares whether users can read or write the file. If the file is application software, the mode shows whether users can execute the application.

The reply returns additional file attributes such as the file size, last time accessed, and last time updated. We would expect these attributes to be maintained in just about any file system.

12.2.8 Dealing With Duplicate Requests

When an RPC service is based on TCP, requests and responses will be delivered reliably. TCP takes care of assuring that nothing gets lost in transmission.

```
RPC:    ----- SUN RPC header -----
RPC:
RPC:    Transaction id = 641815012
RPC:    Type = 1 (Reply)
RPC:    Status = 0 (Accepted)
RPC:    Verifier: authorization flavor = 0 (Null)
RPC:    [Verifier: 0 byte(s) of authorization data]
RPC:    Accept status = 0 (Success)
RPC:
RPC:    [Normal end of "SUN RPC header".]
RPC:
NFS:    ----- SUN NFS -----
NFS:
NFS:    Proc = 4 (Look up file name)
NFS:    Status = 0 (OK)
NFS:    File handle = 0000070A00000001000A000000005AC9
NFS:                  3298621C000A0000000044C018F294BE
NFS:    File type = 1 (Regular file)
NFS:    Mode = 0100644
NFS:      Type = Regular file
NFS:      Owner's permissions = rw-
NFS:      Group's permissions = r--
NFS:      Others' permissions = r--
NFS:    Link count = 1, UID = 303, GID = 1
NFS:    File size = 130, Block size = 8192, No. of blocks = 2
NFS:    File system id = 1802, File id = 23241
NFS:    Access time        = 10-May-90 20:54:32.036785 GMT
NFS:    Modification time =  3-May-90 18:03:54.008032 GMT
NFS:    Inode change time =  3-May-90 18:03:54.008032 GMT
NFS:
NFS:    [Normal end of "SUN NFS".]
NFS:
```

Figure 12.7 Reply to an RPC message containing an NFS request.

If the service is based on UDP, then the client and server must provide their own timeout, retransmission, and duplicate detection strategies. These will vary, depending on the needs of the application. The application developer can adopt either of the following client strategies:

- If no response is received within a timeout, then just return an error message to the end user. Let the end user try the service again.

- If no response is received within a timeout, resend the request. Repeat until a reply is received or a maximum retransmission limit is reached.

If the client resends, the application developer must provide the server with a strategy to deal with duplicates. The server might:

- Keep no record of what was done in the past. If a request arrives, execute its procedure, even though it may be a duplicate. Note that there are services, such as asking for a user's mail identifier, for which this would be a harmless way to proceed. Of course, the client may end up receiving duplicate replies, but can discard duplicates by keeping track of recently completed transactions.

- Keep a copy of the responses that you have sent during the past few minutes. If a duplicate request arrives and you already have performed the procedure and sent back a response, then send back a copy of the original response. If you are currently performing the procedure, discard the request.

Keep in mind that each client/server application can incorporate whichever strategies fit it best.

12.3 XDR

When heterogeneous machines want to operate in a client/server environment, how can they understand one another's data? For example, an NFS client may want to ask a server to read 1000 bytes of data from some position in a file. How are the parameters of that request encoded?

All of the parameters in Sun RPC messages are defined and encoded using XDR, the eXternal Data Representation protocol. Typical data elements include file or directory names, file attributes such as file size, and integers specifying a number of bytes or position in a file.

The XDR data description language is used to define the datatypes that appear in calls and replies. The XDR encoding rules are applied to these definitions to format the data for transmission.

12.3.1 XDR Data Description Language

XDR definitions are similar to programming language datatypes, and they are quite easy to understand. There are a number of basic XDR datatypes such as unsigned and signed integers, enumerated integers, ASCII strings, booleans, and floating point numbers. The *opaque* datatype is used to carry general octet strings. Encrypted information can appear in an opaque field. More complicated array, structure, and union datatypes are built from the basic datatypes.

An enumerated integer type assigns a meaning to each number on a short list of integers. A simple example of an enumerated integer datatype is the message type (*msg_type*), which identifies whether a message is a call or a reply. This datatype appears in the first field in an RPC message:

```
enum msg_type {
   CALL  = 0,
   REPLY = 1
   };
```

Only one of the enumerated values, 0 or 1, may appear in this field. Entering any other integer into the field would be an error.

The structure that defines the next fields of an RPC message is:

```
struct call_body {
    unsigned int rpcvers; /* The version must be equal to two */
    unsigned int prog;    /* This is the program number      */
    unsigned int vers;    /* This is the program version     */
    unsigned int proc;    /* This is the specific procedure  */
    opaque_auth cred;     /* Credentials, e.g., userid       */
    opaque_auth verf;     /* Verifier for the credentials    */
                          /* This might be an encrypted field */
    /* procedure specific parameters start here */
};
```

12.3.2 XDR Encoding

Call and reply messages for a given version of a program and procedure have a fixed format. You know what kind of data will be in a field by its position in the message. The length of every field must be a multiple of four bytes.

There are many parameters represented by unsigned integers, which occupy 4 bytes. For example, *Procedure = 5* is represented by:

```
            00 00 00 05
```

ASCII strings are encoded as a 4-octet integer that contains the string length, followed by the ASCII characters and padded so that the field's length is a multiple of four. For example, the string *README* appears as:

```
(string length=6) R  E  A  D  M  E  (pad)
   00 00 00 06    52 45 41 44 4D 45 00 00
```

The OSI ASN.1 data definition and encoding standard is very likely to replace XDR in RPC implementations within the next few years. The standard encoding for ASN.1 precedes the data contents of a field with an identifier and length for the field. ASN.1 will be described in Chapter 16.

The advantage of XDR is that data is encoded with fewer bytes. The disadvantage of XDR is that each field must be in a predetermined position.

In contrast, since the standard encoding for ASN.1 includes an identifier and length with each field, it is easy to change the number and positions of parameters, and new program versions easily can be written so that they are backward compatible with old programs.

12.3.3 RPC and XDR Programming Interface

RPC client/server applications are developed using a library of subroutines that create, send, and receive RPC messages. Other library routines are used to convert between the local data representation of message parameters and their XDR format. A typical RPC subroutine is:

```
int callrpc(host, prognum, versnum, procnum, inproc, inparams,
outproc, outparams)
```

The *host* parameter identifies the server system, *prognum* identifies the program, and *procnum* is the procedure to be executed. The input parameters to be sent in the call message are in structure *inparams*. The *inproc* routine will convert the input parameters to XDR format. When the reply arrives, the *outproc* routine will convert the XDR reply parameters to a local format and store them in structure *outparams*.

12.3.4 Other Remote Procedure Call Facilities

The Sun microsystems RPC library is widely available today. The Open Software Foundation offers an RPC function as part of its Distributed Computing Environment. There are several TCP/IP products currently available that include both of these programming interfaces. In addition, vendors such as Netwise offer RPC products that run in many different types of environments.

12.4 NFS MODEL

NFS evolved on UNIX computers and the UNIX environment influenced its design. NFS works best with a hierarchical directory structure.[6] Most often, NFS files are treated as unstructured streams of bytes.[7]

Following UNIX conventions, a *file system* is defined to be a (sub)-tree of directories located on a single physical device. On a UNIX computer, file systems located on various devices are glued together to form the computer's overall directory structure, which has a single root. For example, a UNIX computer named "tiger" might have the directory tree structure shown in Figure 12.8.

UNIX directories and files are identified by pathnames that are formed by listing the names along the path from the root, separating the names by a slash (/). For example, */etc/hosts* and */usr/john/abc* are pathnames.

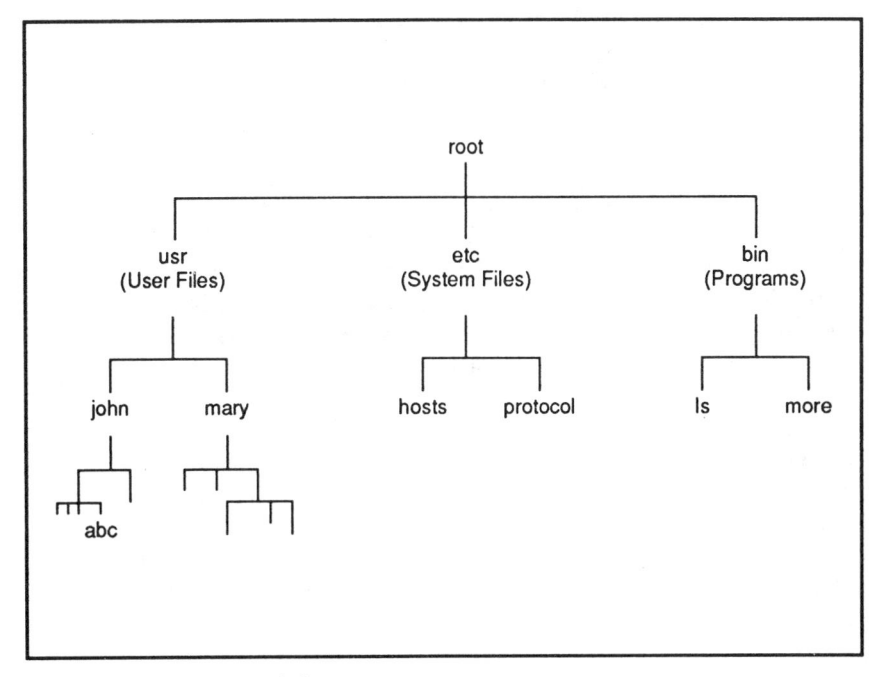

Figure 12.8 Tree-structured directory.

---

[6]There are successful implementations for servers without a hierarchical directory tree. For example, an IBM VM server has a flat file structure.

[7]Version 3 of NFS, which is under current development, uses a slightly more general file system model.

The syntax used to write pathnames on other systems can be different. For example, *E:\WP\LETTER.DOC* is a DOS pathname. NFS assumes that every file can be identified a *pathname*.

Pieces of a UNIX directory system can reside on different hard disks. For example, the root, /, and directory */etc* may be on one physical disk, while */var* and all of its subdirectories are on another. The UNIX *mount* command is used to glue a piece such as */var* into the big tree. A typical UNIX mount command to do this is:

```
mount    /dev/xy0b    /var
```

The files on the physical device *xy0b* are identified with the files in directory */var*.

In designing NFS, it was natural to simply extend the mount command so that remote subtrees also could be glued into a computer's directory tree. For example, suppose a network administrator wants the user files for host *tiger* to be physically located at computer *bighost*, where they will safely be backed up every night. The administrator creates directories for the user's files at *bighost*, say under */tigerUsers*. From *tiger*, the administrator issues the command:

```
mount  -t  nfs  bighost:/tigerUsers    /usr
```

Server directory */tigerUsers* and all of its subdirectories are glued on top of tiger's directory */usr*. To end users, *tiger's* directory system appears as shown in Figure 12.8. However, the file */usr/john/abc* actually is stored in */tigerUsers/john/abc* at server *bighost*. Another way of putting this is that whenever a local user asks for a file that is in a tree under */usr*, the operating system knows that the file really is at *bighost* under */tigerUsers*.

While UNIX directory systems form a single tree, DOS directory systems have multiple trees (a forest?), rooted at devices A:, B:, C:, D:, E:, etc.. DOS computers glue a remote NFS directory onto a device such as E:.

Many other operating systems have hierarchical directories. Those that do not are mapped onto this model by incorporating restrictions on the depth of the tree and on the directory and file name syntax.

12.5 THE MOUNT PROTOCOL

The mount protocol is used to glue a remote directory into the local file system. Mount is RPC program number 100005, and its port is advertised by the portmapper. Mount runs over both UDP and TCP. Before a computer can mount a directory from a server, the server must be configured to *export* the directory. The way that this is typically done is that an administrator creates a file listing the server directories to be exported, the hosts allowed to access them, and the access restrictions to be imposed. For example, a UNIX */etc/exports* configuration file has the form:

```
/man        -ro
/bin        -ro,access=tiger:lion
/tigerUser  -rw,access=tiger
```

The first directory is accessed read-only (ro), and is accessible from any host. Hosts tiger and lion can read the second directory. Host tiger has read-write access to the third directory.

A server can export only its own directories. It cannot export a directory that it has mounted from another NFS server!

A client system can mount directories from as many servers as it likes. Of course, a directory can be mounted only if the server's export restrictions make the directory available to the client.

The client needs to identify all of the remote servers and directories that it wants to mount. Typically, this is done by executing a sequence of mount commands at system startup. Sometimes mount command information is read out of a configuration file. There are many optional parameters for a mount command. The most important select:

- Whether the directory should be mounted read-only or read-write.
- Whether to periodically retry failed mounts in the background and what limit to set on the number of retries.
- Whether a user can interrupt an NFS RPC call that is taking a very long time to complete.
- Whether to use a secure version of NFS that is based on secure remote procedure calls.[8]

A mount command causes an *Add Mount Entry* RPC message to be sent to the server. In the response message, the mount protocol returns the *file handle* that the client will use to identify that directory in all future calls.

Recall that the file handle is a 32-byte string that has meaning for the server system, and enables the server to identify the corresponding

---

[8]To make RPC secure, the client and server first execute a protocol that enables them to securely agree on an encryption key to be used for their interactions. This key is then used to encrypt a timestamp within each client request.

directory. For example, when we mount */tigerUsers* on top of local directory */usr*, the response to the mount request contains a file handle for directory */tigerUsers*.

The full list of procedures supported by a mount server program is:

0. *Null:* Respond showing the program is active.
1. *Add Mount Entry:* An entry for the client is added to the mount list, and a file handle for the mounted directory is returned.
2. *Return Mount Entries:* Reports to the client on the currently mounted pathnames.
3. *Remove Mount Entry:* Removes the mount of a specified directory.
4. *Remove All Mount Entries:* Removes all of the client's mounts.
5. *Return Export List:* Returns a list consisting of directories and the hosts allowed to access each.

12.6 NFS PROTOCOL

The spirit of NFS is that the server should be as *stateless* as possible. What this means is that an NFS server should have a minimum of client information to remember, so that recovery from a client or server crash is painless and simple.

A client knows that the NFS server has completed all of the work for a request when a reply is received. However, what should be done if no reply arrives? NFS usually is built on top of UDP, and UDP is unreliable. Therefore, requests are repeated after a timeout period.

It is possible that the request actually got through to the server but the reply was lost! For this reason, NFS servers usually keep a record of recent transactions so that duplicate requests can be handled correctly.

The current NFS version is 2. The server program number is 100003. By convention, most NFS servers will grab port 2049 when they initialize. However, this is not a well-known port, and the safest course for a client is to check out the NFS port number with the portmapper.

12.6.1 File Handles

Recall that when a client mounts a directory, the mount protocol returns a file handle that identifies that directory in all future calls. The directory that is mounted may have subdirectories, and these may have subdirectories. A file's pathname can be nested several levels deep.

NFS, RPC, and NIS 263

For example, before a user at the client can update the file

/usr/brown/book/chapter3

it is necessary to obtain its file handle from the server. The way that NFS does this is to look up one pathname at a time. For our example, the NFS client would:

- Send a lookup call to the server that includes the file handle for */tigerUser* and pathname component *brown.* The reply contains a handle for */tigerUser/brown.*
- Send a lookup call to the server that includes the file handle for */tigerUser/brown* and pathname component *book.* The server returns a file handle for */tigerUser/brown/book.*
- Send a lookup call to the server that includes the handle for */tigerUser/brown/book* and pathname *chapter3.* The reply contains the file handle that we want!

The result of this long-winded approach to getting to a file handle that we want is that NFS clients issue lots of lookup calls.

12.6.2 NFS Procedures

There are NFS procedures that let a client access, read, and write files. The client can find out about the organization and capacity of the remote file system, and can ask to see the attributes of individual files. The client can delete or rename files. Some of the procedures deal with features provided by the UNIX file system, such as linking an alias name to a file. The NFS procedures include:

0. A null procedure, used to test for server response and timing.
1. Get attributes of a file. The file must be identified by its file handle. File attributes include information such as the owner of the file, access rights of other users, the file size, and the last time that it was modified.
2. Set attributes for a given file. For example, change the access rights of other users.
3. Root procedure – obsolete.
4. Lookup a file. That is, given the file handle for a directory and the name of a subdirectory or file, return the file handle for the subdirectory or file.

5. Get information about a (UNIX) symbolic link, which is an alias pointing to a file.
6. Read a specified number of bytes from a file, starting at a given offset.
7. Write to cache — to be used in the next protocol revision.
8. Write a specified number of bytes to a file, starting at a given offset.
9. Create a file with given attributes in a specified directory.
10. Remove a file from a specified directory.
11. Rename a file.
12. Create a file which is hard-linked to another file. Changes to either file are reflected in both.
13. Create a symbolic link — that is, an alias name for a file.
14. Create a new directory.
15. Remove an empty directory.
16. Read directory entries.
17. Get information about a file system, such as the optimum transfer size, the native block size, and the number of free blocks available.

12.6.3 Special NFS Services

Ideally, NFS should be transparent to a user. Server files are opened, read, written, and closed as if they are local. Ordinary local commands are used to copy, rename, or delete server files.

When the client and server have the same operating system, this is straightforward. Sometimes a few special additional commands make NFS work better when the client and server file conventions are very different. An example may help to clarify this.

When a DOS client uses a UNIX system as a file server, files that are created and named by the DOS client will conform to DOS conventions, and will be a natural part of the client's file system.

If the DOS client wants to read a text file created by a UNIX user, there are some problems. First of all, DOS names consist of up to eight characters optionally followed by a dot and up to three more characters. When a DOS user types a filename, all letters are converted to uppercase. For example, *COMMAND.COM* is a DOS file name. UNIX names can be much longer, and can contain a mixture of upper and lower case letters. For example, *aLongerName.More* is a valid UNIX file name.

How can a DOS user access the UNIX file? Different vendors provide different solutions. For example, FTP Software's *Interdrive* software does an automatic translation of UNIX names so that a DOS *dir* command shows *ALONG~01* for *aLongerName.More*. A DOS user can use this shortened name to work with the file. For example, if server files are attached to disk E:, a user could copy the file to a PC disk with the command:

```
copy e:ALONG~01    c:myfile
```

There are two supplementary FTP Software *Interdrive* commands that make it easier to work with UNIX files. One maps the UNIX name to a name chosen by the user. The other produces a directory listing that shows the true UNIX name of a file as well as its DOS mapped name.

There is still one more hurdle to get over. Lines in a DOS text file end with carriage return and line feed characters while lines in a UNIX text file end with a new line code. Interdrive provides commands *unix2dos* and *dos2unix* to translate between these formats. Other vendors provide similar utilities.

12.6.4 File Locking

There are some files that are accessed by several users. For example, a configuration file may be read by many application processes. A user who needs to update a file will want to obtain exclusive access to the file — that is, lock the file — during the update activity.

File locking in an NFS environment is handled by two RPC services: the lock manager and the status program. The lock manager handles client requests for file locks. A server's status monitor tries to keep track of which client hosts currently hold locks. If a server crashes, it will send notification to the status monitors at registered client hosts, asking them to resubmit their lock requests.

12.6.5 NFS Implementation Issues

A program may repeatedly ask its operating system to read or write a few bytes of data. Accessing a hard disk frequently for small amounts of data is not efficient. Normally, operating systems read in entire blocks of data ahead of time and respond to read calls using data stored in memory. Similarly, writes are saved in memory and periodically written to disk.

Frequent accesses to a remote NFS server for small amounts of data are even more inefficient than local disk accesses. Client NFS implementations perform read-aheads of blocks of data, and perform writes into local memory to reduce the number of RPC write calls.

An NFS server can improve its performance by keeping directory and file attribute information in memory, and reading ahead to anticipate client calls.

12.6.6 Monitoring NFS

The UNIX *nfsstat* command results in a report on NFS activities. Similar commands are available at other operating systems.

In the example shown in Figure 12.9, the local system is acting as both a server and as a client. There is very little server activity reported. However, the system's users are making a large number of client calls.

The display shows the number of uses of each type of call over the monitoring period. Note the large number of lookups. Recall that these calls are used to walk down a file's pathname one step at a time in order to obtain the file handle. Since there are no client writes, it appears that the system has read-only access to its server.

12.7 NETWORK INFORMATION SERVICE

The Network Information Service (NIS) is an RPC-based database directory service designed by Sun Microsystems. NIS has been ported to many UNIX systems. The Open Software Foundation provides a competing database system as part of its Distributed Computing Environment.

NIS databases are called *maps*, and are stored at one or more servers. An NIS map contains a key and some simple information that is matched with the key. Any type of key and information can be stored, but typically a set of NIS maps contains network configuration information. NIS maps are used to translate host names to IP addresses, RPC program names to program numbers, and services (such as FTP) to port numbers.

If an administrator wants to make all of the computers on a LAN appear to be a single machine, then a set of userids and passwords is kept in a central NIS map. The ability to define a network userid and password is extremely helpful in administering a distributed file server/print server environment.

A library of subroutines is installed on a system that is using NIS, so that programs that need to look up information such as IP addresses or RPC program numbers will use NIS maps to replace or supplement the normal configuration files.

```
nfsstat

Server rpc:
calls       badcalls    nullrecv    badlen      xdrcall
160         0           0           0           0

Server nfs:
calls       badcalls
160         0
null        getattr     setattr     root        lookup      readlink    read
0   0%      32  20%     0   0%      0   0%      95  59%     13  8%      7   4%
wrcache     write       create      remove      rename      link        symlink
0   0%      1   0%      1   0%      0   0%      0   0%      0   0%      0   0%
mkdir       rmdir       readdir     fsstat
0   0%      0   0%      3   1%      8   5%

Client rpc:
calls       badcalls    retrans     badxid      timeout     wait        newcred     timers
18825       33          0           1           26          0           0           33

Client nfs:
calls       badcalls    nclget      nclsleep
18799       7           18799       0
null        getattr     setattr     root        lookup      readlink    read
0   0%      5570 29%    0   0%      0   0%      4017 21%    4838 25%    3596 19%
wrcache     write       create      remove      rename      link        symlink
0   0%      0   0%      4   0%      4   0%      0   0%      2   0%      0   0%
mkdir       rmdir       readdir     fsstat
0   0%      0   0%      696 3%      72  0%
```

Figure 12.9 A report of NFS activities.

There also are commands that enable an end user to look up a map entry, or to read the entire contents of a map. NIS used to be called *Yellow Pages*, so the commands characteristically start with *yp*. For example, *ypcat*[9] types out the contents of a database while *ypmatch*

---

[9] On UNIX systems, the *cat* command is used to type out the contents of files.

looks up one entry.

For example, to get a list of names for current maps:

```
ypcat -x
```

```
Use "passwd" for map "passwd.byname"
Use "group" for map "group.byname"
Use "networks" for map "networks.byaddr"
Use "hosts" for map "hosts.byname"
Use "protocols" for map "protocols.bynumber"
Use "services" for map "services.byname"
Use "aliases" for map "mail.aliases"
Use "ethers" for map "ethers.byname"
```

To list out the table of protocols:

```
ypcat protocols
```

```
ospf      89    OSPF      # ospf routing protocol
rdp       27    RDP       # "reliable datagram" protocol
xns-idp   22    XNS-IDP   # Xerox NS IDP
hmp       20    HMP       # host monitoring protocol
udp       17    UDP       # user datagram protocol
egp       8     EGP       # exterior gateway protocol
tcp       6     TCP       # transmission control protocol
ggp       3     GGP       # gateway-gateway protocol
igmp      2     IGMP      # group multicast protocol
icmp      1     ICMP      # internet control msg protocol
```

And finally, to look up the IP address of a host:

```
ypmatch casper hosts
```

```
128.36.12.1      casper.na.cs.yale.edu
```

Implementations of NIS usually can be configured so that if there is no name-to-address translation entry for a particular host in the local NIS map, a call will automatically be sent to a Domain Name Server.

Note that if a host name-to-address translation is entered incorrectly in the local map, the user will just be given the wrong answer. For this reason, administrators should keep only reliable local information in host name maps.

An NIS administrator creates and maintains the maps at a central *master server*. To avoid having a single point of failure for the network, copies of the maps can be exported to one or more *slave servers*. NIS can be configured so that whenever the master maps are

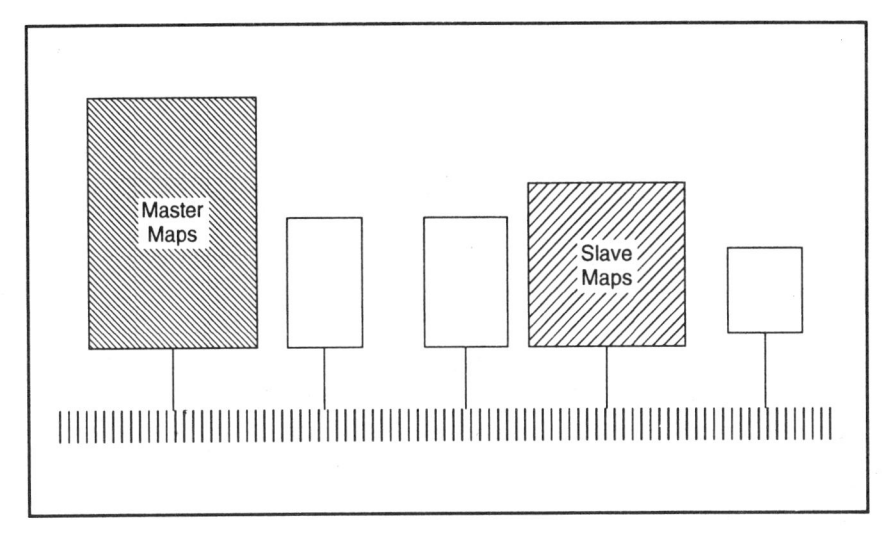

Figure 12.10 NIS master and slave servers.

updated, the revised maps are automatically installed at the slaves.

If a LAN has an NIS server, a client system will broadcast a request during initialization. The first server to answer will be used by the client thereafter. If that server fails, the client just broadcasts a new request for a server. Note that this tends to spread the work around and balance the load across the servers.

12.7.1 Network Information Service Protocol

The NIS protocol is built on top of Remote Procedure Call, External Data Representation, TCP, and UDP. Maps are accessed via RPC program 100004. The primary NIS procedures are:

- Match a key with a value.
- Read the first entry in a map.
- Read the next entry in a map.
- Retrieve all entries in a map.

UDP is used for the first three procedures. TCP is used for the last because it requires a substantial data transfer.

Userids and passwords can be kept in an NIS map. This enables an administrator to control user file access privileges from the master server. There is an RPC program named yppasswd that allows end users to update personal passwords stored at the master NIS server.

12.8 RECOMMENDED READING

NFS is defined in RFC 1094, RPC in RFC 1057 , and XDR in RFC 1014. *Managing NFS and NIS* by Hal Stern is full of useful lore on how to make these protocols work on real systems.

The Open Software Foundation Remote procedure Call facility and Directory Services are described in *Introduction to DCE*, OSF DCE 1.0.

Chapter 13

Telnet

13.1 INTRODUCTION

What use is a network with a rich offering of applications if users cannot login to different computers and use the applications? TCP gives us computer-to-computer connectivity, but there are other obstacles to overcome.

For a long time it seemed as if every computer vendor was determined to market a proprietary environment. An application at a vendor's host could be accessed only by special terminals manufactured by that vendor. The primary purpose of the Telnet protocol is to deal with vendor dissimilarities and let a user connected to any host in a network login to any other host.

The way that this works is that every login session starts off with a simple protocol that lets a client computer talk to a server computer. The client and server proceed to negotiate options that describe the kind of terminal emulation that will be used to access applications at the server. In the years since Telnet was introduced, options for many terminal emulations have been added to the protocol.

13.1.1 Network Virtual Terminal

When a Telnet connection is set up, each end behaves like a very basic *Network Virtual Terminal* (NVT) that has well-defined default characteristics. Eight-bit bytes of data are passed between NVTs. User data consists of streams of 7-bit ASCII characters padded to 8 bits with a 0. Bytes with a 1 in the eighth bit are used for embedded command codes.

Actually, an NVT acts like an old fashioned half-duplex keyboard and printer operating in line-at-a-time mode! (At the time that Telnet was developed, line-at-a-time hardcopy terminals were common.) The protocol is symmetric, so that Telnet also can be used for terminal-to-terminal and application-to-application communications. For example, we already have encountered a hidden subset of Telnet, used to implement the FTP control connection!

In this chapter, we are most interested in Telnet's ability to help a user login to a remote application, so the rest of the discussion will focus on this aspect of Telnet. Although this is a peer-to-peer protocol, for convenience we will refer to the user end of a connection as a *Telnet client* and the application end of a connection as a *Telnet server.*

13.2 TELNET MODEL

As shown in Figure 13.1, a user at a real terminal interacts with its local Telnet client process. The Telnet client exchanges data with the remote Telnet server over a TCP connection. The Telnet server interacts with applications by emulating a native terminal.

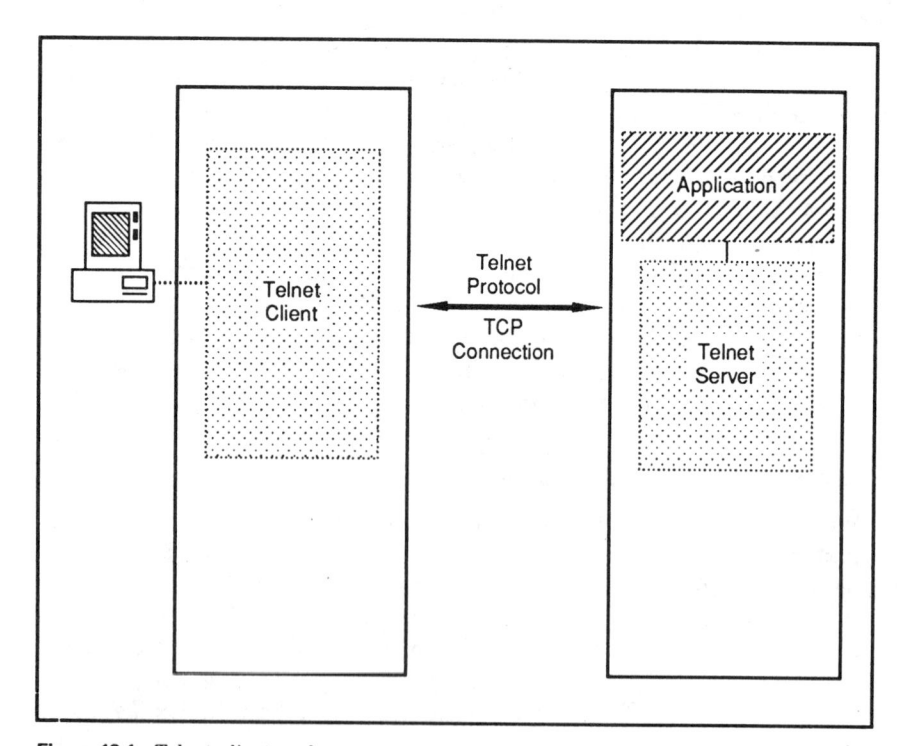

Figure 13.1 Telnet client and server.

13.2.1 NVT Keyboard

A user's terminal appears to be "talking" to a remote application, but input actually is being manipulated by the Telnet client software. The Telnet client translates user input into an appropriate form for the emulation and sends them to the Telnet server.

NVT codes include 7-bit ASCII characters and Telnet commands. At minimum, a user needs a way to enter characters that correspond to all 128 7-bit ASCII codes, as well as control sequences that can be translated to the Telnet commands. After a terminal emulation has been negotiated, the user will need a template that matches local terminal keys to inputs for the emulated terminal.

13.2.2 Dealing With Control Codes

Customarily a user's terminal is monitored by the local operating system, and there are some special control keys that cause the operating system to wake up and take notice. For example, a user may press a backspace key to erase a character while typing a command line. A user may hold down CONTROL key and C at the same time (written ^C) — or some other special function key — to ask the operating system to kill the current application.

During a Telnet session, these control codes need to be passed to the operating system at the *remote* end. The Telnet client must therefore handle all of the raw keystrokes typed by the user, translate them to a standard format, and pass them to the Telnet server. NVT uses control code sequences to support functions such as:

- Send a break or attention signal to the remote process.
- Signal the remote operating system to interrupt the remote process.
- Abort output. Typically, this asks the server application to throw away the rest of the output for the current operation, and take the user back to a prompt.
- Are you there? This means show evidence that the server is still running.
- Erase preceding character. This is used for interactive line editing.
- Erase current line. This is used for interactive line editing.

What if the user's remote session gets very muddled and the user wishes to change the session's characteristics or abort it? *One control code sequence always is reserved to mean "escape to Telnet command mode."* The default sequence frequently is CONTROL and] (^]). This escape sequence can be redefined by the user.

13.2.3 Using Telnet

Most of the time, using Telnet is extremely simple. Below we ask Telnet to connect us to host plum.math.yale.edu. The Telnet client sets up a connection to the Telnet server at well-known port 23 at plum. Telnet reminds us that pressing CONTROL and] (^]) can be used to escape into Telnet command mode. Then the normal login prompt is displayed, and the user proceeds just as if the terminal were directly connected to plum.

```
telnet plum.math.yale.edu
Trying 128.36.12.27 ...
Connected to plum.math.yale.edu.
Escape character is '^]'.
login:
```

That's all there is to it! But read on if you want to know more about what goes on behind the scenes.

13.2.4 Control Codes Sent from the Telnet Server

During a basic NVT session, the Telnet server sends characters and controls to the client's *NVT printer* — that is, the user's display. The output device must be able to represent all 95 ASCII graphics (ASCII codes 32 through 126).

There is a small repertoire of controls for managing an NVT session and manipulating the client's display. A basic NVT interaction is half-duplex, which means that at any time, either the Telnet client or the Telnet server is in charge. After the Telnet client has sent a line terminated by Carriage Return and Line Feed (CR LF), control switches to the server. The Telnet client accepts output from the server, and can enter input again after receiving a *Go Ahead* control code sequence from the server.

At the end of a line of output, the server uses CR and LF to move to the next line of the client's display. The server shapes NVT output using the standard ASCII codes displayed in Table 13.1. In the table, the ASCII codes have been translated to decimal numbers.

Of course, most of the time, the basic NVT is *not* the right terminal to use! The native terminal for a server host may be a VT100, IBM 3270, or other kind of device.

Terminal characteristics are changed by negotiating Telnet *options*. Either side may ask its partner to *DO* a particular option, such as "echo individual characters." The partner can accept or refuse. Either side can volunteer that it *WILL* perform some option. Again, the partner can accept or refuse.

TABLE 13.1 NVT Printer Controls

Description	ASCII Code
Bell, to sound an audible signal	7
Backspace, to move one space left	8
Horizontal tab	9
Line Feed	10
Vertical tab	11
Form Feed (move to top of next "page")	12
Carriage return	13
Null (for filler time)	0

13.2.5 Options

There are four patterns for option negotiation:

DO (option code): Ask partner to perform option.
WILL (option code): Partner agrees. Option now holds.

DO (option code): Ask partner to perform option.
WON'T (option code): Partner refuses. Status unchanged.

WILL (option code): Indicates desire to begin option.
DO (option code): Partner gives permission. Option now holds.

WILL (option code): Indicates desire to begin option.
DON'T (option code): Partner refuses. Status unchanged.
WON'T (option code): Confirms that status will be unchanged.

It usually is at connection startup that a swarm of option requests bounce back and forth between the partners. Occasionally options are exchanged in mid-session.

Some options open the door for later subnegotiations. For example, a client sending WILL TERMINAL TYPE is willing to tell the server about the client's terminal type. If the server wants to see this information, it responds with DO TERMINAL TYPE. At a later time the server can poll for the client's terminal type. The poll can be repeated until either the client provides a type that is acceptable to the server or the client's list of supported types is exhausted. Formal terminal type identifiers such as DEC-VT100, HP-2648, or IBM-3278-2 are defined in the Assigned Numbers RFC.

In the sample dialogue below, we start up Telnet, and use the *toggle options* command to cause Telnet to show us its negotiations. Then the *open* command is used to start a login. The partners negotiate a full-duplex session by suppressing Go Ahead. The client and server agree that they are willing to do terminal type subnegotiations later. The server offers to echo the client's input, and this is accepted.

Neither side waits for an answer to an option request before sending another. A negotiator doesn't even have to respond to options in the same order that they were received. As a result, a series of negotiations sometimes needs to be untangled before it can be understood.

```
telnet
telnet> toggle options
Will show option processing.

telnet> open cantor.cs.yale.edu
Trying 128.36.12.26 ...
Connected to cantor.cs.yale.edu.
Escape character is '^]'.

SENT do SUPPRESS GO AHEAD
SENT will TERMINAL TYPE (reply)
RCVD do TERMINAL TYPE (don't reply)
RCVD will SUPPRESS GO AHEAD (don't reply)
RCVD will ECHO (reply)
SENT do ECHO (reply)

login:
```

13.3 TELNET COMMAND PROTOCOL

Telnet commands are represented by an *Interpret As Command* (IAC) byte followed by one or more code bytes. Interpret As Command is X'FF, or, in decimal, 255.

Table 13.2 lists acronyms for commands discussed earlier, along with the decimal values of their codes. Each would be preceded by 255 when sent across the Telnet connection.

13.3.1 The Telnet Synch

A user who interacts with a local operating system to interrupt a process gets immediate attention. However, an Interrupt Process control sequence may be buried in a Telnet or TCP buffer at the source or destination. How can we distinguish information that needs

TABLE 13.2 Telnet Command Codes

Acronym	Command	Code
BRK	Break	243
IP	Interrupt Process	244
AO	Abort Output	245
AYT	Are You There	246
EC	Erase Character	247
EL	Erase Line	248
GA	Go Ahead	249

to be noticed quickly?

The Telnet *synch* mechanism can do the job. A *Data Mark*, which is the sequence 255 242, is inserted into the data stream. The TCP header carrying the sequence contains an urgent data flag set to one, and its urgent data pointer points to the end of the Data Mark. This tells the server application to quickly scan the data leading to the Data Mark, looking for a control such as *IP*, *AO*, or *AYT*. Normal processing resumes with data past the Data Mark.

13.3.2 Negotiating Options

More than 20 RFCs have been written detailing options that define specialized features such as characteristics of IBM 3270 or 5250 terminals, parameters for X.3 Packet Assembler/Disassemblers (PADs), or properties of data entry stations. An implementation is not required to support all, or even most of these options, but there are several that are important:

- *Transmit Binary:* Begin transmitting 8-bit binary data. If an *IAC* escape character is part of the data stream, it should be doubled in order to be interpreted as data. If an IAC is followed by a command code, then it is interpreted as an embedded command. IBM 3270 sessions are conducted in binary.

- *Terminal Type:* The partners agree that the server can poll later for the types of terminal that the client can emulate. Terminal information is requested and carried in subnegotiation commands.

- *Suppress Go-Ahead:* Abandon Go Ahead control. This is used to enter a full-duplex interaction, or else to switch to some other special control dictated by the terminal type to impose half-duplex operation.

- *Echo:* The server process will echo characters back to the client's display. When operating as an NVT, characters entered at the keyboard are displayed immediately by the local system.

- *Status:* The partners agree that either will be allowed to poll for the current option settings. A status request and response are carried in a subnegotiation exchange.

- *End of Record:* The partner receiving DO END-OF-RECORD will use a standard control code of IAC 239 to denote end of record in its data stream.

- *Window Size:* The partners agree that the client can later send subnegotiation reports informing the server of the width and height of a screen window, measured in characters. This feature is useful when a Telnet session is run at a windowing station.

- *Extended Options List:* This feature prepares for a time in the future when all possible option codes (0 to 254) have been exhausted. It allows new options to be expressed in subnegotiations.

13.3.3 Encoding Option Requests

Option requests are encoded with three bytes consisting of *Interpret as Command* (IAC), the request, and an option code. For example, the decimal representation of the sequence for *WILL TERMINAL TYPE* is:

```
IAC       WILL   TERMINAL TYPE
255       251    24
```

This is one of the options that open the door to subnegotiation. Later on in the session, there could be a subnegotiation exchange:

```
SERVER:
IAC SB    TERMINAL-TYPE    SEND IAC  SE
255 250       24            1   255  240
CLIENT:
IAC SB    TERMINAL-TYPE    IS   DEC-VT220 IAC SE
255 250       24            0   DEC-VT220 255 240
```

TABLE 13.3 Negotiation and Option Codes

Negotiation Codes	
Request	Code
WILL	251
WON'T	252
DO	253
DON'T	254
SB Subnegotiation	250
SE End of subnegotiation	240
Codes for Major Options	
Command Option	Code
Transmit Binary	0
Echo	1
Suppress Go Ahead	3
Status	5
Terminal Type	24
End of Record	25
Window Size	31
Extended Options List	255

Table 13.3 displays the decimal values for the negotiation codes and the codes for the most important options. Subnegotiation parameters are defined in a variety of RFCs dealing with Telnet options, and are listed in the *Assigned Numbers* RFC.

13.4 TELNET DIALOGUES

Most of the time you will use Telnet simply by entering *telnet "hostname"*. From time to time, you may want to interact with Telnet to set or display its parameters, or check the status of your current session.

The dialogue that follows illustrates a typical Telnet user interface. You can find out about your own implementation by entering *telnet*

280   Chapter Thirteen

and typing "?" or "help" to find out about your local commands.

It is a good idea to take note of your keyboard escape sequence. This will allow you to suspend your login session at any time, go into Telnet command mode, and make changes to the environment.

```
telnet

telnet> ?
Commands may be abbreviated.  Commands are:

close           close current connection
display         display operating parameters
mode            try to enter line-by-line or character-at-a-time mode
open            connect to a site
quit            exit telnet
send            transmit special characters ('send ?' for more)
set             set operating parameters ('set ?' for more)
status          print status information
toggle          toggle operating parameters ('toggle ?' for more)
z               suspend telnet
?               print help information

telnet> open plum.math.yale.edu
Trying 130.132.23.16 ...
Connected to plum.math.yale.edu.
Escape character is '^]'.

login: xxxxxxxx
Password: xxxxxxxx
Last login: Sat Dec 28 06:30:44 from golem.cs.yale.ed
Sun UNIX 4.2 Release 3.4 (Plum-EGP) #3: Tue Aug 2 10:25:24 EDT 1988
*****************************************************************
*
*           Welcome to the Yale Mathematics Department's Fabulous
*
*                          ** Plum **
*
*****************************************************************
You have mail.
```

At this point we will enter the escape sequence and look at the attributes that have been established for this session.

```
^]
telnet> status
Connected to plum.math.yale.edu.
Operating in character-at-a-time mode.
Escape character is '^]'.
```

```
^]
telnet> display
will flush output when sending interrupt characters.
won't send interrupt characters in urgent mode.
won't map carriage return on output.
won't recognize certain control characters.
won't process ^S/^Q locally.
won't turn on socket level debugging.
won't print hexadecimal representation of network traffic.
won't show option processing.

[^E]    echo.
[^]]    escape.
[^?]    erase.
[^O]    flushoutput.
[^C]    interrupt.
[^U]    kill.
[^\]    quit.
[^D]    eof.

logout
Connection closed by foreign host.
```

13.4.1 3270 Logons

IBM mainframe applications are written for a terminal type such as IBM-3278-2 or IBM-3279-3. Telnet 3270 emulation uses binary transmission and End of Record codes. There also is an elective 3270-REGIME option that allows a sender to offer a list of supported terminal types.

Often 3270 Telnet access is implemented as a separate program, and must be invoked with a command other than *telnet*, such as *tn3270*. The dialogue below shows option negotiation for a 3270 logon to an IBM VM host.

```
tn3270

tn3270> toggle options
Will show option processing.

tn3270> open uoft.utoledo.edu
Trying...
Connected to uoft.utoledo.edu.

RCVD do TERMINAL TYPE (reply)
SENT will TERMINAL TYPE (don't reply)
Received suboption Terminal type - request to send.
Sent suboption Terminal type is IBM-3278-2.
RCVD do END OF RECORD (reply)
```

```
SENT will END OF RECORD (don't reply)
RCVD will END OF RECORD (reply)
SENT do  END OF RECORD (reply)
RCVD do  BINARY (reply)
SENT will BINARY (don't reply)
RCVD will BINARY (reply)
SENT do  BINARY (reply)

RUNNING
```

13.5 RELATIONSHIP TO OSI

OSI's Virtual Terminal Service supports remote terminal access capability. As might be expected, the OSI standard is far more complex than Telnet, allowing for elaborate virtual terminal environments to be established.

OSI defines:

- An A-mode of operation which resembles full-duplex manipulation of a virtual keyboard and display.
- An S-mode of operation, which models synchronous, two-way alternate dialogues.

The OSI negotiation process has been formalized to a far greater degree than Telnet's. However, the basic OSI negotiation scenario of *invite/accept/reject* is similar to the Telnet DO/DON'T/WILL/WON'T. There is a very large number of options which may be used to describe an OSI virtual terminal.

OSI puts sets of options together into predefined profiles. An entire virtual terminal environment can be established quickly by means of a profile selection. This avoids prolonged negotiation exchanges at the beginning of every session.

13.5.1 Other Technologies

There are well-established technologies that compete with the OSI Virtual Terminal standard. The X Window System designed and developed at the Massachusetts Institute of Technology enables a user to run several concurrent applications in windows at the user's display. X Windows does not care where an application is located. Each application may in fact be running in a different computer on the network.

The X Window protocol provides a uniform way for applications to handle input and output that is restricted to a display window. It is designed to be independent of hardware, operating system and network type. Current implementations run over TCP/IP.

The protocol can run in a workstation or on a multiuser computer that controls bit-mapped displays. There also are dedicated X Window terminal products. X Window support is very widespread, and there are highly functional application development tools available. X Window development tools frequently are bundled with TCP/IP products.

Another current trend dispenses with an application's need to drive a user's terminal. Client/server applications are being developed to totally localize control of the user interface within a process at the user's workstation. A server application exchanges data with a client application without any concern for how input data was entered or how output data will be displayed.

Many vendors offer toolkits for developing client/server applications in a TCP/IP environment.

13.6 RECOMMENDED READING

RFC 854 defines the Telnet protocol. Options defining different terminal types have been published in: RFC 1205 for 5250 emulation, RFC 1096 for X display location, RFC 1053 for the X.3 PAD option, RFC 1043 for data entry terminals, and RFC 1041 for 3270 regimes.

The terminal-type option is explained in RFC 1091, and the window size option can be found in RFC 1073. RFC 1184 describes the Telnet linemode option. RFCs 855 through 861 describe other frequently used options.

Chapter 14

Electronic Mail

14.1 INTRODUCTION

Of all of the TCP/IP applications, electronic mail engages the largest number of people. When an organization offers good access to mail, usage grows explosively. Mail attracts users who never dreamed that they would login to a computer!

Electronic mail is a convenient way to reach people, and normally is easy to use. The dialogue below shows a very simple interaction with a UNIX mail program. The program prompts for the Subject:, and the user signals the end of the message by typing a period as the only character on a line.

```
mail Fred
Subject: New Materials
The manuals have arrived.
Let's discuss them next week.
```

There are mail programs that are far more elegant, with a full screen user interface and point-and-click options. The formal name for a mail program is a *User Agent*. A User Agent is expected to perform several chores: display information about incoming mail messages that are waiting in a user's *mailbox*, save incoming or outgoing messages in local files, prompt a user for the recipients or subject of a message, and provide a good editor for entering message text.

The style of User Agent that an individual prefers has always been viewed as a matter of personal taste, and not subject to standardization. The important thing is that the end result always is the same — mail items are sent and delivered.

Let's return to our original mail transaction. It all looks very easy, but there is a lot of muscle hiding behind the scenes. As it happens, "Fred" is a *nickname* or *alias*, not a real recipient identifier. How will my mail program find out Fred's real identifier?

It will turn out that Fred is not a user at my computer. Where should his mail be sent? How will the mail be moved from computer to computer? When my mail message is delivered, will his program understand its format?

The first problem is solved easily. The User Agent looks up Fred in a file of mail alias names. Aliasing is not standardized, but most mail products let users create private alias files and also support a public alias file that is maintained by a mail administrator. For example, an alias database is one of the maps routinely installed at a Network Information System server.

We shall see that there is a generic format for Internet mail recipient identifiers. However, software vendors and public mail service providers have expressed a lot of individuality in designing their own recipient formats. There are mail gateways that are kept very busy converting between these formats. A widely available mail transfer program named *sendmail* can perform conversions between lots of different name formats.

Usually a recipient identifier contains a strong clue pointing to where the recipient is located. Once we know where Fred is, we have to figure out how to get the mail to him. One way to do this is to transfer the mail across a direct TCP connection between the source host and recipient host. Sometimes it is more convenient to relay the mail via one or more intermediate hosts.

The Simple Mail Transfer Protocol (SMTP) is a recommended Internet standard for moving mail between computers. Over the next few years, we can expect to see mail relayed by means of both SMTP and the new CCITT/OSI X.400 protocols.

When the mail arrives, Fred's User Agent will need to understand message elements such as the sender's identifier, date sent, or subject. The Agent must display the text contents correctly.

The venerable *Standard for the Format of ARPA Internet Text Messages* has provided the durable pattern used for Internet mail messages for a decade. However, this format only supports 7-bit ASCII text messages. Recently defined extensions support multi-part messages that can contain documents created by word processors, images, or encoded audio.

It is very likely that the versatile X.400 message format and message transfer protocol will be phased in gradually over time.

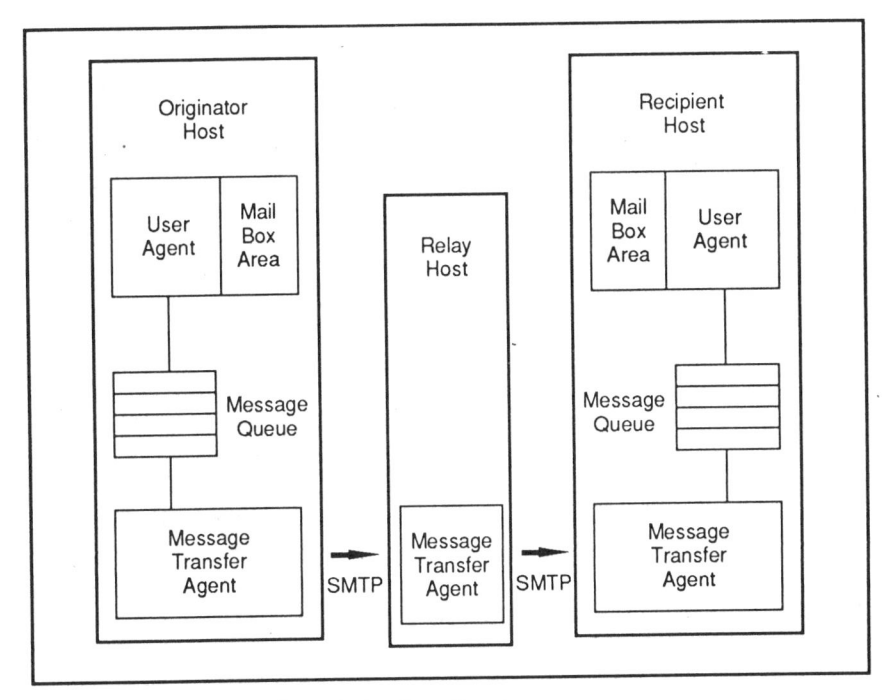

Figure 14.1 Components of an electronic mail system.

14.2 MODEL FOR MAIL OPERATIONS

Figure 14.1 shows the elements of a mail system. Mail is prepared with the help of a User Agent application. The User Agent typically queues mail to a separate application, called a *Message Transfer Agent*, which is responsible for setting up communications with remote hosts and transmitting the mail. *User Agent* and *Message Transfer Agent* are terms used in the X.400 message system standards. These terms denote entities that are valid for SMTP mail as well.

The mail may be sent directly between the source and destination Message Transfer Agents, or relayed via intermediate Message Transfer Agents. When a mail item is relayed, the entire message is transmitted to an intermediate host, where it is stored until it can be forwarded at a convenient time. Mail systems that use relaying are called *store-and-forward* systems.

At the recipient host, mail is placed on an incoming queue, and later is moved to a user's *mailbox* storage area. When a user invokes a User Agent program, the User Agent usually displays a summary of incoming mail that is waiting in the mailbox.

14.2.1 Relaying Mail

Why would a Message Transfer Agent ever want to relay mail rather than connect directly to the recipient host? When a host uses a direct connection, it can be sure that mail has reached its destination. Relayed mail uses intermediate storage resources, and requires multiple connections. To relay mail, we have to design a store-and-forward mail relaying road map, and if we do not do a good job, mail will wander around in an inefficient manner.

14.2.2 A Mail Relay Scenario

Before abandoning store-and-forward, let's look at the scenario illustrated in Figure 14.2. John, who works for ABC Industries, is sending mail items to Mary, Sue, and Philip. John's computer is a LAN workstation that is powered down much of the time. The workstation sends and receives mail via a relay server on the LAN.

Mary works for a JCN Computers, a company that is very security-minded. JCN allows mail to be exchanged with the outside world only via a designated relay host. The company's network is attached to the outside world by a router that blocks all traffic except for connections to the relay computer's mail port.

Sue works for TeleMatique in France. John's company, ABC Industries, relays transatlantic mail to a collection point and batches the mail over during low-cost night hours.

John, Mary, and Sue are connected to TCP/IP networks that use Internet mail standards. However, Philip's company, XYZ Insurance, has an SNA network and has adopted IBM's PROFS electronic mail system. XYZ has connected a host to the Internet, and uses this host as a mail relay gateway that translates between PROFS mail and Internet mail.

This scenario illustrates that relaying offers a number of benefits:

- PCs and workstations can depend on a relay system to forward outgoing mail and hold their incoming mail for them.
- A company can participate in mail while guarding its network.
- Cost savings can be realized by batching mail from a relay at favorable times.
- A mail relay can perform protocol translations.

In the sections that follow, we will look at some of the mechanisms that have evolved within the TCP/IP protocol family to support naming and routing in an expanding electronic mail universe.

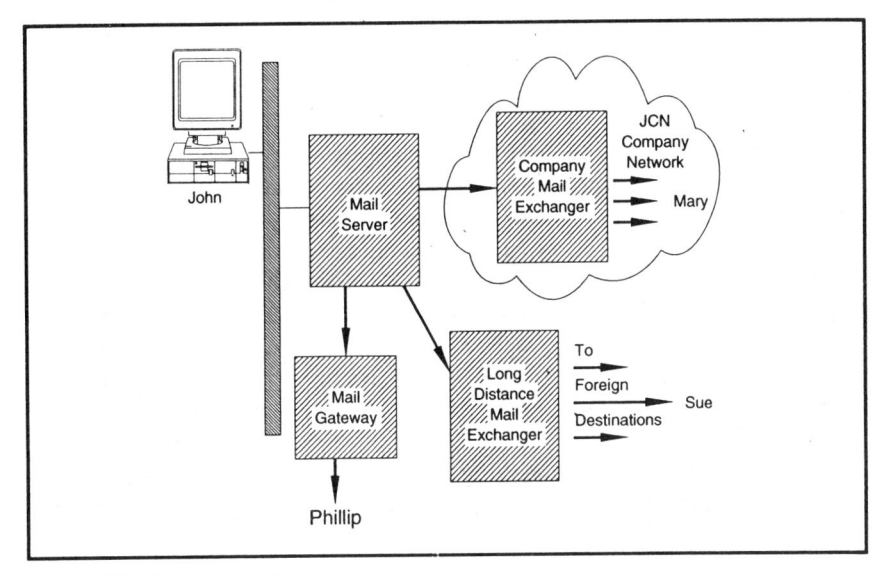

Figure 14.2 Mail relay points.

14.3 NAMES AND MAIL DOMAINS

It is the job of a mail system to deliver messages to a recipient's mailbox. A reply to a message is sent to an originator's mailbox. The Internet mail standards quite properly view mailboxes as the sources and destinations of mail. However, most of us think of mail sources and destinations as human originators and recipients. We will depart a little from the formal language of the Internet standards, and use the terms *originator* and *recipient* instead of *mailbox* in our discussions.

Internet mail recipients are identified by names following the general pattern:

local-part@domain-name

The format of the local-part is allowed to vary depending on the domain.

Returning to our original message, the recipient name Fred turns out to be an alias for *jonesc@tiger.cs.yale.edu*. This is a special case of the general form, and follows the pattern:

userid@host-domain-name

This is a popular pattern for Internet names. However, an organization may not want to advertise its userids and host names to the world. Using a *logical* naming scheme that follows the general pattern, local-part@domain-name, can improve the security of a network. Logical names also permit users to acquire new userids or move to different computers without changing their mail identifiers.

The domain-name part of an Internet mail name may be a logical name that identifies a *mail domain*, rather than a computer. A Message Transfer Agent looks up the domain-name in a database (typically at a Domain Name Server) in order to discover if there is a *mail exchanger* host to which mail should be relayed.

When mail reaches a mail exchanger, the local-part will be looked up in an alias file and converted to a userid and host name — or whatever type of mail identifier is used in the destination network.

In the dialogue below, the *nslookup* command is used to find the identity of a mail exchanger that corresponds to the mail domain name FTP.COM. In order to switch to queries about mail servers, the query type is set to *MX*, meaning *Mail eXchanger*. The Domain Name Server first displays its own name and address, and then prints the host name and IP address of a mail exchanger for FTP.COM.

```
nslookup
> set type=MX

> ftp.com
Server:   DEPT-GW.CS.YALE.EDU
Address:  128.36.0.36

FTP.COM            preference = 10, mail exchanger = babyoil.ftp.com
babyoil.ftp.com    inet address = 128.127.2.105
```

14.3.1 The Mail Domain Tree

Recall that Internet planners created a hierarchical tree for naming administrative domains and hosts. This structure allowed responsibility for naming to be delegated to various subauthorities. A similar tree is used for Mail Domains. Figure 14.3 shows part of the Internet mail domain tree.

14.3.2 Role of a Mail Exchanger

A mail exchanger can buffer incoming mail for PCs and workstations, collect outgoing mail from assorted originators for efficient batching to remote locations, and provide a safe point of entry to the outside world.

The local-part of a name optionally can be a nickname that hides the actual userid and location of the recipient from external partners.

```
                              ROOT
                   ┌────────────┴────────────┐
                  COM                       EDU
          ┌────────┼────────┐        ┌───────┼───────┐
         FTP      SCA     CISCO   BERKELEY PURDUE   YALE
```

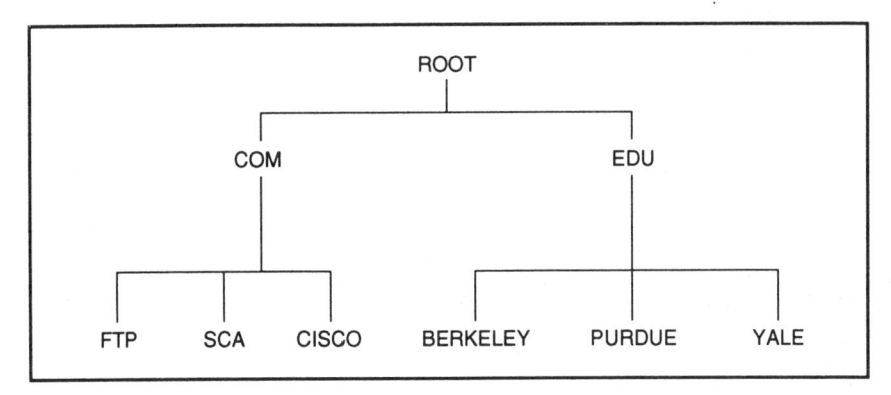

Figure 14.3 Part of a mail domain tree.

At the mail exchanger, the local-part can be translated to the real recipient identifier before the mail is relayed to its true destination.

A mail exchanger also can act as a gateway to external non-Internet style mail services. The proprietary naming formats associated with vendor mail products and commercial mail services can be encapsulated in the local-part of the Internet identifier.

What about mail from the outside world that is directed to an internet-style recipient? Each type of external mail system has its own unique way of letting its users direct mail to a mail exchanger gateway. The gateway needs special software to perform identifier translation.

It is a good idea for an organization to set up backup mail exchangers in order to keep mail transfer active while the primary exchanger is offline.

The following Domain Name System dialogue shows that mail domain PURDUE.EDU has three exchangers. A sender must attempt to connect to the exchangers in order of preference number, starting with the smallest number. Host ARTHUR.CS.PURDUE.EDU is the preferred exchanger for PURDUE.EDU.

```
> purdue.edu
Server:  DEPT-GW.CS.YALE.EDU
Address:  128.36.0.36

purdue.edu          preference = 1, mail exchanger = arthur.cs.purdue.edu
purdue.edu          preference = 2, mail exchanger = ector.cs.purdue.edu
purdue.edu          preference = 5, mail exchanger = merlin.cs.purdue.edu
arthur.cs.purdue.edu    inet address = 128.10.2.1
ector.cs.purdue.edu     inet address = 128.10.2.10
merlin.cs.purdue.edu    inet address = 128.10.2.3
```

14.4 SMTP MAIL TRANSFER PROTOCOL

The Simple Mail Transfer Protocol (SMTP) defines a straightforward way to move mail between hosts. There are two roles in the SMTP protocol: sender and receiver. The sender establishes a TCP connection with the receiver. The well-known port used for a receiver is 25.

During an SMTP session the sender and receiver exchange a sequence of commands and responses. First they identify their host domain names. Then the sender executes a mail transaction by:

- Identifying the mail originator.
- Identifying the mail recipients.
- Transmitting the mail data.
- Transmitting a code that indicates that the item is complete.

At the end of a transaction, the sender can:

- Start another transaction.
- Reverse roles so it becomes the receiver.
- Quit and close the connection.

14.4.1 Mail Scenario

The scenario that follows shows a dialogue in which a sender transfers one message to a receiver. The mail item that is delivered is:

```
From brown@plum.math.yale.edu Mon Dec 30 14:31:28 1991
Received: from Plum.MATH.YALE.EDU by TIGER.CS.YALE.EDU via SMTP; Mon,
 30 Dec 91 14:31:23 -0500
Received: by plum.math.yale.edu; Mon, 30 Dec 91 14:29:47 EST
Date: Mon, 30 Dec 91 14:29:47 EST
From: Herbert Brown <brown@plum.math.yale.edu>
Message-Id: <9112301929.AA19891@plum.math.yale.edu>
To: <whoisit@tiger.cs.yale.edu>
To: <jonesc@tiger.cs.yale.edu>

Good morning.
This is a message from a user at plum.
```

The sender opens a connection to the receiver's mail port, port 25, and the receiver starts the dialogue by transmitting its domain name.

The command/reply model that we have seen in FTP also applies here, and the encoding of the reply messages is similar. To make the dialogue easier to follow, transmissions from the sender and receiver have been marked with S: and R: respectively.

Note that the protocol uses angle brackets to enclose identifiers (e.g., <brown@plum.math.yale.edu>). Host names appear in both upper and lower case. Host names are assumed to be insensitive to case. However, a user name may be case sensitive, depending on the user naming convention for any given type of host.

R: 220 tiger.cs.yale.edu Sendmail 3.2/ ready at Mon, 30 Dec 91 14:31:28 EST

When the connection is opened, the receiving system identifies itself.

S: HELO PLUM.MATH.YALE.EDU

R: 250 tiger.cs.yale.edu Hello PLUM.MATH.YALE.EDU, pleased to meet you

The sender provides an ID and the receiver accepts it, repeating its own ID.

S: MAIL FROM:<brown@PLUM.MATH.YALE.EDU>

The mail originator identifier is sent.

R: 250 <brown@PLUM.MATH.YALE.EDU>... Sender ok

The receiver saves it and responds "OK."

S: RCPT TO:<jonesc@TIGER.CS.YALE.EDU>
R: 250 <jonesc@TIGER.CS.YALE.EDU>... Recipient ok

A recipient is identified. The receiver saves the identifier and responds "OK."

S: RCPT TO:<whoisit@TIGER.CS.YALE.EDU>

A second recipient is identified. The receiver checks.

R: 550 <whoisit@TIGER.CS.YALE.EDU>... User unknown

S: DATA

There is no one by that name at the host.

R: 354 Enter mail, end with "." on a line by itself

S: Good morning.
S: This is a message from a user at plum.
S: .

The mail data consists of lines of ASCII text, each ending with carriage return and line feed. Any of the 128 7-bit ASCII codes can be used (the high-order bit is set to 0).

R: 250 Mail accepted
S: quit
R: 221 tiger.cs.yale.edu delivering mail

14.4.2 Timestamps and Return Address

When you receive mail, there are a number of things that you probably will want to know. Who sent it? What time was it sent? When did it arrive at my computer? SMTP adds this information to your message. SMTP also keeps track of all of the hosts that relayed the message and the time that each received the message.

When a message is passed to an SMTP Message Transfer Agent, the agent inserts a timestamp at the beginning of the message. Each time that an item is relayed, another timestamp is inserted. Each timestamp shows:

- The identity of the host that sent the message.
- The identity of the host that received the message.
- The date and time that the message was received.

Keep in mind that the date and time in a timestamp will be valid for the location where the host resides. Timestamp implementations are notoriously sloppy. Formats vary, and diverse information is included by different vendors. Computer clocks are sometimes inaccurately set, so that some timestamp sequences won't appear to make very good sense. Since network administrators usually are the only people who pay attention to timestamps, the anomalies are tolerated.

When the mail arrives at its final destination, the receiver optionally may add a line that identifies the original sender.

The example that follows illustrates how lines are added at the top of a message. The first line was added by the UNIX mail system and shows the identifier of the originator:

craig@tiger.cs.yale.edu

The timestamps should be read from the bottom up. The first was written by the originating host's SMTP Message Transfer Agent when it received the message from the local mail User Agent. Then the message was shipped to BULLDOG.CS.YALE.EDU, which wrote its stamp. Next the message went to the recipient system, PLUM.MATH.YALE.EDU.

```
From craig@tiger.cs.yale.edu Fri Jan  5 13:46:14 1992
Received: from BULLDOG.CS.YALE.EDU by PLUM.MATH.YALE.EDU;
  Fri, 5 Jan 92 13:45:59 EST
Received: from TIGER.CS.YALE.EDU by BULLDOG.CS.YALE.EDU;
  Fri, 5 Jan 92 13:29:10 EST
Received: by TIGER.CS.YALE.EDU;
  Fri, 5 Jan 92 13:28:12 EST
```

14.4.3 SMTP Commands

The scenario in section 14.4.1 contained the most frequently used SMTP commands. The complete set of SMTP commands is defined below.

A command is transmitted as a 4-character mnemonic. Many commands are followed by a parameter.

A session between SMTP partners employs Telnet Network Virtual Terminal (NVT) conventions such as sending 7-bit ASCII characters in 8-bit bytes and ending a line with carriage return and line feed.

- *HELO:* Identifies the sender to the receiver.
- *MAIL:* Starts a mail transaction and identifies the mail originator.
- *RCPT:* Identifies an individual recipient. The command is repeated in order to identify multiple recipients. If possible, the receiver checks the validity of the recipient name and indicates the result in the reply message. An immediate check is not practical at a relay host. If it later turns out that some recipient was not valid, a brief mail item reporting the error will be sent back to the originator.
- *DATA:* The sender is ready to transmit text. An SMTP implementation must be able to send and receive messages that are up to 64 kilobytes in length. A larger maximum size is desirable, since mail often is used to copy files between users.
- *VRFY:* Asks the receiver to confirm that a name identifies a valid recipient.
- *EXPN:* Asks the receiver to confirm that a name identifies a mailing list, and if so, to return the membership of that list. This command is purely informational, and will not add to the current list of recipients.
- *HELP:* Asks the partner for information about its implementation, such as the list of commands that are supported.
- *NOOP:* Asks the partner to send a positive reply.
- *QUIT:* Asks the partner to send a positive reply and close the connection.
- *TURN:* Asks the partner to switch roles and become the sender. The partner is allowed to refuse.
- *SEND:* If the recipient is logged in, deliver a mail item directly to the recipient's terminal.
- *SOML:* Send or Mail – if the recipient is logged in, deliver direct to the terminal. Otherwise, deliver as mail.

- *SAML:* Send and Mail – deliver to the recipient's mailbox. If the user is logged in, also deliver to the terminal.
- *RSET:* Abort the current mail transaction, clearing out all originator and recipient information.

14.4.4 Reply Codes

The SMTP reply codes are structured in very much the same way as the FTP reply codes. The codes are made up of three digits. The first digit indicates the status of the command:

- 1yz Positive Preliminary reply (currently not used in SMTP)
- 2yz Positive Completion reply
- 3yz Positive Intermediate reply
- 4yz Transient Negative reply ("try again")
- 5yz Permanent Negative reply

The second digit classifies the reply:

- x0z In reply to a problem, this indicates a syntax error or unknown command
- x1z Reply to information request such as help
- x2z Reply referring to the connection
- x3z Unspecified as yet
- x4z Unspecified as yet
- x5z Reply that indicates the status of the receiver mail system

The meaning of the third digit varies depending on the command and the first two digits.

14.5 INTERNET MESSAGE FORMAT

The standard for the format of Internet text messages, defined in RFC 822, is straightforward. It consists of a set of header fields (most of which are optional), followed by a blank line, followed by the text or *body* of the message. A header field has the form:

Field-name: Field-contents

Field names and contents are expressed using ASCII characters. There are many header fields. A representative sample includes:

- Received
- Date
- From
- To
- cc
- bcc (blind cc)
- Message-Id
- Reply-To
- Sender (if not the message creator)
- In-Reply-To
- References (to earlier Message IDs)
- Keywords
- Subject
- Comments
- Encrypted

We expect every message header to include *Date*, *From*, and *To* fields. *Received* fields are constructed using the timestamp information gathered as mail is transferred between Message Transfer Agents. Most mail software can create a message identifier that is included in the message. For example:

Message-Id: <9112301929.AA19891@plum.math.yale.edu>

The Message-Id is designed to be unique across the network. To achieve this, it usually includes the originating host's domain name, along with an alphanumeric identifier. *Resent* fields are added if a message is forwarded. For example, Resent-To, Resent-From, Resent-cc, Resent-bcc, Resent-Date, Resent-Sender, Resent-Message-Id, and Resent-Reply-To.

14.5.1 The Post Office Protocol

The Post Office Protocol (POP) can be used to transfer mail between desktop stations and a mail server. Under POP, a user's outgoing mail is transferred to the server by means of SMTP.

However, POP provides a lot of extra functions when a user retrieves incoming mail. The user can view the list of waiting items and their sizes and can selectively retrieve and delete mail items.

14.6 MAIL ISSUES

14.6.1 Performance

Mail services use memory, disk, processing, and transmission bandwidth resources. A mail service is enormously useful, and traffic can be expected to build steadily.

Messages must be saved while they await transmission or relay. At a recipient host, mail sometimes is kept in a public storage location until users login and access their mailboxes. It can be hard to predict the amount of storage that will be consumed in supporting a mail application.

Since mail handling is automated, items could conceivably sit in a Message Transfer Agent's queue forever. It is important to define timeouts for every mail activity, to prevent black holes from swallowing up computer resources.

14.6.2 Deficiencies in the Internet Standards

The Internet standards define a solid mail service, but users have a right to expect more. ASCII text is fine for short notes, but you might want to send along a picture or a digitally encoded voice message. For important transactions, you may need a delivery confirmation service that indicates whether the mail has reached the recipient system, and whether it has been viewed by a recipient. Business users are accustomed to having a priority mail service that guarantees to get mail to its destination within a fixed time.

The next-generation X.400 mail service is ready to come on stage and perform these functions.

14.7 X.400

The International Telegraph and Telephone Consultative Committee (CCITT) operates under the International Telecommunications Union, an agency of the United Nations. The CCITT is charged with supporting international telegraph, telex, and telephone connectivity. As noted in Chapter 4, the CCITT is responsible for the X.25 data communications standards.

Every four years, the CCITT holds a plenary assembly. At that time, it produces a list of *questions* for study and consideration. The results of four years of deliberation emerge as *recommendations* that can be approved for publication.

The CCITT established a study group that met during the 1981 to 1984 period and developed the X.400 set of recommendations for an international electronic message handling service. These recommendations were comprehensive, and were subsequently adopted by ISO. The standards were updated in 1988, but most current implementations are based on the 1984 specification. Some of the characteristics of X.400 are:

- Definition of a general store-and-forward service that can be used for electronic mail (which they call *interpersonal messaging*) as well as for other applications.
- Global, international scope for message delivery, and support for international alphabets.
- The ability to send many information types besides text, such as binary, image, or digitized voice.
- If the sender wishes, notification of delivery to a recipient system and detailed non-delivery notices. There is an optional feature that can signal that the recipient end user has received[1] the mail.
- Support for mail priority.
- The ability to convert a message to a different medium — for example, deliver via FAX or convert to hardcopy and use postal delivery.
- Definition of user-friendly identifiers for originators and recipients.
- Use of a formal envelope that contains fields that can be used to trace messages and gather other mail management information.

X.400 can be viewed in three ways. It defines a standard for the exchange of mail between administrations recognized by the CCITT.[2] It defines an elegant architecture that can be the basis for a new generation of mail products. It also can be seen as a gateway standard. If every vendor of a proprietary mail system provided software that converted their messages to X.400 messages, then users of any of these products could exchange messages.

14.7.1 X.400 Message

Unlike the Internet standards, X.400 does not rely on 7-bit ASCII and NVT conventions. Fields are formatted using the ISO Basic Encoding

---

[1]What it means to receive a message is deliberately left undefined. This could mean anything from observing a summary of the contents of the mailbox, to pressing a function key to acknowledge receipt.

[2]For example, national Postal, Telephone, and Telegraph (PTT) administrations.

Standard that will be described in Chapter 15. This encoding introduces each field with a hex identifier code and length value. Figure 14.4 shows an outline for a sample message that illustrates general features of the X.400 format.

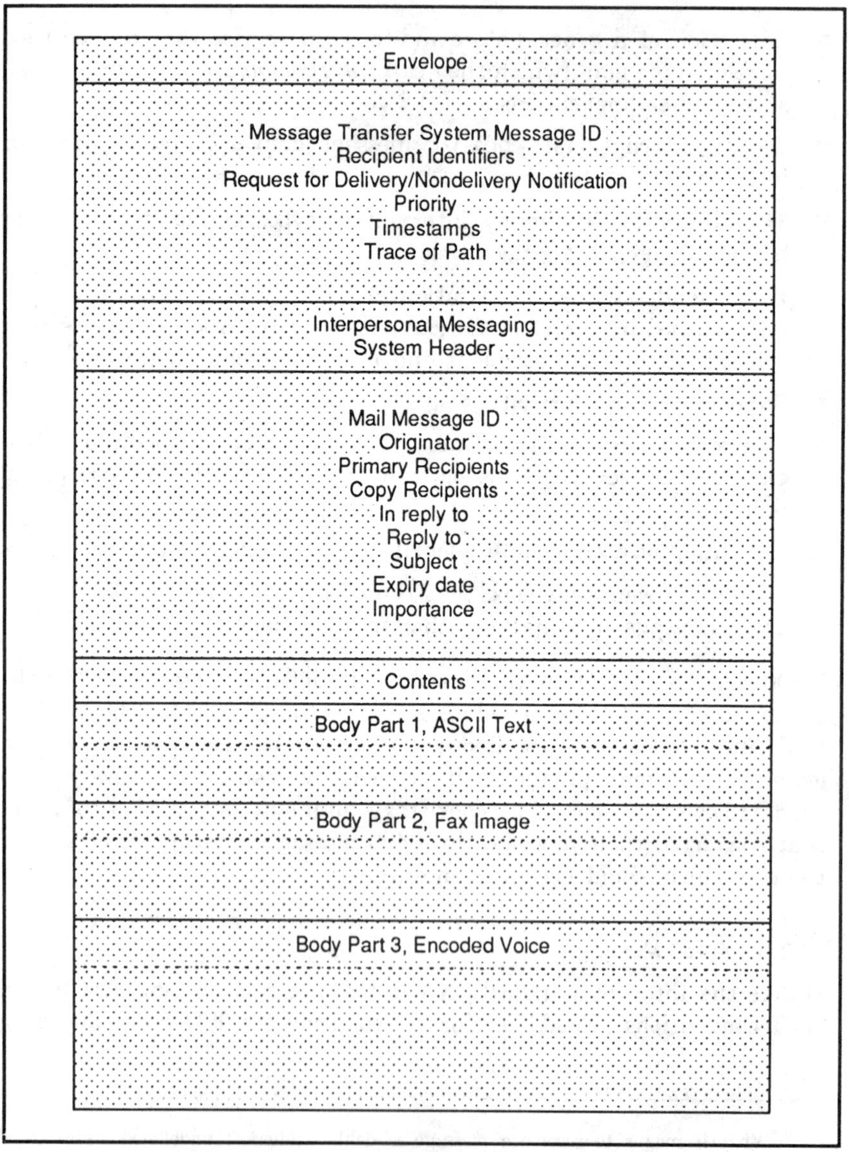

```
┌─────────────────────────────────────────────────┐
│  ┌───────────────────────────────────────────┐  │
│  │               Envelope                     │  │
│  ├───────────────────────────────────────────┤  │
│  │      Message Transfer System Message ID   │  │
│  │              Recipient Identifiers         │  │
│  │    Request for Delivery/Nondelivery Notification │
│  │                  Priority                  │  │
│  │                 Timestamps                 │  │
│  │                Trace of Path               │  │
│  ├───────────────────────────────────────────┤  │
│  │          Interpersonal Messaging           │  │
│  │              System Header                 │  │
│  ├───────────────────────────────────────────┤  │
│  │              Mail Message ID               │  │
│  │                 Originator                 │  │
│  │             Primary Recipients             │  │
│  │              Copy Recipients               │  │
│  │                In reply to                 │  │
│  │                  Reply to                  │  │
│  │                  Subject                   │  │
│  │                Expiry date                 │  │
│  │                Importance                  │  │
│  ├───────────────────────────────────────────┤  │
│  │                 Contents                   │  │
│  │          Body Part 1, ASCII Text           │  │
│  │                                            │  │
│  │          Body Part 2, Fax Image            │  │
│  │                                            │  │
│  │         Body Part 3, Encoded Voice         │  │
│  │                                            │  │
│  └───────────────────────────────────────────┘  │
└─────────────────────────────────────────────────┘
```

Figure 14.4 Format of an X.400 Interpersonal Message.

14.7.2 X.400 Naming

How do you identify people when you refer to them in conversation? You might say "Mary Jones, who is a Technical Consultant at the Milwaukee unit of MCI Telecommunications Corporation." Or you might say "Jacques Brun, who lives at 10 Rue Centrale in Paris, France." The drafters of X.400 wanted to define a universal naming system that would correspond to the natural way that people are identified.

An X.400 originator or recipient name is a list of attributes. The standard defines many optional attributes which may be used in various combinations. The attributes that are expected to be most prevalent in electronic mail systems are:

- Country Name
- Administration Domain Name
- Personal Name (e.g. John H. Jones III)
- Organization Name
- Organizational Unit Names
- Private Domain Name
- Domain Defined Attributes

Private domains include facilities such as commercial electronic mail services and corporate electronic mail systems based on proprietary mail products.

Domain-defined attributes allow names used by existing mail systems to be embedded in an X.400 identifier. This is an important feature. It allows an X.400 gateway to switch mail between proprietary mail systems as well as between a proprietary system and an X.400 compliant system.

14.7.3 Interworking Between X.400 and Internet Mail

Since both X.400 and Internet mail are store-and-forward services, mail can be passed between these services by means of mail gateways. Several RFCs have been written that deal with mapping between the Internet message format and X.400 message format.

Further refinements will be added as experience with real mail gateway implementations grows. Elements of the mapping include:

- Direct translation between elements supported by both services, such as Date, To, From, cc, bcc, Subject, Message-Id, and so forth.

- Definition of additional RFC 822 header fields corresponding to new header fields defined for X.400 such as Converted Indication, Original Encoded Information Types Indication, and Submission Time Stamp.
- Support for X.400 service elements in the RFC 822 network by means of special action by the mail gateway.
- Mapping between X.400 originator and recipient names and the current Internet identifiers.

14.8 ISO/CCITT DIRECTORY

Producing the correct identifier for an X.400 recipient can be difficult. The naming attributes that are selected will vary from user to user. When X.400 was completed, it was realized immediately that a directory service was needed if X.400 was to succeed. The X.500 recommendations, which were prepared during the 1985 to 1988 CCITT study period, define directory services and protocols. Several research and commercial associations have created pilot implementations of X.500.

The directory standard is very broad in scope. The X.500 directory (see Figure 14.5) is a distributed database intended to include many types of information.

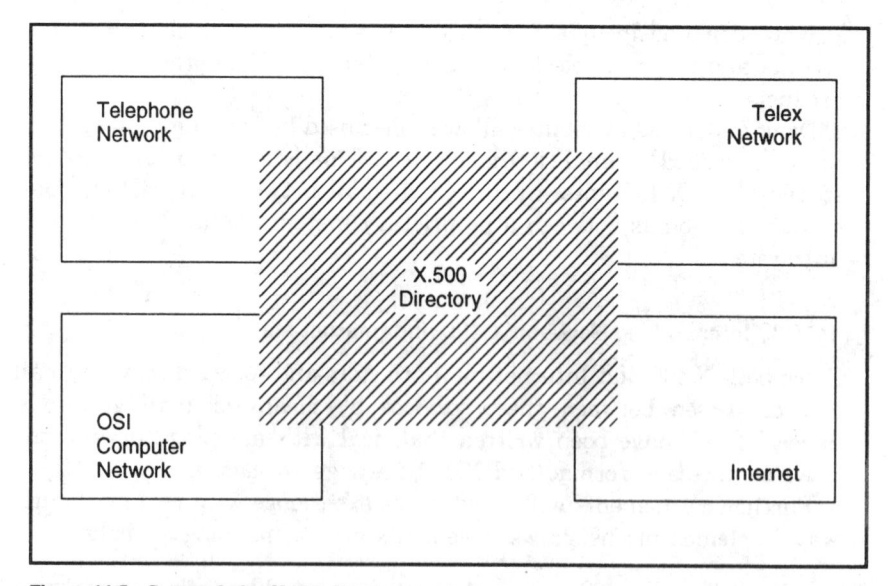

Figure 14.5 Scope of the X.500 directory.

For example:

- Names of people
- Postal addresses
- User identifiers for X.400 mail
- Internet style mail identifiers
- Telex and FAX numbers
- Telephone numbers
- Name-to-address mapping for OSI applications
- Names and locations of printers

There are some similarities between the X.500 directory system and the Domain Name System. Both are distributed databases whose information is maintained within various domains. Both have an overall structure organized as a hierarchical tree.

14.8.1 The X.500 Directory Information Tree

The X.500 directory is made up of entries distributed across a family of servers. The totality of information is called the *Directory Information Base*. The entries are organized as a tree (see Figure 14.6).

Entries higher in the tree describe objects such as countries or organizations, while entries at the bottom of the tree (the *leaves*) describe people, equipment, or application processes. The entries below any node are called its *children*.

Every entry contains a set of attributes. Of course, the attributes depend on the *class* of the entry, such as country, organization, or organizational person.

Entries obtained from a pilot X.500 implementation supported by Performance Systems International illustrate the types of attributes that can be expected in directory entries. The entry for the country node representing the United States starts with:

```
objectClass          - domainRelatedObject & friendlyCountry
                       & quipuNonLeafObject
countryName          - US
description          - Land of the Free and the Home of the Brave
lastModifiedTime     - Mon Dec  9 08:46:25 1991
```

The object class determines the types of attribute values that you might expect to find in an entry. There usually will be a small number of mandatory attributes for an entry and a larger number of

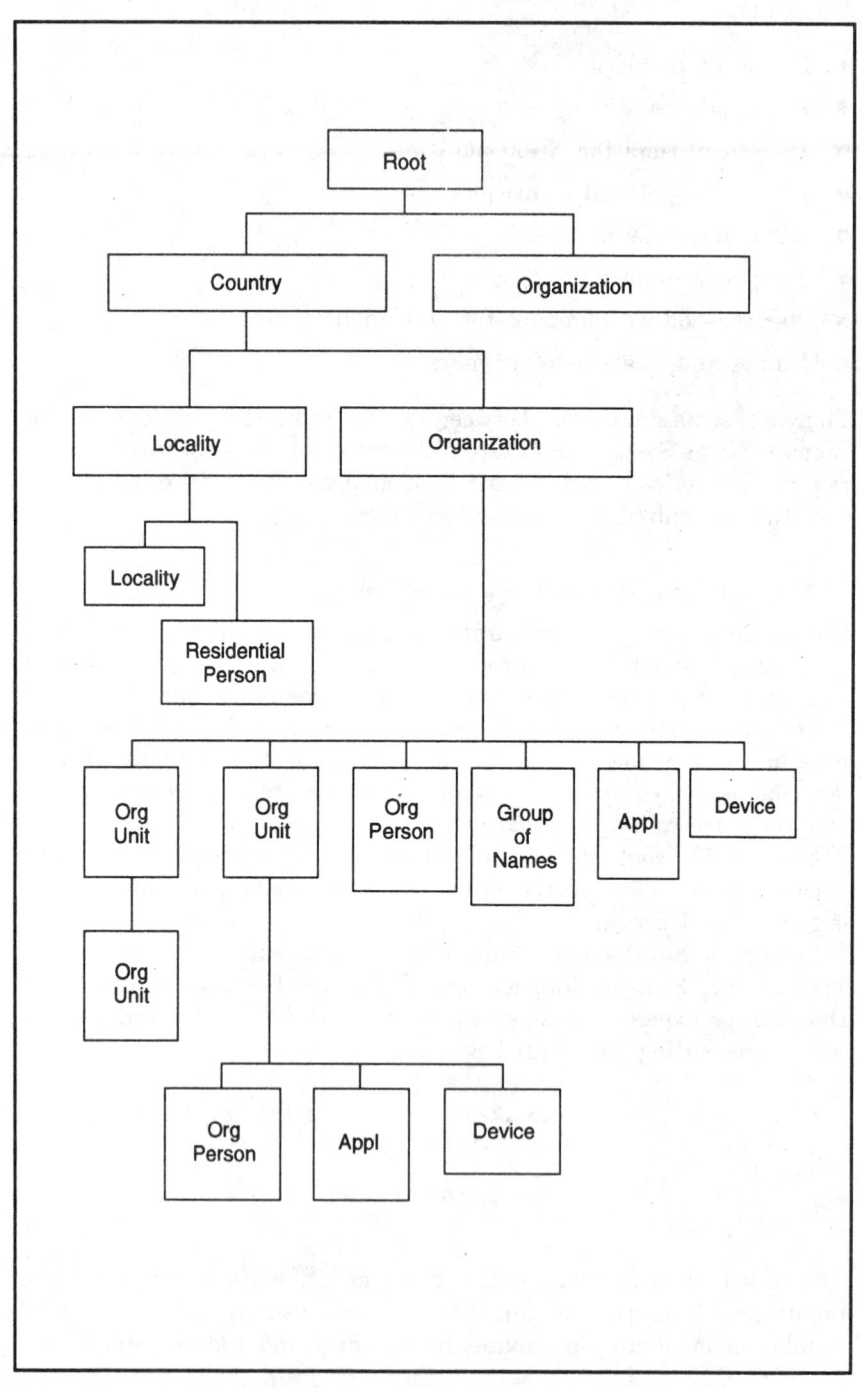

Figure 14.6 Structure of the Directory Information Base tree.

optional attributes which may be present.

An organizational person leaf entry contains attributes such as the person's name, title, address, telephone number, and electronic mail identifier.

A sample entry for an organizational person is displayed in Figure 14.7. This entry includes both a full postal address and a FAX number for the organizational unit — that is, the business — for which this person works.

In addition to its abundant supply of information about the person, note that the entry contains an access control list that spells out who can read or write this entry, who can change its attributes, and the operations for which a password is required. Access rights also can be defined for an entry's children. This is beside the point here, because this entry is a leaf.

How do you identify an entry so that you can ask to have it printed out? Every entry has a unique distinguished name, which is obtained by walking down the tree from the root and concatenating the names passed along the way.

The distinguished name is made up of components such as country, organization, organizational unit, and personal name. Alias names also can be used to make lookups easier.

Figure 14.8 shows the path from the root of the pilot X.500 directory to reach the organizational person entry in Figure 14.7. The path traverses country, organization, and organizational unit nodes to reach the person. The distinguished name would contain the identifiers for these nodes.

14.8.2 Directory Model

The Directory Information Base is distributed across a community of databases controlled by *Directory Service Agents* (DSAs). Users access directory information by means of a *Directory User Agent* (DUA). A DUA provides the user interface for interactive queries and updates, and passes user requests to a DSA.

The X.500 standard defines a formal protocol that governs the interaction between a DUA and a DSA. There also is a DSA-to-DSA protocol that enables DSAs to relay user queries or download copies of parts of the Directory Information Base.

There are a number of structural similarities between the X.500 directory system and the Domain Name System. Both are distributed directory systems. Users of each interact with a local client to reach a designated server, and that server can initiate distributed queries on behalf of the user. X.500 databases eventually are expected to include

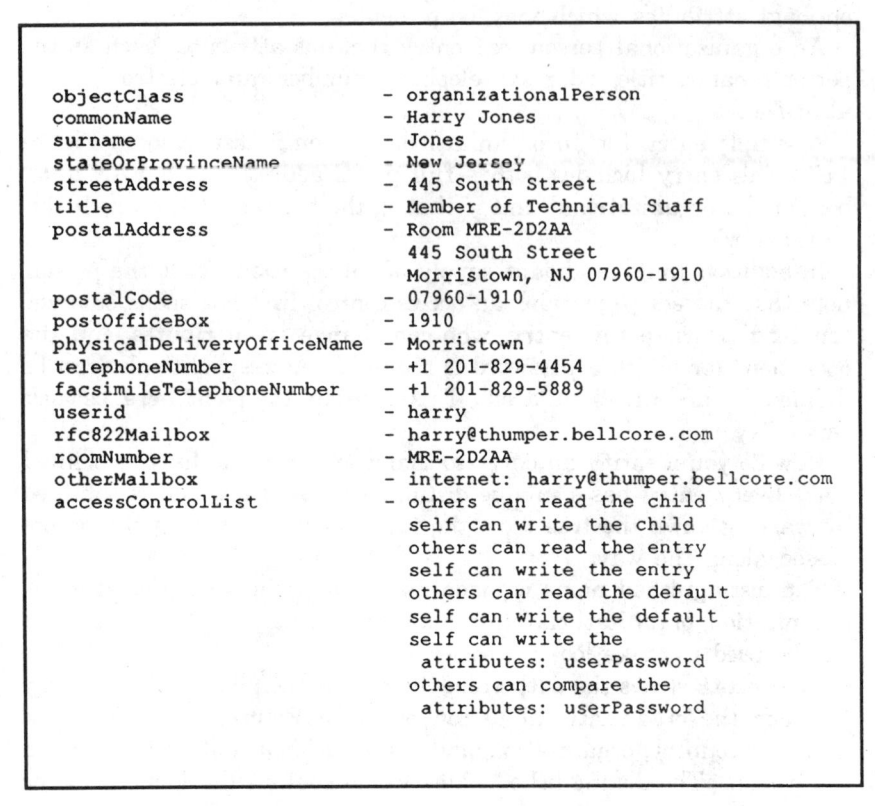

```
objectClass                    - organizationalPerson
commonName                     - Harry Jones
surname                        - Jones
stateOrProvinceName            - New Jersey
streetAddress                  - 445 South Street
title                          - Member of Technical Staff
postalAddress                  - Room MRE-2D2AA
                                 445 South Street
                                 Morristown, NJ 07960-1910
postalCode                     - 07960-1910
postOfficeBox                  - 1910
physicalDeliveryOfficeName     - Morristown
telephoneNumber                - +1 201-829-4454
facsimileTelephoneNumber       - +1 201-829-5889
userid                         - harry
rfc822Mailbox                  - harry@thumper.bellcore.com
roomNumber                     - MRE-2D2AA
otherMailbox                   - internet: harry@thumper.bellcore.com
accessControlList              - others can read the child
                                 self can write the child
                                 others can read the entry
                                 self can write the entry
                                 others can read the default
                                 self can write the default
                                 self can write the
                                  attributes: userPassword
                                 others can compare the
                                  attributes: userPassword
```

Figure 14.7 A sample X.500 directory entry.

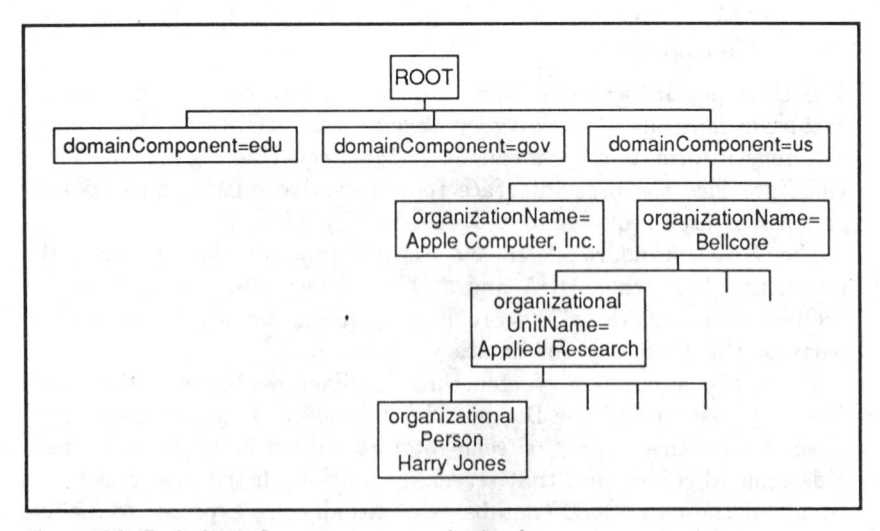

Figure 14.8 Path from the root to an organizational person.

information that helps users to locate network resources.

The specific X.500 database operations that a user can perform (subject to satisfying access controls) are:

- Read information from an entry.
- Compare a value with the value of an attribute in an entry.
- Obtain a list of the subordinates of a node.
- Search for entries of interest using attribute keys.
- Add or remove a directory leaf entry.
- Modify an entry.

Even if a particular DSA does not have the information a user wants, it will know about other servers that might have the data. A DSA may either pass the address of another server to the Directory User Agent, or else may directly contact another server to get the information requested by a user.

Figure 14.9 illustrates DUA-to-DSA and DSA-to-DSA interactions.

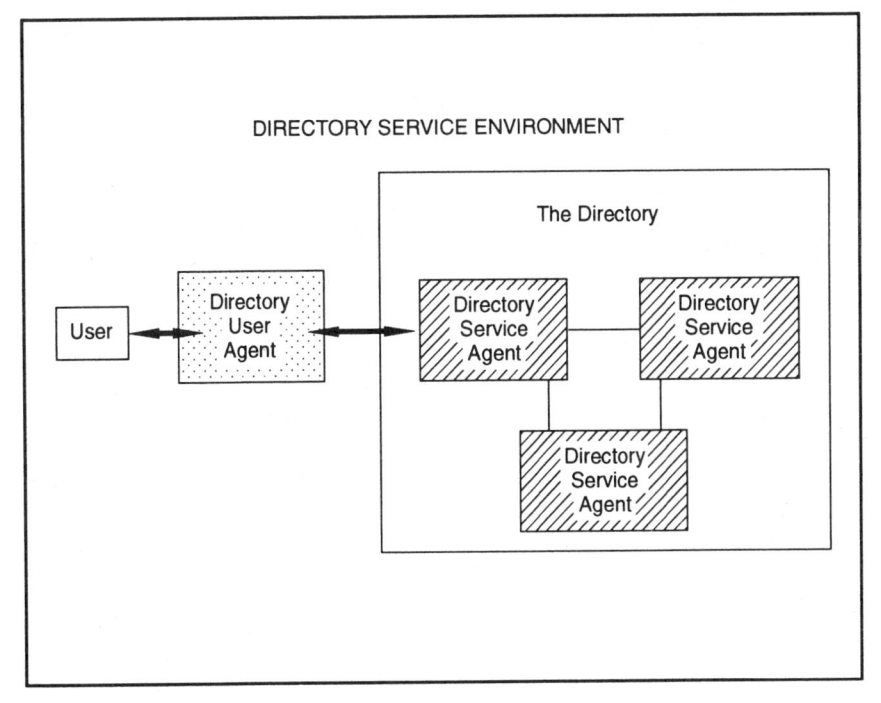

Figure 14.9 Directory service interactions.

14.9 RECOMMENDED READING

RFC 821 defines the Simple Mail Transfer Protocol, and RFC 822 describes the format of Internet messages. RFC 1225 describes the Post Office Protocol used to transfer mail between desktop workstations and a mail server. RFC 1341 expands the scope of Internet mail to include multi-part textual and binary information.

RFC 1148 currently defines the mapping between X.400 elements and the RFC 822 format. This RFC has been updated frequently, so the RFC index should be consulted for the current version.

X.400 was initially published as part of the 1984 CCITT recommendations, and was updated in the 1988 recommendations. ISO published its version of X.400 in ISO 10021, which is made up of several parts. X.500 was an 1988 CCITT recommendation.

Chapter

15

Network Management

15.1 INTRODUCTION

Network management has been a slow runner, lagging far behind other network facilities. Very large TCP/IP networks have operated and functioned quite well, but administration and management of these networks has been a labor-intensive task, requiring experienced personnel with a high level of technical skill.

This especially has been the case for the Internet, with its ever-expanding size and complexity. In the late 1980s, the IAB, which is charged with setting technical policy for the Internet, concluded that there was a critical need to define a network management framework and set of protocol standards, and to turn these into working tools as quickly as possible.

Although some excellent work already had been accomplished by OSI committees responsible for producing network management standards, there was no prospect for quickly translating their draft documents into tools that would fit TCP/IP management needs.

An Internet working group chaired by Marshall Rose had designed, implemented, and tested the Simple Network Management Protocol (SNMP). SNMP was designed to meet TCP/IP needs, but its architecture had been structured to have much in common with OSI's model. The IAB decided on a very practical strategy:

- Adopt the Simple Network Management Protocol (SNMP) as a short term solution.
- Target the OSI network management standards — Common Management Information Services/Common Management Information Protocol (CMIS/CMIP) — as a long term solution.

309

It should be stressed that OSI management standards are not yet complete, and further, OSI management protocols do not have much of an implementation and production use track record.

The Open Software Foundation has selected a framework for a Distributed Management Environment (DME) that combines OSI and SNMP protocols with object-oriented development packages. OSF intends to devote significant effort to integrating a number of technologies in order to create powerful network management tools.

15.1.1 Results of IAB Adoption of SNMP

The initial SNMP specifications established a starting point. The IAB expected that changes and enhancements would evolve rapidly. As stated in RFC 1052, *IAB Recommendations for the Development of Internet Network Management Standards:*

"We will learn what [Inter]Network Management is by doing it.

(a) in as large a scale as is possible

(b) with as much diversity of implementation as possible

(c) over as wide a range of protocol layers as possible

(d) with as much administrative diversity as we can stand."

The results of the IAB policy probably have exceeded their expectations. Since the time that the SNMP specifications and sample source code were made available on the Internet, the protocol has been incorporated into hundreds of products ranging from complex mainframe hosts to the simplest communications devices. The scope of SNMP has steadily been enlarged and strengthened. Recently, data collected by passive monitoring devices has been integrated into the SNMP framework.

Vendors have been able to create network management stations that use a well-defined set of mechanisms. A thriving new market has been created in which vendors compete to enhance their management stations with features such as graphical user interfaces, history databases, and report generation capabilities.

The production of a stream of RFCs devoted to network management is evidence of the dynamic expansion of the scope of the protocol.

15.1.2 CMOT

The IAB's long term goal was to contribute to the development of OSI management standards, and to use those standards in both TCP/IP and OSI networks. Internet research groups have implemented elements of OSI management, and they are accumulating a body of hands-on experience. OSI uses the *Common Management Information Protocol* (CMIP) to transmit network management information. The standard defining the use of OSI management over TCP/IP has the title *Common Management Information Services and Protocol over TCP/IP*, or CMOT for short.

There are important concepts shared by SNMP and CMOT. Both are based on a simple model in which network managers exchange information with agents located at devices. Both use similar frameworks for defining and encoding configuration parameters and performance statistics. Both carefully separate the model for the storage of network management information from the protocols used to access the information. As a result, management information can be read and updated by multiple protocols (see Figure 15.1).

Initially there was an effort to maintain compatibility between OSI and TCP/IP management definitions. However, the immediate needs of operational networks led to abandonment of this effort. In fact, Internet-sponsored management standards are being driven by urgent market requirements, and are rapidly diverging from OSI.

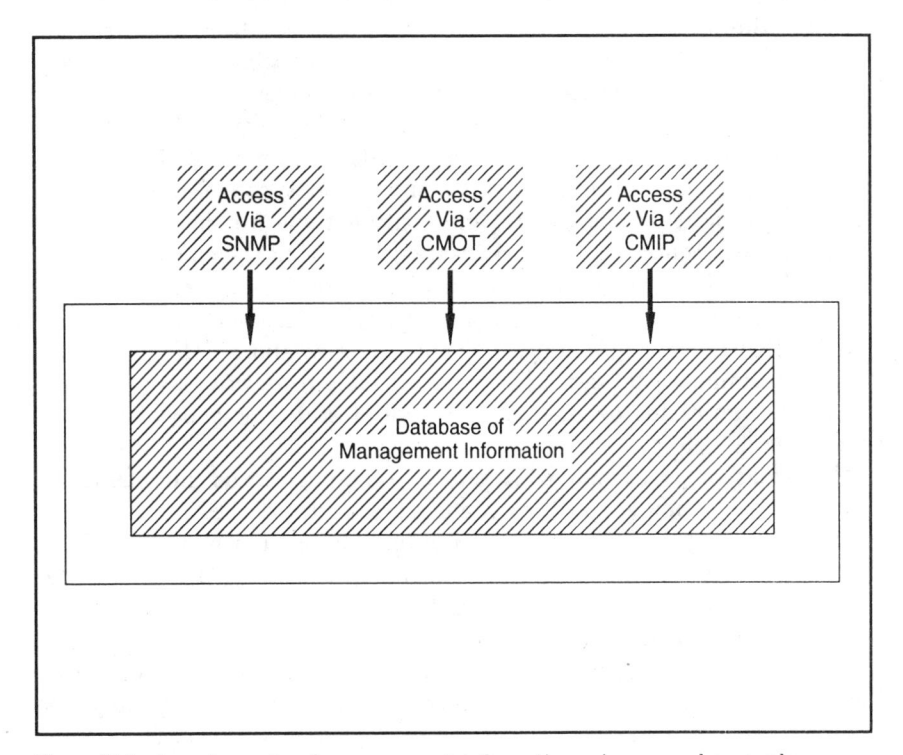

Figure 15.1 Accessing network management information using several protocols.

15.2 SNMP MODEL

An SNMP environment is made up of one or more management stations and a set of network elements. Any elements that participate in communications can be managed: hosts, gateways, hubs, bridges, or even modems, multiplexers, and data switches. Monitor stations, which passively capture information on network traffic, can share their data with an SNMP manager.

A managed element contains *agent* software and a special database — a *Management Information Base* or MIB. A MIB contains:

- System and device status information
- Performance statistics
- Configuration parameters

15.2.1 Roles of Managers and Agents

A management station contains manager software and network management applications. The manager software implements the protocols used to exchange data with agents. Network management applications provide the user interface that enables an operator to invoke network management functions, view the status of components, and analyze data that has been extracted from network elements.

A manager supervises a network element by asking the element's agent to report status and performance data from its MIB. Typical parameters in a MIB include the number and types of physical network interfaces, traffic counts, and routing table information.

A manager controls a network element by asking the element's agent to update MIB status or configuration parameters. A parameter change can be tied to an action. For example, a network interface can be disabled by setting a status variable to *down* and a TCP connection can be terminated by setting a status variable to *delete*. An agent can report a significant event (e.g., a change of status or a problem) to a manager.

Information is exchanged between a manager and an agent by means of the Simple Network Management Protocol (SNMP).

SNMP is lean and flexible. Agents have been implemented with as little as 20 to 64 kilobytes of software. The MIB in a network element contains only those variables that make sense for the element; for example, a bridge does not need TCP-related variables.

There are management station products that run on platforms ranging from a PC to a mainframe. An ever increasing range of devices can be monitored from today's management stations.

Network Management 313

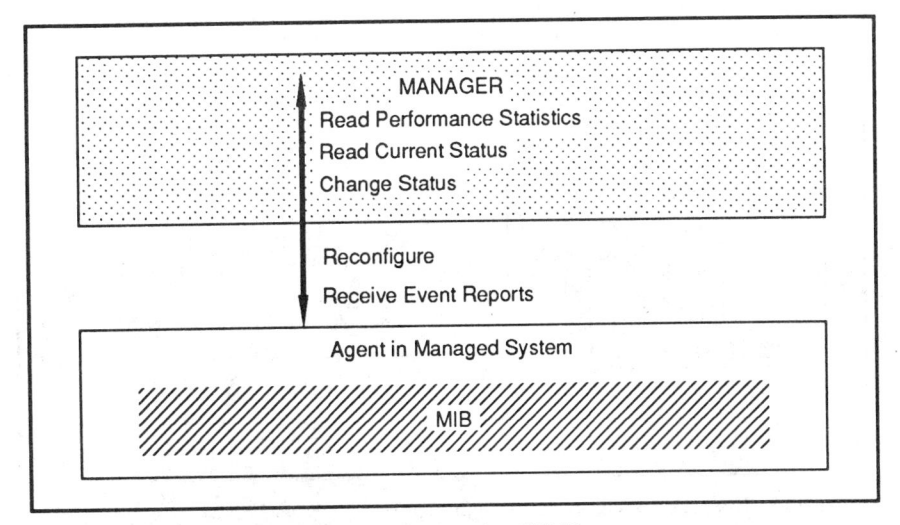

```
+-------------------------------------------------+
|             MANAGER                             |
|             Read Performance Statistics         |
|             Read Current Status                 |
|             Change Status                       |
|                                                 |
|             ↕                                   |
|             Reconfigure                         |
|             Receive Event Reports               |
|                                                 |
|             Agent in Managed System             |
|             ////////// MIB //////////           |
+-------------------------------------------------+
```

Figure 15.2 A manager and an agent exchanging SNMP messages.

Figure 15.2 shows a management station interacting with an agent in a network element to monitor and control the element.

New monitoring and control functions are defined by adding new variables to the MIB database. In fact, vendors are encouraged to define and register MIB variables that are specific to their own products.

Furthermore, many vendors have written portable modules that can be installed on a range of management stations. A number of tools have evolved that make it possible for generic SNMP management stations to monitor and control the vendor's equipment.

MIB definitions are not considered part of the Simple Network Management Protocol. MIB definitions were carefully kept separate with the intention that a MIB could be accessed by future versions of SNMP, or by completely independent protocols, such as OSI network management.

15.2.2 Proxy Agents

In the basic SNMP model, an agent and MIB reside within a device that is being monitored or controlled. A *proxy* management agent extends the model, enabling indirect access to devices. A management station interacts with the proxy, requesting and receiving information. The proxy exchanges information with the device by means of a separate interaction (see Figure 15.3).

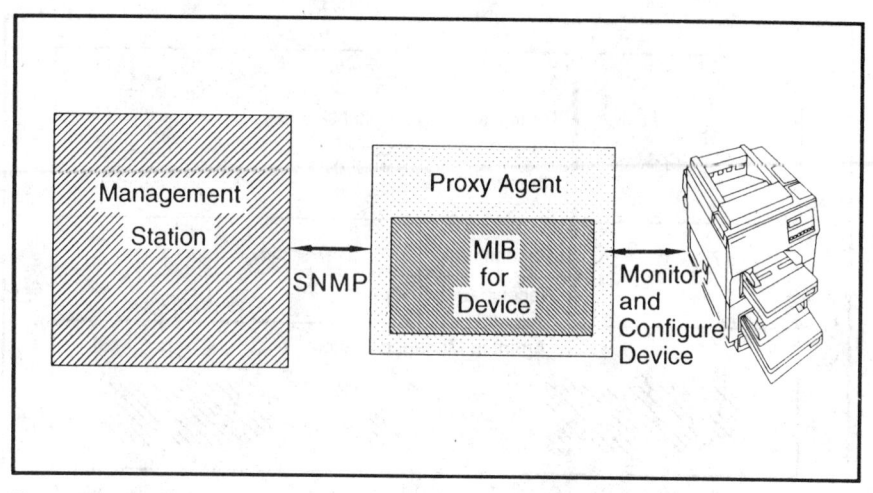

Figure 15.3 Network management through a proxy.

For example, two applications of proxy management are:

- A proxy agent enables an SNMP management station to control and monitor a device that does not support SNMP. The proxy agent translates native device information into a form suitable for a MIB, and communicates with an SNMP manager on behalf of the device.[1]
- A proxy may be used to relay management information from TCP/IP systems that may not be directly accessed for reasons of security.

15.3 SNMP MESSAGES

Managers and network elements communicate with each other by sending SNMP messages. There are only five message types:

- Get Request
- Get Next Request
- Get Response
- Set Request
- Trap

---

[1]This type of architecture was illustrated at an Interop meeting, where a toaster was controlled from an SNMP management station.

Limiting exchanges to these five message types keeps the implementation simple, while not imposing limits on the functionality of SNMP.

A Get Request contains a variable or list of variables that the manager wants to read from a MIB. The Get Next Request provides a way to read sequentially through a MIB. The Set Request is used to set the value of one or more variables. The Get Response is sent to reply to a Get Request, Get Next Request, and Set Request messages.

A Trap is used to report events such as:

- Reinitializing self
- Local link failure
- Link functioning again
- Received message with incorrect authentication
- Neighbor not responding

It is part of the SNMP philosophy that the number of trap messages that are transmitted should be kept as small as possible. Network managers are familiar with the phenomenon that when one thing goes wrong, a lot of other problems get triggered. A flood of alarm messages can clog the network, slowing down recovery procedures.

Typically, a management station will be set up to read statistics at regular periods — such as each fifteen minutes. After each read, the statistics can be reset to zero.

15.3.1 Communities

A group of managers and their network elements make up a *community* and are assigned a community name. The community name, along with optional authentication information, establishes the validity of the message sender.

A device can participate in more than one community; in fact, a community name is used to define the scope of control that a manager has over elements in a community.

For example, a manager using community identifier *netControl* might have the right to read and update every variable in every MIB on a LAN, while a manager whose community name *is helpDesk* might be restricted to read-only access to MIB values at a selected set of devices.

15.3.2 SNMP Message Protocol

Each SNMP message is enclosed within a single UDP datagram, and is sent via IP. A manager receives all messages except traps at UDP port 161. Traps are directed to UDP port 162. An agent receives messages at UDP port 161 (see Figure 15.4).

Every implementation must be able to handle messages of at least 484 octets. Although current implementations use UDP, there is no inherent restriction that will prevent the use of other transports in the future.

It is important to protect access to configuration and status variables. A serious deficiency in current implementations is that they do not provide authentication beyond checking the community name. However, this is expected to change soon with the introduction of encrypted authentication controls.

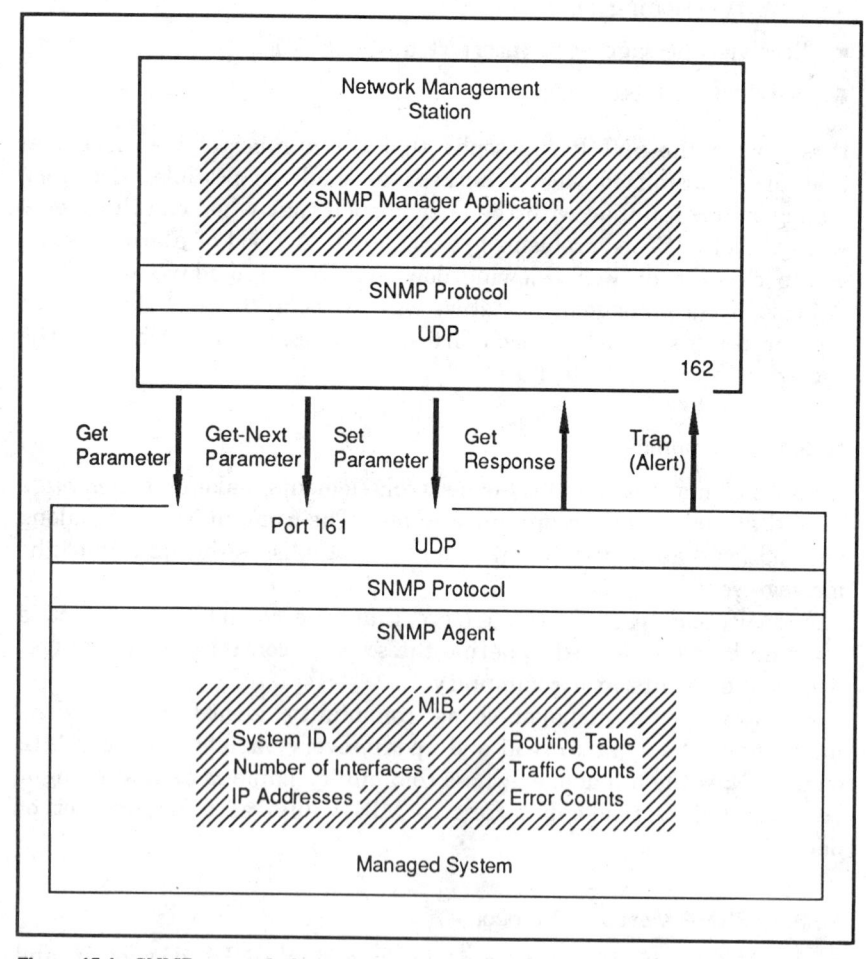

Figure 15.4 SNMP protocol elements.

15.4 STRUCTURE OF MANAGEMENT INFORMATION

In order to read or write a MIB database variable, you first need a way to identify the variable. ISO and CCITT have established a naming tree for assigning unique identifiers to all objects related to communications standards. This tree also defines an administrative structure for assigning identifiers.

15.4.1 Object Identifiers

Every tree node is labeled with an brief text description and an integer number. By convention, the text part of a label is written in lower case, unless it is a compound word. In this case, any word after the first is capitalized, as in "ifOperStatus."

A tree node's identifier, formally called its *Object Identifier*, is the sequence of integers traversed from the root to reach the node.

Many of the nodes represent administrations which are responsible for defining names in the subtrees below their nodes. For example, objects in the subtree under the *internet* node are registered with the Internet Assigned Numbers Authority.

Figure 15.5 shows part of the ISO/CCITT tree. MIB database definitions are under Internet administration. The path 1.3.6.1.2.1.2.8 is the object identifier obtained by traversing the labelled nodes:

Label	Description
iso (1)	ISO
org (3)	National and international organizations
dod (6)	Department of Defense
internet (1)	Internet Activities Board
mgmt (2)	Network management
mib-2 (1)	MIB definition
if (2)	Interfaces
ifOperStatus(8)	Interface operational status

Its text name is iso.org.dod.internet.mgmt.mib-2.if.ifOperStatus. This text name is the variable's *Object Descriptor*.

Elements at the bottom of the tree contained in boxes outlined with dots represent specific entries for a real device. For example, the object identifier 1.3.6.1.2.1.2.8.2 identifies a MIB variable that holds the operational status (up or down) of the second network interface for a network element (assuming the element to have at least two interfaces).

The path 1.3.6.1.2.1.1.1 leads to the *sysDescr* variable. There is a single, unique system description associated with a device. By convention, a uniquely valued variable for a real device is identified using a final 0. Hence, the system description of a real node has object identifier 1.3.6.1.2.1.1.1.0.

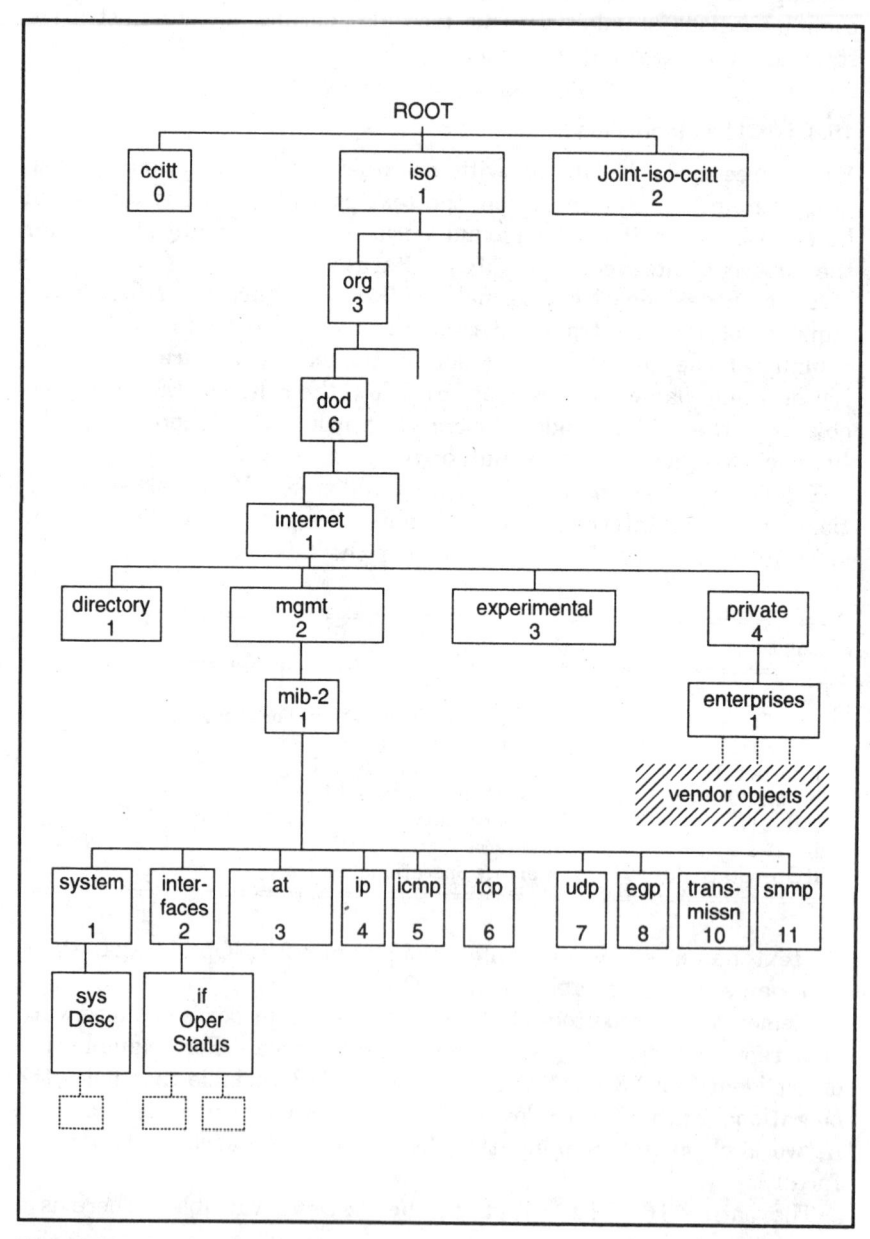

Figure 15.5 The ISO/CCITT Object Identifier tree.

15.4.2 Vendor Variables

A vendor can apply to the Internet Assigned Numbers Authority for a number defining a unique subtree under the *enterprises* node. The vendor subtree contains subnodes for the vendor's products, and for the variables needed to configure and manage each product.

Note that SNMP can be used to manage non-TCP/IP products. For example, a LAN terminal server that speaks the proprietary DEC LAT protocol for terminal I/O traffic can use its single network interface for both LAT traffic and SNMP messages exchanged between a manager and a proxy agent in the terminal server.

15.4.3 Categories of MIB Information

The ten most commonly used categories of network information are listed in Table 15.1, along with some examples of the variables associated with each. A network element needs to support only the categories that make sense for it. For example, a bridge has no need for TCP or EGP.

The address translation category is being phased out. Information relating to IP address translation have been moved under the IP category. The CMOT category, which was assigned identifier 9 in an earlier version of the MIB, has been dropped.

15.4.4 MIB Extensions

Objects which are coming into common use but have not yet been standardized are placed under the *experimental* node of the *internet* subtree. Vendor-defined objects are placed under the *enterprises* node.

15.5 DEFINING MIB VARIABLES

Now that we have a mechanism for identifying variables, we turn to describing their values and characteristics. MIB variables are defined by specifying:

- *SYNTAX:* The datatype for the variable, such as integer or string of characters.
- *ACCESS:* Permission level, which may be read-only, read-write, write-only, or not-accessible.
- *STATUS:* If the variable is in a category that has been included in an element's MIB, this defines whether the variable is mandatory, optional, or obsolete.
- *DESCRIPTION:* A clear text statement describing the variable.

TABLE 15.1 MIB Categories and Examples

Cat	Name	Examples
1	System	Text description of the system Time since management agent was last initialized Contact person for this system Physical location of the system
2	Interfaces	Total number of subnetwork interfaces Table of values for each interface: e.g., type (Ethernet, Token-Ring, etc.), MTU, physical address, operational status, and traffic statistics
3	Address translation	(Being phased out) Table of IP addresses and physical addresses
4	IP	Role as Gateway or host Default Time-To-Live IP traffic statistics IP routing table
5	ICMP	Total number of ICMP messages received Number of attempts to send ICMP messages Number of messages of specific types sent and received (e.g., Destination Unreachable or Time exceeded)
6	TCP	Maximum limit on number of TCP connections Statistics on number of segments sent and received Information about active connections (e.g., IP addresses, ports, current state)
7	UDP	Number of incoming UDP datagrams delivered successfully Number of UDP datagrams sent IP addresses and ports listening for UDP datagrams
8	EGP	Number of EGP messages received without error Number of locally generated EGP messages Table of information about EGP neighbors
10	Transmission	(Currently experimental)
11	SNMP	Number of messages delivered to local SNMP Number of incoming messages of each type Statistics on errors found in incoming messages Total number of outgoing SNMP messages

The sample formal definition below defines a *system location* object whose text label is *sysLocation*. Its *SYNTAX* or datatype is a display string (i.e., a string of printable characters) at most 255 characters in length. Its *ACCESS* is read-write, so a manager can update its value. The variable is mandatory. The last line of the formal definition indicates that *sysLocation* is attached to the tree under *system* and has integer label 6. Therefore, its full object identifier is 1.3.6.1.2.1.1.6.

```
sysLocation OBJECT-TYPE
    SYNTAX   DisplayString (SIZE (0..255))
    ACCESS   read-write
    STATUS   mandatory
    DESCRIPTION
            "The physical location of this system (e.g.,
            'telephone closet, 3rd floor')."
    ::= { system 6 }
```

15.5.1 SNMP Datatypes and Abstract Syntax Notation One

The Internet standards documents define the syntax — i.e. datatype — of variables using the CCITT/ISO formal datatype definition language, *Abstract Syntax Notation One* (ASN.1).

Programmers are very familiar with the concept of datatype definition. Every programming language provides some basic set of datatypes such as integers or octet strings. Most languages provide a mechanism for defining composite datatypes such as records, arrays of records, or complicated data structures.

CCITT and ISO committees need to define many datatypes in the course of writing standards. Initially introduced by CCITT, Abstract Syntax Notation One was subsequently adopted for use by both CCITT and ISO. ASN.1 offers many benefits. It helps standards writers and implementors to:

- Write clear and uniform datatype definitions
- Reuse definitions
- Separate the definition of datatypes used in protocol exchanges from the encoding of the data for transmission across a network

ASN.1 is very powerful, and actually encompasses more than datatype definitions. For example, ASN.1 is used to create templates that describe the structure of MIB object definitions. An ASN.1 template defined the framework for the *sysLocation* definition shown above.

15.5.2 SNMP Datatypes

ASN.1 is a very rich language, making it possible to define very complex datatypes. However, keeping in mind the need for simplicity, good performance, and the immature status of network management protocols, SNMP is based on a few simple datatypes. These include:

- *Integer:* For example, the size of the Maximum Transmission Unit that can be transmitted at an interface is expressed as an integer.
- *Octet String:* A sequence of octets, each of which may take any value in the range 0 to 255. For example, a community identifier is an octet string.
- *Display String:* A display string is a sequence of octets, each of which is restricted to Telnet NVT characters. For example, the physical location for a system is expressed as a Display String.
- *Null:* A value needed as a placeholder.
- *Object Identifier:* The numeric name of an object, obtained by traversing the ISO/CCITT naming tree.
- *IP address:* The IP address is expressed as four octets. Each network element is configured with at least one IP address.
- *Physical address:* A physical address is expressed as an octet string of suitable length. For example, 802.3 and 802.5 physical addresses consist of six octets.
- *Counter:* A non-negative 32-bit integer. The number of octets received at a network interface is measured via a counter.
- *Gauge:* A non-negative integer that increases and decreases, latching at maximum values. The length of a queue of frames waiting to be transmitted by an interface is measured by a gauge.
- *Time Ticks:* A non-negative integer that counts time in hundredths of a second. The current system uptime is measured in TimeTicks.
- *Opaque:* Data, passed as an octet string, but having some special meaning to an application. For example, encrypted security information could be sent in a opaque datatype.
- *List:* A sequence of simple datatypes.
- *Table:* A sequence of lists (entries). For example, an IP routing table is a sequence of entries, each containing information including a destination network address, the interface to use, the local network mask, and the next-hop address.

Counters, Gauges, and Time Ticks all range from 0 to 4294967295.

15.5.3 Sample IP Datatypes

The sample datatypes listed below should give a fairly good sense of the kind of information that is stored in a MIB. Each of these variables is located below the *ip* node (1.3.6.1.2.1.4) in the naming tree. The numbering in the list corresponds to the numeric node label of each that is used in its object identifier.

1. *ipForwarding:* An integer that is set to 1 if the system is a gateway, 2 if it is a host.
2. *ipDefaultTTL:* An integer defining the default Time-To-Live.
3. *ipInReceives:* A counter, registering the total number of datagrams received from all interfaces.
4. *ipInHdrErrors:* A counter equal to the number of input datagrams discarded due to IP header errors.
13. *ipReasmTimeout:* An integer equal to the number of seconds that fragments will be held pending reassembly.
20. *ipAddrTable:* A table containing the system's IP addresses, and associated information, such as the network mask for each address.

15.6 SNMP MESSAGE FORMAT

An SNMP message consists of a sequence of elements:

- Protocol version
- Community name
- Message Protocol Data Unit, which is one of the five types, Get Request, Get Next Request, Get Response, Set Request, or Trap

A request or response Protocol Data Unit consists of:

- A request-id, used to correlate requests with responses.
- An error-status field, set to 0 in requests, and used in responses that report problems in carrying out the request, such as a refusal to update a read-only variable.
- An error-index field, set to 0 in requests, and used to describe problems more fully.
- A sequence of object identifiers and values. In a Get Request, the values are null. In a Set Request or a Get Response, the values are filled in.

A trap Protocol Data Unit contains:

- The type of element generating the trap
- The IP address of the element
- The type of trap, e.g. link down or loss of a neighbor router
- A more specific trap code
- A time stamp
- Parameters relating to the trap

Figure 15.6 shows a Sniffer analysis of an SNMP message requesting the number of unicast (i.e., not broadcast or multicast) packets that were received at physical interface number 1 and delivered to a higher layer protocol.

The material in the sections that follow is very technical. It may be of interest if you have hands-on responsibility for network management, but may be skipped by the general reader.

15.7 ASN.1 ENCODING

Along with the ASN.1 datatype definition language, ISO has defined a set of Basic Encoding Rules that can be applied to encode data values for transmission. The standard encoding for data values has the form:

[*IDENTIFIER*] [*LENGTH (of contents)*] [*CONTENTS*]

The first three bits of the identifier octet are special indicators. The first two indicate whether the datatype is a universal ASN.1 type (00) such as integer, a type defined for general use within an application (01), or a type that will only appear in a single specific context (10).

The third bit indicates whether the type is a *primitive* (0) such as an integer or octet string, or is *constructed* (1), e.g., a sequence.

The remaining five bits of the identifier octet specify a numeric *tag* value. For example, an IP Address has a tag value of 0. Its identifier is encoded as hex 40 because:

- IP Addresses have general use in SNMP. They are used within several SNMP datatypes.
- An IP Address is primitive — i.e., it is not a sequence.
- Binary 0100 0000 is hex 40.

```
                                                    SNMP Get ifInUcastPkts
DLC:   ----- DLC Header -----
DLC:
DLC:   Frame 48 arrived at  12:49:08.3917; frame size is 88 (0058 hex) bytes.
DLC:   Destination = Station DEC    07F2F1
DLC:   Source       = Station Sun   00394E
DLC:   Ethertype   = 0800 (IP)
DLC:
IP:    ----- IP Header -----
IP:
IP:    Version = 4, header length = 20 bytes
IP:    Type of service = 00
IP:           000. .... = routine
IP:           ...0 .... = normal delay
IP:           .... 0... = normal throughput
IP:           .... .0.. = normal reliability
IP:    Total length = 74 bytes
IP:    Identification = 18090
IP:    Flags = 0X
IP:    .0.. .... = may fragment
IP:    ..0. .... = last fragment
IP:    Fragment offset = 0 bytes
IP:    Time to live = 255 seconds/hops
IP:    Protocol = 17 (UDP)
IP:    Header checksum = 6DD4 (correct)
IP:    Source address = [130.128.1.35]
IP:    Destination address = [130.128.1.1]
IP:    No options
IP:
UDP:   ----- UDP Header -----
UDP:
UDP:   Source port = 5103 (SNMP)
UDP:   Destination port = 161
UDP:   Length = 54
UDP:   No checksum
UDP:
SNMP:  ----- Simple Network Management Protocol -----
SNMP:
SNMP:  Version = 0
SNMP:  Community = interop
SNMP:  Command = Get request
SNMP:  Request ID = 591478078
SNMP:  Error status = 0 (No error)
SNMP:  Error index = 0
SNMP:
SNMP:  Object = {1.3.6.1.2.1.2.2.1.11.1} (ifInUcastPkts.1)
SNMP:  Value  = NULL
```

Figure 15.6 A sample SNMP Get Request message.

A Get Request has a tag value of 0. Its identifier is encoded as A0 because:

- A Get Request appears in only one specific position[2] in a message.
- The content of a Get Request is a sequence.
- Binary 1010 0000 is hex A0.

15.7.1 Identifiers Used in SNMP Datatypes

Table 15.2 shows the identifiers that will appear in the encoding of SNMP datatype values.

All of the datatypes in the table whose identifiers start with hex 0 or 4 are primitive. A list (i.e., a record) is encoded as a sequence of primitive types. A MIB table is encoded as a sequence of lists, i.e., a sequence of sequences. Requests, responses, and traps contain lists and tables, and so are referred to as constructed types.

The Display String datatype is encoded with an Octet String identifier. However, the symbols in a display string are restricted to Telnet NVT characters.

15.7.2 Encoding Object Identifiers

The first two numeric labels (x,y) of an object identifier are translated to a single decimal number using the formula $40x+y$. SNMP objects start with 1.3, which translates to decimal 43. This is encoded as hex 2B. The remaining number labels are encoded as follows:

- If a number label is 127 or less, it is binary encoded into the last 7 bits of an octet.
- A 1 flag in the first bit of an octet indicates that the number is continued into the next octet.

For example, 1.3.6.1.1.4.130.129 is encoded:

   2B 06 01 01 04 <u>81 02 81 01</u>

The last two numbers each occupy two hex positions.

---

[2]Since the request appears in only one place, its identifier can be encoded as context-specific.

Network Management 327

TABLE 15.2 Identifiers for ASN.1 Data Types Used in SNMP

	ID In Hex
BASIC ASN.1 TYPES	
Integer	02
Octet String	04
Null	05
Object Identifier	06
Sequence	30
BASIC SNMP APPLICATION TYPES	
IP Address	40
Counter	41
Gauge	42
Time Ticks	43
Opaque	44
CONSTRUCTED SNMP APPLICATION CONTEXT-SPECIFIC TYPES	
Get Request	A0
Get Next Request	A1
Get Response	A2
Set Request	A3
Trap	A4

15.7.3 Format of SNMP Messages

The hex translation of the SNMP part of the Get Request message of Figure 15.6 is shown in Figure 15.7. The entire message consists of 46 octets. The message is encoded as a sequence of items. Recall that each length field indicates the length of the contents part of an item. Note how sequences are nested inside one another.

The *Sniffer* analyzer translation and hex expansions of the corresponding Get Response is displayed in Figure 15.8.

```
SNMP   MESSAGE
Sequence    Length=44
  30          2C

  VERSION
  Integer    Length=1   Value=0
    02          01         00

  COMMUNITY
  Octet String Length=7  Value= i  n  t  e  r  o  p
    04           07             69 6E 74 65 72 6F 70

  GET   REQUEST
  Get request    Length=30
    A0             1E

    REQUEST   ID
    Integer    Length=4    Value=591478078
      02          04           23 41 3D 3E

    ERROR   STATUS          ERROR   INDEX
    Integer   Length=1  Value=0   Integer  Length=1  Value=0
      02         01        00        02        01        00

    SEQUENCE (OF OBJECT IDENTIFIERS AND VALUES)
    Sequence   Length=16
      30          10

      SEQUENCE (= ONLY OBJECT ID/VALUE PAIR FOR THIS MESSAGE)
      Sequence   Length=14
        30          0E

        OBJECT IDENTIFIER FOR ifInUcastPkts.1
        Object ID   Length=10   1.2 .6 .1 .2 .1 .2 .3 .1.11 .1
          06           0A        2B 06 01 02 01 02 02 01 0B 01

        PLACEHOLDER FOR VALUE
        Null
        05 00
```

Figure 15.7 Hexadecimal encoding of a Get Request message.

```
SNMP: ----- Simple Network Management Protocol -----
SNMP:
SNMP: Version = 0
SNMP: Community = interop
SNMP: Command = Get response
SNMP: Request ID = 591478078
SNMP: Error status = 0 (No error)
SNMP: Error index = 0
SNMP:
SNMP: Object = {1.3.6.1.2.1.2.2.1.11.1} (ifInUcastPkts.1)
SNMP: Value  = 58319 packets

S N M P    M E S S A G E
Sequence    Length=47
   30         2F

   V E R S I O N
   Integer    Length=1   Value=0
   02          01          00

   C O M M U N I T Y
   Octet String Length=7  Value=  i  n  t  e  r  o  p
       04           07             69 6E 74 65 72 6F 70

   G E T    R E S P O N S E
   Get response   Length=33
       A2            21

      R E Q U E S T    I D
      Integer   Length=4    Value=591478078
       02         04           23 41 3D 3E

      E R R O R   S T A T U S      E R R O R    I N D E X
      Integer  Length=1  Value=0   Integer  Length=1  Value=0
       02        01        00       02        01        00

      SEQUENCE (OF OBJECT IDENTIFIERS AND VALUES)
      Sequence    Length=19
         30          13

         SEQUENCE (= ONLY OBJECT ID/VALUE PAIR FOR THIS MESSAGE)
         Sequence    Length=17
            30          11

            OBJECT IDENTIFIER FOR ifInUcastPkts.1
            Object ID  Length=10   1.2 .6 .1 .2 .1 .2 .3 .1.11 .1
               06         0A        2B 06 01 02 01 02 02 01 0B 01

            VALUE
            Counter   Length=3     58319 packets
             41         03          00 E3 CF
```

Figure 15.8 Hexadecimal encoding of a Get Response message.

15.7.4 Get Next Requests

Get Next Requests are used to step through a sequence of MIB variables. The requests and responses that follow step through information about network interfaces. The first request asks for the number of interfaces at the network element. The variable that counts the number of interfaces is one-of-a-kind, and the convention is that its full object identifier ends with a 0. Variables like ifOperStatus come in bunches; there will be one for each interface, and their object identifiers will end with 1, 2, etc..

```
Command = Get next request
Object = {1.3.6.1.2.1.2.1} (ifNumber — Report number of interfaces)
Value  = NULL              (This is a placeholder.)

Command = Get response
Object = {1.3.6.1.2.1.2.1.0} (ifNumber.0 — 0 means this is a unique value)
SNMP: Value  = 2            (The value reports two interfaces)
```

The operational status of the nth interface is 1.3.6.1.2.1.2.2.1.8.n. By asking for the operational status of the "next after 0," we mean the operational status of the first.

```
Command = Get next request
Object = {1.3.6.1.2.1.2.2.1.8.0} (ifOperStatus.0)
Value  = NULL

Command = Get response
Object = {1.3.6.1.2.1.2.2.1.8.1} (ifOperStatus.1)
Value  = 1 (up)
```

Now ask about the next after 1:

```
Command = Get next request
Object = {1.3.6.1.2.1.2.2.1.8.1} (ifOperStatus.1)
Value  = NULL

Command = Get response
Object = {1.3.6.1.2.1.2.2.1.8.2} (ifOperStatus.2)
Value  = 1 (up)
```

There only are two. What happens if we ask for the next?

```
Command = Get next request
Object = {1.3.6.1.2.1.2.2.1.8.2} (ifOperStatus.2)
Value  = NULL
```

```
Command = Get response
SNMP: Object = {1.3.6.1.2.1.2.2.1.9.1} (ifLastChange.1)
SNMP: Value  = 0 hundredths of a second
```

The response contains the first entry for the variable that follows in lexicographic sequence, namely ifLastChange. Recall that the community identifier corresponds to the view of the MIB that is available to a requester. When using *Get Next* to traverse a MIB, the next *permitted* variable in the lexicographic order is returned to the requester.

15.7.5 Tables and Get Next Requests

Get Next Requests can be used to step through tables. Tables are defined with an index, and an index value is used to step through the table entries. Each answer contains the index, and so the answer can be used to form the next request.

15.7.6 The RMON MIB

A *network monitor* is a device that passively watches LAN traffic and can be configured to gather data about the traffic. Monitors are configured with error count thresholds that can be used to spot problems before they become critical.

The *Remote Network Monitoring MIB* (RMON MIB) integrates the valuable information collected by monitors into the SNMP framework. This will give a significant boost to the power of SNMP management stations. A remote monitor can independently collect local data, carry out diagnostics, and detect alarm situations. Since problems will be reported as they arise, a network management station can cut back on the frequency of its requests to read MIB data.

There are nine data groups defined for the RMON MIB:

- *statistics:* Records statistics such as number of frames detected.
- *history:* Compiles statistics for a configured polling interval.
- *alarm:* Generates an event if values for an interval exceed a configured threshold.
- *host:* Reports hosts that have been detected by the monitor as well as related statistics, such as how many frames each sent.
- *hostTopN:* Reports statistics for the hosts that top a list sorted on these statistics.
- *matrix:* Reports statistics for conversations between pairs of addresses.

- *filter:* Defines criteria for frame matching.
- *packet capture:* Allows frames satisfying a filter match to be captured.
- *event:* Controls the generation and notification of events. An event may be caused by a local occurrence such as exceeding a threshold. An event can trigger a local activity such as packet capture, or cause a trap message to be sent to a management station.

15.7.7 What Next?

There is bustling activity among vendors and standards writers to expand and refine MIB definitions. The result is that an abundance of raw information will be available to network management stations.

Good software tools are needed in order to use SNMP information effectively for problem detection and long term capacity planning. Developers want standardized toolkits so that they can port new tools across management station products.

An area that is receiving a lot of attention is secure management. It may be acceptable to access statistical information about a network element using only the community name to authenticate management privilege. However, network managers will not allow remote control of a system by means of unauthenticated *set* commands. Secure authentication requires the encryption of some fields in an SNMP message. Note that this will impose some additional processing overhead.

15.8 RECOMMENDED READING

There is a long and growing list of RFCs dealing with SNMP and MIBs. We will cite a few of the most important, and give a sampling of the others. RFC 1157 defines the Simple Network Management Protocol. The original SNMP MIB was defined in RFC 1156. RFC 1213 describes the second version of the TCP/IP Management Information Base, MIB-II. RFC 1271 describes the RMON MIB.

RFC 1155 details the structure and identification of management information — that is, the structure of the tree of management information and the use of object identifiers for network elements. RFC 1212 describes the concise format to be used to define MIB objects.

Several RFCs contain MIBs to be used for specific technologies, such as RFC 1231's Token Ring MIB, RFC 1243's Appletalk MIB, and RFC 1233's list of managed objects for a DS3 interface. RFC 1215 outlines a convention for defining traps.

Chapter 16

Administering a TCP/IP Network

16.1 INTRODUCTION

The range of network technologies, routers, hosts, and software applications that run with TCP/IP make this protocol suite a popular choice for systems integration. But successful integration brings its own new problems. Administrators will find themselves running larger, more diverse, and more complex networks than ever.

Planning a network architecture is especially critical for an internet. The only thing that is certain about a network is that it will change. It is very likely that the number of users and hosts will increase. Users will move around, services will outgrow one processor and will be moved to another, LANs will be split up for better performance or tighter security. New locations will be attached into the network, requiring integration of their LANs and additional wide area links.

It is important to start out with well thought out designs for network topology, naming conventions, and address allocations that can accommodate change and allow for painless expansion.

End users are interested in availability and performance. A network administrator needs to plan the actions that will be taken to ensure continued service when something goes wrong (and it will). It is a good idea to create a diagram showing all of the bridges, routers, and servers in the network, and imagine what will happen if any one of them fails.

Networks are managed by people, and it is important that their responsibilities and span of control are clearly defined. For example, you don't want to find out that only one person is able to access and fix a critical piece of network equipment on the day that it fails and that person is vacationing in the Bahamas.

Network technicians need tools that facilitate fault detection and repair. They must gather the information required to track changing user requirements. This means that performance and capacity measurement should be normal, day-to-day activities.

Network administrators also have to be concerned with security, protecting the network from disruption and guarding user information. They must be able to invoke auditing of resource utilization, and need facilities that help them to monitor network users. There is a growing requirement for encryption services to support secure authentication procedures and to protect the transfer of sensitive data.

Fortunately for users, there has been steady convergence to a reasonably uniform user interface and level of functionality for TCP/IP services. A similar convergence to a uniform administrator user interface and set of tools for configuring, controlling, and monitoring a TCP/IP network would be equally welcome.

Too frequently, management tools are not integrated in any coherent way. Often they just consist of a jumble of unintegrated odds and ends. The advent of SNMP has brought many new network management station products to the marketplace. It is hoped that a more uniform system of network management will grow out of the SNMP products that will be released within the next year or two, or that the OSF Distributed Management Environment will evolve into a coherent framework for network administration.

In this chapter we are going to discuss a number of different areas that are the responsibility of network planners and administrators. In the first part of the chapter, we will examine various options for network topologies, and compare bridge and router capabilities. Next we will tackle configuration issues, covering individual network interfaces, IP routing, use of the Domain Name System, TCP, higher layer services, and SNMP configuration. The section on maintenance, monitoring and troubleshooting contains many examples illustrating widely available tools. The final section discusses some security considerations.

16.2 TOPOLOGY

Over the past few years, organizations have installed dispersed local area networks (LANs), as well as one or more wide area networks (WANs). Migration to TCP/IP offers the opportunity to interconnect these existing facilities, creating an integrated internet. But what kind of topology should this internet have? How does a choice of topology affect performance, reliability, security, and manageability?

Administering a TCP/IP Network   335

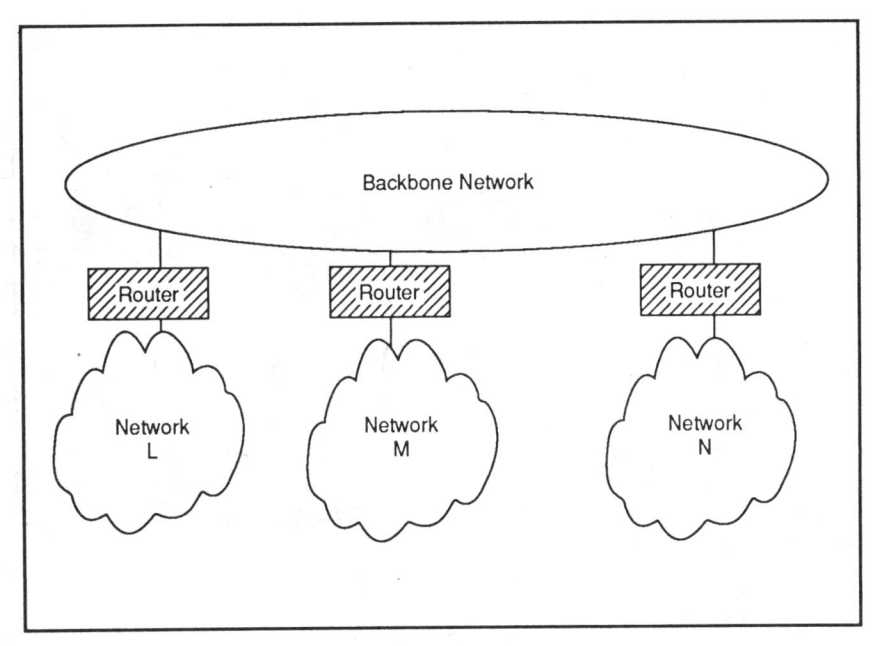

Figure 16.1 Networks connected to a backbone by routers.

A simple, manageable routing design is achieved by building a single backbone and connecting all other networks to the backbone by means of routers. Figure 16.1 shows an example of this type of topology.

This is a good starting point for a network blueprint. The checklist below provides some criteria for modifying this design:

1. Should some of the LANs be combined using bridges? Small LANs whose users share resources may get better performance across a bridge. If a lot of traffic between the LANs can be expected, a direct connection offloads this traffic from the backbone, improving performance for other users.

2. If a network's connection to the backbone is lost, how serious will the consequences be for its users? If this loss is critical, a redundant connection to the backbone or a separate route to the resources needs to be built into the internet.

3. Is there a bottleneck in the backbone? If so, either capacity needs to be increased or a second path should be provided.

4. What are the points of failure on the backbone? Can these be eliminated by means of backup equipment, or do alternative paths have to be provided?

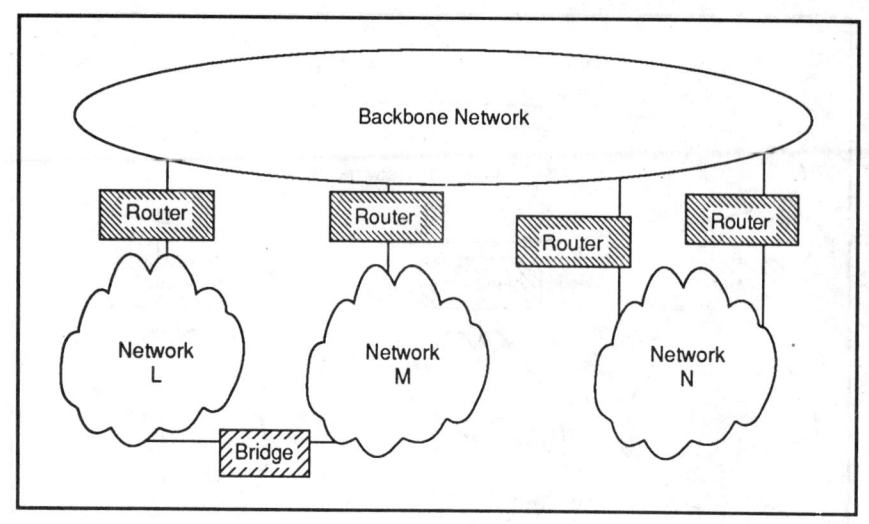

Figure 16.2 Network topology for improved performance.

Figure 16.2 shows a modified network topology. Some of the hosts on LAN L need to access servers on LAN M, and these networks have been connected by a bridge. Users on LAN L and LAN M need to login to critical applications that run on hosts attached to LAN N. A second router improves the reliability of connections to LAN N. The additional bridge and router prevent the backbone from becoming congested. Sensitive information is stored on a host on LAN N, and the routers screen the traffic that passes between the LANs to prevent access to this host.

The sections that follow discuss the characteristics of bridges and routers, and how they can be deployed to improve performance and security.

16.2.1 Connecting LANs with Bridges

A bridge connects two or more LANs that use the same MAC protocol. Bridges operate by absorbing all LAN traffic and examining the source and destination physical addresses in the MAC headers. A bridge carries frames from a source LAN connected to one bridge interface to a destination LAN at another interface (see Figure 16.3).

Since a bridge does not care what higher layer protocols are contained in a frame, a bridge can connect LANs that carry a mix of protocol traffic such as DECnet, LAT (DEC's terminal access protocol) and TCP/IP.

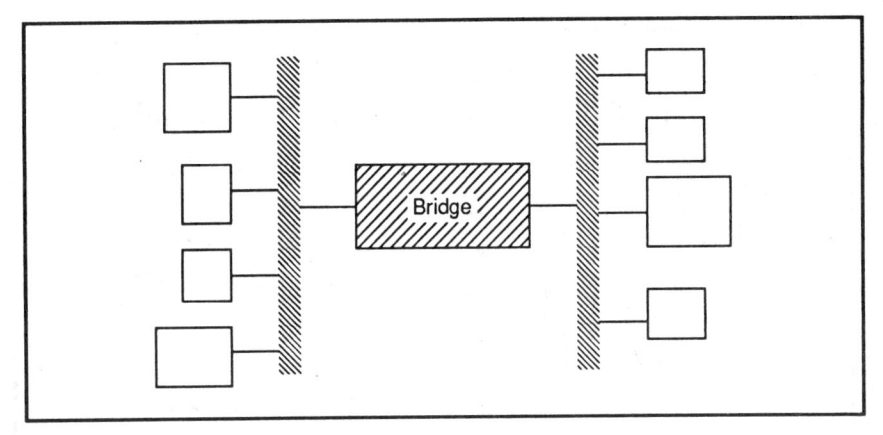

Figure 16.3 LANs connected by a bridge.

There are many situations for which a bridge provides an excellent connectivity solution. For example, bridges can connect LANs that use different media, such as coax, fiber optics, or twisted pair. Bridges can operate at LAN speeds.

Many bridge products are equipped with a self-configuration feature that is very popular with network administrators. To install a self-configuring bridge, you simply connect it to your LANs and plug it in. The bridge listens to traffic, learning the physical addresses of the devices on each LAN. Within a few minutes, the bridge is able to capture and deliver traffic whose destination is not on the same LAN as its source.

There are bridges that can join LANs that are widely separated as well as LANs that are contiguous. Many vendors offer bridging equipment that operates across medium to high speed wide area links (see Figure 16.4).

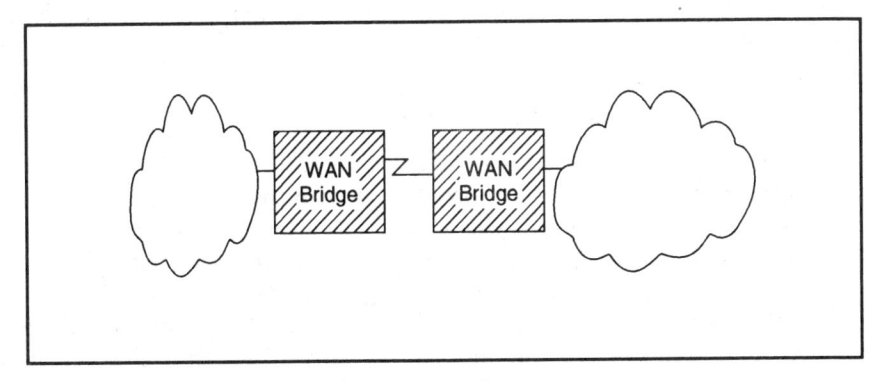

Figure 16.4 Bridging across a wide-area connection.

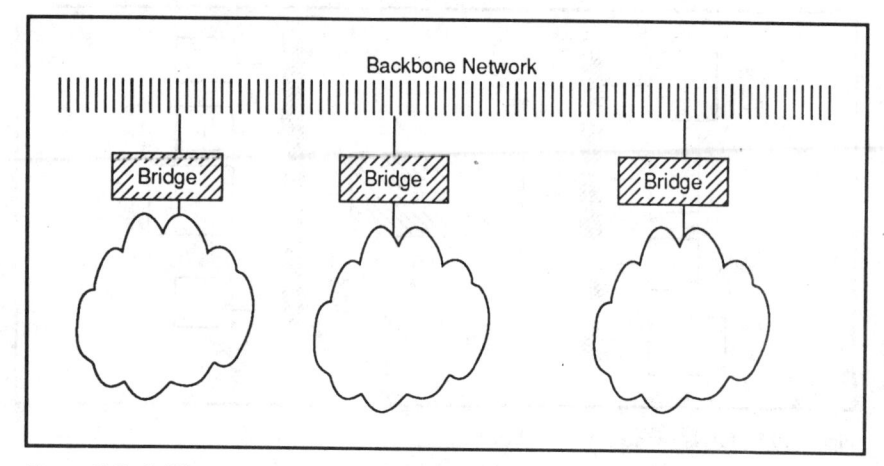

Figure 16.5 LANs connected to a backbone by means of bridges.

16.2.2 Splitting LANS with Bridges

A LAN with too many nodes can become a management nightmare. Performance suffers on an overburdened LAN. A problem with the network medium or with a network interface board can affect many systems, and can be difficult to diagnose. Using bridges, you can split up the oversized LAN and then reconnect the pieces.

Several things are accomplished by splitting an oversized LAN into two or more smaller LANs. Local traffic decreases and so performance improves. Problems are isolated within a smaller unit, affect fewer users and are easier to find and fix. Of course, it helps if you can partition the original LAN so that the 80-20 rule holds. That is, so that local traffic accounts for 80% or more of the load, while 20% or less needs to cross the bridge.

The backbone topology shown in Figure 16.5 is convenient when several LANs are to be bridged. A fiber optic backbone provides for abundant future capacity.

16.2.3 Backup Bridges and Network Loops

One shortcoming of some types of bridges is that they cannot tolerate a looped or multiply-connected topology. A loop confuses such a bridge, making it impossible to tell which side of the bridge a source address belongs to. However, backup bridges can be built into a network.

The spanning tree algorithm lets bridges negotiate in order to turn the network into a loop-free tree. Bridges that would form loops are deactivated, and are brought into service only when an active bridge

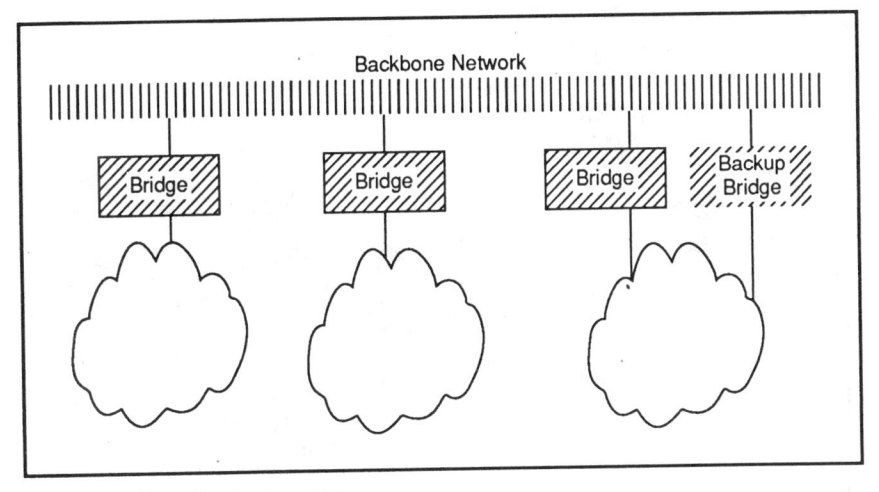

Figure 16.6 Use of a backup bridge.

goes down. After a failure, the spanning tree algorithm enables the bridged network to reconfigure itself automatically. The backup bridge shown in Figure 16.6 becomes active if the operative bridge fails.

16.2.4 Routers

A router operates at the network layer, and is tied to a particular protocol, such as IP.[1] Routers are slightly more costly than bridges, and require a moderate level of effort to install and maintain.

16.2.5 Router Capabilities

What can a router do that a bridge cannot do? A router can connect multiple LANs and WANs that use different MAC or link layer protocols.

Routers control the scope of broadcasts, while bridges generally propagate them.[2] For example, ARP messages need to be carried across a bridge. When the number of systems on the entire bridged network is large, broadcast messages become a nuisance that slows everyone's performance. Splitting up a large network by means of routers reduces broadcast traffic significantly.

---

[1] Vendors also sell multiprotocol routers. These can be viewed as several routers packaged within a single system.

[2] Some bridges can be configured to discard selected types of broadcast messages.

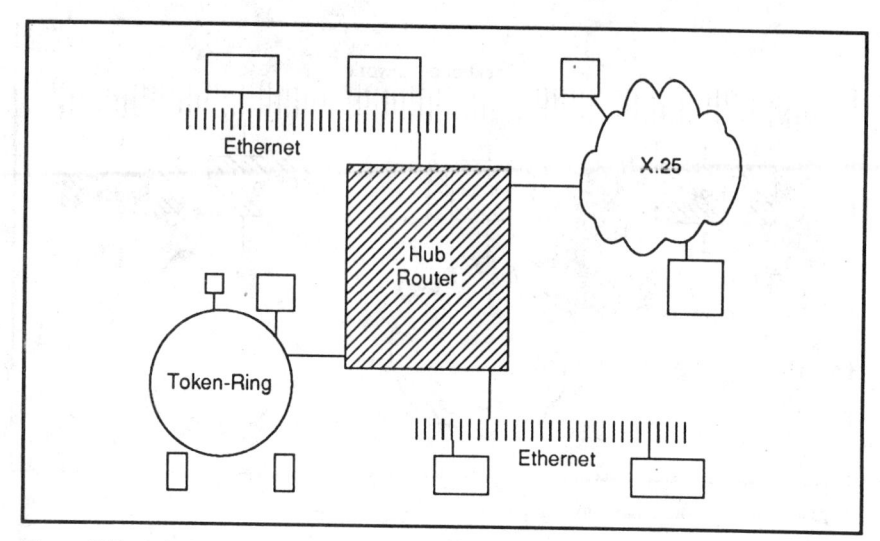

Figure 16.7 A hub router connected to several networks.

Some organizations use a routing hub as a single switching point for their entire network, as shown in Figure 16.7.

IP routers are used to construct large, complex internets (like that shown in Figure 16.8), which may be distributed across many locations. IP routing protocols can discover alternate paths, and adapt to network changes that happen in remote parts of the internet.

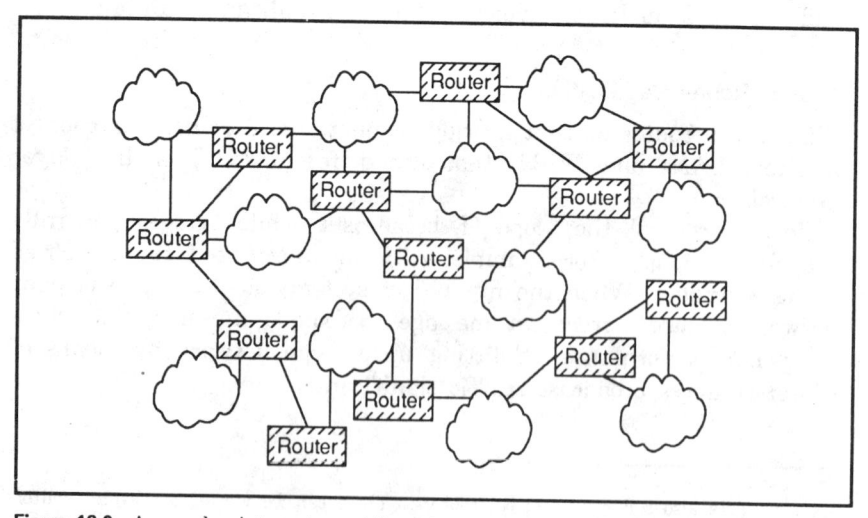

Figure 16.8 A complex internet providing alternate routes to destinations.

When using one of the capable modern IP routing protocols, traffic to a single destination can be split across several available paths, avoiding network congestion.

A bridge checks the source and destination physical addresses of every frame on each connected net. A router looks at traffic that has explicitly been sent to it, and at broadcast frames. Of course, a router must perform far more processing on the traffic that it examines than a bridge would.

16.2.6 Router Security Features

Some vendors have built significant security functions into their IP routers. These functions enable an administrator to restrict the traffic that is allowed to enter or leave a network. For example, a router could:

- Refuse to let any traffic that originates outside of an organization be delivered to a given subnet.
- Allow access to a particular host for file transfers, but bar terminal logins.

More specifically, IP traffic can be permitted or barred from transmission across a router interface based on the source or destination IP address, or based on the source or destination port.[3] Your routers also can prevent outsiders from getting a free ride across your network from an external source to an external destination!

This security feature helps an organization to protect the integrity of its network while enjoying the benefits of Internet services or the commercial advantage of connecting to clients and suppliers.

16.2.7 Routers with Proxy ARP

Many routers are capable of executing the proxy ARP protocol. Proxy ARP lets a host send an ARP request asking for the physical address of a destination that is *not* on its local network. The router that has the best route to the destination replies with an ARP message that contains the destination IP address and its own physical address.

This causes the originator to transmit datagrams to the router's physical address. The router handles the datagram normally, reading the destination IP address and forwarding the datagram towards its destination.

---

[3] Note that the router "cheats" and looks at UDP or TCP headers to check ports.

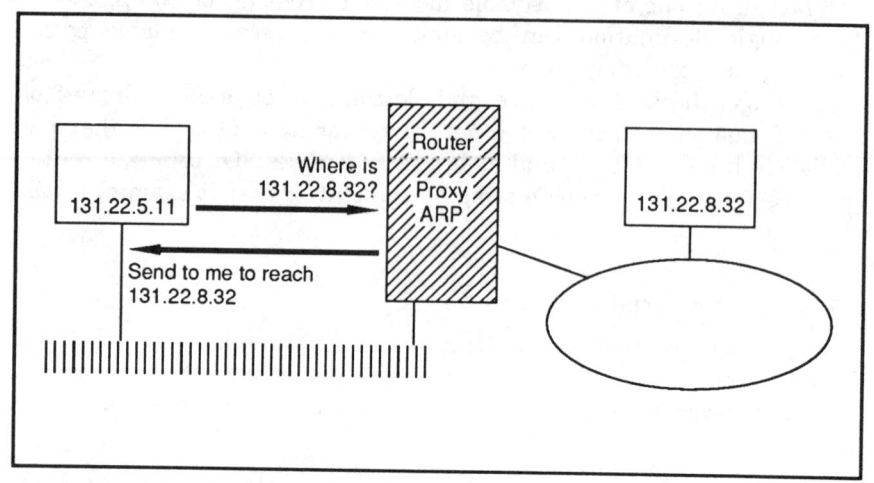

Figure 16.9 A router performing proxy ARP.

Figure 16.9 shows a proxy ARP router responding to a host's ARP request. An originator that wants to use proxy ARP must be configured so that it thinks that a set of remote systems are on its local network. One way to do this is to lie about the subnet mask.

For example, suppose that Class B network 131.22.0.0 is made up of 10 subnetworks. If systems are not configured with a subnet mask, they will believe that all destinations in the network lie on a single LAN. When they use ARP, an appropriate router will see to it that their traffic goes to the right place. What does this buy? A host can function even if it has not been configured with routing information. On the other hand, there is likely to be a hefty price to pay in the form of a lot of extra ARP traffic.

Then why bother? Proxy ARP is very helpful for network devices such as concentrators or bridges that need to receive initialization information or a software download from a server that is not on the local subnetwork. Before initialization these devices will be unaware of the subnet mask.

16.2.8 Brouters and Multiprotocol Routing

Suppose that some of the traffic on your LANs needs to be bridged, while routing is suitable for other traffic? Vendors have obligingly built *brouters*, which flexibly filter the traffic, routing some types while bridging others. Furthermore, today's routers and brouters can route multiple protocols selected from choices such as IP, DECnet, XNS, NetWare, Appletalk, or the OSI connectionless network protocol.

16.3 CONFIGURATION

Network configuration can be very simple. A workstation or server may be delivered with a set of preconfigured defaults that never have to be changed. The only job that you may have to do is to attach the system's interface to the network medium, assign a domain name and choose an IP address.

On the other hand, you may occasionally need to carry out the more complicated task of installing and configuring a network interface board on a host. There always is some work to do when configuring a router, especially if you want to make use of some of its security and performance enhancing features.

The sections that follow give an overview of configuration activities and the types of information that can be configured into TCP/IP systems. Examples that are shown are taken from UNIX systems, which tend to use a lot of small, separate configuration files.

The same type of information is gathered by means of menus in some other systems, while IBM mainframes define almost all TCP/IP configuration parameters in a single file. However, the organization of configuration menus, and the subheadings in the IBM file correspond to similar information in the individual UNIX files and should be easily recognizable from our examples.

16.3.1 Installing Interfaces

To connect to a selected medium, a bridge, router, or host station must be equipped with an interface board that possesses the correct physical attachments and Media Access Control protocol. Interface boards also carry out part of the data link protocol. Typically a simple connectionless link protocol is used to carry IP traffic. That is, datagrams are sent in unnumbered information frames.

Device driver software within a station controls the interface board. This software should be provided either by the station vendor or by the interface board supplier.

Not only hosts and routers need to support IP. Any device (such as a bridge) that contains an SNMP agent also will need to support IP and UDP for network management communications.

Bridge and router vendors customize their products with the selected boards and software before shipping them to customers. However, sometimes a host interface must be installed by the customer. This involves physically installing the board, loading the software, and changing system configuration parameters. In some cases, the system's operating system will have to be regenerated.

TABLE 16.1 Hex Codes Used for Network Masks

Subnet Bits	Hexadecimal Mask	Decimal Mask
8	FF	255
7	FE	254
6	FC	252
5	F8	248
4	F0	240
3	E0	224
2	C0	192
1	80	128

16.3.2 Configuring Interface Addresses and Masks

Several important TCP/IP parameters are associated with an interface. First of all, each interface is assigned an IP address. How do you choose IP addresses? Get in touch with the DDN NIC[4] and let them assign a unique block of addresses for your exclusive use! Making up your own addresses at random is sure to cause trouble for your organization some time in the future.

Each interface has an associated address mask. Table 16.1 shows the decimal and hexadecimal representations for one to eight bits of masking.

If you are not subnetting, the default mask simply covers the network part of the address. For example, the default mask for a Class C network is 255.255.255.0, or hex ffffff00. If you are subnetting, the mask covers the network and subnet fields in the IP address.

For example, if you have a Class A network and are using a 12-bit subnet field, the mask is 255.255.240.0 or hex FFFFF000.[5]

The network part of the address can be viewed as identifying your organization. The subnet part identifies an individual LAN or link. The remaining bits in the address identify an individual host or router

---

[4]See Chapter 1.

[5]Sometimes these configuration values are entered and displayed using a lower case hexadecimal representation: for example, ffffff00.

interface. You may want to reserve a few small numbers on each subnet (e.g., 1, 2, 3, and 4) for assignment to router interfaces. This will provide instant recognition of what type of system an address belongs to.

Each multiaccess interface board (such as an Ethernet or Token-Ring board) is shipped with a physical address that is guaranteed to be unique. It is possible to override the built-in address and replace it with a locally selected value. Of course, this adds the additional chore of physical address administration to the list of network management responsibilities.

The physical address to be used for broadcasts can be explicitly assigned to an interface attached to a multiaccess network or subnet.[6] The use of ARP must be enabled or disabled for the net.

Permanent entries can be configured into an ARP table, cutting down on the amount of broadcast traffic. If hundreds of PCs power up on your LAN every morning, you could preconfigure them with the ARP entries for their frequently used servers and primary router to help them to get off to a fast start!

16.3.3 Other Interface Parameters

As part of the system configuration process, an interface is assigned a metric that reflects the cost of crossing its attached network. For example, an administrator might assign a metric of 1 to crossing an Ethernet, while assigning 10 to crossing a 56-kilobit per second point-to-point link. Recall that these metrics are used in calculating the shortest route to a destination. Slower networks should be assigned larger metrics.

Each multiaccess interface has an associated default Maximum Transmission Unit (MTU), which is the size of the largest datagram that can be sent or received by the interface. For example, the Ethernet MTU is 1500 octets. Some systems allow an administrator to override the default MTU and enter a smaller value.

Point-to-point interfaces usually need to be assigned an MTU. If possible, this should be set to at least 576 octets in order to avoid excessive fragmentation.

The BSD 4.2 implementation introduced a nonstandard format for Ethernet MAC frames that tacked header information onto the MAC trailer. Quite a few commercial products picked up this feature, although now its use is fading away. The use of trailers should be

---

[6] Some old BSD-based systems default to using 0s in broadcasts instead of 1s. If possible, these should be reconfigured to use 1s.

avoided. However, if the use of trailers turns out to be necessary, there is a configuration parameter that turns this feature on.

16.3.4 Running Multiple Subnets on one LAN

Suppose that you are routing using RIP and have run out of addresses for hosts on your LAN? You could split up the LAN by installing an extra router, but if you are not having any performance or maintenance problems, this seems an unnecessary expense.

For example, if you have a type B network address and want to use an 8-bit subnet field, only 254 host addresses can be assigned to a subnet. But suppose that your LAN has 350 stations? If you could use two subnet numbers on the LAN, you would have 508 addresses to work with. Can you do this? The answer is that usually you can.

First, let's deal with the routers that are attached to your LAN. Many routers allow you to assign more than one IP address to an interface. The first address assigned is called the primary address, and any additional addresses are called secondary addresses.

For the LAN in our example, each router interface on the LAN would have to be assigned two addresses. This enables the routers to direct incoming traffic to any system on the LAN.

This leaves us with one more problem. Suppose that host DOUGHNUT with IP address 129.17.10.6 wants to communicate with host BROWNIE with address 129.17.11.23. DOUGHNUT will compare addresses using its subnet mask, which is 255.255.255.0, and come to the conclusion that BROWNIE is a remote system. How do we route to BROWNIE?

Fortunately, there is a common solution that is supported on most systems. You create an entry in DOUGHNUT's routing table that says "route to subnet 129.17.11.0 through me with a metric of zero." A metric of zero means that the destination is actually on the same physical subnet. The only trouble with this solution is that these routing entries must be created at every host on the LAN.

It might be tempting to configure hosts on the LAN with 7-bit masks. Traffic to 129.17.10 and 129.17.11 would then correctly appear to be on the same LAN. If there is only a single router on the LAN, then all external traffic can be exchanged via this default router and routing will function correctly.

If there are multiple routers, eavesdropping on RIP broadcasts will lead to a lot of confusion. Because of the local 7-bit mask, a routing table entry like 129.17.15.0 will appear to be the address of a host on subnet 129.17.14.0. It is a better idea to switch to OSPF, whose routing tables record the subnet mask for each destination subnet.

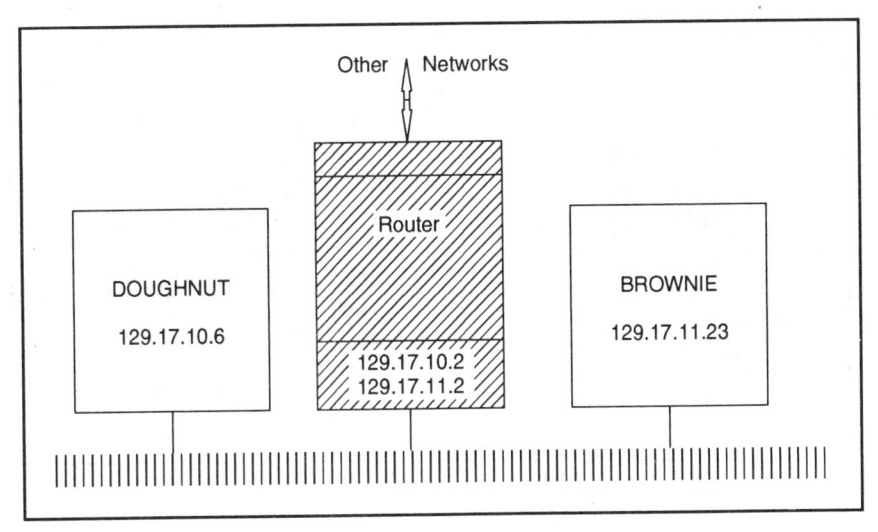

Figure 16.10 Subnets sharing a single physical LAN.

Figure 16.10 shows a LAN whose systems have addresses starting with 129.17.10 and 129.17.11. Each router interface connected to the LAN has two addresses.

16.3.5 Interfaces With More Than One Name

Depending on the system implementation, an administrator may have the option of associating a different name with each interface. That is, if desired, a different name could be assigned to every interface on a multihomed host or on a router.

Why bother? If an administrator wants to test an interface and likes to type user friendly names rather than IP addresses, it is handy to have a unique name to work with. In addition, identifying a destination by choosing a definite host network interface can be used to force data to be routed via that network, and there are times when users may want to do this.

16.3.6 Configuring Point-to-Point Links

Point-to-point links can be configured with their baud rate, Maximum Transmission Unit size, and with other parameters that are associated with the link protocol that is being used. For example, implementations of the Point-to-Point Protocol (PPP) allow a link to be configured so that the address and control fields of the PPP header are omitted, and the protocol field is shrunk to a single byte.

348 Chapter Sixteen

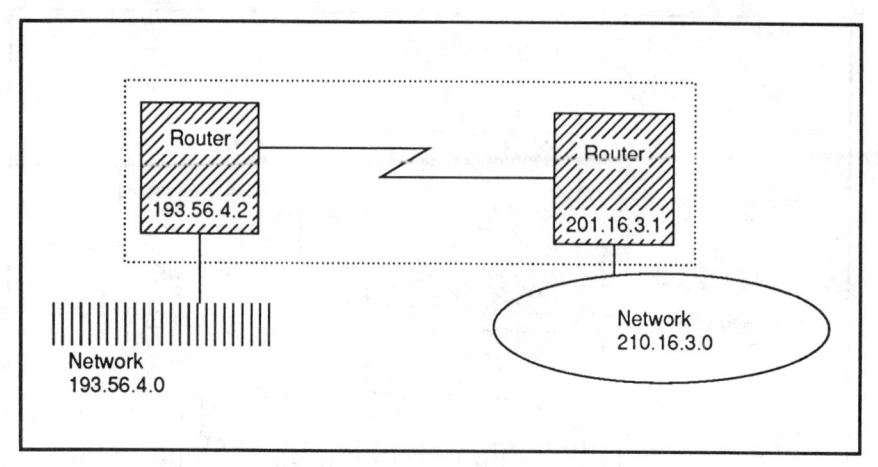

Figure 16.11 Routers connected by a point-to-point link.

16.3.7 Serial Interfaces without IP Addresses

Usually, the only interface parameter that is absolutely required is the IP address. However, there are times when we might not want to assign an IP address to an interface! How could this be? A point-to-point link is a very small subnet — it consists of only two systems. Using up an entire subnet address space for a link is very wasteful.

It is sometimes more convenient to view the two systems as if they are one.[7] Routers generally allow for this type of configuration. Of course, there is one disadvantage. It is not possible to send a ping to a serial interface that has not been assigned an IP address, although SNMP messages can be directed to any of a device's other IP addresses.

Figure 16.11 shows routers connected by a point-to-point link that has no assigned network and subnet addresses. Other systems on the network view them as a single device with one interface onto network 193.56.4.0 and another interface onto network 201.16.3.0.

Although this method saves subnet numbers, invisible interfaces do not support robust network management. An alternative way to be thrifty in your allocation of subnet numbers is to use 14-bit masks for point-to-point links.

16.3.8 Configuration Parameters and Commands

Table 16.2 summarizes frequently used interface configuration parameters.

---

[7]Another solution is to use a subnet mask of 255.255.255.252 for point-to-point lines.

TABLE 16.2 Interface Parameters

MULTIACCESS INTERFACE PARAMETERS	DESCRIPTION
Physical Address	Usually six octets. Easiest to use the default provided by the interface vendor.
IP Address	Required, except for serial links, where it is optional.
Secondary IP Address	An optional feature for routers, used to turn one physical network into two logical networks.
Subnet Mask	The default is a mask that covers the network address only.
Broadcast Address	Should use 1s in the broadcast field.
Protocol(s)	We are interested in IP, sometimes specified as inet.
Use of ARP for interface	Most often is YES.
Timeout for temporary ARP entries	Defaults set by vendors range from minutes to hours!
Use of RARP	Most often NO.
SERIAL INTERFACE PARAMETERS	**DESCRIPTION**
Optional IP Address	Could save a subnet number by not assigning one, or use longer subnet masks for serial lines.
Role as DTE or DCE	Can choose the behavior for the interface.
Baud Rate	Speed for interface.
MTU	Maximum Transmission Unit size.
If PPP used, PPP parameters	For example: addresses to be used in link negotiation, or whether to compress headers.

Many systems follow UNIX conventions, and have an *ifconfig* command that sets and displays network interface parameters. Recall that in Chapter 6 we displayed the current configuration for an Ethernet interface called le0, with the command:

```
ifconfig le0
le0: flags=63<UP,BROADCAST,NOTRAILERS,RUNNING>
     inet 128.36.12.27 netmask ffffff00 broadcast 128.36.12.255
```

Other systems provide menus, interactive dialogues or configuration files that are used to collect or display interface configuration data.

16.3.9 Configuring System Names

First of all, a system must be given its primary name. Unique naming is essential, so here again it is important to obtain a domain name, such as mycompany.com, from the NIC. The hierarchical system of delegation discussed in Chapter 5 can assure that all of the system names created within your organization are unique.

The NIC provides a form that is used to apply for a domain name. This form can be obtained by calling or writing to the NIC. It also is available online at host NIC.DDN.MIL in directory netinfo, in a file called *domain-template.txt*.

RFC 1032, *Domain Administrators Guide*, describes the responsibilities of a domain administrator and describes the rules for forming domain names. This RFC also includes instructions on how to fill out the form and contains a sample completed form.

The primary name assigned to a system usually is configured by means of a command included in the system's startup procedure. Some systems allow additional names to be associated with specific interface addresses.

16.3.10 IP Routing Tables

The primary IP configuration task is to initialize and maintain routing tables. Manual configuration often suffices for host routing tables in any size of network. Frequently, all that a host needs to know is the location of a single default router to be used for non-local destinations.

Tables for routers in a small, stable network also may be entered and maintained manually. However, routers in medium and large networks maintain their routing tables by periodically exchanging information via RIP, OSPF, or a proprietary protocol.

The selection of a routing protocol is an important configuration decision. Once chosen, the protocol's routing process should be started automatically when the system comes up. Note that even when a dynamic protocol is used, an administrator can configure a few static routes. These will be prevented from changing as a result of information learned from the network.

Although dynamic routing information exchange is mainly the concern of routers, hosts on a multiaccess LAN can eavesdrop and update their own tables accordingly, as long as they have the right software. It is not unusual for hosts to use dynamic updates when the RIP routing protocol is used, since RIP software is universally available.

However, note that this is not necessarily a smart thing to do. A host that really needs only two or three entries in its routing table may end up with a long list of extraneous entries. This list will be searched every time an IP address is looked up, which will slow performance.

Some routers support priority routing. They can be configured to assign a priority to traffic based on protocol, Type of Service, or on other criteria. High priority traffic is transmitted more promptly, and is less likely to be discarded under conditions of congestion.

Two global timers are important: one establishes how often routers talk to each other, and the second sets the interval after which a silent router is declared to be dead. Of course, these timers should be the same at all systems in the routing domain.

OSPF is a very complex protocol, and requires quite a lot of specialized configuration. For example, when OSPF is used, an internet needs to be partitioned into areas, and each area must be assigned an area number.

16.3.11 Accessing Routers

There are router products that allow administrators to login across an internet via Telnet in order to perform maintenance tasks. It is very important to configure strict access controls over these logins.

Typically, access control information includes the IP addresses of authorized source hosts, a userid, and a password. If desired, access can be restricted to a permanent or dialup serial connection. The option to perform maintenance via a login based on standard internet protocols gives customers flexibility in designing their own control strategies.

16.3.12 DDN IP Security

Recall that in Chapter 6 we discussed DDN security parameters that optionally may be carried in an IP header. These parameters were established for use in military and government applications, and generally are not used in a commercial environment. In fact, although becoming more available than in the past, there are many TCP/IP products that do not implement the security options.

Basic Security Option parameters include a classification level ranging from Unclassified to Top Secret, and flags that identify the protection authorities whose rules apply to the datagram. A datagram carrying the Basic Security Option may also include an Extended Security Option field. There are several different subformats for this option, depending on the needs of various defining authorities.

Systems that are operating under DDN security must be configured with the range of acceptable classification levels that may appear in the security field of a datagram transmitted or received by the system, the valid protection authorities for incoming datagrams, and the authorities for datagrams generated by the system. Classification and protection values also must be assigned on a per interface level, covering all datagrams transmitted or received by an interface. Security configuration is explained in detail in RFC 1108, *U.S. Department of Defense Security Options* for the Internet Protocol.

A host must discard information that it is not authorized to handle. It is important that secure data be delivered along routes that protect secure information. For this reason, when a router sees a datagram that it is not authorized to carry, it must discard it.

16.3.13 IP Parameters

Table 16.3 outlines parameters used to configure IP.

16.3.14 Dynamic Configuration

Diskless workstations have no way to remember configuration information. How can they get started? There are two protocols that are used.

The simplest is reverse ARP, or RARP, which allows a station to broadcast a request that contains its physical address and asks a server to return its IP address. The more functional bootstrap protocol, BOOTP, enables a BOOTP server to return information including the system's IP address, the address of a local router, and the address of a server that can download initialization files to the workstation via TFTP.

BOOTP also can be used to centralize the administration of PCs. However, if a lot of diskless stations and PCs simultaneously execute BOOTP first thing every morning, the network will be off to a slow start.

TABLE 16.3 IP Configuration Information

GENERAL PARAMETERS	DESCRIPTION
System Name	For example, BLINTZ.MED.YALE.EDU.
Routing Protocol	For example, RIP or OSPF.
Permanent Routing Entries	These will never change.
Initial Temporary Routing Entries	These can be overridden by current information.
DDN Security Parameters	Optional DOD Basic/Extended fields.
ROUTER PARAMETERS	**DESCRIPTION**
Traffic Priorities	For example, based on Type of Service.
Restrictions	For example, accept Telnet connections only from a given list of networks.
DDN Security Parameters	Optional DOD Basic/Extended fields.

16.3.15 External Routing

If you plan to connect to the Internet or to other external networks, you will need to obtain an Autonomous System (AS) number from the Network Information Center. External computers cannot communicate with your systems unless they know the addresses of your border routers and the networks that can be reached through these routers.

To exchange network reachability information with an external network, one or more of your border routers will need to run the Border Gateway Protocol (BGP) or the older Exterior Gateway Protocol (EGP).

A border router that exchanges reachability information must be configured with your Autonomous System number. It will need to know the identities of external neighbors, i.e., the routers with which it will exchange BGP or EGP information. The border router must be provided with the list of the networks that it will advertise. You can prevent external systems from communicating with one of your internal networks by omitting it from the list of advertised networks.

TABLE 16.4 Sample BGP Configuration Values

Parameters	Examples
Local Autonomous System Number	151
Remote Autonomous System Number	172
Neighbor Router	29.16.44.2
Neighbor Router	29.17.99.4
Advertise Network	131.10.0.0
Advertise Network	131.11.0.0
Advertise Network	192.17.2.0
Remote Autonomous System Number	173
Neighbor Router	29.19.33.1
Advertise Network	131.10.0.0
Advertise Network	131.15.0.0

Table 16.4 displays some sample BGP configuration information for an Autonomous System whose number is 151. Local Autonomous System 151 will exchange reachability information with neighbor routers in Autonomous Systems 172 and 173. The IP addresses of two neighbor routers in Autonomous System 172 and one in 173 are shown. The border router will advertise three networks to Autonomous System 172 and two networks to Autonomous System 173.

Recall that BGP supports policy based routing, which means that a BGP router can be configured to select:

- The internal networks that it will advertise to the world.
- The external networks that it will advertise to internal routers.
- The external Autonomous Systems that can send traffic to or through this Autonomous System.
- The external Autonomous Systems that can be crossed or reached by traffic that originates in this Autonomous System.

With policy-based routing, you can refuse to let your network provide free transit services for other organizations' data, and you can prevent your traffic from being carried across an insecure network.

16.3.16 Name to Address Translation

In a small, fairly static network, systems can be configured with a file (usually called *hosts*) that translates names to IP addresses. Some typical entries in a UNIX */etc/hosts* file are listed below. The entries contain the internet number, hierarchical name, and a nickname that can be used locally.

```
130.132.19.31    blintz.med.yale.edu     blintz
130.132.19.32    borscht.med.yale.edu    borscht
130.132.19.33    couscous.med.yale.edu   couscous
```

The administrator of a medium-sized network may prefer to use a server at which names and addresses are maintained. Domain Name System (DNS) servers generally are maintained for medium-sized or large networks.

16.3.17 Using the Domain Name System

Most computer vendors provide Domain Name System resolver software which enables a client to make queries, as well as software that lets a node act as a server and interact with other servers.

Vendors provide several variations on how programs request name translation. Some systems match a name by first looking in a local host table, and then sending a DNS query if this fails. LANs using a Network Information System (NIS) host database[8] consult that first. If no match is found, NIS will send a query to DNS.[9]

Relying on local information can be risky if that information is not kept up to date. Some administrators choose to use DNS exclusively. Alternatively, the software might try DNS first, and if no response can be obtained, try a local host table. This would prevent a host from becoming totally cut off when it is unable to reach a DNS server.

In fact, various TCP/IP implementations use different combinations of local, LAN, and DNS lookups to perform name to address translations.

A DNS resolver needs to know the location of one or more Name Servers. For example, for UNIX systems, this information is contained in the file */etc/resolv.conf*.

---

[8]NIS is the local database service created by Sun Microsystems. See Chapter 12 to review its features.

[9]Persistent automatic queries from NIS cause problems for the Domain Name System.

356 Chapter Sixteen

The sample file below contains three nameserver addresses as well as a domain name. This domain name will be tacked onto the end of names that do not contain a period.[10]

```
domain CS.YALE.EDU
nameserver 128.36.0.36
nameserver 128.36.0.3
nameserver 128.36.0.1
```

Thus, if a user enters "newton," the resolver will send a name query for NEWTON.CS.YALE.EDU to the server at 128.36.0.36. If this server is not available, the resolver will try 128.36.0.3, and if this server is down, the query is sent to 128.36.0.1. DNS servers routinely maintain a cache of recent lookup results that speed performance by cutting down on the number of remote queries that are needed.

If no nameserver is identified in a UNIX resolver configuration file, your system might assume that there is a nameserver at the local host!

16.3.18 Getting All of the IP Addresses for a System

In the *nslookup* dialogues that we have displayed in earlier chapters, it appeared that a Domain Name Server returned a single address to a query. In fact, a system may have multiple addresses, and a server is capable of returning all of them.

In order to see a full response, we can run *nslookup* and turn debug on. We also set nodefname, which prevents our *nslookup* from automatically appending the local domain name components to every query. Note that two addresses are returned under ANSWERS:

```
nslookup
Default Server:  DEPT-GW.CS.YALE.EDU
Address:   128.36.0.36

> set debug
> set nodefname

res_mkquery(0, bulldog.cs.yale.edu, 1, 1)
------------
Got answer:
    HEADER:
    opcode = QUERY, id = 4, rcode = NOERROR
    header flags:   response, auth. answer, want recursion, recursion
```

---

[10] Some implementations tack on the domain name even if there is a dot in the entered name! If this search fails, they retry, removing one component of the domain name at a time.

```
avail.
  questions = 1,  answers = 2,  auth. records = 0,  additional = 0

    QUESTIONS:
    bulldog.cs.yale.edu, type = A, class = IN
    ANSWERS:
    -> bulldog.cs.yale.edu    inet address = 128.36.0.3
    -> bulldog.cs.yale.edu    inet address = 130.132.1.2

------------
Name:    bulldog.cs.yale.edu
Address: 128.36.0.3
```

How does IP route to a system with multiple addresses? The first thing to check is whether any of these addresses is on a locally attached subnet. If not, IP ought to pick the address that corresponds to the smallest metric.

An administrator might want to access a selected interface of a system, e.g., for testing. Recall that we can assign a distinguished name to each interface. This unique name-to-address translation also should be recorded at the DNS server.

Note that an organization connecting a network to the Internet is expected to support primary and backup Domain Name Servers.

16.3.19 Setting Up Domain Name Servers

The Domain Name System is a distributed database system that was designed to provide information about the systems in the Internet. As we already have seen, DNS servers provide name-to-address translation and identify the location of mail exchangers.

An organization can attach its network to the Internet and merge its own servers into the Internet database or can create a set of private DNS databases.

Most TCP/IP vendors provide name server software. Often this software is based on the Berkeley Internet Domain (BIND) implementation. RFC 1033, the *Domain Administrators Operations Guide*, contains detailed descriptions of server configuration and of the structure of a DNS database. Of course, there will be differences across vendor products, and vendor documentation should always be consulted.

The information in a distributed DNS database is divided into *zone* files. A zone file holds information about a subtree or a contiguous piece of a subtree in the domain name space. Zone data is updated by the administrative authority that is responsible for the nodes in the zone. Updates always are applied to a master file, but the master file can be copied to other servers in order to preserve availability.

Chapter Sixteen

The NIC requires at least two distinct servers for each zone. A single server can hold information about several zones. A server does not have to reside within the domain that it describes.

Domain name servers are organized into a hierarchy. A server is configured with information that enables it to locate any server below it in the hierarchy. The Internet maintains 7 root servers. Any of these servers can be consulted to locate any Internet DNS database.

To become part of the Internet DNS, a server will be configured so that it knows the Internet root servers, the servers that are below it in the hierarchy, and the local zone files to be loaded. A list of all of the Internet root servers is maintained at NIC.DDN.MIL in the file /netinfo/root-servers.txt.

Each zone file contains *resource records*. Resource records contain information such as system names, system nicknames, IP addresses, and the locations of mail exchangers. There also are resource records that map domain names to their domain name servers.

In the dialogue below, we use nslookup to find the name servers for the COM domain. The rules specify that because there is only a single label in this domain name, our query must end with a period. Note that the same response would be received for any of the other top level domains, such as EDU.

```
nslookup
Default Server:  DEPT-GW.CS.YALE.EDU
Address:   128.36.0.36

> set type=NS
> COM.
Server:   DEPT-GW.CS.YALE.EDU
Address:   128.36.0.36

COM          nameserver = NS.NIC.DDN.MIL
COM          nameserver = KAVA.NISC.SRI.COM
COM          nameserver = C.NYSER.NET
COM          nameserver = TERP.UMD.EDU
COM          nameserver = NS.NASA.GOV
COM          nameserver = AOS.BRL.MIL
COM          nameserver = NIC.NORDU.NET
NS.NIC.DDN.MIL         inet address = 192.112.36.4
KAVA.NISC.SRI.COM      inet address = 192.33.33.24
C.NYSER.NET            inet address = 192.33.4.12
TERP.UMD.EDU           inet address = 128.8.10.90
NS.NASA.GOV            inet address = 128.102.16.10
NS.NASA.GOV            inet address = 192.52.195.10
AOS.BRL.MIL            inet address = 128.63.4.82
AOS.BRL.MIL            inet address = 26.3.0.29
AOS.BRL.MIL            inet address = 192.5.25.82
```

NIC.NORDU.NET   inet address = 192.36.148.17

Servers can cache the results of recent lookups, and use the cache to respond to subsequent queries. Answers that have been obtained from a cache are labelled as "non-authoritative."

The dialogue below shows the unusual format used to look up the name corresponding to a known IP address. First the type must be set to PTR. Then the IP address is entered in reverse order, followed by "in-addr.arpa." The answer comes from cached data, and so is labelled "non-authoritative."

```
> set type=PTR
> 32.0.9.128.in-addr.arpa

Server:  DEPT-GW.CS.YALE.EDU
Address: 128.36.0.36

Non-authoritative answer:
32.0.9.128.in-addr.arpa host name = venera.isi.edu
Authoritative answers can be found from:
CHARM.ISI.EDU    inet address = 128.9.128.128
VENERA.ISI.EDU   inet address = 128.9.0.32
VAX.DARPA.MIL    inet address = 192.5.18.99
VAX.DARPA.MIL    inet address = 192.48.218.99
```

16.3.20 Configuring TCP

There is not much general configuration to do at the TCP level. One reason for this is that configuration can be tuned on a per-connection basis by means of the programming interface to TCP.

Usually an administrator must select a default receive window size. Another important TCP parameter is the maximum number of *data* bytes that TCP is willing to receive in one segment, called the Maximum Segment Size (MSS).[11] TCP will check whether a destination is on a locally connected network. If it is, TCP will look up the interface for the network, and will calculate the MSS by subtracting 40 from the Maximum Transmission Unit configured for the interface.

If the destination is not local, most TCP software automatically selects a MSS of 536. This matches the Maximum Transmission Unit of 576, which is the standard default datagram size. A few products allow an administrator to tabulate the Maximum Transmission Units to be used for specific destination networks.

---

[11]Although a segment consists of a TCP header and data, by definition Maximum Segment Size measures only the amount of data in a segment.

```
###############################################################
     echo       7/tcp      # Returns any data received.
     echo       7/udp      # Used for testing.
     discard    9/tcp      # Discards any data received.
     discard    9/udp      # Used for testing.
     netstat    15/tcp     # Collects lots of network information
     ftp-data   20/tcp     # File transfer data connection
     ftp        21/tcp     # File transfer control connection
     tftp       69/udp     # Trivial file transfer protocol
     telnet     23/tcp     # Telnet server
     smtp       25/tcp     # Simple mail transfer protocol
     talk       517/udp    # Sets up terminal conversations.
     time       37/tcp     # Used to synchronize time of day
     time       37/udp     # Clocks on a network.
###############################################################
# NIC Services                                                #
###############################################################
     whois      43/tcp     # User information. Queries are
                           # usually sent to the NIC
     domain     53/udp     # Domain Name Server
     domain     53/tcp     # Domain Name Server
     hostnames  101/tcp    # Usually to NIC
###############################################################
# Remote Procedure Call Portmapper                            #
###############################################################
     sunrpc     111/udp    # Portmapper port for RPC services
     sunrpc     111/tcp    # Portmapper port for RPC services
```

Figure 16.12 Internet services and their ports.

16.3.21 Configuring Services

A host needs to be configured with the reserved port numbers used for TCP and UDP services. Usually TCP/IP software includes a standard configuration file that can be edited to include the services that are supported locally. The list in Figure 16.12 is taken from a UNIX */etc/services* file, and contains characteristic information.

Quite a few of the entries are familiar. We see that port 21 is used for file transfer control connections and port 20 is used for data connections. Telnet service is available at port 23 and mail transfer is carried out via port 25. The echo service at port 7 and discard at port 9 are used for testing. The talk server at port 517 sets up a connection between two terminal users on a network who can then have a conversation by typing messages to each other.

Whois, at port 43, accesses a NIC database that provides information about people, such as their Internet mailboxes and telephone numbers. When a new network connects to the Internet, it is normal practice for the NIC staff to add entries that identify the network's administrators.

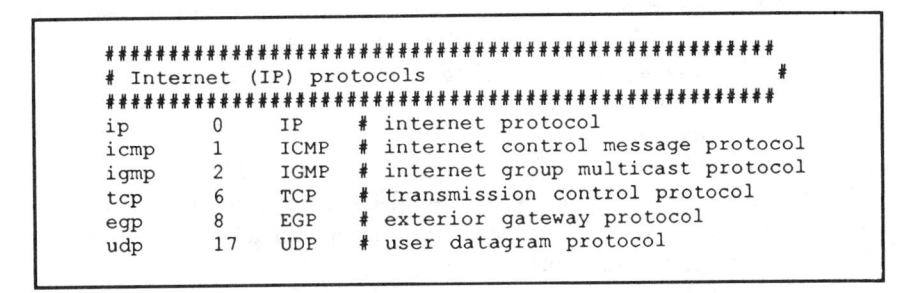

```
###########################################################
# Internet (IP) protocols                                  #
###########################################################
ip      0     IP      # internet protocol
icmp    1     ICMP    # internet control message protocol
igmp    2     IGMP    # internet group multicast protocol
tcp     6     TCP     # transmission control protocol
egp     8     EGP     # exterior gateway protocol
udp     17    UDP     # user datagram protocol
```

Figure 16.13 Protocol configuration file.

We see that Domain Name Servers operate out of port 53 via either TCP or UDP. Port 111 is the home of the portmapper, which is the clearinghouse for port information for Remote Procedure Call services.

Another configuration file translates protocol names to the numbers that appear in the IP protocol field. The UNIX version of this file is called */etc/protocols*. Figure 16.13 shows entries from a sample file.

16.3.22 Configuring Anonymous FTP

Anonymous FTP enables users without accounts at the local system to access selected public directories. The actual configuration of this service varies depending on a computer's operating system. Frequently, an *ftp* userid is created, and logins with a userid of *ftp, anonymous*, or *guest* are accepted. The privileges for the *ftp* user account must be strictly controlled so that anonymous users will not be able to write files, will not have access to files outside of the public directory, and will be unable to run programs apart from the FTP server.

16.3.23 Running Services

How do services get started? How do they handle multiple clients? There are two methods. Let's take file transfer as an example. A vendor might build a multithreaded FTP server that is started as part of system initialization. This single server would handle requests from all clients.

Another popular implementation is to have one process that listens for client requests and starts a fresh FTP process for each client. In fact, in order to avoid having many background processes that spend most of their time sitting around and waiting for clients — and consuming system resources while they wait — many systems let a single process listen on lots of ports. This process creates the right kind of server for each client request.

362   Chapter Sixteen

In UNIX, this super-listener is called *inetd*. The inetd process can invoke services, such as file transfer and Telnet servers, as they are needed. The entries in Figure 16.14 are taken from an inetd configuration file (*inetd.conf*, of course). This file lists and describes the servers that inetd will start.

Let's take a look at the FTP entry. We see that FTP servers use a TCP stream type of socket interface. Nowait means that as soon as inetd has taken care of a client by setting up a new FTP server process, inetd can help another FTP client.

The FTP server program is in file */usr/etc/in.ftpd* and should be run under the ownership of the privileged system manager account, *root*. The entry ends with any arguments to the program. In this case, the only argument is the program's name.

On the other hand, *talk* is a User Datagram server, and once it has been started, the single talk server will handle all talk clients. After the talk server terminates, inetd can resume listening on talk's port, and will restart the server when another client request arrives.

Echo is somewhat different; it also is a datagram service, but inetd performs the echo protocol service internally — that is, inetd acts as the echo server.

A program such as inetd is not used to start all services. For example, NFS and mount servers generally are started at system initiation time, and run continually as background tasks.

```
###############################################
#
# Internet services syntax:
#   <service_name> <socket_type> <proto> <flags>
#       <user> <server_pathname> <args>
#
# Ftp and telnet are standard Internet services.
###############################################
ftp      stream  tcp  nowait  root  /usr/etc/in.ftpd     in.ftpd
telnet   stream  tcp  nowait  root  /usr/etc/in.telnetd  in.telnetd
talk     dgram   udp  wait    root  /usr/etc/in.talkd    in.talkd
echo     dgram   udp  wait    root  internal
```

Figure 16.14 Configuration file for inetd startup function.

16.3.24 Mail

LANs with attached PCs or workstations may want to use a local mail relay system. The relay collects incoming mail for these systems, and delivers it upon request. The relay also accumulates outgoing mail from stations, and sends it at convenient intervals. Sometimes the Post Office Protocol or some other local protocol is used between a relay and its stations.

An organization may want to set up one or more *mail exchangers*. Recall that all mail sent to an organization can be directed to a mail exchanger by means of an entry in the DNS mail exchanger database. Optionally, name translation may take place at the exchanger.

16.3.25 Remote Procedure Call Services

Remote procedure call (RPC) programs are each assigned a number. The program name, program number, and command names for the service are listed in a configuration file. Figure 16.15 shows some entries in the UNIX configuration file, */etc/rpc*. When an RPC program initializes, it registers its program number and port number with the *portmapper* service.

```
################################################
#          rpc                                  #
################################################
portmapper    100000    portmap sunrpc
rstatd        100001    rstat rup perfmeter
rusersd       100002    rusers
nfs           100003    nfsprog
ypserv        100004    ypprog
mountd        100005    mount showmount
walld         100008    rwall shutdown
etherstatd    100010    etherstat
rquotad       100011    rquotaprog quota rquota
sprayd        100012    spray
rexd          100017    rex
llockmgr      100020
nlockmgr      100021
statmon       100023
status        100024
bootparam     100026
pcnfsd        150001
```

Figure 16.15 Sample Remote Procedure Call configuration file.

16.3.26 NFS

NFS is transparent to users — until something goes wrong and part of a user's file system vanishes! Careful planning is required to work out the placement of NFS servers and a coherent system of naming that helps administrators to pinpoint the real location of a lost directory.

Servers need to be configured with export files listing the directories that clients can access. The NFS server background processes should be initiated at server startup time. If the optional file locking protocol is also to be used, then lock manager and status manager processes must also be run.

Similarly, clients need to be configured with import files listing the hosts and directories to be mounted and a set of configuration parameters for each mount. The client system's startup procedure should mount all of the directories listed in the import file. NFS client implementations often include a background process that runs continually and improves file access performance by executing block reads and writes on behalf of all users.[12]

16.3.27 Configuring Network Management

In Chapter 15 we discussed the way that SNMP access privileges are defined by means of a *community name* and a *community profile*. A simple way of setting this up is to define one community profile that allows a manager to read Management Information Base (MIB) data, and another that gives a manager general read/write access.

Allowing write access might be considered risky since current SNMP implementations do not support authentication. However, some systems improve SNMP security by allowing an administrator to restrict the IP address or addresses from which a privileged community name will be accepted.

Perhaps the most important SNMP configuration information is the identity of the host or hosts that should receive the Trap messages that are generated as the result of problems.

16.3.28 General TCP/IP Configuration

Most systems provide reasonable default amounts of memory resources for TCP/IP networking. These values can be changed to tune the system for better performance. This information may take the form of an explicit allocation of buffers of various sizes, or else as a limit on the number of connections that can be supported.

---

[12] For UNIX, this process is called biod.

A default level for precedence and Type of Service can be set. Default Type of Service values can be overridden by values set by applications on a per connection basis.

An administrator will have to identify the name for the local time zone, such as EST or PST, and the offset from universal time (formerly Greenwich Mean Time). If this computer is going to synchronize its time of day clock, the name of a LAN timeserver is needed. It is very helpful to have PCs and workstations on a LAN set the time from a single server. When troubleshooting a problem, consistent timestamps on items such as error log entries and mail messages are essential to figuring out what is going on.

16.3.29 The System Startup Procedure

Your system vendor will provide a sample startup procedure that usually needs only minor tailoring. It is a good idea to stick as close to this procedure as possible.

In particular, it is easy to get in trouble if you shift around the order of the commands in the procedure. For example, a portmapper process needs to be started before an RPC service such as NFS comes up, because an RPC service needs to register with an active portmapper.

16.4 MAINTENANCE, MONITORING, AND TROUBLESHOOTING

An internet is complex, with lots of intelligence distributed across many locations. It is multivendor and multitechnology. The tasks of capacity planning, maintenance, and problem solving are more challenging than ever before.

A network manager needs to monitor traffic on a regular basis to find out normal and peak hour loads, performance levels, and error rates. This data is the basis for long term capacity planning. Even more to the point, knowing the normal condition of the network is the key to recognizing that behavior has become abnormal!

Planning for trouble is probably the most important management function. Important as it is to locate and fix faulty components, what users want is to reach the services that they want to reach. Deploying backup communications equipment and backup servers keeps the telephone quiet while the process of detailed diagnosis goes forward.

What are the tools can help to track down problems?

16.4.1 SNMP Facilities

In Chapter 15 we discussed the Simple Network Management Protocol. SNMP at last provides a critical missing element in TCP/IP network management: a simple, uniform protocol that can be installed in every network device.

Prior to the widespread deployment of SNMP, vendors either insisted that you had to control their devices by means of a local console, or else provided a proprietary remote control protocol. Understanding and maintaining a dozen proprietary network management protocols is itself a management task of large proportions!

Although the technology is new, SNMP managers and agents already provide significant and useful information. An SNMP manager can gather traffic statistics for each hour of the day and collect errors and failures at every protocol level. Information will be concentrated at a central collection point, rather than being dispersed haphazardly through the network. Although this is a new technology, many vendors already offer management stations with graphical network displays and sophisticated report generating capabilities.

Other simple tools that have proved their value through several years of use will be discussed in the sections that follow.

16.4.2 Network Monitors

A dedicated network monitor is a product that passively listens to LAN network traffic. A monitor can get answers to your questions about what is going on across your LAN. It can generate periodic traffic reports broken down by frame size, source, destination, protocol, or just about any other criterion that you can think of.

A LAN monitor can trap and save network traffic based on configured filters. It can display detailed information about every level of a protocol stack. A monitor can be used to look for security violations by capturing all login attempts. It can capture traffic containing some pattern that is associated with a network problem.

As we have seen in the Network General *Sniffer* monitor reports in earlier chapters, protocol header fields are displayed in a simple, interpreted format. Data captured by monitors can be fed into a relational database for general study and report generation.

One of the great advantages of a monitor is that it gathers information without using any network bandwidth. It provides the fastest and most direct information on the instantaneous status of a LAN.

A limited monitoring function can be built into devices such as bridges. Recall that integrating network monitor information into SNMP by means of the RMON MIB was discussed in Chapter 15.

Examples of information that is available include:

- Names and addresses of active stations.
- Traffic to and from each station.
- Number of frames discarded and why.
- Current Telnet, SMTP, or FTP sessions.

A powerful, dedicated monitor should be capable of scanning all LAN traffic. However, if you do not have a dedicated monitor, many UNIX workstations have the capability to listen to their LAN and provide limited, but still useful information.

16.4.3 Ping, Spray, and Traceroute

The simple *ping* command, built on top of the ICMP echo message, is the most universally available monitoring tool. *Ping* can check whether a host is alive. It can test each separate interface of a router to see if it is functioning. A *ping* dialogue is short and succinct:

```
ping flash.bellcore.com
flash.bellcore.com is alive
```

There are several versions of the ping program. The version shown below was invoked with an *-s* flag that caused ping to send one echo message each second. At the end of the sequence, the program prints a brief summary report that states the number of messages that were lost and the minimum, maximum, and average round trip times. Note that either the network or the destination host was congested, and 21% of the "packets" (meaning the ICMP echo messages) were lost.

```
ping -s flash.bellcore.com
PING bellcore.com: 56 data bytes
64 bytes from flash.bellcore.com(128.96.32.20):icmp_seq=3.time=21.ms
64 bytes from flash.bellcore.com(128.96.32,20):icmp_seq=4.time=18.ms
64 bytes from flash.bellcore.com(128.96.32.20):icmp_seq=5.time=17.ms
64 bytes from flash.bellcore.com(128.96.32.20):icmp_seq=6.time=19.ms
64 bytes from flash.bellcore.com(128.96.32.20):icmp_seq=7.time=17.ms
64 bytes from flash.bellcore.com(128.96.32.20):icmp_seq=8.time=17.ms
64 bytes from flash.bellcore.com(128.96.32.20):icmp_seq=9.time=17.ms
64 bytes from flash.bellcore.com(128.96.32.20):icmp_seq=10.time=18.ms
64 bytes from flash.bellcore.com(128.96.32.20):icmp_seq=11.time=17.ms
64 bytes from flash.bellcore.com(128.96.32.20):icmp_seq=12.time=17.ms
64 bytes from flash.bellcore.com(128.96.32.20):icmp_seq=13.time=17.ms

----flash.bellcore.comPING Statistics----
14 packets transmitted, 11 packets received, 21% packet loss
round-trip (ms)  min/avg/max = 17/17/21
```

Spray is a Remote Procedure Call based function that sends a stream of datagrams to a Remote Procedure Call server and displays the result.[13] *Spray* does not wait between messages, and so can be used to check the result of a burst of traffic.

```
spray -c 10 flash.bellcore.com

sending 10 packets of lnth 86 to flash.bellcore.com ...
   in 0.4 seconds elapsed time,

  2 packets (20.00%) dropped by flash.bellcore.com
Sent:    22 packets/sec, 1.9K bytes/sec
Rcvd:    17 packets/sec, 1.5K bytes/sec
```

Failure to reach a host does not necessarily mean that the host is down. There may be a problem with a router or link along the path. The *traceroute* command helps to locate the trouble spot.

Traceroute sends a sequence of probing UDP datagrams to the selected destination. Three initial messages are sent with the Time to Live (TTL) field set to one. This causes the first router on the path to return ICMP messages reporting that the TTL has expired. The TTL value is increased to 2 and three more messages are sent. This causes the second router to return ICMP messages. New messages with larger TTLs are sent until the destination is reached or a preset maximum TTL limit is reached.

Traceroute reports the round trip time of each of its messages. A sample result is shown below. Note that in most cases there is a great difference between the first probe and the ones that follow. This may be due to a need to use ARP for the initial message.

```
traceroute flash.bellcore.com
  1   CASPER.NA.CS.YALE.EDU (128.36.12.1)    64 ms   3 ms    3 ms
  2   SPINE-GW.CS.YALE.EDU (128.36.0.2)      60 ms   6 ms    8 ms
  3   YALE-GATEWAY.JVNC.NET (130.132.1.13)   93 ms   6 ms    6 ms
  4   preppy1-gateway.jvnc.net (130.94.22.9) 63 ms   6 ms    6 ms
  5   bigapple1-gateway.jvnc.net (130.94.15.250) 31 ms  10 ms  10 ms
  6   core-gateway.jvnc.net (130.94.9.26)    50 ms  13 ms   15 ms
  7   128.96.58.2 (128.96.58.2)              91 ms  13 ms   13 ms
  8   flash.bellcore.com (128.96.32.20)      16 ms  25 ms   16 ms
```

Traceroute is widely available as free software. Its use is sometimes restricted to privileged systems staff.

---

[13]There also is an option that causes the spray command to send ICMP echo messages instead.

16.4.4 Netstat for General Networking Status

The *netstat* command, which has been ported to many operating systems, provides a variety of information about the status of network components at the local system. Every implementation of *netstat* is a little different, but the sample displays that follow, obtained using the Sun Microsystems implementation, are representative. The dialogues that follow show some, but not all, of the reporting capabilities that are bundled into *netstat*. The first display shows the first few rows of the current routing table.

```
netstat -nr
Routing tables
Destination          Gateway         Flags   Refcnt  Use     Interface
127.0.0.1            127.0.0.1       UH      , 2     940     lo0
128.36.16.0          128.36.12.1     UG        0     19      le0
default              128.36.12.1     UG        0     48      le0
. . .
```

Recall that any address starting with 127 is a loopback address, used to test communications software. The next display shows summary routing statistics.

```
netstat -nrs
routing:
    0 bad routing redirects
    0 dynamically created routes
    0 new gateways due to redirects
   13 destinations found unreachable
   12 uses of a wildcard route
```

To cut down on configuration chores, a host routing table can be set up with nothing but a loopback address and a single default router. If there are other routers on the LAN, the default router will send an ICMP redirect whenever another router provides a better path to a destination. Redirects can be used to correct the local table. However, no redirects were reported in the above display.

The *netstat -s* command can produce quite comprehensive statistics on the various TCP/IP protocols. The reports in Figure 16.16 and Figure 16.17 show that the protocol software at the local system behaved quite well during the sample period.

UDP had no problems. However, it would be normal to see a certain number of UDP socket overflows. This results from the fact that, unlike TCP, UDP never knows how much data may arrive at any time. A sudden burst of traffic can exhaust all of the buffers that are available.

```
udp:
    0 incomplete headers
    0 bad data length fields
    0 bad checksums
    0 socket overflows

tcp:
    3438 packets sent
            1711 data packets (9687 bytes)
            0 data packets (0 bytes) retransmitted
            1613 ack-only packets (1427 delayed)
            2 URG only packets
            6 window probe packets
            14 window update packets
            92 control packets
    2402 packets received
            1767 acks (for 9753 bytes)
            52 duplicate acks
            0 acks for unsent data
            1847 packets (50639 bytes) received in-sequence
            86 completely duplicate packets (33694 bytes)
            16 packets with some dup. data (5720 bytes duped)
            34 out-of-order packets (0 bytes)
            0 packets (0 bytes) of data after window
            0 window probes
            4 window update packets
            0 packets received after close
            0 discarded for bad checksums
            0 discarded for bad header offset fields
            0 discarded because packet too short
    41 connection requests
    10 connection accepts
    51 connections established (including accepts)
    60 connections closed (including 0 drops)
    1 embryonic connection dropped
    1766 segments updated rtt (of 1807 attempts)
    1 retransmit timeout
            0 connections dropped by rexmit timeout
    0 persist timeouts
    2 keepalive timeouts
            2 keepalive probes sent
            0 connections dropped by keepalive
```

Figure 16.16 UDP and TCP *netstat* protocol statistics.

```
icmp:
    6 calls to icmp_error
    0 errors not generated 'cuz old message too short
    0 errors not generated 'cuz old message was icmp
    Output histogram:
            echo reply: 15
            destination unreachable: 6
    0 messages with bad code fields
    0 messages < minimum length
    0 bad checksums
    0 messages with bad length
    Input histogram:
            echo reply: 1
            destination unreachable: 10
            echo: 15
    15 message responses generated

ip:
    39751 total packets received
    0 bad header checksums
    0 with size smaller than minimum
    0 with data size < data length
    0 with header length < data size
    0 with data length < header length
    11918 fragments received
    0 fragments dropped (dup or out of space)
    0 fragments dropped after timeout
    0 packets forwarded
    0 packets not forwardable
    0 redirects sent
    0 ip input queue drops
```

Figure 16.17 Protocol statistics for ICMP and IP.

There were no outgoing TCP retransmissions, but quite a few duplicate segments were received. There were 51 new connections set up during the period, and 60 connections terminated. ICMP traffic consisted of a few destination unreachables, and some ping echo messages.

IP received a significant number of fragmented datagrams, but managed to put all of them back together.

Finally, Figure 16.18 shows part of the response to the *netstat* command that asks for a display of active TCP and UDP communications. Note the large number of TCP-based servers listening for clients.

```
netstat -a
Active Internet connections (including servers)
Proto Recv-Q Send-Q   Local        Foreign    (state)
                      Address      Address
 udp    0      0      *.daytime    *.*
 udp    0      0      *.discard    *.*
 udp    0      0      *.echo       *.*
 udp    0      0      *.time       *.*
 udp    0      0      *.tftp       *.*
 udp    0      0      *.talk       *.*
 udp    0      0      *.name       *.*
 udp    0      0      *.who        *.*
 udp    0      0      *.688        *.*
 udp    0      0      *.syslog     *.*
 udp    0      0      *.route      *.*
 udp    0      0      *.sunrpc     *.*
 tcp    0      0      plum.login   peach.yale..1023
                                              ESTABLISHED
 tcp    0      0      *.daytime    *.*        LISTEN
 tcp    0      0      *.discard    *.*        LISTEN
 tcp    0      0      *.echo       *.*        LISTEN
 tcp    0      0      *.time       *.*        LISTEN
 tcp    0      0      *.finger     *.*        LISTEN
 tcp    0      0      *.uucp       *.*        LISTEN
 tcp    0      0      *.exec       *.*        LISTEN
 tcp    0      0      *.login      *.*        LISTEN
 tcp    0      0      *.printer    *.*        LISTEN
 tcp    0      0      *.shell      *.*        LISTEN
 tcp    0      0      *.telnet     *.*        LISTEN
 tcp    0      0      *.ftp        *.*        LISTEN
 tcp    0      0      *.725        *.*        LISTEN
 tcp    0      0      *.722        *.*        LISTEN
 tcp    0      0      *.sunrpc     *.*        LISTEN
```

Figure 16.18 *Netstat* report on TCP and UDP connections.

16.4.5 Checking the Status of Computers

SNMP management stations will be able to poll systems for exhaustive status information. In the absence of SNMP agents on older systems, many of these support the remote uptime service, which broadcasts a brief status message once per minute.

The *ruptime* display that follows shows part of an uptime report that the local system has constructed by listening to the uptime broadcasts. The number of hours and minutes that each system has been up (or down) is displayed, along with the number of users and the average number of jobs that have been in the system's queue over

the last 1, 5, and 15 minutes. All of the systems listed are very
lightly loaded.

```
ruptime
zonker      down 121+20:41
blondie       up  42+00:09,    0 users,   load 0.00, 0.00, 0.00
calvin        up  51+23:52,    0 users,   load 0.02, 0.00, 0.00
hobbes        up  52+00:04,    4 users,   load 0.00, 0.00, 0.00
cantor        up  35+23:39,    1 user,    load 0.00, 0.00, 0.00
casper        up   5+21:28,    3 users,   load 0.28, 0.33, 0.44
```

The *finger* command can be used to show exactly who is logged in to
a system on a LAN and where the login originated. Note the @ sign
before the system name. The first "user" on the list is a backup
process that was initiated at the system console. The other two users
have logged in from remote computers.

```
finger @casper.cs.yale.edu
[CASPER.CS.YALE.EDU]
Login   Name            TTY    Idle    When           Where
backup  Jane Q Backup   co     4       Fri 09:58
kimble  John Kimble     p0             Fri 09:08      sun4.eng.yale
swillm  Steve Williams  p1     1:20    Fri 08:04      panda.eng.yale
```

16.4.6 Checking Telnet, Mail, and FTP

The easiest way to find out whether Telnet or FTP is up on a host is
to open a Telnet or FTP connection. Telnet also can be used to verify
that a remote mail server is active. The dialogue that follows shows
how this can be done. A port number can be added to a *telnet* command to open a connection to that port, rather than the Telnet server.
In this case, an interactive connection is opened to port 25, the mail
server's port. A brief exchange verifies that the server is active.

```
telnet plum.cs.yale.edu 25
Trying 130.132.23.16 ...
Connected to plum.cs.yale.edu.
Escape character is '^]'.
220 plum.cs.yale.edu Sendmail 3.2/ ready at Thu, 16 Jan 92 17:36:46
EST
HELO PEACH.CS.YALE.EDU
250 plum.cs.yale.edu Hello PEACH.CS.YALE.EDU, pleased to meet you
QUIT
221 plum.cs.yale.edu closing connection
Connection closed by foreign host.
```

16.4.7 Monitoring Remote Procedure Call Services

The *rpcinfo* command probes local and remote systems to find out which RPC services currently are running. The *rpcinfo* command can be issued from any station that supports the command to probe any other system that runs RPC programs. The first command below checks which services have registered with the local portmapper.

```
rpcinfo -p
   program vers proto    port
   100000   2   tcp      111   portmapper
   100000   2   udp      111   portmapper
   100007   2   tcp      658   ypbind
   100007   2   udp      660   ypbind
   100003   2   udp     2049   nfs
   100005   2   udp      699   mountd
   100005   2   tcp      702   mountd
   100024   1   udp      709   status
   100024   1   tcp      711   status
   100021   3   tcp      717   nlockmgr
   100021   3   udp     1030   nlockmgr
   100020   1   udp     1031   llockmgr
   100020   1   tcp      722   llockmgr
   100001   4   udp     1034   rstatd
   100002   2   udp     1035   rusersd
   100012   1   udp     1036   sprayd
   100008   1   udp     1037   walld
```

The next command asks which RPC services have registered with the portmapper at bulldog.cs.yale.edu.

```
rpcinfo -p bulldog.cs.yale.edu
   program vers proto    port
   100000   2   tcp      111   portmapper
   100000   2   udp      111   portmapper
   100003   2   udp     2049   nfs
   100005   2   udp      748   mountd
   100005   2   tcp      751   mountd
   100026   1   udp      760   bootparam
   100024   1   udp      764   status
   100024   1   tcp      766   status
   100021   3   tcp      771   nlockmgr
   100021   3   udp     1031   nlockmgr
   100020   1   udp     1032   llockmgr
   100020   1   tcp      776   llockmgr
   100011   1   udp     1070   rquotad
   100001   4   udp     1129   rstatd
   100002   2   udp     1130   rusersd
   100012   1   udp     1131   sprayd
   100008   1   udp     1132   walld
```

The command below is a bit like broadcasting a *ping* to a set of servers. It broadcasts a message to the null procedure of every version 2 NFS server on the network. All active servers respond.

```
rpcinfo -b 100003 2
128.36.12.26 cantor.cs.yale.edu
128.36.12.1  casper.cs.yale.edu
128.36.12.4  zonker.cs.yale.edu
128.36.12.20 calvin.cs.yale.edu
128.36.12.16 nancy.cs.yale.edu
128.36.12.23 blondie.cs.yale.edu
```

16.4.8 Monitoring NFS

NFS is without doubt the most important RPC service. A user at a client system can get a quick overview of the list of current servers by typing *showmount:*

```
showmount
cantor.cs.yale.edu
ceres.math.yale.edu
gauss.math.yale.edu
```

The *mount* command can be issued at a client to check up on which directories are currently mounted, as shown below.

```
mount -p
casper:/          /server          nfs ro,bg,intr
casper:/usr       /server/usr      nfs ro,bg,intr
casper:/var       /server/var      nfs rw,bg,intr
casper:/u1        /server/u1       nfs rw,bg,intr
casper:/u2        /server/u2       nfs ro,bg,intr
casper:/u5        /server/u5       nfs ro,bg,intr
```

The client has mounted directories from casper onto local directory */server.* Some are accessed with read-write permission, while others are read only.

All of the mounts are configured so that if the first attempt to mount fails, there will be periodic retries in the background (bg). If a server goes down, a user's program will hang on an attempted remote file access. The *intr* parameter means that users will be able to issue a keyboard interrupt that ends the wait.

We can find out how successful the client's NFS calls have been using the *nfsstat* command. The display that follows shows that all recent calls have been successful. Most of the calls read file attributes, looked up file handles, or read files.

Chapter Sixteen

```
nfsstat -cn

Client nfs:
calls       badcalls    nclget      nclsleep
587         0           587         0
null        getattr     setattr     root        lookup       readlink    read

0   0%      196 33%     0   0%      0   0%      149 25%      57  9%      103
17%
wrcache     write       create      remove      rename       link
symlink
0   0%      0   0%      0   0%      0   0%      0   0%       0   0%      0
0%
mkdir       rmdir       readdir     fsstat
0   0%      0   0%      46  7%      36  6%
```

Another *nfsstat* subcommand shows detailed information about a client's nfs mounts. The command and part of the response follow. Two of the mounts from server casper are shown.

Note that read and write buffer sizes of 8192 bytes are used. These are the usual NFS defaults. The report shows the smoothed round trip time and estimated deviation for lookups, reads and writes. The numbers (e.g., srtt=7) are based on an internal system metric. The values in parentheses translate these numbers to milliseconds.

The initial retransmission timeout is manually configured. The value is doubled after retransmissions. The current backed-off retransmission timeout (e.g., cur=2) is shown for each operation. After a count of five retransmissions have been sent, a warning message will be printed at the client system's console.

```
nfsstat -m

/server from casper:/ (Addr 128.36.12.1)
Flags: hard int  read size=8192, write size=8192,  count = 5
 Lookups: srtt=7 (17ms), dev=4 (20ms), cur=2 (40ms)
 Reads: srtt=5 (12ms), dev=4 (20ms), cur=2 (40ms)
 Writes: srtt=0 (0ms), dev=0 (0ms), cur=0 (0ms)
 All: srtt=7 (17ms), dev=4 (20ms), cur=2 (40ms)

/server/usr from casper:/usr (Addr 128.36.12.1)
Flags: hard int  read size=8192, write size=8192,  count = 5
 Lookups: srtt=7 (17ms), dev=4 (20ms), cur=2 (40ms)
 Reads: srtt=12 (30ms), dev=5 (25ms), cur=4 (80ms)
 Writes: srtt=0 (0ms), dev=0 (0ms), cur=0 (0ms)
 All: srtt=7 (17ms), dev=4 (20ms), cur=2 (40ms)
```

So far, the information has dealt with the local system's role as a client. However, this system also is acting as a server.

Administering a TCP/IP Network   377

The display below shows that there is not very much use of this NFS server's files.

```
nfsstat -sn

Server nfs:
calls      badcalls
5          0
null       getattr    setattr    root       lookup     readlink   read
0   0%     2   40%    0   0%     0   0%     3   60%    0   0%     0   0%
wrcache    write      create     remove     rename     link       symlink
0   0%     0   0%     0   0%     0   0%     0   0%     0   0%     0   0%
mkdir      rmdir      readdir    fsstat
0   0%     0   0%     0   0%     0   0%
```

There are two useful NFS monitoring tools that are available as free UNIX software.[14] The *nfswatch* command monitors all NFS traffic directed at a selected server, and displays detailed breakdowns on a continuously updated display. If desired, traffic counts for up to 256 individual files can be shown. NFS performance can be checked using the *nhfsstone* benchmarking program. An artificial traffic load is generated at a client and server performance is measured.

16.4.9 Simple Troubleshooting

When users cannot reach their services, where can we look to find the trouble? To summarize some of the tools that we have seen in this chapter:

1. Use *nslookup* to check that the local Domain Name Server is active. Users may not be able to get anywhere because name-to-address translation is down.

2. *Ping* the server that users cannot reach.

3. If the server is remote and you cannot reach it, run *traceroute* to the problem destination.

4. If *traceroute* does not return any information, *ping* all of the ports on the local routers.

5. Take a look at a report on recent ICMP messages using *netstat* and/or SNMP.

6. If you suspect that the problem stems from incorrect routing, get

---

[14] See RFC 1147, *Tools for Monitoring and Debugging TCP/IP Internets and Interconnected Devices.*

a printout of the current routing tables on the local routers. SNMP or other tools can be used to get this.

7. For a TCP based service, try a direct Telnet attachment to the service port.
8. If users are having trouble reaching a Remote Procedure Call service, use *rpcinfo* to send a message to the service's null process.
9. If it is an NFS problem, use the *mount* command to check current client mounts, and nfsstat at servers.

Quick checks of what is going on at other systems can be carried out by invoking the *rexec* command, which runs a program at a remote host and returns the result to the user. However, *rexec* sometimes is disabled because of security considerations.

16.5 SECURITY

Occasionally we see stories in the press about a "computer genius" who has broken into far-ranging computer sites. How smart do you have to be to break into a computer?

Unfortunately, breaking into some sites requires no brains at all. Most vulnerabilities are due to simple carelessness. Some administrators forget to change some of the default login identifiers and passwords that were preconfigured before their systems were shipped. Administrators sometimes set up new user accounts with passwords identical to the userid, and there are users who never change these. Too many users select simple, easy to guess passwords, such as their own first names.

These problems are easy to avoid. For example, there are password programs that require users to change their passwords periodically and refuse to accept passwords that are too easy to crack. As we already have seen, a capable router can be used to prevent break-ins by building a firewall that restricts the types or sources of traffic that are permitted to enter a network.

Measures like this are the beginning of security protection, not the end. What else is needed? A clear definition of security requirements is the first step in site protection. Next, an organization needs to decide what its security policies are and how these policies will be implemented.

Finally, a set of procedures for dealing with suspected security violations needs to be thought out ahead of time. The cooperation of several people may be required in order to deal with a problem, and their roles and responsibilities need to be defined.

Also, it should go without saying that network administrators should track down and fix well-known weaknesses that have been detected and cured at other sites.

One problem with TCP/IP security is that, historically, implementations have sacrificed tight security in order to promote interworking. For example, mail ports will accept connections from anywhere.

16.5.1 Audit Trails

Audit trail files can be used to track all successful logins, failed login attempts, and use of services such as file transfer. When tracking a break-in, you may even want to set up a network monitor to centrally record all logins that originate externally to the network. This information can be examined for deviations from normal usage.

File accesses also can be audited, and the audit log can be consulted when unauthorized attempts to read or write data are suspected. Files can be protected against clandestine replacement by recording the last time that they were updated along with a checksum against the file contents. Periodic rechecks can ferret out spurious file versions.

RFC 1244, *Site Security Handbook*, contains a wealth of useful security information, as well as a comprehensive bibliography of other security publications.

16.5.2 Kerberos

One of the most worrisome aspects of modern networks is the ease with which an eavesdropper can tap into a network to read userids and passwords and inject spurious traffic. The Kerberos[15] security protocols were developed under project Athena at MIT to attack this problem.

A pair of Kerberos servers act as go-betweens, helping clients to access services. Think of the Kerberos servers as King Arthur and his brother, chief knight Ted. Arthur is the ruler of authentication and knows all of the clients in his realm. Ted guards the services that clients want to reach. Before a client can access a service, Arthur must introduce the client to brother Ted. Then Ted introduces the client to the service.

Kerberos uses tickets to guard resources. If you are a client who wishes admission to a service, you have to get a ticket as well as an encryption key that you will use to exchange data with the server.

---

[15]Kerberos is named for the mythological three-headed dog who guards the gates of Hades.

Chapter Sixteen

The procedure is somewhat indirect. First you get a ticket from Arthur to meet brother Ted. You also get an encryption key so that your interaction with Ted is secure. Arthur is called the *Kerberos authentication server*. Then you get a ticket and key from brother Ted so that you can use the service. Ted is called the *Kerberos ticket-granting server*. The steps are:

1. Communicate with the Kerberos authentication server, identify yourself, and ask for an initial ticket that lets you talk to the Kerberos ticket granting server.
2. Present your initial ticket to the Kerberos ticket granting server, identify yourself in a secure manner, and ask for a ticket that lets you use a specific service.
3. Present the ticket to the service and use the service. Employ encryption to get whatever level of protection is appropriate.

Figure 16.19 illustrates these steps. The Two Kerberos servers could run on different computers, but in the figure, they are coresident.

In practice, we would expect a user to obtain all of the tickets needed for a computer session at the time of the login procedure. Each ticket is marked with the amount of time that it will be valid, which usually is a period of hours.

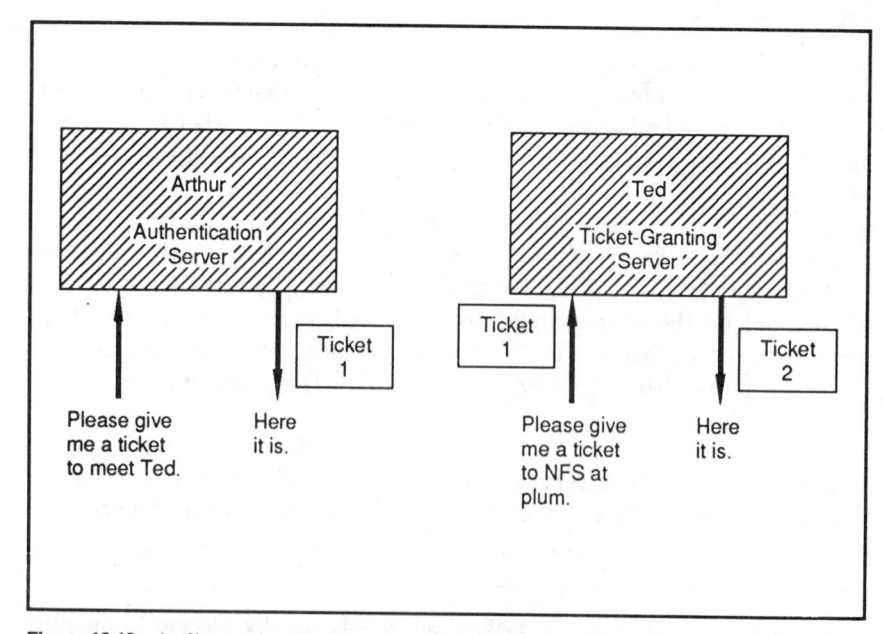

Figure 16.19 A client using Kerberos to obtain a ticket to a service.

Contents of a ticket include:

- The client's identifier and network address
- A new randomly generated session encryption key
- A time stamp
- A lifetime for the ticket
- The name of the requested service
- Optional fields, such as a sequence number

This is complicated, but is it secure? We have to take a closer look at what is going on to see that it is. First of all, tickets are always passed in encrypted form. Secondly, long-term encryption keys only are used to start up an interaction. New, short-term encryption keys are generated and used to protect sensitive network information. Now we can take a more detailed look at the steps:

1. In the clear, the client sends Arthur its identifier and a request for a ticket of introduction to Ted.

2. Arthur knows two important things — a secret key for every client, and a secret key for Ted. Arthur looks up this client's key.

3. Arthur randomly generates a session key, and creates a ticket. Arthur encrypts the ticket using Ted's key.

4. Arthur creates a message containing the session key and the encrypted ticket. Then, as shown in Figure 16.20, Arthur encrypts this whole message in the client's key. Arthur sends the result back to the client.

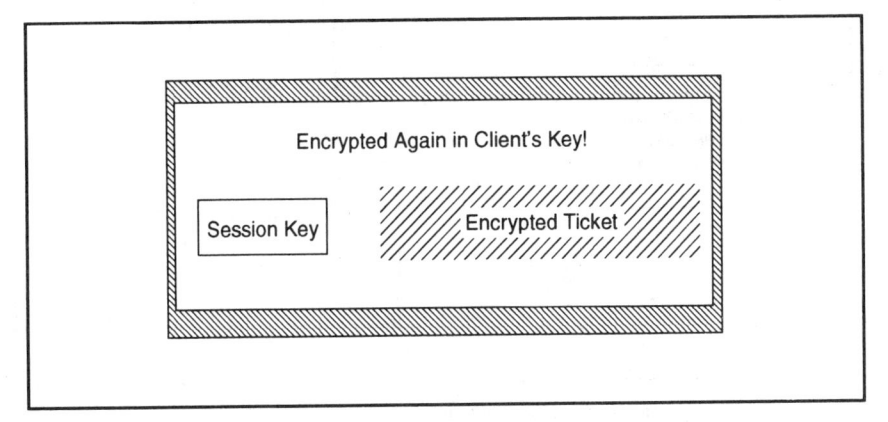

Figure 16.20 Encrypting tickets and keys.

5. The client's software asks the end user to enter a password, which is turned into the key. The client uses this key to decrypt the message. The client now has:
   - A new session key
   - The ticket, still encrypted in Ted's key
6. The client will now send the ticket to Ted. But how will he prove to Ted that he is the true owner of the ticket? The client creates an authenticator containing the client's identifier, network address and a timestamp.
7. The client sends Ted a message containing:
   - The ticket (still encrypted in Ted's key)
   - The authenticator, encrypted in the session key
   - The name and location of the service that the client wants to use
8. Ted decrypts the ticket and finds out the session key. Ted can then use the session key to decrypt the authenticator, as shown in Figure 16.21. Next Ted compares the information extracted from the authenticator with the information in the ticket. If they match, then this client is valid!

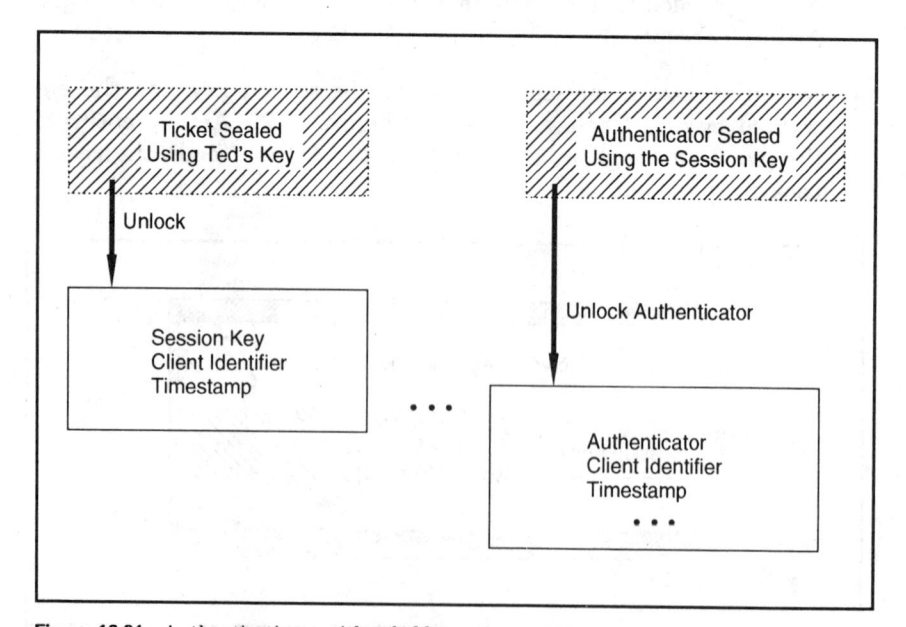

Figure 16.21 Authenticating a ticket holder.

9. The client is half-way to its goal! Ted knows the secret key of every service. Ted looks up the key for the service requested by the client.

10. Ted generates a new session key. Ted creates a ticket containing the new session key, introducing the client to the desired service.

11. Ted builds a message containing the new session key encrypted with the old session key, and the ticket, encrypted in the service's secret key. Ted sends the message to the client.

12. The client uses the old session key to unwrap the new session key. Once again, the client builds an authenticator and then encrypts it with the new session key.

13. The client sends the server a message containing:
    - The ticket (encrypted in the server's key).
    - The authenticator, encrypted in the new session key.

14. At last — the server decrypts its ticket and gets the new session key. It uses this key to unwrap the authenticator. Now it can check the identifier for the client and the timestamp.

15. Now the client is ready to start some real work. Every ticket has an assigned lifetime, and the client might be able to use the service for a period of hours before needing to repeat this authentication procedure.

The client's interaction with the service can be fully encrypted using the new session key, or, to save overhead, may just use encrypted checksums to validate messages.

Many vendors are implementing Kerberos. Issues in using the protocol involve server maintenance and encryption overhead.

16.6 RECOMMENDED READING

James VanBokkelen's summary of the oral tradition for Internet network administrators in RFC 1173, *Responsibilities of Host and Network Managers*, contains guidelines that are useful for any internet.

Charles L. Hedrick's *Introduction to Administration of an Internet-based Local Network* contains a very thorough discussion of LAN issues. It describes a number of problems that crop up when you assign two or more subnet numbers to a single LAN, and suggests solutions. This document is available by request from the author at the Rutgers Center for Computers and Information Services, Laboratory for Computer Science Research. It also can be obtained by anonymous FTP from CS.RUTGERS.EDU. The file is in directory *runet* and is named *tcp-ip-admin.doc*.

RFC 1147, *Tools for Monitoring and Debugging TCP/IP Internets and Interconnected Devices*, lists vendor products as well as free tools that are available via file transfer across the Internet.

The *UNIX System Administration Handbook* by E. Nemeth, G. Snyder, and S. Seebass contains detailed instructions for configuring TCP/IP in a UNIX environment, and unravels the mysteries of UNIX system administration.

RFC 1034 contains an introduction to the Domain Name System. RFC 1033 describes DNS server configuration, while RFC 1032 spells out the responsibilities of a domain administrator.

RFC 1108, *U.S. Department of Defense Security Options for the Internet Protocol*, details the framework and use of security parameters. RFC 1244, *Site Security Handbook*, contains a thorough discussion of security issues, as well as an excellent bibliography of security documents.

The National Institute of Standards and Technology (NIST) is working on a definitive set of system security requirements. The current version of these requirements has been published in the draft document, "Minimum Security Functional Requirements for Multi-user Operating Systems."

Kerberos information is available online at ATHENA.MIT.EDU.

Chapter 17

The Socket Programming Interface

17.1 INTRODUCTION

Communications standards define all of the rules needed to exchange data across a network. However, until recently, the need to standardize Application Programming Interfaces (APIs) for communication has been ignored. How can a programmer write a client/server application if the programs are completely different on every computer?

Fortunately, most TCP/IP implementations offer a programming interface that follows a single model, the *socket programming interface*. The socket programming interface was first introduced with the 1982 4.1c Berkeley Software Distribution version of the UNIX operating system. A number of improvements have been incorporated into the original interface over time.

The socket programming interface was designed for use with several communications protocols, not for TCP/IP alone. However, when the OSI transport layer specification was completed, it was clear that the socket interface was not general enough to satisfy OSI requirements.

In 1986, AT&T introduced the Transport Layer Interface (TLI) for UNIX System V. The TLI can be used to interface to the OSI transport layer, TCP, and other protocols.

Currently, several standards groups have work in progress to define other communications APIs. However, at this time, the socket interface is a de facto standard because it is almost universally available, and in widespread use.

This chapter is intended to provide a general understanding of how the socket interface works. There will be minor differences in the APIs offered on various computers, due to the way that each vendor has implemented communications services within its operating system. The manual for the appropriate system should be consulted for programming details.

17.2 UNIX Orientation

The original socket interface was written for a UNIX operating system. The UNIX architecture provides a framework in which standard file, terminal, and communications I/O all operate in a similar fashion. For example, when a program opens a file, the program is given a small integer called a file descriptor. The program uses this descriptor to identify the file in any subsequent operations. Operations are performed on the file by means of calls such as:

```
read(descriptor, buffer, length)
write(descriptor, buffer, length)
close(descriptor)
```

An identical framework is used for TCP/IP socket communications. The primary difference between the socket programming interface and a UNIX file I/O interface is that a number of preliminary calls are required in order to assemble all of the information that is needed to carry out communications.

17.2.1 Socket Services

The socket interface provides three TCP/IP services. It can be used for TCP stream communication, UDP datagram communication, and for raw datagram submission to the IP layer. Figure 17.1 illustrates these services.

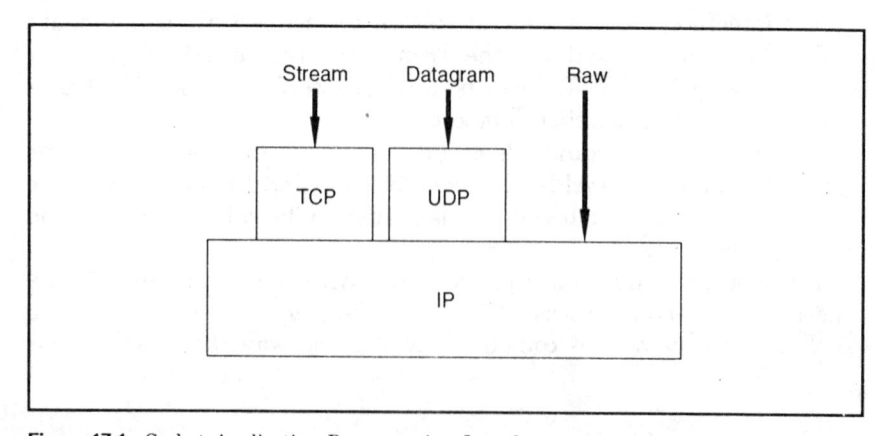

Figure 17.1 Socket Application Programming Interfaces.

Recall that the socket API was not designed for use exclusively with TCP/IP. The original idea was that the same interface could also be used for other communications, such as XNS, and exchange of data between local processes in a single computer.

The result can be slightly confusing. For example, we shall see later that some socket calls contain optional parameters that are not relevant for TCP/IP communications — they are used with some other protocol.

Occasionally, the programmer will be required to spell out the length of a well-known quantity such as an IP address. The reason for this is that although it is obvious that an IP address contains four bytes, the interface can be used for other protocols with different address lengths.

17.3 THE TCP SERVICE INTERFACE

Before going into the specific characteristics of the socket programming interface, let's take a look at the general service interface defined in the TCP standard.

Recall that service interface definitions do not mandate exactly how functions should be implemented, but do provide guidelines for the commands and parameters that need to be passed across the interface between two layers.

In this case, as shown in Figure 17.2, the interface lies between an application and a TCP service provider. The interface commands are: OPEN, SEND, RECEIVE, STATUS, CLOSE, AND ABORT.

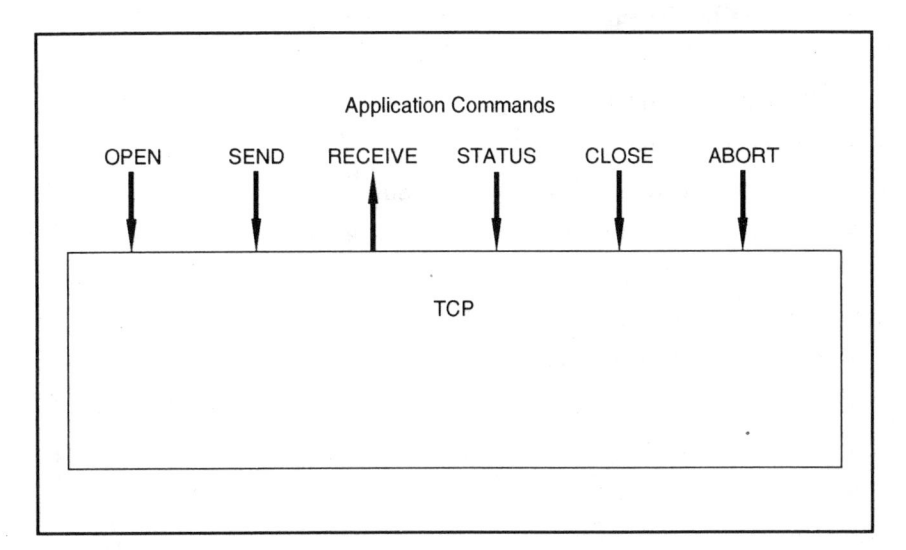

Figure 17.2 The TCP service interface.

388   Chapter Seventeen

The service commands and their parameters will be discussed in the sections that follow. Within each command definition, the command parameters that are optional will be enclosed in brackets.

17.3.1 Opening a Connection

An OPEN command is used to prepare for communication. A server executes a passive open, waiting for a partner. A client executes an active open that initiates communication. The creation of a data structure that will hold communication information is a very important element in the implementation of an OPEN.

17.3.2 Transmission Control Block (TCB)

The data structure in which TCP keeps all of the information that relates to a connection is called a Transmission Control Block (TCB). Typically, there are over 50 parameters in a TCB. We list a few to give an idea of the type of information that is included:

- The local IP address
- The local port
- The protocol (e.g., TCP or UDP)
- The remote IP address
- The remote port
- Send buffer size
- Receive buffer size
- Current TCP state
- Smoothed round trip time
- Smoothed round trip deviation
- Current retransmission timeout value
- Number of retransmissions that have been sent
- Current send window size
- Maximum send segment size
- Sequence number of last byte that was ACKed
- Maximum receive segment size
- Sequence number of next byte to be sent
- Enable or disable tracing

17.3.3 OPEN Command

There are three types of OPEN command. The first two enable a server to get ready for incoming connection requests, while the third is used by a client to actively initiate a connection. An OPEN will cause a TCB data structure to be created.

An OPEN command returns a local connection name. An application uses this name in all future references to the connection. In the socket programming interface, this name is a small integer.

- *Unspecified Passive OPEN:* Allows a server to listen for a connection request from any client.

    Input: Local port, [timeout], [precedence], [security parameters], [maximum segment size]

    Output: Local connection name

- *Fully Specified Passive OPEN:* Allows a server to listen for a connection request from a specific client.

    Input: Local port, remote IP Address, remote port, [timeout], [precedence], [security parameters], [maximum segment size]

    Output: Local connection name

- *Active OPEN:* Allows a client to actively initiate a connection with a server.

    Input: Local port, destination IP address, destination port, [timeout], [precedence], [security parameters], [maximum segment size]

    Output: Local connection name

17.3.4 OPEN Command and the Socket Interface

The OPEN command corresponds to a sequence of socket interface functions that are used to set up a TCB and establish the values of a number of variables.

The optional timeout parameter in OPEN calls is intended to set a limit for the successful delivery of any data submitted to TCP. If the timeout expires, then TCP must abort the connection. There also is an optional timeout parameter in the Send command that is used to change this timeout value. Having said all this, we note that most implementations hard code a fixed default timeout value, so that a programmer using the socket interface probably will never see this parameter.

17.3.5 Sending and Receiving Data

SEND and RECEIVE commands move data between an application and TCP.

- *SEND:* Allows a client or server to pass a buffer of data to TCP for transmission.

    Input: Local connection name, buffer address, byte count, PUSH flag, URGENT flag, [timeout]

- *RECEIVE:* Identifies a receive buffer for incoming data.

    Input: Local connection name, buffer address, size of buffer in bytes

    Output: Number of bytes actually placed into the buffer, PUSH flag, URGENT flag

17.3.6 SEND/RECEIVE Primitives and the Socket Interface

A socket programmer can use a *send()* call, or a *write()* call that looks very much like an ordinary file write.

There also are *sendv()* and *writev()*[1] calls that concatenate data that is stored in a sequence of buffers and send it out. Every one of these sending calls automatically causes its data to be PUSHed.

RECEIVE is implemented by *recv()*, or a *read()* call that looks very much like an ordinary file read. There also are *recvmsg()* and *readv()* calls that fill a sequence of buffers with chunks of the incoming data.

17.3.7 Other Commands

The remaining commands are used to find out about the status of a connection, and to terminate a connection.

- *STATUS:* Gets information about a connection.

    Input: Local connection name

    Output: Depends on implementation, but usually includes local and remote socket address, local connection name, receive window, send window, connection state, number of buffers awaiting acknowledgment, number of buffers pending receipt, urgent state, precedence, security information, transmission timeout

---

[1] Meaning send vector or write vector.

- *CLOSE:* Requests that the connection be closed.

  Input: Local connection name

- *ABORT:* Asks TCP to discard all data currently in send and receive buffers and abort the connection.

  Input: Local connection name

17.3.8 Relation to the Socket Interface

Socket STATUS is obtained by the *getsockopt()* function, as well as by other local system calls. CLOSE and ABORT both are implemented by means of a *close()* call.

17.3.9 Blocking and Nonblocking Calls

The details of exactly how this general service interface should be implemented were intentionally left vague in the TCP standard. One issue left to local choice was whether service calls should be:

- Blocking (Synchronous): Requires the calling program to wait until successful completion of the command before the program can continue with its execution.
- Nonblocking (Asynchronous): Returns to the program immediately. A later call can be used to find out whether the function has completed yet.

Blocking commands force the calling program to wait. They are similar to commonplace I/O statements, in which the calling program is suspended until the I/O has been performed. An example of a nonblocking call is a *receive* that returns immediately with an error code that indicates that TCP has no data to deliver at this time.

Are socket programming interfaces blocking or nonblocking? The answer is yes! The programmer usually can take control of how the calls will behave.

Figure 17.3 shows a sequence of commands that make up a typical TCP dialogue. All of the calls shown are assumed to be synchronous. For example, in the scenario, the server's RECEIVE call blocks until the sender issues a SEND/PUSH and pushed data is actually transmitted to the server.

In the sections that follow, we shall examine the details of how this abstract set of commands is mapped onto the concrete socket programming interface.

```
                    CLIENT              SERVER

   ACTIVE OPEN  ⇒                    ⇐  UNSPECIFIED
                                        PASSIVE
                                        OPEN

         Local  ⇐
connection name
                                    ⇒  Local
                                        connection name

     SEND/PUSH  ⇒                    ⇐  RECEIVE
                                    →  Buffer of data

     SEND/PUSH  ⇒                    ⇐  RECEIVE
                                    →  Buffer of data

       RECEIVE  ⇒
                                    ⇐  SEND/PUSH
 Buffer of data ⇐

         CLOSE  ⇒                    ⇐  CLOSE
        Closed  ⇐
                                    →  Closed
```

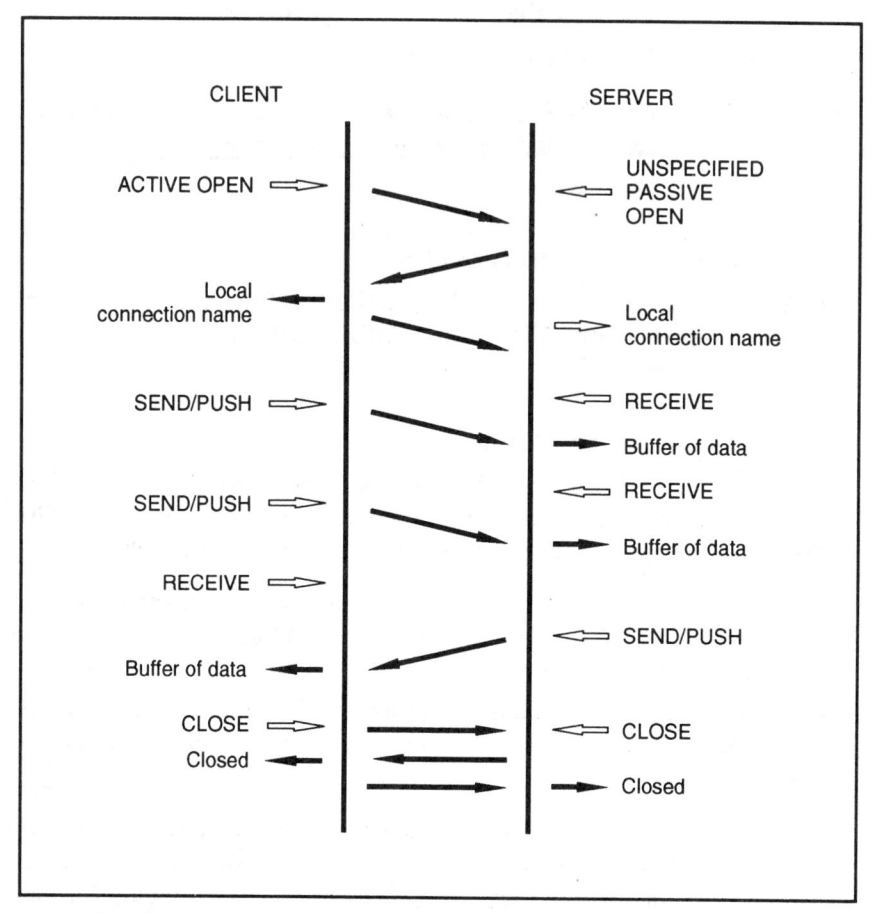

Figure 17.3 A typical sequence of TCP primitives.

17.4 THE TCP SOCKET PROGRAMMING INTERFACE

In this section, we will examine the socket programming calls that are used to interface with TCP. For simplicity, we will omit the input and output parameters for the calls at this stage, and concentrate on their major functions and relation to one another. The details will be provided later.

17.4.1 TCP Server Model

A typical scenario for a TCP server is that there is a master process that spends most of its time listening for clients. When a client connects, it often is the case that the server creates a new process that does the actual work for the client, passes the client over to the new process, and then goes back to listening.

Sometimes clients arrive faster than the master process can get to them. What should be done with them? The standard mechanism is that when the master starts up, it tells TCP to create a queue that can hold a specific number of requests. Clients that can't be served immediately are put on the queue and served in turn. Suppose that the queue fills up and another client arrives? The new client's connection request will not be accepted.

17.4.2 TCP Server Passive Open

A server's passive open command is implemented by the series of calls:

- *socket()*: The server identifies the type of communication (TCP in this case). The local system creates an appropriate TCB data structure for the communication, and returns a local connection name. The connection name is a small integer called a *socket descriptor*.

- *bind()*: The server establishes the local IP address and port that it wants to use. Recall that a host may have multiple IP addresses. The server may specify one IP address, or else indicate that it is willing to accept connections arriving at any local IP address. The server may ask for a specific port, or else let the bind call obtain a free port that it can use.

- *listen()*: The server sets the length of the client queue.

- *accept()*: The server is ready to accept client connections. If the queue is not empty, the first client connection request is accepted. The *accept()* call creates a *new socket descriptor* that will be used for this client's connection and returns this new descriptor to the server.

Usually a synchronous form of *accept* is used, so that if the queue is empty, *accept()* will wait for the next client to show up before returning.

17.4.3 TCP Client Active OPEN

A client's open command is mapped to:

- *socket()*: The client identifies the type of communication (TCP in this case). The local system creates an appropriate TCB data structure for the communication, and returns a local socket descriptor.

- *connect()*: The client identifies a server's IP address and port. TCP will attempt to establish a connection with the server.

If the client wishes to specify exactly which local port it wants to use, the client must call *bind()* before calling *connect()*. If the port is available, the *bind* will assign it to the client.

If the client does not call *bind()* to ask for a port, then the *connect* call will assign an unused port to the client. The port number will be entered into the TCB.

17.4.4 Other Calls

The remaining calls are used in the same way by both the client and the server.

The input parameters in *send* and *recv* calls are specific to sockets, and support sending and receiving urgent data as well as ordinary data. The *write* and *read* calls are designed to look like ordinary file I/O, and cannot recognize urgent data.

- *send()*: Writes a buffer of data to the socket. Alternatively, write() may be used.
- *sendv()*: Passes a sequence of buffers to the socket. Alternatively, writev() may be used.
- *recv()*: Receives a buffer of data from a socket. Alternatively, read() may be used.
- *recvmsg()*: Receives a sequence of buffers from a socket. Alternatively, readv() may be used.
- *close()*: Ends a connection and closes down the socket.
- *getsockopt()*: Reads information out of the Transmission Control Block. Optionally, a system may provide additional I/O system calls that can be used to read various parts of the TCB.

Later, when we examine the input parameters for the opening calls, sends, and receives, we shall see that only a subset of the service interface parameters listed earlier are included in these calls. The reason is that a set of default values normally are used for the missing parameters.

For example, by default, all data is sent or written with a push. Default values also are preset for important environment information such as the receive buffer size, whether event logging is enabled, and use of blocking or nonblocking processing for calls such as *recv*.

Some defaults can be changed by using the functions:

- *setsockopt()*: Sets a number of TCB parameters such as input and output buffer sizes, use of logging, whether urgent data should be received in the normal sequence order, and whether a close should block until all outstanding data has been safely sent.
- *ioctnl()* or *fcntl()*: Sets socket I/O to blocking or nonblocking.

Figure 17.4 translates the TCP dialogue of Figure 17.3 into a sequence of socket calls. *Socket()*, *bind()*, and *listen()* calls complete quickly and have an immediate return.

The accept(), *send()* and *recv()* calls shown are assumed to be blocking, which is their normal default.

17.4.5 A TCP Server Program

Now we are ready to take a close look at a sample server program. The server is designed to run forever. The server will:

1. Create its master socket - i.e., create a TCB and return an integer called the socket descriptor which will identify this TCB in future calls.

2. Enter the server's local socket address information into a data structure.

3. Call bind. The system will assign a free port to the server and copy the socket address into the TCB.

4. Retrieve the port that was assigned to the server and print it.

5. Set up a queue that can hold up to five clients.

The remaining steps are repeated over and over:

6. Wait for a client. When a client request arrives, create a new TCB for the client. The new TCB is constructed by making a copy of the master TCB and writing the client's socket address and other client parameters into the new TCB.

7. Create a child process to serve the client. The child will inherit the new TCB and handle all further communication with the client. The child will wait for a message from the client, write the message, and exit.

396 Chapter Seventeen

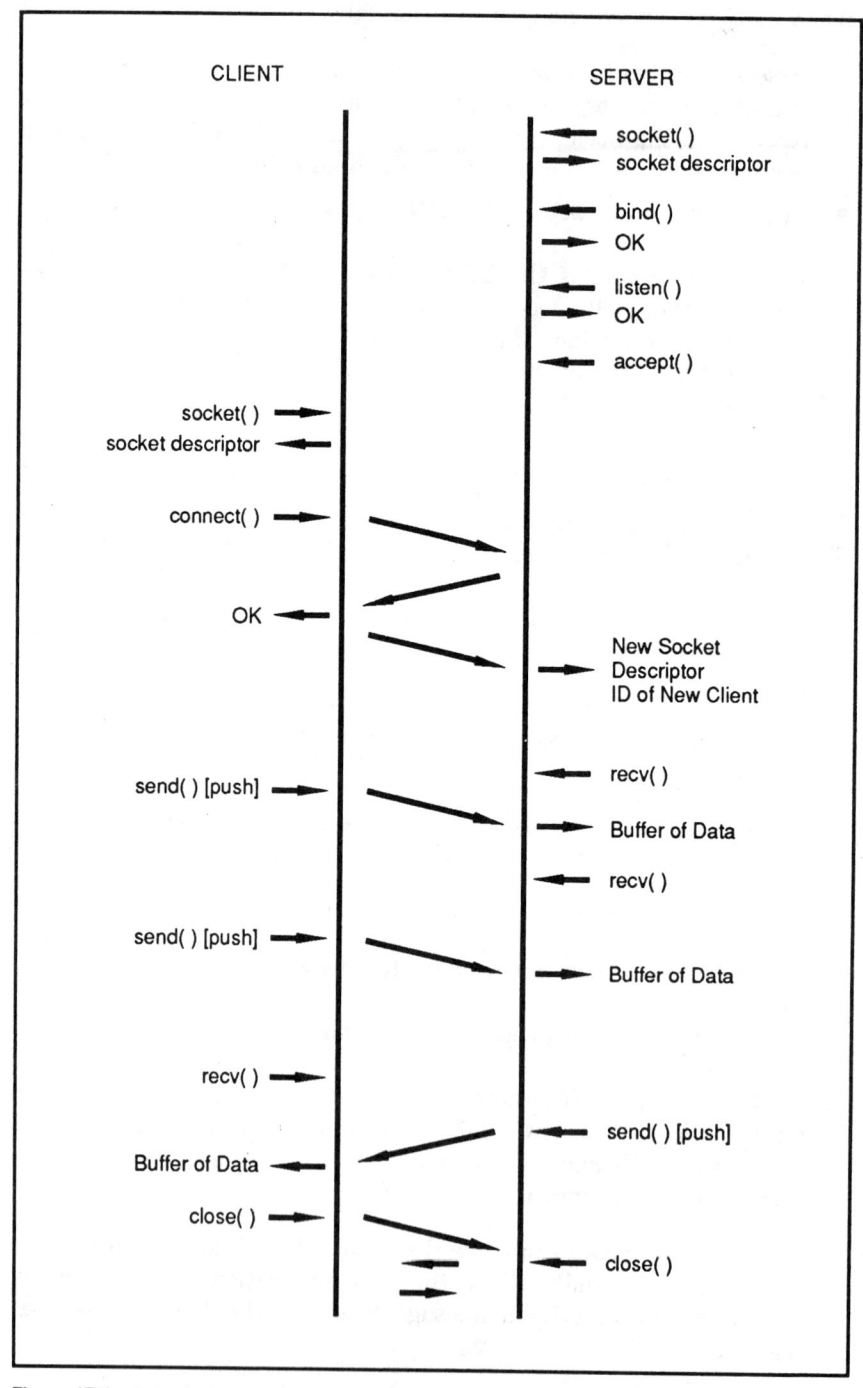

Figure 17.4 A typical sequence of socket programming calls.

The Socket Programming Interface   397

Each step in the program will be explained in the section that follows.

```c
/* tcpserv.c
 * To run the program, enter "tcpserv".
 */

/* First we include a bunch of standard header files.
 */
#include <sys/types.h>
#include <sys/socket.h>
#include <stdio.h>
#include <netinet/in.h>
#include <netdb.h>
#include <errno.h>

main()
{
int sockMain, sockClient, length, child;
struct sockaddr_in servAddr;

/* 1. Create the master socket.
 */

if ( (sockMain = socket(AF_INET, SOCK_STREAM, 0)) < 0 )
    {perror("Server cannot open main socket.");
     exit(1);
    }

/* 2. Create a data structure to hold the local IP address
 *    and port that we will use. We are willing to accept
 *    clients connecting to any local IP address (INADDR_ANY).
 *    Since this server will not use a well-known port,
 *    set the port=0. The bind call assign the server a port
 *    and write it into the TCB.
 */
bzero( (char *) &servAddr, sizeof(servAddr));
servAddr.sin_family = AF_INET;
servAddr.sin_addr.s_addr = htonl(INADDR_ANY);
servAddr.sin_port = 0;

/* 3. Call bind. Bind will pick a port number and write it
 * in the TCB.
 */
if ( bind(sockMain, &servAddr, sizeof(servAddr)) )
    { perror("Server;s bind failed.");
     exit(1);
    }

/* 4. We want to look at the port number. We use the
 * getsockname() function to copy the port into servAddr.
 */
```

398 Chapter Seventeen

```
length = sizeof(servAddr);
if ( getsockname(sockMain, &servAddr, &length) )
    { perror("getsockname call failed.");
      exit(1);
    }

printf("SERVER: Port number is %d\n", ntohs(servAddr.sin_port) );

/* 5. Set up a queue that can hold up to five clients.
 */
listen(sockMain,5);

/*  6. Wait for an incoming clients.  Accept will return
 *      a NEW socket descriptor that will be used for this client.
 */
for ( ; ; ) {

if ( (sockClient = accept(sockMain, 0, 0)) < 0)
    { perror("Bad client socket.");
      exit(1);
    }

/* 7. Create a child process to handle the client.
 */
if ( (child = fork()) < 0)
    {perror("Failed to create child.");
      exit(1);
    }
else if (child == 0)    /* This is code for the child to execute */
    { close(sockMain); /* The child is not interested in sockMain.*/
      childWork(sockClient);
      close(sockClient);
      exit(0);
    }

/*  8. This is the parent.  It is no longer interested in
 *      the client socket.  The parent closes its entry to
 *      the client socket and loops back to issue a new accept().
 */
  close(sockClient);
    }
}

/* The child reads one incoming buffer, prints a message and quits.
 */
#define BUFLEN 81
int childWork(sockClient)
int sockClient;
{
char buf[BUFLEN];
int msgLength;
```

```
/*  9. Zero out the buffer.  Then issue a recv to get a message
 *     from the client.
 */
bzero(buf, BUFLEN);
if ( (msgLength = recv(sockClient,buf, BUFLEN, 0)) < 0)
    { perror("Bad receive by child.");
      exit(1);
    }
printf("SERVER: Socket used for this client is %d\n", sockClient);
printf("SERVER: Message length was %d\n", msgLength);
printf("SERVER: Message was: %s\n\n", buf);
}
```

17.4.6 Calls Used in the TCP Server Program

1. *sockMain = socket(AF_INET, SOCK_STREAM, 0)*

The socket call has the form:

```
socket_descriptor = socket(address_domain,
                           communications_type, protocol)
```

Recall that the socket interface can be used for other kinds of communications, such as XNS. AF_INET selects the Internet Address Family. SOCK_STREAM requests a TCP socket. This variable is set to SOCK_DGRAM to create a UDP socket and SOCK_RAW to interface directly to IP.

We do not have to specify any other protocol information for TCP (or for UDP). However, the protocol parameter is needed for the raw interface, and for some of the other families that use sockets.

2. *struct sockaddr_in servAddr;*

  . . .

  bzero((char *) &servAddr, sizeof(servAddr));
  servAddr.sin_family = AF_INET;
  servAddr.sin_addr.s_addr = htonl(INADDR_ANY);
  servAddr.sin_port = 0;

The *servAddr* structure is used to hold server address information. The *bzero()* call just initializes *servAddr* by putting 0s into all parameters. The first variable in the *servAddr* structure indicates that the rest of the values contain internet Address Family data.

The next variable holds the local IP address at which this server can be reached. For example, if the server is attached to an Ethernet LAN and to an X.25 network, it might want to restrict access to clients reached through the Ethernet interface. In this program, we don't care. INADDR_ANY means that clients can connect through any interface.

The *htonl()* or host-to-network-long function is used to translate a 32-bit integer stored in the local computer to the Internet format for a 32-bit IP address. Internet standards represent integers with the most significant byte first. This is called the Big Endian style of data representation. Some computers store data with the least significant byte first, in a Little Endian style. If the local computer is Big Endian, then *htonl()* will have no work to do.

If this server were operating at a well-known port, we would fill that port number into the next variable. Since we want the operating system to assign us a port for this test program, we just enter a zero value.

3. *bind(sockMain, &servAddr, sizeof(servAddr));*

The *bind* call has the form:

```
return_code = bind(socket_descriptor,
                   address_structure, length_of_address_structure)
```

If the address structure identifies a desired port, *bind* will try to get it for the server. If there is a 0 in the port variable, *bind* will obtain an unused port. *Bind* will enter the port number and IP address into the TCB.

4. *getsockname(sockMain, &servAddr, &length);*

The getsockname call has the form:

```
return_code = getsockname(socket_descriptor, address_structure,
                          length_of_address_structure)
```

We asked *bind* to get us a port, but *bind* does not tell us what port it got. If we want to find out, we have to read it out of the TCB. The *getsockname()* function retrieves information from the TCB and copies it into the address structure where we can read it. The port number is extracted and printed in the statement:

```
printf("SERVER: Port number is %d\n", ntohs(servAddr.sin_port) );
```

The *ntohs()* or network-to-host-short function is used to convert the network byte order of the port number to local host byte order.

5. *listen(sockMain,5);*

The *listen* call is used by connection-oriented servers, and has the form:

```
return_code = listen(socket_descriptor, queue_size)
```

The *listen* call indicates that this will be a passive socket, and creates a queue of the requested size.

6. *sockClient = accept(sockMain, 0, 0);*

The *accept* call has the form:

```
new_socket_descriptor = accept(socket_descriptor,
    client_address_structure, length_of_client_address_structure)
```

By default, the call will block until a client connects to this server. If a client_address_structure variable is provided, the client's IP address and port will be entered into this variable when a client connects. In this sample program, since we are not checking up on the client's IP address and port number, we just fill 0s into the last two parameter fields.

7. *child = fork();*

. . .

close(sockMain);

This is the C language *fork* command that creates a new child process. The child process will inherit all of the parent program's I/O descriptors, and will have access to *sockMain* and *sockClient*. The operating system keeps track of the number of processes that have access to a socket.

A connection is closed when the last process accessing the socket calls *close()*. When the child closes *sockMain*, the parent will still have access to this socket.

8. *close(sockClient);*

This call is made within the parent part of the program. When the parent closes *sockClient*, the child will still have access to this socket.

9. *msgLength = recv(sockClient,buf, BUFLEN, 0);*

. . .

close(sockClient);

The *recv* call has the form:

```
message_length = recv(socket_descriptor, buffer,
                    buffer_length, flags)
```

By default, the *recv* call blocks. (The fcntl() or iocntl() function could be used to change the status of a socket to nonblocking.)

After the child has received data and printed its messages, it closes its access to *sockClient*. This will cause the connection to enter its termination phase.

17.4.7 A TCP Client Program

The client connects to the server, sends a single message, and terminates. The program steps will be explained in the next section. To run this program, an end user inputs the server host's name and port, and a message to be sent to the server. For example:

    tcpclient plum.cs.yale.edu 1356 hello

```
/* tcpclient.c
 *   Start the server before starting a client.  Find out
 *   the server's port.
 *   To run the client, enter:
 *      tcpclient hostname port message
 */
#include <sys/types.h>
#include <sys/socket.h>
#include <netinet/in.h>
#include <netdb.h>
#include <stdio.h>
#include <errno.h>

main(argc, argv)   /* The client program has input arguments. */
int argc;
char *argv[];
{
int sock;
struct sockaddr_in servAddr;
struct hostent *hp, *gethostbyname();

/* Args are 0:program-name, 1:hostname, 2:port, and 3:message   */
if (argc < 4)
   {printf("ENTER tcpclient hostname port message\n");
    exit(1);
   }

/* 1. Create a socket.   */
if ( (sock = socket(AF_INET, SOCK_STREAM, 0)) < 0)
   {perror("Could not get a socket\n");
    exit(1);
   }

/* 2. We will fill the server's address and port into the servAddr.
 *    First we fill the address structure with 0s.
 *    Next we look up the IP address for this host name and
 *    fill it in.
 *    Finally, we fill in the port number, which is in argv[2].
 */
bzero( (char *) &servAddr, sizeof(servAddr) );
servAddr.sin_family = AF_INET;
hp = gethostbyname(argv[1]);
```

```
bcopy(hp->h_addr, &servAddr.sin_addr, hp->h_length);
servAddr.sin_port = htons(atoi(argv[2]) );

/* 3. Connect to the server.  We do not have to call bind.
 *    The system will assign a free port while performing the
 *    connect function.
 */

if ( connect(sock, &servAddr, sizeof(servAddr) ) < 0)
    {perror("Client cannot connect.\n");
     exit(1);
    }

/* 4. The client announces that it is ready to send the message.
 *    It sends and prints a goodbye message.
 */

printf("CLIENT: Ready to send\n");

if (send(sock, argv[3], strlen(argv[3]), 0) < 0)
    {perror("problem with send.\n");
     exit(1);
    }
printf("CLIENT: Completed send.  Goodbye.\n");
close(sock);
exit(0);
}
```

17.4.8 Calls Used in the TCP Client Program

1. *sock = socket(AF_INET, SOCK_STREAM, 0);*

The client creates a TCP socket, just as the server did.

2. The server had to initialize an address structure to use in its *bind* call. This structure had space for its local IP address and port number. The client also initializes an address structure — and again it contains information about the *server's* IP address and port. This structure will be used by the connect call to identify the destination.

The *bzero()* call below just puts 0s into the server address structure, *servAddr*. Then we again identify the Address Family as Internet.

Next we must convert the host name entered by the user to an IP address. The *gethostbyname* function does this, returning a pointer to a *hostent*, i.e., host entry structure. This structure contains the server's name and IP address.

The *bcopy* function is used to copy the IP address (which is in *hp->h_addr*) into *servAddr*.

The second argument entered by the end user was the server's port. This was read as an ASCII text string, so it must first be converted to an integer via *atoi()* and then converted to network byte order by *htons()*. Finally, the port number is copied into the address variable in *servAddr*.

```
bzero( (char *) &servAddr, sizeof(servAddr) );
servAddr.sin_family = AF_INET;
hp = gethostbyname(argv[1]);
bcopy(hp->h_addr, &servAddr.sin_addr, hp->h_length);
servAddr.sin_port = htons(atoi(argv[2]) );
```

3. *connect(sock, &servAddr, sizeof(servAddr));*

The *connect* call has the form:

```
connect(socket_descriptor, address_structure,
        length_of_address_structure)
```

The client will open a connection with the server whose IP address and port are contained in the address_structure.

4. *send(sock, argv[3], strlen(argv[3]), 0);*

The *send* call has the form:

```
return_code = send(socket_descriptor, buffer, buffer_length, flags)
```

Recall that the third argument entered by the end user (which appears in the program as *argv[3]*) is a text message. A common use for the flags parameter is to signal urgent data. In this instance, the flags parameter is set to 0.

5. *close(sock);*

The client issues a *close* to terminate the connection.

17.4.9 A Simpler Server

Many servers have the form shown in the earlier example. However, a simpler model can be used when the server needs to perform only a simple task for a client, as was the case in the example above.

Instead of creating a child process for each client, the server can directly perform the task and then close the connection to the client. The server queue enables a few other clients to wait until the server is ready for them.

Code for a simpler server follows. This server also can be accessed by clients running the tcpclient program discussed above.

```c
/*  tcpsimp.c
 *  To run the program, enter "tcpsimp".
 */

/* First we include a bunch of standard header files.
 */
#include <sys/types.h>
#include <sys/socket.h>
#include <stdio.h>
#include <netinet/in.h>
#include <netdb.h>
#include <errno.h>

main()
{
int sockMain, sockClient, length, child;
struct sockaddr_in servAddr;

/* 1. Create the master socket.
 */

if ( (sockMain = socket(AF_INET, SOCK_STREAM, 0)) < 0 )
    {perror("Server cannot open main socket.");
     exit(1);
    }

/* 2. Enter information into a data structure used to hold the
 *    local IP address and port.  The "sin" in the variable names is
 *    short for "socket internet."
 */
bzero( (char *) &servAddr, sizeof(servAddr) );
servAddr.sin_family = AF_INET;
servAddr.sin_addr.s_addr = htonl(INADDR_ANY);
servAddr.sin_port = 0;

/* 3. Call bind.  Bind will write a usable port number into servAddr.
 */
if ( bind(sockMain, &servAddr, sizeof(servAddr)) )
    { perror("Server;s bind failed.");
      exit(1);
    }

/* 4. We want to look at the port number.  We use the
 *    getsockname() function to copy the port into servAddr.
 */

length = sizeof(servAddr);
if ( getsockname(sockMain, &servAddr, &length) )
    { perror("getsockname call failed.");
      exit(1);
    }
```

```
printf("SERVER: Port number is %d\n", ntohs(servAddr.sin_port) );

/* 5. Set up a queue that can hold up to five clients.
 */
listen(sockMain,5);

/* 6. Wait for an incoming clients. Accept will return
 * a new socket descriptor that will be used for this client.
 */

for ( ; ; ) {
    if ( (sockClient = accept(sockMain, 0, 0)) < 0)
        { perror("Bad client socket.");
          exit(1);
        }

/* 7'. Serve the client and close the client's connection.
 */
    doTask(sockClient);
    close(sockClient);
    }
}

/* Read one incoming buffer, print some information and quit.
 */

#define BUFLEN 81
int doTask(sockClient)
int sockClient;
{
char buf[BUFLEN];
int msgLength;

/* 8'. Zero out the buffer, and then issue a recv
 * to get a message from the client.
 */

bzero(buf, BUFLEN);
if ( (msgLength = recv(sockClient,buf, 80, 0)) < 0)
    { perror("Bad receive.");
      exit(1);
    }

printf("SERVER: Socket used for this client is %d\n", sockClient);
printf("SERVER: Message length was %d\n", msgLength);
printf("SERVER: Message was: %s\n\n", buf);
}
```

The Socket Programming Interface 407

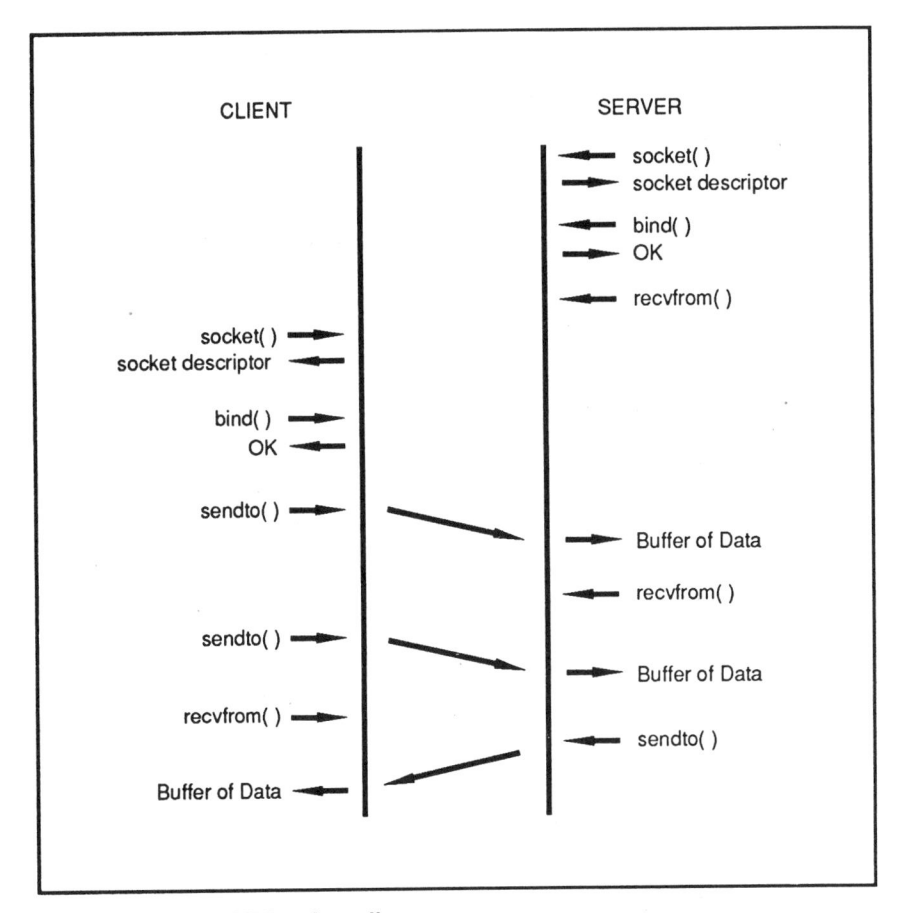

Figure 17.5 Typical UDP socket calls.

17.5 THE UDP SOCKET PROGRAMMING INTERFACE

We have tackled the TCP programming interface, which is the most complex, first. Now let's take a look at programming a UDP server and client. Figure 17.5 shows an outline of a UDP dialogue between a client and server. The *socket()* and *bind()* calls complete quickly and have an immediate return. All of the calls shown are assumed to be blocking, which is their normal default. They can be changed to non-blocking (i.e., asynchronous) mode.

17.5.1 A UDP Server Program

The program that follows creates a UDP socket, binds to a port, and then begins to receive and print messages that are sent to its port.

```c
/* udpserv.c
 * To run the program, enter "udpserv".
 *
 * First we include a bunch of standard header files.
 */
#include <sys/types.h>
#include <sys/socket.h>
#include <stdio.h>
#include <netinet/in.h>
#include <netdb.h>
#include <errno.h>
#define BUFLEN 81

main()
{
int sockMain, addrLength, msgLength;
struct sockaddr_in servAddr, clientAddr;
char buf[BUFLEN];

/* 1. Create a UDP socket.
 */

if ( (sockMain = socket(AF_INET, SOCK_DGRAM, 0)) < 0)
    {perror("Server cannot open UDP socket.");
     exit(1);
    }

/* 2. Enter information into a data structure used to hold the
 *    local IP address and port.  We will let bind get a free
 *    port for us.
 */
bzero( (char *) &servAddr, sizeof(servAddr) );
servAddr.sin_family = AF_INET;
servAddr.sin_addr.s_addr = htonl(INADDR_ANY);
servAddr.sin_port = 0;

/* 3. Call bind.  Bind will write a usable port number into the TCB.
 */
if ( bind(sockMain, &servAddr, sizeof(servAddr)) )
    { perror("Server;s bind failed.");
      exit(1);
    }

/* 4. We want to look at the port number.  We use the
 *    getsockname() function to copy the port into servAddr.
 */
addrLength = sizeof(servAddr);
if ( getsockname(sockMain, &servAddr, &addrLength) )
    { perror("getsockname call failed.");
      exit(1);
    }
printf("SERVER: Port number is %d\n", ntohs(servAddr.sin_port) );
```

```
/* 5.  Loop forever, waiting for messages from clients.
 */
for ( ; ; ) {

   addrLength = sizeof(clientAddr);
   bzero(buf, BUFLEN);
   if ( (msgLength = recvfrom(sockMain, buf, BUFLEN, 0,
                     &clientAddr, &addrLength)) < 0)
      { perror("Bad client socket.");
        exit(1);
      }

/* 6.  Print the client's IP address and port, and the message.
 */
   printf("SERVER: Client's IP address was: %s\n",
                  inet_ntoa( clientAddr.sin_addr) );

   printf("SERVER: Client's port was: %d\n",
                  ntohs(clientAddr.sin_port));
   printf("SERVER: Message length was %d\n", msgLength);
   printf("SERVER: Message was: %s\n\n", buf);
   }
}
```

17.5.2 Calls Used in the UDP Server Program

1. *sockMain = socket(AF_INET, SOCK_DGRAM, 0);*

The Address Family is again Internet.

2. *bzero((char *) &servAddr, sizeof(servAddr));*
   servAddr.sin_family = AF_INET;
   servAddr.sin_addr.s_addr = htonl(INADDR_ANY);
   servAddr.sin_port = 0;

The calls initializing the server address structure are the same as those used in the TCP programs.

3. *bind(sockMain, &servAddr, sizeof(servAddr));*

As before, *bind* will get a port for the server and write values into a Transmission Control Block. Of course, UDP has a very small amount of control information compared to TCP.

4. *getsockname(sockMain, &servAddr, &length);*

We use *getsockname* to extract the port assigned to the socket.

5. *msgLength = recvfrom(sockMain, buf, BUFLEN,*
       0, &clientAddr, &length);

The recvfrom call has the form:

```
recvfrom(socket_descriptor, receive_buffer, buffer_length,
        flags, source_address_structure,
        pointer_to_length_of_source_address_structure)
```

The flags parameter can be set to allow the caller to peek at a message without actually receiving it.

On return, the address_structure will be filled with the client's IP address and port number. A pointer to the length of the source address is used, because this length may be changed when the actual client address fields are received and filled in.

6. *inet_ntoa(clientAddr.sin_addr);*

This call converts the client's 32-bit Internet address to the familiar dot notation for IP addresses.

17.5.3 A UDP Client Program

The client connects to the server, sends a single message, and terminates. To run this program, an end user inputs the hostname and port of the server and a message to be sent to the server. For example:

```
udpclient plum.cs.yale.edu 2315   "This is a message."
```

```
/* udpclient.c
 * Start the server before starting a client.
 * Find out the server's port.
 * To run the client, enter:
 *    udpclient hostname port message
 */
#include <sys/types.h>
#include <sys/socket.h>
#include <netinet/in.h>
#include <netdb.h>
#include <stdio.h>
#include <errno.h>

main(argc, argv)
int argc;
char *argv[];   /* These are the arguments entered by the end-user. */
    /* argv[0] is the program name.  argv[1] points to a hostname. */
        /* argv[2] points to a port, */
        /* and argv[3] points to a text message. */
```

```
{
int sock;
struct sockaddr_in servAddr, clientAddr;
struct hostent *hp, *gethostbyname();

/* Should be four args.   */
if (argc < 4)
    {printf("ENTER udpclient hostname port message\n");
     exit(1);
    }

/* 1. Create a UDP socket.   */
if ( (sock = socket(AF_INET, SOCK_DGRAM, 0)) < 0)
    {perror("Could not get a socket\n");
     exit(1);
    }

/* 2. We will fill the server's address and port into the servAddr.
 *    First we fill the address structure with 0s.
 *    We use the gethostbyname function to look up the host name
 *    and get its IP address.  Then we copy the IP address
 *    into servAddr using the bcopy function.
 *    Finally, we fill in the port number, which is in argv[2].
 */
bzero( (char *) &servAddr, sizeof(servAddr) );
servAddr.sin_family = AF_INET;
hp = gethostbyname(argv[1]);
bcopy(hp->h_addr, &servAddr.sin_addr, hp->h_length);
servAddr.sin_port = htons(atoi(argv[2]) );

/* 3. We have to call bind to get a UDP port.  The system
 *    will assign a free port.
 */
bzero( (char *) &clientAddr, sizeof(clientAddr) );
clientAddr.sin_family = AF_INET;
clientAddr.sin_addr.s_addr = htonl(INADDR_ANY);
clientAddr.sin_port = 0;
if ( bind(sock, &clientAddr, sizeof(clientAddr)) < 0)
    {perror("Client cannot get a port.\n");
     exit(1);
    }

/* 4. The client announces that it is ready to send the message.
 *    It sends and prints a goodbye message.
 */
printf("CLIENT: Ready to send\n");
if (sendto(sock, argv[3], strlen(argv[3]), 0, &servAddr,
    sizeof(servAddr)) < 0)
    {perror("problem with sendto.\n");
     exit(1);
    }
```

```
printf("CLIENT: Completed send.  Goodbye.\n");
/*  Close the connection    */
close(sock);
}
```

17.5.4 Calls used in the UDP Client Program

1. *sock = socket(AF_INET, SOCK_DGRAM, 0);*

The UDP client creates a UDP socket.

2. *bzero((char *) &servAddr, sizeof(servAddr));*
servAddr.sin_family = AF_INET;
hp = gethostbyname(argv[1]);
bcopy(hp->h_addr, &servAddr.sin_addr, hp->h_length);
servAddr.sin_port = htons(atoi(argv[2]));

The *servAddr* structure is filled in using values entered by the end user, just as was done for the TCP client.

3. *bind(sock, &clientAddr, sizeof(clientAddr);*

The client calls *bind* to get a port.

4. *sendto(sock, argv[3], strlen(argv[3]), 0, &servAddr, sizeof(servAddr));*

The *sendto* call has the form:

```
sendto(socket_descriptor, buffer, buffer_length, flags,
       destination_address_structure,
       length_of_destination_address_structure)
```

Note that this call contains all of the destination information required to send a User Datagram.

17.6 RECOMMENDED READING

Any UNIX Programmer's Manual contains descriptions of socket program calls. *UNIX Network Programming* by W. Richard Stevens provides an in-depth discussion of socket programming. TCP/IP programmer's manuals for other operating systems describe the socket calls, and often include sample programs. The manual for the TCP/IP product in use should be consulted, since there are small variations due to differences between operating systems.

Appendix A

Abbreviations and Acronyms

ACK	An Acknowledgement
AF	Address Family
ANSI	American National Standards Institute
API	Application Programming Interface
ARP	Address Resolution Protocol
ARPA	Advanced Research Projects Agency
AS	Autonomous System
ASA	American Standards Association
ASCII	American National Standard Code for Information Interchange
ASN.1	Abstract Syntax Notation One
BBN	Bolt, Beranek, and Newman, Incorporated
BER	Basic Encoding Rules
BGP	Border Gateway Protocol
BSD	Berkeley Software Distribution
CCITT	International Telegraph and Telephone Consultative Committee
CMIP	Common Management Information Protocol
CMIS	Common Management Information Services
CMOT	Common Management Information Services and Protocol over TCP/IP

CR	Carriage Return
CRC	Cyclic Redundancy Check
CSMA/CD	Carrier Sense Multiple Access with Collision Detection
DARPA	Defense Advanced Research Projects Agency
DCE	Data Circuit-terminating Equipment, Distributed Computing Environment
DDN	Defense Data Network
DEC	Digital Equipment Corporation
DES	Data Encryption Standard
DEV	Deviation
DFS	Distributed File Service
DISA	Defense Information Systems Agency
DIX	Digital, Intel, and Xerox Ethernet protocol
DME	Distributed Management Environment
DNS	Domain Name System
DSA	Directory System Agent
DSAP	Destination Service Access Point
DTE	Data Terminal Equipment
DUA	Directory User Agent
EBCDIC	Extended Binary-Coded Decimal Interchange Code
EGP	Exterior Gateway Protocol
EOF	End of File
EOR	End of Record
FCS	Frame Check Sequence
FDDI	Fiber Distributed Data Interface
FIN	Final Segment
FTAM	File Transfer, Access, and Management
FTP	File Transfer Protocol
FYI	For Your Information
GGP	Gateway-to-Gateway Protocol
GMT	Greenwich Mean Time
GOSIP	Government Open Systems Interconnection Profile
HDLC	High Level Data Link Control Protocol

IAB	Internet Architecture Board (Internet Activities Board)
IAC	Interpret As Command
IANA	Internet Assigned Numbers Authority
IBM	International Business Machines
ICMP	Internet Control Message Protocol
ID	Identifier
IEEE	Institute of Electrical and Electronics Engineers
IEN	Internet Engineering Notes
IESG	Internet Engineering Steering Group
IETF	Internet Engineering Task Force
IGMP	Internet Group Management Protocol
IGP	Interior Gateway Protocol
IP	Internet Protocol
IRTF	Internet Research Task Force
ISDN	Integrated Services Digital Network
ISN	Initial Sequence Number
ISO	International Organization for Standardization
ISODE	ISO Development Environment
LAN	Local Area Network
LAPB	Link Access Procedures Balanced
LAPD	Link Access Procedures on the D-channel
LF	Line Feed
LLC	Logical Link Control
MAC	Media Access Control Protocols
MAN	Metropolitan Area Network
MIB	Management Information Base
MS	Millisecond
MSS	Maximum Segment Size
MTA	Message Transfer Agent
MTU	Maximum Transmission Unit
MX	Mail Exchanger
NETBIOS	Network Basic Input Output System

NFS	Network File System
NIC	Network Information Center
NIS	Network Information System
NREN	National Research and Education Network
NSAP	Network Service Access Point
NSFNET	National Science Foundation Network
NVT	Network Virtual Terminal
OSF	Open Software Foundation
OSI	Open Systems Interconnect
OSPF	Open Shortest Path First
PAD	Packet Assembler/Disassembler
PC	Personal Computer
PDU	Protocol Data Unit
PI	Protocol Interpreter
POP	Post Office Protocol
PPP	Point-to-Point Protocol
RARP	Reverse Address Resolution Protocol
RFC	Request For Comments
RIP	Routing Information Protocol
RMON	Remote Network Monitor
RPC	Remote Procedure Call
RST	Reset
RTT	Round Trip Time
SDEV	Smoothed Deviation
SDLC	Synchronous Data Link Protocol
SLIP	Serial Line Interface Protocol
SMDS	Switched Multimegabit Data Service
SMTP	Simple Mail Transfer Protocol
SNA	Systems Network Architecture
SNAP	Sub-Network Access Protocol
SNMP	Simple Network Management Protocol
SONET	Synchronous Optical Network

SPF	Shortest Path First
SRTT	Smoothed Round Trip Time
SSAP	Source Service Access Point
SYN	Synchronizing Segment
TCB	Transmission Control Block
TCP	Transmission Control Protocol
TCU	Trunk Coupling Unit
TELNET	Terminal Networking
TFTP	Trivial File Transfer Protocol
TLI	Transport Layer Interface
TP4	OSI Transport Class 4
TSAP	Transport Service Access Point
TTL	Time-To-Live
UA	User Agent
UDP	User Datagram Protocol
ULP	Upper Layer Protocol
WAN	Wide Area Network
XDR	External Data Representation
XNS	Xerox Network Systems

Appendix B

RFCs and Other NIC Documents

Appendix C contains dialogues showing how to use the file transfer protocol or mail service to access files stored at the Network Information Center. The sections that follow describe some of these files.

THE NETINFO DIRECTORY

There are several useful documents in the netinfo directory. Some of these are described below.

asn.txt	A list of assigned autonomous system numbers.
domain-template.txt	Form used to register a domain with the NIC.
hosts.txt	A list of Internet hosts. This is a large file!
ien-index.txt	Index of IEN documents.
internet-number-template.txt	How to request an internet number.
nic-pubs.txt	Publications available from the NIC.
nug.doc	DDN new user guide, ASCII version.
protocols-dod.bib	Bibliography of TCP/IP articles, ASCII version.
protocols-dod.ps	Postscript version of the bibliography.
rfc-by-author.txt	Brief RFC index sorted by author.
rfc-by-title.txt	Brief RFC index sorted by title.
rfc-index.txt	Full RFC index sorted by RFC number.
rfc-sets.txt	Major RFCs, organized by topic.

420   Appendix B

root-servers.txt   The list of Domain Name Service root servers.
vendors-guide.doc   TCP/IP Vendors Guide. This is a large file.
what-the-nic-does.txt   An informative description of NIC functions.

THE RFC DIRECTORY

A selected set of documents is listed below, by category. Consult the NIC document */netinfo/rfc-index.txt* for a complete and up-to-date list. These documents are stored in directory */rfc*. Most of the documents are in ASCII format and have names ending in .txt: for example, *rfc1250.txt*. Some documents also are provided in a postcript version, with names ending in .ps.

The endings (.txt or .ps) are omitted in the lists that follow.

Parameters, Requirements, and Useful Information

rfc1340	Assigned numbers. Reynolds, J.K.; Postel, J.B.; 1992 July
rfc1250	IAB official protocol standards. Postel, J.B., ed.; 1991 August
rfc1208	Glossary of networking terms. Jacobsen, O.J.; Lynch, D.C.; 1991 March
rfc1180	TCP/IP tutorial. Socolofsky, T.J.; Kale, C.J.; 1991 January
rfc1178	Choosing a name for your computer. Libes, D.; 1990 August
rfc1175	FYI on where to start: A bibliography of internetworking information. Bowers, K.L.; LaQuey, T.L.; Reynolds, J.K.; Roubicek, K.; Stahl, M.K.; Yuan, A.; 1990 August
rfc1173	Responsibilities of host and network managers: A summary of the "oral tradition" of the Internet. VanBokkelen, J.; 1990 August
rfc1166	Internet numbers. Kirkpatrick, S.; Stahl, M.K.; Recker, M.; 1990 July
rfc1127	Perspective on the Host Requirements RFCs. Braden, R.T.; 1989 October
rfc1123	Requirements for Internet hosts — application and support. Braden, R.T., ed.; 1989 October

Appendix B 421

rfc1122	Requirements for Internet hosts — communication layers. Braden, R.T., ed.; 1989 October
rfc1118	Hitchhikers guide to the Internet. Krol, E., 1989 September
rfc1011	Official Internet protocols. Reynolds, J.K.; Postel, J.B.; 1987 May
rfc1009	Requirements for Internet gateways. Braden, R.T.; Postel, J.B.; 1987 June
rfc980	Protocol document order information. Jacobsen, O.J.; Postel, J.B.; 1986 March

Lower Layers

rfc1236	IP to X.121 address mapping for DDN IP to X 121 address mapping for DDN. Morales, L.F., Jr.; 1991 June
rfc1220	Point-to-Point Protocol extensions for bridging. Baker, F.,ed.; 1991 April
rfc1209	Transmission of IP datagrams over the SMDS Service. Piscitello, D.M.; Lawrence, J.; 1991 March
rfc1201	Transmitting IP traffic over ARCNET networks. Provan, D.; 1991 February
rfc1188	Proposed standard for the transmission of IP datagrams over FDDI networks. Katz, D.; 1990 October
rfc1172	Point-to-Point Protocol (PPP) initial configuration options. Perkins, D.; Hobby, R.; 1990 July
rfc1171	Point-to-Point Protocol for the transmission of multi-protocol datagrams over Point-to-Point links. Perkins, D.; 1990 July
rfc1149	Standard for the transmission of IP datagrams on avian carriers. Waitzman, D.; 1990 April 1
rfc1055	Nonstandard for transmission of IP datagrams over serial lines: SLIP. Romkey, J.L; 1988 June
rfc1044	Internet Protocol on Network System's HYPERchannel: Protocol specification. Hardwick, K.; Lekashman, J.; 1988 February
rfc1042	Standard for the transmission of IP datagrams

over IEEE 802 networks. Postel, J.B.; Reynolds, J.K.; 1988 February

rfc1027 — Using ARP to implement transparent subnet gateways. Carl-Mitchell, S.; Quarterman, J.S.; 1987 October

rfc903 — Reverse Address Resolution Protocol. Finlayson, R.; Mann, T.; Mogul, J.C.; Theimer, M.; 1984 June

rfc895 — Standard for the transmission of IP datagrams over experimental Ethernet networks. Postel, J.B., 1984 April

rfc894 — Standard for the transmission of IP datagrams over Ethernet networks. Hornig, C.; 1984 April

rfc893 — Trailer encapsulations. Leffler, S.; Karels, M.J., 1984 April

rfc877 — Standard for the transmission of IP datagrams over public data networks. Korb, J.T., 1983 September

Bootstrapping

rfc1084 — BOOTP vendor information extensions. Reynolds, J.K.; 1988 December

rfc951 — Bootstrap Protocol. Croft, W.J.; Gilmore, J.; 1985 September

rfc906 — Bootstrap loading using TFTP. Finlayson, R.; 1984 June

IP and ICMP

rfc1219 — On the assignment of subnet numbers. Tsuchiya, P.F.; 1991 April

rfc1112 — Host extensions for IP multicasting. Deering, S.E.; 1989 August

rfc1088 — Standard for the transmission of IP datagrams over NetBIOS networks. McLaughlin, L.J.; 1989 February

rfc950 — Internet standard subnetting procedure. Mogul, J.C.; Postel, J.B.; 1985 August

Appendix B

rfc932	Subnetwork addressing scheme. Clark, D.D.; 1985 January
rfc922	Broadcasting Internet datagrams in the presence of subnets. Mogul, J.C.; 1984 October
rfc919	Broadcasting Internet datagrams. Mogul, J.C; 1984 October
rfc886	Proposed standard for message header munging. Rose, M.T.; 1983 December 15
rfc815	IP datagram reassembly algorithms. Clark, D.D.; 1982 July
rfc814	Name, addresses, ports, and routes. Clark, D.D.; 1982 July
rfc792	Internet Control Message Protocol. Postel, J.B.; 1981 September
rfc791	Internet Protocol. Postel, J.B.; 1981 September
rfc781	Specification of the Internet Protocol (IP) timestamp option. Su, Z.; 1981 May

Routing Protocols

rfc1267	A Border Gateway Protocol 3 (BGP-3). Lougheed, K.; Rekhter, Y.; 1991 October
rfc1247	OSPF version 2. Moy, J.; 1991 July
rfc1222	Advancing the NSFNET routing architecture. Braun, H.W.; Rekhter, Y. 1991 May
rfc1195	Use of OSI IS-IS for routing in TCP/IP and dual environments. Callon, R.W.; 1990 December
rfc1164	Application of the Border Gateway Protocol in the Internet. Honig, J.C; Katz, D.; Mathis, M.; Rekhter, Y.; Yu, J.Y.; 1990 June
rfc1163	Border Gateway Protocol (BGP). Lougheed, K.; Rekhter, Y.; 1990 June
rfc1074	NSFNET backbone SPF based Interior Gateway Protocol. Rekhter, J.; 1988 October
rfc1058	Routing Information Protocol. Hedrick, C.L.; 1988 June
rfc904	Exterior Gateway Protocol formal specification.

	Mills, D.L.; 1984 April
rfc827	Exterior Gateway Protocol (EGP). Rosen, E.C; 1982 October
rfc823	DARPA Internet gateway. Hinden, R.M.; Sheltzer, A.; 1982 September
rfc1136	Administrative Domains and Routing Domains: A model for routing in the Internet. Hares, S.; Katz, D.; 1989 December
rfc911	EGP Gateway under Berkeley UNIX 4.2 EGP Gateway under Berkeley UNIX 4 2. Kirton, P.; 1984 August 22
rfc888	"STUB Exterior Gateway Protocol". Seamonson, L.; Rosen, E.C.; 1984 January

Routing Performance and Policy

rfc1254	Gateway congestion control survey. Mankin, A.; Ramakrishnan, K.K.,eds.; 1991 August
rfc1246	Experience with the OSPF protocol. Moy, J.,ed.; 1991 July
rfc1245	OSPF protocol analysis. Moy, J.,ed.; 1991 July
rfc1125	Policy requirements for inter Administrative Domain routing. Estrin, D.; 1989 November
rfc1124	Policy issues in interconnecting networks. Leiner, B.M.; 1989 September
rfc1104	Models of policy based routing. Braun, H.W.; 1989 June
rfc1102	Policy routing in Internet protocols. Clark, D.D.; 1989 May

TCP and UDP

rfc1072	TCP extensions for long-delay paths. Jacobson, V.; Braden, R.T.; 1988 October
rfc896	Congestion control in IP/TCP internetworks. Nagle, J.; 1984 January
rfc879	TCP maximum segment size and related topics. Postel, J.B.; 1983 November
rfc813	Window and acknowlegement strategy in TCP.

	Clark, D.D.; 1982 July
rfc793	Transmission Control Protocol. Postel, J.B.; 1981 September
rfc768	User Datagram Protocol. Postel, J.B.; 1980 August 28

File Transfer and File Access

rfc1094	NFS: Network File System Protocol specification. Sun Microsystems, Inc.; 1989 March
rfc1068	Background File Transfer Program (BFTP). DeSchon, A.L.; Braden, R.T.; 1988 August
rfc959	File Transfer Protocol. Postel, J.B.; Reynolds, J.K.; 1985 October
rfc949	FTP unique-named store command. Padlipsky, M.A.; 1985 July
rfc783	TFTP Protocol (revision 2). Sollins, K.R.; 1981 June
rfc775	Directory oriented FTP commands. Mankins, D.; Franklin, D.; Owen, A.D.; 1980 December

Terminal Access

rfc1205	Telnet 5250 interface. Chmielewski, P.; 1991 February
rfc1198	FYI on the X window system. Scheifler, R.W.; 1991 January
rfc1184	Telnet Linemode option. Borman, D.A.,ed.; 1990 October
rfc1091	Telnet terminal-type option. VanBokkelen, J.; 1989 February
rfc1080	Telnet remote flow control option. Hedrick, C.L.; 1988 November
rfc1079	Telnet terminal speed option. Hedrick, C.L.; 1988 December
rfc1073	Telnet window size option. Waitzman, D.; 1988 October
rfc1053	Telnet X.3 PAD option. Levy, S.; Jacobson, T.; 1988 April

rfc1043	Telnet Data Entry Terminal option: DODIIS implementation. Yasuda, A.; Thompson, T.; 1988 February
rfc1041	Telnet 3270 regime option. Rekhter, Y.; 1988 January
rfc1013	X Window System Protocol, version 11: Alpha update. Scheifler, R.W. 1987 June
rfc946	Telnet terminal location number option. Nedved, R.; 1985 May
rfc933	Output marking Telnet option. Silverman, S.; 1985 January
rfc885	Telnet end of record option. Postel, J.B.; 1983 December
rfc861	Telnet extended options: List option. Postel, J.B.; Reynolds, J.K.; 1983 May
rfc860	Telnet timing mark option. Postel, J.B.; Reynolds, J.K.; 1983 May
rfc859	Telnet status option. Postel, J.B.; Reynolds, J.K.; 1983 May
rfc858	Telnet Suppress Go Ahead option. Postel, J.B.; Reynolds, J.K.; 1983 May
rfc857	Telnet echo option. Postel, J.B.; Reynolds, J.K.; 1983 May
rfc856	Telnet binary transmission. Postel, J.B.; Reynolds, J.K.; 1983 May
rfc855	Telnet option specifications. Postel, J.B.; Reynolds, J.K.; 1983 May
rfc854	Telnet Protocol specification. Postel, J.B.; Reynolds, J.K.; 1983 May
rfc779	Telnet send-location option. Killian, E.; 1981 April
rfc749	Telnet SUPDUP-Output option. Greenberg, B.; 1978 September
rfc736	Telnet SUPDUP option. Crispin, M.R.; 1977 October
rfc732	Telnet Data Entry Terminal option. Day, J.D.; 1977 September

rfc727	Telnet logout option. Crispin, M.R.; 1977 April
rfc726	Remote Controlled Transmission and Echoing Telnet option. Postel, J.B.; Crocker, D.; 1977 March
rfc698	Telnet extended ASCII option. Mock, T.; 1975 July

Mail

rfc1341	MIME (Multipurpose Internet Mail Extensions) Mechanisms for Specifying and Describing the Format of Internet Message Bodies. Borenstein, N.; Freed, N.; 1992 June
rfc1143	Q method of implementing Telnet option negotiation. Bernstein, D.J.; 1990 February
rfc1090	SMTP on X.25. Ullmann, R.; 1989 February
rfc1056	PCMAIL: A distributed mail system for personal computers. Lambert, M.L.; 1988 June
rfc974	Mail routing and the domain system. Partridge, C.; 1986 January
rfc822	Standard for the format of ARPA Internet text messages. Crocker, D.; 1982 August 13
rfc821	Simple Mail Transfer Protocol. Postel, J.B.; 1982 August

Domain Name System

rfc1035	Domain names – implementation and specification. Mockapetris, P.V.; 1987 November
rfc1034	Domain names – concepts and facilities. Mockapetris, P.V.; 1987 November
rfc1033	Domain administrators operations guide. Lottor, M.; 1987 November
rfc1032	Domain administrators guide. Stahl, M.K.; 1987 November
rfc1101	DNS encoding of network names and other types. Mockapetris, P.V. 1989 April
rfc974	Mail routing and the domain system. Partridge, C.; 1986 January

Appendix B

rfc920 — Domain requirements. Postel, J.B.; Reynolds, J.K.; 1984 October

rfc799 — Internet name domains. Mills, D.L.; 1981 September

Other Applications

rfc1196 — Finger User Information Protocol. Zimmerman, D.P.; 1990 December

rfc1179 — Line printer daemon protocol. McLaughlin, L.; 1990 August

rfc1129 — Internet time synchronization: The Network Time Protocol. Mills, D.L.; 1989 October

rfc1119 — Network Time Protocol (version 2) specification and implementation. Mills, D.L.; 1989 September

rfc1057 — RPC: Remote Procedure Call Protocol specification: Version 2. Sun Microsystems, Inc.; 1988 June

rfc1014 — XDR: External Data Representation standard. Sun Microsystems, Inc.; 1987 June

rfc954 — NICNAME/WHOIS. Harrenstien, K.; Stahl, M.K.; Feinler, E.J.; 1985 October

rfc868 — Time Protocol. Postel, J.B.; Harrenstien, K.; 1983 May

rfc867 — Daytime Protocol. Postel, J.B.; 1983 May

rfc866 — Active users. Postel, J.B.; 1983 May

rfc865 — Quote of the Day Protocol. Postel, J.B.; 1983 May

rfc864 — Character Generator Protocol. Postel, J.B.; 1983 May

rfc863 — Discard Protocol. Postel, J.B.; 1983 May

rfc862 — Echo Protocol. Postel, J.B.; 1983 May

Network Management

rfc1271	Remote network monitoring management information base. Waldbusser, S.; 1991 November
rfc1253	OSPF version 2: Management Information Base. Baker, F.; Coltun, R.; 1991 August
rfc1243	Appletalk Management Information Base. 1991 July
rfc1239	Reassignment of experimental MIBs to standard MIBs. Reynolds, J.K.; 1991 June
rfc1238	CLNS MIB for use with Connectionless Network Protocol (ISO 8473) and End System to Intermediate System (ISO 9542). Satz, G.; 1991 June
rfc1233	Definitions of managed objects for the DS3 Interface type. Cox, T.A.; Tesink, K.,eds.; 1991 May
rfc1232	Definitions of managed objects for the DS1 Interface type. Baker, F.; Kolb, C.P.,eds.; 1991 May
rfc1231	IEEE 802.5 Token Ring MIB. McCloghrie, K.; Fox, R.; Decker, E.; 1991 May
rfc1230	IEEE 802.4 Token Bus MIB. McCloghrie, K.; Fox, R.; 1991 May
rfc1229	Extensions to the generic-interface MIB. McCloghrie, K.,ed.; 1991 May
rfc1228	SNMP-DPI: Simple Network Management Protocol Distributed Program Interface. Carpenter, G.; Wijnen, B.; 1991 May
rfc1227	SNMP MUX protocol and MIB. Rose, M.T.; 1991 May
rfc1224	Techniques for managing asynchronously generated alerts. Steinberg, L.; 1991 May
rfc1215	Convention for defining traps for use with the SNMP. Rose, M.T.,ed.; 1991 March
rfc1214	OSI internet management: Management Information Base. LaBarre, L.,ed.; 1991 April
rfc1213	Management Information Base for network management of TCP/IP-based internets: MIB-II. McCloghrie, K.; Rose, M.T.,eds.; 1991 March

rfc1212	Concise MIB definitions. Rose, M.T.; McCloghrie, K.,eds.; 1991 March
rfc1187	Bulk table retrieval with the SNMP. Rose, M.T.; McCloghrie, K.; Davin, J.R.; 1990 October
rfc1157	Simple Network Management Protocol (SNMP). Case, J.D.; Fedor, M.; Schoffstall, M.L.; Davin, C.; 1990 May
rfc1156	Management Information Base for network management of TCP/IP-based internets. McCloghrie, K.; Rose, M.T.; 1990 May
rfc1155	Structure and identification of management information for TCP/IP-based internets. Rose, M.T.; McCloghrie, K.; 1990 May
rfc1147	FYI on a network management tool catalog: Tools for monitoring and debugging TCP/IP internets and interconnected devices. Stine, R.H., ed.; 1990 April
rfc1089	SNMP over Ethernet. Schoffstall, M.L.; Davin, C.; Fedor, M.; Case, J.D.; 1989 February

Security

rfc1244	Site Security Handbook. (Also FYI 8)
rfc1115	Privacy enhancement for Internet electronic mail: Part III — algorithms, modes, and identifiers [Draft]. Linn, J.; 1989 August
rfc1114	Privacy enhancement for Internet electronic mail: Part II — certificate-based key management [Draft]. Kent, S.T.; Linn, J.; 1989 August
rfc1113	Privacy enhancement for Internet electronic mail: Part I — message encipherment and authentication procedures [Draft]. Linn, J.; 1989 August
rfc1108	Security Options for the Internet Protocol.; 1991 November

Tunneling

rfc1241	Scheme for an internet encapsulation protocol: Version 1.

Appendix B   431

rfc1234	Tunneling IPX traffic through IP networks. Provan, D.; 1991 June
rfc1088	Standard for the transmission of IP datagrams over NetBIOS networks. McLaughlin, L.J.; 1989 February
rfc1002	Protocol standard for a NetBIOS service on a TCP/UDP transport: Detailed specifications. NetBIOS Working Group; 1987 March
rfc1001	Protocol standard for a NetBIOS service on a TCP/UDP transport: Concepts and methods. NetBIOS Working Group; 1987 March

OSI

rfc1240	OSI connectionless transport services on top of UDP: Version 1. Shue, C.; Haggerty, W.; Dobbins, K.; 1991 June
rfc1237	Guidelines for OSI NSAP allocation in the internet. Collela, R.; Gardner, E.P.; Callon, R.W.; 1991 July
rfc1169	Explaining the role of GOSIP. Cerf, V.G.; Mills, K.L.; 1990 August
rfc1148	Mapping between X.400(1988) / ISO 10021 and RFC 822. Kille, S.E.; 1990 March
rfc1142	OSI IS-IS Intra-domain Routing Protocol. Oran, D.,ed.; 1990 February
rfc1086	ISO-TP0 bridge between TCP and X.25. Onions, J.P.; Rose, M.T.; 1988 December
rfc1085	ISO presentation services on top of TCP/IP based internets. Rose, M.T.; 1988 December
rfc1070	Use of the Internet as a subnetwork for experimentation with the OSI network layer. Hagens, R.A.; Hall, N.E.; Rose, M.T.; 1989 February
rfc1069	Guidelines for the use of Internet-IP addresses in the ISO Connectionless-Mode Network Protocol. Callon, R.W.; Braun, H.W.; 1989 February
rfc1008	Implementation guide for the ISO Transport Protocol. McCoy, W.; 1987 June
rfc1006	ISO transport services on top of the TCP: Ver-

Appendix B

	sion 3. Rose, M.T.; Cass, D.E.; 1987 May
rfc995	ISO End System to Intermediate System Routing Exchange Protocol for use in conjunction with ISO 8473. International Organization for Standardization; 1986 April
rfc994	ISO Final text of DIS 8473, Protocol for Providing the Connectionless-mode Network Service. International Organization for Standardization; 1986 March
rfc982	Guidelines for the specification of the structure of the Domain Specific Part (DSP) of the ISO standard NSAP address. Braun, H.W.; 1986 April
rfc941	International Organization for Standardization; ISO Addendum to the network service definition covering network layer addressing. 1985 April
rfc905	ISO Transport Protocol specification ISO DP 8073. McKenzie, A.M.; 1984 April

Miscellaneous

rfc1251	Who's who in the internet: Biographies of IAB, IESG and IRSG members. Malkin, G.S.; 1991 August
rfc1207	FYI on Questions and Answers: Answers to commonly asked "experienced Internet user" questions. Malkin, G.S.; Marine, A.N.; Reynolds, J.K.; 1991 February
rfc1206	FYI on Questions and Answers: Answers to commonly asked "new Internet user" questions. Malkin, G.S.; Marine, A.N.; 1991 February

OTHER DIRECTORIES

The /ietf directory contains reports and minutes detailing ietf activities. The /iesg directory contains minutes of the IETF Steering Group. The /netprog directory contains source code for whois and nicname services.

The /ien directory contains the *Internet Engineering Notes*, written in the time period spanning 1977 to 1982. Several notes are still of interest. For example, ien-109, entitled *How to Build a Gateway*, and ien-137, *On Holy Wars and a Plea for Peace*, which discusses big-endian versus little-endian data formats. The */scc* directory contains several documents on Internet security problems which may provide insight into general security issues.

Appendix C

Dialogues

This appendix contains dialogues that illustrate how to obtain online information. Text that is entered by the end user will be in boldface.

C.1 NIC FILE TRANSFER

Below, we access the NIC file transfer server with userid anonymous and password guest. We switch to directory /ien and get file ien-137.txt. See Chapter 11 for a retrieval of an rfc file.

```
ftp nic.ddn.mil
Connected to nic.ddn.mil.
220-*****Welcome to the Network Information Center*****
     *****Login with username "anonymous" and password "guest"
     *****You may change directories to the following:
        ddn-news         - DDN Management Bulletins
        domain           - Root Domain Zone Files
        ien              - Internet Engineering Notes
        iesg             - IETF Steering Group
        ietf             - Internet Engineering Task Force
        internet-drafts  - Internet Drafts
        netinfo          - NIC Information Files
        netprog          - Guest Software (ex. whois.c)
        protocols        - TCP-IP & OSI Documents
        rfc              - RFC Repository
        scc              - DDN Security Bulletins
220 And more.
Name (nic.ddn.mil:feit): anonymous
331 Guest login ok, send "guest" as password.
Password:
230 Guest login ok, access restrictions apply.
ftp> cd ien
```

435

436   Appendix C

```
250 CWD command successful.
ftp> get ien-137.txt
200 PORT command successful.
150 Opening ASCII mode data connection for ien-137.txt (35861 bytes).
226 Transfer complete.
local: ien-137.txt remote: ien-137.txt
36677 bytes received in 4.2 seconds (8.6 Kbytes/s)
ftp> quit
221 Goodbye.
```

C.2 WHOIS SERVICE

The NIC offers an online database service that contains information about administrators, domains, domain name servers, networks, and computers. The dialogue below illustrates the use of the *whois* service.

```
telnet nic.ddn.mil
Trying 192.112.36.5 ...
Connected to nic.ddn.mil.
Escape character is '^]'.

SunOS UNIX (nic)
*
* -- DDN Network Information Center --
*
* For user and host information, type: WHOIS <return>
*
. . .

@ whois
Connecting to id Database . . . . . .
Connected to id Database
NIC WHOIS Version: 1.26 Tue, 31 Dec 91 07:10:59 , load 0.67

   Enter a handle, name, mailbox, or other field, optionally preceded
   by a keyword, like "host sri-nic". Type "?" for short, 2-page
   details, "HELP" for full documentation, or hit RETURN to exit.
   ---> Do ^E to show search progress, ^G to abort a search or output
   <---

Whois: vanbokkelen, james
VanBokkelen, James B. (JBV2)           jbvb@FTP.COM
   FTP Software, Inc.
   26 Princess Street
   Wakefield, MA 01880-3004
   (617) 246-0900
   Record last updated on 24-Oct-90.

Whois: domain yale.edu
Yale University (YALE-DOM)
```

```
Department of Computer Science
P.O. Box 2158 Yale Station
New Haven, CT 06520
Domain Name: YALE.EDU

Administrative Contact, Technical Contact, Zone Contact:
    Watt, Alan S.   (ASW3)    watt-alan@CS.YALE.EDU
    (203) 432-6600 ext 394

Record last updated on 21-Oct-90.
Domain servers in listed order:

YALE.EDU                  128.36.0.1, 130.132.1.1
CS.YALE.EDU               128.36.0.3, 130.132.1.2
RA.DEPT.CS.YALE.EDU       128.36.16.1
SERV1.NET.YALE.EDU        130.132.1.9
SERV2.NET.YALE.EDU        130.132.1.10
SERV3.NET.YALE.EDU        130.132.1.11
NISC.JVNC.NET             128.121.50.7
```

C.3 NIC ELECTRONIC MAIL

NIC documents can be requested and received by means of electronic mail. Requests should be sent to mailbox:

SERVICE@NIC.DDN.MIL

The desired document must be identified in the SUBJECT field! Example SUBJECT lines are:

```
HELP
RFC 822
RFC INDEX
RFC 1119.PS
FYI 1
```

C.4 ARCHIE

The McGill School of Computer Science has developed a database server named Archie that can be used to find documents and software at open file transfer sites. Archie became so popular that it has been replicated at several other sites.

Access to services like Archie, or use of public file transfer facilities, should be restricted to low traffic hours. Most sites are happy to make their facilities available between 7 P.M. and 6 A.M. on weekdays (local time), or on weekends. When outside users abuse a public database, the site is very likely to simply close its service.

Appendix C

In the dialogue below, we contact the main Archie server via Telnet, and login as *archie*. No password is requested. Archie is very talkative, and some of Archie's messages have been omitted from the dialogue.

In the dialogue, we find out the location of other Archie servers and invoke *help*. We then use the *prog* command to look up *traceroute*. It is a good idea to use "set maxhits" to limit the number of responses before using *prog*.

Note that Archie also provides a mail interface at mailboxes named *archie@archiehost*. A mail message sent to Archie can contain a sequence of Archie commands.

In choosing an Archie server, check the domain name, and try to pick one that is fairly close to you. For example, using the Australian Archie is not the most efficient choice from the U.S.!

```
telnet 132.206.2.3
Trying 132.206.2.3 ...
Connected to 132.206.2.3.
Escape character is '^]'.

SunOS UNIX (quiche.CS.McGill.CA)

login: archie
ARCHIE: The McGill School of Computer Science Archive Server

   ** 'help' for help
   ** corrections/additions to archie-admin@archie.mcgill.ca
   ** bug reports, comments etc. to archie-l@archie.mcgill.ca

=================================================================
archie> servers

Current archie servers (as of Jan 3 1992):

   archie.mcgill.ca      (132.206.2.3)      McGill University,
                                            Montreal, Canada
   archie.sura.net       (128.167.254.179)  SURAnet, College Park,
                                            Maryland, USA
   archie.ans.net        (147.225.1.2)      ANS, New York, USA
   archie.unl.edu        (129.93.1.14)      Lincoln, Nebraska, USA
   archie.rutgers.edu    (128.6.18.15)      Piscataway, New Jersey, USA
   archie.funet.fi       (128.214.6.100)    FUnet, Helsinki, Finland
   archie.au             (128.184.1.4)      Deakin University, Geelong,
                                            Australia
   archie.doc.ic.ac.uk   (146.169.3.7)      Imperial College, London,
                                            UK
```

Whenever possible, please avoid the use of trans-oceanic links since these tend to have limited bandwith and are already heavily congested.

```
To access the email interface: mail to
    archie@archiehost
Where "archiehost" is one of the hosts listed above.
All archie hosts support the Prospero interface for the use of archie
clients.

archie> help

Help gives you information about various topics, . . .
Currently, the available help topics are:

        about     - a blurb about archie
        bugs      - known bugs and undesirable features
        bye       - same as "quit"
        email     - how to contact the archie email interface
        exit      - same as "quit"
        help      - this message
        list      - list the sites in the archie database
        mail      - mail output to a user
        nopager   - *** use 'unset pager' instead
        pager     - *** use 'set pager' instead
        plans     - future plans for archie
        prog      - search the database for a file
        quit      - exit archie
        servers   - display a list of all currently available archie servers
        set       - set a variable
        show      - display the value of a variable
        site      - list the files at an archive site
        term      - *** use 'set term ...' instead
        unset     - unset a variable
        whatis    - search for keyword in the software description database
. . .

archie> set maxhits 5
archie> prog traceroute
Host clouso.crim.ca    (192.26.210.1)
Last updated 06:09 17 Feb 1992

    Location: /pub
        FILE       rw-r--r--      22567   Apr 26  1990   traceroute.tar.Z
. . .
```

C.5 ANONYMOUS FTP SITES

There is a large and ever-changing set of Internet sites that will admit anonymous FTP. A list of these sites is maintained as part of the Archie database. To see a complete list, just login to Archie and give the *list* command. Note that the list currently includes more than 1000 sites!

C.6 EVOLVING INFORMATION ORGANIZERS

There is an abundance of information resources on the Internet and on users' private networks. The problem for users is to find and organize the resources that they need.

Prospero is a distributed directory system, file system, and index service that enables a user to impose a logical structure on a virtual file system constructed of both local and remote directories. The *Internet Gopher* provides a single, simple user interface that can be used to apply a query to multiple information sources. Both of these services are described in the July 1992 Issue of *ConneXions*.

Appendix

D

Review of Commands

In this appendix, we review the commands that were used in the text. Examples of *finger, mount, netstat, nfsstat, nslookup, ping, rpcinfo, ruptime, showmount, spray,* and *traceroute* can be found in Chapter 16. There are ftp dialogues in Chapter 11 and in Appendix C. The *telnet* command is illustrated in Chapter 13. The *arp* command is used in Chapter 5 and *ifconfig* is illustrated in Chapter 6. Sample dialogues using *ypmatch* and *ypcat* may be found in Chapter 12.

Sun Microsystems SunOS 4.1 commands were used in this text. However, identical or similar versions have been ported to many operating systems. Check your manuals for the commands or menus at your own system that provide a corresponding function.

arp	View or update the Address Resolution Protocol table, which maps IP addresses to physical network addresses.
finger	View the list of users logged into systems on the network.
ftp	Invoke an ftp client in order to access ftp servers.
ifconfig	View or configure parameters for a network interface.
mount	Mount directories into the local file structure, or view the list of mounts that have been configured.
netstat	View a variety of network statistics.
nfsstat	View statistics on the usage of NFS procedures, or details about the configuration parameters for mounted systems.
nslookup	Access a Domain Name server to look up IP addresses, the location of mail exchangers, and host information.

ping   Send an ICMP echo message to a remote system to test whether it is up. A sequence of messages also may be sent.

rpcinfo   View information about active programs at the local host or at remote hosts.

ruptime   View a report showing how long systems on the network have been up, and how heavily each is loaded.

showmount   View servers currently mounted at a client.

spray   Send a batch of UDP datagrams to a system to check the throughput that the network and remote system can handle.

telnet   Login to remote hosts.

traceroute   Send a sequence of datagrams with varying Time-to-Live fields. ICMP messages will be returned from each router along the path to the destination.

ypcat   List the contents of a Network Information Service database.

ypmatch   Look up an entry in an Network Information Service database. Typical databases provide lookups that match domain names to IP addresses, protocol numbers to protocols, and mail aliases to mailbox names.

Glossary

Abstract Syntax Notation One (ASN.1). A language used for defining datatypes. ASN.1 is used in OSI standards, and also is used in TCP/IP network management specifications.

Access Control. A facility that defines each user's privileges to access computer data.

Acknowledgement. TCP requires that data be acknowledged before it can be considered to have been transmitted safely.

Active Open. Action taken by an application to initiate a TCP connection.

Address Mask. A 32-bit binary number used to identify the parts of an IP address that are used for network and subnet numbers. Every bit in the network and subnet fields is set to 1.

Address Resolution Protocol (ARP). A protocol that dynamically discovers the physical address of a system, given its IP address.

Agent. In the Simple Network Management Protocol, the process within a device that responds to get and set requests, and sends trap messages.

American National Standards Institute (ANSI). Organization responsible for coordinating United States standardization activities. ANSI is a member of ISO.

Application Programming Interface (API). A set of routines that enable a programmer to use computer facilities. The socket programming interface and the transport layer interface are both APIs used for TCP/IP programming.

ARPANET. The world's first packet-switching network, which for many years functioned as an Internet backbone.

ASCII. American National Standard Code for Information Interchange. Seven of the eight bits in an octet are required to define a ASCII character.

Autonomous System (AS). A collection of routers under the control of a single administrative authority, and using a common Interior Gateway Protocol.

Basic Encoding Rules (BER). The rules for encoding datatypes specified using ASN.1 into their transmission format.

Glossary

Baud. A unit of signaling speed equal to the number of times per second that a signal changes state. If there are exactly two states, the baud rate equals the bit rate.

Berkeley Software Distribution (BSD). UNIX software that included TCP/IP support.

Big Endian. A format for the storage or transmission of data that places the most significant byte (or bit) first.

Border Gateway protocol (BGP). A protocol used to advertise the set of networks that can be reached within an Autonomous System. BGP enables this information to be shared with other Autonomous Systems. BGP is newer than EGP, and offers a number of improvements.

Bridge. A device that connects two or more physical network components and forwards frames which have source and destination addresses on different network components.

Brouter. A device that performs both bridging and routing functions. Some traffic is selected for routing, while the rest is bridged.

Buffer. An area of storage used to hold input or output data.

Carrier Sense Multiple Access with Collision Detection (CSMA/CD). A simple media access control protocol. All stations listen to the medium. A station wanting to send may do so if there is no signal on the medium. When two stations transmit simultaneously, both back off and retry after a random time period.

Common Management Information Protocol (CMIP). A central OSI network management protocol.

Common Management Information Services and Protocol over TCP/IP (CMOT). A specification for using OSI management protocols on a TCP/IP network.

Connection. A logical communication path between TCP users.

Core Gateway. A router operated by the Internet Network Operations Center. Core gateways distribute reachability information among the Autonomous Systems attaching to the Internet backbone.

Cyclic Redundancy Check (CRC). A mathematical function applied to the bits in a frame, and appended to the frame. The CRC is recalculated when the frame is received. If the result differs from the appended value, then the frame is discarded.

Data Circuit-terminating Equipment (DCE). Equipment required to connect a DTE to a line or to a network.

Data Encryption Standard (DES). Encryption protocol officially sanctioned by the United States government.

Data Terminal Equipment (DTE). A source or destination for data. Often used to denote terminals or computers attached to a wide area network.

Directory System Agent (DSA). An facility that accepts queries from Directory User Agents and extracts information from a database. A DSA interacts with a Directory User Agent by means of X.500 protocols.

Directory User Agent (DUA). A facility enabling a user to send queries to an X.500 directory server. A DUA interacts with a Directory Service Agent (DSA).

Distributed Computing Environment (DCE). A set of technologies selected by the Open Software Foundation to support distributed computing.

Distributed File Service (DFS). A file server technology adopted by the Open Software Foundation.

Distributed Management Environment (DME). A set of technologies selected for network and system management by the Open Software Foundation.

Domain Name System (DNS). A set of distributed databases providing information such as the IP addresses corresponding to system names, and the location of mail exchangers.

Exterior Gateway Protocol (EGP). A protocol used to advertise the set of networks that can be reached within an Autonomous System. EGP enables this information to be shared with other Autonomous Systems. See core gateway and BGP.

eXternal Data Representation (XDR). A standard developed by Sun Microsystems to define datatypes used as parameters, and to encode these parameters for transmission.

Fiber Distributed Data Interface (FDDI). A standard for high speed data transfer across a dual ring.

File Transfer, Access, and Management (FTAM). The OSI file transfer and management protocol. FTAM allows users to copy whole files or part of a file, such as an individual record.

File Transfer Protocol (FTP). The TCP/IP protocol that enables users to copy files between systems and perform file management functions, such as renaming or deleting files.

Flow Control. A mechanism that allows a receiver to limit the amount of data that a sender may transmit at any time. Flow control prevents a sender from exhausting the receiver's memory buffers.

For Your Information (FYI). A set of documents including useful information, such as answers to frequently asked questions about TCP/IP. FYI documents also are published as RFCs.

Fragmentation. Partitioning of a datagram into pieces. This is done when a datagram is too large for a network technology that must be traversed to reach the destination.

Frame Check Sequence (FCS). A mathematical function applied to the bits in a frame, and appended to the frame. The FCS is recalculated when the frame is received. If the result differs from the appended value, then the frame is discarded.

Gateway. An IP router. Many RFC documents use the term gateway rather than router.

Gateway to Gateway Protocol (GGP). A protocol formerly used to exchange routing information between Internet core routers.

Government Open Systems Interconnection Profile (GOSIP). Specification of a set of OSI protocols to be preferred in government procurements of computer equipment.

High Level Data Link Control Protocol (HDLC). A standard that is the basis for several link layer protocols.

Initial Sequence Number (ISN). A sequence number defined during TCP connection setup. Data octets sent over the connection will be numbered starting from this point.

Integrated Services Digital Network (ISDN). A set of CCITT standards aimed at integrating voice and data services. ISDN provides end-to-end digital services.

Interior Gateway Protocol (IGP). Any routing protocol used within an Autonomous System.

Intermediate System to Intermediate System protocol (IS-IS). A protocol that can be used to route both OSI and IP traffic.

International Organization for Standardization (ISO). An international body founded to promote international trade and cooperative progress in science and technology.

International Telegraph and Telephone Consultative Committee (CCITT). An organization formed to facilitate connecting communications facilities into international networks.

internet. A set of networks connected by IP routers and appearing to its users as a single network.

Internet. The world's largest network, the Internet is based on the TCP/IP protocol suite.

Internet Architecture Board (IAB). Formerly the Internet Activities Board. An independent group responsible for promoting protocol development, selecting protocols for Internet use, and assigning state and status to protocols.

Internet Assigned Numbers Authority (IANA). The authority responsible for controlling the assignment of a variety of parameters, such as well-known ports, multicast addresses, terminal identifiers, and system identifiers.

Internet Control Message Protocol (ICMP). A protocol that is required for implementation with IP. ICMP specifies error messages to be sent when datagrams are discarded or systems experience congestion. ICMP also provides several useful query services.

Internet Engineering Notes (IEN). A set of documents discussing features of the TCP/IP suite. These documents are available online at the Network Information Center.

Internet Engineering Steering Group (IESG). A group that coordinates the activities of the IETF working groups.

Internet Engineering Task Force (IETF). A group directed by the IAB, charged with solving short-term Internet problems.

Internet Group Management Protocol (IGMP). A protocol that is part of the multicast specification. IGMP is used to carry group membership information.

Internet Protocol (IP). The TCP/IP layer 3 protocol responsible for transporting datagrams across an internet.

Internet Research Task Force (IRTF). A group directed by the IAB, charged with long-term research on Internet protocols.

IP Address. A 32-bit quantity that identifies a network interface.

IP Datagram. The unit of data routed by IP.

ISO Development Environment (ISODE). A research effort that has produced software enabling OSI protocols to run on top of TCP/IP.

Kerberos. An authentication service developed at the Massachusetts Institute of Technology. Kerberos uses encryption to prevent intruders from discovering passwords and gaining unauthorized access to files or services.

Little Endian. A format for the storage or transmission of data that places the least significant byte (or bit) first.

Logical Byte. A logical byte is a specified number of bits in length. In a file transfer, it is sometimes necessary to specify a logical byte size in order to preserve the integrity of data that is transferred.

Logical Link Control (LLC). A layer 2 (data link layer) protocol that governs the exchange of data between two systems connected to a single physical medium, or connected via a sequence of bridged media.

Mail Exchanger. A system used to relay mail into an locally administered internet.

Management Information Base (MIB). A database that contains configuration and statistical performance information. A MIB may be stored at any type of networking element, such as a host, router, or bridge.

Maximum Segment Size. The maximum permissible size for the data part of any segment sent on a particular connection.

Maximum Transmission Unit (MTU). The largest datagram that can be sent across a particular network technology, such as an Ethernet or Token-Ring.

Media Access Control (MAC). A protocol governing a station's access to a network. For example, CSMA/CD provides a set of MAC rules for sending and receiving data across a local area network.

Message Transfer Agent (MTA). An entity that moves messages (such as electronic mail) between computers.

Metropolitan Area Network (MAN). A technology supporting high speed networking across a metropolitan area. IEEE 802.6 defines a MAN protocol.

Multi-homed Host. A host attached to two or more networks, and therefore requiring multiple IP addresses.

National Education and Research Network (NREN). A planned high capacity network to be used as part of a future backbone for the Internet.

National Institute of Standards and Technology (NIST). A United States standards organization that has promoted communications standards. NIST formerly was the National Bureau of Standards.

National Science Foundation Network (NSFnet). A network used as part of the current Internet backbone.

NETBIOS. A network programming interface and protocol developed for IBM-compatible personal computers.

Network Address. The 32-bit IP address of a system.

Network File System (NFS). A set of protocols introduced by Sun Microsystems, enabling clients to mount remote directories onto their local file systems, and use remote files as if they were local.

Network Information Center (NIC). A central administration facility for the Internet. The NIC supervises network names and network addresses, and provides several information services.

Network Information Service (NIS). A set of protocols introduced by Sun Microsystems, used to provide a directory service for network information.

Network Service Access Point (NSAP). An identifier used to distinguish the identity of an OSI host, and to point to the transport layer entity at that host to which traffic is directed.

Network Virtual Terminal (NVT). A set of rules defining a very simple virtual terminal interaction. The NVT is used at the start of a Telnet session, but a more complex type of terminal interaction can be negotiated.

Open Shortest Path First (OSPF). An internet routing protocol that scales well, can route traffic along multiple paths, and uses knowledge of an internet's topology to make accurate routing decisions.

Open Software Foundation (OSF). A consortium of computer vendors cooperating to produce standard technologies for open systems. The MOTIF user interface and Distributed Computing Environment are OSF technologies.

Open Systems Interconnection (OSI). A set of ISO standards relating to data communications.

Packet. Originally, a unit of data sent across a packet-switching network. Currently, the term may refer to a protocol data unit at any layer.

Packet Assembler/Disassembler (PAD). Software that converts between a terminal's stream of traffic and X.25 packet format.

Page Structure. A file organization supported in FTP for use with older Digital Equipment Corporation computers.

Passive Open. Action taken by a TCP/IP server to prepare to receive requests from clients.

Pathname. The character string which must be input to a file system by a user in order to identify a file.

Point-to-Point Protocol (PPP). A protocol for data transfer across serial links. PPP supports extensive link configuration capabilities, and allows traffic for several protocols to be multiplexed across the link.

Port. A 2-octet binary number identifying an upper level user of TCP.

Protocol Data Unit (PDU). A generic term for the protocol unit (e.g., a header and data) used at any layer.

Protocol Interpreter (PI). An entity that carries out FTP functions. FTP defines two PI roles: user and server.

Proxy ARP. Use of a router to answer ARP requests. This will be done when the originating host believes that a destination is local, when in fact it lies beyond a router.

Push Service. A service provided by TCP that lets an application specify that some data should be transmitted and delivered as soon as possible.

Receive Window. The valid range of sequence numbers that a sender may transmit at a given time during the connection.

Record Structures. Common structure for data files. During a transfer of a file that is organized as a sequence of records, records can be delimited by End-of-Record markers.

Remote Network Monitor (RMON). A device that collects information about network traffic.

Remote Procedure Call (RPC). A protocol that enables an application to call a routine that executes at a server. The server returns output variables and a return code to the caller.

Requests For Comments (RFCs). A set of documents containing Internet protocols and discussions of related topics. These documents are available online at the Network Information Center.

Resolver. Software that enables a client to access the Domain Name System databases.

Retransmission Timeout. If a segment is not ACKed within the period defined by the retransmission timeout, then TCP will retransmit the segment.

Reverse Address Resolution Protocol (RARP). A protocol that enables a computer to discover its IP address by broadcasting a request on a network.

Round Trip Time (RTT). The time elapsed between sending a TCP segment and receiving its ACK.

Router. A system used to connect separate LANs and WANs into an internet, and to route traffic between the constituent networks.

Routing Information Protocol (RIP). A simple protocol used to exchange information between routers. The original version was part of the XNS protocol suite.

Segment. A protocol data unit consisting of a TCP header and optionally, some data.

Send Window. The range of sequence numbers between the last octet of data that already has been sent and the right edge of the receive window.

Sequence Number. A 32-bit field of a TCP header. If the segment contains data, the sequence number is associated with the first octet of the data.

Serial Line Interface Protocol (SLIP). A very simple protocol used for transmission of IP datagrams across a serial line.

Shortest Path First. A routing algorithm that uses knowledge of a network's topology in making routing decisions.

Silly Window Syndrome. Inefficient data transfer that results when a receiver reports small window credits and a sender transmits correspondingly small segments. This problem is easily solved using algorithms cited in RFC 1122.

Simple Mail Transfer Protocol (SMTP). A TCP/IP protocol used to transfer mail between systems.

Simple Network Management Protocol. A TCP/IP protocol that enables a management station to configure, monitor, and receive trap (alarm) messages from network devices.

Smoothed Deviation. A quantity that measures deviations from the smoothed round trip time, and used to calculate the TCP retransmission timeout.

Smoothed Round Trip Time (SRTT). An estimate of the current round trip time for a segment and its ACK, used in calculating the value of the TCP retransmission timeout.

Socket Address. The full address of a communicating TCP/IP entity, made up of a 32-bit network address and a 16-bit port number.

Socket Descriptor. An integer that an application uses to identify a connection. Socket descriptors are used in the Berkeley socket programming interface.

Source Quench. An ICMP message sent by a congested system to the sources of its traffic.

Source Route. A sequence of IP addresses identifying the route a datagram must follow. A source route may optionally be included in an IP datagram header.

Subnet Address. A selected number of bits from the local part of an IP address, used to identify a specific local area network or wide area network.

Subnet Mask. A 32-bit quantity, with 1s placed in positions covering the network and subnet part of an IP address.

Switched Multimegabit Data Service (SMDS). A data transfer service based on the IEEE 802.6 Metropolitan Area Network protocol.

SYN. A segment used at the start of a TCP connection. Each partner sends a SYN containing the starting point for its sequence numbering, and, optionally, the size of the largest segment that it is willing to accept.

Synchronous Data Link Protocol (SDLC). A protocol similar to HDLC that is part of IBM's SNA communications protocol suite. SDLC is used for point-to-point and multipoint communications.

Synchronous Optical Network (SONET). A standard for the transmission of information fiber optic channels.

Systems Network Architecture (SNA). The protocol suite developed and used by IBM.

Telnet. The TCP/IP protocol that enables a terminal attached to one host to login to other hosts and interact with their applications.

Time-to-Live (TTL). A limit on the length of time that a datagram can remain within an internet. The Time-to-Live usually is specified as the maximum number of hops that a datagram can traverse before it must be discarded.

Token-Ring. A local area network technology based on a ring topology. Stations on the ring pass a special message, called a token, around the ring. The current token holder has the right to transmit data for a limited period of time.

Transmission Control Block (TCB). A data structure used to hold information about a current TCP or UDP communication.

Transmission Control Protocol (TCP). The TCP/IP protocol that provides reliable, connection-oriented data transmission between a pair of applications.

Transport Class 4 (OSI TP4). An OSI transport layer protocol that is functionally similar to TCP.

Transport Layer Interface (TLI). An application programming interface introduced by AT&T that interfaces to both TCP/IP and OSI protocols.

Transport Service Access Point (TSAP). An identifier that indicates the upper layer protocol entity to whom a protocol data unit should be delivered.

Trivial File Transfer Protocol (TFTP). A very basic TCP/IP protocol used to upload or download files. Typical uses include initializing diskless workstations or downloading software from a controller to a robot.

Trunk Coupling Unit (TCU). A hardware element connecting a Token-Ring station to the backbone of a ring.

Urgent Service. A service provided by TCP that lets an application indicate that specified data is urgent and should be processed by the receiving application as soon as possible.

User Agent (UA). An electronic mail application that helps an end user to prepare, save, and send outgoing messages and view, store, and reply to incoming messages.

User Datagram Protocol. A simple protocol enabling an application to send individual messages to other applications. Delivery is not guaranteed, and messages need not be delivered in the same order as they were sent.

Virtual Circuit. A term derived from packet-switching networks. A virtual circuit is supported by facilities which are shared between many users, although each circuit appears to its users as a dedicated end-to-end connection.

Wide Area Network (WAN). A network that covers a large geographical area. Typical WAN technologies include point-to-point, X.25, and frame relay.

Well-known Port. A TCP or UDP port whose use is published by the Internet Assigned Numbers Authority.

X.121. A CCITT standard describing the assignment of numbers to systems attached to an X.25 network. These numbers are used to identify a remote system so that a data call can be set up over a virtual circuit.

X.25. A CCITT standard for connecting computers to a network that provides reliable, virtual circuit based data transmission.

X.400. A series of protocols defined by the CCITT for message transfer and interpersonal messaging. These protocols were later adopted by ISO.

Xerox Network System (XNS). A suite of networking protocols developed at Xerox Corporation.

X-Window System. A set of protocols developed at MIT that enable a user to interact with applications which may be located a several different computers. The input and output for each application occurs in a window at the user's display. Window placement and size are controlled by the user.

Bibliography

American National Standards Institute, *Fiber Distributed Data Interface (FDDI) – Token Ring Physical Layer Protocol (PHY)*, ANS X3.148-1988, (also ISO 9314-1, 1989).
———, *Fiber Distributed Data interface (FDDI) – Token Ring Media Access Control (MAC)*, ANS X3.139-1987, (also ISO 9314-2, 1989).
———, *T1.602 – Telecommunications – ISDN – Data Link Layer Signalling Specification for Application at the Network Interface*, 1990.
———, *T1.606 – Frame Relaying Bearer Service – Architectural Framework and Service Description*, 1990.
———, *T1S1/90-175 – Addendum to T1.696 – Frame Relaying Bearer Service – Architectural Framework and Service Description*, 1990.
———, *T1S1/90-214 – DSS1 – Core Aspects of Frame Protocol for Use with Frame Relay Bearer Service – Architectural Framework and Service Description*, 1990.
Bellcore TA-TSV-00160, *Exchange Access SMDS Service Generic Reqiuirements*, December 1990.
Bellovin, S., and M. Merritt, *Limitations of the Kerberos Authentication System*, Computer Communications Review, October 1990.
Black, Uyless D., Data Communications, *Networks, and Distributed Processing*, Reston, 1983.
Bolt, Beranek, and Newman, *A History of the ARPANET: The First Decade*, Technical Report, 1981.
Borman, D., *Implementing TCP/IP on a Cray Computer*, Computer Communication Review, April 1989.
Brand, R., *Coping with the Threat of Computer Security Incidents: A Primer from Prevention through Recovery*, at cert.sei.cmu.edu in /pub/info/primer, June 1990.
Callon, Ross, *An Overview of OSI NSAP Addressing in the Internet*, ConneXions, The Interoperability Report, December 1991.
CCITT Recommendation I.22, *Framework for providing additional packet mode bearer services*, Blue Book, ITU, Geneva, 1988
CCITT Recommendation X.25, *Interface between data terminal equipment (DTE) and data-circuit-terminating equipment (DCE) for terminals operating in the packet mode on public data networks*, 1980 and 1984.
CCITT Recommendation X.400, *Message Handling System*, 1984 and 1988.
CCITT Recommendation X.500, *The Directory*, 1988.
Cerf, V., *A History of the ARPANET*, ConneXions, The Interoperability Report, October 1989.
Cerf, V., and R. Kahn, *A Protocol for Packet Network Intercommunication*, IEEE Transactions on Communication, May 1974.
Cheswick, B., *The Design of a Secure Internet Gateway*, Proceedings of the Summer Usenix Conference, Anaheim, CA, June 1990.
cisco, StrataCom, Digital Equipment Corporation, *Frame Relay Specification with Extensions*, Draft, 1990.
cisco Systems, *Gateway System Manual*, 1991.

Coltun, Rob, *OSPF: An internet routing protocol*, ConneXions, August 1989.
Comer, Douglas E., *Internetworking With TCP/IP, Volume I Principles, Protocols, and Architecture*, Second Edition, Prentice Hall, 1991.
Comer, Douglas E., and Stevens, David L., *Internetworking With TCP/IP, Volume II, Design, Implementation, and Internals*, Prentice Hall, 1991.
Cooper, J., *Computer and Communications Security: Strategies for the 1990s*, McGraw-Hill, 1989.
Deering, S., *IP Multicasting*, ConneXions, February 1991.
Dern, Daniel P., *Standards for Interior Gateway Routing Protocols*, ConneXions, July 1990.
Digital Equipment Corporation, Intel Corporation, and XEROX Corporation, *The Ethernet: A Local Area Network Data Link Layer and Physical Layer Specification*, September 1980.
Frey, Donnalyn and Adams, Rick, *!%@: A Directory of Electronic Mail Addressing and Networks*, 2nd Edition, O'Reilly & Associates, 1989.
Fricc, *Program Plan for the National Research and Education Network*, Federal Research Internet Coordinating Committee, US Department of Energy, Office of Scientific Computing Report ER-7, May 1989.
FTP Software, *PC/TCP Kernel Installation and Reference Guide*, Version 2.05 for DOS, 1990.
———, *PC/TCP User's Guide*, Version 2.05 for DOS, 1990.
GOSIP, *U.S. Government Open Systems Interconnection Profile Version 2.0*, Advanced Requirements Group, National Institute of Standards and Technology (NIST), April 1989.
Green, James Harry, *The Dow Jones-Irwin Handbook of Telecommunications*, Dow Jones-Irwin, 1986.
Hedrick, Charles L., *Introduction to Administration of an Internet-based Local Network*, Rutgers, The State University of New Jersey, 1988, at cs.rutgers.edu, in /runet/tcp-ip-admin.doc.
———, *Introduction to the Internet Protocols*, Rutgers, The State University of New Jersey, 1987, host cs.rutgers.edu, /runet/tcp-ip-intro.doc.
Hoffman, L, *Rogue Programs: Viruses, Worms, and Trojan Horses*, Van Nostrand Reinhold, 1990.
IBM GG24-3442, *IBM AS/400 TCP/IP Configuration and Operation*, 1991.
IBM GG24-3696, *Managing TCP/IP Networks Using NetView and the SNMP Interface*, 1991.
IBM SC31-6081, *TCP/IP Version 2 Release 2 for VM: User's Guide*, 1991.
IBM SC31-6084, *TCP/IP Version 2 Release 2 for VM: Programmer's Reference*, 1991.
IBM, *Vocabulary for Data processing, Telecommunications, and Office Systems*, 1981.
Institute of Electrical and Electronics Engineers, *Draft Standard P802.1A – Overview and Architecture*, 1989.
———, *Local Area Networks – CSMA/CD Access Method*, ANSI/IEEE 802.3, (ISO 8802-3).
———, *Local Area Networks – Distributed Queue Dual Bus (DQDB) Subnetwork of a Metropolitan Area Network (MAN)*, ANSI/IEEE 802.6 (ISO DIS 8802-6, 1991).
———, *Local Area Networks – Higher Layers and Interworking*, ANSI/IEEE 802.1, 1990 (ISO DIS 8802-1D, 1990).
———, *Local Area Networks – Logical Link Control*, ANSI/IEEE 802.2, 1989 (ISO 8802-2, 1989).
———, *Local Area Networks – Network Management. Draft IEEE 802.1B*, 1990.
———, *Local Area Networks – Token-Bus Access Method*, ANSI/IEEE 802.4, (ISO 8802-3).
———, *Local Area Networks – Token Ring Access Method*, ANSI/IEEE 802.5, 1989 (ISO 8802-5, 1989).
International Organization for Standardization, *Information Processing Systems – Common Management information Protocol (CMIP)*, ISO 9596, 1990.
———, *Information Processing Systems – Common Management information Service (CMIS)*, ISO 9595, 1990.

———, *Information Processing Systems — Data Communications — Addendum to the Network Service Definition*, ISO 8348 AD1.
———, *Information Processing Systems — Data Communications — High-Level Data Link Control Procedures — Consolidation of Classes of Procedures*, ISO 7809.
———, *Information Processing Systems — Data Communications — High-Level Data Link Control Procedures — Consolidation of Elements of Procedures*, ISO 4335.
———, *Information Processing Systems — Data Communications — High-Level Data Link Control Procedures — Frame Structure*, ISO 3309.
———, *Information Processing Systems — Data Communications — Network Service Definition*, ISO 8348.
———, *Information Processing Systems — Data Communications — Protocol for Providing the Connectionless-Mode Network Service*, ISO 8473.
———, *Information Processing Systems — Open Systems Interconnection — Basic Connection Oriented Session Protocol Specification*, ISO 8327.
———, *Information Processing Systems — Open Systems Interconnection — Basic Connection Oriented Session Service Definition*, ISO 8326.
———, *Information Processing Systems — Open Systems Interconnection — Connection Oriented Presentation Protocol Specification*, ISO 8823.
———, *Information Processing Systems — Open Systems Interconnection — Connection Oriented Presentation Service Definition*, ISO 8822.
———, *Information Processing Systems — Open Systems Interconnection — Connection Oriented Transport Protocol*, ISO 8073.
———, *Information Processing Systems — Open Systems Interconnection — Intermediate System to Intermediate System Intra-Domain Routing Exchange Protocol for use in Conjunction with the Protocol for Providing the Connectionless-Mode Network service*, ISO DIS 10589.
———, *Information Processing Systems — Open Systems Interconnection — Message Handling System*, ISO 10021/CCITT X.400.
———, *Information Processing Systems — Open Systems Interconnection — Protocol Specification for the Association Control Service Element*, ISO 8650.
———, *Information Processing Systems — Open Systems Interconnection — Remote Operations: Model, Notation, and Service Definition*, ISO 9072-1.
———, *Information Processing Systems — Open Systems Interconnection — Remote Operations: Protocol Specification*, ISO 9066-2.
———, *Information Processing Systems — Open Systems Interconnection — Service Definition for the Association Control Service Element*, ISO 8649.
———, *Information Processing Systems — Open Systems Interconnection — Specification of Abstract Syntax Notation One (ASN.1)*, ISO 8824.
———, *Information Processing Systems — Open Systems Interconnection — Specification of Basic Encoding Rules for Abstract Syntax Notation One (ASN.1)*, ISO 8825.
———, *Information Processing Systems — Open Systems Interconnection — Transport Service Definition*, ISO 8072.
———, *OSI Routing Framework*, ISO TC97/SC6/N4616, June 1987.
Jacobson, V., *Congestion Avoidance and Control*, ACM SIGCOMM-88, August 1988.
Jain, R. and K. Ramakrishnan, and D-M Chiu, *Congestion Avoidance in Computer Networks With a Connectionless Network Layer*, Technical Report, DEC-TR-506, Digital Equipment Corporation, 1987.
Kapoor, Atul, *SNA, Architecture, Protocols, and Implementation*, McGraw-Hill, 1992.
Karn, P. and C. Partridge, *Improving Round Trip Time Estimates in Reliable Transport Protocols*, Proceedings of the ACM SIGCOMM, 1987.
Kernighan, Brian W., and Dennis M. Ritchie, *The C Programming Language: Second Edition*, Prentice-Hall, 1988.
Kessler, Gary C., and Train, David A., *Metropolitan Area Networks*, McGraw-Hill, 1992.
Kessler, Gary C., *ISDN*, McGraw-Hill, 1990.
Kochan, Stephen G. and Wood, Patrick H., Consulting Editors, *UNIX Networking*, 1989.
Laquey, T. L., *User's Directory of Computer Networks*, Digital Press, 1989.
Lippis, Nick, and James Herman, *Widening Your Internet Horizons*, ConneXions, October 1991.

Malamud, Carl, *DEC Networks and Architectures*, McGraw-Hill, 1989.
———, *STACKS–The INTEROP Book*, Prentice-Hall, 1991.
McKenney, P., *Congestion Avoidance*, ConneXions, February 1991.
Medin, Milo, *The Great IGP Debate – Part Two: the Open Shortest Path First (OSPF) Routing Protocol*, ConneXions, October 1991.
Mills, D., and H-W. Braun, *The NSFNET Backbone Network*, Proceedings of the ACM SIGCOMM, 1987.
Mogul, Jeffrey C., *Efficient Use Of Workstations for Passive Monitoring of Local Area Networks*, Proc. SIGCOMM '90 Symposium on Communications Architectures and Protocols, September 1990.
Narten, T., *Internet Routing*, Proceedings of the ACM SIGCOMM, 1989.
Nemeth, Evi, Garth Snyder, and Scott Seebass, *UNIX System Administration Handbook*, Prentice-Hall, 1989.
Perlman, Radia, and Ross Callon, *The Great IGP Debate – Part One: IS-IS and Integrated Routing*, ConneXions, October 1991.
Pfleeger, C., *Security in Computing*, Prentice-Hall, 1989.
Postel, J. B., C. A. Sunshine, and D. Chen, *The ARPA Internet Protocol*, Computer Networks, 1981.
Postel, J, B., C. A. Sunshine, and D. Cohen, *The ARPA Internet protocol*, Computer Networks, Vol. 5, No. 4, July 1981.
Postel, J. B., *Internetwork Protocol Approaches*, IEEE Transactions on Communications, 1980.
Quarterman, John S., and Hoskins, J. C., *Notable Computer Networks*, Communications of the ACM, October, 1986.
Quarterman, John S., *The Matrix*, Computer Networks and Conferencing Systems Worldwide, Digital Press, 1990.
Romkey, John, *The Packet Driver*, ConneXions, July 1990.
Rose, Marshall T., *The Little Black Book: Mail Bonding with OSI Directory Services*, Prentice-Hall, 1990.
———, *The Open Book: A Practical Perspective on OSI*, Prentice-Hall, 1990.
———, *The Simple Book: An Introduction to Management of TCP/IP-based Internets*, Prentice-Hall, 1990.
St. Amand, Joseph V., *A Guide to Packet-Switched, Value-Added Networks*, Macmillan, 1986.
Schwartz, Michael F., *Resource Discovery and Related Research at the University of Colorado*, ConneXions, May 1991.
Seeley, D., *A Tour of the Worm*, Proceedings of 1989 Winter USENIX Conference, Usenix Association, San Diego, CA, February 1989.
Spafford, E., *The Internet Worm Program: An Analysis*, Computer Communication Review, Vol. 19, No. 1, ACM SIGCOM, January 1989.
Stallings, William, *Data and Computer Communications*, Macmillan, 1984.
———, *Handbook of Computer Communications Standards*, Department of Defense Protocol Standards, 1988.
Stern, Hal, *Managing NFS and NIS*, O'Reilly and Associates, 1991.
Stevens, W. Richard, *UNIX Network programming*, Prentice Hall, 1990.
Stoll, C., *The Cuckoo's Egg*, Doubleday, 1989.
Tannenbaum, Andrew S., *Computer Networks*, Prentice Hall, 1981.
Vitalink, *Building and Managing Multivendor Networks using Bridge and Router Technologies*, 1990.
Tsuchiya, Paul F., *Inter-domain Routing in the Internet*, ConneXions, January 1991.
XEROX, *Internet Transport protocols, Report XSIS 028112*, Xerox Corporation, 1981.

Index

10BASE5 53
10BASEF 53
10BASET 53
10BROAD36 53
3270 emulation 277, 281
802 standards 51
802.2 57
802.3 41, 51-55
  frame header 55
802.4 42, 57
802.5 56
  Media Access Control 57
802.6 57, 59

Abstract Syntax Notation One (ASN.1) 321, 322
accept() 393
ACK (Acknowledgment) 179, 192
Acknowledgment (ACK) 179, 192
Active open 388, 389
Adaptive routing 97
Address formats 69
Address mask 74, 94
Address Mask message 134, 135
Address Resolution Protocol (ARP) 78-81, 94
  ARP Table 81, 94
Address space 73
Advanced Research Projects Agency (ARPA) 5
Advertise 143, 147, 156, 159-161
Agent 312
Alias 305
Anonymous 218, 361
API (Application Programming Interface) 385
Application Programming Interface (API) 385

Archie Archive Server 15, 437-439
ARCNET 42
Area 150, 351
ARP (Address Resolution Protocol) 78-81, 94
  ARP Table 81, 94
  reverse ARP 81
ARPA (Advanced Research Projects Agency) 5
ARPANET 5, 6
ASN.1 (Abstract Syntax Notation One) 321, 322
  encoding 324
Assigned Numbers 11
Asynchronous 391
Audit trail 379
Autonomous System 34, 139, 150, 152
  number 353
  reachability information 354

Backbone 152, 335, 338
Basic Encoding Rules 324
Basic Security option 107, 352
bcopy() 403
Berkeley Internet Domain (BIND) 77, 357
Berkeley Software Distribution (BSD) 7
BGP (Border Gateway Protocol) 164, 353
  policy based routing 354
Big Endian 3
BIND (Berkeley Internet Domain) 77, 357
bind() 393
Bit-stuffing 44
Blocking 391
Bolt Beranek and Newman 7
BOOTP (Bootstrap protocol) 168, 352

457

458 Index

Bootstrap protocol (BOOTP) 168, 352
Border Gateway Protocol (BGP) 164, 353
Border router 156, 353
Boundary router 157
Bridge 335-338, 341
Broadcast 60, 75, 76
Brouter 342
BSD (Berkeley Software Distribution) 7
Byte 3
bzero() 397

Carrier Sense Multiple Access with Collision Detection (CSMA/CD) 54
CCITT 47, 48, 298
Checksum 99, 170, 191
Class A address 70, 72
Class B address 70, 72
Class C address 70, 72
Class D address 70, 85
Class E address 70
Client/server 18, 244, 283
close() 394
CMIP (Common Management Information Protocol) 309, 311
CMIS (Common Management Information Services) 309
CMIS/CMOT over TCP/IP (CMOT) 310, 311
CMOT (CMIS/CMIP over TCP/IP) 310, 311
Coaxial cable 52
Common Management Information Protocol (CMIP) 309, 311
Common Management Information Services (CMIS) 309
Community 315
Configure
  access controls in routers 351
  ARP table 345
  BGP router 354
  DDN security 352
  diskless workstations 352
  DNS 358
  Ethernet 350
  inetd 362
  IP 352
  IP address 95
  monitor filters 366
  MSS 359
  name to address translation 355, 358
  network management 364
  NFS 364, 375, 376
  point-to-point links 347
  primary host name 350
  proxy ARP 342
  reserved ports 360

Configure (Cont):
  router with Autonomous System number 353
  routers for priority traffic 351
  RPC 363
  static routes 351
  TCP/IP defaults 365
Congestion 204
Congestion window 204
connect() 394
Connection setup 181
Connection-oriented communication 17
Connectionless communication 17
Counter 322
Counting to infinity 145
CSMA/CD (Carrier Sense Multiple Access with Collision Detection) 54

DARPA (Defense Advanced Research Projects Agency) 1
Data circuit-terminating equipment (DCE) 48
Data Encryption Standard (DES) 252
Data Link header 39
Data Link layer 26
Data terminal equipment (DTE) 48
Database Description message 155
Datagram 38, 90, 92, 94
  header 100, 101
DCA (Defense Communications Agency) 5
DCE (Data circuit-terminating equipment) 48
DCE (Distributed Computing Environment) 10, 242
DDN (Defense Data Network) 7
DDN Network Information Center (DDN NIC) 8
DDN NIC (DDN Network Information Center) 8
DECnet 55
Default address 96, 97
Defense Advanced Research Projects Agency (DARPA) 1
Defense Communications Agency (DCA) 5
Defense Data Network (DDN) 7
Defense Information Systems Agency (DISA) 8
DES (Data Encryption Standard) 252
Designated Router 154, 155, 159, 160
Destination Service Access Point (DSAP) 58
Destination Unreachable message 127
DFS (Distributed File Service) 242, 243
Directory Information Base 305
Directory Service 302

Index   459

Directory Service Agent (DSA)   305, 307
Directory User Agent (DUA)   305, 307
DISA (Defense Information Systems Agency)   8
Distance vector algorithm   142, 143, 162
Distinguished name   305
Distributed Computing Environment (DCE)   10, 242
Distributed File Service (DFS)   242, 243
Distributed Management Environment (DME)   310
DME (Distributed Management Environment)   310
DNS (Domain Name System)   20, 29, 76, 77, 355
  cache   359
  in-addr.arpa   359
  non-authoritative   359
  resolver   355
  root server   358
  setting up   357
  zone   357
Domain   65, 67
Domain name   65, 66, 69, 350
  label   68
Domain Name System (DNS)   20, 29, 76, 77, 355
Dot notation   69, 94
DSA (Directory Service Agent)   305, 307
DSAP (Destination Service Access Point)   58
DTE (Data terminal equipment)   48
DUA (Directory User Agent)   305, 307

EBCDIC (Extended Binary-Coded Decimal Interchange Code)   222
Echo Request message   132
EGP (Exterior Gateway Protocol)   163, 164, 353
Electronic mail   285, 363
  domains   290
  identifiers   289
  mail exchanger   290
  model   287
  performance   298
  relay scenario   288
  X.400   298
Encoding Options   108
Ethernet   41, 51-54
  frame header   54
Ethernet type code   55
Extended Binary-Coded Decimal Interchange Code (EBCDIC)   222
Extended Security   107
Extended Security Option   352
Exterior Gateway Protocol (EGP)   163, 164, 353

External Data Representation (XDR)   243, 254, 256, 258
External routing   353

FCS (Frame check sequence)   39, 44, 46, 50
FDDI (Fiber Distributed Data Interface)   41, 59
Fiber Distributed Data Interface (FDDI)   41, 59
Fiber media   41
File handle   254, 261-263
File server   241
File systems   217
File Transfer Protocol (FTP)   19, 29, 217, 218
File Transfer, Access, and Management (FTAM)   235
File-structure   226, 227
FIN   187, 195
finger   373
Flag   44
Flow control   173, 188, 210
For Your Information (FYI)   13
Fragment Offset field   103
Fragmentation   98, 103
Fragmented datagram   103
Frame   39
Frame check sequence (FCS)   39, 44, 46, 50
Frame header   39
Frame Relay   41, 47, 49, 50
FTAM (File Transfer, Access, and Management)   235
FTP (File Transfer Protocol)   19, 23, 29, 217, 218
  anonymous   361
  block mode   226
  commands   231-234
  compressed mode   227
  data type   225
  debug   223
  error recovery and restart   227
  file structure   226
  get   222
  globbing   222
  help   223
  ls   224
  mget   222
  mput   222
  open   223
  performance   234
  protocol   225
  put   222
  quit   224
  reply codes   228
  scenario   219

FTP (File Transfer Protocol) (*Cont*):
    session trace 228-231
    status 223
    transmission mode 226
FYI (For Your Information) 13

gated 143, 163
Gateway 4, 32
Gauge 322
get 219, 222
Get Next Request 314, 315
    example 330
    tables 331
Get Request 314, 315, 326
Get Response 314, 315
getsockopt() 394
Globbing 222
GOSIP (Government OSI Profile) 15
Government OSI Profile (GOSIP) 15

HDLC (High-level Data Link Control) 41, 44-46
Header Checksum 104
Hello message 154, 155, 158, 163
High-level Data Link Control (HDLC) 41, 44-46
Hold down 148
Hop 140-145
Hop count 142
Hops 92
Host 3
Hosts 355
HYPERchannel 42

IAB (Internet Architecture Board) 8, 309, 310
IAC (Interpret as Command) 278
IANA (Internet Assigned Numbers Authority) 11, 61, 166-168, 177, 317
ICMP (Internet Control Message Protocol) 118, 123
    Address Mask message 134, 135
    Destination Unreachable message 127
    Echo Request message 132
    error message format 126
    error messages 124-126
    Parameter Problem message 128
    query messages 131
    Redirect message 130
    Source Quench message 129
    Time Exceeded message 128
    Timestamp message 134
ICMP error messages 124
Identification field 102

IEEE (Institute of Electrical and Electronics Engineers) 41, 51
IEN (Internet Engineering Notes) 13
IESG (Internet Engineering Steering Group) 9
IETF (Internet Engineering Task Force) 9
ifconfig 95, 350
IGMP (Internet Group Management Protocol) 85, 86
IGP (Interior Gateway Protocol) 34, 139, 149
IGRP (Inter-Gateway Routing Protocol) 162
in-addr.arpa 359
inetd 362
Initial sequence number (ISN) 181, 190, 192, 194
Institute of Electrical and Electronics Engineers (IEEE) 41, 51
Integrated Services Digital Network (ISDN) 41
Inter-Gateway Routing Protocol (IGRP) 162
Interface
    address mask 344
    assigning names 347
    configuration 344
    ifconfig command 95, 350
    installation 343
    metric 345
    MTU 345
    physical address 345
    use of trailers 345
    without IP address 348
Interior Gateway Protocol (IGP) 34, 139, 149
Intermediate System (IS) 162
International Organization for Standardization (ISO) 2, 15
International Telegraph and Telephone Consultative Committee 47, 298
internet 6, 8, 32, 89, 340
Internet Architecture Board (IAB) 8, 309, 310
Internet Assigned Numbers Authority (IANA) 11, 61, 166, 177, 317
Internet Control Message Protocol (*See* ICMP)
Internet Engineering Notes (IEN) 13
Internet Engineering Steering Group (IESG) 9
Internet Engineering Task Force (IETF) 9
Internet Group Management Protocol (IGMP) 85, 86
Internet message format 296, 297
Internet name 66

Index

Internet Protocol (IP) 28, 33, 89, 90, 92-94
Internet Research Task Force (IRTF) 9
Interpret as Command (IAC) 278
iocntl() 395
IP address format 69
IP (Internet Protocol) 28, 33, 89, 90, 92-94
  Basic Security option 107
  datagram header 100, 101
  Extended Security option 107
  Flags field 102, 103
  Fragment Offset field 102, 103
  fragmented datagram 103
  Header Checksum 104
  Identification field 102, 103
  Loose Source Route option 106
  options 99, 105
  performance 115
  Protocol field 104
  Record Route option 106
  routing table 350
  Sample IP Header 111
  security 351
  service interface 119, 120
  Strict Source Route option 105
  Time-to-Live field 104
  Timestamp option 107
  Total Length field 102
  Type of Service field 101
IP route 140
IPX 61
IRTF (Internet Research Task Force) 9
IS (Intermediate System) 162
IS-IS 162
ISDN (Integrated Services Digital Network) 41
ISN (Initial sequence number) 181, 190, 192, 194
ISO (International Organization for Standardization) 2, 15
ISO Development Environment (ISODE) 15
ISODE (ISO Development Environment) 15

Jacobson's Algorithm 200

Karn's algorithm 200
Kerberos 252, 379-383

LAN (Local Area Network) 1, 20, 27, 97, 335, 336
LAPB (Link Access Procedures Balanced) 45

LAPD (Link Access Procedures on the D-channel) 45
Layer N PDU 38
Layering 26
Link Access Procedures Balanced (LAPB) 45
Link Access Procedures on the D-channel (LAPD) 45
Link state routing 142, 143, 149, 152
Link State Update message 159
listen() 393
Little Endian 3
LLC (Logical Link Control) 57, 58
Local Area Network (LAN) 1, 20, 27, 97, 335, 336
Logical byte 3, 225
Logical Link Control header 39
Loopback address 76, 96, 97
Loose Source Route 99, 106
Lower layers 27

MAC (Media Access Control) 51, 54
Mail alias 286, 289, 290
Mail alias names 286
Mail Domains 290
Mail exchanger (MX) 290, 363
  role 290, 291
Mail gateway 286, 288, 291, 299
Mailbox 285, 287, 289, 296
MAN (Metropolitan Area Network) 57
Management Information Base (MIB) 312, 313
Manual routing 142
Manufacturing Automation Protocol 57
Maximum datagram size 60, 63
Maximum frame size 60
Maximum Segment Size (MSS) 187, 188, 192
Maximum transmission unit (MTU) 92
Media Access Control (MAC) 51, 54
Message Transfer Agent 287
Metropolitan Area Network (MAN) 57
mget 222
MIB (Management Information Base) 312, 313
  categories 319
  definitions 319
  extensions 319
  sample datatypes 323
  sample definition 321
  structure of information 317
Mount 243, 246, 260, 375
  procedures 262
  protocol 260
mput 222
MSS (Maximum Segment Size) 187, 188, 192

462 Index

MTU (Maximum transmission unit) 92
   802.3 92
   802.4 92
   Ethernet 92
   FDDI 92
   SMDS 92
Multicast 60, 61, 70, 84-86
   Physical Multicast Addresses 86
Multicast group 84
Multihoming 82
MX (Mail exchanger) 290, 363
   role 290, 291

Nagle algorithm 199, 200
Name server 77, 356
National Research and Education Network (NREN) 8
National Science Foundation Net (NSFNET) 8
Neighbor acquisition 163
Neighbor reachability 163
NETBIOS 21
netstat 95, 135, 136, 141, 172, 210, 369
Network administration 333
Network configuration 343
Network File System (NFS) 20, 29, 241, 243, 260
Network Information Center (NIC) 10, 11, 13, 14, 350
Network Information Service (NIS) 241, 266, 267, 355
Network interface 61, 62
Network layer 28
Network management 309
Network management station 312
Network monitor 366
Network topology 334, 336
Network Virtual Terminal (NVT) 271
NFS (Network File System) 20, 29, 241, 243, 260
   file handle 254, 261, 262
   file locking 265
   implementation issues 265
   lookup 263
   model 259
   procedures 263, 264
   protocol 262
   special services 264
nfsstat 266, 376, 377
NIC (Network Information Center) 8, 10, 11, 13, 14, 350
NIS (Network Information Service) 241, 266, 267, 355
   maintain maps 268
   map 266
   protocol 269
   server 269

Nonblocking 391
Notational Conventions 4
NREN (National Research and Education Network) 8
NSFNET (National Science Foundation Net) 8
nslookup 23, 78, 166, 290, 356, 358
ntohs() 398, 400
NVT (Network Virtual Terminal) 271
   keyboard 273

Object descriptor 317
Object identifier 317, 318, 321-323, 332
   encoding 326, 330
Octet 3
Open Shortest Path First (OSPF) 34, 139, 149-152, 154, 351
Open Software Foundation (OSF) 10, 242, 310
Open Systems Interconnection (OSI) 2, 15, 28, 63, 120, 136, 162, 210, 212, 235, 282, 310
OSF (Open Software Foundation) 10, 242, 310
OSF/1 242
OSI (Open Systems Interconnection) 2, 15, 63
   comparison with FTP 235
   comparison with IP 120
   comparison with TCP 210
   comparison with Telnet 282
   Connection Request PDU 212
   error messages 136, 137
   network layer PDU 121
   network management 310
   presentation layer 28
   routing 162
   session layer 28
   TP4 212, 214
   TP4 Acknowledgment 215
   Transport Class 4 211
   transport layer 28, 210
   Virtual Terminal Service 282
OSPF (Open Shortest Path First) 34, 139, 149-152, 154, 351
   area 150
   backbone 152
   Designated Router 154
   external link message 161
   Hello messages 154
   Link State Request message 155
   Link State Update message 155, 159
   network link message 160
   protocol 158
   router link message 160
   Routing Database 155
   summary link message 160

Packet network 47
Packet radio 42
Packet-switching 47
Parameter Problem message 128
Passive open 389
Pathname 259, 260, 262
PDU 38
Peer 38
Performance 115, 206
Permanent virtual circuit 48, 50
Physical address 53, 60, 61
Physical layer 26
ping 133, 200, 367
Point-to-point link 42
Point-to-Point Protocol (PPP) 41, 45, 46, 347
Poisoned reverse 147
POP (Post Office Protocol) 297
Port 166-168, 177-179, 181, 192
Portmapper 247-249, 363
Ports 180
Positive acknowledgment with retransmission 179
Post Office Protocol (POP) 297
PPP (Point-to-Point Protocol) 41, 45, 46, 347
Priority routing 351
Protocol 3
  states 11
  status 11
Protocol stack 3
Protocol suite 3
Proxy agent 313, 314
Proxy ARP 341, 342
put 222

RARP (Reverse ARP) 81, 352
RBOC (Regional Bell operating company) 59
Reassembly 103
Reassembly timeout 115
Receive window 188
Record Route 106
Record Route option 99
recv() 394
Redirect message 130
Regional Bell operating company (RBOC) 59
Remote Network Monitoring MIB (RMON MIB) 331, 366
Remote Procedure Call (RPC) 18, 29, 242-245, 257, 363
Repeater 52
Request For Comments (RFC) 10
Requirements for Internet Gateways 12
Requirements for Internet Hosts 12

Reserved ports 167
Reset (RST) 187, 192, 195
Resolver 355
Resource records 358
Restart recovery 218
  restart markers 227
Retransmission timeout 179, 200, 203
Reverse ARP (RARP) 81, 352
rexec 378
RFC (Request For Comments) 10, 420-432
RIP (Routing Information Protocol) 34, 139, 143-146, 346
  counting to infinity 145
  hold down 148
  Message Protocol 148
  poisoned reverse 147
  split horizon 147
  Triggered updates 148
  unreachable routers 146
RMON MIB (Remote Network Monitoring MIB) 331, 366
Router 3, 32, 33, 89-91, 152, 339-341
  multiple protocols 342
  proxy ARP 341, 342
  router processing 114
  security 341
  Telnet login 351
Routing 139
  manual 142
  metric 142
  Type of Service 152
Routing Information Protocol (RIP) 34, 97, 139, 143-146, 346
Routing procedure 92
Routing protocol 141, 341
Routing table 34, 95, 140, 141, 350
  default address 96
RPC (Remote Procedure Call) 18, 29, 242-245, 257, 363
  authentication 250, 252
  message format 250
  portmapper 247-249
  procedure 246
  program 246, 250
  programming interface 258
  Secure 252
  structure with NFS 243, 244
  transaction identifier 250
  typical programs 246
  version 246
rpcinfo 248, 249, 374, 375
RST (reset) 187, 192, 195
ruptime 373
rusers 246

SDEV (Smoothed deviation) 203

464 Index

SDLC (Synchronous Data Link Protocol) 45
Security 351, 378
   Audit trail 379
   classification 352
   Kerberos 379
Security option 99
Segment 38
Send window 190
send() 394
sendmail 286
Serial Interface 348
Serial Line Interface Protocol (SLIP) 42, 46, 47
Set Request 315
SetRequest 314
setsockopt() 395
Shortest Path First 143
showmount 375
Silly Window Syndrome 199
Simple Mail Transfer Protocol (SMTP) 19, 29, 286, 292
Simple Network Management Protocol (SNMP) 21, 309, 310, 334, 366
Slow start 205
SMDS (Switched Multimegabit Data Service) 41, 59
Smoothed deviation (SDEV) 203
Smoothed Round Trip Time (SRTT) 202
SMTP (Simple Mail Transfer Protocol) 19, 29, 286, 292
   commands 295, 296
   dialogue 293
   reply codes 296
   scenario 292
   timestamps 294
SNAP (Sub-Network Access Protocol) 58
SNMP (Simple Network Management Protocol) 21, 309, 310, 334, 366
   agent 312
   authentication 316
   community 315
   datatype identifiers 326
   datatypes 321, 322
   Get Next Request 314, 315, 330
   Get Request 314, 315, 326
   Get Response 314, 315
   manager 312
   message format 323, 327
   message protocol 315
   messages 314
   MIB 312
   model 312
   Object descriptor 317
   object identifier 317, 318, 321-323, 332
   proxy agent 313, 314
   Set Request 314, 315

SNMP (Simple Network Management Protocol) (*Cont.*):
   Trap 314, 315, 324
   vendor-defined objects 319
Socket
   program 397
   raw 386
   stream 386
   UDP datagram 386
   XNS 387
Socket address 178
Socket programming interface 18, 29, 385, 386, 389, 391, 392
   active open 393
   passive open 393
   sample TCP client program 402, 403
   sample TCP server program 395, 397-399
   sample UDP program 407
   send and receive 394
   Simple TCP server program 405, 406
   UDP client program 410, 411
   UDP server program 408, 409
socket() 393
SONET 59
Source Quench message 129
Source Service Access Point (SSAP) 58
Spanning tree algorithm 338
Special addresses 75
Split horizon 147
Spray 246, 368
SRTT (Smoothed Round Trip Time) 202
SSAP (Source Service Access Point) 58
Store-and-forward 287, 288
Strict Source Route 99, 105
Structure of Management Information 317
Subnet 73
Subnet mask 74, 94
Subnets
   multiple on one LAN 346
Sub-Network Access Protocol (SNAP) 58
Switched Multimegabit Data Service (SMDS) 41, 59
Switched virtual circuit 48
SYN 181, 192
Synchronous 391
Synchronous Data Link Protocol (SDLC) 45
System startup procedure 365

T1 41, 59
TCB
   definition 388
   parameters 388
TCP (Transmission Control Protocol) 28, 35, 36, 173, 388

Index 465

TCP (Transmission Control Protocol) (Cont.)
  ACK field 192
  acknowledgment 179
  Acknowledgment Number field 194
  checksum 191
  client/server 174
  close 185
  configuring 359
  connection setup 181
  Data Offset field 192
  data streams 175
  data transfer 183, 185
  FIN 187
  flow control 188
  functions 207
  header 180
  initial sequence number 192, 194
  length 192
  Maximum Segment Size 187
  MSS 188
  performance 197, 198, 206
  pseudo header 191
  push 175, 176
  PUSH flag 194
  receive window 188, 189
  reset 187
  retransmission 195
  retransmission timeout 200
  sample segment 195
  segments 175
  send window 190
  Sequence Number field 192
  service interface 387, 389-391
  Silly Window Syndrome 199
  socket address 178
  SRTT 202
  states 208, 210
  SYN 181
  timeout 184
  URG flag 194
  urgent data 175, 176, 195
  Window field 192
TCP program 397
TCU (Trunk Coupling Unit) 56
Telnet 19, 29, 271
  3270 logon 281
  command protocol 276
  dialogue 274, 276, 280, 281
  display control codes 274
  extended options 278
  Interpret as Command 278
  keyboard control codes 273
  model 272
  options 275, 277
  subnegotiation 278
  synch 276, 277
TFTP (Trivial File Transfer Protocol)
  218, 235, 236, 352

TFTP (Trivial File Transfer Protocol) (Cont.)
  protocol 236, 237
  scenario 238
Third party transfer 218
Time Exceeded message 128
Time Ticks 322
Time-to-Live (TTL) 98, 104, 368
Timestamp 107
Timestamp message 134
Timestamp option 99
TLI (Transport Layer Interface) 385
tn3270 281
Token-Ring 41, 56
Topology 31
Total Length field 102
TP4 212, 214, 215
traceroute 368
Trailer 39, 42, 49, 54, 59, 63
Transmission Control Block (TCB) 388
Transmission Control Protocol (TCP) 28,
  35, 36, 173
Transport Layer Interface (TLI) 385
Trap 314-316, 324
Triggered updates 148
Trivial File Transfer Protocol (TFTP)
  218, 235, 236, 352
Troubleshooting 377, 378
Trunk Coupling Unit (TCU) 56
TTL (Time-to-Live) 98, 104, 368
Tunneling 61
Twisted pair 41
Type of Service 98
Type of Service field 101

UDP (User Datagram Protocol) 18, 28,
  37, 165, 166
  checksum 170
  header 169, 171
  protocol 168, 169
  pseudo header 170
  services 167
  socket overflows 172
Urgent data 194, 195
User Agent 285-287
User Datagram 38
User Datagram Protocol (UDP) 18, 28,
  37, 165, 166

Virtual circuit 48, 49, 63

WAN (Wide Area Network) 27
Wide Area Network (WAN) 27

X Window System 282, 283

Index

X.25 41, 47-49
X.400 286, 287, 298
   characteristics 299
   domain-defined attributes 301
   interworking with Internet mail 301
   message format 300
   originator or recipient name 301
X.400 Gateway 299
X.500 302
   database operations 307
   Directory Information Base 305
   directory information tree 303, 305
   Directory Service Agent 305
   Directory User Agent 305
   distinguished name 305
   information 303
XDR (External Data Representation)
   243, 254, 256, 258
   datatypes 257
   encoding 257

ypcat 268
ypmatch 165, 268

Zero-bit insertion 44
Zone 357, 358